PUNISHMENT
and AVERSIVE BEHAVIOR

THE CENTURY PSYCHOLOGY SERIES

Richard M. Elliott, Kenneth MacCorquodale,
Gardner Lindzey, and Kenneth E. Clark

EDITORS

PUNISHMENT
and AVERSIVE BEHAVIOR

EDITED BY

Byron A. Campbell
PRINCETON UNIVERSITY

Russell M. Church
BROWN UNIVERSITY

New York

APPLETON-CENTURY-CROFTS
EDUCATIONAL DIVISION
MEREDITH CORPORATION

PRINTED IN THE UNITED STATES OF AMERICA

390-16865-3

Preface

This volume is a direct outgrowth of a conference on punishment which was held at the Nassau Inn in Princeton, N.J. from May 31 through June 4, 1967. As a result of a resurgence of interest in the effects of punishment on behavior during the mid 1960's, we believed that the time was appropriate for such a conference. Many people who were initiators of the current work on punishment were still active, and it seemed appropriate to bring these people together, if at all possible, in order to get their views of current trends in the field. The aim of the conference was to bring together many of the diverse approaches to the problem in the hope that such a conference would (1) summarize a substantial portion of the research accomplished in the past few years, (2) achieve some resolution of diverse beliefs in the course of face-to-face discussion, and (3) help to restructure the field and stimulate new approaches to old problems.

The focus of this volume is upon the experimental psychology of punishment, but its range is broader. Punishment refers to noxious stimulation that is contingent upon a response, but a complete treatment of the effects of punishment on behavior necessarily involves consideration of emotion, attention, abnormal behavior, etc. Although most, if not all, of the work contained in the volume had its historical roots in the early studies of punishment, it was frequently pointed out during the course of the conference that the research under discussion did not conform to the punishment paradigm. Subsequent to the conference we discussed several possible titles, but in the end we decided upon a title that would encompass the scope of research contained in the volume.

This volume may serve as a supplementary textbook for advanced undergraduate courses in learning and for graduate seminars in learning and motivation. Psychologists, and others with some psychological training, should find it a valuable reference to the present state of knowledge of the varied effects of punishment on behavior.

Although the editors bear joint responsibility for all stages of the conference and the volume, we have divided our primary concerns so that one of us (B. A. C.) concentrated on the details of organizing and conducting the conference and the other (R. M. C.) concentrated on the details of preparing the manuscripts for publication. We wish to express our appreciation to Carol Wooten, Lynn Wojtowicz, and Helen Donnelly for invaluable assistance in the preparation of manuscripts. This book could not have appeared without the conference, which was supported by Grant No. GB-5785 from the National Science Foundation. Finally, we wish to express our appreciation to the authors of the chapters of this book who were remarkably conscientious in submitting their manuscripts on schedule.

Byron A. Campbell
PRINCETON UNIVERSITY

Russell M. Church
BROWN UNIVERSITY

Contents

I

QUANTIFICATION of PUNISHMENT

Psychophysics of Punishment[1]

Byron A. Campbell

PRINCETON UNIVERSITY

Fred A. Masterson

UNIVERSITY OF PENNSYLVANIA

"An eye for an eye, a tooth for a tooth." Thus primitive man declared punishment to be an effective deterrent of unwanted behavior. Yet philosophers, educators, and humanitarians of all ages have hotly contested this adage and even today the issue is unresolved. In California, Governor Reagan has reinstituted the death penalty, while in New York State a law has just been passed prohibiting the death sentence.

Where do psychologists stand on this issue? Most of us believe punishment to be a powerful determinant of behavior. Cats will starve to death rather than expose themselves to a physically harmless tone that signals impending severe pain (Masserman, 1943), and dogs will respond hundreds if not thousands of times to escape from a not-unpleasant buzzer that signals a forthcoming sub-tetanizing shock (Solomon et al., 1953). Similarly, conditioned reflex therapy is predicated primarily on the premise that punishment can temporarily if not permanently suppress unwanted behaviors.

Upon what empirical foundations are those views based? Surprisingly substantial ones, considering the uneven state of our science. Hundreds of studies document the pervasive and long-lasting effects of punishment. But, with the exception of an occasional slap or burst of loud noise, the entire literature on punishment is based on one of psychology's most variable and uncontrollable stimuli, the electric shock. The reason for its extensive use is simply that the advantages of shock far outweigh its

1 This research was supported in part by NSF Grants, G 9979, GB 235, GB 5628, and by NIH Grant MH 01562. The authors wish to thank Dr. James R. Misanin for his invaluable assistance in designing, analyzing, and supervising the experiments. We also wish to thank Mrs. Stephie Orsi for running the majority of animals used in this research.

disadvantages. Since its introduction as a motivating stimulus in the early 1900's, shock has remained the only simple method of producing pain in animals, an impressive record when viewed in the context of 60 years of explosive technological and scientific advancement.

Electric shock remains an inherently variable stimulus when used to motivate free-moving animals, primarily because the electrical resistance of the subject varies enormously as he moves about on a shock grid. This variation in resistance, which can range from a few thousand ohms to several million, causes proportional variations in either current flow, power dissipation, or voltage drop, depending upon the type of stimulator used. An imaginary analogy from human psychophysics might be a vision experiment where subjects could move about the room, view the distal stimulus from different distances and angles, and even look away from the stimulus from time to time.

Given that all shock procedures must entail some variability, the fact remains that some procedures will have less variability than others, and the problem before us is to find those procedures which entail the least amount. Before reporting our own progress with this problem, we shall review some of the previous attempts to refine electric shock techniques.

Historical Background

According to Watson (1914), Elmer Gates in 1895 was the first to use electric shock as a punishing stimulus. But the history of research on shock-induced punishment really begins a few years later with Yerkes' use of electric shock to study the sensory capacities of infra-primate vertebrates. Yerkes was apparently led to the use of electric shock as a behavior-modifying technique through his early training in zoology, a field in which electrical stimulation was used extensively to study nerve conduction, muscle contraction, and similar processes. Yerkes first used electric shock in a paper entitled "The instincts, habits, and reactions of the frog" (1903), in which he punished incorrect responses in a color discrimination problem using current from two dry cell batteries. Current flow in the circuit was naturally dependent upon the frog's skin resistance, and Yerkes reports that he frequently had to moisten the frog's skin in order to maintain good contact. Shortly after that experiment, Yerkes switched to the inductorium as his source of electrical stimulation, probably because of Martin's research quantifying the stimulating properties of the induction coil (Martin, 1908). Martin not only specified the electrical characteristics of the coil, but also attempted to quantify the stimulating properties of electricity by relating current flow to strength of contraction in the frog's gastrocnemius muscle. Thus began the attempt to specify and quantify electrical stimulation. Watson (1914), some years later, wrote: "His [Yerkes'] work on behavior, coupled with that of Martin on the standardization of the Porter inductorium, gives us our first approach to a real control of incentives" (p. 204).

The inductorium remained the standard and widely used source of electrical stimulation until the 1920's when externally generated alternating current and electronic sophistication became commonplace in psychological laboratories. The inductorium, while far superior to the low DC voltages generated by dry cells, was a cumbersome stimulator for two main reasons. First, it produced a shock only once with each activation, meaning that some electromechanical means of rapidly making and breaking contact with the coil had to be employed to produce a continuous shock, and second, the current flow characteristics were difficult to control and calibrate because of the brief pulse and high voltages involved.

One of the first to employ alternating current as a punishing stimulus was Moss (1924) in his early study using the obstruction technique as a measure of motivation. For that work he used a constant voltage 20- or 28-volt shock with no resistor in series with the rat. A few years later Jenkins, Warner, and Warden (1926), in an improved version of the obstruction technique, developed an AC constant current source essentially similar to those in use today. It consisted of a step-up transformer with an output voltage of 1200 volts and a high resistance in the secondary to control current flow through the rat. In this type of circuit, variations in current flow are held to a minimum because variations in the animal's tissue resistance (resulting from changes in contact area, dehydration, or skin moisture, or the like) are small compared to the total resistance in the circuit. The greater the resistance in series with the rat, the less the variation in current flow. As circuit resistance is increased, the source voltage (output voltage of the step-up transformer) must be increased to provide sufficient potential to force the current through the high resistance. Figure 1–1 illustrates the problem graphically. With a 5000-volt source it requires a 49.8-megohm resistor in series with the rat to limit current flow to .1 ma., assuming the rat's resistance is approximately 200K ohms (Campbell & Teghtsoonian, 1958). With a 500-volt source, a series resistance of 4.8 megohms limits current flow to .1 ma. In the former case variations in the rat's resistance from 50–1000K ohms (which approximate the range of resistances possible at this current level) produce a maximum variation of 1.7% in current flow, while the 500-volt source allows a variation in current of over 14%.

Since the high voltage–high resistance source clearly offers superior current regulation, why not adopt it or even higher source voltages along with higher series resistances to achieve superior current regulation? Knight Dunlap (1931, p. 135) was the first to point out the potential weakness of this approach when he noted in comparing two source

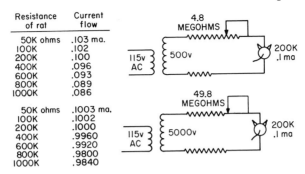

Resistance of rat	Current flow
50K ohms	.103 ma.
100K	.102
200K	.100
400K	.096
600K	.093
800K	.089
1000K	.086

Resistance of rat	Current flow
50K ohms	.1003 ma.
100K	.1002
200K	.1000
400K	.9960
600K	.9920
800K	.9800
1000K	.9840

FIG. 1–1.   Two hypothetical constant current shock stimulators with 500-volt and 5000-volt source potentials. The current level is adjusted to 0.1 ma. with a dummy load resistor approximating the resistance of the rat in the circuit. The tables beside each figure show hypothetical variations in current flow as the rat's resistance changes from 50 to 1000K ohms $(I = V/R_1 + R_{rat})$.

voltages (450 and 1500 volts) that when the "rat makes contact with the 'live' grid, the higher voltage has entirely different effect from the lower, in that, at the higher voltage, the . . . current employed (.00015 amp), will jump nearly a millimeter. The result is that the rat's foot receives a spark just before it touches the grid." This observation and subsequent similar observations had a profound influence on the proliferation of different types of shock sources that were soon to appear.

Shortly after Dunlap's observations, Muenzinger and Walz (1934) reported an entirely new way of generating and controlling electric shock. Their new apparatus made full use of the then rapidly expanding field of electronics. It consisted of a pentode vacuum tube and appropriate control circuitry which produced a constant direct current stimulus as opposed to the previous AC constant current source. The major advantage of this circuit was that it regulated current accurately without high source voltages. The regulation achieved by this type of constant current DC source approximates that achieved by a constant current AC stimulator with a source voltage of over 5000 volts, yet the peak voltage applied to the rat remains well below 500 volts.

In theory and probably in practice the greatest disadvantage of the constant current sources, both AC and DC, is the possibility that current density is a major determinant of the perceived severity of the shock stimulus. Current density refers to the relative density of current flow per unit area of skin tissue (current/area). When the animal has a firm contact with the grid with all four paws, current flows relatively evenly throughout the entire skin area, although depending on the position of the scrambler, current may be entering the animal through either 1, 2, or 3 paws and leaving through the inverse number. Movements influence current density, particularly when the current flow is concentrated through one paw. If the shock source is a constant current source with a high source voltage (e.g., 1500 volts), then lifting the paw will concentrate current into a smaller and smaller area. Furthermore, if the conditions are optimal, a small arc will be drawn out between the paw and the grid. In contrast, if the shock source is a fixed impedance source, lifting the same paw simply causes a decrease in current flow without undue concentration of current. It is quite likely that the concentration of current into a small area is more painful than the same current spread out over the entire paw. As a result, it was hypothesized that animals learn to avoid this increase in painful stimulation by remaining relatively immobile on the grid, thus avoiding the higher current density associated with movement. This theoretical analysis was substantiated by frequent observations that animals tended to freeze on shock grids, particularly at low current levels.

During the next decade relatively little research was carried out using electric shock, primarily because the learning theorists of that time (Hull, Guthrie, Tolman, and Skinner) were mainly concerned with the analysis of appetitive conditioning. Later, World War II disrupted all basic research. After the war, the Hull-inspired contingent of Miller, Brown, and Mowrer turned to a full-scale analysis of fear conditioning. In the course of their work they introduced a new class of shock sources which we would like to call fixed impedance sources. A schematic of this type of source is shown in Fig. 1–2.

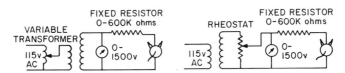

FIG. 1–2.   Two fixed impedance sources. Voltage applied to the rat is adjusted by means of a variable transformer in the left-hand schematic and by a potentiometer in the right schematic. Shock level is specified as the voltage at the output of the step-up transformer in the source using a variable transformer or as the voltage at the output of the rheostat in the source using a voltage divider.

Shock intensity in this source is controlled by the voltage applied to the rat through the fixed series resistor either by varying the input voltage to a step-up transformer (left schematic) or by adjusting a voltage divider across the secondary of the step-up transformer (right schematic). The two are nearly electrically equivalent since the resistance of the voltage divider is usually small compared to the fixed series resistor. The former circuit is preferred, however, since the total resistance in series with the rat is known and remains constant at all voltages. When the fixed resistor is 0 ohms, the source becomes a constant voltage source, because the voltage applied to the rat remains constant regardless of the rat's resistance.

The fixed impedance source was widely adopted in the late 1940's and is still one of the two most widely used types of shock generators, the other being the constant current AC source. Adoption of the fixed impedance source was spurred by two major considerations: First, it minimizes the current density problem, particularly at low shock levels since the source voltages necessary to produce mild levels of motivation are on the order of 30–100 volts far below the source voltage necessary to produce an arc or severe concentration of current. The second and perhaps more historically important reason for its wide-spread adoption was its inherent simplicity. All that is needed is an old radio transformer, either a variable transformer or a few high wattage resistors for a voltage divider, a series resistor, and a simple volt-ohmeter to specify the voltage. The constant current AC source requires a slightly more complicated series of potentiometers or fixed resistors to adjust current, and also requires a vacuum tube voltmeter to measure low current levels.

The fixed impedance source was given a further boost in a paper published by Campbell and Teghtsoonian in 1958, which demonstrated that some fixed impedance sources approximately matched the impedance of the rat at low to moderate shock levels. Since the power variations are minimal when the source impedance equals the average load impedance, fixed impedance sources in the 50–200K-ohm range approximate constant power stimulators. It was thought at that time that there might be some advantage to a constant power source, or at least to a matched impedance source, particularly since the current density problem is minimized at low shock levels with this type of source. At high shock levels, the "matched impedance" source begins to approach a constant current source since the 150K-ohm fixed resistor is on the order of 3–10 times larger than the rat's resistance at those intensities.

Another important result of that study was the finding that the electrical resistance of the rat (skin and tissue resistance) decreased as a function of shock intensity. Since this relationship between shock intensity and the animal's resistance will be important to some of our later discussion, these data are presented in Fig. 1–3. The left-hand panel shows the resistance of rats at six intensities of a constant current AC source and the right-hand panel shows the resistance of rats at five intensities of a fixed impedance 150K-ohm source. The interquartile range of resistance variation is shown by the vertical lines at each data point. Later research has shown that skin resistance measured in this way also varies quite considerably depending upon humidity and type of cage the animals are housed in. Animals housed directly on dry sawdust or

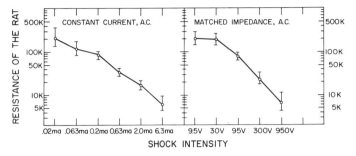

FIG. 1-3.   Electrical resistance of rats shocked by a 150K-ohm fixed impedance source (right panel) and a constant current AC source (left panel). The vertical bars represent the interquartile range of resistance variations.

shavings have a higher skin resistance than animals housed on wire mesh cages where dirt and moisture accumulate on the mesh. These various local conditions can change the overall height of the function substantially in either direction, but the overall slope of the function remains constant regardless of the absolute levels. This finding that tissue conductance varies as a function of current flowing through the tissue was known for some time in biological circles, but the effect had not previously been demonstrated to hold with externally applied electric shock. Prior to this research, psychologists believed that skin resistance remained relatively constant at all shock levels on the basis of Muenzinger and Mize's (1933) measurements of skin resistance using a Wheatstone bridge.

When the source impedance is 0 ohms, the stimulator becomes a constant voltage source. That is, variation in the rat's resistance has no effect whatsoever on the voltage applied to the rat. Hence the rat's own tissue resistance determines entirely current flow through the circuit. The lower the rat's resistance, the greater the current flow. This characteristic of the constant voltage source leads, even at moderate shock intensities, to serious consequences because of the effect of current flow on skin resistance described above. With the constant voltage source set at a moderate intensity, a low level of current flows through the animal. This small current lowers the skin resistance which in turn increases current flow, which in turn further lowers skin resistance. This positive feedback action ultimately produces tetanization and death, even though the initial reaction to the shock may have been quite mild (see Campbell & Teghtsoonian, 1958, for a further description of this process).

In the two decades since the introduction of the fixed impedance source as a major type of stimulator still another general class of shock generators, the constant power stimulators, has emerged (Hurwitz & Dillow, 1966). These attempt to regulate the amount of power dissipated in the rat electronically. They have only recently been developed, however, and they are neither widely used nor likely to be widely used because the electrical characteristics of the constant power source are quite similar to those of the constant voltage source. In order to regulate power the following occurs. Assume that the power dissipated in the rat decreases. To compensate for the drop, current flow through the rat has to be increased ($P = I^2R$). When current flowing through the rat is increased, skin resistance drops and a further increase in current is required to hold power constant. As with the constant voltage source, this positive feedback action will soon lead to tetanization and death.

The major occurrence of the past 20 years has been the incredible elaboration or varieties of constant current and fixed impedance sources. Because there have been no standards and because no extensive comparisons have been made between different types of shock stimulators, each investigator and each manufacturer of behavioral equipment has devised his own slightly unique circuit rendering precise comparison between two stimulators (and the work of any two investigators) virtually impossible. The source voltages used in constant current AC stimulators, for example, range from a minimum of around 350 volts (Grason-Stadler) to a maximum of 3900 volts (Lehigh Valley Model No. 1311), despite the general knowledge that high source voltages produce extreme current density effects. Fixed impedance shockers, on the other hand, range from constant voltage sources to around 600K ohms.

In short, this proliferation of types of shock stimulators led us to conclude a number of years ago that it was high time to initiate a thorough psychophysical study of the properties of electric shock as a behavioral stimulus, a project that was first recommended by Forbes, Muenzinger, and Wendt (1935) in their "Report of round tables on use of electric shock" over 30 years ago.

We shall examine the following for several major types of shock sources:

1. Detection, aversion, tetanization, and death thresholds
2. Equal aversion functions
3. Aversion difference limen functions
4. Electrical model of shock-induced pain
5. Validation of psychophysical measures of aversiveness using other behavioral techniques.

The major assumption underlying this research is that painful stimulation arising from different types of electric shock, which may differ qualitatively in several respects, can nonetheless be reduced to a single ordinal scale of aversiveness. As such, this work is intended to be a step in the direction of developing mathematical scales of motivation, as well as a solution to the practical problem of how to control and specify shock applied to infra-primate mammals, such as the rat.

Method

In this section we would like to present the major experimental details that are common to the forthcoming experiments.

Subjects

The subjects used in the following research were all female albino rats. Because of the large number of rats necessary for this research, the rats obtained were discarded breeders from two sources, Dierolf Farms in Boyerstown, Pa., and Perfection Breeders in Douglassville, Pa. Most of the rats weighed between 250–400 gm., although a few rats fell outside of those extremes. This exclusive use of female rats may raise some concern about the generality of the forthcoming research, but we have carried out a number of extensive studies comparing males and females on several different measures and found no differences. We have also compared animals of different ages and found no differences except that very young animals tended to tetanize at somewhat lower shock intensities (Campbell, 1967). In all of the experiments eight rats were used in each group unless otherwise specified.

Apparatus and Procedure

The basic behavioral measure used in the research was a simple spatial preference technique in which the animal is allowed to choose between two aversive stimuli, or between the absence or presence of a stimulus. The behavioral apparatus consisted of a small, rectangular cage 7 inches wide, 7 inches high, and 14 inches long. The top and sides were aluminum, and the floor consisted of $\frac{3}{32}$-inch stainless steel grids spaced $\frac{1}{2}$ inch apart center to center. The grids were supported in a Plexiglas frame mounted on a central pivot so that when the animal crossed from one side of the cage to the other a microswitch either opened or closed, which in turn controlled the intensity of shock applied to the grids as well as recording the location of the animal. The ends of the shock grids were covered with Teflon tubing and then inserted into the ends of the Plexiglas frame. The Teflon coating on the ends of the grids eliminated partial short circuiting caused by dirt and moisture adhering to the Plexiglas. The cage itself was housed in a file-drawer type cabinet with an exhaust fan and a low level of illumination.

Shock was applied to the grids through a 12-level stepping switch which was advanced two times per second. Each position of the switch presented a different pattern of shock polarity to the grids. The grids were checked with an insulation tester before each rat was run. If partial short-circuiting was indicated, the Plexiglas frame holding the grids was washed and then dried by a high intensity heat gun.

The test period for each subject was 15 minutes unless otherwise specified. The time the subjects spent on each side of the cage was recorded in seconds. The 15-minute session was divided into 10 equal periods of 90 seconds each, and most analyses were made on the last 6 minutes of the 15-minute session. The last 6 minutes was selected as the time interval representing asymptotic preference. The 15-minute period was chosen as a compromise between a longer period which might produce more stable preferences between the two aversive stimuli and a shorter period which would be less traumatic to the animal. Of the eight rats run for a given comparison of two stimuli, four rats received the standard (or reference) shock on the right side of the cage and four on the left side to balance out any position preferences that might occur.

Shock Sources

The shock sources used in this research are essentially those described in the introduction. For each major study to be reported, six to eight fixed impedance sources, a constant current AC source, and a constant current DC source were typically used. The fixed impedance sources ranged in value from 0 to 1200K ohms. Shock intensity was specified by the voltage of the output of the step-up transformer as shown in Fig. 1–2. A variable transformer was used to control the output voltage. The constant current AC source consisted of a step-up transformer set to 500 volts (Fig. 1–1), and current was measured by a vacuum tube voltmeter which read the voltage dropped across a precision 1K-ohm resistor in series with the rat. The constant current DC stimulator was a modernized version of Muenzinger and Walz's (1934) early circuit which has been previously described (Campbell & Teghtsoonian, 1958). It is also similar to a circuit described by Davidon and Boonin (1956). The source voltage was 500 volts DC.

The current levels for both AC and DC constant current sources were set with a load resistor across the output approximating the resistance of the rat at that current level. The load resistance values were derived from Fig. 1–3.

Detection, Aversion, Tetanization, and Death Thresholds

One of the pieces of information that has long been missing from the literature on electric shock is the range over which various types of shock stimuli can influence behavior. With a powerful stimulus like electric shock, the potential range of stimulation is from the detection threshold (i.e., the minimal intensity of shock that the animal can perceive) to the intensity of shock that is fatal. Another relevant parameter for electric shock stimulation is the aversion threshold, namely the minimal intensity of shock that an animal will avoid or escape. The purpose of our first series of experiments was to determine these functions for a wide range of fixed impedance sources and for two types of constant current sources.

Detection Thresholds

To determine the minimally detectable intensity of electric shock, weak electrical stimuli were used as conditioned stimuli in a standard avoidance conditioning experiment. The apparatus was a two-compartment shuttle box identical to that described by Brush and Knaff (1959) and the unconditioned stimulus was a 185 volt shock from a 150K-ohm fixed impedance source. The CS-US interval was 5 seconds. The experiment was divided into a training and a testing phase. During training a 40-volt 150K-ohm, supra-threshold shock was used as conditioned stimulus to train the animal in an avoidance task. Eight animals were given 5 days of training with 80 trials per day to assure that all animals reached a high level of avoidance responding. Following training, each rat had eight successive daily sessions, one for each shock source studied (0, 17.5, 35, 75, 150, 300, 600, and 1200K ohms). At each impedance, seven voltages (including 0) were used as conditioned stimuli, and were presented to the rats in a fixed random order for 80 trials. The first 30 trials of each 80-trial session were warm-up trials and were excluded from the data analysis. After a rat completed these eight test sessions, it was cycled back through the test schedule two more times (16 more daily sessions). Thus the total test schedule (24 days) can be split into three 8-day replications. The left panel of Fig. 1–4, showing one subject's data for the 150K-ohm source, is representative. Percent avoidance increases with CS intensity. This plot typifies the unfortunate fact that we had a good-sized "false alarm" rate (avoidance rate on the no-shock or 0-volt trials), which reflects a high rate of intertrial responding.

A few words concerning our definition of "threshold" are now in order. In view of the arbitrary nature of this concept, we have adopted a completely atheoretical interpretation. When dealing with percent performance indices, which start out at a chance level at 0 stimulus intensity and rise to a 100% level as stimulus intensity increases, the "threshold" will be defined as the behavioral halfway point between chance performance and 100% performance. As such, thresholds give a rough indication of where the major behavioral changes take place.

Consider the animal whose data appear in Fig. 1–4. As you can see,

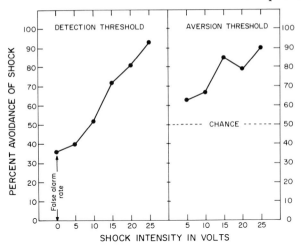

FIG. 1–4.   Sample detection and aversion threshold functions for the 150K-ohm source.

at the zero intensity end of the voltage scale this animal has an avoidance rate of 36%. Using percent avoidance as the behavioral index, our definition sets the threshold near 14 volts since at this level the index is about 68%, midway between 36% and 100%.

How does this method compare with the traditional threshold analysis? Suppose we want the voltage which is detected 50% of the time. The "false alarm" percentage at 0 volts is considered to be a "guessing percentage" which is used to "correct" the rest of the percentages (i.e., to partial out the guessing effect from data at voltages greater than 0). In this case, the resulting threshold occurs where the observed percentage is halfway between the false alarm rate and 100%, and the results are consistent with our atheoretical definition. We note in passing that this correction involves a rather strong theoretical assumption concerning the independence of the false alarm mechanism from the sensory detection mechanism (Luce et al., 1963, p. 126). Although this assumption is often contraindicated in human psychophysics, it may be an appropriate representation for the spontaneous responding occurring in the present experiment.

In practice, we used traditional psychophysical procedures to interpolate threshold values from our data. The present avoidance scores were corrected for false alarms by the formula

$$P_c = 100 \frac{P - b}{100 - b}$$

where P_c is the corrected percentage, P is the observed percentage, and b is the false alarm rate (percentage of avoidances with 0-volt CS). The corrected percentages were transformed to normal deviate scores which were then least squares fitted with straight lines. The lines were used to estimate the 50% threshold points. One difficulty with this method is that scores falling below the false alarm rate must be discarded; fortunately, this occurred only once in the present data.

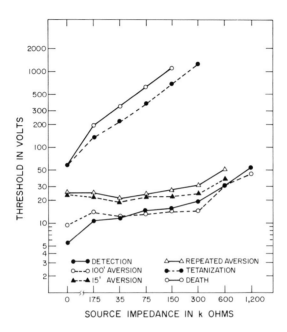

FIG. 1–5.   Detection, aversion, tetanization, and death thresholds as a function of source impedance.

The detection thresholds are shown in the lower line of Fig. 1–5. As might be expected, the minimally detected voltage increased as resistance in series with the rat increased. At 0 ohms (the constant voltage source) the detection threshold is only 5 volts and then rises gradually to 53 volts at 1200K ohms.

Aversion Thresholds

By aversion thresholds we mean the stimulus intensity which the animal avoids 75% of the time in our spatial preference apparatus when the alternative choice is a stimulus of 0 intensity. The apparatus is arranged so that when the animal stands on one side of the cage no shock is present, but when it is on the opposite side, a specified level of shock is switched on and stays on as long as the animal remains there.

When the electrical stimulus is not aversive, the animals spend approximately 50% of the time on both sides of the cage (when averaged over groups); but as the stimulus becomes more and more aversive, the animals spend proportionately more time on the nonshock side of the cage. This percentage approaches 100% as the shock intensity increases. The right-hand panel of Fig. 1–4 shows this relationship for the 150K-ohm fixed impedance source. Each point in this figure represents the mean percent preference of eight rats for the no-shock side over the shock side for the last 40 minutes of a single 100-minute session.

The figure illustrates one of the major problems associated with determining aversion thresholds. At subthreshold intensities, where shock does not compel a discrete preference, variability is high since animals typically settle on one side and stay there under conditions of low motivation. If five out of eight animals settle on one side and do not move from that side for the last 6 minutes, for example, the resulting preference is 62.5%. Hence, it is quite common for the variability to be high at low stimulus intensities.

Our general definition of threshold corresponds in this case to the shock intensity producing 75% preference, since 75% is halfway between the 0 intensity score (50%) and the maximum score (100%). Alternatively, one may imagine our procedure as correcting the observed preference scores for an *a priori* 50% response bias, since the rats cannot indicate a "no, it isn't aversive" judgment, but communicate such a judgment by randomly settling down on one side or the other ("guessing"). One may then use the correction procedure to estimate the intensity perceived as aversive 50% of the time. It turns out to correspond to an observed preference of 75%, in line with our interpretation.

Aversion thresholds determined by three procedures are shown in Fig. 1–5. In the first procedure we simply placed animals in our above-described preference apparatus and measured percent time spent on the nonshock side as a function of intensity for a 15-minute period and used the last 6 minutes as an estimate of asymptotic preference. As can be seen in Fig. 1–5, the aversion thresholds measured in this manner are relatively consistent across source impedances from 0K–300K, and are followed by a slight rise at the higher impedances.

On the basis of more recent data, we next inferred that the 15-minute preference data might not be asymptotic, and consequently we ran the same experiment using a 100-minute session. The sample data shown in Fig. 1–4 were obtained with this procedure. Here the last 40 minutes of the session were used to calculate the aversion thresholds. It is clear that the longer test period resulted in a much lower aversion threshold. Examination of the period-by-period scores (time spent on the nonshock side was recorded in 10-minute periods) showed no apparent decrease in threshold after the first 40–50 minutes. The preference data for the last 40 minutes of the 100-minute session were analyzed as described above, and the resulting thresholds are shown by the open circles–dashed line in Fig. 1–5. The aversion thresholds range from approximately 9 volts for the 0 ohm source to 44 volts at 1200K.

What is most striking about these data is that there is no appreciable difference between the detection and aversion thresholds. Assuming our detection thresholds are not biased upward, this result suggests that a rat will avoid any shock it is able to detect, no matter how small. It is not necessary to infer, however, that small detectable shocks cause pain since it is equally possible that the weak shocks produce a tingle or vibrating sensation that is qualitatively different from the pain produced by high shocks but is still aversive. This contrasts the situation with visual and auditory stimuli where there is a range of neutral intensities which are large enough to be detected by rats, yet not large enough to motivate escape or avoidance (e.g., Campbell, 1957).

Incidentally, we did not find any significant tendency for low intensities of shock to be reinforcing as has been occasionally reported (Harrington & Linder, 1962). We did, however, note occasional brief periods of apparent preference for mildly aversive shock levels during the middle portions of the 100-minute session. At shock levels producing 90–100% asymptotic avoidance of the shock side, the rats would typically develop a high level of preference for the nonshock side of the cage within the first 10 or 15 minutes, then after 30–60 minutes on the nonshock side many rats showed what appeared to be an active exploration of the shock side for as long as 10–15 minutes with repeated crossings from one side to the other. This period of active exploration was then followed by complete avoidance of the shock side. While these observations were casual at best, our conclusion is that no intensity of electrical stimulation is innately positively reinforcing and that any activity sustained in the presence of such stimulation is motivated by curiosity.

Returning to the measurement of aversion thresholds, we carried out a third procedure in which each subject was run repeatedly through all of the shock levels for one of the fixed impedance sources. For each source impedance, seven shock levels ranging from below to above threshold were selected, and each subject received the seven intensities in a random order for three successive replications all in a single daily session lasting approximately 5½ hours.

The 5½-hour session was organized as follows. The rat was placed in the apparatus for a 15-minute period with no shock present. Then one of the shock intensities from the random order was applied to the side of the cage occupied by the rat. The rat had to move to the opposite side of the cage and stay there to escape the shock. Fifteen minutes later the next intensity was presented in the same manner, and so on, so that the rat was tested with a new intensity every 15 minutes. Aversion thresholds were calculated on the basis of preference during the last 6 minutes of each 15-minute period. With this procedure percent preference for the no-shock side of the cage ranged from 0 to 100% rather than from approximately 50 to 100%. Accordingly, the aversion threshold was defined as the intensity of shock producing a 50% preference for the nonshock side of the cage. The aversion thresholds obtained in this manner are considerably higher than those obtained using the 100-minute session, but they are not appreciably different from those obtained using a single 15-minute session.

Just as in human psychophysics the method used to determine the aversion threshold exerts a strong influence on the threshold obtained. The extended session gives more sensitive results than the 15-minute session probably because competing exploratory responses, which would mask preference for the absence of shock, have more opportunity to habituate during the longer session. Individual results are harder to compare because of the basic procedural differences that were needed to extract meaningful thresholds from individual rats. We imagine that the exploratory activity level plays a role here also. The rats in the individual threshold experiment have generally settled down on one side for a nap when a new shock is turned on. These rats should be harder to budge than freshly introduced rats that have yet to commit themselves to one side or the other.

Tetanization and Death Thresholds

It goes without saying that the upper limits of usefulness of electric shock as a psychological stimulus are defined by the intensities of shock producing either tetanization or death. In fact, the investigation of these processes is one that should be undertaken only after serious consideration of the scientific value of the findings that may be obtained. In the present case we felt that the systematic determination of these functions would provide a quantitative guideline for future research in the field. In the absence of such information in the past, the research worker desiring to use the highest possible nonlethal shock had to determine, through pilot research, the upper limits of tolerance for his particular stimulator. The present research, since it covers all major types of electric shock stimulators, should eliminate the need for this redundant pilot work by individual investigators.

Tetanization and death thresholds were determined in a single experiment for a range of fixed impedance sources and for two constant current sources. The experiment was carried out in the same preference apparatus equipped with a Plexiglas lid rather than the usual aluminum lid so that the animal could be observed. For each shock source five to seven intensities of shock were used, ranging from a subtetanizing level to a level producing at least 75% mortality. The test period was the usual 15 minutes and shock was present on both sides of the cage.

An animal was scored as tetanized when completely immobilized and unable to release the stainless steel grids. Tetanization was characterized by active struggling to free the paws from the grids, followed by clonic grasping of the grids, which in turn was followed by extreme debilitation, coma, or death. Thresholds were defined as the point at which 50% of the animals tetanized or died.

The results are shown in Fig. 1–5. Except for the 0 ohm source there is a clear separation between the intensity of shock producing tetanization and the intensity producing death. At 0K ohms, tetanization and death probably occur at the same level because, as tetanization occurs, skin resistance is minimized and current flow maximized in the absence of any current-limiting resistor. At lethal shock levels the tissue resistance levels are well below 10K ohms (Campbell & Teghtsoonian, 1958). At the higher impedance sources (300K and up) tetanization and death thresholds were not determined because the voltages required exceeded the insulation properties of our scrambling and switching circuits.

In addition to the fixed impedance sources we also determined aversion, tetanization, and death thresholds for several constant current sources. The results of the research to date are shown in Table 1–1.

TABLE 1–1. *Aversion, Tetanization, and Death Thresholds for the Constant Current Sources*

Behavioral Measure	Type of Source	
	Constant Current AC	Constant Current DC
Aversion Threshold	0.041	0.015
Tetanization Threshold	5.5 ma.	6.1
Death Threshold	7.5 ma.	15.8

Equal-Aversion Functions

Ever since the unveiling of shock as a motivating stimulus, experimental psychologists have searched for the optimal shock source to adopt as a standard for their work. The goal was a source that could produce stimuli of nearly constant discomfort for all subjects under all conditions. Meanwhile, a great proliferation of different types of shockers was viewed as an unpleasant but temporary phase preceding the discovery of this ideal source.

The search was usually initiated by posing the question, "What aspect of electric shock—voltage, power, or current—determines the degree of pain experienced by the animal?" Only one of these aspects can be held constant at any given time, since when one is constant all the others will vary with changes in the animal's contact with the grids.

The problem of controlling shock was thus reduced to that of finding the underlying physical correlate of shock-induced pain, and then designing a source that would hold it constant.

It now appears that the search for *the* underlying physical parameter was a blind alley. It seems likely that several dimensions of electric shock influence the aversiveness of a shock stimulus, and that no one source will ever constitute the "perfect" source. In line with this, we will offer our own formulation of the "variability" problem in the next section. Looking ahead a little bit, we shall show that, while there is no perfect source, there are several *optimal* sources. It thus appears that the proliferation of shock sources is a permanent, rather than temporary, feature of this field. The only alternative is a rather arbitrary adoption of one of the optimal sources by most experimenters.

Therefore, the main task in measuring and controlling shock stimuli is the construction of a common scale of aversiveness for all sources. With such a scale it will no longer be a matter of concern that different investigators use different sources (so long as they use optimal sources), since it will be possible to translate back and forth between sources.

We have used the preference technique described earlier to construct a common scale of shock aversiveness. Two shock stimuli will be called *equal in aversiveness* (or equally aversive) when rats spend 50% of their time on either side of a preference cage programmed to compare the two stimuli. In practice, several comparisons were made and the 50% point was estimated by interpolation. This will be illustrated by means of the following example. What current from a constant current AC source is equal in aversiveness to a 115-volt shock from a 150K-ohm fixed impedance source? To answer this, the 115-volt shock was compared in the preference situation with shocks of .35, .40, .45, .50, .55, and .60 ma. from the constant current source. The results are shown in Fig. 1–6. Each point represents the behavior of the eight rats that were given a choice between the 115-volt, 150K-ohm shock and the constant current shock listed directly under the point on the abscissa; the ordinate value of the point is the mean percentage of time the eight rats spent on the 115-volt, 150K-ohm shock side, during the last 6 minutes of the 15-minute period. As the intensity of the constant current shock increases, rats spend more of their time on the 150K-ohm shock side. The curve describing this change resembles the S-shaped curves commonly encountered with psychophysical data. To determine the point at which the two stimuli were equally aversive, the preference scores were first transformed to normal deviate scores in order to eliminate most of the curvature. The transformed points were then least squares fitted with a straight line, and the line was used to interpolate the current level at which the preference is 50%. Using this procedure, we estimate that a .51-ma. shock from the constant current source is equally aversive with the 115-volt, 150K-ohm shock.

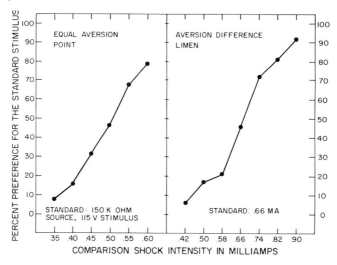

FIG. 1–6.   Sample equal aversion and aversion difference limen plots. The left panel shows an equal aversion plot comparing the constant current AC source with the 115-volt reference level (150K-ohm source). The right panel shows an aversion difference limen plot for the AC constant current source, where the standard intensity is 0.66 ma.

Equal-aversion comparisons were made for eight different shock sources, six fixed impedance sources (0, 35, 75, 150, 300, and 600K ohm), an AC constant current source, and a DC constant current source. The source voltage for both constant current sources was 500 volts.

The 150K-ohm fixed impedance source was chosen as a "reference" shock source against which the seven other sources were compared. This source was selected on the basis of previously reported research (Campbell & Teghtsoonian, 1958) which indicated that it had several desirable features as a shock source. Five intensities (45, 72, 115, 185, and 300 volts) of the 150K-ohm source were selected as reference intensities. These intensities are approximately equidistant on a log-voltage scale, and they range from near the aversion threshold to near the tetanization threshold (see Fig. 1–5).

The plan for the equal-aversion experiment was to determine for each of the seven other sources the intensity of shock (measured as free-load voltage for the fixed impedance sources or as current flow for the constant current sources) that was equal in aversiveness to each of the five reference levels of the 150K-ohm source. Each estimate involved an interpolation from the results of five to seven comparisons (as in Fig. 1–6). In practice, the 0 ohm source was compared with the 150K-ohm source only for the reference intensities of 45, 72, and 115 volts because of the premature upper limit to the voltages which may safely be used with the 0 ohm source. Above this limit 0 ohm shocks are initially below tetanization but over time drift up to tetanization by means of the positive feedback mechanism described previously. We also were not able to compare the 600K-ohm source with the 300-volt reference intensity because the voltages needed to produce equal preference exceeded the capacity of the present equipment.

In summary, the plan of the equal-aversion experiment was to determine for each of seven other sources the intensity of shock that was equal in aversiveness to each of the five levels of the 150K-ohm reference source. This design parallels the procedure used by Fletcher and Munson (1937) in developing equal loudness contours for different frequencies of sound in which they had subjects match the loudness of a wide range of frequencies to a 1000-hz. reference tone.

The results for the fixed impedance sources are shown in Fig. 1–7. Using this plot one may locate a reference voltage from the 150K-ohm source, V_{150} and a particular source impedance Z on the bottom two axes, then read up the vertical axis to find the equally aversive voltage, V_Z, from a fixed impedance source of impedance Z (impedances are expressed in units of 1K ohm). For example, let us use this plot to determine the voltage from the 600K-ohm source which is equal in aversiveness to 115 volts from the reference source. First, we find the intersection of $Z = 600K$ ohm and $V_{150} = 115v$ on the bottom plane, and then we read up to the appropriate data point. At this point we are in line with about $V_Z = 350v$ on the vertical axis. Thus, about 350 volts from the 600K-ohm source is equivalent to 115 volts from the reference source.

The smooth surface shown in Fig. 1–7 was fitted to the data according to the following considerations. It had been noted that V_Z was a nearly linear function of V_{150} provided Z was held constant. Similarly, V_Z appeared to be a nearly linear function of Z provided V_{150} was held constant. The smooth surface having these properties is a paraboloid:

$$V_Z = \alpha + \beta V_{150} + aZ + bZV_{150}$$

where α, β, a, and b are constants.

Figure 1–7 shows the actual data points obtained when the 150K-ohm source was compared to itself; however, we ignored these points when we fitted the paraboloid surface, using instead our *a priori* knowledge that $V_Z = V_{150}$ when $Z = 150K$ ohms. How does this affect the form of the paraboloid equation? Substituting V_{150} for V_Z and 150 for Z in the equation yields

$$(\alpha + 150a) + (\beta + 150b - 1)V_{150} = 0$$

This relation can be satisfied for all values of V_{150} only by setting the coefficients equal to zero:

$$\alpha + 150a = 0$$
$$\beta + 150b - 1 = 0$$

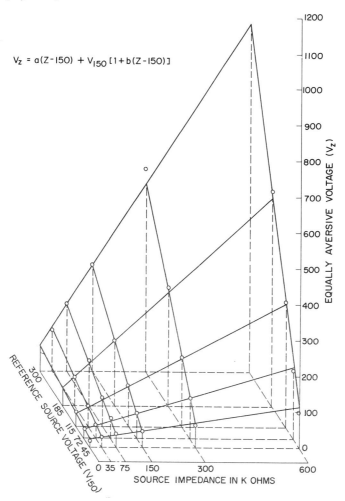

$$V_Z = a(Z-150) + V_{150}[1+b(Z-150)]$$

FIG. 1–7.   Equal aversion surface for the fixed impedance sources. The surface shown is the fitted function, and the points are the actual data obtained.

Using these constraints to eliminate α and β from the general paraboloid equation, we get

$$V_Z = a(Z - 150) + V_{150}[1 + b(Z - 150)] \qquad (1)$$

A modified method of least squares was used to fit equation 1 to the data of Figure 1–7. Consider a particular observed value of V_Z which we shall call $V_{Z,o}$, and the corresponding value predicted by the surface, $V_{Z,P}$. The deviation $V_{Z,P} - V_{Z,o}$ is a poor index or error since, for example, a 10-volt error would be negligible if $V_{Z,o}$ were 300 volts, but would be quite significant if $V_{Z,o}$ were 20 volts. Therefore, instead of minimizing the summed squares of the deviations, we selected parameters a and b to minimize the summed squares of the proportional deviations,

$$\frac{V_{z,\,o}}{V_{z,\,p} - V_{z,\,o}}.$$

These parameters are

$$a = -.0872$$
$$b = .00530$$

yielding an average proportional deviation of about .078 or 7.8% (by "average" is meant the root-mean-square, which in this case corresponds to the square root of the mean of the squared proportional deviations).

We may derive from equation 1 a general formula giving the conditions when shocks from two fixed impedance sources are equally aversive. This will be true when the value of

$$\frac{V_z + .0872\,(Z - 150)}{1 \; + .0053\,(Z - 150)}$$

is the same for both sources.

Equal-aversion points for the AC and DC constant current sources are shown in Fig. 1–8 where both the abscissa (150K-ohm reference voltage) and the ordinate (equally aversive current) have log spacing. Straight lines were fitted to log-log plots of these variables, yielding the corresponding power functions:

$$I = .000268(V_{150})^{1.56} \tag{2a}$$

for the AC source, and

$$I = .000183(V_{150})^{1.70} \tag{2b}$$

for the DC source. Here currents are expressed in units of 1 ma.

A given current from the DC constant current source appears to be somewhat less aversive than the same current from the AC constant current source. In terms of Fig. 1–8, it takes more current from the DC source than from the AC source to match a given reference voltage from the 150K-ohm source.

A relevant question at this point is whether or not the preferences measured in our apparatus have the property of transitivity. This is the property that, whenever rats prefer A over B, and they prefer B over C, then they also prefer A over C. We made implicit use of this property in deriving the last condition for equally aversive shocks from any two fixed impedance sources since we did not make all possible comparisons but only compared each source with the 150K-ohm source. Transitivity appears to hold when shocks A, B, and C are delivered by the same source, but has not been empirically tested for the case when A, B, and C are produced by different sources.

Another question, of perhaps greater relevance, deals with temporal

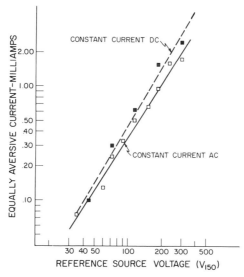

FIG. 1-8.   Equal aversion functions relating the AC and DC constant current sources to the 150K-ohm reference source.

changes in aversiveness with the different sources. Is it possible that our equal aversion function applies only to the last 6 minutes of a 15-minute test period? If that were so, the generality of findings would be greatly restricted. Fortunately, an examination of the ten consecutive 90-second periods reveals that the equal aversion points are remarkably constant over time. Fig. 1–9 shows a period-by-period analysis of the equal aversion points for the 150K-ohm source (the reference source compared with it-self). Quite clearly, the estimates settle down almost immediately and tightly cluster about a central value. All of the sources were compared in this manner by computer analysis and no appreciable time changes were found for any source.

A related question concerns the accuracy of the equal aversion esti-mates. Obviously the greater the accuracy of these estimates, the greater our confidence in the overall equal-aversion functions. Fortunately a simple technique of estimating the accuracy of the equal-aversion esti-mates can be derived from the research on the aversion difference limens to be reported in a forthcoming section. In that research each shock source was compared with itself to determine the change in intensity producing 75 and 25% preference respectively. Accuracy of the equal-aversion preference technique can be estimated from these functions by interpolating the 50% point exactly as we would in an equal-aversion plot. In this case it is known where the 50% point should occur since the same source provides both the standard and comparison shocks. Rats should spend 50% of their time on either side when the comparison level equals the standard level.

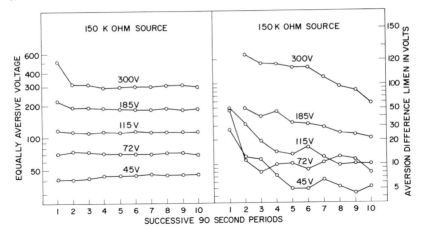

FIG. 1–9.   Equal aversion levels (left panel) and aversion difference limens (right panel) as a function of 90-second periods during the 15-minute period. (The first period estimates of the difference limens for 185 volts and 300 volts were too large to fit on the figure.)

Fifty-two comparisons of shock sources with themselves are reported in the aversion difference limen section. Of the 52 error estimates obtained, 26 were less than 2.5%, 14 were between 2.5% and 5%, 9 were between 5% and 10%, and the remaining 3 were each about 20%. When an *a priori* criterion exists, the equal-aversion technique proves to be quite accurate.

In summary, the equal-aversion equations may be listed as follows:

1. Translation of the reference source into another fixed impedance source.

$$V_Z = [1 + .00530 \, (Z - 150)] \, V_{150} - .0872 \, (Z - 150)$$

2. Translation of the reference source into the constant current AC source.

$$I = .000268 \, (V_{150})^{1.56}$$

3. Translation of the reference source into the constant current DC source.

$$I = .000183 \, (V_{150})^{1.70}$$

These equal-aversion functions give us a means of comparing the relative aversiveness of electrical stimulation produced by all of the major classes of shock generators. For the first time it will be possible to compare the work of different investigators using any of the above-described shock sources. There are naturally some limitations to the extent to which the various types of shock sources can be interchanged, since there are considerable differences in variability between some shock sources as we will show subsequently. In addition, we have not systematically investigated the effect of source voltage in constant current sources (which influences the current density parameter), which therefore restricts the comparison between fixed impedance sources and constant current sources to constant current stimulators with source voltages in the neighborhood of 500 volts (e.g., 350–650 volts).

A Mathematical Model for the Equal-Aversion Results

The orderliness of the preceding data suggests that the factors determining the severity of the shock stimulus might be further explicated by means of a mathematical model. To this end we constructed a preliminary model to describe the equal-aversion data. Our intent was to determine the feasibility of the general approach rather than to construct a detailed theoretical structure.

The first assumption of the model is that the electrical parameters—current, voltage, and skin resistance—remain constant over time. This is clearly an oversimplification since the entire problem of controlling shock stimuli stems from the inherent variability of these parameters. Our second assumption is that the aversiveness of shock stimulation is proportional to the current flowing through the rat. This assumption is based on the finding reported in the next section that the variability in aversiveness decreases the more fixed impedance sources approximate constant current sources. The third assumption states that the resistance of the rat decreases as shock current increases, an assumption suggested by the data presented in Fig. 1–3.

Let us apply the assumptions to a group of equally aversive shocks from fixed impedance sources. By the second assumption, the currents induced by the equally aversive shocks must all be the same, and therefore, by the third assumption, the skin resistance of rats subjected to these shocks must be the same. In other words, current, I, and skin resistance, r, are invariant over all the shocks in the group. Therefore, the voltage of a particular shock in the group of equally aversive shocks is a linear function of the impedance of the source delivering the shock, in accordance with Ohm's Law:

$$V_z = IZ + Ir$$

where Z is the impedance, V_z the voltage, and I and Ir may be regarded as constant coefficients. These coefficients may be estimated by fitting a straight line to the above equation, using the empirically derived values of V_Z. We thus obtain estimates of the values of I and r appropriate to the group of equally aversive shocks under consideration. These estimates may then be compared to Campbell and Teghtsoonian's empirical determination of r and I in order to evaluate the adequacy of the model.

We performed the above analysis for the five groups of equally aversive shocks from fixed impedance sources. Straight lines were fitted in order to minimize the sum of the squared proportional deviations of the predicted from the observed values of V_Z. The average percent error was 6.7%, slightly lower than the 7.8% obtained with the fitted paraboloid surface of Fig. 1–7.

The resulting values for r and I have been plotted as solid circles in the left panel of Fig. 1–10. The Campbell and Teghtsoonian resistance data (Fig. 1–3) have been replotted in the same panel for comparison (the 150K-ohm currents were derived from the specified voltages and measured resistances by means of Ohm's Law). For a given current, the resistance predicted by the model fall above those measured although the

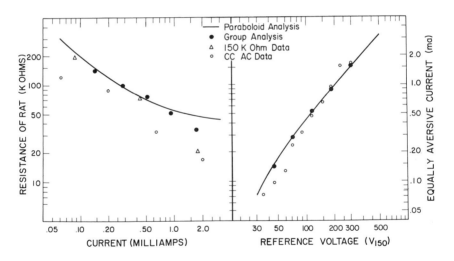

FIG. 1–10.   Comparison of model predictions to data. Left panel: Resistance of the rat as a function of current. Right panel: Equally aversive AC constant current source level as a function of reference voltage.

trends are similar. It is extremely difficult to say where the error lies, since any of the model's assumptions can be called into question. The most flagrant assumption is the one that brushes aside the problem of statistical fluctuations. It is worth noting that this same problem confounds the interpretation of Campbell and Teghtsoonian's data in the present context, since their measured resistance values were averaged across time (within a given rat) with medians, then across rats with arithmetic means. Different averaging techniques could have produced different results. The problem is made acute by the asymmetry of the resistance distribution, which has a long tail on the high side. In the light of all these difficulties, the model's prediction seems close enough to motivate further investigations along these lines.

The model may also be checked against the equal-aversion data for the constant current AC source. For example, the model predicts that a shock of 115 volts from the reference source causes a current flow of .52 ma. Therefore a .52 ma. shock from the constant current AC source should be equivalent to the 115-volt standard source shock. The value measured in the equal-aversion experiment was .49 ma. Comparisons of this type are shown as solid circles in the right panel of Fig. 1–10. Again, the model is in line with the data, considering the oversimplification involved.

How does the present approach relate to the parabaloid surface in Fig. 1–7? It can be shown that the model will predict this surface if the third assumption is augmented by the equation

$$r = \frac{16.5}{I} + 38.8$$

which gives the rats' resistance (K ohms) as a function of current (ma.). This equation has been drawn as a smooth curve in the left panel of Fig. 1–10. The corresponding prediction for the constant current AC source equal-aversion data is given by

$$I = .00530 \, V_{150} - .0872$$

which appears as a smooth curve in the right panel of the same figure. It will be noted that these equations, while quite realistic within the range of stimuli studied ($45 \leqq V_{150} \leqq 300$; $.1 \leqq I \leqq 2$), break down outside the range. For example, the resistance equation predicts infinite resistance for $I = 0$. This simply means that the parabaloid formula should only be applied to stimuli falling in the range covered by the equal-aversion experiment.

We conclude that our simple model is worth refining. The most obvious refinement would involve allowing the electrical quantities to vary. This will raise two interesting problems. First, how does the rat temporally integrate its momentary impressions of shock discomfort in order to arrive at an overall estimate of aversiveness? Put in more objective language, what sort of averaging operation should be applied to the distribution of momentary current values in order to best predict the aversiveness of a shock stimulus? This is obviously an empirical question.

The second problem concerns the striking changes in the rat's resistance caused by shock. What is the temporal structure of these changes—are they rapid or slow? There is indication that these changes are, for all practical purposes, instantaneous (Gibson, 1965).

Another refinement would involve the assumption that current is the physical correlate of aversiveness. Our aversion difference limen results (see the following section) suggest that current is a good predictor of aversiveness, and a better one than voltage. However, a contact surface area variable probably should be added to current in order to account for current density effects. This will be a complicated undertaking since contact area depends on the animal's locomotion pattern, which depends in turn on shock intensity (and may depend on the type of source employed).

A further improvement in the model might be made by allowing the rat's impedance to have a reactive (nonresistive) component. Phase shift measurements made in the Princeton Laboratory with 60-hz. AC shocks indicate that the rat's impedance acts like a resistor and a small capacitor wired in parallel. Unlike the resistor, which gets smaller as shock increases, this capacitor remains at a constant value in the neighborhood of .01 micro-farads. This finding is probably related to Gibson's observation that the resistance of human skin and the current flowing through it adjust instantaneously to sudden pulses of constant current shock, while the voltage across the skin requires on the order of a millisecond to stabilize (Gibson, 1965). Such a voltage lag suggests the presence of a capacitative component.

Aversion Difference Limens

In a preceding section we presented a method of relating the majority of different types of shock stimuli to a common scale of aversiveness. This scale, however, provides no quantitative indication of the differences in variability inherent in the various types of sources. That differences in variability do exist between the shock sources is documented by the positive feedback action of the constant voltage (0 ohm) source, where in the course of a single session an initially subtetanizing shock ultimately causes tetanization and death. The aim of the following section is to compare experimentally the variability in aversiveness produced by the previously described shock sources.

While there are a variety of ways one could assess stimulus variability, the classic measure in psychophysics has been the difference limen or just noticeable difference. By analogy, we shall define the aversion difference limen (ADL) or the just aversive difference (JAD) as the difference in intensity between two aversive stimuli when one of them is preferred over the other 75% of the time.

The procedure for determining ADL's was essentially the same as that used in the equal-aversion study, except that here different intensities of each source were compared with each other. For each shock source several "standard" intensities covering the usable range of stimulation were selected, and five to seven "comparison" stimuli were paired with each standard in the spatial preference apparatus. To illustrate, the ADL for a .66 ma., constant current stimulus was determined by comparing the "standard" stimulus (.66 ma.) with .42, .50, .58, .66, .74, .82, and .90 ma. shocks from the same source. The results are shown in Fig. 1–6. Each point shows the behavior of the eight rats given a choice between the standard (.66 ma.) shock and the comparison shock listed under the point on the abscissa. The ordinate of the point is the mean percent preference of the eight rats for the standard shock during the last 6 minutes of the 15-minute period. A straight line was least squares fitted to normal deviate scores, and used to interpolate the current levels producing 25% and 75% preference. We then took half the difference between these currents as the estimate of the ADL. This procedure is analogous to that used in human psychophysics where the DL is defined as one half of the distance between the upper and lower limens (Guilford, 1954, Torgerson, 1958).

We determined ADL's for several standard intensities of shock for each of six different shock sources. Each estimate involved five to seven comparisons of neighboring intensities with the standard intensity (as in Fig. 1–6). Figure 1–11 gives the results. The left panel shows the aversion difference limen functions in volts for four fixed impedance sources (0, 35, 150, and 600K ohms). For any one source, the ADL's are generally an increasing function of standard shock intensity. The right-hand panel of Fig. 1–11 presents the ADL's for the constant current sources, which also increase as a function of standard stimulus intensity.

Comparison of the relative variability of the different sources is not easy with this plot, however, because the aversion difference limens are

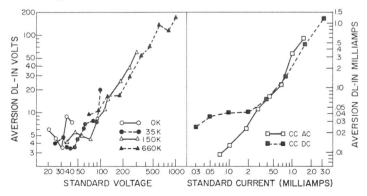

FIG. 1–11.   Aversion difference limens for the fixed impedance sources (left panel) and the constant current sources (right panel).

not plotted on a common behavioral scale. Accordingly, to interrelate the different AC sources, we transformed all of the aversion difference limens and standard shock intensities into equivalent current units. The ADL's were transformed by converting the interpolated 25% and 75% intensities into equivalent currents and setting the ADL's equal to half the difference between the equivalent 25% and 75% currents. Voltages from the 150K-ohm source were transformed into currents by equation 2a. Voltages from the other fixed impedance sources were first converted to equally aversive 150K-ohm source voltages by equation 1, and then transformed into currents by equation 2a.

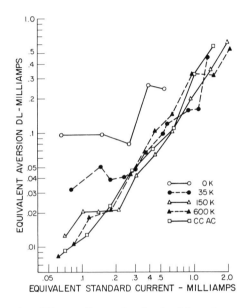

FIG. 1–12.   Aversion difference limens for the fixed impedance and constant current AC sources when related to a common scale (AC milliamps).

The transformed ADL's are shown in Fig. 1–12 which plots the ADL's and standard intensities for all of the AC sources in terms of equivalent current. For example, the equivalent current for the 35K, 100-volt standard level is 1.3 ma. and the ADL is .46 ma. (A careful comparison of Figs. 1–11 and 1–12 reveals that the transformed ADL's are not always monotonically related to the original ADL's. These departures from monotonicity always involve original ADL's that are close together in value, and are a consequence of the nonlinearity of the transformations required to convert voltages to equivalent currents.)

This transformation procedure relates the ADL data to a common scale via a behavioral preference test. The transformed ADL's appear to be the same for all the shock stimuli, except that the 35K-ohm ADL's are larger below .3 ma., and all the 0 ohm ADL's are larger. For example, 35 volts from the constant voltage source (0 impedance) is equivalent to .4 ma. from the AC constant current source. Yet the equivalent ADL's for these equally aversive shocks are .25 ma. for the constant voltage source and .07 ma. for the constant current source. Therefore, shock from the constant voltage source is more variable than the equivalent constant current shock in the sense that it must undergo a larger displacement on the equivalent current scale to produce the same discriminable difference.

Similarly, the low level shocks from the 35K-ohm source, while less variable than the equivalent constant voltage shocks, are more variable than the equivalent shocks from the 150K-ohm, 600K-ohm, or AC constant current sources. The ADL's for the constant current DC source are also large at low shock intensities, but here the cause is probably different. With all DC sources the capacitance inherent in the shock source, scrambler, leads, and shock grids is charged to the maximum plate voltage potential whenever the rat is on safe grids and discharged when the rat returns to live grids (cf. Campbell & Teghtsoonian, 1958). It is likely that this characteristic remains constant at low shock levels, accounting for the large and relatively constant ADL's in that region. Aside from these exceptions, all other equally aversive shocks display about the same variability as measured by the difference limens.

Another aspect of the aversion difference limen which is of considerable importance is the manner in which it changes over the course of the 15-minute period. It was previously shown that the equal-aversion functions were virtually constant throughout the 15-minute test period. This is not the case for the ADL's, which are shown in the right-hand panel of Fig. 1–9. Here it is immediately apparent that asymptotic preference levels are not rapidly attained, and, in fact, the ADL's at high intensities are still falling at the end of the session. In terms of the normal deviate plots used to interpolate the aversion difference limens this means: (1) that the fitted line almost always crosses 0 (corresponding to 50%) in the same place throughout the session, and (2) that the slope of the line (which determines the ADL) increases over time. Why does it take so long for the high intensity ADL's to reach an asymptote? First, the higher intensity shocks may be more difficult to discriminate. Second, the high level shocks tend to interfere with muscular coordination, and it may take some time for a rat to learn how to remain on what it already perceives as the less painful side. In any event it is clear that future research should examine the ADL functions over longer time periods.

At this juncture some discussion of the aversion difference limen and its implications for the analyses of different types of shock sources is in order. In human psychophysics the difference limen or just noticeable difference is generally taken as an index of how well subjects can discriminate changes in a given stimulus dimension. In the typical experiment every effort is made to minimize variations in the stimulus reaching the receptor; and the subject is asked to judge whether the two stimuli are the same or different on some precisely specificable physical continuum. Errors in the subject's judgments are then taken to reflect limitations in sensory capacity and/or momentary variations in sensory sensitivity. In our aversion threshold and aversion difference limen experiments the situation is quite different because we are unable to control or specify the moment to moment variability in the physical stimulus. Thus in our aversion-measuring apparatus there are two sources of perceived stimulus variability. One is the random fluctuation in sensory sensitivity that is typical of all sensory modalities, and the other is the variation in intensity of the physical stimulus reaching the receptor produced by movement of the animal on the grid floor, the scrambler, and other apparatus characteristics. The latter are undoubtedly the larger source of perceived variability.

It follows from this analysis that the aversion difference limens are in fact primarily a measure of the variability of the stimulus reaching the receptor rather than a measure of "noise" in the sensory system. Hence, we can use the aversive difference limens as one criterion for evaluating the precision with which different types of shock sources stimulate pain receptors in the rats' paws. The larger the ADL, the greater the variability in the dimension of the shock stimulus responsible for producing pain. Applying this reasoning to the problem of determining optimal shock stimulators for the rat and other mammals, it follows that the most desirable sources are ones in which the ADL values are smallest.

Summation of Just Aversive Differences

A Simple Index of Shock Source Variability

In pursuing the parallels between human psychophysics and the present research, it follows that the contributions of Fechner to the measurement of sensation should be considered next. As has just been demonstrated, the just aversive difference cannot be considered a measure of differential receptor sensitivity to aversive stimulation, and hence to use the JAD as a unit of aversiveness in a Fechnerian scale, which in itself has not had wide acceptance as a measure of sensation, is totally unjustified. Yet this same basic procedure of integrating differences can be adapted to form an index of the desirability of various types of shock sources.

At an intuitive level the optimal shock source is one which has the greatest number of discriminable differences in aversiveness. Hence we would like to propose an index for assessing the overall desirability of shock sources based on the Fechnerian principle of integrating JAD's. The index simply states that the desirability of a source is directly proportional to the number of just aversive differences between the aversion and tetanization thresholds—the useful range for any source. The procedure for determining the number of JAD's is essentially the integration technique proposed by Fechner, but in practice we used the graphical accumulation method recommended by Luce and Edwards (1958).

Turning to the present research, the number of JAD's between the aversion and tetanization thresholds was determined for all sources by first fitting a smooth curve to the ADL data by eye and then marking off successive JAD's. For convenience we used the transformed ADL plots to accumulate JAD's and assumed a common regression line for all sources at the higher intensities. The results with this procedure are virtually identical with those obtained from the original ADL plots, the advantage of the transformed plots being that the combined data give a more reliable estimate of the general form of the functions involved.

Figure 1–13 shows the number of just aversive differences lying between the aversion and tetanization thresholds for all sources used in the present study except the constant current DC source. It is clearly evident that the number of JAD's increases as source impedance increases. Moreover it is apparent that the function becomes asymptotic at approximately 150K ohms. Therefore, judged by this criterion, the constant

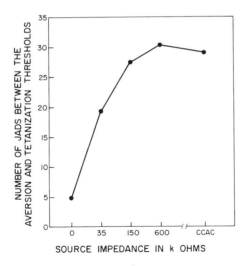

FIG. 1–13.   Number of just aversive differences between the aversion and tetanization thresholds as a function of source impedance.

current sources and the fixed impedance sources of 150 K ohms or greater all offer equally precise control of the shock stimulus, each having approximately 30 JAD's within its useful range.

When these findings are compared with an earlier study (Campbell, 1956) it is evident that the number of JAD's obtained for the 150K-ohm fixed impedance source is approximately double that previously reported. The primary difference between the two studies was the design of the cage and the use of a scrambler in the present study. Both changes increased the proportion of time the subject was exposed to the shock stimulus and decreased the possibility of the subject acquiring responses to reduce or eliminate shock.

This criterion for evaluating the desirability of different types of shock sources should always be considered in the context of the other characteristics which may make the source unsuitable for some specific purpose or within some specified range of intensities. The constant current DC source is a case in point. At low shock intensities the aversion difference limens for that source are disproportionately large, suggesting that it is not suitable for use in that range. For this reason we did not include the constant current source in the figure portraying the number of JAD's between the aversion and tetanization thresholds.

Transsituational Generality of the Equal-Aversion Functions

A major question stemming from the preceding research concerns the extent to which equal aversiveness, as defined by preference, predicts equal performance in other experimental settings. If the above-described equal-aversion functions are to be useful tools in interrelating different types of shock, they should extend to a majority of behavioral techniques. Previous comparisons between shock sources, as noted in the introduction, have focused on the varying effects different types of shock stimuli have on behavior, particularly on the tendency to produce crouching with constant current sources. No doubt these behaviors still occur at some intensities of some shock sources, but no comparisons of different sources have ever been made at equally aversive levels of stimulation.

We now report three experiments which were addressed to this problem. The shock apparatus used in these studies was of the same general design as that employed in the measurement investigations.

In the first experiment (Masterson, 1965) rats were trained to traverse a 30-inch runway to avoid shock of several different equally aversive intensities from either a 35K-, 150K-, or 600K-ohm fixed impedance source. Each rat received 30 trials separated by a 40-second intertrial interval. The CS was the opening of the start box door and a 70-db

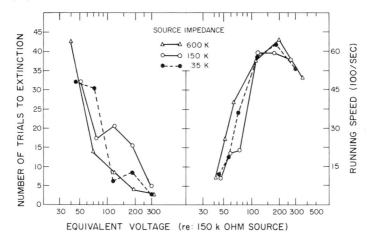

FIG. 1–14.   Left panel: Effect of equally aversive shock punishments on resistance to extinction of an avoidance response. Right panel: Asymptotic running speeds of animals trained in an avoidance-conditioning task using equally aversive shock stimuli.

clicking sound. The CS-US interval was 5 seconds, and the CS terminated when the subject reached the goal box.

The running speeds are shown in the right panel of Fig. 1–14 for the last five trials. Separate performance vs. shock voltage curves have been plotted for each of the three shock sources. The abscissa gives the measured shock voltage for the 150K-ohm source, or the equally aversive 150K-ohm voltage for the 35K- and 600K-ohm sources (determined from equation 1). Consequently, equally aversive shocks from the three sources should appear directly over one another on the curves. In light of this, you will immediately note that our shock stimuli are grouped in six clumps of three *nearly* (but not exactly) equally aversive shocks. This is because our present equal-aversion formula (equation 1) is an improved version of the one available at the time this experiment was performed. For purposes of analysis we shall pretend the three shocks in each clump are exactly equivalent. Returning to Fig. 1–14, it is apparent that the curves for the three sources are in close agreement, and an analysis of variance (equivalent shock voltage × shock source) confirms this evaluation.

In the second validation experiment rats were punished by various shock stimuli in order to facilitate the extinction of a shuttle response. In the first phase of the experiment rats learned a standard shock-avoidance problem in a two-compartment shuttle box (Brush & Knaff, 1959). Training extended until a rat made four successive avoidances (animals which did not reach this criterion in 50 trials were omitted from the experiment). The CS was a clicking noise plus the activation of a light in the compartment occupied by the rat, and the US was a 185-volt shock from the 150K-ohm source. The CS-US interval was five seconds. Following this standard training procedure each rat received 80 extinction trials where the shuttle response was punished by a 0.15-seconds shock of different equally aversive intensities from either the 35K-, 150K-, or 600K-ohm source. Both phases of the experiment, acquisition and extinction-punishment, occupied a single session in which trials were spaced by a 30-second variable interval.

The number of "avoidance" responses (latency less than 5 seconds) made during extinction are recorded in the left panel of Fig. 1–14. This plot is similar to the other panel, with separate performance vs. equivalent voltage curves for each shock source (again one may note that the shocks are grouped in clumps of three nearly equivalent intensities). The only visible trend is simply that the more aversive shocks are more effective punishments. An analysis of variance confirms this impression.

In a final experiment we measured the amount of activity elicited by several intensities of shock from the 35K-, 150K-, 300K-, and 600K-ohm fixed impedance sources and both constant current sources. The 0K-ohm source was not included because of the extreme variability of that source.

The apparatus was the same as that used in the previous preference studies, but it was wired so that the shock intensity did not change as the subject moved from side to side in the cage. Instead of recording preference, we recorded the total number of crossings elicited during 15 minutes of unescapable shock. Some counts were also recorded when the subject leaped into the air and shook the tilting floor.

The shock levels for each source were selected before the equal-aversion experiment was completed and analyzed, hence the shocks were not equally spaced along a common continuum of aversiveness. This experiment is essentially a replication and an extension of a previous study (Campbell & Teghtsoonian, 1958).

To compare the effects of different intensities of different shock sources on spontaneous activity, the various voltages and current levels used were transformed to a common scale. Fixed impedance source voltages were transformed to reference source voltages (equation 1) and then to equally aversive current levels (equation 2a). Constant current DC current levels were also transformed to equally aversive AC current levels. For illustrative purposes both the equally aversive current scale and the fixed impedance reference source scale are shown in Fig. 1–15. Here it is quite clear that the activity elicited by equally aversive shocks is remarkably constant. Shocks that were found to be equally aversive using preference as the criterion of equality also produce approximately equal amounts of activity. At low and intermediate shock intensities the similarity of the functions is striking, but at the highest intensities some divergence is apparent. This is to be expected since variance increases as a function of shock intensity and only eight subjects were run per group. There is also a tendency for some subjects to tetanize partially at the higher levels accounting for the inflection in some functions.

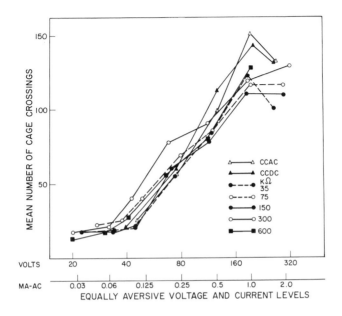

FIG. 1–15. Amount of activity elicited by three fixed impedance sources and two constant current sources as a function of shock intensity. All shock intensities were transformed to a common scale (equation 1). Also shown for comparison purposes is the equally aversive constant current AC scale.

One striking feature of the data shown in Fig. 1–15 is the extent to which they differ from the activity functions previously reported in the Campbell and Teghtsoonian paper. An attempt was made in that paper to plot the activity on a common scale by expressing shock intensity as a ratio of the behavioral threshold intensities. For convenience these ratios were expressed as decibels, paralleling the procedure in human psychophysics. When activity is plotted in this fashion, activity for a 150K-ohm source increases linearly as a function of intensity, but the constant current AC and DC sources show either no increment or a decrement in activity at low shock intensities. Thus intensities that are equal on a decibel scale, with the aversion threshold as a reference level, do not produce equal increments in activity. Whereas when behavioral preference is used as the criterion for developing a common scale, equally aversive shock intensities produce equal amounts of activity.

In summary, the equal aversion functions shown in Figs. 1–7 and 1–8 predict with remarkable accuracy the behavior motivated by shock in three different types of apparatus: the number of avoidances in a straight runway, the number of responses to extinction in a punishment-avoidance experiment, and spontaneous activity.

These findings, taken in conjunction with the previous aversion difference limen findings, suggest that for all practical purposes shock sources with internal impedances of 150K ohms or more can all be used interchangeably. Moreover, it is now possible to relate the various sources to a common scale. Voltages from fixed impedance sources can be transformed into equivalent current units and vice versa.

At this point a final word of caution is in order. While the present research demonstrates a remarkable equivalence between the types of sources tested, this by no means implies that this equivalence will apply with the same precision to other types of apparatus, different scrambling devices, different grid shapes and sizes, etc. There is always the possibility, if not the likelihood, that some apparatus parameter will interact in some fashion with a particular shock source to make it more or less aversive. Long leads with high interlead capacitance may attenuate constant current stimuli more than fixed impedance stimuli, and large or flat grids may reduce the intensity of fixed impedance stimuli more than constant current stimuli. Moreover, we have neglected one major variable in this research, namely the source or compliance voltage used in constant current stimulators. Substantial pilot work in our laboratory clearly indicates that constant current generators with source potentials over 1000 volts are far more aversive than stimulators with moderate source potentials in the 500-volt range. Hence the findings of the present study are limited to constant current sources in this class. We hasten to add, however, that high source voltages in constant current stimulators are unnecessary for adequate current regulation, and that they should be avoided because of the extreme variations in current density they produce. On the positive side, it is our opinion that the present equal-aversion functions apply to the majority of shock stimulators currently in use, and that the equal-aversion functions will therefore yield good estimates of relative aversiveness for the majority of different shock stimuli.

Summary and Conclusions

The principal aim of this chapter has been to examine the characteristics of electric shock as a behavioral stimulus using basic concepts and experimental techniques derived from human psychophysics.

Over the course of the present century a great proliferation of types of electric shock stimulators has occurred. As a result, two very important yet unresolved problems emerged. First, how can the results of experiments using different types of shock sources be compared with each other? Second, which type or class of source is the most suitable for behavioral research?

We attacked these problems by first determining the useful range of shock intensities for a wide variety of sources. Detection, aversion, tetanization, and death thresholds were measured for each source. The useful range (for motivating rats) was defined as the span of intensity lying between the aversion and tetanization thresholds. Next we attacked the problem of comparing different types of shock sources with each other by constructing a series of equal-aversion functions using techniques analogous to Fletcher and Munson's procedure for deriving equal loudness contours. A simple preference measure was used to place different shock stimulators on a common scale of aversiveness. With this scale, it is now possible to translate back and forth between experiments performed with different sources.

Our approach to the second problem was to express the variability in aversiveness of shock stimulation in terms of "aversion difference limens," an obvious analogy to the traditional psychophysical estimate of sensation variability—the difference limen or JND. Comparison of aversion difference limens for several types of sources led to the delineation of a class of "optimal" shock sources.

The final series of experiments demonstrated that shocks which were equal in aversiveness as defined by behavioral preference also produced equal learning in a straight alley, equal resistance to shock-punishment extinction, and equal amounts of random activity.

REFERENCES

BRUSH, F. R., & KNAFF, P. R. A device for detecting and controlling automatic programming of avoidance-conditioning in a shuttle-box. *American Journal of Psychology*, 1959, **72**, 275–278.

CAMPBELL, B. A. The reinforcement difference limen (RDL) function for shock reduction. *Journal of Experimental Psychology*, 1956, **52**, 258–262.

CAMPBELL, B. A. Auditory and aversion thresholds of rats for bands of noise. *Science*, 1957, **125**, 596–597.

CAMPBELL, B. A. Developmental studies of learning and motivation in infra-primate mammals. In H. W. Stevenson (Ed.) *Early Behavior: Comparative and developmental approaches*. Wiley, 1967. Pp. 43–71.

CAMPBELL, B. A., & TEGHTSOONIAN, R. Electrical and behavioral effects of different types of shock stimuli on the rat. *Journal of Comparative and Physiological Psychology*, 1958, **51**, 185–192.

DAVIDON, R., & BOONIN, N. A constant current stimulus-generator. *American Journal of Psychology*, 1956, **69**, 466–468.

DUNLAP, K. Standardizing electric shocks for rats. *Journal of Comparative Psychology*, 1931, **12**, 133–135.

FLETCHER, H., & MUNSON, W. A. Relation between loudness and masking. *Journal of the Acoustical Society of America*, 1937, **9**, 1–10.

FORBES, T. W. MUENZINGER, K. F., & WENDT, G. R. Report of round tables on use of electric shock. *Psychological Bulletin*, 1935, **32**, 185–196.

GIBSON, R. H. Communication by electrical stimulation of the skin. *Space Research Coordination Center Report*, No. 21, University of Pittsburgh, 1965.

GUILFORD, J. P. *Psychometric methods*. New York: McGraw-Hill, 1954.

HARRINGTON, G. M. & LINDER, W. K. A positive reinforcing effect of electrical stimulation. *Journal of Comparative Psysiological Psychology*, 1962, **55**, 1014–1015.

HURWITZ, H. M. B., & DILLOW, P. V. The effect of constant power shock on the acquisition of a discriminated avoidance response. *Psychonomic Science*, 1966, **5**, 111–112.

JENKINS, T. N., WARNER, L. H., & WARDEN, C. J. Standard apparatus for the study of animal motivation. *Journal of Comparative Psychology*, 1926, **6**, 361–382.

LUCE, R. D., BUSH, R. R., & GALANTER, E. (Eds.) *Handbook of mathematical psychology*. Vol. 1. New York: Wiley, 1963.

LUCE, R. D. & EDWARDS, W. The derivation of subjective scales from just noticeable differences. *Psychological Review*, 1958, **65**, 222–237.

MARTIN, E. G. A quantitative study of faradic stimulation. II. The calibration of the inductorium for break shocks. *American Journal of Physiology*, 1908, **22**, 116–132.

MASSERMAN, J. H. Behavior and neurosis. Chicago: University of Chicago Press, 1943.

MASTERSON, F. A. Equal aversion functions as predictors of instrumental responding. Unpublished doctoral dissertation, Princeton University, 1965.

MOSS, F. A. Study of animal drives. *Journal of Experimental Psychology*, 1924, **7**, 165–185.

MUENZINGER, K. F., & MIZE, R. H. The sensitivity of the white rat to electric shock: Threshold and skin resistance. *Journal of Comparative Psychology*, 1933, **15**, 139–148.

MUENZINGER, K. F., & WALZ, F. C. An examination of electrical-current-stabilizing devices for psychological experiments. *Journal of Genetic Psychology*, 1934, **10**, 477–482.

SOLOMON, R. L., KAMIN, L. J., & WYNNE, L. C. Traumatic avoidance learning: the outcomes of several extinction procedures with dogs. *Journal of Abnormal and Social Psychology*, 1953, **48**, 291–302.

TORGERSON, W. S. *Theory and methods of scaling*. New York: Wiley, 1958.

WATSON, J. B. *Behavior: An introduction to comparative psychology*. New York: Holt, 1914.

YERKES, R. M. The instincts, habits, and reactions of the frog. I. Associative processes of the green frog. *Harvard Psychology Studies*, 1903, **1**, 579–638.

2

The Negative Incentive Value of Punishment[1]

Frank A. Logan

UNIVERSITY OF NEW MEXICO

Among what still were billed in 1954 as *"Modern Learning Theories"* (Estes et al., 1954), substantial agreement existed about the essential role of rewarding stimuli. They reinforced responses. Much as in the older theory of Thorndike (1911), where rewarding stimuli "stamped in" stimulus-response connections, they then served to protect responses from unlearning (Guthrie), to increase habit strength (Hull), or to build a reflex reserve (Skinner). Rewarding stimuli acted mechanically and automatically to affect the learning process directly. Rewarded responses were learned.

Aversive stimuli trod a considerably rockier road during this era. It may be intuitively obvious that aversive stimuli play the opposite role from rewarding stimuli, and indeed Thorndike initially proposed that they served to "stamp out" stimulus-response connections, but he quickly abandoned this position in favor of an equivocal neutrality. Subsequently, Guthrie (1934) evaluated aversive stimuli entirely in terms of their response-evocation property, Hull (1952) adopted the notion of response conflict, and Skinner (1953) favored transitory response suppression. Aversive stimuli had effects, to be sure (Estes, 1944), but they were circumspect. Certainly responses followed by aversive stimuli were not unlearned and hence their role was not simply the opposite of rewarding stimuli.

While the conceptual and experimental analysis of aversive stimuli lay largely dormant, rewarding stimuli have since had their own difficulties. During the ensuing decade, one after another theorist has abandoned the notion that rewards affect learning in any direct manner. Rewarding stimuli are currently given a less mechanical and more flexible motivational role. Stimuli or responses become associated with any subsequent

[1] This research was supported in part by a grant from the National Science Foundation. I am indebted to William Candelaria, Albert Gonzales, and Eli Padilla for assistance in running subjects.

rewards and give rise to what Hull (1952) and Spence (1956) called "incentive motivation." Although this language will be used, it might be noted that reasonably comparable terms among contemporary theorists are: "go" (Miller, 1963), "hope" (Mowrer, 1960), "excitement" (Sheffield, 1966), and other such terms (Cofer & Appley, 1964; Miller, Galanter, & Pribram, 1960; Seward, 1956). Indeed, it would be unfair to ignore Tolman's (1932) role in this brief history, although his notion of "expectation of goal objects" was embedded in cognitive maps of mazes. The essential communality among these approaches is the image that rewards do not simply strengthen habits; they excite habits.

Incentive theory has not yet been fully elaborated, and the differences among the several versions have not yet been reconciled. But the fundamental approach is clear enough. The organism is assumed to be choosing, continuously overtime, from among the available stimuli and responses. Insofar as these stimuli or responses have historically been associated with rewarding stimuli, they will provoke incentive motivation favoring their selection. Incentive motivation guides the organism toward optimal behavior, perhaps through a cybernetic feedback mechanism, by exciting habits to their previously experienced outcomes.

These developments set the stage for viewing again the role of aversive stimuli as opposite to that of rewarding stimuli. To recapitulate briefly: initially, learning was thought to be stamped in by rewarding stimuli and stamped out by aversive stimuli; it then became clear that aversive stimuli do not stamp out responses, and it has recently become clear that rewarding stimuli do not stamp in responses. If rewarding stimuli potentiate habits through incentive motivation, then aversive stimuli may inhibit habits in a corresponding manner. In short, aversive stimuli may produce *negative* incentive motivation.

Experimental Background

The program of research within which this work is embedded has bypassed some of the unresolved problems of incentive theory and proceeded toward quantification in spite of them. A brief review of this background will provide a context for the preliminary data to be reported.

Because incentive motivation is a principal basis for response selection, and because attempts to measure it in any absolute manner via response speed or rate run afoul of the fact that such response dimensions are themselves learnable (e.g., Logan, 1960), we have employed a single choice procedure in an attempt at *relative* quantification. Specifically, rats may be given a choice between two alternatives, one of which contains a larger reward but entails a longer delay before its delivery. Now it is well known that rats prefer larger rewards and shorter delays; but in this context, the rat must make a decision between these dimensions of the reward. By parametrically studying different amounts and delays within this paradigm, it is possible to find combinations between which the rat is indifferent and in this way to estimate the incentive effects of different amounts of reward relative to the incentive effects of different delays of reward.

If aversive stimuli produce negative incentive, then a comparable procedure should enable us to encorporate such events into a quantification of net incentive motivation. Specifically, if one of two alternatives contains a larger reward but also entails receipt of an aversive stimulus, and if punishment produces negative incentive that subtracts from the positive incentive based on reward, then preference should be correspondingly affected. In general one should be able to offset a differential in reward by an equivalent differential in punishment.

Preliminary evidence consistent with this approach was obtained in my laboratory by Sears (1964). Two groups of rats were first trained to choose the larger of two rewards, but for one group the differential in reward was greater than for the other. Although both groups thus preferred the larger reward, the incentive analysis would presume that there was a greater incentive motivational basis for this preference for the group with a larger differential in reward. Then both groups were given electric shock punishment in the alternative containing the larger reward, at first at a very weak level and then at progressively increased intensities. During all of this time, preference was monitored. As one would expect from incentive theory including the notion that punishment produces negative incentive, Sears found that the larger the differential in reward, the stronger the electric shock that was necessary to reverse preference from the larger reward to the smaller reward alternative.

The present research utilized the same basic procedure but used parameters of reward that permit a more precise quantitative evaluation of the hypothesis that aversive stimuli can be conceptualized in terms of negative incentive. Our previous researches (Logan, 1965a, 1965b) have indicated that the positive incentive differential between one and three pellets reward is approximately equal to that between three and seven pellets reward. The basis for that statement is that both of these differences in amount of reward were approximately equal to the difference between 1 and 12 seconds in delay of reward when pitted against those amounts. In effect then, we have three differences in reward which are presumably based on the same differential in positive incentive motivation. If electric shock punishment can properly be viewed in terms of negative incentive, then the intensity of shock necessary to offset the reward differential should be the same in all three cases. This was the primary hypothesis under test, although several additional conditions,

including partial punishment, were included to indicate some of the
directions in which further work along these lines might proceed.

Method

Subjects

Subjects were 64 hooded rats bred in the colony at the University of New
Mexico. They were 90–120 days of age at the beginning of the study and
were housed individually with water freely available. Males and females
were assigned equally to the different conditions. Daily diet of 14 gms.
laboratory chow was given immediately after each day's experimental
session.

Apparatus

The apparatus was a pair of parallel alleys, 8 feet long, one of which was
black and the other white. The gray start box was positioned in front of
the appropriate alley for forced trials, and was centered between the
alleys for free-choice trials. The start door opened vertically by a spring
when released by a solenoid. Goal-box doors were lowered manually,
enclosing the last two feet of the alleys. This section also contained a
grid-floor insert through which shock could be delivered when the rat
broke a photobeam 2 inches in front of the foodcup. Reward consisted of
45 mg. Noyes pellets delivered by Davis feeders pulsed at a rate of about
five per second. Delay of reward, where appropriate, was timed from
breaking a photobeam within the foodcup.

Shock was provided 120 volts AC passed through a variac into a
step-up transformer with 150K ohms resistance in series with the rat. Grid
floors were $\frac{1}{16}$ inch stainless rods separated by $\frac{1}{8}$ inch so that each paw
would normally make contact with both sides of the adjusted line voltage.
Shock duration was .2 second.

Procedure

Rats were run in squads of four providing an intertrial interval of 3–4
minutes. The first four trials of each six-trial block were forced according
to one of the following rotated sequences: LLRR, LRRL, RLLR, RRLL.
The fifth trial was a free-choice trial and the sixth trial was then forced
opposite to that chosen on the free trial. Partial punishment was scheduled over four blocks of trials (12 trials to each alley) so that each trial
including the choice trials would receive the 50% schedule of punishment.

Design

Four basic conditions of reinforcement were employed (where A stands for amount in pellets and D for delay in seconds): 3A,OD vs. 1A,OD; 7A,OD vs. 3A,OD; 7A,OD vs. 1A,OD; and 3A,1D vs. 3A,12D. Twenty-eight blocks of trials were run under these conditions prior to the introduction of shock punishment. Thereafter, half of the rats received shock on every trial in the preferred-reward alternative and the other half received shock on half of the trials in that alternative. An initial shock level of 75 volts was maintained for 20 blocks of trials, followed by 10 blocks of trials at 85, 100, and for the partial punishment rats, 115 volts. The last five days at each level were used to determine terminal performance, speeds being computed from the first four forced trials and choice from the fifth trial.

Results

The choice data are shown in the two panels of Fig. 2–1. The left panel shows the effect of 100% shock punishment given in the preferred-

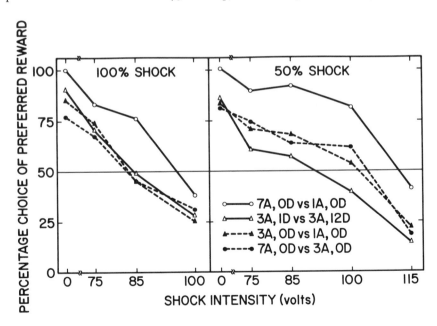

FIG. 2–1. Percentage of choice of the preferred reward as a function of shock intensity in that alternative.

reward alternative at progressive levels of intensity. The three lower curves refer to the reward conditions expected to be essentially equivalent in the difference in positive incentive. The correspondence among these curves is apparent, all beginning with a strong but not complete preference for the better reward condition and declining steadily as shock was increased. (It should be noted that these averages reflect more the number of rats that had reversed preference at each shock intensity rather than intermediate percentages for individual rats.) On the average, by linear interpolation, about 83 volts of shock punishment produced indifference.

That the correspondence among these three groups did not result from a universal effect of shock but was indeed related to the incentive differential can be seen by the choice performance of the group receiving a larger differential in reward (7-vs.-1 Group). This group was consistently above the other three groups, their total number of choices of the preferred reward over all punishment trials significantly exceeding the groups with a smaller reward differential ($t = 2.1$, $df = 31$, $p < .05$). Again by linear interpolation, the indifference value for the 7-vs.-1 Group was about 95 volts of shock punishment. Since the difference in incentive was presumably twice as large for this group as for the other three, a first approximation quantifying the negative incentive value of shock punishment is that a 95-volt shock (with this system) is approximately twice as aversive as an 83-volt shock.

The results of partial punishment are shown in the right panel of Fig. 2–1. The correspondence among the three presumably equivalent conditions was less striking in this case, the group for which the reward differential was based on delay reversing somewhat more rapidly than the other two groups. Although this difference was not statistically significant, it may nevertheless indicate a possible interaction when partial punishment is combined with delayed reward. It is also possible, however, that the number of trials given at each shock intensity was too small to reach complete stability because of the reduced number of shocks encountered. The two differential amount groups were reasonably similar and again, the group receiving the large differential in reward maintained significantly greater preference during the punishment series ($t = 2.8$, $df = 31$, $p < .02$).

Because of the discrepancy among the three equal differential-incentive conditions, only a very tentative, illustrative comparison can be made between the negative incentive value of partial as compared with continuous punishment. From inspection of the two panels of Fig. 2–1, it is clear that partial punishment was less effective in reversing preference, but it would be desirable to estimate how much less effective. Were 50% punishment exactly half as aversive as 100% preference, then the indifference point for the three comparison groups should be at about 95 volts. This inference is based on the assumption that doubling the positive incentive by increasing the differential in reward should be equivalent to halving the negative incentive by reducing the frequency of punishment. Although no strong conclusion can be reached because of the between-group differences, it would appear on the average that over

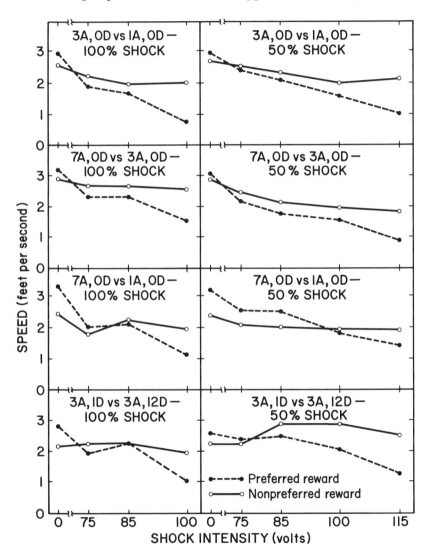

FIG. 2–2.   Speeds to the preferred (dashed lines) and nonpreferred (solid lines) rewards for each group at the different levels of punishment.

95 volts was required to reach indifference with partial punishment. This would indicate that the negative incentive value of 50% shock is less than half that produced by 100% shock.

The speed data for each group are shown in the eight panels of Fig. 2–2. Several points about these data may be noted. First, all groups ran faster to the preferred reward before the introduction of shock punishment and, thereafter, speed in the punished alternative decreased as shock intensity increased. This pattern of results is consistent with expectation of incentive theory in this situation where faster speeds get the reward and punishment sooner. It is interesting to note that, in every case, reversal in the difference in speeds occurred at a lower shock intensity than required to reverse preference.

It can also be seen that there were no indications of incentive contrast. That is to say, speed to three pellets was the same whether pitted against seven pellets or one pellet, and speeds to the latter were equivalent whether pitted against each other or against three pellets. There does, however, appear to be a generalization effect in the data because speeds generally declined in the nonpunished alley as shock intensity increased in the punished alley.

Discussion

The results of the research reported are generally consistent with the hypothesis that aversive stimuli given as punishers for selecting one response in preference to another can be understood in terms of a negative incentive construct. That is to say, choice is based upon the *net* incentive motivation associated with each alternative, including not only the parameters of reward but also the parameters of punishment. However, it is appropriate to note that, in addition to further parametric research, there are a number of conceptual difficulties to be resolved before this approach is fully elaborated.

One difficulty concerns the use of a gradually increasing shock intensity. There are data (N. E. Miller, 1960) which clearly indicate that the disruptive effects of electric shock are importantly dependent upon prior exposure to shock. Rats tolerate a strong shock better if they have been gradually introduced to this stimulus than if it is suddenly imposed upon an instrumental response. This could mean that the negative incentive value of an aversive stimulus is not an absolute property of that stimulus but depends also upon how it is presented. A related finding has been reported with respect to delay of reward (Harker, 1956) indicating that the detrimental effects of delay are dependent upon whether delay is suddenly or gradually introduced. It is possible that these effects will be understood solely in terms of the response evocation or other properties of rewarding and aversive stimuli, but it is also possible that a quantification of incentive motivation will need to include specification of the prior experiences of the subjects with those events.

A second problem concerns the fact that we used a particular shock source, and, therefore, little quantitative generality may be presumed. Because this topic is discussed at length by others, it can only be noted here that a choice measure of negative incentive may be necessary to evaluate the specificity of our results to the characteristics of the aversive stimulus employed.

A more critical problem concerns the procedure of giving the aversive stimulus immediately preceding the goal and the subsequent rewarding stimulus. There are reasons to believe that any stimulus preceding a rewarding stimulus acquires some secondary rewarding properties; if that stimulus is aversive, its negative incentive value could be attenuated. It is well known that Pavlov (1927) used, among other things, aversive stimuli as conditioned stimuli for classical salivary conditioning, and reported that these stimuli ultimately lost their tendency to elicit emotional responses indicative of pain–fear. In the present work, electric shock always preceded the preferred reward, and the incentive estimates made in this context might be materially affected by this temporal sequence.

This difficulty can be accentuated if one considers the larger domain including delay of both reward and punishment. In some such combinations reward would precede punishment and in that temporal order, the rewarding stimulus would be expected to acquire some secondary motivating properties which might attenuate its positive incentive effect. In other combinations, punishment would precede reward and the aversive stimulus might acquire secondary reinforcing properties. In general, reward and punishment may not simply combine as positive and negative incentive, but may interact with each other in such a way as to affect their separate incentive values. This possibility can be evaluated empirically, but may constrain the conclusions of the data reported.

Conceptually, the most difficult problem is whether incentive motivation is mediated. This problem arises with both positive and negative incentive but is perhaps more conspicuous in the former case. Briefly, the position is this: when an organism responds, the resulting feedback stimuli may have become associated with fractional components of the consequent events as previously encountered. Incentive motivation is then mediated by the properties of these anticipatory responses.

There are several difficulties with such an approach to positive incentive which have been described elsewhere (Logan, 1968). The most critical was anticipated earlier (Logan et al., 1955) but may be briefly recapitulated here. This problem concerns response selection. It is clear enough that a response may produce feedback stimuli which in turn elicit anticipatory responses $(r_g - s_g)$, but it is not clear how these latter can enter into the selection of that response itself. The organism, in effect, would have to scan the entire range of alternatives, receiving tentative feedback from each so as to make the associated fractional anticipatory responses, store the values of $r_g - s_g$ during this time, and then choose on the basis of some comparison procedure. While complex human decisions may indeed be described in this manner, it seems unlikely that the moment-to-moment behavior of all organisms follows so complex a path.

The problem is equally applicable to negative incentive. In this case, the mediating response would presumably be fear associated with the feedback from the response on the basis of prior punishment. Indeed, one could further assume that fear is incompatible with $r_g - s_g$ and that their competition results in a compromise producing what we have called net incentive. Appealing as this approach is, however, the problem remains that responses must be initiated, at least in surrogate form, for the mechanism to operate. The development of a cybernetic analysis of incentive motivation remains to be formalized.

A negative incentive approach toward punishment does not necessarily deny other possible effects of aversive stimuli. Such stimuli normally elicit overt responses which may become anticipatory and affect instrumental performance accordingly. Indeed, such an effect can be inferred from the difference between the choice and speed data of the present studies. Speed in the punished alternative became slower than that in the nonpunished alternative at a level of shock below that which produced a reversal of preference. Accepting choice behavior as a measure of relative net incentive, we must conclude that the greater relative effect on instrumental running speed presumably arose from some other performance factor. A reasonable suggestion comes from competing-response theory. Since the withdrawal responses elicited by foot shock are incompatible with the approach response, their anticipatory form would reduce speed more than indicated by the effect on net incentive. This same principle could also account for the observed generalization of slower running in the nonpunished alley. Accordingly, the role of aversive stimuli as stimuli and elicitors of responses need to be included in a complete account of punishment. Nevertheless, the choice data provide encouraging preliminary evidence that aversive stimuli given consequent upon a response affect the net incentive motivation for selecting that response.

In short, the parameters of reward determine the value of positive incentive motivation and the parameters of punishment determine the value of negative incentive motivation, and these combine to determine preference for one response over another. Both reward and punishment may have other properties, but they give rise to opposing motivational effects. Conjointly, they determine preference.

Summary

The assumption that the effects of punishment are symmetrically opposite to the effects of reward, first stated with respect to learning in the original law of effect, is here proposed with respect to incentive motivation. The assumption is that rewards and punishments do not affect learning directly, their effect on performance being motivational in nature. The net value of an alternative thus depends jointly on the positive incentive associated with the reward and the negative incentive associated with the punishment.

This approach was evaluated experimentally by first training hungry rats in a choice between two alternatives that differed in food reward, and then introducing punishment in the preferred alternative. More specifically, two differences in amount of reward and one difference in delay of reward, all of which had previously been shown to be approximately equivalent in differential positive incentive, were pitted against gradually increasing intensities of shock punishment. In general, the expectation that the same intensity of punishment would be required to reverse the preference based on these differentials in reward was confirmed. Furthermore, partial (50%) punishment was less effective in reversing preference, and it was tentatively estimated that its negative incentive value is less than half that of continuous punishment. Finally, larger reward differentials required stronger shock intensities.

Several problems for further development of incentive theory were noted. In addition to the fundamental problem of response selection, the negative incentive value of gradually increasing punishment and of punishment in temporal relation to reward require analysis. Classical response effects of punishment must be included since punishment decreased running speed sooner than it reversed preference. Overall, however, the results were consistent with incentive theory and provide preliminary integration of negative incentive into a quantification of net incentive motivation.

REFERENCES

Cofer, C. N., & Appley, M. H. *Motivation: Theory and research.* New York: Wiley, 1964.

Estes, W. K. An experimental study of punishment. *Psychological Monographs,* 1944, **57**, (3, Whole No. 263).

Estes, W. K., Koch, S., MacCorquodale, K., Meehl, P. E., Mueller, C. G., Schoenfeld, W. N., & Verplanck, W. S. *Modern learning theory.* New York: Appleton-Century-Crofts, 1954.

GUTHRIE, E. R. Reward and punishment. *Psychological Review,* 1934, **41**, 450–460.

HARKER, G. S. Delay of reward and performance of an instrumental response. *Journal of Experimental Psychology,* 1956, **51**, 303–310.

HULL, C. L. *A behavior system.* New Haven: Yale University Press, 1952.

LOGAN, F. A. *Incentive: How the conditions of reinforcement affect the performance of rats.* New Haven: Yale University Press, 1960.

LOGAN, F. A. Decision-making by rats: Delay versus amount of reward. *Journal of Comparative and Physiological Psychology,* 1965, **59**, 1–12. (a)

LOGAN, F. A. Decision-making by rats: Uncertain outcome choices. *Journal of Comparative and Physiological Psychology,* 1965, **59**, 246–251. (b)

LOGAN, F. A. Incentive theory and changes in reward. In K. W. Spence & J. T. Spence (Eds.), *The psychology of learning and motivation.* Vol. II. New York: Academic Press, 1968. Pp. 1–30.

LOGAN, F. A., OLMSTED, D. L., ROSNER, B. S., SCHWARTZ, R. D., & STEVENS, C. M. *Behavior theory and social science.* New Haven: Yale University Press, 1955.

MILLER, G. A., GALANTER, E., & PRIBRAM, K. H. *Plans and the structure of behavior.* New York: Holt, Rinehart, and Winston, 1960.

MILLER, N. E. Learning resistance to pain and fear: Effects of overlearning, exposure and rewarded exposure in context. *Journal of Experimental Psychology,* 1960, **60**, 137–145.

MILLER, N. E. Some reflections on the law of effect produce a new alternative to drive reduction. In M. R. Jones (Ed.), *Nebraska symposium on motivation.* Lincoln: University of Nebraska Press, 1963. Pp. 65–112.

MOWRER, O. H. *Learning theory and behavior.* New York: Wiley, 1960.

PAVLOV, I. P. *Conditioned reflexes.* (Tr. G. V. Anrep). London: Oxford University Press, 1927. (Reprinted, New York: Dover, 1960.)

SEARS, D. O. Punishment and choice in the rat. *Journal of Comparative and Physiological Psychology,* 1964, **57**, 297–299.

SEWARD, J. P. Drive, incentive, and reinforcement. *Psychological Review,* 1956, **63**, 195–203.

SHEFFIELD, F. D. A drive induction theory of reinforcement. In R. N. Haber (Ed.), *Current research in motivation.* New York: Holt, 1966. Pp. 98–121.

SKINNER, B. F. *Science and human behavior.* New York: Macmillan, 1953.

SPENCE, K. W. *Behavior theory and conditioning.* New Haven: Yale University Press, 1956.

THORNDIKE, E. L. *Animal intelligence.* New York: Macmillan, 1911.

TOLMAN, E. C. *Purposive behavior in animals and men.* New York: Century, 1932.

II

SUPPRESSIVE EFFECTS of PUNISHMENT

3

Outline of a Theory of Punishment[1]

W. K. Estes[2]

STANFORD UNIVERSITY

Introduction

A rather striking characteristic of the literature on punishment is the large and still growing disparity between the volumes of theoretical and experimental contributions. For example, one finds in Boe's bibliography (Appendix B of this volume) that the greatly accelerated output of research on punishment during recent years is not accompanied by a similar trend with respect to theoretical or interpretive articles. Also, in most of the major learning theories of the past few decades, treatments of punishment are either brief and casual (Guthrie, 1952; Skinner, 1938) or missing altogether (Hull, 1943; Spence, 1956; Tolman, 1932). The reason for this curious state of affairs may be in part that, whereas the interpretation of such processes as acquisition and retention is universally taken to be a primary task for learning theory, the treatment of punishment is frequently regarded as secondary, or derivative.

The concept of punishment is defined, not with respect to any unique class of events involved, but only with respect to a particular relationship of contingency. The types of stimuli used as punishers all occur in other situations as unconditioned stimuli for classical defense, escape, or avoidance conditioning. Ordinarily we speak of punishment only if the stimulus which could serve as a basis for one of these types of conditioning is instead made contingent upon occurrence of some specified response. Although it is a logical possibility that punishing stimuli have some basic and unique property, for example that of reducing associative strength, which appears only when they are made contingent upon response occurrences, theories based on such an assumption have not

[1] Preparation of this article was supported in part by Contract Nonr 225(73) between the Office of Naval Research and Stanford University.
[2] Now at Rockefeller University.

fared well. The principal alternative view is that the effects of punishment should be entirely predictable from properties of punishing stimuli which can be determined independently in studies of conditioning which do not involve punishment contingencies. The series of experimental studies of punishment which led to my earlier monograph (Estes, 1944) seemed to call for an interpretation of the latter type. While some interpretations of this type have proven viable, all, including my own first attempt, have in the course of time revealed major shortcomings.

In attempting to assimilate the factual input from the effervescence of research on punishment during the last few years, I have come to feel that converging lines of evidence triangulate quite specifically the point at which current interpretations of punishment require revision. What I should like to accomplish in the present paper is to indicate the nature of this needed revision and to sketch in outline how it leads to my own second approximation to a theory of punishment.

By way of general organization, I propose firstly to review the main experimental facts leading to my 1944 interpretation; secondly, to evaluate and criticize that formulation in the light both of facts available at the time and of others which have come to hand subsequently; thirdly, to offer a revised interpretation; and finally, to make at least a start on the job of assaying the merits of my second approximation for handling the much larger body of data now available.

Empirical Context of Original Formulation

Like most psychologists of my generation I was educated on an interpretation of punishment growing out of Thorndike's development of the law of effect. However, I was not at all comfortable with the asymmetry of Thorndike's later formulation, which held that rewards have a direct positive effect on the strength of the preceding response whereas punishments act only indirectly by somehow increasing variability of behavior (Thorndike, 1931, 1935). My dissatisfaction arose from both theoretical and empirical considerations. On the one hand, it was hard to see why qualitatively different mechanisms should have evolved to mediate the influences of the two kinds of aftereffects on learning; on the other, the various stages of development and modification of the law of effect as it pertains to punishment were based almost exclusively on studies using punishments which involved little or no element of pain or trauma, usually merely indications of incorrectness of response. The one published study of punishment in an operant situation prior to 1940, that of Skinner (1938), yielded results in seeming agreement with Thorndike's conclusions, but it also involved only very mild punishment.

Thus my own studies on punishment, which led to the 1944 monograph, were initiated to see whether more severe punishments would not yield effects comparable in uniformity and magnitude to those of rewards. These experiments unequivocally showed that a more traumatic stimulus, electric shock, administered immediately after bar-pressing responses by rats, yielded reliable and uniform suppression of responding, the degree and duration of suppression being directly related to the intensity of the shock and the duration of the period of punishment. These results, which have been replicated many times by other investigators, led me to feel that I might have been wrong and that the effect of punishment was simply the opposite of that of reward; namely, to exert a direct weakening effect on the strength of the punished response.

Just one bit of evidence from these studies did not quite jibe with this conclusion and ultimately led to my principal series of studies on punishment. In all respects but one the effects of punishment seemed to be simply an amplification of the usual effects of nonreward on a previously food-rewarded response. The exception has to do with recovery from punishment. If, following training of a response with food reinforcement, a series of sessions of extinction is given, frequency of responding simply declines in regular fashion from one session to the next as seen, for example, in the control curve of Fig. 3–1. If, however, responses during the first extinction period are punished, then, under some condi-

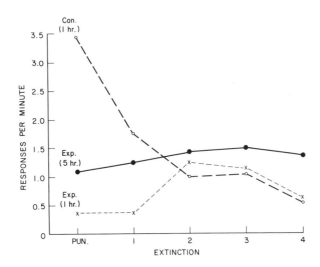

FIG. 3–1.   Suppressive effect of a period of punishment (Pun.) upon subsequent extinction responding in relation to number of hours of previous training under partial reinforcement.

From: W. K. Estes, "An Experimental Study of Punishment," *Psychological Monographs,* **57** (3, Whole No. 263), 1944, Fig. 8, p. 18. Copyright 1944 by the American Psychological Association and reproduced by permission.

tions, the curve of response frequency per period does not decline regularly during subsequent sessions of unpunished extinction but rather exhibits recovery, sometimes rejoining the control curve at some point, as in the case of the lower experimental curve in Fig. 3–1, and sometimes exceeding it (compensatory recovery) as in the case of the upper experimental curve in Fig. 3–1. This figure is based on data from Experiment F of my 1944 monograph. The essentials of the experiment are that the control group and one experimental group received 1 hour of 4-minute, fixed-interval food reinforcement for bar pressing after initial conditioning and the other experimental group, 5 hours; then all groups received a 40-minute period of extinction during which both experimental groups were punished with shock for all responses; finally, on 4 consecutive days all groups received 1-hour periods of extinction.

Aside from the partial recovery from the effects of punishment, another feature of this result bears emphasis, namely the fact that resistance to the effects of punishment varies directly with the amount of previous training. This relationship has been somewhat obscured by later studies which have shown in some instances that resistance to punishment is essentially unaffected by different amounts of training under conditions of 100% reinforcement. I do not know of any results in the literature, however, which throw any doubt on the generalization that resistance to punishment is an increasing function of the amount of training when training is given with intermittent reinforcement.

The findings concerning recovery suggested strongly that punishment must involve a process distinct from simple extinction and following a different time course. If punishment and extinction were two alternative conditions yielding the common result of weakening response strength (so that the addition of punishment simply accelerated the course of extinction), then the curves for the experimental groups should have continued to decline following the period of punishment and, in particular, should never have crossed the control curve. One parsimonious interpretation can be formulated in terms of stimulus generalization effects. Since the introduction of punishment involves a novel stimulus, electric shock, which was not present during acquisition, the shift from punishment plus extinction to simple extinction returns the organism from a stimulus situation differing drastically from that of acquisition to one more similar to that of acquisition. However, this hypothesis would imply a greater relative recovery effect following more intense punishment. Another superficially plausible interpretation involves the effects of changes in relative reward value of the outcomes of responses. Presumably the combination of punishment and absence of food reward would be the outcome of lowest reward value; thus a shift from punishment plus extinction to simple extinction would involve an increase in rate of responding. As in the case of the generalization hypothesis, however, this interpretation would imply greater relative recovery following more severe punishment, which is certainly contrary to fact.

A more promising interpretation was suggested by some independent sources of evidence which came to hand at just about the time of my studies of punishment and recovery. I refer to the initial experiments on the establishment of the conditioned emotional response (CER) (Estes & Skinner, 1941) which showed that a stimulus which precedes a non-contingent shock acquires the capacity of suppressing ongoing behavior. In view of this finding, it appeared that the effects of punishment must be due at least in part to the establishment of a CER to cues which were normally part of the discriminative stimulus complex for the response, and thus necessarily paired with shock on punishment trials.

Two major testable implications of this assumption came immediately to mind. The first was that it should be possible to mimic the effects of punishment to some extent simply by giving periodic electric shocks, uncorrelated with the animal's behavior, during a period when it was engaged in responding for food reward. Experiments of this type were done and the results were generally confirmatory, the effects of non-contingent shocks being to generate a suppression of operant behavior with time courses of suppression and recovery generally similar to those of response-contingent punishment. More importantly, it should be possible following a period of response-contingent punishment to acceler-

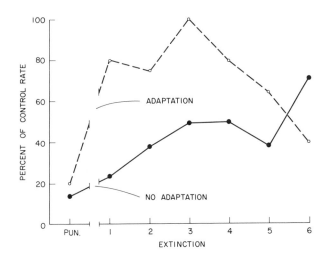

FIG. 3–2. Recovery from effects of punishment of a previously rewarded response in relation to opportunity for adaptation to apparatus cues between the period of punishment and the first period of extinction.

From: W. K. Estes, "An Experimental Study of Punishment," *Psychological Monographs*, **57** (3, Whole No. 263), 1944, Fig. 13, p. 28. Copyright 1944 by the American Psychological Association and reproduced by permission.

ate greatly the course of recovery by giving a period of adaptation in the apparatus with the manipulandum for the operant response removed but with opportunity for extinction of the CER to other cues normally a part of the discriminative stimulus complex for the response. Results of experiments of this type are exemplified by the one portrayed in Fig. 3–2 (from Experiment J of my 1944 monograph). Following training on 4-minute fixed interval food reward for bar pressing, both groups were given a 10-minute period of response-contingent punishment for all responses, reward being discontinued; then the adaptation group was placed in the boxes with the levers removed for two 1-hour periods in order to permit extinction of the CER to cues of the experimental situation, the no adaptation group not being exposed to the apparatus during these periods. During the subsequent six-hour periods of simple extinction, recovery from the effects of punishment was very greatly accelerated in the case of the adaptation group, providing rather cogent support for the idea that at least a major portion of the normal effect of punishment may be accounted for in terms of the establishment of a CER.

First Approximation to a Theory of Punishment

The set of results just described, together with those of the classical experiments already in the literature concerning effects of delay of punishment and the like, all seemed to point to an interpretation in terms of a theory which assumes the primary mechanism in punishment to be the establishment of a CER. Upon an occurrence of punishment of a response, the punishing stimulus provides a basis for establishing a CER to any cues immediately preceding the evocation of the punished response, such as experimentally controlled discriminative stimuli, cues associated with the manipulandum involved, and to a lesser extent general background stimuli. Then on subsequent occasions, when the animal is exposed to these same cues, the CER will be evoked, leading to suppression of ongoing operant behavior, including, in particular, the previously punished response. The differences between effects of response-contingent and noncontingent punishment would be interpreted simply as a matter of differential opportunities for establishing a CER to cues closely associated with occurrence of the punished response: in the case of lever pressing, cues associated with the lever and the movement of the lever itself.

This mechanism by itself would appear to account for the usual suppressive effects of punishment and their functional relationships to intensity of the punishing stimulus, duration of period of punishment, delay of punishment, and differences between contingent and noncontingent punishing stimuli. Further, it allows for different rates of recovery following different amounts of punishment and also for the acceleration of recovery by adaptation to stimuli in the experimental situations during a period when the punished response is prevented from occurring.

The principal limitation of the CER interpretation, relative to the facts available at the time of its formulation, was the difficulty of accounting for instances in which recovery from effects of punishment could evidently be delayed indefinitely by a prolonged period of severe punishment. What seemed to me at that time the most parsimonious augmentation of the theory to handle this observation was to assume that with adequate opportunity a withdrawal response, incompatible with execution of the punished response, might become conditioned to the cues previously leading to the former; that is, the organism would establish a conditioned-avoidance response (CAR).

Evaluation of the CER–CAR Theory

The two factors, CER and CAR, in varying combination, seem to characterize most interpretations of punishment espoused by other investigators down to the present. Both are prominent, for example, in the major recent reviews of the field by Church (1963), and by Solomon (1964). The most popular version seems to be a two-stage combination: The first instances of punishment lead by classical conditioning to establishment of a CER; then some response which terminates the conditioned stimuli for the CER, or removes the animal from them, is reinforced by this termination (i.e., by reduction of fear or anxiety). The instrumental avoidance response thus established being in direct competition with the punished response, results in its suppression. Different versions of this interpretation have been presented by Dinsmoor (1954), though in somewhat different terms, and Solomon (1964), among others.

The CAR component of the dual-process interpretation has proven, in my estimation, to be the weak link. Firstly, the notion that suppression of a response by punishment is primarily the result of its displacement by a competing avoidance response was never founded in direct observation of the supposed process of avoidance conditioning. Secondly, the uniformity with which a response is suppressed by punishment of sufficient intensity does not jibe with the extreme difficulty observed in many situations in establishing avoidance responses with similar shocks as unconditioned stimuli. Further, the time courses of the two classes of phenomena are not at all similar. Only under a very few special circumstances does one ever observe rates of avoidance conditioning comparable to the rates at which suppressive effects of punishment appear under a wide range of conditions. Finally, the effects of the same punishing stimulus are often observed to be quite different depending upon whether the punished response has been maintained by a positive reward, such as food, or by escape or avoidance. Frequently responses previously reinforced on an avoidance schedule are not suppressed by punishment and may even be facilitated. All this is not to say that in some situations involving punishment active avoidance responses may not ultimately be established. However, the weight of the evidence seems to me to indicate that the conditioning of active avoidance responses cannot be a necessary condition for suppression of a response by punishment, and further, that probably the immediate suppression of ongoing behavior by punishment is a facilitating, if not necessary, condition for the establishment of active avoidance responses in the same situation.

The notion of suppression of ongoing behavior by a CER consequent upon the occurrence of punishment seems descriptively sound so far as it goes. The conditions under which prompt and uniform suppression of responding by punishment occurs are precisely those known to be favorable for establishment of a CER. However, there is a basic conceptual weakness; namely, it has never been spelled out in detail why and how a CER suppresses ongoing behavior. Most investigators in this area have been content to note that the animal "freezes" upon occurrence of a stimulus which has preceded shock. However, the notion of freezing simply describes a behavioral phenomenon without elucidating the process or mechanism involved.

My own original assumption, though not spelled out either in the Estes and Skinner (1941) article or in my 1944 monograph, was that a CER exerts its effects on ongoing behavior essentially via stimulus generalization decrement. A stimulus which precedes shock will become a CS for a variety of visceral and skeletal reactions all carrying characteristic interoceptive and perhaps also proprioceptive stimuli. Then upon the occurrence of that CS in an operant situation, this barrage of stimuli, novel to that situation, will suddenly be elicited and, simply by changing the stimulus conditions under which the operant behavior has been learned, will lead to a decrement in response rate.

In hindsight I can see three major weaknesses in this interpretation. Firstly, as in the case of the avoidance interpretation, independent evidence for the assumed process has not been forthcoming. Secondly, the time course of suppression of behavior by a CER or by punishment does not prove similar to the time course of a disturbance of behavior by simple extraneous stimulation. In the case of the latter, the maximum effect is always manifest upon the very first trial in which the extraneous stimuli are introduced, with a monotone course of recovery as the new stimuli become conditioned under the continuing reinforcing schedule. Contrariwise, the effects of punishment generally increase with repetitions and, if the stimulus is of sufficient intensity, no recovery is observed so long as punishment is continued. Third, the effects of CER have turned out to depend upon the nature of the base-line behavior, the stimulus for the CER suppressing ongoing behavior if it has been maintained on a positive reward schedule but facilitating ongoing behavior if it has been maintained on an avoidance schedule (Herrnstein & Sidman, 1958; Waller & Waller, 1963). This last result could be brought into harmony with a generalization decrement hypothesis by means of some plausible additional assumptions, but I think it may be better simply to take it as a straw in the wind pointing toward a more satisfactory interpretation of a somewhat different character.

Second Approximation to a Theory of Punishment

In order to simplify the following exposition, I shall begin with a few demurrers, for the theory to be outlined is not intended to be complete enough to provide a full and detailed interpretation of a wide range of experiments on punishment. Firstly, the conditioning of active avoidance responses in punishment situations is not an integral part of my interpretation; however, this is not to deny that such conditioning may occur. When conditions are such as to facilitate establishment of a CAR, the effects of punishment will naturally be prolonged, but I believe it possible to account for the main facts about punishment without appeal to the learning of competing responses. Secondly, let us understand that, as Church has brought out nicely in his 1963 review, the punishing stimulus has properties of stimuli in general as well as those peculiar to its class, and, further, that in most situations punishing stimuli will have greater weight than ordinary background cues or discriminative stimuli. The notion of "weight" may be equated roughly with "attention value" or, in the context of stimulus-sampling theory, the number of associated stimulus elements. (The ideas involved are precisely those that I have previously developed in connection with drive stimuli [Estes, 1958].) Thus, the interpretation to be sketched in the sequel will be limited to the primary process believed to mediate the distinctive effects of punishment which cannot be accounted for simply by the effects of the punishing stimulus per se.

In the light of the ensuing quarter century of research, I believe now that I was right back in the early 1940's, both in assuming that the effects of reward and punishment should be essentially symmetrical, and also in concluding that interpretation of punishment requires a separate process rather than a simple weakening of associative strength. I think that where I went wrong, in the illustrious company of Thorndike, Skinner, and Hull, among others, was in assuming the effects of reward to involve a simple, direct strengthening of associative connections, and thus in looking for the wrong kind of symmetry. What I wish now to outline is a dual-process interpretation of both reward and punishment,

with an associative process common to both but with reward and punishment each involving separate, though symmetrical, effects upon
performance.

Unfortunately for convenience of exposition, the organism's behavior is not so compartmentalized that one can present a theory of
punishment without reference to other processes having to do with
discrimination, drive, and reward, among others. As a compromise for
our present purposes, I shall begin by sketching some modifications in
the general statistical theory of learning presented in earlier papers
(e.g., Estes, 1950, 1959) that seem to be called for by new sources of evidence on reward and punishment and then shall indicate how some
of the principal phenomena of punishment can be treated within the
new framework.

A convenient point of departure is my paper concerned with the
stimulus-sampling interpretation of drive (Estes, 1958). The primary
assumption was that the organism's behavior at any time is jointly controlled by stimuli of external origin, discriminative stimuli or cues, and
by stimuli of internal origin, drive stimuli. At any moment the stimulus
population available for sampling by the organism was assumed to
comprise elements of both types, the number of cue elements being a function of such experimental manipulations as the presentation of discriminative stimuli and the number of drive elements being a function
of such variables as deprivation time. Any individual stimulus element
of either type was assumed to be associated with (or "connected to")
exactly one response at any given time and the probability of a response
was assumed to be equal to the proportion of the elements currently
sampled, regardless of origin, associated with the given response. That is,
cues and drive-stimulus elements were assumed to be strictly interchangeable and to combine additively in their effects on behavior. Further, the determination of response probability by the stimulus sample
was assumed to be exhaustive. That is, given the makeup of the stimulus
sample, response probability was fully specified; variables having to do
with drive or motivation could influence behavior only insofar as they
might control the set of stimuli in the current sample.

Within that framework, there were basically only two ways in which
punishment could modify behavior: (1) by directly changing the state of
conditioning of stimulus elements previously associated with the punished response; or (2) by evoking behaviors incompatible with the
punished response under conditions conducive to counterconditioning.
But the many lines of accumulating evidence briefly surveyed above have
convinced me that the former of these conceptions is incorrect and the
latter insufficient. Rather, it appears that the effects of punishment must
primarily be exerted via the weakening of motivational support for the
punished response in a manner not provided for by earlier association-
istic theories.

I now propose to replace the assumption of simple, additive stimulus–response connections with what may be termed a summation, or stimulus amplifier, hypothesis. In the reformulation, it will be assumed that the occurrence of a response requires a summation of input from stimulus and drive sources. Regarding the latter, the primary function of drives and rewards is to act, so to speak, as stimulus amplifiers. Except perhaps in the case of certain reflexes, response evocation requires that the stimuli associated with the given response as a result of previous learning or innate organization summate with internally generated *amplifier elements*. It would be natural to refer to these as "drive elements," but a new term without so many associations may help avoid confusion with the closely related conception of ordinary discriminative elements which arise from drive-related operations such as eating and fasting.

The principal addition to the structure of earlier stimulus-sampling theory is that of a source, or generator, of amplifier elements associated with each of the principal drive systems; e.g., hunger, thirst, pain. It will be assumed that each of these generating sources provides a certain base rate of input of amplifier elements under a given deprivational or stimulating condition and that local changes in the input are evoked by the occurrence of traumatic stimuli, stimuli for consummatory behaviors, and the like.

Although the precise form of quantification is not of central importance for our present purposes, the response evocation process conceived in the new theory may be most easily clarified by comparing it with that of earlier versions of stimulus-sampling theory. In the former (see, e.g., Estes, 1959; LaBerge, 1959) it is assumed that on any trial of a learning experiment the organism draws ("perceives") a sample of the available discriminative cues, some of which may be connected to the reference response as a result of preceding learning, some to competing responses, and perhaps some to neither. Elements which are not connected either to the reference response or to alternative competing responses which may occur in the given situation are customarily termed "neutral" elements (LaBerge, 1959). Having drawn a sample of elements, the organism scans these singly, the scanning continuing until an element is processed which is connected with a permissible response, and then that response is made overtly. Thus, response latency depends upon the density of neutral elements in the sample, and the probability of a given reference response is equal to the proportion of nonneutral elements in the sample which are connected with that response.

In the revised theory, the sampling and scanning processes are assumed to proceed in the same way, but with one major qualification; namely, when a nonneutral element in the stimulus sample is processed, it will evoke a response only if an amplifier element is sampled simultaneously. Under any given drive–reward condition there is some probability that any given element in the sample will be processed simultaneously with an amplifier element. The latency of the evoked response will vary inversely with this probability, but the probability of a given reference response relative to competing responses will be unaffected. However, as will be developed in more detail in the sequel, different stimuli in an experimental situation may, as a result either of innate organization or of learning, have different probabilities of being accompanied by amplifier inputs; thus, in effect, the stimuli will have different weights in response determination.

The way in which amplifier elements enter into learning can be elucidated in terms of one of the positive drive systems, say that associated with hunger, and a negative system, say that associated with pain. It will be assumed that prior to any learning experiences the amplifier input of a given system is connected to a family of stimulus–response units, those having to do with consummatory behavior in the case of hunger, those having to do with escape, attack, and other defensive behaviors in the case of pain. When, for example, an animal becomes hungry, the base rate of input of amplifier elements to the appropriate family of responses increases; this in itself does not lead to overt response occurrences, but it provides a basis for summation of amplifier elements with any unconditioned or conditioned stimuli for consummatory responses which may become available.

Although we cannot go into detail in this paper, it may be seen that the proposed mechanism for combining effects of discriminative and drive inputs will account in a natural way for a number of phenomena which were awkward to handle in the earlier theory. One of these is the commonly observed disparity between the strong control of rate and speed of responding in simple operant situations by deprivation conditions and the difficulty of developing discriminations based upon different deprivation conditions. The former relation results, in the present model, from the direct relationship between input of drive amplifier elements and the probability that currently available discriminative cues will receive the summation necessary to lead to response evocation. The difficulty of discrimination arises from the fact that, although the amplifier inputs associated with two drive conditions, say hunger and thirst, may be quite distinct, they do not by themselves evoke overt responses, and the populations of interoceptive or proprioceptive cues associated with different deprivations have high proportions of elements in common. Secondly, the covariation in strength, or probability of occurrence, of families of responses as a function of such operations as deprivation is more readily handled in the revised theory, since it is no longer assumed that any particular amplifier element can be associated with only one response at a given time. Thirdly, the dissociation between thresholds determined electrophysiologically and thresholds determined by behavioral preference tests fits naturally into the present schema. For example, adrenalectomized rats show a markedly reduced threshold for salt in preference tests but no difference from normals in electrophysiological determinations (Pfaffmann & Bare, 1950); in the present terms, the result of adrenalectomy is to increase the input of amplifier elements to a consummatory-response system involved in the ingestion of salt solutions while the sampling probabilities of gustatory stimuli are unaffected.

The two additional revised assumptions of greatest import have to do with reciprocal inhibition and with conditioning. Regarding the former, it is assumed that the activity of the negative, flight–attack system results in reciprocal inhibition of the activity of generators belonging to positive-drive systems. Thus, whereas in many extant theories (including Thorndike's formulation of the law of effect, 1931; Guthrie's contiguity theory, 1952; previously published accounts of statistical learning theory, as Estes, 1959; and perhaps also Hull's theory, 1943, 1952) an account of the suppression of positively motivated behavior by punishment must involve appeal to competing responses, in the present theory the immediate effect of punishment is to reduce the supply of amplifier elements needed for maintenance of the positively motivated behavior. This I am inclined to regard as a considerable advantage in view of the long history of meagre success on the part of many investigators in attempting to pin down the specific competing responses evoked by various punishing stimuli.

The assumed conditioning process needs to be spelled out in some detail. Considering first a positive system, such as that involved in hunger and food ingestion, the generation of amplifier elements is assumed to be jointly controlled by deprivation conditions, which by themselves provide a relatively steady base rate of amplifier input, and by stimuli, gustatory in this instance, which initiate consummatory behavior. Occurrence of the latter yields a momentary increase in amplifier input. Through conditioning by contiguity, the capacity of certain stimuli to evoke changes in drive input is transferred to other stimuli which immediately precede them; over a series of occasions the facilitatory effects move backward, that is begin to occur anticipatorily. At a later stage in the conditioning process, cues which occurred prior to those evoking the rewarded response will generate an input of amplifier elements facilitating approach to the latter, and so on. Thus, after establishment of the behavior chain leading to reward, the first member occurs when the organism is exposed to the appropriate discriminative stimulus and this summates with amplifier elements generated by the existing deprivation condition to evoke the first response of the chain. The feedback consequence of this response is to generate an increase in amplifier input which provides a basis for summation, and thus facilitates occurrence of the behaviors which follow in the chain.

In the case of a negative system, say that associated with an electric shock stimulus, the generation of amplifier elements is originally controlled only by the painful stimulation itself, the consequence of this input being to provide a basis for summation and thus to facilitate the occurrence of members of the flight–attack family of behaviors which might occur in the presence of the shock. As a result of conditioning by contiguity, this control of what may be termed negative amplifier input is transferred from the shock to stimuli immediately preceding it. The anticipatory occurrence of the negative input entails facilitation of the family of initial responses to shock and at the same time inhibition of the activity of any positive drive systems which might have been controlling the organism's behavior just prior to the shock.

Thus the consequences of variations in drive input are quite different in the two types of situations. When the hungry animal tastes food, the result is a generation of facilitative feedback that locks the animal in on the stimulus which initiated the consummatory activity and helps insure that the chain of consummatory behavior will run to completion. When the animal makes a response which brings it into contact with a painful stimulus, the result is the generation of feedback which increases the probability that the organism will break contact with the painful stimulus.

It should be noted that conditioning can occur between as well as within positive- and negative-drive systems. Thus, if a shock is followed by food, the result will be that the increase in amplifier input to consummatory behaviors normally following food intake will come to be evoked by the shock as a conditioned stimulus, attenuating the normally negative effects of the shock. Conditioning will occur, of course, only if shock is not so intense as to inhibit entirely the normally positive response to food which follows. Conversely, if food precedes shock, the negative drive input evoked by shock will come to be evoked by stimulation from food, thus leading on subsequent occasions to inhibition of the facilitative support for the hunger motivated behavior which initially led to approaching and ingesting food. A qualitative implication of this assumed conditioning process is that if a response is followed by both reward and punishment, say food and shock, and the shock is not so severe as to inhibit hunger-motivated behavior entirely, the animal should learn to delay the ingestion of food until after the shock occurs.

Interpretations of CER and Punishment in the Revised Theory

In order to give a full account of experiments involving punishment it would be necessary to discuss the representation of acquisition and extinction within the revised stimulus sampling theory in more detail than is feasible in the present paper. Thus in order to bring out some of the distinctive implications of the new theory for phenomena of punishment, specifically, let us simply assume an experimental situation in which a positively motivated operant response has been established and is occurring at some stable rate under the joint control of discriminative stimuli and deprivation-produced amplifier input. If, now, the organism is subjected to the usual CER conditioning procedure in a different situation, an originally neutral CS being presented and followed by a noncontingent shock, conditioning will occur such that after this training the CS will evoke the negative amplifier input originally produced by the shock. When, now, the CS is tested in the operant situation, the consequent generation of negative elements will have two effects. Firstly, via the summation process assumed in the theory, the probability of occurrence of responses belonging to the flight–attack family will be increased. Secondly, regardless of whether any specific overt responses occur which would be incompatible with the ongoing operant behavior, the increase in activity of the negative drive system will reciprocally inhibit the positive system which had provided facilitation for the positively motivated operant response, thus producing a decrease in probability of the latter. The degree of response suppression will be a joint function of the intensity of the shock and the prevailing level of positive-drive input.

An aspect of the CER experiment which has generally escaped explicit comment needs discussion in view of the recent study by Rescorla (1968), who has demonstrated the importance of the discriminative contingencies involved. During CER training a CS is followed by shock; and after conditioning has occurred, negative-drive activity is increased during CS presentations with the consequent inhibition of positive amplifier input. However, termination of the CS and shock are in consequence uniformly followed by a decrease in negative input, with the resulting elimination of the reciprocal inhibition and an increase in positive amplifier input to the prevailing level. Thus termination of the CS and shock become a conditioned signal for increase in the positive input, and over a series of occasions the suppression of behavior by the CS becomes progressively more sharply confined to the period during which the CS and shock are present. If, on the contrary, training were entirely nondiscriminative—that is, shocks simply being given intermittently in the experimental situation without a preceding signal—then the activity of the negative amplifier system would become conditioned to a variety of cues in the experimental situation, all of which would come to have suppressive effects; on the other hand, no stimuli would be uniformly correlated with shock termination and the recovery of positive input. The result to be expected in this case would be a diffuse suppression of responding throughout the experimental session.

As in the earlier theory, the primary mechanism of punishment is assumed to be the establishment of a CER, the role of the CS being taken on by cues which were originally involved in the occurrence of the punished response and thus were temporally contiguous with the onset of the punishing stimulus and its attendant increase in negative drive input. In this interpretation the well-known importance of temporal contiguity between response and punishment is simply a corollary; the critical relation is that between the cues originally initiating the punished response and the onset of the punishing stimulus. Experimental arrangements which insure that the punishing stimulus will follow closely upon the response also improve the temporal contiguity between the punishing stimulus and the discriminative cues.

As soon as conditioning has occurred, so that cues originally leading to a punished response have taken on the function of a CS for a CER, the occurrence of these cues will lead to an increase in negative amplifier activity. During presentation of this CS, the organism will suffer inhibition of the positive input which must be available to summate with discriminative stimulation in order to evoke the response. Whereas effects of noncontingent shocks may be expected to be eliminated entirely during a period of adaptation to the experimental situation without shock, when conditioned associations between various apparatus cues and negative amplifier activity can extinguish, recovery will generally be incomplete during a similar period of adaptation following response contingent punishment. In the latter case, not all of the cues involved in the initiation and execution of the response will be present during the adaptation period, so that the CER will be protected from complete extinction. For example, in the studies of this type that I reported earlier (Estes, 1944) the punished response was bar pressing and the adaptation period involved exposure to the apparatus with the bar removed. During this period the animals might explore the vicinity of the bar and make some of the movements normally involved in approaching it, but could not expose themselves to all of the stimulation previously entailed in bar pressing.

Unlike the earlier theory, the new formulation predicts quite different effects if CER or punishment procedures are imposed on a baseline of negatively rather than positively motivated behavior. Suppose, for example, that a CER is established in the usual way but that the effects of the CS are then tested during a period when the animal is operating a response manipulandum in order to escape shock rather than in order to obtain food. In this case, the increase in negative amplifier input during the period of the CS will add to, rather than subtract from, the level of facilitative input supporting the response. Although just as in the case of a hunger-motivated response, the CS for the CER will lead to inhibition of any prevailing positive drive input, the only relevant effect of this will be to reduce further the probability of occurrence of positively motivated responses which might otherwise occur in this situation in competition with the escape response.

The effects of response-contingent punishment of an escape response are too complex to be handled in any general way at a qualitative level. It is clear that the suppressive effects of punishment would be less than for an otherwise comparable positively motivated response and that the degree of suppression would depend on the relative intensities of the stimulus being escaped and the punishing stimulus. Specification of the functional relationships involved and of the conditions under which facilitation rather than suppression of the punished response might be expected (as observed in studies of "vicious circle" behavior by Brown, Martin, & Morrow, 1964; Martin & Melvin, 1964) must wait upon further examination of the new theory by mathematical or computer simulation methods.

Similarly the effects of shock for correct responses in discrimination learning (Muenzinger, 1934; Fowler & Wischner, Chapter 12 of this volume) depend upon a balance of parameter values and cannot be satisfactorily analyzed at a qualitative level. If the shock is sufficiently intense, so that its effects persist into the subsequent consummatory activity and reduce the positive drive stimulus input that would normally occur, then the probability of the correct response would necessarily be reduced as compared to an otherwise similar case in which correct responses were not followed by shock. However, if the intensity of the shock were lowered sufficiently and its effects did not diminish the positive input associated with subsequent ingestive behavior, then the shock would become a CS for activity of the positive system. The net result in this instance would be amplification of the effects of discriminative cues associated with the correct choice and a consequent improvement in performance.

Phenomena having to do with recovery from effects of punishment are of special interest in relation to alternative theories. Although, again, detailed account of the implications of the present formulation cannot be given without mathematical analysis, some major qualitative predictions can be indicated and the importance of a major distinction between two types of experimental situations elucidated by means of the illustrative curves presented in Figs. 3–3 and 3–4. Although the curves were derived from a quantitative formulation of the ideas presented in this paper, they can be understood without reference to the derivations. Let us consider first an experiment conducted with discrete trials, for example, a runway experiment in which each trial terminates with the occurrence of the reference response. If, following a period of positively rewarded training, simple extinction is initiated, the probability of the previously rewarded response should decline along a negatively accelerated curve of the form indicated for the control condition in Fig. 3–3. The associative relationship previously established between discriminative

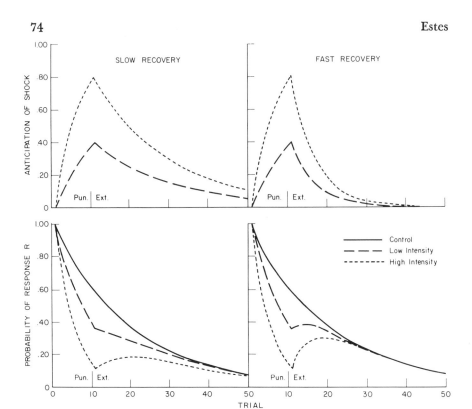

FIG. 3–3.   Illustrative extinction curves for discrete trial experiment, with a pre-viously rewarded response (R) receiving 10 trials of punishment by electric shock fol-lowed by simple extinction. Upper panels show the acquisition and extinction of anticipation of shock; lower panels, changes in probability of R during punishment and extinction (extinction throughout for the control condition). The two punishment conditions in each panel represent different intensities of the punishing stimulus. The left and right sides of the figure differ only with respect to the parameter governing rate of extinction of shock anticipation following discontinuation of punishment.

cues for the response and stimuli for consummatory behavior extin-guishes over the sequence of trials when reward no longer follows the response; and, as the organism's tendency to anticipate positive amplifier activity following a response decreases, so also does the input of positive elements needed to facilitate response occurrence. If, during the initial portion of the extinction series, each response is punished, then, as in-dicated in the upper panels of Fig. 3–3, the animal learns to anticipate shock following response occurrences. Conditioning of the tendency to an-ticipate shock follows a negatively accelerated course at a rate which is directly related to intensity of the punishing stimulus. The immediate consequence of this learning is that negative amplifier activity comes to be evoked by the cues which formerly led to the punished response,

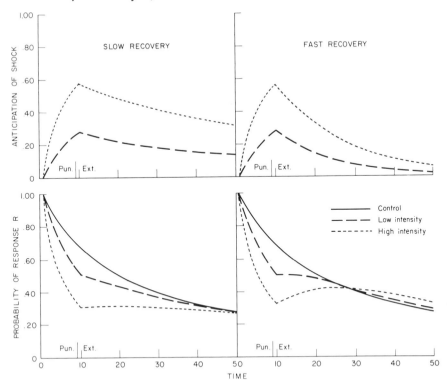

FIG. 3-4. Illustrative extinction curves for free-responding experiment. All conditions and parameter values are the same as for corresponding curves in Fig. 3-3, but response probability is plotted as a function of time rather than trials.

reducing the level of facilitative support for the response, and thus its probability of occurrence, below that of the control group. The value of response probability on any trial n for a given punishment curve in Fig. 3-3 is obtained by multiplying the value of the control curve on trial n by $1 - a_n$, where a_n denotes the value of the corresponding anticipation of shock function in the upper panel.

If at some point, following Trial 10 in the example, punishment is discontinued, then the tendency to anticipate shock also undergoes extinction as shown in the right-hand side of each of the upper panels of Fig. 3-3. As this extinction lowers the activity of the negative system which inhibited the positive input during the period of punishment, the input of positive elements again becomes available and the curves of response probabilities for the punished animals approach those of the controls, as shown in the right-hand side of each of the lower panels. The general qualitative predictions for this situation are that, following the discontinuation of punishment, recovery will occur but that the rate and extent of recovery will be a function of the intensity of punishment. Further, recovery will be delayed according as experimental conditions during punishment (e.g., intermittency of shock) favor resistance to extinction of the anticipation of the punishment. The left and right panels of Fig. 3–3 differ only with respect to the parameter governing rate of extinction of shock anticipation (decrease in a_n) following the termination of punishment. Conversely, recovery will be accelerated according as previous conditions of reinforcement favor resistance to extinction of the punished response. It should be noted, in particular, that for the discrete trial situation, with the assumption that each trial continues until the reference response occurs, there can never be compensatory recovery, that is, recovery which would carry the curves for the previously punished animals above the curve for the control condition.

A comparable analysis is presented in Fig. 3–4 for a typical free-responding operant situation in which probability of the reference response is recorded as a function of time in the experimental situation (all parameter values being the same as those of the corresponding curves of Fig. 3–3). The course of conditioning of anticipation of shock and the effects of this upon response probability are essentially the same as in the discrete-trial case. The important differences appear following the discontinuation of punishment. The predictions of the theory [3] are that, as illustrated in the figure, for the same parameters of reward and punishment, recovery will in general be delayed longer following the termination of punishment in the free-responding situation; but on the other hand compensatory recovery may occur, with the curve of response probability for previously punished animals ultimately crossing the control curve and running above it for a time before they ultimately converge to a common asymptote.

The reason for these differences in the free-responding case is that extinction of the conditioned associative relationship between cues involved in the response occurrence and the activity of the negative-drive system evoked by shock can be extinguished only on occasions when a response occurs so that the cues are present in the absence of shock. In the free-operant situation the punished animal may cease responding for a considerable period, during which the tendency to anticipate punishment following responses is protected from extinction, thus delaying recovery; but at the same time the tendency to anticipate reward following occurrences of the reference response is protected from extinction, thus setting the stage for compensatory recovery when the effects of punishment do ultimately extinguish. Both the delay in recovery and the compensation will be functions of the frequency and intensity of the

---

[3] Derivations are more difficult than in the discrete trial case, and the illustrative curves of Fig. 3–4 were obtained by computer-simulated runs of groups of 100 "statistical subjects."

punishing stimulus during the preceding period of punishment; with punishment of low intensity recovery may be early with substantial compensation; with punishment of high intensity, recovery may be so delayed that no appreciable compensation is ever observed.

Comparison of the Present Approach with Others

In one respect the present theory represents a simplification of the currently most widely accepted interpretation of punishment, since the two principal factors of CER–CAR theory come down to one in the present formulation. In the currently influential two-phase theory, the principal effect of punishment is to set the stage for reinforcement of avoidance responses, the basis of reinforcement being either fear reduction (Solomon, 1964) or escape from stimuli which have acquired aversive properties (Dinsmoor, 1954). In the present theory the establishment of a CER to cues associated with the initiation and execution of a punished response is the primary mechanism and it is assumed to be a sufficient basis for the characteristic phenomena of punishment. Although under suitable circumstances active avoidance responses may indeed be learned in situations involving punishment, I believe that these are not necessary to account for the suppressive effects of punishment. Rather than accounting for the suppressive effects in terms of avoidance learning, I would say that the suppression normally occurs first and sets the stage for avoidance learning. The main contribution of the latter is to delay or prevent recovery from the effects of punishment if the avoidance response keeps the organism from re-exposing itself to the stimuli which originally evoked the punished response.

The present interpretation of drive differs in one major respect from my own earlier formulations (Estes, 1958). In the initial development of a stimulus-sampling theory of drive, I remained carefully noncommittal as to whether drive-inducing operations, such as deprivations, affect the probabilities of occurrence only of interoceptive or of both interoceptive and exteroceptive stimuli. Now I propose specifically to assume the latter. The immediate effect of an increase in activity of any drive system is the generation of an input of facilitative or amplifier elements which summate with (in the terminology preferred by some investigators, e.g., Campbell & Sheffield [1953], "lower the thresholds of") the set of stimuli, internal or external in origin, associated with the system. One consequence of this facilitative input will be increased sampling probabilities of visceral cues which provide the basis for drive discriminations. Another will be the increased probability that behaviors associated with the system, e.g., consummatory responses, will be evoked by their discriminative stimuli.

Unlike Hull's (1943) theory, the present formulation assumes no general energizing factor. Rather, activity from a particular drive system will "energize"—that is, facilitate the occurrence of—some classes of responses and suppress others. The innate organization of the organism's drive systems is assumed to be such that activity in any one system originally leads to facilitation of a family of responses: consummatory responses in some cases, flight and attack responses in others. Then through conditioning these facilitative effects are extended to other stimuli and additional stimulus–response units are, so to speak, assimilated into the system. On the other hand, one of the divergences between my original formulation and that of Hull has been reduced. Whereas, in the model sketched in my 1958 paper, effects of drive variables and discriminative stimuli can only combine additively in the determination of response probability, the present assumption is that the facilitative effect of drive input upon stimulus sampling probabilities is multiplicative, as is the combination of drive and habit factors in Hull's theory. There is no basic distinction in the present theory corresponding to that between drive and incentive (D and K) in Hull's system except, perhaps, the recognition that variations in activity of drive systems are influenced both by long-term conditions such as deprivation and by more local ones such as unconditioned stimuli for consummatory behaviors.

The idea of a reciprocal interaction between mechanisms of reward and punishment has been put forward, with considerable supporting evidence, by several recent investigators working within a more physiological framework, notably Miller (1963) and Stein (1964). In each of these proposals, it has been tentatively assumed that rewards arouse a "go," or activating mechanism, possibly hypothalamic in locus, which intensifies ongoing behaviors; that punishments arouse a "stop" mechanism, which exerts precisely the opposite effect; and that these mechanisms are to some extent mutually inhibiting. These notions have impressed me as extremely promising, and the analyses advanced by Miller and Stein have influenced the direction of my own reformulation. However, as indicated in preceding sections, a model differing in some specific assumptions from those hitherto proposed appears to have some advantages with regard to simplicity and the range of phenomena that can be handled. Concerning the suppressive effects of punishment, in particular, it seems to me that a "stop" mechanism operating directly on responses would have a more disorganizing effect on behavior than is ordinarily observed, and would not readily yield the qualitatively different effects of punishing stimuli that are well known to occur under different motivating conditions.

Finally, the notion of feedback is important in the present theory, as in a number of other contemporary approaches. However, the primary feedback relation in the present theory is different in important respects from that assumed by, e.g., Mowrer (1960) and Stein (1964). In both of the latter approaches, it is assumed that, as a result of a learning process, responses which have been followed by rewards or punishments come to evoke facilitatory or inhibitory feedback; however, the critical relation is that between the feedback and the response which evoked it. Thus, Mowrer's approach has been criticized by Miller (1963) on the grounds that this type of feedback does not account for the effects of reward or punishment upon response selection, since the response must occur before it can generate the positive or negative feedback. In the present theory, the feedback operates primarily in a forward rather than a backward direction; that is, a response which has previously been rewarded comes to instigate the activity of a positive-drive system which facilitates the occurrence of behaviors that normally follow in the consummatory chain.

Upon being returned to a situation in which reward has been obtained, the organism is not required by the present model to search its entire response repertoire until it finds a response carrying positive feedback, as is apparently the case in Mowrer's scheme. Rather, when the organism samples some cue in the situation, the last associated response is activated, simply as a result of conditioning by contiguity. If this response is a member of a sequence leading to reward, facilitative feedback will be generated, increasing the probability that the given sequence will run to completion. If not, the stimulus-sampling process continues. The stimulus-amplifier theory assumes a major role for a scanning or VTE process in response selection, but it is the set of available stimuli which is scanned, not the set of possible responses. The function of rewards occurring on previous trials is, in effect, to alter the relative weights of the various available stimuli, and thus to bias the scanning process in favor of stimuli whose associated responses have led to reward.

Summary

The theories of punishment considered in this chapter fall into three main categories which may be denoted, for brevity, as (1) unlearning, (2) new learning, and (3) suppression theories. Accumulating evidence appears to support the decision, arrived at through various routes by most theorists from Thorndike onward, against a theory of the first type, which would attribute to response-contingent punishing stimuli a unique property of weakening stimulus response associations. The most influential theory of the second type in recent years has been one assuming a two-stage process, the immediate effect of punishment being to establish a conditioned emotional state which in turn leads to the reinforcement of avoidance responses through fear or anxiety reduction. Although the learning of avoidance responses, as envisaged in this interpretation, doubtless occurs in some situations involving punishment, I believe no satisfactory case has been made for such a process as a necessary condition for the principal phenomena of punishment. According to the third view, cues originally evoking a punished response become conditioned stimuli for a conditioned emotional reaction which suppresses the ongoing behavior directly, the effect not necessarily being mediated by any type of direct competition between approach and avoidance responses. The conclusion of the present review is that the suppression theory is descriptively adequate, but that earlier versions are incomplete in that they provide no adequate theoretical basis for the suppressive effects.

In the revised suppression theory outlined in this paper, the primary mechanism of punishment is not a competition of responses but rather a competition of motives. The principal assumptions are (1) that maintenance of any type of nonreflex behavior involves the summation of discriminative or conditioned stimuli with the input of amplifier, or facilitative, elements from drive sources, and (2) that the activation of negative drive systems by pain or the anticipation of pain reciprocally inhibits amplifier input from positive-drive sources. Thus, a stimulus which has preceded a traumatic event, e.g., shock, as in the typical CER or punishment paradigm, acquires the capacity of inhibiting the input of amplifier elements from sources associated with hunger, thirst, and the like. If, then, while the animal is performing an instrumental response for, say, food reward, this conditioned stimulus is presented, the facilitative drive input will be reduced and so also the probability or rate of the instrumental response. If, on the other hand, the same stimulus is introduced while the animal is performing a response for escape from shock, there will be no similar reciprocal inhibition between drive sources and thus no suppressive effect.

The revised theory accounts for the classical parametric relationships of punishment studies, including effects of delay and intensity of punishment, and amount of previous training of the punished response, the differences between response-contingent and noncontingent punishment, and the attenuation of punishment by adaptation to stimuli in the absence of opportunity for responding. Also, detailed predictions are derivable regarding the course of recovery from punishment following different types of training, including specifications of conditions under which compensatory recovery may be expected. Finally, the revised formulation appears to represent a distinct advance over my earlier one in that it provides a means of interpreting temporal and order effects in situations involving both reward and punishment, and a rationale for the differential effects of punishment upon behaviors maintained by appetitive and aversive sources of motivation.

REFERENCES

BROWN, J. S., MARTIN, R. C., & MORROW, M. W. Self punitive behavior in the rat: Facilitative effects of punishment on resistance to extinction. *Journal of Comparative and Physiological Psychology,* 1964, **57**, 127–133.

CAMPBELL, B. A., & SHEFFIELD, F. D. Relation of random activity to food deprivation. *Journal of Comparative and Physiological Psychology,* 1953, **46**, 320–322.

CHURCH, R. M. The varied effects of punishment on behavior. *Psychological Review,* 1963, **70**, 369–402.

DINSMOOR, J. A. Punishment: I. The avoidance hypothesis. *Psychological Review,* 1954, **61**, 34–46.

ESTES, W. K. An experimental study of punishment. *Psychological Monographs,* 1944, **57** (3, Whole No. 263).

ESTES, W. K. Toward a statistical theory of learning. *Psychological Review,* 1950, **57**, 94–107.

ESTES, W. K. Stimulus–response theory of drive. In M. R. Jones (Ed.), *Nebraska symposium on motivation.* Lincoln, Neb.: Nebraska University Press, 1958. Pp. 35–68.

ESTES, W. K. The statistical approach to learning theory. In S. Koch (Ed.), *Psychology: A study of a science.* Vol. 2. New York: McGraw-Hill, 1959. Pp. 380–491.

ESTES, W. K., & SKINNER, B. F. Some quantitative properties of anxiety. *Journal of Experimental Psychology,* 1941, **29**, 390–400.

GUTHRIE, E. R. *The psychology of learning.* (Rev. ed.) New York: Harper, 1952.

HERRNSTEIN, R. J., & SIDMAN, M. Avoidance conditioning as a factor in the effects of unavoidable shocks on food-reinforced behavior. *Journal of Comparative and Physiological Psychology,* 1958, **51**, 380–385.

HULL, C. L. *Principles of behavior.* New York: Appleton-Century, 1943.

HULL, C. L. *A behavior system.* New Haven: Yale University Press, 1952.

LABERGE, D. L. A model with neutral elements. In W. K. Estes and R. R. Bush (Eds.), *Studies in mathematical learning theory.* Stanford, Calif.: Stanford University Press, 1959. Pp. 53–64.

MARTIN, R. C., & MELVIN, K. B. Vicious circle behavior as a function of delay of punishment. *Psychonomic Science,* 1964, **1**, 415–416.

MILLER, N. E. Some reflections on the law of effect produce a new alternative to drive reduction. In M. R. Jones (Ed.), *Nebraska symposium on motivation.* Lincoln, Nebr.: Nebraska University Press, 1963. Pp. 65–112.

MOWRER, O. H. *Learning theory and behavior.* New York: Wiley, 1960.

MUENZINGER, K. F. Motivation in learning: II. The function of electric shock for right and wrong responses in human subjects. *Journal of Experimental Psychology,* 1934, **17**, 439–448.

PFAFFMANN, C., & BARE, J. K. Gustatory nerve discharges in normal and adrenalectomized rats. *Journal of Comparative and Physiological Psychology,* 1950, **43**, 320–324.

RESCORLA, R. A. Probability of shock in the presence and absence of CS as determinants of fear conditioning. *Journal of Comparative and Physiological Psychology,* 1968, **66,** 1–5.

SKINNER, B. F. *The behavior of organisms.* New York: Appleton-Century, 1938.

SOLOMON, R. L. Punishment. *American Psychologist,* 1964, **19,** 239–253.

SPENCE, K. W. *Behavior theory and conditioning.* New Haven: Yale University Press, 1956.

STEIN, L. Reciprocal action of reward and punishment mechanisms. In R. G. Heath (Ed.), *The role of pleasure in behavior.* New York: Harper & Row, 1964. Pp. 113–140.

THORNDIKE, E. L. *Human learning.* New York: Appleton-Century, 1931.

THORNDIKE, E. L. *The psychology of wants, interests, and attitudes.* New York: Appleton-Century, 1935.

TOLMAN, E. C. *Purposive behavior in animals and men.* New York: Appleton-Century, 1932.

WALLER, M. B. & WALLER, P. F. The effects of unavoidable shocks on a multiple schedule having an avoidance component. *Journal of the Experimental Analysis of Behavior,* 1963, **6,** 29–37.

4

Hedonism Revisited: On the Negative Law of Effect[1]

Howard Rachlin

R. J. Herrnstein

HARVARD UNIVERSITY

Hedonism, the theory that organisms seek to gain pleasure and avoid pain, is the venerable antecedent of the positive law of effect, identifying pleasure with increases in responding, and of the negative law of effect, identifying pain with decreases in responding. Although the positive law of effect has been the cornerstone of a portion of American psychology since the beginning of the century, the negative version has been under almost continuous attack. Early objections to the negative law, including one by its formulator, Thorndike (1932), maintained simply that it did not work, that aversive stimulation did not really alter behavior, but only suppressed it temporarily as physical restraint might do. Later objections were sometimes more elaborate. Estes (1944), for example, said that aversive stimulation affects a response upon which it is contingent in the same way that it affects a response with respect to which its occurrence is random. The reduction of punished responding then, while seeming to be an instrumental effect, would actually be a kind of negative pseudo-instrumental conditioning. Pseudoinstrumental conditioning is certainly conceivable for the positive law of effect, as when a stimulant, such as caffeine, adrenalin, or cocaine, increases responding even though administered independently of the response.

To qualify as a positive reinforcer, a stimulus contingent on a response must not only increase responding, but this increase must be greater than that obtained when the stimulus is presented independently of responding. Food and water will qualify under the appropriate circumstances, even though caffeine or adrenalin might not. According to Thorndike and Estes, no stimulus should pass the analogous test for punishers. However, a series of experiments by Azrin (1956, 1958) has

[1] The research reported here was supported by National Science Foundation Grants No. GB-3121 and GB-3723 to Harvard University. We wish to thank Richard Schuster for permission to include unpublished data.

suggested that aversive stimuli such as shock and loud noise do suppress responding more when contingent, than when noncontingent, upon responding. By the above criterion alone they would qualify as true punishers. Theories of punishment, however, have become more complex since Thorndike's day.

While it is now generally recognized that punishment involves some sort of true instrumental conditioning (Solomon, 1964), the need for a negative law of effect has not been established. Instead, several theorists (e.g., Dinsmoor, 1954; Mowrer, 1947; Skinner, 1953) have argued that the suppressive effects of punishment are to be accounted for by two processes, neither of which is the negative law of effect in the original sense of a response-decrementing mechanism. These two-process theories of punishment are extensions of the familiar two-process theories of avoidance, according to which a stimulus becomes aversive or fearsome because it is paired with a primary aversive event like electric shock, and then a response increases in frequency because it removes the conditioned aversive or fearsome stimulus. In punishment procedures the apparent *decrease* in responding frequency is thereby explained by a postulated *increase* in the nonpunished alternatives to the directly measured behavior. For Thorndike and Estes, the theoretical issue concerning the negative law of effect hinged on the empirical characteristics of response suppression. With two-process theories available, the issue no longer seems to depend on the outcome of direct experimental test, for even an unequivocal demonstration of response suppression based on a punishment contingency is open to other interpretations than the negative law of effect.

This poses a problem for the experimenter who studies punishment. How is he to describe his experiments? The vocabulary of the two-process theory is quite different from that implied by a negative law of effect or from that used in ordinary language. For instance, the two-process theory holds that the effect of punishment is a by-product of an increase in nonresponding, not a manifestation of a basic phenomenon in behavior-response suppression. Although one should be willing to abandon an old terminology or common parlance, there should be something gained by doing so. The earlier discussions of punishment do not seem to have made a compelling case for the change.

The present experiments are offered as contributions to the solution of the problem of a suitable vocabulary for the effects of punishment, insofar as matters of vocabulary can be subjected to the test of data. The experiments study the effect of contingent and noncontingent schedules of shock on two dependent variables: rate of responding during a schedule of shock, and choice between various schedules of shock. The results will be initially described in terms of response suppression since that vocabulary is the one the authors are used to. Afterward, this description of the results will be compared with one based on a two-process account of punishment.

The Concurrent-Chain Procedure

All but one of the following experiments maintained the key-pecking of hungry pigeons on a variation of concurrent-chain procedure developed by Autor (1960) and Herrnstein (1964a, 1964b). The purpose of this procedure is to measure preference for one schedule over another as well as performance while the schedule is imposed.

A diagram of the two-key concurrent-chain schedules is shown in Fig. 4–1. Each session began with a choice period during which both keys were illuminated with white light. Pecks on the left key occasionally changed the left key-light from white to red and darkened the right key. While the left key-light was red, pecks on the left key produced food reinforcement (3.5 sec. access to mixed grain) on a 1-minute variable-interval schedule (VI 1) while pecks on the darkened right key had no programmed consequences. The left key remained red for 5 minutes, after which both keys were again white, signalling a new choice period. Pecks on the right key during the choice period had corresponding consequences; they occasionally changed the color of the right key from white to red and darkened the left key. Again, while the right key was red, a 1-minute schedule of positive reinforcement was in effect thereon, while pecks on the other key had no effect. And again, after 5 minutes the choice period was restored.

The asymmetry between the two keys lay in various schedules of aversive stimulation superimposed on the 1-minute variable-interval positive reinforcement schedules. Numerous rates, intensities, and contingencies upon responding of electric shock (35-msec. pulses of 60 cps AC delivered through two gold wires implanted around the pigeon's two pubis bones) were compared by presenting them during opposing 5-minute reinforcement periods. The red light, therefore, was a signal for both reinforcement and punishment.

The change from the choice period to each of the 5-minute reinforcement periods was programmed by separate 3-minute variable-interval (VI 3) schedules for the two keys. With these schedules during the choice period, low response rates on either key increased the probability that the few pecks made on the key would produce a reinforcement period and insured approximately equal exposures to the two reinforcement periods, even when one key was strongly preferred.

The difference between a simple concurrent program and a concurrent-chain program is that the former studies choice between essentially instantaneous events while the latter studies choice between temporally extended events. Because both responses are always available in simple concurrent programs, the subject is constantly making choices. In the concurrent chain, on the other hand, the alternatives are not always

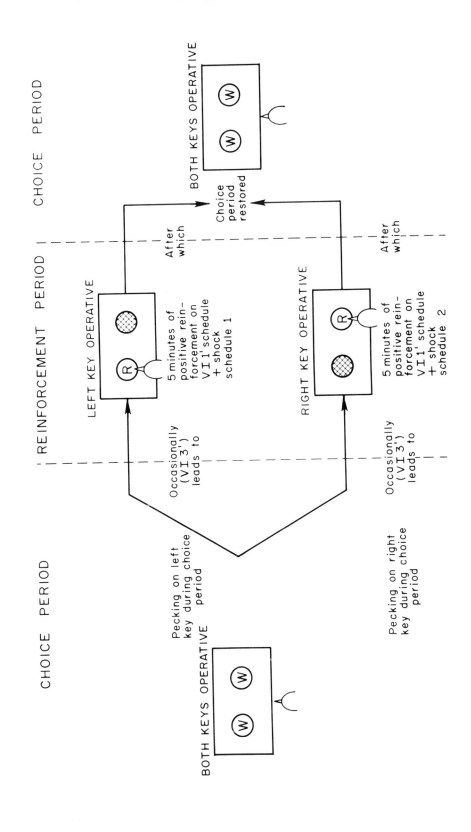

accessible and the subject must abide (for 5 min.) by the consequences of a choice. The procedure is analogous to having a rat choose between two arms of a T maze and then press a lever located at the end of each arm. The present arrangement, however, has the further advantage of exposing the subject equally to the two schedules without forced choice and of requiring anatomically equivalent responses for both choice of a schedule and responding during that schedule.

Independent Variables

The independent variables for the first three experiments were the intensity and frequency of shock and whether the shock was contingent upon, or independent of, responding. The standard procedure was to train responding without shock, then to increase frequency or intensity of shock in steps and maintain shock at a given step for seven to fifteen sessions. After increasing the independent variable to its maximum, it would be decreased in steps back to zero.

Dependent Variables

The following are measures of behavior in the three experiments.

Suppression.   Suppression of ongoing responding by shock is always shown as a ratio of the rate of suppressed responding to the rate of responding before shock was introduced, with all other variables, such as key location, color, and reinforcement schedule, held constant. This measure is appropriate where shock is introduced and then varied in rate or intensity. The denominator of the fraction is the preshock rate, and the numerator is the presumably suppressed rate.

Relative rate.   While *suppression* is a comparison between rates during the reinforcement period on a single key before and after shock is introduced, *relative rate* is a comparison between rates during the reinforcement periods on the two keys. In a two-key concurrent chain, the relative rate on Key 1 is the rate of responding on Key 1 divided by the sum of the rates on Key 1 and Key 2. The relative rates on the two keys are, then, necessarily complementary.

FIG. 4–1.   Diagram of the concurrent chain procedure. During the choice period both keys are illuminated with white light and operative. Pecking on either key leads on a 3-minute variable-interval schedule (VI 3) to a reinforcement period during which the key just pecked is illuminated with red light and the other is dark and inoperative. Pecking at the red key during the reinforcement period is rewarded with food on a 1-minute variable-interval schedule. Various schedules of shock are also delivered during the reinforcement period.

Choice.   Choice is the percentage of total pecks on a given key during the choice period. For example, in a two-key concurrent chain, choice of Key 1 is the number of pecks on Key 1 divided by the sum of the pecks on Key 1 and Key 2 during choice periods only.

The measures of behavior reported are medians of the last 3 to 5 days at each condition.

Experiment I: Punishment versus No Punishment

In this experiment (Rachlin, 1967) with a two-key concurrent chain such as the one just described, three subjects were punished for each response during one reinforcement period and not punished during the other reinforcement period. Over the course of the experiment, the intensity of the shock during the reinforcement period on the left key was increased from zero to 9.0 ma. and back to zero in steps of 3 ma. Then the intensity was similarly varied during the reinforcement period on the right key. This cycle of increase and decrease on one key, then increase and decrease on the other, was repeated three times.

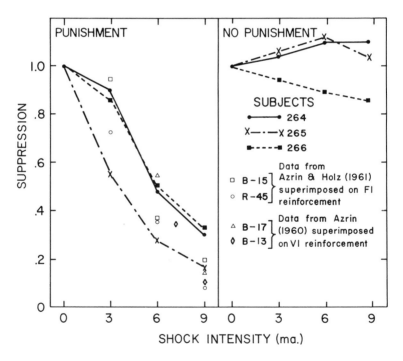

FIG. 4–2.   Suppression as a function of intensity of punishment during reinforcement period when pecks were punished and during reinforcement period when pecks were not punished. The closed symbols are data for the three subjects of the present experiment. The open symbols are data from other experiments.

Figure 4–2 shows the ratio of response rate during punishment to response rate without punishment (suppression) for the punished and unpunished reinforcement periods.

The connected points are averages of six exposures at each point for each of three subjects. The unconnected points are data reported by Azrin (1960) and Azrin and Holz (1961) who superimposed punishment of various intensities on variable- and fixed-interval schedules of reinforcement in pigeons. For the Azrin (1960) data, the rates were estimated from cumulative records. The lower set of curves clearly shows the strong and consistent suppressive effect of punishment on key-pecking in pigeons. All subjects showed large increments in suppression as shock intensity increased. During the other, unpunished, reinforcement period, two subjects showed slight but consistent increases in responding, while the third showed consistent decreases in responding. This consistency within subjects and inconsistency between subjects with respect to their behavior

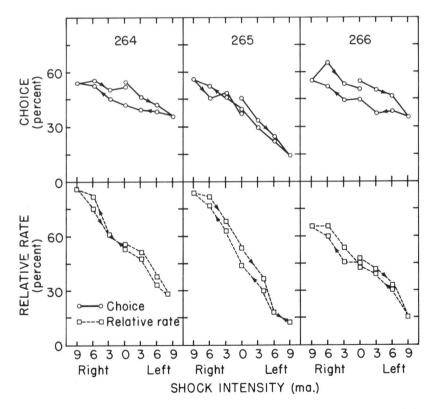

FIG. 4–3.   Choice of the left key (upper curves) and relative rates on the left key during the reinforcement period (lower curves) as intensity is varied. Increasing and decreasing intensities are superimposed for each curve. Starting at zero and following the arrows, intensity increased on the left key, decreased on the left key, increased on the right key, and decreased on the right key.

during unpunished components while punishment is varied in another component confirms previous observations (Rachlin, 1966) of mild punishment in a multiple schedule.

Figure 4–3 (bottom curves) shows relative rates during the reinforcement period on the left key, as a function of punishment intensity, as it was increased on the left key, decreased on the left key, increased on the right key, and decreased on the right key. All subjects show a steep, nearly linear, variation in relative rate as a function of intensity, in accordance with the suppression functions in Fig. 4–2. The top curves of Fig. 4–3 show choice over these same variations in punishment intensity. The choice functions in all cases are flatter and more irregular than the relative rate functions. There is no necessity that this be so. In fact, in concurrent-chain studies where positive reinforcement was varied (Autor, 1960; Fantino, 1967; Herrnstein, 1964a, 1964b), the choice functions were invariably steeper and more regular than the relative rate functions. Steeper choice functions would also be expected in the light of other evidence (Azrin & Holz, 1966) that ongoing rate in successive exposures to various punishment intensities is less sensitive to intensity of punishment than choice in a simple concurrent procedure where both punished and unpunished responses are simultaneously available.

One way to account for the relatively shallow functions for choice is to assume that choice is a function of rate of shock pulses as well as intensity of shock. Since shock was being delivered as punishment, rate of shock was strictly dependent on rate of responding, the one necessarily equaling the other. As Fig. 4–2 shows, high intensities of shock result in low rates of responding and, hence, of shock. A high intensity with a low rate of shock might be only slightly more aversive than a low intensity with a higher rate. While the intensity of shock could be controlled by the experimenter, the rate of shock was determined by the subjects, who had a clear tendency to counteract high intensities of shock with low rates of responding. Having balanced off the large differences in intensity with the appropriate differences in rate of responding, the animals show in the flatness of their choice functions that relative aversiveness is jointly determined by intensity and frequency of shock.

A stronger way to state this suggestion is to raise the possibility that the relative aversiveness of a schedule of shock, as measured by choice, is determined by the intensity and rate of shock actually obtained, and not by the nature of the contingency producing the shock nor by the emotional state of the animal. Fears, expectations, and contingencies may, however, play a role in determining ongoing rate of responding.

Experiment I is by no means a test of any of these notions. Several questions remain to be answered. Among them are (1) whether relatively steep choice functions can be obtained when both intensity *and* rate of shock are controlled by the experimenter, and (2) whether the dependence or independence of shocks on responding has any influence on the aversiveness of a schedule. Experiments II and III deal with these questions.

Experiment II: Rate of Noncontingent Shock

In this experiment (Rachlin, 1967) with a three-key concurrent-chain, trains of shock pulses were superimposed on 1-minute variable-interval reinforcement independently of the pigeon's pecking. The three reinforcement periods, associated with Keys 1, 2, and 3, differed with respect to the frequency of shock pulses (120, 30, or 6 pulses per min.) imposed on each. Three keys were used to provide a wider, but at the same time more detailed, range of shock pulse frequencies than two keys would allow.

Experiment II, then, differed from Experiment I in two respects: (1) each of three (instead of two) choices led to a reinforcement period accompanied by a different schedule of shock; (2) the shock was delivered independently of responding during all three reinforcement periods instead of as punishment during one reinforcement period. Whereas, in Experiment I, a reinforcement period unaccompanied by shock was always available, in Experiment II, all reinforcement periods were accompanied by shock, although at different frequencies. The intensity of the shock, always equal in each of the three reinforcement periods, was varied in steps from zero to 10 ma. and back down to 3 ma.

Figure 4–4 shows suppression as a function of intensity of shock for the four subjects at the three frequencies of shock pulses. Only two of the subjects (355 and 356) showed consistent suppression and only one of these (355) showed maximal suppression for the highest frequency of shock. Another subject's (426) responding was suppressed by the two low frequencies of shock, but its responding increased with the highest frequency. The fourth subject (441) showed increased responding at all frequencies.

Notwithstanding this variety of effects, an overall average of the data would show something like a direct relation between suppression and both intensity and frequency of shock. The experiment, in other words, confirms and extends previous studies showing some suppressive effect of response-independent shock. Comparison with Experiment I clearly shows, however, that much greater suppressive effects result from response-produced shock.

Figure 4–5 shows average relative rate and choice for the keys corresponding to the highest and lowest frequencies of shock (the middle-key data is strictly dependent on the other two and is not shown). The arrows

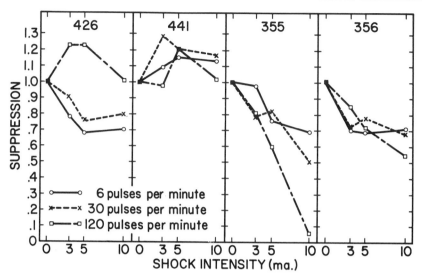

FIG. 4–4.   Suppression as a function of intensity of noncontingent shock during reinforcement periods for shock-pulse frequencies of 6, 30, and 120 pulses per minute for the four subjects.

show the order in which the data were obtained. The slope of the choice function is steeper than the slope of the relative-rate function. While the individual subjects varied considerably in suppression, as Fig. 4–4 shows, they were consistent in the fact that all choice functions (not shown for individuals) were steeper than all relative-rate functions. For example, subject 441 showed the least preference during the choice period for the lower shock frequencies. Yet, this preference for low versus high shock frequency, slight as it was, was always greater than the difference in relative rates of responding during the corresponding reinforcement periods. On the other hand, 355's responding was a good deal more suppressed for high shock frequencies than for low ones; at 10 ma., for instance, the difference in relative rates of responding between the highest and lowest shock frequencies was 50%. Yet, no matter how great the difference in relative rates was, the corresponding difference in choice was greater. This was true for all subjects and is reflected by the wide spread between the choice curves at the top of Fig. 4–5 and the narrow spread between relative rate of responding curves at the bottom.

The relatively large preferences for low frequencies of shock over high, despite the fact that different frequencies had little consistent effect on ongoing responding, indicates that frequency and intensity of shock can affect the relative aversiveness of a schedule, independent of its correlation with responding. The further conclusion that a given frequency

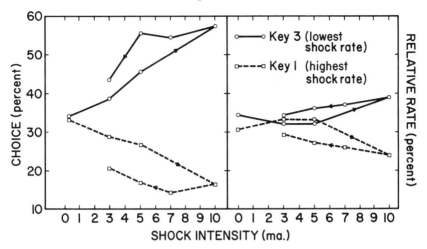

FIG. 4–5.   Average choice (left panel) and relative rate (right panel) on two of the
three keys as a function of intensity of noncontingent shock. The arrows follow the
increase and subsequent decrease of intensity.

and intensity of shock endows a situation with a given aversiveness,
whether or not the shock is dependent on responding, is not yet either
affirmed or denied. Experiment III is addressed to this final question.

A tentative conclusion that seems to be justified by Experiments I
and II is that shock affects the responding of the subject in proportion to
the degree that responding is allowed to affect shock. In Experiment I,
responding could affect the frequency of shock significantly during the
reinforcement period, but only slightly during the choice period, hence
the greater variation in responding was found during the reinforcement
period. In Experiment II, responding could not affect shock frequency at
all during the reinforcement period, but it had the same slight effect
during the choice period as in Experiment I, hence the greater variation
was found during the choice period.

Experiment III: Punishment versus Noncontingent Shock

This experiment (Schuster & Rachlin, 1968) comprised a two-key
concurrent chain with one reinforcement period in which responding was
punished and another reinforcement period in which the shock was not
contingent on responding but presented at a steady pulse rate. The intensity of the shock was held constant (7 ma.) throughout the experiment.
The independent variable, the frequency of noncontingent shock pulses,
was increased in steps from zero to 120 pulses per minute, then decreased
back to zero. This experiment bears quite directly on the notion, ex-

pressed in connection with Experiments I and II, that shock must be contingent on responding in order to suppress responding significantly, but that both contingent and noncontingent shock affect choice. It also should bear on the question whether the aversiveness of a situation is determined solely by the parameters of the aversive event itself or whether the nature of the correlation with behavior is also involved. In Experiment III, in which the pigeons chose between alternatives involving contingent and noncontingent shocks, it might be expected that although preference will tend to shift away from noncontingent shocks as the rate of shock presentation is raised, the shift in choice is likely not to be accompanied by a corresponding change in the magnitude of suppression. The notions outlined earlier suggest that the contingent procedure is the more suppressive of the two, even when it is clearly the preferred.

Figure 4–6 shows suppression during the reinforcement period containing noncontingent shock as a function of the rate of presentation of

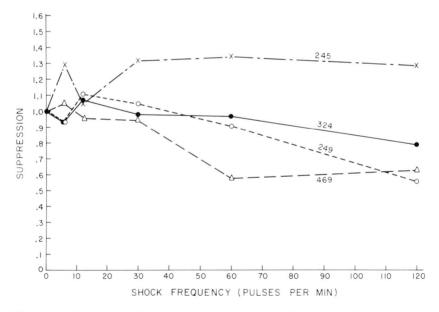

FIG. 4–6.   Suppression during the reinforcement period accompanied by noncontingent shock as a function of frequency of noncontingent shock.

the noncontingent shock (ascending and descending shock frequency, averaged). One subject (469) showed strong and consistent suppression. The responding of two subjects (324 and 249) was suppressed at only high frequencies of shock with one of them (324) suppressed only slightly. The **fourth subject (245)** had its responding increased at all frequencies of shock. Once again, it may be said that noncontingent shock has at best only a small suppressive effect on responding, regardless of whether its intensity (Experiment II) or, in this case, its frequency is varied.

Figure 4–7 shows choice and relative rate of responding for the four subjects. All subjects preferred noncontingent shock to punishment at

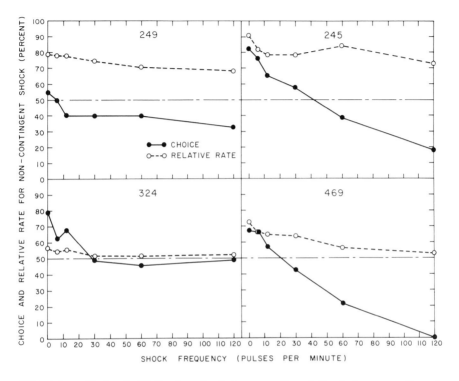

FIG. 4–7.   Choice (solid lines) and relative rate (dotted lines) for noncontingent shock as opposed to contingent shock of the same intensity as a function of the pulse frequency of noncontingent shock.

low frequencies of noncontingent shock. As frequency increased, preference passed through indifference and, finally, all subjects preferred punishment. With regard to relative rate of responding, all subjects responded faster during noncontingent shock than they did during punishment as long as frequency of noncontingent shock was low. As frequency increased, the rates during noncontingent and contingent shock tended to equalize; but even at the rate of 120 pulses of noncontingent shock per minute, all of the four subjects responded faster during the noncontingent than during the contingent shock. For all four subjects, the overall slope of the choice function was steeper than that of the relative rate function. It was not unusual for the relative rate to be above

50% at the same time as the choice was below 50%. This showed that the subjects often responded faster on one key during the choice period and faster on the other key during the reinforcement period. Such a reversal is an argument against response theories of reinforcement (such as Premack's [1959]) that attempt to infer an ordering of strengths of reinforcers from the ordering of rates of response.

Another fact made clear by this experiment is that the ongoing rate of response is not a reliable measure of the aversiveness of a schedule of shock unless shock is contingent on responding. It is not clear how this unreliability bears on the so-called "conditioned emotional response," which is a suppression of responding by noncontingent shock. It may well be, however, that changes in the magnitude of the CER, such as those produced by "tranquilizing" drugs (e.g., Brady [1956]) and widely thought of as a change in the underlying state of anxiety, would not be reflected in a measure of aversion based on a choice procedure.

If choice does depend only on the rate and intensity of shock and not upon whether it is contingent on responding, then, in the present experiment, the subjects should be indifferent between punishment and noncontingent shock when the frequency of noncontingent shock equals the frequency of punishment. Figure 4–8 shows the rate of punished responding (necessarily equal to rate of shock during periods of punishment) as a function of rate of noncontingent shock. The diagonal lines cross the functions at the point where rate of contingent shock equals rate of noncontingent shock. The rates of noncontingent shock at this point are shown in Table 4–1 for each of the four subjects. Each rate of non-

TABLE 4–1

Subject	Rate of Noncontingent Shock Equal to Rate of Punishment (*shocks per minute*)	Choice of Noncontingent Shock at This Point (from Fig. 4–7) (*percent*)
249	31	40
245	33	55
324	52	49
469	22	50

contingent shock corresponds in Fig. 4–7 to a particular choice value, shown in the right column of Table 4–1. The choice values average to 48.5% which, given the range of experimental variation, may be taken as close to indifference (50%). The pigeons were, in other words, indifferent between equal frequencies of contingent and noncontingent shock. To the extent that there was departure from 50%, two out of the four subjects showed a preference for contingent shock and one, a preference for noncontingent shock.

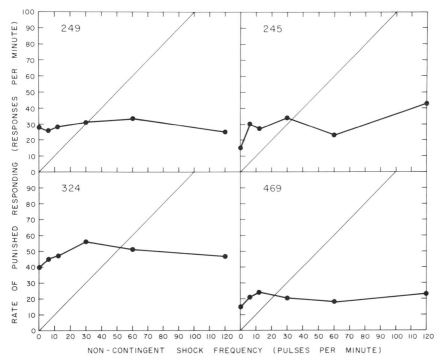

FIG. 4–8.   The points show rate of pecking (equal to the rate of shock) during the reinforcement period when each peck was punished by a single shock, as a function of rate of the pulse frequency of noncontingent shock during the other reinforcement period. The diagonal lines are the loci of equal overall rates of shock during the two reinforcement periods.

It may be worthwhile to note that while the contingency of shock was different during the two reinforcement periods, the predictability of shock need not have been different. The contingent shock was predictable because it was controlled by the subject; the noncontingent shock was predictable because of its regular periodicity.

Figure 4–9 shows the entire function for which the data in Table 4–1 constitute a single point. The proportion of choices are here plotted against the relative rates of shock actually received in the two periods for each of the four pigeons. Table 4–1 showed that this function passed close to the 50% point on both ordinate and abscissa, as it must if choice is determined by aversive stimulation and not by the nature of the contingency. Figure 4–9 shows that the remainder of the function is monotonically decreasing, but that the variability from animal to animal prohibits any more precise characterization. It might be noted that the average slope of this function should bear some relation to the relative strengths of the food and shock factors in the situation. If the animal

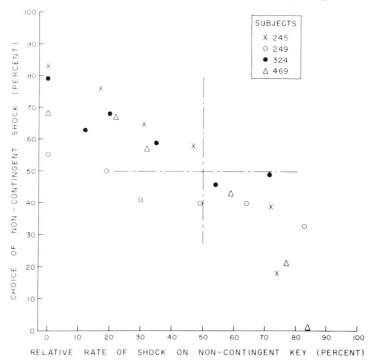

FIG. 4–9.   Choice of noncontingent shock as a function of the relative rate of shock on the noncontingent key. The abscissa values were determined by dividing the rate of noncontingent shock (the shock-pulse frequency) by the sum of the rate of noncontingent shock and the rate of contingent shock during the other reinforcement period.

was indifferent to the frequency of shock, the function would have a slope of zero and an intercept of 50%. On the other hand, if the animal was indifferent to the frequency of food reinforcement, the function might be expected to be a step function with a jump from zero to 100% at 50% on the abscissa. The intermediate slope in Fig. 4–9 says that neither of these limiting conditions prevail here, but it would be premature to try to quantify these notions further at the present time.

The three experiments reported here confirm previous findings on the suppressive effects of shock in two respects:

1. *Responding is barely, if at all, suppressed by noncontingent shock, except at high levels of intensity or rate of presentation.*

2. *Contingent shock suppresses responding more than noncontingent shock of equal intensity, even when noncontingent shock is more frequent.*

In addition, the present experiments add a generalization about the effects of shock on choice:

Given a pair of alternative conditions for responding, involving equal positive reinforcement and different aversive stimulation, choice depends on the intensity and frequency of aversive stimulation and is independent of the rate of responding and the correlations between the aversive stimulation and responding.

Although this last generalization may seem counterintuitive, it appears to be supported by analogous findings in situations in which positive reinforcement was the independent variable. Autor (1960) used the concurrent chain with one reinforcement period comprising a conventional schedule of intermittent food reinforcement while the other presented food *ad libitum*. He found that the distribution of choices was governed solely by the relative frequencies of reinforcement without regard to whether the reinforcer was contingent on responding or not. Herrnstein (1964a) further substantiated this general notion in another experiment involving the concurrent chain. He showed that even when the schedules of reinforcement in the two reinforcement periods were of different basic types (interval versus ratio), so that the rates of reponding for given frequencies of reinforcement were different, the distribution of choices was still governed by the relative frequencies of reinforcement without regard to the rates of responding.

A number of surprising predictions follow from the idea that the choices among situations involving aversive stimulation depend upon the amounts of such stimulation actually received, rather than upon the degree of suppression produced therein. For instance, we would predict that if punishment were presented on an interval schedule (on which changes in the rate of responding cause only small changes in the frequency of shock) and intensity were increased, choice would vary steeply with intensity. If, on the other hand, shock were presented on a ratio schedule (on which frequency of shock is directly proportional to frequency of responding) and intensity were increased, choice would vary slightly with intensity, as it did in Experiment I. Not quite a prediction, but rather an interesting possibility, is that the preference for an unshocked reinforcement period over one involving the CER procedure would remain intact even if a suitable drug succeeded in eliminating the suppression. Such a finding would show that the drug had acted on nothing so general as an underlying state of "anxiety," but on whatever it is that accounts for the localized suppression in the presence of noncontingent shock.

A Theoretical Epilogue

As far as new information is concerned, this report could have ended one or two paragraphs ago. However, in discussing the experiments, we have used such terms as "response reduction" and "suppression," expressions that connote a negative law of effect. Since this law, in the sense of implying a *reduction* of responding, is still unaccepted by many psychologists, it behooves us to clarify our position.

It is useful here to distinguish between two notions: the avoidance theory of punishment and the punishment theory of avoidance. The distinction can be understood with reference to Table 4–2, showing the instrumental relations between responses and aversive stimulation. The diagonals set forth the familiar procedures. Avoidance paradigms call for

TABLE 4–2.   *Instrumental Relations Between Responding and Aversive Stimulation*

		consequence	
		punishment	nonpunishment
behavior	response	$R \longrightarrow P$	$R \longrightarrow \overline{P}$
	nonresponse	$\overline{R} \longrightarrow P$	$\overline{R} \longrightarrow \overline{P}$

the contingencies, $R \rightarrow \overline{P}$ and $\overline{R} \rightarrow P$. Punishment paradigms call for contingencies, $R \rightarrow P$ and $\overline{R} \rightarrow \overline{P}$. The noncontingent procedure is given by the column on the left, $R \rightarrow P$ and $\overline{R} \rightarrow P$.

An avoidance theory of punishment takes a theory designed to account for the facilitation of responding in an avoidance procedure and applies it to the reduction of responding in a punishment procedure. In terms of Table 4–2, this type of theory states that the explanation for the effects of one diagonal can be applied to the effects of the other. In avoidance procedures, a specific response (shuttling, jumping, lever pressing, etc.) is increased; in punishment procedures, the increased response must be defined nonspecifically (i.e., $\overline{R}$), which is to say, as anything the subject does except the specified response (R). Besides this difference in the degree of specificity of the response, an avoidance theory of punishment is an assertion that avoidance and punishment are equivalent procedures in that both involve a version of the law of effect that deals in response increments. Here, the law of effect is saying that when behavior eliminates a disagreeable state of affairs, it increases in frequency. In terms of Thorndike's original two laws, this one belongs with the positive case. In Skinner's terminology (1953), both avoidance and punishment procedures are treated as negative reinforcement, since both involve response increments resulting from the removal of a stimulus. For avoidance conditioning, the response increment is a matter of observation; for punishment procedures, it is a matter of interpretation. Although an avoidance theory of punishment is obviously suited to explain the response decrement in a punishment procedure, it is unable to explain any response decrement (slight as it may be) resulting from noncontingent

aversive stimulation. As noted earlier, the left column of Table 4–2 con·
tains no entry leading to $\overline{P}$, which is to say that neither responding nor
its absence can be reinforced by the removal of aversive stimulation. If
there is learning with noncontingent shock, it must be attributable to
factors falling outside the scope of an avoidance theory of punishment.

In contrast to avoidance theories of punishment would be any punishment theory of avoidance. Such a theory would be based on a fundamental process stated in terms of response decrements, like those observed
in a punishment procedure, and would be extended to account for the
response increment of an avoidance procedure by once again invoking
the fundamental effect on the nonspecific response ($\overline{R}$). As before, the
noncontingent procedure would pose a problem; but here it would be
because both responding and nonresponding would be reduced, presumably cancelling each other out and leaving the observed behavior
intact.

Notwithstanding the fact that avoidance theories of punishment
abound, while punishment theories of avoidance are virtually unheard of,
the difference between the two is entirely a matter of personal preference.
As long as responding and nonresponding are viewed as mutually exclu·
sive and exhaustive classes of behavior, equally susceptible to instrumen·
tal conditioning, the two theories make identical predictions about
behavior. It is a curious fact that these two sides of a single coin have
turned up with such different frequencies. The punishment theory of
avoidance is simply a form of the negative law of effect, that often
repudiated principle, adapted to account for the response increment of
avoidance procedures. If it is unacceptable, it must be for reasons that are
neither empirical nor logical, since it is easy to show that at both levels
it is virtually identical with the avoidance theory of punishment, a long-
standing favorite.

Any theory of active avoidance could be extended, in principle, as
an avoidance theory of punishment. In practice, however, only one theory
of avoidance, the two-process theory, has been extended in this way. The
reason is obviously the almost complete ubiquity of some version of two-
process theory in discussions of avoidance. Two-process theories of avoidance are conceptual devices that convert what appear to be avoidance
procedures into seemingly more explainable escape procedures. Thus,
according to the theory, the animal does not learn to respond to forestall
an aversive event; it responds to eliminate a signal that has acquired aversive properties through some process of association. In discriminated
avoidance, the warning stimulus becomes aversive because it is at first
invariably followed by shock. Any change from the now-aversive warning
stimulus to a safe stimulus is reinforcing. If such a change is made contingent on responding, the responding will increase. The discriminated
avoidance procedure is a way of making the change from the warning

stimulus to the safe stimulus contingent on a specific response and, therefore, a way of increasing responding.

It is not hard to extend this theory to punishment as, in fact, Mowrer (1947), Skinner (1953), and Dinsmoor (1954, 1955) have already done. Because these theorists have not always spelled out the details of the extension, it might be useful to review them here. First of all, the specific act leading to punishment must be assumed to be something like a chain of several responses, each with its own feedback stimuli. For example, bar pressing may be analyzed into the subunits of approaching the bar (R_1), raising the paw (R_2), and lowering the paw onto the lever (R_3), each with its distinctive proprioceptive stimuli, S_{R_1}, S_{R_2}, and S_{R_3}. A chain of events, then, consisting of:

takes place when each response is made. If punishment follows R_3, then S_{R_3}, S_{R_2}, and S_{R_1} become aversive through contiguity conditioning. Suppose, after punishment has occurred and the stimuli S_{R_1}, S_{R_2}, and S_{R_3} have become aversive, the chain is modified in the following manner:

$$R_1 \nearrow^{S_{R_1}} \longrightarrow R_2 \nearrow^{S_{R_2}} \longrightarrow R_3' \nearrow^{S_{R_3'}}$$

where R_3' means any response other than R_3 (pressing the bar) and $S_{R_3'}$ is the complex of stimuli resulting from this new response, a complex that is not aversive since it has not been paired with shock. Since S_{R_2} *is* aversive while $S_{R_3'}$ is not, any change from S_{R_2} to $S_{R_3'}$ is reinforcing. And since this change is contingent on the response R_3', which is anything except bar pressing, it follows that the frequency of bar pressing must decrease. In this way, two-process theory, which deals in response increments, can be adapted to handle punishment, which ostensibly entails response decrements. The reputed virtue of the extension is parsimony in conception. Instead of two laws of effect, one accounting for increases in responding and the other for decreases in responding, a two-process theory of punishment obviates the need for a fundamental mechanism to account for response decrements. An equivalent measure of parsimony would be had by the inverse formulation in which avoidance behavior is viewed as a consequence of the reduction of alternative responses.

A disadvantage of either stratagem is that it postulates complicated chains of events which, if they are not observed, must be assumed to occur within the organism. For instance, the two-process theory of punishment allows no mechanism for reducing the frequency of the first response in the chain, the one we arbitrarily called "approaching the bar." No matter how intense the punishment, the first response cannot be displaced by an R_1' simply because there is, by definition, no S_{R_0} whose removal would be reinforcing. The absence of a mechanism to produce response decrements means that the initial stages of the response must remain unaffected by punishment. It may be true that incipient responding is observed in punishment situations, but the theory implies that there is no change whatever in the frequency of initiations of the response. An animal actually responding at half of its normal rate in a punishment experiment must be assumed to be making as many approaches to the manipulandum as it did before the punishments were begun. It cannot be claimed that R_1 is extinguished through lack of reinforcement because, with variable-interval schedules of reinforcement, the reinforcement rate stays constant even when responding is considerably suppressed. If these frequent incipient responses are not observed (as indeed they are not), they must be moved into the organism, out of reach of empirical scrutiny. Of course, this is no disproof of two-process theory. In fact, it would be difficult to state the conditions for a disproof as long as the free postulation of unobserved behavior is considered acceptable.

Notwithstanding these problems, it is our judgment that the choice data are still more troublesome for conventional theories of aversive control. According to the two-process theory, the chief difference between avoidance and punishment is in the locus of the secondary aversive stimuli, which are external for avoidance and internal (i.e., proprioceptive feedback from the response) in punishment. But in the present experiments, the response (of key pecking) and the proprioceptive feedback from it are presumably the same whether during choice periods or reinforcement periods. Why, then, is the extent to which shock affects behavior so different (in some instances virtually reversed) during the two kinds of periods? By the conventional theory, the answer would seem to be that the *external* stimuli, which are different during the two periods, signal differential responding, based on differing levels of aversiveness arising from proprioceptive stimulation. And in order to be able to endow proprioceptive stimulation with different aversive values in the choice and reinforcement periods, one must postulate a four-fold process of conditioned inhibition with the external stimuli of the two keys during the two periods serving as conditioned inhibitors of various strengths for the learned response of nonresponding. All of this complexity grows out of the notion that punishment is really a tacit form of response increment, in which everything except the recorded response benefits from negative reinforcement.

It seems to us that such complicated accounts of behavior, so tenuously linked to the data, are too high a price to pay for the convenience of a single law of effect. It may be argued that only complicated accounts could serve for the present experiments because the experiments themselves are so complicated. But consider the following simple experiment: A subject is reinforced with food for every occurrence of some response and, in addition, punished for it only when a red light is present. At other times, the light is green and responding is not punished, but still reinforced. It may be assumed that responding is slowed when the light is red and unchanged (or even increased) when the light is green. One account of this result might assert the negative law of effect and hold that the red light serves as a discriminative stimulus for the response decrement resulting from punishment, just as the positive law of effect is used to explain increases in responding in comparable procedures involving the differential reinforcement of behavior. A two-process account cannot handle this result so simply. The red light might seem to qualify as the required conditioned aversive stimulus, but the red light's aversiveness is immaterial since it is not affected by responding. Rather the stimuli from the proprioceptive feedback of responding must be implicated if a response decrement is to be explained. These feedback stimuli, however, are only aversive when the red light is on and unaversive when the green light is on, otherwise there is no basis for the difference in rates of responding. When external stimuli are shown to control responding during avoidance, the stimuli themselves are held to be aversive by virtue of having been paired with shock. During punishment, however, the aversiveness of these same stimuli, also paired with shock, becomes irrelevant and the stimuli serve only as conditioned inhibitors.

Let us emphasize again that in no sense do we claim to have found evidence against a two-process theory of punishment, nor against any of its formal equivalents. There is, as we have suggested, some doubt about the possibility of finding such evidence, given the acceptability of certain kinds of postulated behaviors. What we have done, rather, is to show that responding is controlled by contingent and noncontingent punishment in a way that is analogous to the control of responding by positive reward, except that the direction of the control is reversed. At the most general level, the present results may be subsumed under the simple notion that the effect of punishment on behavior depends upon the effect of behavior on the frequency of punishment. From this simple idea the various findings of the three experiments are readily derived, predicting that choice will be influenced by the actual amount of shock obtained without regard to whether the shock is contingent on responding or not, and that the suppressive effects of shock are primarily limited to situations in which the responding controls the occurrence of the shock. The literature of positive reinforcement contains ample support for our assertion of an analogy between the two kinds of consequence. We are, in other words, suggesting that Thorndike's statement of a two-part law of effect seems a reasonable theoretical framework for the present findings.

The attempt to achieve even greater economy in theory by postulating a common mechanism for avoidance and punishment is, in our opinion, indefensible. As indicated previously, the attempt can only work (and then with considerable difficulty) if the theory tacitly assumes that responding and nonresponding are essentially equivalent kinds of behavior as regards susceptibility to conditioning and that each of the two classes of behavior can be treated as a discrete and specifiable form of response. Thus, for avoidance theories of punishment, the contingency between nonresponding and nonpunishment is the operative one, producing a rise in the frequency of nonresponding and therefore a decrement in the frequency of responding. A comparable equation of responding and nonresponding is made by the other possible attempt for maximum parsimony, which the reader can easily provide.

Whether the two classes of behavior—responding and nonresponding—are, in fact, thus equivalent might be thought of as an empirical question rather than one to be asserted as a postulate. Viewed empirically, the prospect for this extreme parsimony is discouraging. For instance, the pigeon shows a sensible readiness to have its nonresponses increased by aversive stimulation, which is to say that it rapidly stops engaging in punished behavior. Yet, it has proved to be peculiarly intractable when it is the key-pecking response which is to be increased by the removal of aversive stimulation (see Hoffman & Fleshler, 1959). To some extent, rats show a similar asymmetry as regards the contingency between aversive stimulation and responding or nonresponding (see Meyer, Cho, & Wesemann, 1960). For both rats and pigeons, on the other hand, the same specific response (lever pressing and key pecking) is quite easily increased by contingencies with positive reinforcers. It is actually quite simple to test directly the presumed equivalence of responding and nonresponding as the following demonstration experiment shows. A period during which responding was both rewarded and punished was alternated with a period during which nonresponding was both rewarded and punished. Whichever was rewarded (responding or nonresponding) might be expected to be predominant during the period in which it was rewarded as long as the intensity of punishment was low. An increase in punishment intensity should decrease the rewarded act and increase its complement. The question is whether the decrease in responding when responding is punished is paralleled by a decrease in nonresponding when nonresponding is punished. A negative answer to this question would reveal a basic asymmetry between the effects of aversive stimulation on responding and nonresponding.

Four pigeons at 80% of normal weight were trained to peck a key whose color alternated between red and green every 2 minutes regardless of the pigeons' behavior. For the purposes of this experiment, a nonresponse was defined as 5 seconds without a peck. When the key was red, pecks at the key occasionally produced reinforcement (3 sec. of access to grain) and occasionally produced electric shock punishment (delivered as in the previous experiments). Figure 4–10 is a diagram of the conditions of delivery of food and shock. With the key red, an average 30-second interval would prime the apparatus so that the next peck would produce either reinforcement or punishment (randomly determined). However, if a nonpeck occurred after priming before a peck, the reinforcement (or punishment) was lost and future pecks had no effect until the next priming. When the key was green, the situation was reversed. That is, after priming, a nonpeck produced reinforcement (or punishment) unless a peck occurred first, in which case the reinforcement (or punishment) would be lost.

After initial training to peck the key with shock intensity at zero, the intensity was increased by 0.5 ma. every session for 30 sessions. Figure 4–11 (solid line) shows the average suppression of responding during red

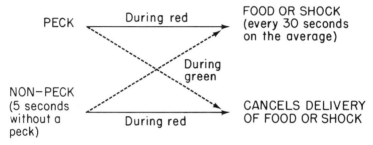

FIG. 4–10.   Diagram of the conditions of delivery of food and shock.

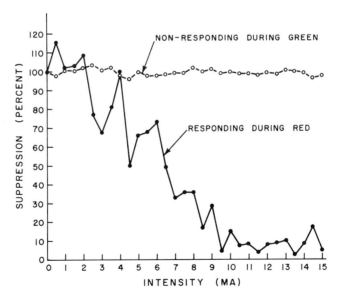

FIG. 4–11.   Suppression as a function of shock intensity for punishment of responding (solid line) and nonresponding (dotted line). The curves shown are the medians of values for four pigeons.

as intensity increased. Since, during red, shock was delivered as punishment for responding, the greater suppression with increased shock intensity confirms previous experiments in which suppression of a response was found to increase with intensity of punishment. Figure 4–11 (dotted line) shows the average suppression of nonresponding during green as intensity increased. Even though the relation of nonresponding to shock during green was identical to the relation of responding to shock during red, no suppression of nonresponding was observed to parallel the suppression of responding, revealing a clear asymmetry between the two. We hold that such an asymmetry, in addition to those suggested by previous workers, cited earlier, argues against a two-process interpretation of punishment and in favor of the negative law of effect as originally conceived.

Summary

Thorndike originally described instrumental conditioning in terms of two laws of effect: a positive law according to which reward increases responding, and a negative law according to which punishment decreases responding. A more popular contemporary view, however, considers the decrements in responding as increments in a nonspecific response defined simply as not-responding. The two older laws are thereby reduced to one having to do only with response increments. The present paper shows that this gain in simplicity of theoretical conception, if it is a gain, involves considerable sacrifice in simplicity in the description of experimental results and perhaps in predictive power.

The experiments described measure the rate of responding of pigeons which are being shocked, as well as their preferences for various schedules of shock presentation. It was found that the factors that govern the amount of response suppression by shock are not identical with those which govern preference for one shock schedule over another. In one instance, the pigeons preferred a schedule during which their responding was greatly suppressed over a schedule during which their responding was only slightly or not at all suppressed. In general, rate of responding varies consistently with shock parameters only when shock is contingent on responding, while preference for various schedules of shock varies with shock parameters irrespective of whether shock is contingent on responding. To fit results such as these, and others reported herein, into the contemporary version of the law of effect takes the postulation of unobserved stimuli and responses whose properties match precisely what the theory calls for. Even at that, however, the contemporary version makes predictions that may be contrary to fact, as the text spells out.

The contemporary version of the law of effect assumes that not-responding is manipulable by positive and negative reinforcement in the same way that responding is. An experiment was done in which the responding and not-responding of pigeons produced identical environmental effects. However, as the intensity of the aversive effect increased, responding and not-responding varied differently, with not-responding showing little sensitivity to a punishment contingency that reduced responding drastically.

Based on these findings and theoretical considerations, the authors recommend a return to Thorndike's first formulation of the law of effect, in which two mechanisms lead to opposite effects on behavior.

REFERENCES

AUTOR, S. M. The strength of conditioned reinforcers as a function of frequency and probability of reinforcement. Unpublished doctoral dissertation, Harvard University, 1960.

AZRIN, N. H. Some effects of two intermittent schedules of immediate and non-immediate punishment. *Journal of Psychology,* 1956, **42**, 3–21.

AZRIN, N. H. Some effects of noise on human behavior. *Journal of the Experimental Analysis of Behavior,* 1958, **1**, 183–200.

AZRIN, N. H. Effects of punishment intensity during variable-interval reinforcement. *Journal of the Experimental Analysis of Behavior,* 1960, **3**, 123–142.

AZRIN, N. H., & HOLZ, W. C. Punishment during fixed-interval reinforcement. *Journal of the Experimental Analysis of Behavior,* 1961, **4**, 343–347.

AZRIN, N. H., & HOLZ, W. C. Punishment. In W. K. Honig (Ed.), *Operant behavior: Areas of research and application.* New York: Appleton-Century-Crofts, 1966. Pp. 380–447.

BRADY, J. V. Assessment of drug effects on emotional behavior. *Science,* 1956, **123**, 1033–1034.

DINSMOOR, J. A. Punishment: I. The avoidance hypothesis. *Psychological Review,* 1954, **61**, 34–46.

DINSMOOR, J. A. Punishment: II. An interpretation of empirical findings. *Psychological Review,* 1955, **62**, 96–105.

ESTES, W. K. An experimental study of punishment. *Psychological Monographs,* 1944, **57** (3, Whole No. 263).

FANTINO, E. Preference for mixed- versus fixed-ratio schedules. *Journal of the Experimental Analysis of Behavior,* 1967, **10**, 35–44.

HERRNSTEIN, R. J. Secondary reinforcement and rate of primary reinforcement. *Journal of the Experimental Analysis of Behavior,* 1964, **7**, 27–36. (a)

HERRNSTEIN, R. J. Aperiodicity as a factor in choice. *Journal of the Experimental Analysis of Behavior,* 1964, **7**, 179–182. (b)

HOFFMAN, H. S. & FLESHLER, M. Aversive control with the pigeon. *Journal of the Experimental Analysis of Behavior,* 1959, **2**, 213–218.

MEYER, D. R., CHO, C., & WESEMANN, A. F. On problems of conditioning discriminated lever-press avoidance responses. *Psychological Review,* 1960, **67**, 224–228.

MOWRER, O. H. On the dual nature of learning—A re-interpretation of "conditioning" and "problem-solving." *Harvard Educational Review*, 1947, **17**, 102–148.

PREMACK, D. Toward empirical behavior laws: I. Positive reinforcement. *Psychological Review*, 1959, **66**, 219-233.

RACHLIN, H. C. Recovery of responses during mild punishment. *Journal of the Experimental Analysis of Behavior*, 1966, **9**, 251–263.

RACHLIN, H. C. The effect of shock intensity on concurrent and single-key responding in concurrent-chain schedules. *Journal of the Experimental Analysis of Behavior*, 1967, **10**, 87–93.

SCHUSTER, R., & RACHLIN, H. Indifference between punishment and free shock: Evidence for the negative law of effect. *Journal of the Experimental Analysis of Behavior*, 1968, **11**, 777–786.

SKINNER, B. F. *Science and human behavior.* New York: Macmillan, 1953.

SOLOMON, R. L. Punishment. *American Psychologist*, 1964, **19**, 239–253.

THORNDIKE, E. L. *The fundamentals of learning.* New York: Teachers' College, Columbia University, 1932.

5

Response Suppression[1]

Russell M. Church
BROWN UNIVERSITY

This chapter will identify some of the major determinants of the magnitude of response suppression produced by punishment. As implied by the term "response suppression," punishment puts down a response by force and tends to conceal it from public view. Neither punishment, nor any other technique, serves to eliminate a response after it has been established. Thus, for example, extinction may reduce the frequency of some behavior; but a test of spontaneous recovery or relearning would indicate that the effects of the previous learning had not been wiped out. Reduction in the frequency of some unwanted behavior is the major purpose of punishment in the practical control of behavior. Although there has been considerable interest in the paradoxes of punishment, a response that is punished is usually suppressed, and this is the case in all of the situations described in this chapter.

In general, a noxious stimulus and a reward affect a response in opposite directions. Positive reinforcement increases the tendency to respond, and punishment decreases the tendency to respond. If it is correct to say, at least metaphorically, that positive reinforcement strengthens a response or "adds" response strength, then it is equally correct to say that punishment weakens a response or "subtracts" response strength.

The major determinants of the effectiveness of a punishment and of a positive reinforcement are identical. The influence of a noxious event or a rewarding event upon a response will depend upon such factors as (1) the characteristics of the event, (2) the relationship between the response and the event, and (3) the presence of a discriminative stimulus. For example, the magnitude of the event is relevant both in the case of a reward (e.g., a pellet of food) and a noxious stimulus (e.g., a brief electric shock). A large reward is more effective than a small one, and an intense noxious stimulus is more effective than a mild one. Similarly, the

[1] The investigations reported in this chapter were supported by PHS Research Grant MH-08123 from the National Institute of Mental Health.

dependence of the event upon a response is an important determinant of the effectiveness of the event. If a reward or a noxious stimulus is dependent upon a response, it will be more effective than if it is independent of the response. As a final example, a discriminative stimulus for a positive reinforcement or for a punishment increases the effectiveness of the event in the presence of the signal and decreases its effectiveness in the absence of the signal.

The Reference Experiment

All of the experiments described in this chapter are variations on a single theme: A subject was trained to press a lever for positive reinforcement, and then it was punished for the performance of that act. Such punishment resulted in suppression of the response. To identify the major determinants of the magnitude of response suppression produced by punishment, many variations of the basic reference experiment were utilized. These included variations in severity of the punishment, in the strength of the positive instrumental act, in the relationship between response and punishment, etc. Before the description of the results of these experiments, it would be useful to examine the general method employed in a basic reference condition.

Subjects

The subjects in all of the studies were experimentally naive, male, Norway albino rats of the Sprague–Dawley strain. In all of the recent experiments they were Charles River CD rats, a hysterectomy-derived, barrier-sustained stock. The development of specific pathogen-free (SPF) strains of rats has led to the elimination of certain problems of animal health that had been a hazard with previous open stock. The SPF animals have been free of respiratory ailments, middle ear disease (PPLO infection), internal parasites (e.g., worms), external parasites (e.g., lice), and infectious skin diseases (e.g., ringworm). In contrast to our experiences of some years ago with conventional rats, no SPF animal has had to be eliminated from an experiment as a result of disease.[2]

The rats were delivered to the Hunter Laboratory of Psychology when they were 7 weeks old. After one week of unrestricted feeding they were placed in individual cages with water always available, and they were given a daily ration of 14 gm. of ground Purina chow mixed with 25 cc of water. During a 4-week period prior to the experiment each subject was handled (removed from its home cage, stroked for about 15

2 I am indebted to Dr. Morris Povar for advice on matters of animal health and care.

sec., and then returned to its cage). Although, in most cases, rats were handled daily, intensive handling for a relatively brief period is generally sufficient to lead to a tame animal.

Apparatus

The apparatus consisted of a standard lever box, enclosed in an ice chest with an acrylic window that permitted observation of the subject. The lever box was approximately 9 inches in each dimension, and its floor consisted of 16 stainless steel bars ($\frac{5}{32}$ in. in diameter). Although in some experiments these bars were inserted through the acrylic walls of the box, in more recent experiments the bars passed below the side wall and into an insulating support that was inaccessible to the subject, an arrangement that reduced grid leakage. An electric shock, delivered through the bars of the floor for fixed periods of time, served as a punishment. Some of the experiments used a constant current source, with intensity specified in milliamperes; other experiments used a matched impedance source (150K ohms in series with the subject) with intensity specified in terms of source voltage. A grid scrambler, located next to the lever box, was used in experiments that had one or more groups with punishments of long duration. The lever was made of stainless steel, and it was reasonably large (2 in. wide), low (2 in. above the floor) and light (25 gm. would activate the microswitch). A rotary solenoid pellet dispenser delivered 45-mg. rat food tablets to the subject. To eliminate possible cues or sources of distraction, the control and recording apparatus was located in a separate room.

Procedure

Pretraining consisted of one session of training to eat pellets of food when the dispenser delivered them (magazine training), and one session of training to press the lever (crf). On the first session the subject received a pellet once a minute for 30 minutes. Lever responses were counted, but they were otherwise ineffective. On the second session the subject was allowed to make 30 reinforced lever responses. About 95% of the subjects learned to press the lever within 30 minutes, and the remaining subjects learned to do so during an additional session on the following day, or with a "shaping" procedure. Training can proceed rapidly when an active, hungry, fearless, and magazine-trained subject is introduced into a situation where it is likely to emit the response. The median time to complete the first 30 responses was about 13 minutes.

Reinforcement training consisted of five 30-minute daily sessions with positive reinforcement on a 1-minute variable-interval schedule (VI 1), a rectangular distribution with a range from 15 to 105 seconds. Punishment training consisted of ten 30-minute daily sessions with a schedule of

response-contingent shock (punishment) added to the positive reinforcement schedule (VI 1). The punishment became available on a 2-minute
variable-interval schedule (VI 2), a rectangular distribution with range
from 30 to 210 seconds. Thus a subject that continued to respond
throughout an experimental session of 30 minutes would receive about
30 reinforcements and 15 punishments.

The Measure of Response Suppression

The introduction of punishment resulted in a reduction in response rate,
and some of the experimental treatments produced substantially greater
response suppression than others. Figure 5–1 shows the response rate of
two subjects during the five sessions of reinforcement training and the ten
sessions of punishment training. The subject in the experimental condition (punishment of .25 ma. for 0.5 sec.) shows considerable reduction in
its response rate followed by partial recovery; the subject in the control
condition (no punishment) continued to increase its rate during the additional sessions of training. Gross differences between experimental treatments could have been easily ascertained with a small number of subjects
and almost any reasonable measure. To distinguish between experimental
treatments that produced only subtle differences in performance, however, it was necessary either to use large groups of subjects or to employ a

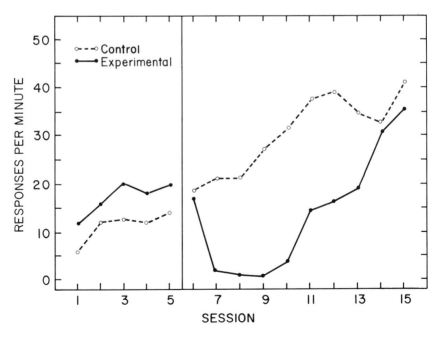

FIG. 5–1.   Response rate of two individual subjects during five sessions of reinforcement training and ten sessions of punishment training.

measure that was particularly sensitive to the experimental treatments under study. The primary criterion for such a measure was that the behavior of subjects given any particular treatment should be much alike, but the behavior of subjects given different treatments should be substantially different. In more exact terminology, the variance of the measure for subjects within a given treatment should be small relative to the variance of the measure for subjects in different treatment groups. The following paragraphs describe the search for such a sensitive measure of response suppression.[3]

Method of evaluation of the sensitivity of a measure. To evaluate a proposed measure of response suppression the performance records of a large number of subjects under a wide variety of conditions of punishment were reanalyzed. In each of these experiments the subject was trained to press a lever for food reinforcement on a variable-interval schedule of reinforcement, and then it was given ten sessions of punishment training. During this punishment training the conditions of positive reinforcement were maintained but some punishment contingency was added. Altogether the data for 505 subjects in 49 treatments were reexamined. The conditions included wide variations in intensity, duration, and schedule of punishment; variations in the frequency of positive reinforcement, the interval between response and punishment, etc. For each proposed measure of response suppression, a one-way analysis of variance was calculated with the conditions of punishment as the independent variable and the proposed measure of response suppression as the dependent variable. These analyses provided the basic information for estimates of ω^2, the strength of the relationship between the independent variable and the various measures of response suppression (Hays, 1963, pp. 381–384). Reliable differences among the values for ω^2 reflect differences in the sensitivity of the various measures of response suppression to variations in the conditions of punishment. In general, the proportion of the variance of a dependent variable (Y) that is accounted for by an independent variable (X) is defined as

$$\omega^2 = \frac{\sigma^2_y - \sigma^2_{y|x}}{\sigma^2_y}$$

In this case, ω^2 may be defined as the percentage of variation in the measure of response suppression that could be accounted for by variation in the treatment.

Response rate during the treatment. Perhaps the simplest measure of response suppression is the response rate during the experimental treatment. The more effective the punishment condition, the lower should be

[3] I am grateful for the detailed comments that Dr. J. E. Keith Smith made on an earlier draft of this section.

the response rate. Some of the treatments involved relatively intense punishing shocks that produced a rapid and nearly complete response suppression; other treatments involved mild punishment near a threshold of detection, or even control treatments without any punishment. Therefore, it is not at all surprising that the F ratio was significant ($F = 9.9$, $df = {}^{48}\!/_{455}$, $p < .001$). The major problem was to compare the sensitivity of this measure of the effectiveness of the treatments to several alternative measures of response suppression. An estimate of ω^2 indicated that about 46% of the variance in the response rate was accounted for by variations in the treatments.

A set of scores is "transformed" when some arithmetic operation is applied to each of the original numbers as recorded by some device. Whether the skin resistance (in ohms) or the skin conductance (in mhos) is a transformed score depends upon the meter that was originally used to record the data. Running speed is normally a transformed score because of the nature of clocks that are typically employed to measure it. Although the number that is directly recorded by the apparatus may provide a measure that is easier to comprehend than a measure that is derived from these observations, the particular equipment that we choose to use should not overly constrain our choice of response measure. The square root transformation, or a closely related transformation, is often applied to frequency data. Although this measure may be used primarily to equalize the variance among the treatment groups, it may also serve to increase the sensitivity of the measure. An estimate of ω^2 based on a reanalysis of the same 505 subjects in the 49 groups, indicated that about 50% of the variance of the square root of the response rate was accounted for by variations in the treatments. Thus the mean square root of response rate contained more information about the treatment than the mean response rate.

A combination of response rate during the treatment and response rate prior to the treatment. For maximum sensitivity a measure of the effectiveness of a treatment should involve a measure of the performance prior to treatment, whenever there is a substantial correlation between the performance prior to treatment and that during (or following) treatment. Although the correlation between the response rate during the ten sessions of punishment (B) with the response rate on the last session of training (A) was essentially zero for subjects within groups that were nearly totally suppressed, there was a substantial positive correlation for those groups that were least suppressed. The slope of the regression line for successive seven groups (from least to greatest suppression) was .90, .90, .96, .60, .33, .18, and .00.

Perhaps the simplest combination of the response rate prior to treatment (A) and the response rate during treatment (B) is the difference

$A - B$. Although, of course, the F ratio resulting from this measure was significant ($F = 7.9$, $df = {}^{48}\!/_{455}$, $p < .001$), the strength of association of this measure with the treatments was even smaller than that of the B measure taken alone ($\omega^2 = .40$). Therefore, this difference measure of the effectiveness of a punishment treatment was rejected.

The basic measure that was used in the analysis of the previous experiments on the effectiveness of various conditions of punishment was $B/(A + B)$, a measure that is called the "suppression ratio." A subject that continued to respond during punishment treatment (B) at the same rate that it did prior to treatment (A) would have a ratio of .500. A subject that reduced its rate by half ($B = A/2$) would have a suppression ratio of .333; a subject that did not respond at all during punishment treatment ($B = 0$) would have a suppression ratio of .000. We might expect that more information regarding the treatment would be contained in the suppression ratio than in the absolute response rate or in the change in response rate. Regardless of a subject's initial response rate, a suppression ratio of .333 is far more consistent with a moderate punishment than with a severe punishment or none at all. A response rate of 10 responses per minute does not convey this much information. Such a rate is consistent with a fairly severe punishment (if the response rate had been 50 responses per minute), but it is also consistent with no punishment at all (if the response rate had been 10 responses per minute). Similarly, a reduction of response rate by 10 responses per minute is consistent with a mild punishment (if the subject had a response rate of 50 responses per minute prior to punishment), or with a strong punishment (if the subject had a response rate of 10 responses per minute prior to treatment). The index ω^2 may be considered as the relative reduction in uncertainty about a treatment given a particular response measure. The results of the reanalysis of the data of subjects in the 49 punishment treatments support the expectation that the suppression ratio $[B/(A + B)]$ is more sensitive to treatment differences than the response rate (B) or the change in response rate ($A - B$). About 55% of the variance of the suppression ratio was accounted for by the treatments. How large an increase in efficiency or power is obtained by the use of the suppression ratio ($\omega^2 = .55$) instead of the response rate ($\omega^2 = .46$)? To obtain the same efficiency or power from the response rate measure (B), it would be necessary to use about 44% more observations (Hays, 1963, pp. 384–385).

No other measure that was evaluated was found to be superior to the suppression ratio, although various other measures were equally sensitive. The measures B/A, $\sqrt{B/A}$, and θ where $\tan \theta = B/A$ gave values of ω^2 that were roughly comparable (53%, 54%, and 55%, respectively). A new measure, however, should not replace an old one unless it is demonstrably superior. The traditional measure yields data that are comparable to the existing information and such comparability should not be sacrificed without compensation. Furthermore, because of its familiarity, the implications of a traditional measure are generally easier to comprehend than those of a new measure.

The criterion for selection of a measure of response suppression.   The major consideration in choosing a measure of the effectiveness of a treatment should be its sensitivity to the effects of the treatment. For the application of certain statistical tests it would be convenient if a transformation equalized the variance of the measure within each treatment group. In the present data, there was a substantial linear correlation between the mean and standard deviation of B ($r = .60$, $p < .01$). There was a substantial curvilinear correlation between the mean and standard deviation of $B/(A + B)$, B/A, $\sqrt{B/A}$, and θ. At intense punishment (when nearly all subjects suppressed), and at extremely mild punishment (when no subjects suppressed), the variability of the measure within groups was less than at moderate punishment when some subjects suppressed far more than others. The mean and standard deviation of the measure $A - B$ were essentially independent ($r = .20$, $p > .05$), but this certainly would not be the measure of choice because it is far more important to reduce the variance than to equalize it. The various obtained relations between the mean and the variance of the suppression measures underscore the essential dependence of this relationship upon the suppression measure chosen.

Psychologists often have the opportunity to choose from among a number of alternative measures of the effectiveness of a treatment, and there are a number of legitimate bases for making the choice. A measure may be well established by precedent, it may be directly readable from standard recording devices, or it may be distributed in a fashion that meets the assumptions of standardized statistical tests. The overriding consideration in the selection of a measure, however, is the amount of information it provides regarding a treatment. The suppression ratio $[B/(A + B)]$ was demonstrated to be more sensitive to differences among various punishment treatments than certain other measures (B and $A - B$), and no alternative measure was found that was more sensitive to the treatment differences. Therefore, this measure was used routinely in the experiments to be described.

The Noxious Stimulus

Quality of the Noxious Stimulus

The punishment procedure is one in which a noxious stimulus is contingent upon the occurrence of a response, and in a large majority of studies of punishment the noxious stimulus has been a brief electric shock. The simple assumption is that all of the principles of aversive behavior based on electric shock are valid for other noxious stimuli, but this assumption has not been thoroughly tested. The primary need for research with noxious stimuli other than electric shock is to test and extend the generality of the principles of aversive behavior. Various alternative noxious stimuli are available for use, e.g., loud noise, bright light, pinch, heat, cold water, blasts of air, and a variety of other unpleasant stimuli. For generality, particular attention should be focussed on those noxious stimuli that arouse emotional responses other than pain and fear, e.g., anger, nausea, and annoyance. Presumably, a breeze from a fan is an "annoying" rather than a "fear-arousing" stimulus to a rat in a refrigerator set at $0°$ C. Nonetheless, the subject readily learns to perform an instrumental act to turn off the breeze, and response suppression may occur if the onset of the fan is contingent upon a response. Further research with such a stimulus may serve to integrate the basic principles of aversive behavior (based primarily upon experiments with electric shock) with those of positive reinforcement (based primarily upon experiments with food reward). In the case of a breeze, the same physical event (air movement) can serve as a noxious stimulus or a reward, depending upon the ambient temperature. (A breeze is a noxious stimulus to a subject in a cold environment, but it is a rewarding stimulus to a subject in a hot environment.) Similar considerations also apply to the physical event of reduction of ambient temperature by K degrees. Certain experiments necessarily require the use of two qualitatively different aversive stimuli to separate the discriminative from the aversive aspects of a punishing stimulus (Melvin & Martin, 1966). Of course, there may be some specific advantages to a noxious stimulus other than electric shock. For example, compared with the elicited behavior to a shock, the elicited behavior to a breeze may compete less with instrumental responding, so that a temporal or ratio requirement for escape may be more readily acquired or performed.[4]

In the experiments described in this chapter, the noxious stimulus was a brief electric shock. Although the physical characteristics of this stimulus are particularly easy to measure and control, considerable precision is lost when the stimulus makes contact with the subject. Especially in the case of an animal that is free to move about on a grid floor, the severity of the electric shock is influenced by several uncontrolled factors. The area of contact affects the current density, the sensitivity of the part of the body in contact with the grid affects the apparent intensity of the shock, and leaping influences the duration of the shock. Despite such un-

---

[4] Dr. John Corbit called my attention to the relevance of behavioral thermoregulation for the study of aversive behavior. T. J. Matthews is currently investigating some of the problems described in this paragraph.

controlled factors, shock is not an unreliable punishing stimulus, and parametric studies of the intensity of electric-shock punishment do not require large groups. In fact, it is much simpler to demonstrate a graded behavioral effect of five intensities of electric-shock punishment than of five magnitudes of food reward.

Severity of the Noxious Stimulus

Intensity. Probably the most thoroughly documented finding in the studies of punishment is that the degree of response suppression is a function of the intensity of the punishment (e.g., Azrin, 1960; Karsh, 1962). One example is shown in Fig. 5–2 (adapted from Camp, Raymond, & Church, 1967). After eight sessions of training to press a lever for food reinforcement on a 1-minute variable-interval schedule, 48 rats were randomly divided into six groups that were given punishment at intensities

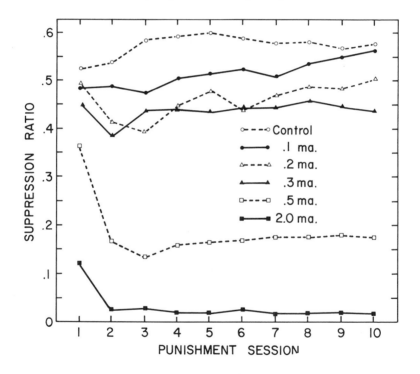

FIG. 5–2.   Mean suppression ratio as a function of intensity of punishment.

From: D. S. Camp, G. A. Raymond, & R. M. Church, "Temporal Relationship Between Response and Punishment," *Journal of Experimental Psychology,* **74**, 1967, Fig. 1, p. 117. Copyright 1967 by the American Psychological Association and reproduced by permission.

of 0, 0.1, 0.2, 0.3, 0.5, or 2.0 ma. The punishment was 2.0 seconds in duration and delivered according to a fixed-ratio schedule calculated for each subject so that it would receive an average of one punishment per minute if its response rate remained unchanged. The mean suppression ratio for the ten sessions of punishment training was inversely related to punishment intensity (Kruskal–Wallis one-way analysis of variance by ranks, $H = 28.8$, $df = 4$, $p < .001$). There was a small but significant recovery from the initial suppressive effects of punishment, particularly in groups with moderate intensity of punishment.

Resistance to extinction is also a function of the intensity of punishment (Boe, 1964; Boe & Church, 1967; Estes, 1944). In a replication of the procedure used by Estes (1944) in Experiment A, 60 rats were given three 1-hour sessions of acquisition of a lever response (on a 4-min. fixed-interval schedule of food reinforcement) and then nine 1-hour sessions of extinction (Boe & Church, 1967). During a 15-minute period of the first extinction session (the 5th through the 20th minute) subjects in the experimental groups were given a brief (.1 sec.) electric shock contingent upon responses on a 30-second fixed-interval schedule of punishment. The source voltages were 0, 35, 50, 75, 120, and 220 volts AC, with a matched impedance circuit (150K ohms in series with the subject). During the remainder of this first extinction session, and during the subsequent eight 1-hour extinction sessions, responses were neither reinforced nor punished. The problem was to determine whether or not the brief 15-minute period of punishment reduced the number of responses to extinction. The results, shown in Fig. 5–3, demonstrate that punishment produced both an immediate decrease in responding during the punishment period and a permanent decrease in responding during the nine sessions of extinction. Both the magnitude of the response suppression during punishment and the extent that punishment decreased the total number of responses during extinction were a function of punishment intensity ($H = 44.9$ and $H = 25.2$, respectively; $df = 5$, $p < .001$).

In the punishment procedure a noxious stimulus is contingent upon the occurrence of a response, but there has been no satisfactory definition of the key concept of a noxious stimulus. In their review of the operant literature on punishment, Azrin and Holz (1966) define a punishment as a "consequence of behavior that reduces the future probability of that behavior." A brief shock following a response and a brief change in illumination following a response may both result in a reduction in the future probability of the behavior. Some consequences of a response, such as a kick-back of a lever combined with a fairly loud click (Skinner, 1938), may be a mild punishment or may serve merely as an external inhibitor (a novel, distracting, curiosity-arousing, investigative stimulus). There is a continuum from stimuli that are clearly neutral (the external

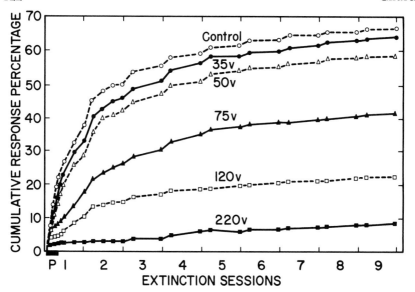

FIG. 5–3.   Cumulative median response percentage during nine sessions of extinction. (Response percentage is the ratio of response rate during a segment of extinction to response rate during the last session of reinforcement training, multiplied by 100.) Punishment (P) was contingent upon lever pressing from the fifth through the twentieth minute of the first extinction session.

From: E. E. Boe & R. M. Church, "Permanent Effects of Punishment During Extinction," *Journal of Comparative and Physiological Psychology*, **63**, 1967, Fig. 1, p. 487. Copyright 1967 by the American Psychological Association and reproduced by permission.

inhibitors) to those that are clearly noxious (the punishers), and the effects of a punishment procedure appear to be temporary only if a response-produced external inhibitor is used to reduce the response rate. An external inhibitor, unlike a punishment, may merely distract a subject, but not subtract from the number of responses it will make during extinction.

Duration.   An increase in the duration of a punishment has an effect that is remarkably similar to an increase in the intensity of a punishment on the degree of response suppression (e.g., Seligman & Campbell, 1965; Storms, Boroczi, & Broen, 1963). One example is shown in Fig. 5–4 (adpated from Church, Raymond, & Beauchamp, 1967). After five sessions of training to press a lever for food reinforcement on a 1-minute variable-interval schedule, 42 rats were randomly divided into six groups that were given punishment for durations of 0.00, 0.15, 0.30, 0.50, 1.00, or 3.00 seconds. The punishment was .16 ma., and it was delivered according to a 2-minute variable-interval schedule. (The reinforcement and the punish-

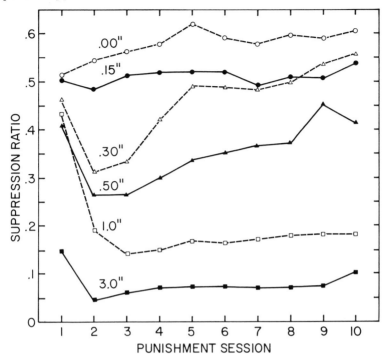

FIG. 5–4.   Mean suppression ratio as a function of duration of punishment.

From: R. M. Church, G. A. Raymond, & R. D. Beauchamp, "Response Suppression as a Function of Intensity and Duration of a Punishment," *Journal of Comparative and Physiological Psychology*, **63**, 1967, Fig. 1, p. 40. Copyright 1967 by the American Psychological Association and reproduced by permission.

ment schedules were independent, except for the restriction that they were never made available to a subject within 7.5 sec. of each other.) The mean suppression ratio for the ten sessions of punishment training was inversely related to punishment duration ($H = 24.4$, $df = 5$, $p < .001$). As the duration of a punishment is increased there is first (1) no suppressive effect, then (2) partial suppression with complete recovery, then (3) partial suppression without complete recovery, and finally, (4) total suppression without recovery. Similar statements may be made about increases in the intensity of a punishment.

The combination of intensity and duration.   The intensity and duration of a shock combine in a simple fashion to determine the "severity" of a punishment, and the magnitude of response suppression is directly related to the severity of the punishment. Over a considerable range, the magnitude of response suppression is a linear function both of the logarithm of the intensity (I) of a punishment and of the duration (D) of a punishment. In cases where the slopes of the linear functions are equal, the magnitude of response suppression is a function of the sum of log I and log D, i.e., log $(I \times D)$. In one experiment (Church, Raymond, & Beauchamp, 1967) the mean suppression ratio was a linear function of the logarithm of the product of the intensity and duration of the punishment, within the limits of .05 to .25 ma. and .25 to 2.0 seconds.

An increase in the intensity and duration of a punishment may produce similar effects for entirely different reasons. For example, if a subject does not perform the instrumental response during a shock, a long-duration punishment may be more effective than a short one because (1) it reduces the effective length of the session, or (2) it introduces a delay between response and reward. The gross differences in the suppression ratio as a function of duration of punishment, however, could not be accounted for in terms of the small difference in the total number of seconds of shocks under the infrequent schedule of punishment employed (VI 2), and the use of a schedule of positive reinforcement that was uncorrelated with the schedule of punishment minimized the number of reinforced responses that were also punished. Of course, the subjects can discriminate between a brief intense shock and a longer moderate shock. The motor responses elicited by a brief intense shock are radically different from those elicited by a longer moderate shock. Nonetheless, some elicited responses (e.g., vocalization thresholds, shock-elicited aggression) are linearly related to the logarithm of the duration of a shock as well as to the logarithm of its intensity. Perhaps escape latency is related to shock intensity partly because the subject begins the response when the shock exceeds some level of severity. Further studies are necessary to assess the extent to which increases in intensity and duration of an electric shock produce equivalent behavioral effects.

Prior Exposure to Shock

The magnitude of response suppression is not only a function of the severity of the punishment that is presently being administered but also a function of the prior experience of the subject with shock. What is the influence of prior exposure to shock on the magnitude of response suppression produced by response-contingent punishment? There are two basic results, both of them amply documented. The first is (1) prior exposure to a noxious stimulus *decreases* the effectiveness of a punishment (e.g., Karsh, 1963); the second is (2) prior exposure to a noxious stimulus *increases* the effectiveness of a punishment (e.g., Pearl, Walters, & Anderson, 1964). These phenomena have sometimes been referred to as adaptation and sensitization, respectively.

Such labels not only fail to explain the results, but they are absolutely misleading. One should not falsely conclude that a phenomenon has been explained when, in fact, it only has been named. There is little contribution to be made from additional examples of either an increase or decrease in reactivity to punishment following prior exposure to shock unless they lead to the isolation of a relevant variable. In this section, four experiments will be described. The first two demonstrate conditions under which prior exposure to a noxious stimulus decreases the effectiveness of a punishment; the next experiment demonstrates a set of conditions under which prior exposure to a noxious stimulus increases the effectiveness of a punishment. The final experiment in this section attempts to reconcile these apparently contradictory results.

Miller (1960) demonstrated that the effectiveness of a punishment is attenuated if subjects have prior exposure to a series of punishments that gradually increase in intensity. In that experiment rats were trained to run to the goal compartment of a runway for food reinforcement and then were subjected to a punishment training procedure in which both food and punishment were administered. The group that received a gradually increasing intensity of punishing shock on successive blocks of trials was much less affected by a relatively intense punishment than groups that had no previous experience with punishment. This result was replicated by Feirstein and Miller (1963), and Karsh (1963) also found that previous experience with a relatively mild punishment reduced the effectiveness of a relatively intense punishment. If, as suggested in the previous section, the severity of a punishment is a function of its duration as well as of its intensity, prior exposure to relatively brief punishing events should attenuate the effectiveness of a punishment of longer duration.

Gradual increases in the duration of a punishment.   Prior exposure to punishments of gradually increasing duration does reduce the effectiveness of subsequent long-duration punishments. Twenty-four rats were trained to press a lever for food reinforcement on a 1-minute variable-interval schedule. After five 30-minute sessions half of the subjects (experimental) continued to receive the VI-1 food reinforcement but, in addition, received a punishment of .16 ma. on a 2-minute variable-interval schedule. On successive pairs of sessions, the punishments increased in duration (0.15, 0.30, 0.50, and 1.0 sec.). The other half of the subjects (control) continued to receive VI-1 reinforcement, but no punishment. After eight sessions of this differential training all subjects were treated alike on the final three sessions. These were 30-minute sessions of punishment training with a 1-minute variable-interval schedule of positive reinforcement and a 2-minute variable-interval schedule of punishment. For all subjects, the intensity of the punishing shock was .16 ma., and its duration was 3.0 seconds.

During the first eight sessions of punishment training the subjects in the control group had a mean suppression ratio of .55 while the subjects in the experimental group that received punishment of gradually increasing duration had a mean suppression ratio that was only slightly lower, .45. Figure 5–5 shows that during the last three sessions, when the two groups were treated alike, the amount of response suppression was considerably different. On the final two sessions, the subjects with previous experience with punishment in the lever box had much less response suppression than subjects without previous experience with shock (Mann–Whitney test, $U = 15$, $p < .002$).

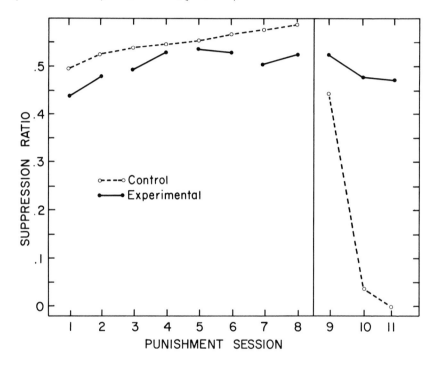

FIG. 5–5.   Mean suppression ratio of subjects with punishment of gradually increasing duration (Experimental) or no prior exposure to shock (Control). Both groups received the same punishment condition on Sessions 9 through 11.

Various explanations have been proposed to account for the attenuation of response suppression produced by punishment of gradually increasing intensity. These include sensory adaptation, counterconditioning, and conditioning of competing responses. None of these explanations are sufficient. *Sensory adaptation* is not a sufficient explanation since a series of shocks in another situation is less effective than the same series of shocks in the situation where punishment will be administered. For example, a group of 12 subjects that received the same shocks of increasing duration in another box without a lever had a mean suppression ratio that was intermediate between the experimental and control groups shown in Fig. 5–5, and significantly different from either of them. Because of the independence of the punishment and reinforcement schedule in this experiment, it was unusual for a reinforcement to occur immediately after a punishment so the opportunity for *counterconditioning* was slight. Presumably, attenuation could be obtained even under conditions of a punishment extinction procedure, i.e., without reinforcement following any of the punishments. The *competing response* hypothesis suggests that the punishments of brief duration may have elicited certain responses that were compatible with lever-pressing, and that these elicited responses maintained themselves even when the duration of the shock was increased. Subjects, however, never appeared to make responses during the 3.0-second punishment that were similar to their responses during short-duration shocks. To a punishment of short duration the subjects made a response that may best be described as a "twitch," and at 3.0-second duration they usually made several complete circles around the lever box. Further evidence against a competing response interpretation would be provided if a gradual increase in one aspect of a shock (intensity, duration, frequency, or delay) attenuated the effect of an abrupt increase in another aspect of the shock.

The "incomplete shift" hypothesis.   Some of the explanations that have been proposed for prior exposure results have an ad hoc flavor, and a different set of explanations is used if the prior exposure increases the effectiveness rather than decreases the effectiveness of subsequent punishment. Ideally, both effects should be produced by variation of a single parameter. The identification of such a parameter should lead to greater theoretical understanding of the prior exposure phenomenon. Raymond (1968) has made some important progress on this problem, and the following three of his experiments suggest that the previous results are not necessarily in conflict.

The same general procedure was used in all three experiments. Rats were given ten 30-minute sessions of training to press a lever on a 22-response fixed-ratio (FR 22) schedule of reinforcement, and this reinforcement schedule was in effect during the remainder of the experiment. After this initial training, subjects were assigned to an experimental group that received exposure to a noncontingent shock or a control group that did not receive this treatment. The shocks were administered on the average of every 2 minutes independently of responding. Then, to equate the response rate of groups prior to the beginning of punishment training, all subjects were given additional sessions of training without shock. Finally, subjects were tested under conditions of punishment, with punishment on a VI-2 schedule. These same four phases were used in each experiment: training, prior exposure to noncontingent shock, retraining, and punishment testing.

The results of the first experiment are shown in Fig. 5–6. The non-contingent shock employed on Sessions 11 through 15 was relatively mild (110 v. for .2 sec.) and it produced only slight response suppression. There was no shock on Sessions 16 through 20, and the median response rates of the experimental group ($N = 10$) and control group ($N = 10$) were equivalent at the beginning of punishment testing. Both groups received punishment of 145 volts for .1 second on Sessions 21 through 25. Most of the subjects that had received prior exposure to shock appeared to be immune to the effect of this punishment, while most of the subjects that had not had prior exposure to shock were almost totally suppressed ($U = 18$, $p < .02$). This may be labelled, but not explained, as a case of adaptation.

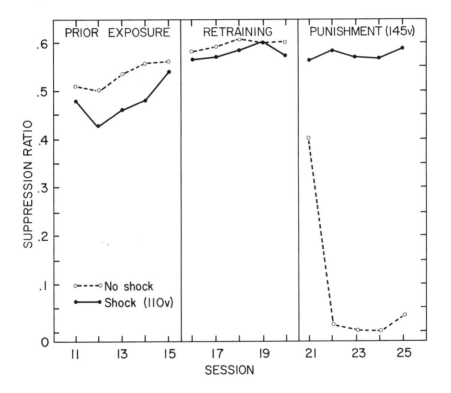

FIG. 5–6.   Median suppression ratio to a punishment of 145 volts as a function of prior exposure to noncontingent shock of 110 volts.

The results of the second experiment are shown in Fig. 5–7. The non-contingent shock employed on Sessions 11 through 15 was relatively severe (220 v. for .2 sec.), and it resulted in nearly complete response suppression. During the five sessions of retraining the response rates became nearly equivalent. Both the experimental group ($N = 21$) and control group ($N = 21$) received a punishment of 110 volts for .1 second on Sessions 21 through 25. Most of the subjects that had not had prior exposure to shock appeared to be immune to the effect of this punishment, while most of the subjects that had prior exposure to shock were almost totally suppressed ($U = 55$, $p < .001$). This may be labelled, but not explained, as a case of sensitization.

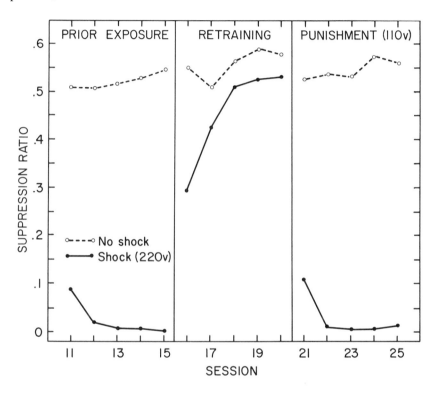

FIG. 5–7.   Median suppression ratio to a punishment of 110 volts as a function of prior exposure to noncontingent shock of 220 volts.

What is the relevant difference between the two experiments? First of all, it may be the intensity of the shock that is used for prior exposure. A weak shock may produce adaptation and an intense shock may produce sensitization. The third experiment demonstrated that the same experience of prior exposure can lead to an attenuation or a magnification of the effect of subsequent punishment. In this experiment 40 experimental subjects received prior exposure to noncontingent shock and 20 control subjects did not receive this treatment. The results are shown in Fig. 5–8. The noncontingent shock used for prior exposure was adjusted for each subject on each session so that it would produce a suppression ratio of about .30. During the retraining phase there was no shock so that the subjects in the experimental group began punishment training with a response rate equivalent to that of the control group. Two intensities of punishment were used, and half of the experimental and control subjects were randomly assigned to each intensity. Prior exposure to shock magnified the effect of a mild (110-volt) punishment, but it attenuated the effect of an intense (180-volt) punishment ($U = 44$, $p < .02$, and $U = 3$, $p < .002$, respectively).

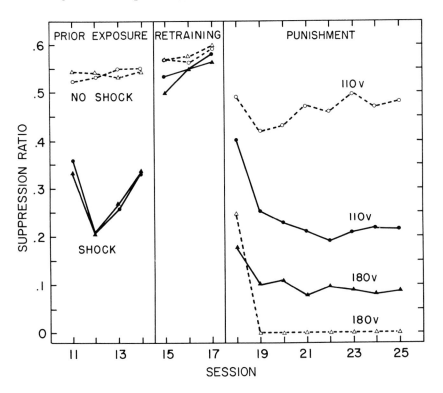

FIG. 5–8.   Mean suppression ratio to punishment of 110 volts and 180 volts as a function of prior exposure to shock.

Why does prior exposure to nonescapable shock increase the effectiveness of mild punishment but decrease the effectiveness of intense punishment? Apparently a given intensity of prior exposure neither sensitizes nor adapts a subject to subsequent exposures to shock. Under conditions of punishment the subject behaves in a manner intermediate between that appropriate to the punishment (as determined by control subjects without prior exposure to shock) and the rate it had previously adopted during the prior exposure condition. This "incomplete shift" or "inertia" hypothesis suggests that many of the previous observations of adaptation and sensitization may, in fact, be examples of generalization.

That is to say, if a subject has learned to perform in a certain manner in the presence of one stimulus configuration, it will perform in a similar manner in the presence of a similar stimulus configuration. Thus, in the presence of a second intensity of shock, a subject has a tendency to persist in the performance it has learned in the context of the first intensity of shock. Generalization can also occur from a shock of one duration to that of another duration. Although the stimulus aspects are less clear, prior exposure to an infrequent punishment can attenuate the response suppression to relatively more frequent punishment (Banks, 1966), and a punishment that is temporally distant from a response can attenuate suppression to a punishment that is temporally closer to the response (Karsh, 1966). It is not known whether or not generalization occurs from one dimension of a punishment to another (e.g., from intensity to duration). This emphasis upon the generalization of a response tendency from one condition to another is consistent with the observation that the effectiveness of prior exposure depends upon the similarity between the conditions of training and the conditions of testing (Miller, 1960). The present experiments do not serve to distinguish between a "primacy" and a "recency" effect, since only one condition of prior exposure was employed.

The Relationship Between Response and Punishment

In many situations punishment clearly leads to suppression of an instrumental lever-pressing response, but there are numerous alternative explanations regarding the mechanism through which it may exert this effect. In the punishment procedure the noxious stimulus is contingent upon the occurrence of a specified response, but is this response of any consequence? There are four types of stimuli that may be readily identified. First of all, there are the situational cues (e.g., the lever box with its grid floor and food cup). These environmental, context, or apparatus cues are the relatively fixed aspects, neither under the control of the experimenter nor of the subject. Secondly, there are the experimenter-controlled stimuli, often referred to as "external stimuli," or simply "stimuli" (e.g., a tone and, when a retractable lever is used, the lever). Such stimuli may be described in terms of their presence or absence, onset or termination, or in terms of the time since their onset or termination. As a signal for inevitable occurrence of a noxious event, an experimenter-controlled stimulus is a conditioned stimulus (CS); as a signal for the occurrence of a noxious event only if a specified response occurs, it is a discriminative stimulus (S+). Thirdly, there are the response-produced, or subject-controlled, stimuli (e.g., proprioceptive feedback of the lever response, and the visual and auditory consequences of the response). Finally, there are the events of positive reinforcement (e.g., food to a hungry subject) and punishment (e.g., electric shock), both of which have obvious stimulus properties. The observed response suppression can be a result of the association of the noxious stimulus with the situation cues (generalized anxiety), the experimenter-controlled stimuli (CER), the response-produced stimuli (punishment), or any combination of these stimuli.

Although a response-contingent shock may produce response suppression, a brief electric shock that is independent of any particular response may also disrupt the performance of a positive instrumental act. For example, a shock that is not contingent upon a response may result in a decrease in the response rate of a subject that is pressing a lever for food reinforcement (Estes, 1944, Experiment I). An illustration of this phenomenon from our laboratory is shown in Fig. 5–9. Sixty subjects were given five sessions of training to press a lever for food reinforcement (VI 1), and then, while the 1-minute variable-interval schedule of food reinforcement used for original training was continued, the subjects were exposed to noncontingent shocks of 2.0-second duration that occurred on the VI-2 schedule. The subjects were randomly partitioned into five groups of 12 subjects each, and each group received noncontingent shocks of 2.00, 0.50, 0.15, 0.05, or 0.00 ma. The greater the intensity of the noncontingent shock, the greater the response suppression ($H = 45.2$, $df = 4$, $p < .001$).[5]

If the mean suppression ratio is a function of the severity of noncontingent shock as well as of response-contingent shock, what is the assurance that the response is relevant? Direct comparisons of the two procedures have led to the empirical generalization that the magnitude of suppression of a positive instrumental response is greater if the punishment is contingent upon the response than if it is not (e.g., Azrin, 1956; Camp, Raymond, & Church, 1967). An additional example of this result from our laboratory is shown in Fig. 5–10. Twenty-four rats were trained

[5] This influence of noncontingent shocks on the "baserate" is a familiar problem in studies of the conditioned emotional response (CER), and most studies of the CER use procedures that minimize the effect of treatment differences on the baserate. Although the noncontingent shock may continue to elicit a motor response, it has relatively little effect on the overall response rate if it is presented infrequently and if it is not severe. In a typical study of the CER, shocks might be presented at a rate of 2 per hour instead of 30 per hour, and the duration of the shock might be about .5 second instead of 2.0 seconds. Finally, the influence of noncontingent shocks on the baserate is less pronounced if a signal is introduced prior to the shock.

to press a lever for food reinforcement (VI 1) and were then randomly partitioned into three groups of eight subjects each. During the next ten sessions, when the 1-minute variable-interval schedule of food reinforcement remained in effect, one group received a .25 ma. shock on a VI-2 schedule of response-contingent shock. A second group (punishment) received a .25 ma. shock on a VI-2 schedule of noncontingent shock, and

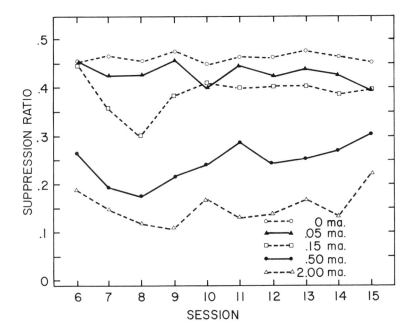

FIG. 5–9.   Median suppression ratio as a function of intensity of noncontingent shock.

the third group received no shock (control). The results of this experiment were as follows: The group with contingent shock was significantly more suppressed than the group with noncontingent shock ($U = 8$, $p < .01$), and the group with noncontingent shock was significantly more suppressed than the control group ($U = 2$, $p < .001$).[6] It should be noted

[6] Although the group with .25-ma. noncontingent shock received the same treatment as groups with noncontingent shocks in the previous experiment, and its mean suppression ratio was between that of groups with .15- and .50-ma. shock, no attempt has been made to compare groups in different experiments. In the studies reported in this chapter, treatment effects have not been reversed in replications of experimental groups, but the absolute magnitude of the effects and the absolute level of response suppression have been influenced by various unknown and uncontrolled variables that may simply be called "replication effects." Any attempt to compare one group from one replication with another group from another replication is, of course, subject to the confounding of treatment and replication effects.

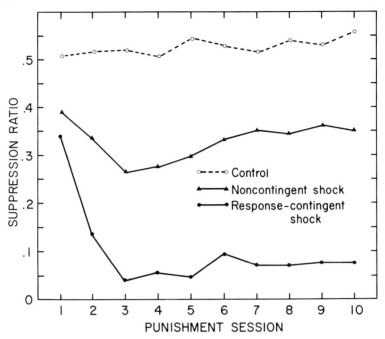

FIG. 5–10.   Mean suppression ratio of subjects with response-contingent shock (punishment) and noncontingent shock, and of an unpunished control group.

that all subjects in the noncontingent group received 15 shocks in each 30-minute session, while subjects in the contingent group markedly reduced the shock frequency by response suppression. Despite this difference in shock frequency, the contingent procedure resulted in greater response suppression.

Why is a shock that immediately follows a response more effective in suppressing that response than a shock that occurs independently of responding? Two variables are potentially relevant, (1) the temporal proximity between the response and punishment (contiguity), and (2) the probabilistic dependence of the punishment upon the response (contingency). The previous experiment confounds these two factors. In the punishment group all shocks immediately followed a lever response (i.e., close temporal contiguity), and the rate of occurrence of shock was dependent upon the response rate (i.e., high contingency). On the other hand, in the noncontingent shock group, many shocks did not follow shortly after a lever response (i.e., remote temporal contiguity), and the rate of occurrence of a shock was independent of the response rate (i.e., no contingency).

Temporal Interval Between Response and Punishment

The magnitude of response suppression is a function of the temporal contiguity between response and punishment, even when the dependence of punishment upon response is held constant. Consider the following two conditions. Under both conditions, on the average of once every 2 minutes, a situation arises such that the subject "earns" a punishment for its next response. Under one condition the shock is delivered immediately; under the other condition the shock is delivered sometime later (delay procedure). Thus the contingency between response and punishment is the same under the two conditions, but the temporal interval between response and punishment (i.e., the contiguity) is different. The delayed-punishment procedure and the immediate-punishment procedure lead to identical treatment of subjects with identical behavior with respect to (1) the number of aversive events received, (2) the distribution of time intervals between aversive events, and (3) the number of aversive events received. The two procedures differ with respect to the temporal interval between a specified response (the one that "earns" the punishment) and the aversive event.

The results from a representative experiment that compared the magnitude of response suppression produced by contingent shock delivered immediately after a response with contingent shock delivered 30 seconds following the specified response are shown in Fig. 5–11 (adapted from Camp, Raymond, & Church, 1967). The punishment was .25 ma. for 1.0 second, the specified response was the first response following a variable interval of 2 minutes, and there were 15 subjects in each group. Contiguity between response and shock significantly increased the effectiveness of punishment ($U = 9$, $p < .002$).

Of course, the time interval between the shock and the immediately-preceding response in the 30-second delay group was rarely as long as 30 seconds. (The requirement of a 30-sec. pause for a shock to occur would introduce an avoidance contingency, i.e., Sidman avoidance.) The specified duration of the delay merely set the maximum interval between a shock and the preceding response. In the present situation it was not possible to distinguish between the distribution of intervals between shock and the immediately preceding response of the 30-second delay procedure and the noncontingent procedure (see Fig. 5–12). Of course, there is no evidence that the response immediately preceding the shock is the only relevant response. Presumably, a subject could learn to space its responses if punishment were to follow a response that had been preceded by another response within t seconds (i.e., the subject could

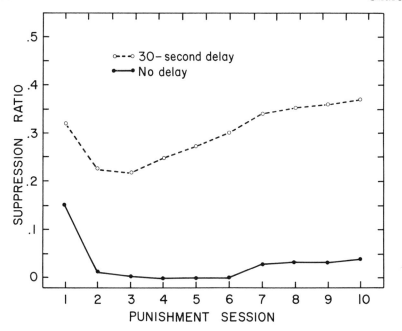

FIG. 5–11.   Mean suppression ratio of subjects with contingent shock delivered immediately (0 sec.) after a specified response or 30 seconds after a specified response.

From: D. S. Camp, G. A. Raymond, & R. M. Church, "Temporal Relationship Between Response and Punishment," *Journal of Experimental Psychology,* **74,** 1967, Fig. 3, p. 119. Copyright 1967 by the American Psychological Association and reproduced by permission.

learn an association between a shock and the response prior to the final one).

Systematic variations in the delay between a response that met a particular criterion (VI 2) and a punishment result in a delay-of-punishment gradient (Camp, Raymond, & Church, 1967). Such a gradient has also been reported in the discrete-trial situation (e.g., Kamin, 1959; Renner, 1966b). Since a trial must be begun by some experimenter-controlled stimulus, which can serve as the basis for the formation of a conditioned emotional response, observed suppression in a delay-of-punishment experiment with discrete trials could be a result of the interval between the experimenter-controlled stimulus and shock rather than the interval between response and shock. The gradient obtained in a free-responding situation, however, eliminates this confounding effect of the temporal interval between discriminative stimulus and shock.

Why is a delayed punishment less effective than a punishment immediately following a response? The effectiveness of a punishment is presumably a function both of its certainty and of its severity. If a re-

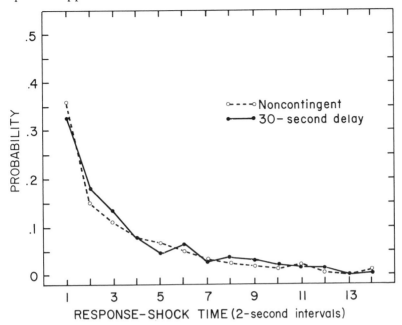

FIG. 5–12.   Probability distribution of times between shock and preceding response (in 2-sec. intervals) for subjects with noncontingent shock and 30-second delay of punishment.

From: D. S. Camp, G. A. Raymond, & R. M. Church, "Temporal Relationship Between Response and Punishment," *Journal of Experimental Psychology,* **74**, 1967, Fig. 3, p. 120. Copyright 1967 by the American Psychological Association and reproduced by permission.

sponse that is always followed by punishment is more suppressed than one that is only occasionally followed by punishment, the differential effectiveness could be attributed to certainty. If a response that is followed by an intense punishment is more suppressed than one that is followed by a mild punishment, the differential effectiveness could be attributed to severity. Are the effects of variations in the temporal interval between response and punishment more analogous to variations in probability or in intensity of punishment? In some cases, delay must introduce uncertainty, particularly if the interval between response and punishment is very long; in other cases, a delayed punishment may be less effective than an immediate one even when punishment is known to be inevitable. A consequence that is certain, but that will not occur for a while, may be effectively less severe than a consequence that will occur immediately. Of course, this statement requires some qualification since, under some conditions, a subject will prefer a signalled to an unsignalled shock (Lockard, 1963) and an immediate to a delayed punishment (Renner, 1966a). By an extension of the principle of momentary maximization (Shimp, 1966), however, a subject may be more influenced by the momentary probability of a punishment than by the overall probability of a punishment.

One interpretation of the greater suppression observed in an immediate punishment group than in a 5-second delay punishment group is that the subject can associate the shock with the response more clearly in the former case than in the latter. The introduction of a signal filling the gap of time between the occurrence of a to-be-punished response and the punishment might be expected to improve the association, and thus to reduce the difference in the magnitude of response suppression between subjects in a 5-second delay punishment group and an immediate punishment group. In the following experiment, which Raymond and I performed, the opposite result occurred.

Forty-eight rats were given the standard pretraining procedure, and ten sessions of training for food reinforcement (VI 1) with exposure to the stimulus that was later to be used as a signal for punishment. Subjects were then randomly partitioned into four groups of 12 subjects. One group received punishment immediately following a response on a VI-2 schedule. A second group, also on a VI-2 schedule, received a 5-second, 70-db, white noise signal that terminated with the onset of a punishment; a third group received the same treatment as the second, but without the signal. The final group was an unpunished control group. Punishment was 110 volts (through 150K ohms) for .2 second during Punishment Sessions 1 through 11, and 220 volts during Punishment Sessions 12 through 17.

Figure 5–13 shows the mean suppression ratio as a function of sessions for the four groups. There were reliable differences in the mean suppression ratio during Sessions 1 through 11 at 110 volts ($H = 18.1$, $df = 3$, $p < .001$) and during Sessions 12 through 17 at 220 volts ($H = 32.6$, $df = 3$, $p < .001$). The group that received punishment immediately following a specified response was most suppressed, and the unpunished control group was least suppressed. The group that received punishment 5 seconds following a specified response had an intermediate degree of suppression. Compared with this group, a group with a signal that bridged the 5-second interval between the response that earned the punishment and the punishment, was overall less suppressed. Although this result was not reliable at 110 volts ($U = 48$, $p > .05$), it was reliable at 220 volts ($U = 19$, $p < .002$). Presumably, the introduction of a signal that invariably preceded the noxious stimulus released subjects from generalized anxiety during most of the session (only 15 signals of 5-sec. duration were used in a 30-min. session). This resulted in an overall increase in the response rate.

Of course, subjects responded slowly during the 5-second signal that

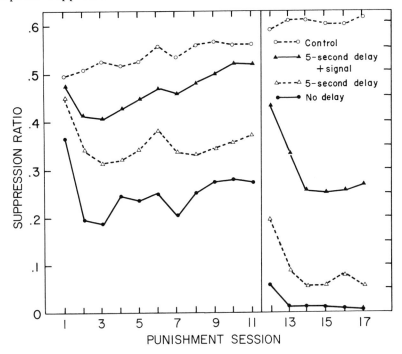

FIG. 5–13.   Mean suppression ratio of subjects with immediate punishment, punishment delayed by five seconds after a specified response, punishment delayed by five seconds after a specified response with a signal between response and punishment, and of an unpunished control group.

was invariably followed by a shock (CER). To assess the effects of the signal on the response rate during the signal a comparison was made between the two groups with the 5-second delay between response and shock. For each subject in these two groups a signal suppression ratio, $B/(A + B)$ was calculated in which B = response rate during the 5-second intervals preceding each shock and A = response rate during the 30-minute sessions. With punishment of 110 volts the mean response rate for B and A, respectively, was 9.3 and 19.0 for subjects with the signal, and 23.6 and 19.9 for subjects without the signal. (The group without the signal was reliably faster during the 5-second intervals prior to a punishment than overall since a response was necessary to produce the punishment and successive responses tended to be positively correlated.) During the 5-second intervals preceding the punishment, subjects with the signal had a significantly lower mean suppression ratio than subjects without the signal ($U = 10$, $p < .002$). At a greater intensity of punishment (220 v.) a reliable measure of suppression during the signal could not be obtained since the overall response rate (baserate) of many subjects was extremely low. In this experiment, the CER in the presence of the signal emerged prior to the relief in the absence of the signal, and it occurred at a lower intensity of the noxious stimulus.

The response-produced signal that preceded the occurrence of a noxious stimulus may be called a "secondary punishment," but the addition of such a signal resulted in an increase rather than a reduction in the overall response rate. In this experiment, and in several related ones involving a signal preceding a noxious stimulus, there was response suppression in the presence of a signal and, relative to a group without the signal, there was an increase in the response rate in the absence of the signal. The introduction of a signal led to conditioning of anxiety to the signal, but it permitted the absence of the signal to produce relief. Thus the primary function of the signal was to lead to a discrimination between those portions of the session in which shock was likely to occur from those in which it was not.

Dependence of a Noxious Stimulus upon a Response

Is the magnitude of response suppression a function of the dependence of the noxious stimulus upon a response, even when the temporal interval between response and noxious stimulus is constant? The degree of dependence is the extent to which the occurrence of a response affects the probability of a noxious stimulus. A noxious stimulus is dependent upon a response if the probability of the noxious stimulus given a response is not equal to the probability of the noxious stimulus given a nonresponse [(i.e., if $p(sh|R) \neq p(sh|\overline{R})$]. If the two conditional probabilities are equal, then the noxious stimulus is independent of the response (see Fig. 5–14). Consider the following experimental situation: At the end of some short interval of time a noxious stimulus is presented with one probability if one or more responses occur in that interval [($p(sh|R) = X$)] and a noxious stimulus is presented with a second probability if no responses occur in that interval [($p(sh|\overline{R}) = Y$)]. All situations in which $X > Y$ may be considered to be conditions of punishment; all situations in which $X < Y$ may be considered to be conditions of avoidance. The ideal punishment case is represented by a point in the lower righthand corner (1.0, 0.0); the ideal avoidance case is represented by a point in the upper lefthand corner (0.0, 1.0). The diagonal between these points would represent a continuum of procedures between punish-

ment and avoidance. The index $\dfrac{X - Y}{X + Y}$ serves as a measure of the degree

of dependence between the response and the noxious stimulus. It varies

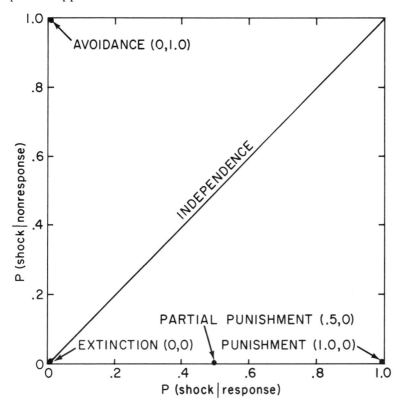

FIG. 5–14.   Diagrammatic representation of the degree of dependence of a noxious stimulus upon a response.

from + 1.0 to − 1.0, with 0.0 (the diagonal with origin in the lower left-hand corner) representing the cases of independence. All points on a straight line with a *Y* intercept of 0 receive the same value of the index of dependence, although, of course, they differ with respect to the frequency of occurrence of noxious stimuli.

A punishment procedure is often defined as one in which a noxious stimulus is contingent upon the occurrence of a response (Church, 1963). Nonetheless, there has been far greater attention to contiguity of response and noxious stimulus than the contingency between response and noxious stimulus. A similar emphasis in classical conditioning has been well documented by Rescorla (1967). Although no such experiments have yet been reported, one can be virtually certain that contingency, as well as contiguity, is an important variable in the determination of the magnitude of suppression produced by punishment.

Discriminative Punishment and the CER

In the discriminative punishment procedure the noxious stimulus is conditional upon (1) an experimenter-controlled stimulus, and (2) a response; in the conditioned emotional response (CER) procedure the noxious stimulus is conditional only upon an experimenter-controlled stimulus. Although a specified response always intervenes between the discriminative stimulus and the noxious stimulus in the discriminative punishment procedure, the first problem is to determine if the occurrence of this response is of any consequence. The reference condition for the discriminative punishment situation is one in which each response in the presence of a signal is followed by a brief aversive event (e.g., Dinsmoor, 1952). The reference condition for the CER situation is one in which a signal is followed by a single, brief, aversive event, whether or not any responses have occurred during the signal (e.g., Estes & Skinner, 1941).

Hunt and Brady (1955) made a direct comparison of the behavior of subjects under the discriminative punishment and CER procedures. All subjects were trained to press a lever on a 1-minute variable-interval schedule of food reinforcement, and then they were exposed to an auditory stimulus of 3-minute duration. For subjects in the Discriminative Punishment Group, each response during the auditory stimulus was accompanied by an electric shock that remained on as long as the lever was depressed; for subjects in the CER Group, two brief 1.5-ma. shocks occurred at the time of CS termination. At this intensity, both groups showed almost complete suppression of the lever responding during the auditory stimulus. The CER Group, however, showed greater response suppression in the absence of the auditory stimulus and greater resistance to extinction than the Discriminative Punishment Group. Furthermore, subjects in the CER Group showed more general signs of anxiety (e.g., crouching, freezing, and defecating), while subjects in the Discriminative Punishment Group often showed abortive lever-pressing. At least four differences between the treatments of the two groups can be identified: (1) the dependence of response and aversive event, (2) the temporal interval between response and aversive event, (3) the number of aversive events, and (4) the duration of each aversive event. By definition, the only essential difference between the procedures is the dependence of response and aversive event.

In the following experiment, Beauchamp (1966) attempted to evaluate the influence of the dependence between response and noxious event in the CER and discriminative punishment situations. After the standard pretraining and reinforcement training conditions (VI 1), subjects were given four additional sessions with a 10-second white noise signal (70 db) on a VI-2 schedule. Then subjects were randomly assigned to one of two groups, Discriminative Punishment or CER. Subjects in the Discriminative Punishment Group were given a shock at the termination of the signal only if they had made one or more responses during that signal; subjects in the CER Group received a shock at the termination of the signal whether or not they had made a response during the signal. Thus the subjects in the Discriminative Punishment Group, but not the subjects in the CER Group, could avoid the shock. (The shock was .25 ma. for 0.5 sec.) To assess the effects of the signal on the response rate, a signal suppression ratio, $B/(A + B)$, was calculated with B = response rate during the 150 seconds of signal and A = response rate during the 30-minute session. The mean signal suppression ratio during the last five sessions of the treatment was lower for the Discriminative Punishment Group than for the CER Group ($F = 11.6$, $df = \frac{1}{32}$, $p < .005$), despite

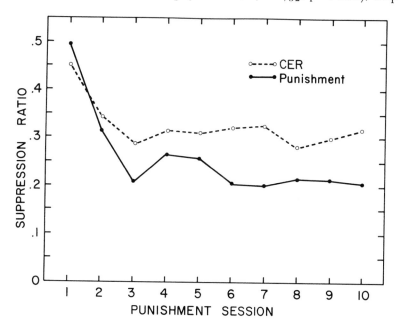

FIG. 5-15.   Mean signal suppression ratio of the Discriminative Punishment Group and the CER Group.

From: R. D. Beauchamp, *A Comparison of the Degree of Suppression Following Either a Discriminative Punishment Treatment or a Conditioned Emotional Response Treatment.* Unpublished master's thesis, Brown University, 1966. Reproduced by permission.

the fact that the former group received only about half as many shocks (see Fig. 5-15).

This experiment provided support for an avoidance interpretation for some of the suppression produced by punishment. The CER and discriminative punishment procedures were identical on those occasions that a subject made one or more responses during the signal; they differed only on those occasions that a subject did not make any response. Apparently, the greater dependence of shock upon response in discriminative punishment conditions more than compensated for the greater number of aversive events in the CER condition. Although one should guard against the circularity of upholding an avoidance interpretation of punishment at the same time as a punishment interpretation of avoidance, one plausible explanation of the results of this experiment is that a successful avoidance of shock resulted in greater suppression than a CER trial.

In a series of five additional experiments comparing a discriminative punishment procedure with a CER procedure, the magnitude of suppression in the two groups has been roughly comparable. The critical variables responsible for the Beauchamp (1966) results have not yet been identified. In one case, the magnitude of suppression produced by CER was even greater than that produced by discriminative punishment. In that experiment subjects were trained under VI-1 schedule of food reinforcement and then were given sessions with a 5-second white noise signal on a VI-2 schedule. In the CER Group ($N = 12$) the termination of each signal was invariably followed by a shock; in the Discriminative Punishment Group ($N = 10$) the first response in the presence of the signal was immediately followed by shock. (The shock was 120 v. for 0.2 sec.) During the last five of the ten sessions of differential training, the magnitude of suppression during the signal was greater for the CER Group than for the Discriminative Punishment Group ($U = 22$, $p < .02$). Presumably, under CER conditions, subjects remained relatively suppressed throughout the signal, but if a subject in the Discriminative Punishment Group made a response during the signal (and received its only punishment) it would be free to make several more responses during the remainder of the signal.

In all the previous experiments comparing the magnitude of suppression produced by the CER and the discriminative punishment procedures, the proportion of signals that have been followed by shock have been unequal (i.e., the subjects in the CER condition have received one shock per signal, and the subjects in the discriminative punishment procedure have received a shock only on those signals during which they made one or more responses). Because of the systematic effects of random error in the yoked control design (Church, 1964), the yoking method to equate the number of shocks would have produced results that would be difficult to interpret. One approach is to compare the response suppression during the signal of subjects under the discriminative-punishment procedure with that of subjects that receive a shock at the end of a signal if they made one or more responses during some previous signal. In one experiment with that design, subjects were trained to press a lever on a 1-minute variable-interval schedule of food reinforcement, and then given additional sessions of this training with a 5-second white noise stimulus on a VI-2 schedule. The Discriminative Punishment Group ($N = 18$) received the shock at the end of the signal if it made one or more responses during the signal; the Control Group ($N = 18$) received a shock at the end of the signal if it made one or more responses during the previous signal. (The shock was 120 v. for 0.1 sec.) The mean signal suppression ratio was indistinguishable under these two conditions, about .250 in both cases. This, however, does not imply that the subjects could not learn this contingency between the response and the shock. Without the signal, this procedure is similar to that employed in the study of the temporal interval between response and punishment (see pp. 135–140). In the Discriminative Punishment Group each shock was preceded by a response within the past 5 seconds; in the Control Group some shocks were not preceded so closely by a response. Thus, when the stimulus was omitted from this procedure (and the shock intensity raised to 240 v. for 0.2 sec.), the subjects in the Discriminative Punishment Group had a significantly lower mean suppression ratio than subjects in the Control Group ($U = 75$, $p < .01$). Apparently, the occurrence of a strong association between the signal and the shock reduced the effectiveness of the association between response and shock in the Discriminative Punishment Group.

Punishment of Various Responses in a Behavior Sequence

The effect of punishment depends, in part, upon which response in a behavior sequence is punished. A behavior sequence may be defined as a series of responses that lead to a reinforcement. Each of the responses may be similar to each other (homogeneous chain), or they may be different from each other (heterogeneous chain). The problem is to determine, and to explain, the differential effect of a punishment delivered immediately after the 1st, 2nd, . . . , Nth instrumental response in a behavior sequence.

Punishment of the initial response. Punishment of the first response in a behavior sequence often produces greater response suppression than punishment of other responses in the sequence. In one experiment in our laboratory 30 rats were trained to press a lever for a ten-response fixed-ratio schedule of reinforcement (FR 10). They were then randomly assigned to three groups to receive punishment (.25 ma. for 0.5 sec.) of the response prior to the reinforcement ($N - 1$), the reinforced response

(N), or the first response after the reinforcement (N + 1). The particular response in the behavior sequence that was punished influenced the mean suppression ratio during the ten sessions of punishment training ($H = 11.1$, $df = 2$, $p < .01$). Punishment of the first response in the ratio (N + 1) produced greater response suppression than punishment of other responses in the behavior sequence (see Fig. 5–16, left panel).

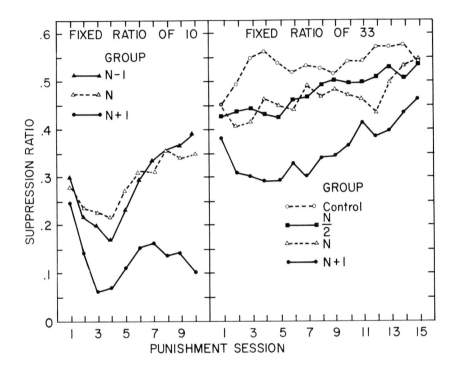

FIG. 5–16. Mean suppression ratio as a function of the response in a behavior sequence that is followed by punishment. (N is the reinforced response.) Fixed ratio of 10 in left panel; fixed ratio of 33 in right panel.

In a similar experiment, 48 rats were given the standard pretraining and reinforcement training conditions (VI 1), and then during the next 15 sessions they were reinforced on a 33-response fixed-ratio schedule (FR 33). The subjects were randomly partitioned into three experimental groups and an unpunished control group of 12 subjects each. One group received punishment of the same response that was reinforced (N), one group received punishment of the response immediately following the reinforced response (N + 1), and the remaining experimental group received punishment of the 16th response after a reinforcement, about half-way between successive reinforcements (N/2). Each punishment was

.10 ma. for 1.0 second. Subjects in all experimental groups, then, received exactly one reinforcement and one punishment for each 33 responses. The results are shown in Fig. 5–16, right panel.

The mean suppression ratio during the 15 sessions of punishment training was a function of the particular response in the fixed ratio that was selected for punishment ($H = 15.6$, $df = 3$, $p < .01$). Although all of the experimental groups showed some response suppression in comparison with the control group, punishment of the first response in the ratio (the response immediately after the reinforced response) resulted in substantially greater suppression than punishment of a response in the middle or end of the ratio.

Discriminability of the punished response. Why does punishment of the first response in a behavior sequence produce greater response suppression than punishment of some later response in that sequence? Two possible explanations are (1) that the distance from punishment to reinforcement is greater, and (2) that the punishment for a particular response is more certain. Regardless of which response in a behavior sequence is punished the subject is certain to receive a punishment before its next reinforcement. Nonetheless, the subject may be primarily influenced by the probability that its next response will be punished (i.e., the principle of momentary maximization). The group that received a punishment for the response immediately after a reinforcement should have had no difficulty in anticipating the punished response. The punished response is (1) the first response after the noise that accompanies the delivery of the food, (2) the first response after the consummatory response, and (3) the first response after a long pause after reinforcement. The $N - 1$, $N/2$, and Nth response are not so discriminable from unpunished responses. Of course, the subject may anticipate the occurrence of punishment by keeping track of the time since the last punishment or by keeping track of the number of responses since the last punishment, but such anticipation is greatly facilitated by external stimuli that are correlated with the punishment.

The addition of an experimenter-controlled stimulus prior to the response that is punished should increase the magnitude of response suppression. In one experiment, subjects were given the standard pretraining and reinforcement training conditions (VI 1), and then during the next 15 sessions they were reinforced on a FR-33 schedule. During these sessions the response prior to the reinforced response was punished. (Punishment was .10 ma. on Sessions 6–8; .16 ma. on Sessions 9–11; and .25 ma. on Sessions 12–20.) In the case of subjects in the Signalled Group, the $N - 2$ response produced a signal that lasted until the punished response occurred. Thus the subject, after receiving a reinforcement, could perform 31 responses in the absence of a signal, punishment, or reinforcement. The next three responses, however, produced signal, punishment, and reinforcement, in that order. The mean suppression ratio of the Signalled Group on Sessions 12 through 20 was significantly lower than that of an equivalent group without the signal ($U = 8$, $p < .01$) (see Fig. 5–17).

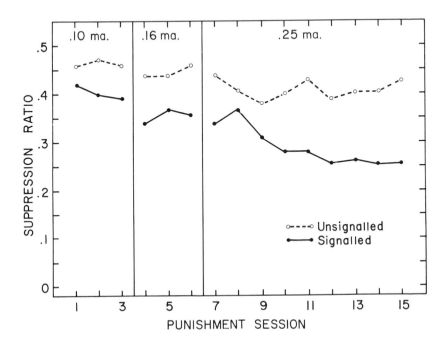

FIG. 5–17.   Mean suppression ratio as a result of punishment of the N-1 response. Under signalled conditions the N-2 response produced a warning signal.

In a free-responding situation, punishment may suppress response rate for two different reasons. In the first place, the subject may reduce its response rate in anticipation of punishment; secondly, the subject may reduce its response rate in reaction to punishment. After the signal the subject was required to make only two additional responses to receive a reinforcement, and with a relatively mild punishment located only a short distance from a reinforcement there was little reaction to the punishment (i.e., only a brief pause following the punishment). Nonetheless, subjects with a signal providing clear anticipation of the punishment were extremely reluctant to press the lever during the signal. The major function of the introduction of the response-produced signal was to reduce the response latency during the signal and thus to reduce the overall response rate.

The anticipation of punishment.   Subjects may show an anticipation of punishment when an instrumental response in a behavior sequence is followed by a noxious event. Such anticipation may be noted by a reduction in response rate shortly before the punishment is due to occur. This is particularly marked whenever the punished response is clearly discriminable from other responses (e.g., the first response in a sequence, or a response preceded by a signal). Of course, to the extent that a group has considerable bound fear, it should have less free-floating anxiety. In one experiment, subjects were trained to press a lever in a FR-10 schedule of food reinforcement in a discrete-trials (retractable-lever) situation with an intertrial interval of 2 minutes. To supplement the inspection of cumulative records, and to permit quantitative analysis of the results, the total time spent on various responses of the fixed ratio was recorded on each session. Figure 5–18 shows the mean time in seconds (on a log scale)

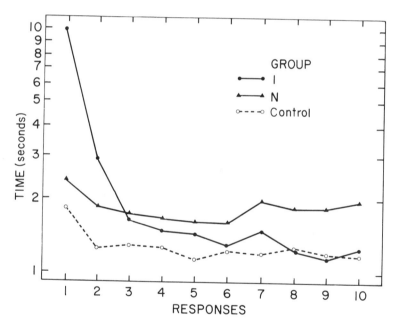

FIG. 5–18.   Mean time in seconds (on a log scale) spent following each of ten responses in a discrete-trial situation as a result of punishment of various responses of a behavior sequence.

spent on each of the responses of the ratio. Punishment of the Nth (10th) response resulted in generally slow responding (relative to the rate of unpunished control subjects). Punishment of the first response in the behavior sequence, however, resulted in an extremely long latency to the first response, but then a rapid acceleration to a rate as fast as that of unpunished control subjects. The fact that the latency to the second response was greater if the first response was punished than if the Nth response was punished may reflect a reaction to the punishment.

The reaction to punishment. Subjects sometimes show a reaction to punishment when an instrumental response in a behavior sequence is

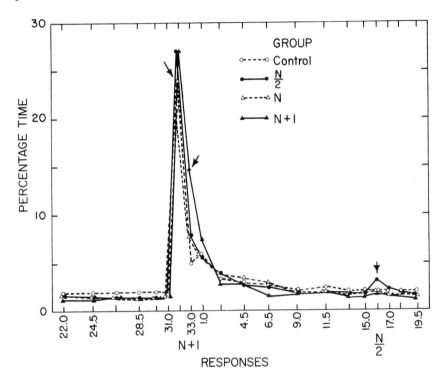

FIG. 5–19.   Percentage of time spent following each of 33 responses in a free-responding situation as a result of punishment of various responses of a behavior sequence. (Arrows indicate responses that were followed by punishment.)

followed by a noxious event. This may be noted by a pause after the punishment. The basic result was that the shorter the distance from punishment to reinforcement, the shorter the pause after the punishment, relative to that of an unpunished control group on the equivalent response (see Fig. 5–19). For example, subjects trained to press a lever on a FR-33 schedule of reinforcement showed a pause after reinforcement, and a rapid acceleration of rate to an asymptotic level. Punishment of the $N + 1$ response (the one of greatest distance from the reinforcement) produced the greatest relative increase in latency to the next response; punishment of the $N/2$ response (the one of intermediate distance from the reinforcement) produced a small relative increase in latency to the next response; punishment of the Nth response (the one with least distance from the reinforcement) produced no detectable relative increase in latency. Further studies are necessary to determine if the relevant dimension of distance is relative or absolute, and whether it is based on time to reinforcement or the number of responses to reinforcement. The general result, however, is consistent with the principle of counterconditioning (e.g., Williams & Barry, 1966).

Punishment of a consummatory response. The behavior sequences that have been considered in this section have been composed of a series of instrumental elements (lever responses). Another behavior sequence would involve alternation between instrumental and consummatory elements. For example, under conditions of continuous reinforcement a rat will press the lever and then eat the food. A punishment may immediately follow pressing the lever or eating the food. If the results from purely instrumental sequences of behavior may be generalized to sequences of behavior that involve a consummatory response, more suppression should be produced by punishment of the instrumental response than by punishment of the consummatory response.

Eighteen rats were trained to press a lever in a box that was modified from the standard box in two ways: (1) the food cup was located on the opposite wall from the lever to separate the two elements of the behavior sequence, and (2) a photocell and source of light was added to the sides of the food cup to provide a definition of the consummatory response. The first lever response, and every other lever response that was preceded by the subject's breaking the beam of light in the food cup, resulted in a pellet of food. After pretraining, subjects were given ten 10-minute sessions and then the conditions of punishment were introduced. Subjects were randomly assigned to one of two punishment training groups. The conditions of positive reinforcement remained in effect and, in addition, there was a punishment of .16 ma. for 0.5 second. For one group the punishment followed each instrumental response that delivered food to the cup, for the other group punishment occurred when a subject broke the beam of light in the food cup that contained a pellet of food. Records were kept of (1) the number of behavior sequences, (2) the number of instrumental and consummatory responses, and (3) the total time between instrumental and consummatory responses and the total time between consummatory and instrumental responses.

Punishment of the instrumental response produced greater response suppression than punishment of the consummatory response ($U = 17$, $p = .05$) (see Fig. 5–20). The most obvious effect of the punishment treatment, however, was that subjects showed great hesitation in making that

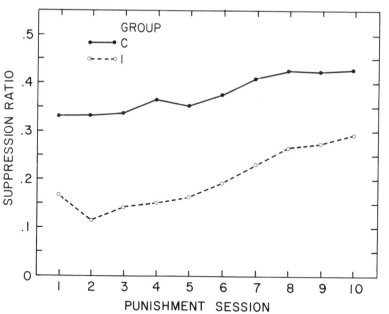

FIG. 5–20.   Mean suppression ratio as a result of punishment of an instrumental response (I) or punishment of a consummatory response (C).

part of the behavior sequence that led to punishment. Punishment of the consummatory response resulted in an increase in the percentage of the 10-minute session spent between instrumental and consummatory responses; punishment of the instrumental response resulted in an increase in the percentage of the session spent between consummatory and instrumental responses (see Fig. 5–21). The difference between the mean percentage I–C time for the two groups during the ten sessions of punishment was reliable ($U = 4$, $p < .002$).

Further research with punishment in this situation should include the investigation of punishment of intentional or anticipatory response (i.e., approach to the lever or to the food cup), and punishment delayed following the instrumental or consummatory response. Although punishment of the "consummatory" response in this experiment may have been punishment for approach to the food cup, subjects typically had the pellet of food in the mouth at the time of punishment. A short delay of punishment after the subject breaks the beam of light in the food cup, however, might be more likely to punish the act of eating. At the present time, however, these studies have produced no evidence to suggest that the principles involving punishment of various responses of a behavior sequence need to be modified when one of the responses is consummatory.

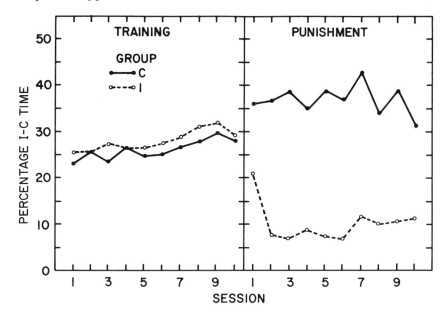

FIG. 5–21. Mean percentage of a ten-minute session spent between performance of an instrumental response and a consummatory response as a result of punishment of an instrumental response (I) or punishment of a consummatory response (C).

Summary

Punishment of a positive instrumental response typically produces suppression of that response, and the magnitude of suppression is a function of (1) characteristics of the noxious stimulus, and (2) the relationship between the response and the noxious stimulus. The experimental evidence described in this chapter was based upon the response rate of rats that were trained to press a lever for food reward and then punished for the performance of that response. A suppression ratio was used as the measure of the effectiveness of punishment. This suppression ratio was demonstrated to be more sensitive to differences among various punishment treatments than several other reasonable measures, and no alternative measure was found to be more sensitive to the treatment differences.

Results of the experiments described in this chapter support the following statements:

1. Severity of the noxious stimulus. The magnitude of response suppression is a direct function of the severity of the punishment, both its intensity and duration.

2. Prior exposure to the noxious stimulus. In the presence of a noxious stimulus of a particular severity a subject has a tendency to per-

sist in the performance it has acquired in the context of previous exposure to noxious stimuli. Therefore, prior exposure to a noxious
stimulus may either increase or decrease the effectiveness of subsequent
punishment.

3. Contingency between response and noxious stimulus. At any given
severity of a noxious stimulus, the magnitude of response suppression is
greater if the noxious stimulus occurs immediately following a response
than if it occurs independently of the response.

4. Contiguity between response and noxious stimulus. The magnitude of response suppression decreases as the temporal interval between
response and punishment increases, even when the dependence of punishment upon response is constant.

5. Discriminative stimulus prior to the noxious stimulus. A warning
signal preceding a punishment reduces the magnitude of suppression in
the absence of the warning signal.

6. Punishment of various responses in a behavior sequence. Punishment of the first response in a behavior sequence produces greater response suppression than punishment of later responses in the behavior
sequence. The decrease in response rate prior to the punished response
(anticipation of punishment) is a function of the discriminability of the
punished response; the decrease in response rate following a punished
response (reaction to punishment) is a function of the number of responses between the punished response and the reinforced response.

These empirical studies may contribute to a theoretical formulation
of the basis for the response suppression produced by punishment. Such
a theory should be closely related to a theory of instrumental training
with reward since the major determinants of the effectiveness of punishment are identical to the major determinants of the effectiveness of positive reinforcement.

REFERENCES

Azrin, N. H. Some effects of two intermittent schedules of immediate and non-
    immediate punishment. *Journal of Psychology,* 1956, **42,** 3–21.
Azrin, N. H. Effects of punishment intensity during variable–interval reinforce-
    ment. *Journal of the Experimental Analysis of Behavior,* 1960, **3,** 123–142.
Azrin, N. H., & Holz, W. C. Punishment. In W. K. Honig (Ed.), *Operant
    behavior: Areas of research and application.* New York: Appleton-Century-
    Crofts, 1966. Pp. 380–447.
Banks, R. K. Persistence to continuous punishment following intermittent pun-
    ishment training. *Journal of Experimental Psychology,* 1966, **71,** 373–377.
Beauchamp, R. D. A comparison of the degree of suppression following either
    a discriminative punishment treatment or a conditioned emotional re-
    sponse treatment. Unpublished MA thesis, Brown University, 1966.
Boe, E. E. Extinction as a function of intensity of punishment, amount of

training, and reinforcement of a competing response. *Canadian Journal of Psychology*, 1964, **18**, 328–342.

BOE, E. E., & CHURCH, R. M. Permanent effects of punishment during extinction. *Journal of Comparative and Physiological Psychology*, 1967, **63**, 486–492.

CAMP, D. S., RAYMOND, G. A., & CHURCH, R. M. Temporal relationship between response and punishment. *Journal of Experimental Psychology*, 1967, **74**, 114–123.

CHURCH, R. M. The varied effects of punishment on behavior. *Psychological Review*, 1963, **70**, 369–402.

CHURCH, R. M. Systematic effect of random error in the yoked control design. *Psychological Bulletin*, 1964, **62**, 122–131.

CHURCH, R. M., RAYMOND, G. A., & BEAUCHAMP, R. D. Response suppression as a function of intensity and duration of a punishment. *Journal of Comparative and Physiological Psychology*, 1967, **63**, 39–44.

DINSMOOR, J. A. A discrimination based on punishment. *Quarterly Journal of Experimental Psychology*, 1952, **4**, 27–45.

ESTES, W. K. An experimental study of punishment. *Psychological Monographs*, 1944, **57** (3, Whole No. 263).

ESTES, W. K., & SKINNER, B. F. Some quantitative properties of anxiety. *Journal of Experimental Psychology*, 1941, **29**, 390–400.

FEIRSTEIN, A. R. & MILLER, N. E. Learning to resist pain and fear: Effects of electric shock before versus after reaching goal. *Journal of Comparative and Physiological Psychology*, 1963, **56**, 797–800.

HAYS, W. L. *Statistics for psychologists*. New York: Holt, Rinehart, & Winston, 1963.

HUNT, H. F., & BRADY, J. V. Some effects of punishment and intercurrent "anxiety" on a simple operant. *Journal of Comparative and Pysiological Psychology*, 1955, **48**, 305–310.

KAMIN, L. J. The delay-of-punishment gradient. *Journal of Comparative and Physiological Psychology*, 1959, **52**, 434–437.

KARSH, E. B. Effects of number of rewarded trials and intensity of punishment on running speed. *Journal of Comparative and Physiological Psychology*, 1962, **55**, 44–51.

KARSH, E. B. Changes in intensity of punishment: Effect on running behavior of rats. *Science*, 1963, **140**, 1084–1085.

KARSH, E. B. Resistance to punishment resulting from training with delayed, partial, and increasing shock. *Proceedings of the 74th Annual Convention of the American Psychological Association*, 1966, 51–52.

LOCKARD, J. S. Choice of a warning signal or no warning signal in an unavoidable shock situation. *Journal of Comparative and Physiological Psychology*, 1963, **56**, 526–530.

MELVIN, K. B., & MARTIN, R. C. Facilitative effects of two modes of punishment on resistance to extinction. *Journal of Comparative and Physiological Psychology*, 1966, **62**, 491–494.

MILLER, N. E. Learning resistance to pain and fear: Effects of overlearning, exposure, and rewarded exposure in context. *Journal of Experimental Psychology*, 1960, **60**, 137–145.

PEARL, J., WALTERS, G. C., & ANDERSON, D. C. Suppressing effects of aversive stimulation on subsequently punished behaviour. *Canadian Journal of Psychology,* 1964, **18**, 343–355.

RAYMOND, G. A. Accentuation and attenuation of punishment by prior exposure to aversive stimulation. Unpublished doctoral dissertation, Brown University, 1968.

RENNER, K. E. Temporal integration: Relative value of rewards and punishments as a function of their temporal distance from the response. *Journal of Experimental Psychology,* 1966, **71**, 902–907. (a)

RENNER, K. E. Temporal integration: The relative utility of immediate versus delayed reward and punishment. *Journal of Experimental Psychology,* 1966, **72**, 901–903. (b)

RESCORLA, R. A. Pavlovian conditioning and its proper control procedures. *Psychological Review,* 1967, **74**, 71–80.

SELIGMAN, M. E. P., & CAMPBELL, B. A. Effect of intensity and duration of punishment on extinction of an avoidance response. *Journal of Comparative and Physiological Psychology,* 1965, **59**, 295–297.

SHIMP, C. P. Probabilistically reinforced choice behavior in pigeons. *Journal of the Experimental Analysis of Behavior,* 1966, **9**, 443–455.

SKINNER, B. F. *The behavior of organisms.* New York: Appleton-Century, 1938.

STORMS, L. H., BOROCZI, G., & BROEN, W. E., JR. Effects of punishment as a function of strain of rat and duration of shock. *Journal of Comparative and Physiological Psychology,* 1963, **56**, 1022–1026.

WILLIAMS, D. R., & BARRY, H., III. Counter conditioning in an operant conflict situation. *Journal of Comparative and Physiological Psychology,* 1966, **61**, 154–156.

6

Frustrative Nonreward: A Variety of Punishment[1]

Allan R. Wagner
YALE UNIVERSITY

In common language one may refer to the withholding of usual rewards, as well as the application of a noxious stimulus as "punishment." Although such designation may not involve a precise criterion of usage, there is no doubt that either event may be usefully employed to produce a subsequent decrement in behaviors upon which it is made contingent.

Since very different operations are involved in the withholding of reward and, for example, the application of a noxious electric shock, it is not surprising that systematic experimental analyses should reveal significant differences in the behavioral effects of the two events (e.g., Leitenberg, 1966). Yet it is as important to an adequate treatment of punishment to recognize also those similarities which exist. In fact, inspection of the experimental literature during the last 20 years indicates an increasing tendency for theorists to emphasize the aversive character of nonreward and the similarity between the behavioral products of nonreward and other events acknowledged to be "punishing."

The purpose of the present paper is to evaluate certain theoretical and empirical relationships between nonreward and punishment within the context of instrumental reward learning. While it could be argued that the very pervasiveness with which nonreward has been characterized as aversive, in quite diverse behavioral situations, most forcefully attests to the utility of this conception, no attempt will be made to survey the massive literature related to this question which has now accumulated. Excellent summaries of various portions of that literature may be found in Amsel (1958, 1962), Mowrer (1960), Leitenberg (1965), Terrace (1966), Spence (1960), and elsewhere. Rather, the discussion will center around a specific theory of *frustrative nonreward* and, in this already restricted context, around a limited number of studies that might be viewed as

[1] Preparation of the present paper and portions of the research reported were supported in part by grants from the National Science Foundation.

especially relevant to the question of whether frustrative nonreward is similar to punishment.

Theory of Frustrative Nonreward

A major class of interpretations of the effects of reward and punishment is based upon certain presumably active properties of anticipatorily occurring, conditioned components of the goal response (e.g., Spence, 1956; Miller, 1959; Mowrer, 1947). Thus instrumental response chains terminating in reward are assumed to be motivated and/or mediated by fractional anticipatory reward responses ($r_r - s_r$, hope), while the stimuli in an S–R sequence ending with noxious stimulation are presumed to elicit fractional components ($r_p - s_p$, fear) of the primary emotional response to punishment.

The decremental effects of response-contingent noxious stimulation are then attributed, at least in part, either to unlearned or previously learned responses elicited by fear, which are incompatible with the punished response (Estes, 1944; Miller, 1959), or to the acquisition of new incompatible (avoidance) responses which are reinforced, when they occur, by a reduction in fear-associated cues (e.g., Mowrer, 1947).

Working within such a general framework, Amsel (e.g., 1951, 1958) was the first to emphasize that some of the effects associated with the nonreward of a previously rewarded instrumental response might be similarly understood in terms of a fractional goal-response mechanism. Thus, it has been assumed that following some number of rewards of an instrumental behavior, necessary to build up anticipatory reward responses to cues in the S–R chain, nonreward will elicit a primary, aversive emotional reaction. This emotional response, termed *frustration,* is assumed to be directly related in intensity to the magnitude of anticipatory reward. It has further been assumed that components of the frustration reaction become conditioned to antedating stimuli so that an anticipatory form will be elicited by cues in a stimulus–response chain that regularly precedes frustrative nonreward. If anticipatory frustration occurs as a conditioned aversive reaction to cues which have preceded frustrative nonreward, then part of the decrement in an instrumental behavior produced by the withholding of reward might be attributed (1) to the "suppressing" effects of unlearned, or previously learned, incompatible behavior mediated by anticipatory frustration, or (2) to the acquisition of avoidance responses which are reinforced by a reduction in frustration-associated cues.

It is clear that this conceptualization treats frustrative nonreward as though it were but an identifiable variety of aversive stimulation. The distinction between fear and anticipatory frustration could be viewed as simply labeling the source of aversiveness, since the two are presumed to be similarly capable of mediating competing responses and motivating avoidance behavior. To the extent that such is the case, the term "punishment" would appear to be as appropriately used to refer to response-contingent frustrative nonreward, as to the response-contingent application of other aversive stimulation.

Is Nonreward Aversive?

The central assumption of the frustration theory which has been outlined is that, under certain conditions, nonreward (as well as the exposure to cues previously associated with nonreward) may be an aversive event. While the usefulness of frustration theory, as that of any set of theoretical propositions, must be judged according to the total set of deductions which it allows (see e.g., Amsel, 1958, 1962; Amsel & Ward, 1965), the reasonably direct demonstrability of such presumed aversive characteristics can be viewed as particularly crucial to the theory.

An "aversive event" is basically one which organisms will behave so as to terminate or prevent. If the escape from, or avoidance of, an event is reinforcing, the event in question may be classified as "aversive" (see e.g., Keller & Schoenfeld, 1950; Solomon, 1964).

Granting this usage of the term, nonreward might be said to be aversive on the basis of any demonstration that organisms will acquire responses which are followed by a nonreward-to-reward transition. That is, whenever it is arranged, for example, that a food-deprived animal is placed in an experimental environment with the absence of food, but food is delivered consequent to some response, such as bar pressing, the response-contingent event is a change from the condition of nonreward to the condition of reward. That such a change is found to be reinforcing is generally ascribed to the initiation of reward; but it could as well be attributed to the cessation of, or escape from, nonreward. The basic fact is that a nonreward–reward *transition* is reinforcing. The two descriptions of the transition, either in terms of cessation of nonreward or initiation of reward, are completely synonymous, and any choice between the two at this level would appear to be based only on semantic preferences.

The issue is not considerably different if one applies an avoidance criterion of "aversive event." Suppose an animal is in the presence of a rewarding stimulus or is periodically presented with such a stimulus, but that the reward occasions are withdrawn unless the subject makes some designated response. If the designated response is acquired under such a contingency, we might attribute the reinforcement to the "avoidance of nonreward," but it could synonymously be ascribed to the "prolonging of reward." Over some period, more reward and less nonreward occurs if the organism engages in the specified behavior than if it does not.

One reason for pointing out this obvious covariance of escape or avoidance of nonreward and receipt or prolonging of reward is that a reasonably large number of studies (e.g., Morse & Herrnstein, 1956; Ferster, 1958; Thomas, 1965; Kaufman & Baron, 1966) have now been conducted in which the investigators have described the reinforcing transitions in terms of the escape or avoidance of nonreward, but in which the alternative description in terms of the initiation or prolonging of reward would appear to be as appropriate. For example, Ferster (1958, Exp. IV) trained chimpanzees in a two-lever situation. Responses on one lever were alternately scheduled to be followed by food (on a variable-interval 3-min. schedule) for 45 seconds, and then nonrewarded for 3 minutes. A response on the second lever during the 45-second reward period was scheduled, however, such that it produced a 1-, 2-, 5-, or 10-minute delay of the next transition from reward to a nonreward period. Of significance is the fact that the latter contingencies maintained responding on the second lever. Ferster described the effective contingency in terms of an avoidance of time-out from reward, but it could have been as well described as a prolonging of the reward condition. To mention another example, Kaufman and Baron (1966) trained hungry rats to drink milk from a dipper which was periodically presented (every 15 or 60 sec.) without a response requirement. The animals were then subjected to irregularly presented periods of nonoperation of the dipper, each preceded by 10 seconds by an auditory stimulus and the insertion of a lever into the chamber. If five lever presses were made in the first 10 seconds of the auditory stimulus, the stimulus terminated and the transition from dipper operation to nonoperation did not occur. If five presses were not made before such transition occurred, the return transition, back-to-dipper operation, was made contingent on completing the five presses. As a result of such contingencies, the subjects gradually acquired the lever-press response, although the five presses were relatively infrequently completed in the first 10 seconds of the auditory stimulus. While Kaufman and Baron described the effective contingency in terms of escape and avoidance of nonreward, they also concurred with the present position, that there is little or no reason to choose such language in preference to a description in terms of the initiation and prolonging of reward.

It is instructive to appreciate that nonreward can, in such manner, be said to satisfy the criteria of an aversive event. It is also worth recognizing that theories of motivation have frequently stressed the aversiveness of conditions associated with the absence of reward, as in the case of Miller's (1959) drive–stimulus reduction theory. Still, from the vantage point of a systematic treatment otherwise stressing the positive aspects of reward, as long as experimental outcomes are interpretable in conventional terms, there is little if anything to be gained by acknowledging that, in the sense of the preceding discussion, nonreward, can be termed aversive. Leitenberg (1965), for example, after reviewing the available operant conditioning studies similar to those of Ferster and Kaufman and Baron on the avoidance of time-out from reward, suggests that, "the concept of aversiveness seems unnecessary. Rather it seems adequate and more parsimonious to explain these findings by just saying: the pattern of behavior followed by most positive reinforcement is most strengthened" (p. 431).

In view of the above discussion it is important to recognize those specific expectations of frustration theory concerning the aversiveness of nonreward that would not be readily interpretable in terms of conventional reward treatments. It should be noted that frustrative nonreward was introduced as referring to a particular nonreward occasion, namely, the nonreward of a previously rewarded instrumental response, and that such nonreward was assumed to have active aversive properties to the degree that $r_r - s_r$ has been conditioned to the cues in the instrumental response chain. Thus the important implication of frustration theory in the present context is that nonreward is frustrating and aversive *in proportion to the degree of anticipation of reward.*

Reconsidering the escape criterion of aversiveness as previously applied to nonreward, the unique expectation of frustration theory is that a nonreward–reward transition would be *more* reinforcing given a constant size reward, the greater the frustration occasioned by the nonreward, i.e., the greater the anticipation of reward at the time of nonreward. While it could be assumed that any such increased reinforcement would be due, not to the greater aversiveness of nonreward, but to the greater "attraction" of rewards which follow frustrative-nonreward, such is not at least a common assumption of reward theory.

Should the reinforcement occasioned by a nonreward–reward transition depend on the prior history of reward and the degree that reward was anticipated, there would be more than semantic justification for designating the nonreward involved as aversive. Unfortunately only a modest number of studies have attempted to evaluate the aversiveness of frustrative-nonreward in such a way that the presumably special aversiveness associated with the anticipation of reward might be revealed.

One set of investigations which, for present purposes, is lacking in certain aspects of design is, however, particularly informative as to the conditions under which nonreward may have active properties as prescribed by frustration theory.

Figure 6–1 presents a schematic diagram of an apparatus similar to that first employed by Amsel and Roussel (1952) to evaluate the effects of frustrative nonreward. It consists essentially of two runways in succession, the goal box of the first serving as start box for the second. Wagner (1959) trained one group of rats in such an apparatus to run to Goal Box 1, where they received .1-gm. food reward, and then, following the opening of a guillotine door, to run to Goal Box 2, where they received an additional .2-gm. reward. A second group was similarly trained to run both alleys in succession, receiving .2-gm. reward in Goal Box 2, but was

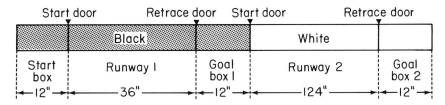

FIG. 6–1.   Floor plan of the double runway apparatus, employed by Wagner (1959), and similar to that used by Amsel and Roussel (1952), McHose (1963) and others.

From: A. R. Wagner, "The Role of Reinforcement and Nonreinforcement in an 'Apparent Frustration Effect,'" *Journal of Experimental Psychology*, **57**, 1959, Fig. 1, p. 132. Copyright 1959 by the American Psychological Association and used by permission.

never rewarded in Goal Box 1. The latter animals were simply retained in Goal Box 1 for a 15-second period, equivalent to the detention time of the rewarded subjects. Following 76 training trials, the group usually fed in Goal Box 1 was nonrewarded for the first time in that goal box, and over subsequent trials received nonrewarded test trials interspersed among usual rewarded trials. The major comparison of interest was the running speed in Runway 2 of the two groups on trials when they were similarly nonrewarded in Goal Box 1. For one group such nonreward should have been frustrating since they had previously been rewarded in Goal Box 1, and should have built up $r_r - s_r$ to the cues encountered; for the other group nonreward should not have been frustrating since they had never experienced reward in Goal Box 1.

Figure 6–2 presents the Runway 2 running speeds during training and test for the two groups described. Of particular interest is the fact that the speeds following nonreward in Goal Box 1 were considerably faster for the group previously rewarded in Goal Box 1 than for the consistently nonrewarded group. Traversing Runway 2 on such trials involved a similar transition in the two groups between nonreward and reward (or, while executing the response, between nonreward and cues increasingly similar to those associated with reward in Goal Box 2). That the presumably frustrated group ran faster is consistent with the view that nonreward was in that group more aversive and better motivating of escape behavior from Goal Box 1.

If the aversiveness of nonreward is dependent upon the magnitude of anticipatory reward, then it should also be possible to show that while a group previously rewarded in Goal Box 1 would escape faster on initial nonrewarded test trials than a never-rewarded group, this difference should eventually disappear if the groups are given sufficient subsequent experience with only nonreward in Goal Box 1. As anticipatory reward extinguishes with continued nonreward experience, the aversiveness of the nonreward should also be reduced. McHose (1963) has recently confirmed this expectation.

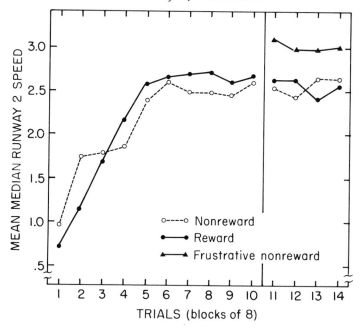

FIG. 6–2. Runway 2 running speeds in a double runway over blocks of eight total trials. The open circle curve refers to a group never rewarded in Goal Box 1 throughout training. The filled circle curves described the speeds of a group always rewarded in Goal Box 1 until the point marked by the vertical line, after which half of the trials were (frustratively) nonrewarded.

From: A. R. Wagner, "The Role of Reinforcement and Nonreinforcement in an 'Apparent Frustration Effect,'" *Journal of Experimental Psychology*, **57**, 1959, Fig. 2, p. 133. Copyright 1959 by the American Psychological Association and used by permission.

It is of further interest that only a very small number of prior rewards may be required to produce evidence of frustration. McCain and McVean (1967) trained rats in a double runway for 44 trials with no reward in Goal Box 1. Half of the animals then continued consistently to receive nonreward while the remaining subjects were shifted to 50% reward in Goal Box 1. The latter subjects on the first block of postshift trials, involving four rewarded and four nonrewarded exposures to Goal Box 1, ran faster in Runway 2 following nonreward than they did prior to shift or than did the consistently nonrewarded animals on the same trials.

Amsel and his associates have reported a sizable number of studies (e.g., Amsel, 1958; Amsel & Ward, 1965) employing such a double-runway apparatus, which make it evident that running speed from a nonrewarded Goal Box 1 varies in a manner which is understandable, in terms of the dependence of frustration upon the anticipation of reward; when conditions obtain which are presumably associated with more vigorous $r_r - s_r$, nonreward is more activating or aversive. In a recent investigation Peckham and Amsel (1967) trained rats concurrently in two double runways having similar grey terminal alleys and goal boxes, but dissimilar initial alleys and goal boxes. The initial portion of one was painted black, the other white. Each subject was rewarded with two .037-gm. food pellets in either terminal goal box, but consistently received different rewards in the two initial goal boxes. Thus some subjects received two pellets on trials in the white initial alley and eight pellets on trials in the black initial alley, while others had the reverse magnitudes in the two alleys. Following 128 trials in each runway, test trials were introduced in which nonreward occurred in both initial goal boxes. In either runway, such trials involved the subjects running from a nonrewarded Goal Box 1 to a rewarded Goal Box 2. The only difference was in the history of reward which the subject had experienced in the nonrewarded goal box: in one, it had previously received eight pellets, in the other two pellets. The findings were that the subjects ran faster following nonreward in the eight-pellet goal box, than they did following nonreward in the two-pellet goal box. The authors point out that, this difference "can be understood only associatively; the N_8 trials occur in the presence of a stimulus signaling eight pellets and the N_2 trials occur when the other stimulus signals two pellets. Presumably two discriminable stimuli each associated with a different magnitude of food as UCS can control within the same organism two different strengths of r_r, each in turn producing its own appropriate value of frustration when reward is withheld" (p. 192).

The results of the above studies are informative in demonstrating variation in the active properties of nonreward as a result of the prior reward history. Their discussion should have served to make clear the general conditions under which the assumptions of frustration theory concerning the aversiveness of nonreward might be especially useful. Since the measured response in these studies involved locomotion *away from* the nonreward situation, it is probably not entirely inappropriate to discuss the findings, as has been done, in terms of escape from nonreward. The situation does not, however, allow an evaluation of the *reinforcing* effects of such escape, in the sense of its increasing the likelihood of some new contingent response. A previously well-learned locomotor behavior was simply observed to have been increased in vigor following the presumably frustrating conditions. Consequently, these studies have never been interpreted as necessarily demonstrating more than a nonspecific energizing effect of frustrative nonreward (e.g., Amsel & Roussel, 1952; Wagner, 1959; McHose, 1963; Peckham & Amsel, 1967). Whether or not the escape feature plays any important role in this situation is simply not known.

An unpublished study conducted in our laboratory by Mary Church goes somewhat further in implicating an aversive factor associated with frustrative nonreward. In essence, rats were trained in an apparatus similar to a double runway, but were provided for the first time during testing with an alternative to entering and remaining in a nonrewarded initial goal box while en route to a terminal rewarded goal box.

The question was whether subjects would be more likely to adopt the alternative behavior if they had previously been rewarded in the initial goal box than if they had never been rewarded there.

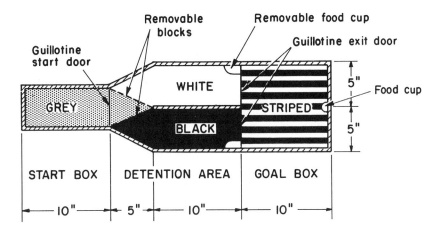

FIG. 6–3.   Floor plan of apparatus employed by Church.

Figure 6–3 presents a schematic diagram of the experimental environment, consisting of a start box, detention area, and terminal goal box. Training trials were run by placing an animal in the start box, raising the door between the start and detention areas, and then exactly 30 seconds later, raising the final guillotine door, allowing the subject to enter the striped goal box, where it received five .045-gm. food pellets. During such trials each subject had the entrance to one of the two compartments in the detention area blocked, half consistently having access to only the black and half to only the white compartment. The important treatment difference was that, during the 30-second detention interval, half of the subjects in each of the above groups were rewarded with four .125-gm. pellets of wet mash, while the remaining subjects were never fed in the detention chamber. There were in all, 12 rats in each treatment group.

Following 70 such training trials distributed over 8 days, testing was begun during which the food cups were removed from the detention area, and all animals were similarly nonrewarded. In addition at the time of testing, the blocks at the entrance to the two compartments of the detention area were removed, allowing the subjects free movement into either side. As in training, 30 seconds after opening the start door, the goal box door was raised and all subjects received reward in the terminal goal box. Access to the terminal goal box was now possible, however, either from that compartment of the detention area with which the subject had been trained or from the novel compartment. Twenty-five test trials, preceded by a single regular training trial, were given in one session, with an average intertrial interval of 12 minutes.

The interesting possibility suggested by frustration theory was that the subjects previously rewarded in one detention chamber would eventually exhibit an aversion to that chamber when presumably frustrated during testing. The behavior of the previously nonrewarded animals should, in comparison, reflect the effects of other available factors influencing approaching and remaining in the alternate chamber, besides escape and avoidance of frustrative nonreward, such as exposure to novel stimuli. Any observation of a lesser tendency on the part of the previously rewarded subjects to expose themselves to the training detention compartment would be the more interesting in view of the fact that the cues of that compartment would generally be emphasized to elicit anticipation of reward and to be secondarily reinforcing, without acknowledging that continued exposure to such cues in the absence of reward may also be frustrating and aversive.

Of primary interest was the detention compartment initially entered, over successive blocks of test trials. On this measure the previously non-rewarded group exhibited stable performance throughout the test session. For example, eight of the twelve subjects in this group entered initially the same compartment on four or five of the trials in every block of five tests. For four of these subjects, however, the detention compartment first entered was the training side, while for the other four it was the novel side. This choice behavior, which was not correlated overall with which of the two compartments the subjects had been trained, suggests the operation of individual brightness or position preferences. In comparison, all 12 of the previously rewarded subjects began testing with a predominant choice of the training compartment. The number of such subjects systematically diminished over testing, however, until by the last block of five test trials only three of the previously rewarded subjects were still predominantly first entering the training compartment. The graph to the left in Fig. 6–4 summarizes these findings by presenting the number of subjects in each group that made three or more of their initial entrances into the training detention compartment in successive blocks of five test trials.

The frequencies depicted clearly indicate that on this measure there was no reliable evidence of a greater avoidance of the training compart-

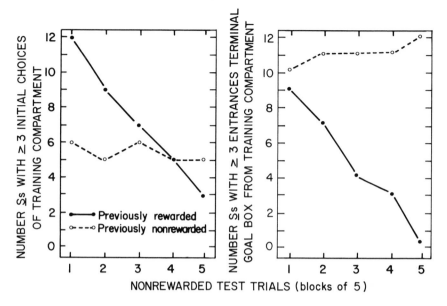

FIG. 6–4.   Preferences exhibited during nonrewarded test trials by two groups of subjects, either previously rewarded or previously nonrewarded in one detention compartment of the apparatus depicted in Fig. 6–3.

ment by the previously rewarded group, although the slight trend in this direction on the last block of test trials suggests that further testing might have been of interest.

In contrast to the initial choice measure, the behavior of the two groups during the 30-second detention interval suggested that continued exposure to the training compartment in the absence of reward was more aversive for the previously rewarded subjects. All subjects invariably exposed themselves to both compartments during the detention interval and typically made numerous entrances into each. Yet, it was observed that most of the previously nonrewarded subjects consistently spent the majority of the detention time in the training compartment, while most of the previously rewarded subjects, at least by the end of te ting, spent the majority of the detention time in the alternate chamber. This pattern was reflected in a second performance index; namely, the detention compartment from which subjects entered the terminal goal box.

The graph to the right in Fig. 6–4, presents the number of subjects in each of the groups that entered the terminal goal box from their training detention compartment on three or more of the trials in successive blocks of five tests. This measure thus indicates the number of subjects in the two groups that in each block of trials were predominantly

in the training compartment at the termination of the 30-second detention interval. In this case it is apparent that, although both groups began
testing with a relatively similar high number of subjects being predominantly in the training compartment and that this number was maintained in the previously nonrewarded group, all 12 of the previously
rewarded subjects eventually came on the last block of trials to enter the
terminal goal box predominantly from the alternate compartment.

As in the case of the simple double-runway studies described above,
nonreward was found in the Church study to have differential effects depending upon the subjects' prior history of reward. The last two blocks
of testing were especially informative in that the two groups contained
an approximately equal number of subjects first entering the training
detention compartment, but grossly different numbers of subjects in that
compartment at the end of the detention interval. Although there was
thus no evidence of avoiding initial exposure to the training compartment in the previously rewarded group, the findings are consistent with
an assumed aversiveness of continued exposure to frustrative nonreward.

In this choice situation, it is still impossible, however, to evaluate
uniquely the degree of reinforcement resulting from escape or avoidance
of the training detention compartment. The degree to which the two
groups exposed themselves to the training compartment over test trials
should have complexly mirrored the changing net aversiveness (or attraction) of each of the compartments and the cumulative reinforcing effects
of the prior numbers of subject-determined entrances of the terminal
goal box from each of the detention chambers.

One study which did attempt rather directly to evaluate the added
reinforcing effects of the escape from frustrative nonreward was reported
by Adelman and Maatsch (1956). The design of the investigation was
similar to that of the studies previously described, in that rats were exposed to a nonrewarded goal box either with or without a prior history
of reward in that box. A major difference, however, was that all subjects
were required to learn a new specified response to escape from the nonrewarded goal box.

One group received 37 training trials in which they ran to an
enclosed goal box containing a .2-gm. food pellet. A second group was
simply placed an equal number of times in the goal box and retained
for a 20-second period, equal to the time the rewarded subjects were
allowed in the goal box. All subjects were then given a series of nonrewarded exposures to the goal box, at which time they were allowed to
jump out onto a 2-inch ledge surrounding the goal box, from which they
were returned after 20 seconds to an individual cage. Whatever the rewards and aversive stimulation otherwise occurring as a result of jumping
(e.g., from novel stimuli, handling, and return to the individual cage), it

should be expected that the contingent transition would be more rein-forcing for the previously rewarded subjects, since for them the non-rewarded goal box should have been more aversive and the escape from nonreward should have contributed more to reinforcement.

According to the data presented by Adelman and Maatsch, the frus-trated group came persistently to make the jump-out response, with a median latency of less than 5 seconds, whereas the previously non-rewarded group after a few trials consistently failed to jump within a 5-minute period. Although these data indicate a substantial difference in the behavioral effects of nonrewarded goal box confinement, depending on the subject's history of reward, they are unfortunately not much more informative concerning the reinforcing value of the escape contingency upon a new response than were the previously reported double-runway studies. The authors reported that on the very first nonrewarded jump–acquisition trial, seven out of the ten frustrated subjects but only two out of the ten previously nonrewarded subjects spontaneously jumped within a 5-minute criterion period. The subjects which did not spontaneously jump on this and later trials were "aided in climbing to the ledge by the [experimenter] inserting a hand into the box to serve as a step" (p. 312). Without knowledge of the transfer of training between such aided "climbs" and unaided "jumps," it is necessary to question whether the subsequent group differences in jumping are a product of more than the different initial likelihoods of making a spontaneous jump.

Jumping in the Adelman and Maatsch study, as running from Goal Box 1 in the double-runway studies, was an "escape" activity, but it is not clear that the differences in the measured behavior should be attrib-uted to differential reinforcing effects consequent to the escape from non-reward, or to nonspecific activating effects of frustrative nonreward that increase the initial likelihood of the escape response. If escape from frustrative nonreward has the special reinforcing effects suggested, it should be possible to reinforce any of a variety of behaviors. Studies are needed of the Adelman and Maatsch variety in which the to-be-acquired escape response has some definite and more nearly equal initial likeli-hoods in frustrated and nonfrustrated subjects.

One attempt has been made in our laboratory (Wagner, 1963) specifically to compare the acquisition of a new response when reinforced by the escape from frustration, as compared to simple nonreward. A major advantage of the design, for present purposes, as compared to the Adelman and Maatsch experiment, was that the to-be-reinforced re-sponse (of hurdle-crossing) was initially performed unaided by all sub-jects. The design also differed from those of the previously described investigations in that it was concerned with the aversiveness of isolatable cues previously paired with frustrative nonreward. Such cues, according to frustration theory, should come to elicit a fractional aversive response of anticipatory frustration, and hence their cessation should be reinforcing.

Two groups of rats received experience in a U-shaped runway and in a circular retaining cage, both located within the same experimental enclosure. All subjects received daily training in the runway on a random 50% reward schedule (for a total of 116 trials) and daily confinement periods in the retaining cage. All subjects were also similarly subjected to a flashing light and interrupted noise cue during this phase. The treatment of the two groups of subjects differed only in when the latter cue was presented. For one group the cue was presented after the runway response was initiated on nonreward trials, so as to just precede and overlap the subject's entrance into the presumably frustrating goal box. For the subjects in the other group, the cue was presented for the same duration while they were in the retaining cage in which they were never rewarded. Thus it was designed that both groups received the light and noise during a period of nonreward, but only in one of the two groups was the cue presumably associated with frustrative nonreward.

Immediately following such training each subject was tested to determine whether the cessation of the light and noise would serve to reinforce a new response. The test apparatus consisted of an aluminum box with two identical compartments. The compartments were separated by a door which could be partially dropped through the floor to provide a 1-inch hurdle. A subject was placed in one compartment with the door closed. Two minutes later the door was opened, presenting the light and noise and allowing the subject to cross to the opposite side. When the subject crossed the hurdle, the cues terminated and the door was raised. Ninety seconds later the door was again opened, presenting the light and noise and allowing the subject to return to its original side which again terminated the cues. Sixteen successive trials were run in this shuttle fashion with the response time recorded on each.

Figure 6–5 presents the mean hurdle-crossing speeds over the first and last half of the test series for the two groups. The frustration group responded faster than the nonfrustration group over both blocks of trials, but this difference was reliably more pronounced in the last half than in the first half of the test series. That the performance of the two groups so diverged over trials is to be expected if cue cessation was especially reinforcing for the frustration group. The divergence may be seen, however, to have been largely a result of a decrease in speeds of the nonfrustration group; the small increase observed in the speeds of the frustration group during testing did not approach statistical reliability.

This pattern of results presents no necessary problem for the frustration theory: reinforcement associated with escape from the light and noise served to maintain the hurdle-crossing response for frustrated

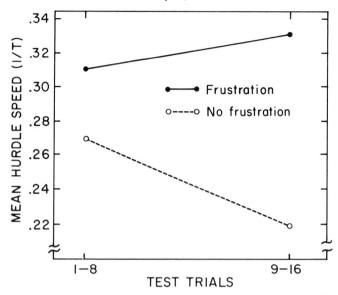

FIG. 6–5.   Mean hurdle-crossing speeds for two groups in which cessation of a noise and light were response contingent. For one group the cues had previously been paired with frustration.

From: A. R. Wagner, "Conditioned Frustration as a Learned Drive," *Journal of Experimental Psychology,* **66,** 1963, Fig. 3, p. 146. Copyright 1963 by the American Psychological Association and used by permission.

subjects in spite of the tendency observed in nonfrustrated subjects for speeds to decrease across trials. Still, the failure to find an absolute increase in the speeds of the frustration group indicates that the magnitude of this reinforcing effect cannot be considered large in comparison to other variables inherent in the test situation. More serious is the fact that failure to demonstrate such an absolute increase allows the possibility that the obtained results may yet be the product of different activating properties of the cue, rather than different reinforcement resulting from cue cessation.[2]

The data thus far reviewed would appear to support strongly the more general contention of the frustration theory that nonreward has special active properties as a result of a history of reward. Concerning the more specific assumption that this is an aversive property in the sense

[2] Since the completion of this paper, Daly (1967) reported a replication and extension of the Wagner (1963) findings in which the cessation of cues associated with frustrative nonreward, as compared to simple nonreward, appeared uniquely to reinforce a hurdle-jumping response. In her study, which employed a one-way hurdle-jumping procedure, the critical increase in hurdle speeds over trials was obtained in the frustrative-nonreward condition.

of its reduction or avoidance being reinforcing, it must be acknowledged that the studies directly addressed to the question are both meager in number and problematic in their interpretation. Nonetheless, the results of the above hurdle-crossing experiment are at least consistent with, and to that degree encouraging to, this more specific assumption as well.

The Similarity of Fear and Anticipatory Frustration

Frustration theory not only assumes that frustrative nonreinforcement is an aversive event, but also that the mechanism by which it produces a response decrement is, in part, like that of other response-contingent aversive events, i.e., via the action of anticipatory aversive emotional responses. A major theoretical advantage of such treatment would be apparent if there were reason to view fear and anticipatory frustration as similar in properties other than their presumably common aversiveness. To such extent, frustrative nonreward and other aversive stimulation might be expected to interact similarly with a variety of experimental manipulations.

One useful research strategy is thus to examine the catalogue of empirical effects associated with conventional punishers, and for which some property of fear is presumably responsible, and to ask whether the same effects will occur if frustrative nonreward is employed as the aversive event.

This approach is exhibited in an investigation reported by Barry, Wagner, and Miller (1962). It is well known that the administration of alcohol and sodium amytal will increase responding previously inhibited by electric shock punishments, and it is common (e.g., Miller, 1959) to attribute this effect to fear-reducing properties of the drugs. Here, then, is an empirical effect (drug-induced recovery) associated with a conventional punisher, for which some property of fear (a special susceptibility to the drugs' depressant action) is presumably responsible. If anticipatory frustration were similar to fear in also being especially susceptible to alcohol and sodium amytal, it would be expected that these drugs would also increase responding previously inhibited by frustrative nonreward. Barry, Wagner, and Miller, in fact, obtained such disinhibiting effects, thus providing evidence of one possible similarity between fear and anticipatory frustration.

Another dimension of potential similarity between fear and anticipatory frustration that could be of appreciable importance allows a somewhat different research strategy for its evaluation. It is assumed that both fear and anticipatory frustration produce characteristic stimuli (s_p and s_f) and that these stimuli come to elicit learned behaviors. Suppose there is some measure of similarity between s_p and s_f, as stimuli. One implication of such similarity is that it should, according to principles of stimulus generalization, lead to a transfer of behaviors learned in the presence of one emotional response to occasions on which the other is aroused.

This possibility has received very little research attention but one experimental approach has been proposed by Rescorla and Solomon (1967). They cite several studies (e.g., Rescorla & LoLordo, 1965) in which cues, which could be assumed to elicit fear as a result of prior Pavlovian pairings with electric shock, were found to enhance an animal's rate of responding on a Sidman avoidance schedule also maintained by shock. If such avoidance responding is mediated by fear, then the introduction of a cue which elicits fear should increase response likelihood. Rescorla and Solomon then suggest that it would be informative to give subjects appetitive Pavlovian discrimination training and then to insert the non-rewarded CS— during a Sidman avoidance session in the same fashion as has been done with CS's from Pavlovian fear conditioning. They enter-tained the possibility that perhaps "all CS—'s for *appetitive* differential conditioning and all CS+'s for *aversive* differential conditioning, can enhance *all* instrumental responses reinforced by the avoidance of *aversive* US's of *any* type" (p. 177).

Since that writing LoLordo (1967) has reported that a CS previously paired with intense noise will increase Sidman avoidance responding maintained by shock, and that this effect shows an orderly increase and decrease as a function of the stage of Pavlovian acquisition and extinction training in which the CS is involved. It might then be assumed that the emotional response resulting from noise training (i.e., fear of noise) is similar enough to that resulting from shock training (i.e., fear of shock) that a response mediated by the latter will also be cued by the former. If a CS— from appetitive classical conditioning can be assumed to elicit anticipatory frustration, and if anticipatory frustration is similar to fear in its cue properties, then the suggestion of Rescorla and Solomon con-cerning the possible enhancing effect of such CS—'s on Sidman avoidance behavior would also be expected.

In terms of the present argument, however, there is no reason to restrict this possibility to a transfer from Pavlovian to instrumental training. It might be expected that any stimulus capable of eliciting anticipatory frustration would tend to enhance avoidance responding based on fear, regardless of whether the tendency of a cue to elicit the aversive emotional response originated in a Pavlovian or instrumental training situation.

In fact, experiments in which stimuli signaling nonreward were drawn from either Pavlovian or instrumental training situations and inserted in a Sidman avoidance situation might be useful toward answer-ing an interesting question of whether frustration requires the nonreward of an instrumental response, or simply the nonoccurrence of reward in any context in which reward is anticipated. If both kinds of signals were found to increase the rate of avoidance responding, the importance of an instrumental behavior per se would obviously be depreciated.

A matter of some theoretical and practical significance, however, within any such experiment involves the relative intensities of $r_p - s_p$ and $r_f - s_f$. It is probably reasonable to assume that $r_f - s_f$ is generally less intense than the $r_p - s_p$ generated by moderate or intense electric shock. It is not then clear what should be expected if, for example, a relatively weak $r_f - s_f$ were introduced into a situation in which avoidance responding is maintained by intense electric shock. If in such a situation the subject is chronically fearful, i.e., is always in the presence of some level of $r_p - s_p$, and avoidance responding is cued only by relatively intense s_p cues, the net effect of a CS eliciting a weaker $r_f - s_f$ might be to decrease the level of emotionality and consequently the likelihood of making the avoidance response. It would be of initial interest at least to know the effects of inserting a CS+ previously paired with very weak noxious stimulation on any Sidman baseline onto which a frustration arousing stimulus were to be inserted.

While experimental designs similar to those described should be especially informative as to the usefulness of assuming that s_f and s_p are similar, studies incorporating them have yet to be run. The only approach to this general problem that has been attempted is based upon an additional set of theoretical propositions.

It is normally expected that fear and anticipatory frustration will come to mediate responses which are incompatible with an instrumental response upon which aversive stimulation or frustrative nonreward has been contingent. To the degree that animals can be trained so that fear or anticipatory frustration will elicit responses that are *compatible* with the instrumental response, these emotional consequences of punishment and frustrative nonreward should have less of a decremental effect. This is what Amsel (e.g., 1958, 1962) has suggested may occur in the case of anticipatory frustration during partial reinforcement training, and what has been the basis for integrating numerous findings concerning the persistence of partially rewarded responses.

Since anticipatory reward, $r_r - s_r$, should be expected to increase with increasing numbers of prior rewards, and the intensity of frustration occasioned by a nonrewarded response is assumed to be directly related to the magnitude of $r_r - s_r$, a partially rewarded subject should experience a schedule of frustrations which increase gradually in intensity. A reasonable consequence of such experience is that $r_f - s_f$ would be introduced in the instrumental chain initially at a weak enough value so as to have negligible tendency to elicit competing responses. As it is gradually increased in intensity, at the same time that the instrumental response continues to be rewarded on a portion of the trials, it is possible that $r_f - s_f$ may become conditioned to the instrumental response itself. Such a process would contribute to the fact that partially rewarded subjects are more resistant to extinction than are continuously reinforced subjects, since the latter subjects, without benefit of such training, would be expected to have incompatible (avoidance) responses elicited by the presumably intense $r_f - s_f$ which occurs during extinction.

Miller (1960) entertained the possibility that rats can be trained to persist in responding to the cues of fear in an analogous fashion. That is, if electric-shock punishments are introduced at a rewarded goal, initially at a very weak value, but are then gradually increased in intensity while the subject continues to be rewarded, the increasingly intense fear aroused may come to elicit the instrumental response rather than avoidance behaviors. Such a process would contribute to the fact (e.g., Miller, 1960) that subjects receiving such gradually increasing shocks are more resistant to the decremental effects of intense shock than are subjects that have received only reward training.

If rats that have been trained to traverse a runway under a partial reward schedule are persistent in responding during nonreward because they have learned to approach to $r_f - s_f$, and if rats which have been similarly trained with gradually increasing shocks are persistent in responding in the face of intense punishment because they have learned to approach to $r_p - s_p$, then one way to evaluate the similarity of s_f and s_p is to ask whether there will be a transfer of the acquired persistance. That is, will the performance of partially rewarded subjects also be resistant to response-contingent noxious stimulation and will the performance of subjects that have received gradually increasing punishment also be resistant to nonreward.

To test this possibility Brown and Wagner (1964) trained three groups of rats in a straight runway. Group C received a simple continuous reward schedule, with food (.135 gm., dry weight, wet mash) alone on all trials. Group N received exposure to nonreward during acquisition on a random 50% reward schedule. Group P received exposure to punishment during acquisition, with electric shock on 50% of the trials in addition to food reward on all trials. All groups received 114 acquisition trials, during which time the shock intensity was gradually increased from 75 volts to 235 volts in Group P. Following training, each of the three training groups was divided into two subgroups. One subgroup was then tested with consistent frustrative nonreward (extinction), the other with consistent 235-volt shock punishments and food reward.

Several additional considerations in the experimental design should also be noted. The rationale was, as indicated, to train Group P to be resistant to punishment and Group N to be similarly resistant to nonreward, both as compared to Group C, and then to determine whether, in addition, Group P would be resistant to nonreward and Group N would be resistant to punishment. The value of the terminal test shocks, the rate of increase in shock intensity in Group P, and the magnitude of food reward were selected such that roughly similar rates of decrease in responding would be observed in the two Group C subgroups tested with nonreward and punishment, and that the comparative resistance to punishment in Group P and resistance to nonreward in Group N would be similar in magnitude. Such conditions appeared important so as to try to equate the likelihoods of detecting transfer in either direction if such occurred, and to attempt to produce two anticipatory aversive emotional responses during testing which might be thought to be not grossly different in intensity.

It would be expected that intense enough shock could be employed during testing such that training to respond to weaker s_f cues would have little effect on resistance to punishment. Likewise with very small magnitudes of reward, anticipatory frustration apparently contributes very little to the response decrement in extinction, such that training to respond to s_p might have little effect on resistance to extinction (Wagner, 1961).

Furthermore, it was deemed important to administer the shock after the subjects contacted and consumed the food pellet. Quite different processes than those discussed here might be involved in training persistance to punishment if the shocks preceded, and hence signaled, the food or if shock were administered and terminated before the completion of the instrumental response chain.

Test trial performance of the several groups may be seen in Fig. 6–6. Exposure to either nonreinforcement or punishment during acquisition successfully produced resistance to the decremental effects of the respective training event; the running speeds of Group P subjects tested with punishment and Group N subjects tested with nonreward decreased only negligibly over the 6-day test period. Of major interest, however, was the transfer of the effects of the two experimental training conditions; Group N subjects were less slowed by punishment and Group P subjects were less slowed by nonreward than were the corresponding Group C subjects. Granting the theoretical context, these results would appear to provide reasonable encouragement to the view that there is some degree of commonality in the emotional responses of fear and anticipatory frustration.

A number of additional studies (e.g., Logan, 1960; Martin & Ross, 1964; Karsh, 1964, 1966) have been reported which are similar in certain of their findings to the Brown and Wagner study but because of procedural differences may be more hazardous to interpret in terms of the similarity of fear and anticipatory frustration. It may be worth re-emphasizing that the issue in the Brown and Wagner study was whether an acquired resistance to shock or nonreward would transfer to the other

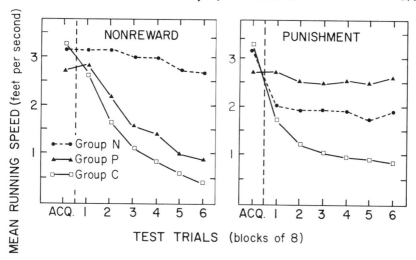

FIG. 6–6.   Mean runway speeds on last day of acquisition and subsequent blocks of eight test trials for groups trained with nonreward (N) or punished (P) trials interspersed during acquisition, as compared to a continuously rewarded (C) group. Separate graphs are presented for the halves of each treatment group tested with nonreward and with punishment.

From: R. T. Brown & A. R. Wagner, "Resistance to Punishment and Extinction Following Training with Shock and Nonreinforcement," *Journal of Experimental Psychology*, **68**, 1964, Fig. 2, p. 505. Copyright 1964 by the American Psychological Association and reproduced by permission.

event. It was thus crucial, for example, that not only did Group P receive experience with punishment during training, but that the experience in fact produced a persistance in responding in the face of punishment. It was then possible to inquire whether such training would also produce a persistance in responding during extinction. Church and Raymond (1967) have recently contrasted the Brown and Wagner data with their own failure to obtain an increased resistance to extinction when punishment was experienced during one phase of acquisition. Their data were obtained with a bar-press response, rewarded on either a 5-minute variable-interval schedule or a ⅕-minute variable-interval schedule and a constant intensity of punishment on a 2-minute variable-interval schedule. While it may be of interest in itself whether such conditions produce an increased resistance to extinction, whether they do or not is beside the point of the present issue, unless it can first be shown that they do produce a resistance to punishment.

It is now known (Terris and Wechkin, 1967) that persistence acquired to electric shock may transfer to loud noise, and that persistence acquired to loud noise may transfer to electric shock. A special advantage of those theories which emphasize the mediating properties of conditioned emotional responses is that such transfers, as well as that demonstrated by LoLordo (1967), are anticipated. It need only be assumed that the fear of loud noise is similar to the fear of electric shock. The Brown and Wagner findings in such context must additionally suggest that the fear of nonreward (anticipatory frustration) is also similar to the fear of electric shock.

Conclusions

Apart from the studies described, the frustration theory, as developed by Amsel and others, which treats frustrative nonreward as an aversive punishment-like event, has proved to be quite useful in deriving a sizable number of findings (see e.g., Amsel, 1958, 1962; Spence, 1960) from inconsistant reward situations. It also may be appreciated as a systematic nicety, in that rather than introducing an additional conceptual network to deal with certain of the effects of nonreward, a set of theoretical principles already useful in dealing with punishment has in large measure simply been translated to a new sphere of behavior.

The issue dealt with in the present paper has essentially been whether the similarity between frustrative nonreward and punishment extends beyond the purely formal characteristics of their associated theories. Does frustrative nonreward have special aversive characteristics, such that it might be said to satisfy the definition of punishment as a response-contingent aversive event? Is there reason from transfer studies to view fear and anticipatory frustration as being more than conceptually similar? To both questions it would appear that cautious affirmative answers are justified, although the need for additional data and the direction in which such might be sought have also been indicated.

It is a truism, pointed out by many authors, that our systematic knowledge of punishment is based almost entirely on the effects of electric shock. It is thus important to an adequate treatment of punishment not only to identify other events which have similar aversive properties, but to determine the degree to which current generalizations about response-contingent aversive stimulation apply equally to the range of such events.

In evaluation of the similarity of various aversive events it may be especially instructive that subjects may transfer a behavior acquired with one aversive stimulus to occasions involving quite different aversive events (e.g., LoLordo, 1967; Terris & Wechkin, 1967) and that this fact apparently holds for the case of frustrative nonreward and shock (Brown & Wagner, 1964). As pointed out, such results find ready interpretation by those treatments which emphasize the mediational properties of conditioned aversive emotional responses. In general, to the degree that subjects such as those in the LoLordo (1967), Terris & Wechkin (1967), and

Brown and Wagner (1964) studies fail to distinguish between the aversive events employed, neither should our theories.

REFERENCES

ADELMAN, H. M., & MAATSCH, J. L. Learning and extinction based upon frustration, food reward, and exploratory tendency. *Journal of Experimental Psychology,* 1956, **52**, 311–315.

AMSEL, A. A three-factor theory of inhibition: An addition to Hull's two-factor theory. Paper read at Southern Society for Philosophy and Psychology, Roanoke, Va., 1951.

AMSEL, A. The role of frustrative nonreward in noncontinuous reward situations. *Psychological Bulletin,* 1958, **55**, 102–119.

AMSEL, A. Frustrative nonreward in partial reinforcement and discrimination learning: Some recent history and a theoretical extension. *Psychological Review,* 1962, **69**, 306–328.

AMSEL, A., & ROUSSEL, J. Motivational properties of frustration: I. Effect on a running response of the addition of frustration to the motivational complex. *Journal of Experimental Psychology,* 1952, **43**, 363–368.

AMSEL, A., & WARD, J. S. Frustration and persistence: Resistance to discrimination following prior experience with the discriminanda. *Psychological Monographs,* 1965, **79** (4, Whole No. 597).

BARRY, H., III, WAGNER, A. R., & MILLER, N. E. Effects of alcohol and amobarbital on performance inhibited by experimental extinction. *Journal of Comparative and Physiological Psychology,* 1962, **55**, 464–468.

BROWN, R. T., & WAGNER, A. R. Resistance to punishment and extinction following training with shock or nonreinforcement. *Journal of Experimental Psychology,* 1964, **68**, 503–507.

CHURCH, R. M., & RAYMOND, G. A. Influence of the schedule of positive reinforcement on punished behavior. *Journal of Comparative and Physiological Psychology,* 1967, **63**, 329–332.

DALY, H. B. Learning of a hurdle-jump response to escape cues paired with reduced reward or frustrative nonreward. Paper presented at the meeting of the Psychonomic Society, Chicago, October, 1967.

ESTES, W. K. An experimental study of punishment. *Psychological Monographs,* 1944, **57** (3, Whole No. 263).

FERSTER, C. B. Control of behavior in chimpanzees and pigeons by time out from positive reinforcement. *Psychological Monographs,* 1958, **72** (8, Whole No. 461).

KARSH, E. B. Punishment: Effect on learning and resistance to extinction of discrete operant behavior. *Psychonomic Science,* 1964, **1**, 139–140.

KARSH, E. B. Resistance to punishment and extinction resulting from training with increased reward in a discrete operant situation. Paper presented at meeting of the Psychonomic Society, St. Louis, 1966.

KAUFMAN, A., & BARON, A. Use of withdrawal of reinforcement with the escape–avoidance paradigm. *Psychological Reports,* 1966, **19**, 959–965.

KELLER, F. S., & SCHOENFELD, W. N. *Principles of psychology.* New York: Appleton-Century-Crofts, 1950.

LEITENBERG, H. Is time-out from positive reinforcement an aversive event? A review of the experimental evidence. *Psychological Bulletin,* 1965, **64**, 428–441.

LEITENBERG, H. Conditioned acceleration and conditioned suppression in pigeons. *Journal of the Experimental Analysis of Behavior,* 1966, **9**, 205–212.

LOGAN, F. A. *Incentive: How the conditions of reinforcement affect the performance of rats.* New Haven: Yale University Press, 1960.

LoLORDO, V. M. Similarity of conditioned fear responses based upon different aversive events. *Journal of Comparative and Physiological Psychology,* 1967, **64**, 154–158.

MARTIN, B., & ROSS, L. E. Effects of consummatory response punishment on consummatory and runway behavior. *Journal of Comparative and Physiological Psychology,* 1964, **58**, 243–247.

McCAIN, G., & McVEAN, G. Effects of prior reinforcement or nonreinforcement on later performance in a double alley. *Journal of Experimental Psychology,* 1967, **73**, 620–627.

McHOSE, J. H. Effect of continued nonreinforcement on the frustration effect. *Journal of Experimental Psychology,* 1963, **65**, 444–450.

MILLER, N. E. Liberalization of basic S-R concepts: Extension to conflict behavior, motivation and social learning. In S. Koch (Ed.), *Psychology: A study of a science.* Vol. II. New York: McGraw-Hill, 1959. Pp. 196–292.

MILLER, N. E. Learning resistance to pain and fear: Effects of overlearning, exposure, and rewarded exposure in context. *Journal of Experimental Psychology,* 1960, **60**, 137–145.

MORSE, W. H., & HERRNSTEIN, R. J. The maintenance of avoidance behavior using the removal of a conditioned positive reinforcer as the aversive stimulus. *American Psychologist,* 1956, **11**, 430. (Abstract)

MOWRER, O. H. On the dual nature of learning—A re-interpretation of "conditioning" and "problem-solving." *Harvard Educational Review,* 1947, **17**, 102–148.

MOWRER, O. H. *Learning theory and behavior.* New York: Wiley, 1960.

PECKHAM, R. H., & AMSEL, A. Within-subject demonstration of a relationship between frustration and magnitude of reward in a differential magnitude of reward discrimination. *Journal of Experimental Psychology,* 1967, **73**, 187–195.

RESCORLA, R. A., & LoLORDO, V. M. Inhibition of avoidance behavior. *Journal of Comparative and Physiological Psychology,* 1965, **59**, 406–412.

RESCORLA, R. A., & SOLOMON, R. L. Two-process learning theory: Relationships between Pavlovian conditioning and instrumental learning. *Psychological Review,* 1967, **74**, 151–182.

SOLOMON, R. L. Punishment. *American Psychologist,* 1964, **19**, 239–253.

SPENCE, K. W. *Behavior theory and conditioning.* New Haven: Yale University Press, 1956.

SPENCE, K. W. *Behavior theory and learning.* Englewood Cliffs: Prentice-Hall, 1960.

TERRACE, H. Stimulus control. In W. K. Honig (Ed.), *Operant Behavior:*

Areas of research and application. New York: Appleton-Century-Crofts, 1966. Pp. 271–344.

TERRIS, W., & WECHKIN, S. Learning to resist the effects of punishment. *Psychonomic Science,* 1967, **7,** 169–170.

THOMAS, J. R. Discriminated time-out avoidance in pigeons. *Journal of the Experimental Analysis of Behavior,* 1965, **8,** 329–338.

WAGNER, A. R. The role of reinforcement and nonreinforcement in an "apparent frustration effect." *Journal of Experimental Psychology,* 1959, **57,** 130–136.

WAGNER, A. R. Effects of amount and percentage of reinforcement and number of acquisition trials in conditioning and extinction. *Journal of Experimental Psychology,* 1961, **62,** 234–242.

WAGNER, A. R. Conditioned frustration as a learned drive. *Journal of Experimental Psychology,* 1963, **66,** 142–148.

III

THE CONDITIONED EMOTIONAL RESPONSE

7

Stimulus Factors in Conditioned Suppression[1]

Howard S. Hoffman

THE PENNSYLVANIA STATE UNIVERSITY

When an initially neutral stimulus consistently precedes an unavoidable noxious event, subsequent presentations of the stimulus will often disrupt or otherwise interfere with ongoing behavior. This phenomenon, conditioned suppression, was initially investigated by Estes and Skinner (1941) and, because of its relevance to the broad problem of learned anxiety, it has since been the subject of many experiments (see Brady & Hunt, 1955; Sidman, 1960). The bulk of the work described here has concerned itself with the manner in which conditioned suppression is mediated by stimuli which are like but not identical to the stimulus that was involved in the original conditioning. This later phenomenon, the stimulus generalization of conditioned suppression, commanded special attention because it represents one of the mechanisms by which a history of aversive controls can affect large segments of an organism's behavior (Mednick, 1958).

Procedural Factors in the Development of Conditioned Suppression

The approach in our laboratory has been to employ pigeons as subjects and key pecking on a variable-interval (VI) schedule of food reinforcements as the base-line (ongoing) behavior. The choices were based upon practical considerations. Under properly arranged circumstances the key peck in pigeons can be a remarkably stable behavior. Moreover, sub-

1 This research was supported by PHS Research Grants MH-02433-08 and MH-23824 from the National Institute of Mental Health. I wish to acknowledge the assistance of the several members of my laboratory who over the years have made substantial contributions to both the research and my thoughts about it. These are Lee McBride, Warren Selekman, Roger Marsh, Norman Stein, James Stratton, Phillip Jensen, and Morton Fleshler. The work of the first three persons was supported by National Science Foundation undergraduate research participation grants. Phillip Jensen's work was made possible by an NSF grant for research participation by college teachers.

stantial response rates can be readily generated. Both factors are obviously important when one seeks to establish a base line for the assessment of suppression.

Like the decision to use pigeons as subjects, the decision as to the nature of the warning signal was also derived from practical considerations. We wanted a signal that did not require specific orienting behavior for its perception. Auditory signals seemed especially appropriate for this function. In addition, at the time, Jenkins and Harrison (1960) had just reported a study of auditory stimulus generalization in the pigeon using positive reinforcement only, and they had obtained very clean gradients. For these reasons we decided to use auditory signals as a warning of impending electric shock; and like Jenkins and Harrison, we chose to measure stimulus generalization along the dimension of tonal frequency.

As a preliminary step the subjects were trained to peck a standard Gerbrand's key on a VI schedule of food reinforcement and were concurrently adapted to the wing bands and swivel connector through which shocks would subsequently be delivered. (See Hoffman, 1960, for a description of the wing band technique for administering shock to pigeons and Fleshler & Hoffman, 1962, for a discussion of the type of schedule used to maintain key pecking.) Once the base-line rate of pecking was stable, the subjects were periodically presented with the tone which, during conditioning, would be paired with shock. They also heard the several tones which subsequently would be employed in the tests for stimulus generalization. During this "adaptation" phase the tones were presented in random order (without shock) while the pigeon pecked the key for food, and the schedule of food reinforcement was independent of the schedule of tone presentation. Thus reinforcement might occur at any time during either tone or silence. The purpose of this phase of the procedure was to mitigate any suppression which might be produced by the presentation of novel stimuli (i.e., the several different tones) during the subsequent tests for stimulus generalization. When the base-line rate was unaffected by the presence or absence of tone, regardless of tone frequency, conditioning procedures were begun. In a given session the subject ordinarily received two 1000-cps tones that ended with unavoidable electric shock. Each tone had a duration of 2 minutes, with shock presented during the final 5 seconds. As during tone adaptation procedures, the schedule of food reinforcement was independent of other experimental events. Thus reinforcement might occur at any time during the session. In developing conditioned suppression, the typical session lasted approximately 70 minutes with tone presentations separated by at least 10 minutes.

Figure 7–1 shows sample cumulative recordings from a single subject (Bird 35) during the acquisition of conditioned suppression to a 1000-cps tone. It illustrates the changes in performance that are observed during several stages of conditioning. For a given stimulus the index of suppression is quantified as a ratio where:

$$\text{Suppression Ratio} = \frac{\text{Pretone R's minus Tone R's}}{\text{Pretone R's}}$$

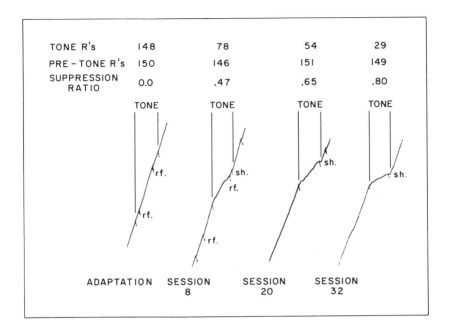

TONE R's	148	78	54	29
PRE-TONE R's	150	146	151	149
SUPPRESSION RATIO	0.0	.47	.65	.80

FIG. 7–1. Sample cumulative recordings during the acquisition of conditioned suppression to a 1000-cps tone. Tone R refers to the number of responses during the 2-minute tone period. Pretone R refers to the number of responses in the 2-minute period that ended with tone onset. Adaptation refers to the final preacquisition session during which tone was presented without shock. The narrow, diagonal markings on the cumulative records indicate the beginning and end of the preshock warning interval; the broader markings reflect food reinforcements. Sh. refers to the point at which a 5-second pulsing shock was delivered.

As illustrated in Fig. 7–1, at the end of tone adaptation the peck rate is unaffected by tone presentation. Thus the suppression ratio is typically very close to zero. In Session 8 the tone tends to disrupt the ongoing rate, and in the cumulative record shown, the suppression ratio equals .47. By Session 20 the suppression ratio has increased to .65, and by Session 32 the suppression ratio is .80. As illustrated in Fig. 7–1 and documented in several papers (Hoffman & Fleshler, 1961; Hoffman, Selekman, & Fleshler, 1966a), the major effect of presenting a tone ending with electric shock is that the rate during tone undergoes a decrease. Although there may be some disruption in the base line during the initial stages of acquisition, after several sessions the base line returns to its preacquisition level and thereafter stays relatively stable.

The stability of the base rate was illustrated in an experiment in which a sequence of tests for stimulus generalization of conditioned suppression was interrupted for 1.5 years (Hoffman, Selekman, & Fleshler, 1966a). Both before and after the interruption the several birds exhibited wide individual differences in base rate, but for a given bird the rate after the rest was within a few responses per minute of what it had been just prior to the initiation of the rest period (Hoffman & Selekman, 1967). The stability of the base rate and its insensitivity to the operations employed in generating and assessing conditioned suppression suggests that changes in rate during tone could readily be employed as an index of the effects of a given conditioning procedure. The present use of a ratio for this index, however, provides a convenient control for the persistent individual differences in base rate among birds.

There are several details in Fig. 7–1 that deserve attention. Although the overall effect of repeated pairings of tone and shock is a reduction in the rate of pecking during tone, there is very little evidence of temporal discrimination. Tone onset is typically accompanied by an immediate reduction in rate, but thereafter the rate during tone tends to be relatively constant. In the early stages of conditioning, however, when reinforcement is delivered during tone (i.e., as occurred in Session 8), the rate following the reinforcement may return to the pretone level. Later on in conditioning this effect is seldom seen.

Finally, as seen in Fig. 7–1 and as will be more fully documented later in this chapter, it is especially noteworthy that the development of conditioned suppression is a slow but nonetheless systematic process. On an intuitive basis one might expect that the subjects would rapidly form the connection between tone presentation and the occurrence of electric shock. Thus, they might be expected to exhibit suppression in an all-or-nothing fashion. Clearly this is not the case. The tone slowly acquires the capacity to suppress behavior, and it does so in a fashion that suggests the gradual development of some form of S–R bond. When Estes and Skinner first developed the conditioned suppression paradigm, they described it as a technique for obtaining a quantitative measurement of anxiety. Subsequent investigators (for example, Brady & Hunt, 1955) have tended to agree with this proposition, but they have preferred to identify the learned reaction as a conditioned emotional response (CER). Our own inclination is to interpret conditioned suppression as a reflection of a CER. Thus, through its repeated pairing with shock the warning signal acquires the capacity to evoke an anxietylike CER, and the magnitude of the suppression effect on a given trial is conceived to be a reflection of the strength of the S–R bond between the warning signal and the CER.

A certain degree of caution must, however, be exercised in seeking to equate CER level with the magnitude of the suppression ratio. In general, the suppression ratio is a direct, simple measure of relative performance decrement. However, measurement by relative suppression presupposes that under constant experimental conditions the warning signal will produce the same relative decrement independent of the rate of the responding at the moment of the warning signal presentation. The validity of this assumption has not been assessed.

A second factor of importance is that at some constant level of ongoing behavior, the suppression ratio is sensitive only to a particular range of variation in the emotional reaction controlled by the stimulus. While the ratio can assume negative values, it has a maximum of 1.00 and beyond this it does not vary with the strength of the CER. Moreover, within its range, the scale that best characterizes variation in the suppressing ability of a stimulus is at present unknown; and the same scale might be adequate for different levels of ongoing behavior or for behaviors that are maintained by different schedules and kinds of positive reinforcement. Clearly additional research is needed to reveal these scales. In the meantime it is convenient, if not altogether correct, to conceptualize the suppression ratio as a reflection of an underlying CER, and in this sense suppression ratios with values near 1 are conceived to reflect a strong CER, whereas ratios with values near zero are conceived to reflect weak CER's.

The Gradient of Stimulus Generalization after Conditioning to a 1000-cps Tone

Tests for stimulus generalization are typically begun at the completion of conditioning procedures. In a given test session, tones with frequencies above, at, and below the frequency of the tone used in conditioning are presented without shock while the subject pecks the key on the previously established schedule of food reinforcement. In a given test session, the entire series of generalization test tones is presented with the order of tones randomized and the interval between tones approximately 10 minutes. The test tones ordinarily have the same duration as during conditioning, and their intensities are equated with each other and with the intensity of the tone used in conditioning (in most studies 88 db re. .0002 dynes per cm^2).

Figure 7–2 shows the gradients of stimulus generalization produced by a single subject (Bird 5) from one of our first experiments (Hoffman & Fleshler, 1961). For this bird the conditioning procedures were essentially as described above, except that the warning period (i.e., the interval from the onset of the 1000-cps tone to the onset of the unavoidable

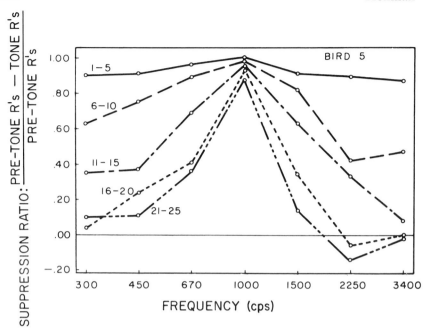

FIG. 7–2.   Generalization gradients for Bird 5. The number spans (1–5, 6–10, etc.) of each gradient indicate the sessions included.

From: H. S. Hoffman & M. Fleshler, "Stimulus Factors in Aversive Control: The Generalization of Conditioned Suppression," *Journal of the Experimental Analysis of Behavior*, 4, 1961, Fig. 2, p. 374. Copyright 1961 by the Society for the Experimental Analysis of Behavior, Inc., and reproduced by permission.

shock) was 40 seconds. This subject received approximately 70 sessions of tone-shock pairings before shock was disconnected and tests for stimulus generalization were begun. Each gradient in Fig. 7–2 is averaged across five successive sessions. At the beginning of testing, generalization of suppression was broad. As testing proceeded, however, the gradient narrowed severely. Since no shocks occurred once testing began, the changes in the shape of the gradient during testing must reflect differences in the extinction of the suppressing capacity of the several stimuli. Because the broad gradients systematically narrowed as testing continued, it must be concluded that there were differences in the rate of extinction of the behavioral control exercised by the several stimuli, a finding which is consistent with the results of several other investigators (Hovland, 1937a, 1937b, 1937c; Brown, 1942; Littman, 1949; Wickens, Schroder, & Snide, 1954; Jenkins & Harrison, 1960).

This sharpening of the gradient of generalization with extinction is a peculiar effect in that it seems to represent the development of discriminated behavior without either previous or concurrent differential reinforcement. Such sharpening might be expected if there were differences in the equation form of the extinction functions for the several stimuli. In general, however, the formalization of such differences would form a relatively unpalatable addition to the several theoretical treatments of generalization, because it would greatly complicate these theories and thus tend to reduce their value as conceptual models. Fortunately, an alternative and far simpler process can be postulated to account for these effects. The generalization gradient can sharpen during extinction if the extinction curve is initially convex and if the several stimuli exercised different degrees of stimulus control at the start of testing. Brady (1955) found that the extinction curve for suppression was in fact initially convex when the ongoing behavior was maintained on a VI schedule, and the results of our early work (as in Fig. 7–2) also suggest convexity. More direct evidence of such convexity appears in Fig. 7–3.

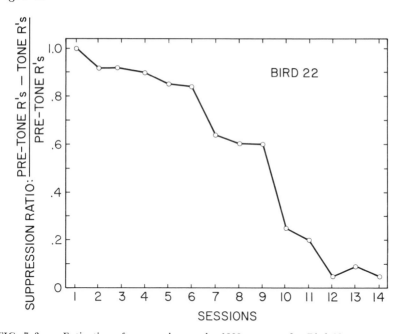

FIG. 7–3.   Extinction of suppression to the 1000-cps tone for Bird 22.

This figure shows the extinction of suppression for Bird 22 which received the same conditioning procedures as Bird 5 but which was extinguished on the 1000-cps tone without either prior or concurrent tests for stimulus generalization. During each session, seven 1000-cps tones were presented without shock. Each point in the figure represents the mean suppression ratio per session. The tone lost its capacity to suppress very slowly, and the curve representing the extinction of suppression was initially convex. In view of these data, the question then becomes: Can the extinction curves for the various tones be derived from one convex extinction function, when the only differences among the tones is the amount of initial suppression and not a difference in the rate of extinction (slope of the curve)? The crucial evidence on which to evaluate this question derives from the comparison of the extinction curves of the conditioning tone and the test tones in the same range of suppression. Unfortunately, the degree to which the extinction curve for the conditioning tone overlapped with that of the test tones was small. Consequently, the question must be left open for now.

Motivational Factors in Conditioned Suppression

In one of our early studies (Hoffman & Fleshler, 1961), we sought to examine the effects of motivation for the base-line behavior on the generalization gradient. Figure 7–4 illustrates the kinds of gradients that were produced by manipulation of the bird's body weight during testing. All gradients in Fig. 7–4 are from Bird 21. Conditioning procedures for this subject were identical to those for Bird 5 (reported previously). Like Bird 5, during conditioning, this subject was maintained at 80% of its previously established *ad libitum* weight level. However, following conditioning but prior to testing, the bird's weight was gradually reduced to 70% of its *ad libitum* level. Once the subject's body weight had stabilized at 70%, it was exposed to three sessions of testing. Finally, the bird's weight was gradually increased back to 80% of its *ad libitum* level; and when the weight was stable, testing was resumed.

The upper graph shows the gradients at the two different levels of body weight, and the lower one shows the continued performance at 80% body weight. The 70% body weight gradient is fairly sharp, showing only a moderate degree of generalization. The first gradient produced after the body weight increase is much broader. As noted in Fig. 7–4, the 70% gradient represents the mean value for the first three sessions of testing, whereas the 80% gradient is for Sessions 4–6. It should again be recalled that no shock occurred once testing had begun. The bottom graph shows that with continued testing at 80% the gradient slowly sharpens in a manner similar to that of birds tested solely at 80% body weight.

Since the broadening of the gradients with increased body weight was in a direction opposite to that which would be expected from continued extinction, it was concluded that the degree to which suppression generalized was an inverse function of the motivation for the ongoing, positively reinforced behavior.

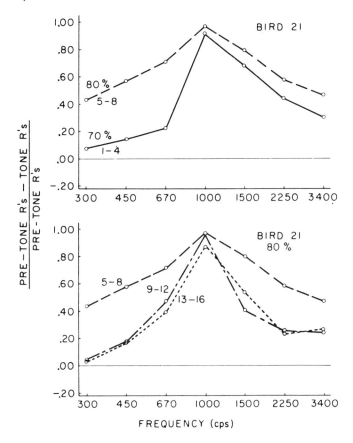

FIG. 7–4. Generalization gradient for Bird 21. The upper graph presents the gradient at 70% body weight and the initial gradient at 80% body weight. The lower graph presents the gradients obtained during continued testing at 80% body weight (with the initial 80% gradient repeated). The number spans (1–4, 5–8, etc.) of each gradient indicate the sessions included.

From: H. S. Hoffman & M. Fleshler, "Stimulus Factors in Aversive Control: The Generalization of Conditioned Suppression," *Journal of the Experimental Analysis of Behavior*, 4, 1961, Fig. 8, p. 376. Copyright 1961 by the Society for the Experimental Analysis of Behavior, Inc., and reproduced by permission.

One effect of the changed deprivation level was a modification of the overall rate of responding. The magnitude of this effect was estimated by averaging the response rates during the pretone periods of test sessions conducted under the two different deprivation levels. For Bird 21, the average pretone response rate during Test Sessions 1–4 (70% free-feeding weight) was 110 responses per minute; however, during Sessions 5–8 (80% free-feeding weight), the bird's average rate was 55 responses per minute. In general, this finding is consistent with those of several other studies (e.g., Clark, 1958) in which VI rate was found to be an inverse function of percentage body weight. Because response rate changed with the modification in the percentage body weight, it could not be determined whether motivation level or its effects on response rate produced the change in the generalization gradient. Regardless of which factor is responsible for the change, however, the results of this phase of the work made it clear that the generalization of suppression is determined in part by the motivational variables which control ongoing behavior, and that manipulation of these variables can profoundly influence the magnitude of such generalization.

The Retention of Conditioned Suppression

The birds used in our initial studies of stimulus generalization were not discarded at the end of testing since we felt that at some later time we might explore the long-term effects of the original conditioning procedures by simply reinstating the test procedures. At the time, the question seemed especially attractive because none of the birds had completely extinguished during the original tests, and maintaining the birds was a relatively simple matter.

The first retention test occurred approximately 2.5 years after the initial tests were completed. The second retention test occurred 1.5 years after the completion of the first retention test. During the two interruptions the birds were maintained on an *ad libitum* feeding schedule and were never subjected to any experimental procedures. At the conclusion of each interruption, the birds were subjected to restricted feeding until their body weights dropped to 80%. They were then run on the previously established VI schedule for ten sessions, each of which lasted approximately 2 hours. This was done in order to reestablish a stable base rate of pecking. No tones were presented during these sessions, and during these sessions as well as during the test sessions which followed, the shock connector was in place but no shocks were presented.

Tests for stimulus generalization were then reinstated. The procedures for these tests were identical to those employed in the initial experiments. The seven different test tones were presented in random order without shock while the subject pecked the key for food. The first retention series involved 20 test sessions. At the end of this series the birds were exhibiting very little suppression to any of the tones (i.e., extinction of suppression to all tones was very nearly complete). At the time, however, it seemed possible that the level of suppression might in part depend upon the subject's general level of emotionality, and that if the birds were exposed to some form of emotional stress they might again exhibit suppression to the several tones. Accordingly, we initiated an additional series of tests under conditions that were designed to "stress" the birds.

The stress condition consisted of eight test sessions in which a series of unsignaled electric shocks was administered during a sequence of time-outs (periods of total darkness) interspersed among tone presentations. Since all pecking ceased during time-outs, the administration of shock during these periods minimized the tendency for the birds to form a direct association between shock and either the tones or the pecking behavior itself. Moreover, since the time-outs with shock were distributed evenly throughout the test sessions, the relationship of tone to shock was uniform across tones. (See Hoffman, Fleshler, & Jensen, 1965, for a more detailed description of the stress condition.)

Following the stress condition, testing was continued as prior to shock stress for eight more sessions. Then after a second 1.5-year interruption, testing proceeded for four more sessions.

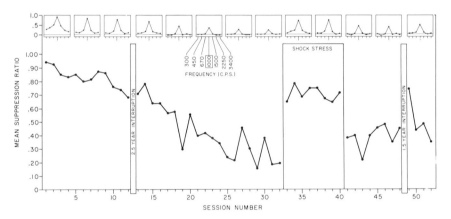

FIG. 7–5.   Successive tests for stimulus generalization during extinction of conditioned suppression. The large curve shows the mean suppression ratio (across four birds) for each presentation of the 1000-cps tone during the several test sessions. The insets at the top show successive gradients of stimulus generalization where each gradient is based on the data from the four sessions which the inset spans. Shock stress refers to a sequence of test sessions in which electric shocks were presented during a series of interpolated periods of darkness. (After Hoffman & Fleshler, 1961)

Figure 7–5 collates the data from the initial studies (Hoffman & Fleshler, 1961) and also summarizes the results of the several tests over the years. The larger function in Fig. 7–5 shows the mean suppression ratio (across the four birds that survived the lengthy interruptions) for each presentation of the tone that had been previously paired with electric shock (1000 cps). The insets at the top show successive gradients of stimulus generalization where each gradient is based upon the data from the four test sessions spanned by its inset.

Since in the initial experiments before the 2.5-year interruption (Hoffman & Fleshler, 1961) different birds received different numbers of test sessions (12–25), only the last 12 sessions of those tests are shown. Thus, Fig. 7–5 summarizes the data from the last 12 sessions before the first interruption as well as the data obtained in the 40 test sessions administered thereafter. As can be seen, the behavioral effects of the original conditioning procedures were extremely inert. Suppression to the tone which had been paired with shock (the large function in Fig. 7–5) extinguished very slowly, and in general the form of the extinction curve is ogival. Indeed, the extinction function for the 1000-cps tone obtained during the first 32 sessions in Fig. 7–5 is quite similar to the function obtained when subjects were extinguished on suppression to a 1000-cps tone with no concurrent or prior generalization testing (i.e., compare Fig. 7–5 to Fig. 7–3). Neither the initial 2.5-year interruption nor the later 1.5-year interruption yielded any loss in suppression. Rather, suppression after the interruptions was, if anything, slightly higher than just before the interruptions.

As seen in the insets, as testing proceeded the slope of the gradient of stimulus generalization gradually increased despite the fact that the birds had never been subjected to discrimination procedures. By Session 32, however, extinction of suppression had proceeded to the point where only the 1000-cps tone produced any suppression at all, and the degree of suppression it controlled was slight. Shock stress was introduced at this point, and it immediately increased the tendency for the several tones to suppress key pecks. In general, however, the birds continued to exhibit maximum suppression to the tone that had originally been paired with shock. Finally, suppression after the stress condition was slightly higher than just before it and remained higher across the final 1.5-year interruption.

It is important to reemphasize once more that except when specifically mentioned the changes in suppression ratios in this and in all subsequent figures in this chapter represent changes in response rate during the warning signal, but not during the pretone periods. In general, neither extended interruption nor any of the other conditions (generalization tests, shock stress, or discrimination procedures) ever changed a given bird's base-line rate by more than four or five responses per minute (as measured by peck rate in the several pretone periods of a given condition). Moreover, such changes as did occur were never reliable.

Razran (1939) and Wendt (1937) have found that classically conditioned responses are retained over interruptions as long as those employed here. Moreover, Thomas, Ost, and Thomas (1960) have found that the gradient of stimulus generalization of responses based on positive reinforcement exhibits negligible changes over a 21-day interruption in testing. Our results extend the implications of the earlier studies by simultaneously demonstrating the longevity and the specificity of the behavioral consequences of conditioned suppression procedures.

The overall picture that emerges from these data seems quite clear. When an initially neutral stimulus has consistently preceded a noxious event, it acquires the capacity to suppress ongoing behavior; and stimuli which are similar to it also exhibit this capacity, but to a lesser degree.

This effect is remarkably resistant to change with the passage of time, and in the absence of specific experimental procedures, the stimuli retain their capacity to suppress behavior for a significant portion of the subject's life. (Pigeons live for approximately 15 yrs. The interruptions in the present study totaled 4 yrs.) Obviously, time in and of itself does not contribute to the elimination of conditioned suppression, nor does it dull the subject's tendency to discriminate between the stimulus involved in the original conditioning and other similar stimuli. Rather, extinction occurs when stimulus presentation no longer leads to a noxious event, but even then the process is quite slow and the stimulus involved in the original conditioning is much more resistant to extinction than the stimuli on the wings of the generalization gradient. Finally, even when extinction is very nearly complete, a period of stress can lead to partial recovery of conditioned suppression, and the effect can persist long after the stress has ended.

The Role of Punishment in Conditioned Suppression

Punishment can be defined as a procedure in which the advent of noxious stimulation (for example, electric shock) is contingent upon the occurrence of a given response. In the conditioned suppression paradigm used here, a warning signal ending with unavoidable electric shock is presented while the subject engages in key pecking for food. With this arrangement, there is no explicitly programmed relationship between the subject's pecks and the presentation of electric shock; but if the subject is pecking at a moderately high rate, the shock is likely to occur either during or shortly after a response. Thus, the procedure used here incorporates the possibility of accidental punishment, especially during the early stages of conditioning.

In one sequence of studies (Hoffman & Fleshler, 1965) we sought to evaluate the effects of this punishment phenomenon. Of course, Brady and his co-workers (see Church, 1963, for a review of that work) had already demonstrated that the suppression effect does not depend upon the explicit pairing of a noxious event with the ongoing behavior. A warning signal that ends with shock will suppress ongoing behavior when the signal has been paired with shock prior to the initial development of the base-line behavior, and it will also do so even if these pairings occur in a separate and distinctive chamber from the one used to develop the base-line behavior (Geller, Sidman, & Brady, 1955).

Still, as noted above, in the paradigms used in our laboratory, shock occasionally occurs in close temporal proximity to a response, and it seemed worthwhile to explore the effects of this accidental response–shock relationship. To do so, a yoked design was employed in which the key pecks of one of two birds initiated shock for itself and for a second (paired) subject who was in a different experimental apparatus. Both members of a given pair periodically received a warning signal while they pecked a key for food on a VI schedule. For the punished member of the pair a key peck at any time after the initial 2 minutes of the warning signal (a 1000-cps tone) simultaneously caused the termination of the warning signal and the delivery of electric shock, and it did so for both himself and his yoked partner. As a result, both members of a pair received exactly the same distributions of shocks and warning signals, but for the punished bird the occurrence of shock was contingent upon the emission of a key peck during the terminal portion of the warning signal, whereas for the yoked bird shock presentation was independent of its ongoing behavior.

Striking differences in the behavior produced by the two procedures were seen in the cumulative records. Figure 7–6 shows sample records for the second stimulus in the second session of each block of four sessions for one pair of subjects. The marks above the recordings indicate the onset of the pretone, tone, and shock-contingency periods, respectively. During the early stages of the procedures, the yoked subject's base-line response rates (as revealed by pretone rate) became somewhat depressed and variable. This tendency persisted with continued shock presentations, but eventually the base rate returned to its previous level. The onset of tone for this subject initiates a short period of negative acceleration, which quickly brings response rate to a low level, and a rough grain, low response rate then prevails throughout the tone. The punished subject showed little change in base-line behavior throughout the aversive procedures. The effects of punishment on behavior during the tone are first seen as very rough grain, sudden oscillations from high rates to low or zero rates of responding. With continued tone-shock presentations, the pauses in responding become longer. Rate changes seldom occur with the onset of tone and aside from very short periods of negative acceleration,

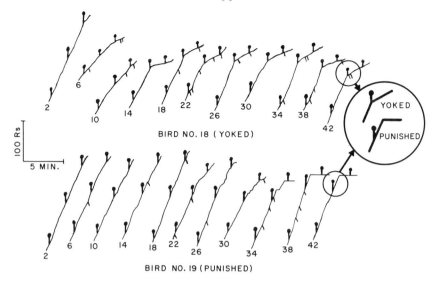

FIG. 7-6.   Sections from the cumulative records from a punished subject and his yoked partner, showing the second trial from the second session of each block of four sessions. The heavy vertical lines above the records indicate the onsets of the pretone, tone, and shock contingency periods respectively. The numbers below the records indicate the session in which the trial occurred.

From: H. S. Hoffman & M. Fleshler, "Stimulus Aspects of Aversive Controls: The Effects of Response Contingent Shock," *Journal of the Experimental Analysis of Behavior*, 8, 1965, Fig. 2, p. 92. Copyright 1965 by the Society for the Experimental Analysis of Behavior, Inc., and reproduced by permission.

no intermediate rates are seen. The insets illustrate the basic features of the differences in suppression during the warning period.

Although explanations of these differences must at present be somewhat speculative, the work suggested that the inclusion of a specific response–shock contingency in the suppression paradigm served to modify the influence of the warning signal. In particular, it seemed to establish a situation in which the necessary condition for suppression to occur was that the subject be responding in the presence of the warning signal. Thus, for punished subjects, the onset of the warning signal was not ordinarily accompanied by a change in response rate. Rather, these subjects typically responded through the initial segment of the warning signal and then abruptly showed a complete cessation of pecking. It was as if the stimulus which gained control over the subject's emotional reaction consisted of a compound in which one element was stimulation provided by the warning signal and the other element was stimulation provided by proprioceptive feedback from the behavior of pecking the key. When either element was missing, as during the intervals between tones (when the tone was missing) and during the first few seconds of tone (when feedback from key pecks during tone was missing), no suppression occurred.

Although further research would be necessary to validate these speculations more fully; the large and consistent differences in performance exhibited by punishment versus conditioned suppression subjects make it apparent that in the conditioned suppression paradigm used here accidental punishment of ongoing responses is not a critical factor in generating the overall effects.

The Effects of Conditioning to Two Signals: The Issue of Summation in Stimulus Generalization and in Conditioned Suppression

One sequence of studies (Hoffman, Selekman, & Fleshler, 1966b) sought to examine the consequences of a conditioning procedure that involved presentation of two tones (having different frequencies), both of which ended with electric shock. In addition to its implications for the interpretation of conditioned suppression, the investigation of stimulus generalization after conditioning to two stimuli is relevant to the theoretical issue of summation in stimulus generalization.

When interpreted in the present context, the summation hypothesis (Hull, 1943) holds that the gradient of stimulus generalization that results from conditioning to two stimuli represents an interactive sum of the gradients produced by conditioning to each stimulus separately. Thus, at points along the stimulus continuum where the separate gradients overlap, the stimuli have two sources of generalized response tendency. The summation hypothesis asserts that these tendencies interact to produce a combined response tendency which is greater than either one alone. The main alternative to the summation hypothesis is that when a stimulus has two sources of generalized response tendency, the resulting tendency is equal to that of the stronger one alone.

Past investigations of the generalization gradient after conditioning to two stimuli have employed positive reinforcement only and have failed to confirm or deny either of these alternatives (Kalish & Guttman, 1957). Our investigation differed from the above primarily in its focus on aversive procedures. Here the question of summation was evaluated by assessing the relative level of conditioned suppression to the tone which lies midway between the tones used in conditioning procedures. According to the summation hypothesis, when the tones used in conditioning are close to each other, the gradients around each of them would be expected to overlap in the middle. As a result, suppression to the tone midway between them should be elevated relative to the suppression controlled by tones that are equally remote from the conditioning stimulus but are located in parts of the stimulus continuum where the gradients do not overlap. When, however, the tones used in conditioning are more widely separated, the overlap of the separate gradients would be either reduced or eliminated. As a result, suppression to the tone midway between the conditioning tones should be relatively reduced.

Figure 7–7 shows the gradients of stimulus generalization that were obtained during a series of tests (without shock) after the subjects had been exposed to a sequence of conditioning sessions in each of which both a 670- and a 1500-cps tone served as a warning of impending electric shock. The subjects received six 2-minute tones per conditioning session, three with frequencies at 670 cps and three with frequencies at 1500 cps. All tones ended with shock, and the order of tones was randomized. Figure 7–8 shows the gradients that were obtained following a similar conditioning history, except that the tones paired with shock had frequencies at 450 and 2250 cps.

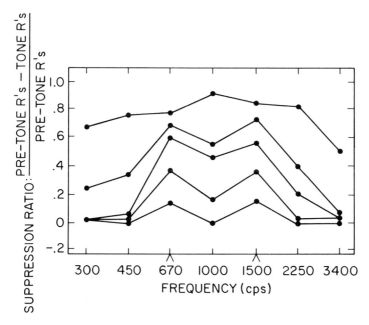

FIG. 7–7.   Stimulus generalization gradients after conditioning to 670- and 1500-cps tones. Each gradient represents data averaged across four test sessions and the sequence of gradients show successive blocks of sessions in descending order.

From: H. S. Hoffman, W. Selekman, & M. Fleshler, "Stimulus Factors in Aversive Controls: Conditioned Suppression After Equal Training on Two Stimuli," *Journal of the Experimental Analysis of Behavior,* **9,** 1966, Fig. 1, p. 651. Copyright 1966 by the Society for the Experimental Analysis of Behavior, Inc., and reproduced by permission.

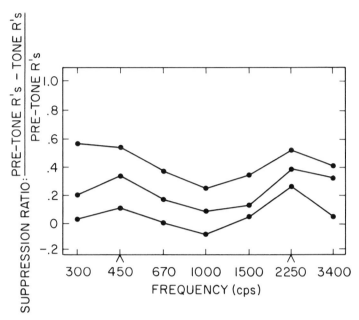

FIG. 7–8.   Stimulus generalization gradients after conditioning to 450- and 2250-cps tones. Each gradient represents data averaged across four test sessions and the sequence of gradients show succesive blocks of sessions in descending order.

From: H. S. Hoffman, W. Selekman, & M. Fleshler, "Stimulus Factors in Aversive Controls: Conditioned Suppression After Equal Training on Two Stimuli," *Journal of the Experimental Analysis of Behavior*, **9**, 1966, Fig. 2, p. 651. Copyright 1966 by the Society for the Experimental Analysis of Behavior, Inc., and reproduced by permisison.

As applied to the present study, the summation hypothesis predicts that when conditioning involves tones with similar frequencies, the test tone intermediate between the conditioning tones will exhibit more suppression than test tones which are also one step removed but on opposite sides of the gradient. When, however, conditioning involves tones that are widely spaced on the stimulus continuum, little or no summation should occur, and the tone intermediate between the conditioning tones should exhibit less suppression than other test tones. As seen in Figs. 7–7 and 7–8, both of these effects occurred. Indeed, in the initial gradient of Fig. 7–7, the 1000-cps tone exhibited even more suppression than either of the tones used in conditioning.

Although these findings were in close accord with predictions based on the summation hypothesis, they did not in and of themselves provide an unequivocal answer to the question of whether or not summation actually occurred. To demonstrate summation unequivocally, it was necessary to show that in Fig. 7–7 suppression to the 1000-cps tone was greater than would have occurred had subjects been conditioned on either 670 or 1500 cps alone. That is, it was necessary to show that the generalization gradients around both 1500 and 670 cps are not asymmetrical with heightened suppression occurring in the region of 1000 cps. Although a laboratory analysis of this issue was possible, several indirect lines of evidence suggested that asymmetrical gradients with heightened suppression at or near 1000 cps were most unlikely.

First, as seen in Fig. 7–8, when conditioning involved more widely separated tones (450 and 2250 cps), suppression to the 1000-cps tone was lower than to any other tone. This would not be expected if the birds were especially likely to suppress to tones with frequencies that approximate 1000 cps. Second, at equal levels of suppression to the tone paired with shock, the slope of the generalization gradients for birds conditioned at 1000 cps only are almost identical to the slopes at the extremes of the gradients in Fig. 7–7 (also see Hoffman, Fleshler, & Jensen, 1963). Third, it is unlikely that the tones with frequencies near 1000 cps are differentially loud, since the tones were equated for intensity (80 db) and, at intensities this high, the equal loudness contour is almost certainly quite flat. Finally, when Jenkins and Harrison (1960) investigated auditory stimulus generalization using positive reinforcement only, they found no evidence of asymmetrical gradients after training to either 1000 cps or to 450 and 2500 cps. Indeed, the gradients around 1000 cps were almost identical to the gradients around 450 and 2500 cps. In short, all of the available data pointed to the notion that conditioning at stimuli other than 1000 cps was not especially likely to produce an asymmetrical generalization gradient. Hence, it was reasonable to conclude that the finding of heightened suppression at 1000 cps (in Fig. 7–7) reflected the summation of generalized conditioned suppression tendencies.

When Kalish and Guttman (1957) used positive reinforcement procedures to examine the gradient of stimulus generalization after equal training to two stimuli, their data exhibited conspicuous (and statistically reliable) departures from the quantitative predictions derived from both the summation and the nonsummation hypotheses; for this reason, both hypotheses were rejected. Examination of their gradients, however, reveals that in every case the departures from the gradients predicted by the nonsummation hypothesis are in the direction predicted by the summation hypothesis. That is, the nonsummation hypothesis was rejected because the response tendency in the region where the separate gradients overlapped was greater than the response tendency expected from either gradient alone. The departures from the predictions based on the summation hypothesis, on the other hand, occurred in both directions; and in two of the three cases these departures were in the direction of a greater, rather than a lesser, response tendency. Thus, the summation hypothesis was rejected largely because the empirical gradients exhibited an even greater summation effect than predicted by the derived theoretical func tion. These considerations suggest that although the quantitative predictions derived by Kalish and Guttman may be untenable, the principle of summation nonetheless received strong support. That principle requires only that overlapping gradients produce a combined response tendency greater than the response tendency expected from either gradient alone. This is what Kalish and Guttman found.

Our study involved aversive procedures, but its findings were almost identical to those of Kalish and Guttman. Suppression in the region of the stimulus continuum where the separate gradients overlap was greater than the suppression expected from either gradient alone. Since those findings agreed with the basic contention of the summation hypothesis, it was concluded that in general the available data provides support for the principle of summation.

Discrimination Training and the Gradient of Generalization

One sequence of recent experiments has focused on an analysis of the manner in which the subject learns to discriminate between a "safe" stimulus and one which serves as a warning of an impending noxious event. Our first experiment (Hoffman & Fleshler, 1964) utilized a straightforward discrimination procedure. After establishing a base-line behavior (key pecking on a VI schedule of food reinforcement), each of three otherwise experimentally naive subjects was subjected to a sequence of 32 discrimination sessions. In each session the bird received two 1000-cps tones, each of which had a duration of 2 minutes and ended with shock (hereafter the tone ending with shock will be called the CS+) and five safe stimuli (a 2-min. 900-cps tone) that never ended with shock (hereafter the safe stimuli will be referred to as CS−).[2] In that initial experiment we also ran a group ($N = 3$) of control birds. In each of 32 sessions the control birds received two 1000-cps tones ending with shock in the same temporal positions as the discrimination birds, but for these subjects the "safe" signals were omitted from the sessions.

---

[2] In our earlier study of the effects of discrimination procedures on conditioned suppression we identified the tone paired with shock as an S_D and the safe signal as an S_Δ. At the time we were concerned with the possible comparisons between our work and studies of stimulus generalization using positive reinforcement only, and the use of the terms S_D and S_Δ seemed appropriate for that purpose. We have come to feel, however, that the terms CS+ and CS− represent a better terminological convention because those terms emphasize that the final operations employed in the development of suppression are those of respondent (i.e., classical) rather than operant (instrumental) conditioning. In essence, the phenomenon of conditioned suppression is the outcome of a procedure in which the experimenter arranges that an initially neutral stimulus is consistently paired with a second (noxious) stimulus. The use of CS+ and CS− reflects the use of these Pavlovian operations.

Figure 7–9 shows the mean suppression ratio across blocks of four conditioning sessions for the subjects that were exposed to the CS+ only (the control birds) and for those exposed to CS−'s as well as CS+'s (the discrimination birds).

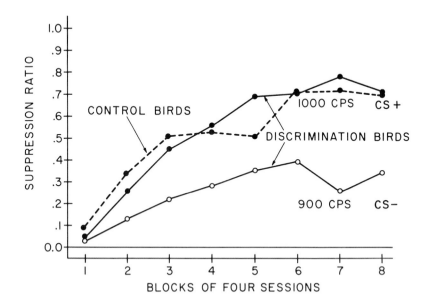

FIG. 7–9.   The development of suppression during conditioning to a 1000-cps tone (the control birds) and during discrimination procedures in which CS+ was a 1000-cps tone that always ended with electric shock and CS− was a 900-cps tone that never ended with shock.

From: H. S. Hoffman & M. Fleshler, "Stimulus Aspects of Aversive Controls: Stimulus Generalization of Conditioned Suppression Following Discrimination Training," *Journal of the Experimental Analysis of Behavior,* **7**, 1964, Fig. 1, p. 235. Copyright 1964 by the Society for the Experimental Analysis of Behavior, Inc., and reproduced by permission.

The development of conditioned suppression to the CS+ proceeded quite slowly and appeared to be approaching an asymptote that was well below the potential upper limit, i.e., complete suppression. The acquisition function for the birds conditioned on the CS+ only (control birds) overlapped the function for the CS+ in the discrimination group. Thus, there was no indication that the exposures to CS−'s during discrimination conditioning had a substantial effect on the development of suppression to the CS+. The CS−'s were not, however, behaviorally neutral for, as discrimination procedures progressed, the CS− exhibited an increasing capacity to produce suppression despite the fact that it was never directly associated with shock. These data were for the most part consistent with expectations. Their general trends are comparable to those found in experiments involving differential reinforcement of classically conditioned responses (e.g., Gynther, 1957). As Kimble (1961, p. 366) has suggested: "This result has typically occurred in studies of differential . . . conditioning and theoretically can happen under circumstances where (1) the excitatory process conditioned to S+ is greater than the inhibitory process conditioned to S−, and (2) the positive and negative stimuli are close together on the stimulus dimension."

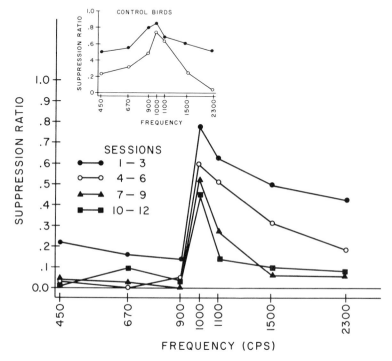

FIG. 7–10.   The gradient of stimulus generalization after discrimination procedures. During conditioning the CS+ was a 1000-cps tone which ended with unavoidable shock. The CS− was a 900-cps tone which was never accompanied by shock. The inset to the left shows the gradients for birds conditioned on the 1000-cps tone only.

Figure 7–10 shows the generalization gradients produced by the subjects with prior discrimination conditioning. The inset to the left shows the gradients generated by the control birds. A comparison between the

initial gradients for the two groups reveals that the discrimination procedures produced a marked reduction in suppression to stimuli on the
side of the gradient occupied by the CS— (900 cps), but that these procedures had little, if any, observable effect on the suppression controlled by
tones with frequencies at and above the frequency of the CS+ (1000 cps).
The effects of the discrimination conditioning were quite permanent, for
they persisted throughout the 12 sessions of testing. During these tests,
the slope of the gradient progressively increased, a finding consistent with
previous results (Hoffman & Fleshler, 1961; Hoffman et al., 1963). Indeed, the data from the control group in the present study provide a
replication of the earlier experiments.

The overall configuration of the generalization gradient differs from
the performances typically generated by comparable procedures involving
appetitive controls (Hanson, 1959; Honig, Thomas, & Guttman, 1959;
Jenkins, Harrison, & Terrace, 1962). When a given stimulus sets the
occasion for positive reinforcement, discrimination training usually leads
to a relative increase in the response rate controlled by that stimulus, to
increased slopes on both sides of the generalization gradient, and to a
shift in the peak of the gradient away from the training stimulus. None
of these effects are visible in Fig. 7–10. At the time we did not understand
why these effects failed to appear, and it was only after completing
several additional studies that the responsible factors began to reveal
themselves.

Schedule Factors in the Discrimination Process

The first of these studies consisted of an attempt to use the schedule of
base-line reinforcement as an instrument to sharpen the discrimination
between CS+ and CS—. Brady and Hunt (1955) have called attention to
the fact that the rate of conditioning and extinction of suppression is,
in part, a function of the positive reinforcement schedule used to maintain the ongoing operant behavior. They reported that if the ongoing
behavior was maintained by continuous reinforcement or by a ratio
schedule of reinforcement, suppression was more difficult to condition
than if the operant was reinforced on an interval schedule. Similarly,
Brady (1955) found that extinction of suppression occurred more rapidly
for subjects whose behavior was reinforced on a ratio schedule than for
those on an interval schedule. He interpreted this finding as indicating
the development of a stronger competing response tendency resulting
from the higher response rates generated by the ratio schedules.

Later studies in this area focused on the frequency of the base-line
reinforcement as a parameter influencing the extent of conditioned sup-

pression. In a study originally designed to investigate the effects of the duration of the conditioned stimulus and the duration of the inter-stimulus interval on conditioned suppression, Stein, Sidman, and Brady (1958) found that the extent of suppression was inversely related to the proportion of the testing session occupied by the conditioned stimulus. More directly relevant to the present material, however, was the additional finding that the number of reinforcements the subject received remained fairly constant, irrespective of the duration programs. "This finding suggested that, after sufficient conditioning, animals will suppress in the stimulus period only to an extent that does not markedly reduce opportunities for positive reinforcement" (Stein, Sidman, & Brady, 1958, p. 160). In addition, they hypothesized that the subject's rate of response varied so as to minimize the loss in the total number of reinforcements obtainable. In the same vein, Carlton and Didamo (1960) hypothesized that the critical variable was the rate at which reinforcements were presented rather than the animals' assumed ability to discriminate between the total number of reinforcements accumulated during the conditioning sessions. They found that when the total number of reinforcements delivered was held constant, there was still a loss in suppression when the duration of the tone was increased relative to its off-time. The experimenters concluded that "changes in response output which minimize the decline in reinforcement rate may account for the observed loss of suppression" (Carlton & Didamo, 1960, p. 257).

A recent series of studies conducted by Lyon (1963, 1964, 1966) has contributed to the clarification and extension of the relationship between the frequency of reinforcement and its effect on the degree of conditioned suppression. In the first experiment, Lyon (1963) trained pigeons on a 1-minute variable-interval schedule in the presence of one stimulus and a 4-minute variable-interval schedule in the presence of a second stimulus (a multiple VI-1 VI-4 base-line schedule), and superimposed a conditioned suppression procedure on each component of the schedule. He found that the initial level of suppression was less on the VI-1 base line than on the VI-4 and that extinction occurred more rapidly with the VI-1 schedule. Lyon (1964) employed the same general procedure but measured the degree of conditioned suppression on a 150-response fixed-ratio schedule of reinforcement. He found that if the conditioned stimulus occurred within the early stages of the ratio runs (0–20), complete suppression resulted. If the conditioned stimulus occurred within an intermediate range (20–60), the extent of suppression was unpredictable. If the onset of the conditioned stimulus occurred during the later stages of the runs (60–150), the subject would not suppress until responding resulted in the presentation of reinforcement. In the final study to date, Lyon and Felton (1966) measured the degree of conditioned suppression on three variable ratio (VR) schedules of base-line reinforcement (VR 50,

100, 200). They concluded that all three schedules were largely insensitive to the conditioned suppression procedure.

In general then, there is substantial agreement that the frequency with which reinforcement is presented is a crucial feature of the conditioned-suppression effect. More specifically, it appears that the degree of suppression during a conditioned stimulus is less severe when the baseline performance is maintained by a high reinforcement frequency than when reinforcement frequency is low. However, whether it is a function of the total number of reinforcements missed in a single session or the rate at which reinforcements are delivered is still an open question.

On the basis of the foregoing material it had seemed possible that if the safe stimulus in a discrimination context was also associated with a heightened reinforcement frequency, the level of suppression during that stimulus would be reduced and, consequently, the subject might form a sharper discrimination than was seen in Fig. 7–9. We thought that such a procedure might yield the peak shift effect that is obtained in positive reinforcement studies. As will be seen, we were wrong.

The procedures were similar to those of our earlier studies. A group of pigeons ($N = 3$) were run on a food-reinforced variable-interval schedule (mean interval 2 min.) until the base line rates were stable. Next, they were subjected to a period of adaptation to a 1000-cps tone, followed by adaptation to the entire series of generalization test tones. After behavior was indifferent to the presence of tone, the discrimination conditioning procedure was introduced. In each session seven tones were presented. Each tone had a 2-minute duration. Two of these (the CS+'s) had frequencies of 1000 cps and ended with a 2.5-second electric shock. The other five were CS−'s (900 cps) and never ended with shock. During three of the CS−'s a continuous reinforcement (CRF) schedule was in effect either 20, 40, or 80 seconds after the onset of the tone. The two other CS−'s were probe trials, during which the base line reinforcement schedule remained in operation. Following the completion of 32 conditioning sessions, shock was discontinued and generalization tests were conducted.

Figure 7–11 shows the mean suppression ratios across blocks of four conditioning sessions. The CS− function is comprised of the suppression ratios obtained during the probe trials. Hence, each point on both the CS+ and CS− curves represents the mean from an equivalent number of tone presentations.

The development of conditioned suppression during the CS+ initially followed an irregular yet statistically reliable pattern. It was characterized by a temporary increase in suppression followed by an abrupt reduction back to its early level. Subsequent conditioning resulted in a gradual increase in the suppression ratio, with the asymptotic level well below the potential upper limit (i.e., complete suppression).

The function produced by the CS− followed a similar, but attenu-

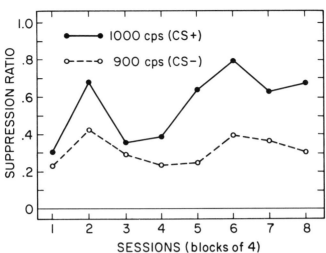

FIG. 7–11.   The development of conditioned suppression during discrimination procedures when the "safe" stimulus (900 cps) was associated with a heightened frequency
of food reinforcement. During conditioning the 1000-cps tone always ended with electrical shock, whereas the 900-cps tone never ended with shock.

ated, course of development. That is, as conditioning progressed, the
gross fluctuations in the suppression level during the CS+'s were accompanied by similar, statistically reliable changes in suppression during
the CS−'s.

As revealed in Fig. 7–9, our earlier experiment had found that the
acquisition functions of the two stimuli were negatively accelerated so
that, as discrimination-conditioning progressed, the CS+'s and CS−'s
both exhibited an increasing capacity to produce suppression. In distinction, the present study revealed a complex interaction between the levels
of suppression controlled by CS+ and CS−, but the interaction was not
understood at the time.

A second salient aspect of Fig. 7–11 relates to the failure of the conditioning procedures to minimize the occurrence of suppression during the
CS−. Indeed, by the end of the first four sessions the CS− had acquired a
statistically significant capacity to suppress behavior, and this capacity
persisted throughout acquisition. This finding suggested that even when
the schedule of reinforcement was such as to maximize the density of
reinforcement during CS−, its effect was not sufficient to compensate persistently for the suppression tendencies that generalized from the CS+.

Figure 7–12 shows the generalization gradients that resulted from this
conditioning procedure. The overall configuration of the initial gradient
is, for the most part, comparable to the initial gradient found in our

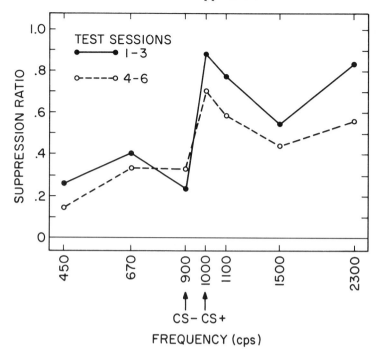

FIG. 7–12.   The gradient of stimulus generalization after discrimination procedures in which the 900-cps safe stimulus also served as a cue for heightened frequency of positive reinforcement.

previous experiment where discrimination conditioning was administered against a constant (VI) base line (e.g., Hoffman & Fleshler, 1964). Both procedures resulted in a marked reduction in suppression to stimuli on the side of the gradient occupied by the CS− (900 cps), but neither had a substantial effect on the suppression controlled by tones with frequencies at and above the CS+. Apparently we had merely replicated our earlier discrimination experiment. We had yet to observe either a peak shift effect or anything remotely like it.

Discrimination Training Using Fade-In Procedures

One characteristic feature of the acquisition functions that were seen in Figs. 7–9 and 7–11 was that the CS− consistently yielded suppression even though the CS− was never itself paired with electric shock. Our next line of investigation sought to determine whether or not we could establish a sharper discrimination between CS+ and CS— by using a variation of the fade-in procedures which, in a different context, had been investigated by Terrace (1966), and which had been found to yield a performance in which the subject forms a discrimination without ever responding to CS— at all.

Our basic approach was identical to that of our initial discrimination experiment (Hoffman & Fleshler, 1964) except that instead of presenting CS— at full intensity (88 db) throughout the conditioning procedure, CS— was gradually faded-in (increased in intensity) from a level that was just barely audible during the initial conditioning session to a level that was equal to that of CS+ (88 db) at the end of the conditioning process. While the subject pecked the key on a VI schedule of reinforcement, seven tones were presented. Each tone had a duration of 2 minutes, and two of them (1000 cps) had an intensity of 88 db and ended with electric shock. The other five tones had a frequency of 900 cps and a duration of two minutes and never ended with shock.

At the start of discrimination conditioning the 900-cps tone had an intensity of 70 db. Although in silence a tone of this intensity would clearly be audible to the pigeon, the ventilation system within the experi-

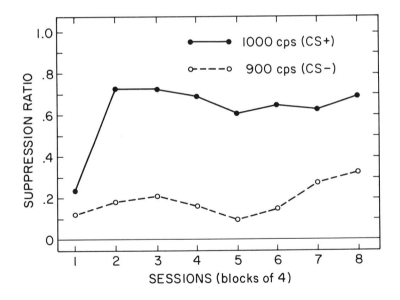

FIG. 7–13.   The development of conditioned suppression during discrimination pro-cedures in which CS— (900 cps) was gradually faded-in along the dimension of acoustic intensity. The intensity of CS— in successive blocks of sessions was 70, 70, 72, 74, 75, 77, 82, and 88 db re 0.0002 dynes per cm². The intensity of CS+ (1000 cps) was 88 db throughout these procedures.

mental chamber was such that the noise level was itself at approximately 70 db. Thus, in the initial conditioning session we were presenting a 70-db tone against a background of 70-db noise. Under those conditions the tone is audible to the human observer, but it sounds quite weak when compared to an 88-db tone presented under the same conditions. As in the earlier discrimination experiments the subjects received 32 sessions of conditioning.

Figure 7–13 shows the mean acquisition function for the four birds that were subjected to this conditioning sequence. In general, the fade-in procedure did not eliminate the tendency to suppress in the presence of CS−, and by the end of the conditioning series the several subjects were suppressing to CS− at a level that was comparable to that exhibited by birds conditioned without the use of fade-in procedures. Because the acquisition performance of the birds conditioned with fade-in was so similar to that of birds conditioned without fade-in, we were quite unprepared for the generalization gradients that were obtained subsequently. Figure 7–14 shows the generalization gradients from six test sessions.

In each session the entire sequence of seven tones was presented in

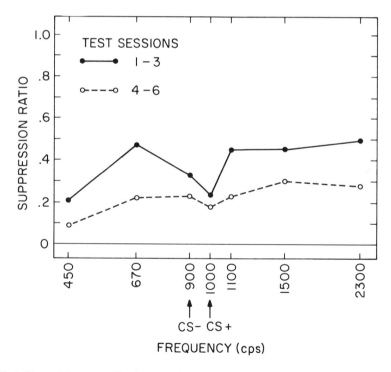

FIG. 7–14. The generalization gradient after discrimination procedures in which the CS− (900 cps) was faded-in along the dimension of acoustic intensity.

random order (without shock) while the subject pecked the key on the previously established VI schedule of food reinforcement. As in previous studies, during generalization tests all tones had an intensity of 88 db. The gradients are low, relatively flat, and exhibit minima in the region of CS— and CS+. Moreover, extinction of suppression appears to proceed much more rapidly than in any of our earlier studies.

Our initial reaction in the face of these unusual gradients was to check carefully our testing procedure. At first we thought that the shape of the gradients might reflect the ordering of the tones during the several test sessions. However, the order of tone presentations was obtained by randomly selecting successive rows from a 7 × 7 Latin square, and the initial three sequences used in the fade-in study happened to be identical to those used in the previous discrimination experiment in which the subjects were exposed to continuous reinforcement during CS—. On this basis it seemed apparent that the sequence of test tone presentations could not be the sole factor responsible for the shape of the gradients.

Our next thought was that perhaps the fade-in birds had experienced some form of acoustical trauma and as a result they had incurred an auditory deficit in the region of 900 to 1000 cps. This seemed most unlikely, but partly as a check and partly in an effort to obtain additional data, we decided to recondition the birds and then test them again. This time, however, the subjects were conditioned to suppress to a 1000-cps tone, and were not exposed to CS—. In a given session they received seven 1000-cps tones each ending with electric shock. After six sessions of reconditioning, the use of shock was again discontinued, and the seven test tones were presented while the birds pecked the key for food. Figure 7–15 shows the resulting generalization gradient. As can be seen, the gradient was comparable to the symmetrical ones usually obtained from subjects conditioned on 1000 cps only, and there are no residual effects of the prior discrimination procedures.

At the time, these results seemed to make it clear that the unusual gradients of Fig. 7–14 were probably a consequence of the procedures used to condition the subjects, but in the absence of specific experimental evidence it was impossible to say what aspect of the conditioning procedures was the critical factor. For a period, we entertained the hypothesis that our data was somehow a mirror image of the kind of data obtained when comparable procedures are applied using positive reinforcement only. Terrace (1966) had found that discrimination training using fade-in does not yield the peak shift phenomenon, whereas Hanson (1959) had found that discrimination training using standard procedures typically produces shift in the peak of the gradient.

In contrast, our data seemed to suggest that in the context of a conditioned suppression experiment, discrimination conditioning using

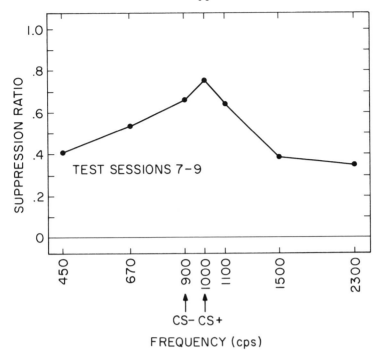

FIG. 7–15.   The generalization gradient after fade-in procedures were followed by 6 sessions of reconditioning on the 1000-cps tone only.

fade-in leads to peak shift, whereas standard discrimination procedures do not. This mirror-image notion was seductive because Hanson and Terrace's work had employed rate of response as a measure of stimulus control whereas our own work employed suppression of rate as the measure of stimulus control. There were certain difficulties, however. First, our data (Fig. 7–14) did not really exhibit a peak shift so much as a general depression of the gradient with minimum suppression occurring in the region of 900 to 1000 cps. Second, Terrace (1966) had argued the peak shift is intimately associated with the phenomenon of behavior contrast (i.e., an increase in response tendency during CS+ that occurs when the subject makes unreinforced responses to CS−). Nowhere in our data did we see any signs of contrast, or even contrastlike processes.

All of this suggested that the explanation of our findings would probably reflect variables quite different from those presumably responsible for peak shift in experiments involving positive reinforcement. In essence, it seemed that if we were to explain our data, it would be necessary to scrutinize more carefully the conditions that were specific to the kinds of aversive procedures that we were employing.

The Effects of Late Discrimination Conditioning

One distinctive feature of the fade-in procedure used in the previous experiment was that subjects were first exposed to the CS— that subsequently would be employed in tests for stimulus generalization near the end of the acquisition process. All of the earlier CS—'s were at a lower intensity and hence, strictly speaking, they were not identical to the ones used during the tests for stimulus generalization. In order to examine the effects of this variable, a group of birds ($N = 3$) were conditioned to suppress to a 1000-cps tone using procedures identical to those for the control birds whose data were shown in Fig. 7–9. In the present experiment the subjects received two 1000-cps tones (2-min. duration) that ended with electric shock while they pecked the key for food; and like the procedure for the control birds in the earlier experiment, the tones were located in the same temporal positions as the CS+'s for birds subjected to conditioned discrimination with fade-in. In the present case, however, no CS—'s were presented at any time during the initial acquisition. After 32 sessions of conditioning, shock was disconnected and the birds were tested for stimulus generalization for three sessions. They then were placed on discrimination procedures for eight sessions during each of which they received two 1000-cps tones ending with shock and five 900-cps tones without shock. Both tones had an intensity of 88 db throughout this phase of the conditioning. A second test for stimulus generalization was then given. Following the second generalization test, the birds were given eight more sessions of discrimination conditioning, and finally they received a third generalization test. Figure 7–16 shows the acquisition function during the initial conditioning to suppress to a 1000-cps tone and during the later conditioning on the discrimination between the 1000-cps warning signal and the 900-cps "safe" stimulus.

Figure 7–17 shows the generalization gradients obtained in the three tests. The initial gradient of stimulus generalization following acquisition to 1000 cps only is essentially the same as obtained in earlier experiments. When discrimination conditioning was finally begun, the birds (as might be expected) showed very little initial tendency to discriminate, but, unexpectedly, they showed no signs of subsequently acquiring the discrimination (see Fig. 7–16). Moreover, as seen in Fig. 7–17 the discrimination conditioning had essentially no effect on the gradient of stimulus generalization. This finding made it clear that late contact with the CS— was not the sole factor in determining the unusual gradient that was seen in Fig. 7–14. In addition, the results provided us with an insight into the nature of discrimination formation in aversive controls. Apparently, if CS— is close to CS+ on the generalization gradient and CS+ already

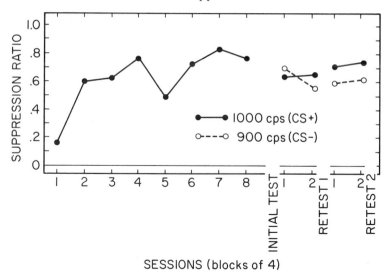

FIG. 7–16.   The development of conditioned suppression to a 1000-cps tone (the solid line) and the levels of suppression to the 1000-cps tone and to a 900-cps safe stimulus (the dashed lines) during late discrimination conditioning. The legends indicate the points at which generalization gradients were assessed.

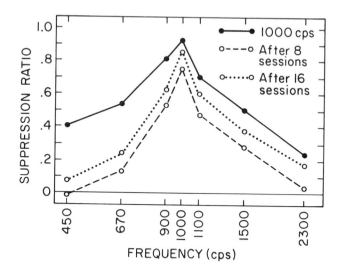

FIG. 7–17.   The gradient of stimulus generalization following late discrimination procedures. The solid line indicates the gradient following conditioning to 1000 cps only. The dashed line shows the gradient after eight sessions of late discrimination procedures. The dotted line shows the gradient after a total of 16 sessions of late discrimination procedures.

generates substantial suppression, the formation of a discrimination is extremely difficult. Of course, it is possible that if conditioning had been continued for a large number of additional sessions these birds might have learned the discrimination, but it is also clear that the formation of the discrimination would require many more sessions than were necessary to develop the same discrimination when the CS− was introduced in the beginning of conditioning.

A Partial Replication of Discrimination Conditioning Using Fade-In Procedures

In order to understand better the events which transpire during discrimination conditioning with fade-in (and to convince ourselves more fully that the resulting gradient was not, in fact, artifactual), we conditioned a new group of four birds on the discrimination using fade-in procedures, but in the present instance, the CS− was faded-in from noise. As in our previous discrimination experiment, the warning signal was a 2-minute 1000-cps tone, and the fade-in procedure was designed to establish a 2-minute 900-cps tone as the safe stimulus.

In each of the early conditioning sessions the subject received two 88-db 1000-cps tones ending with shock, and five 88-db noise signals that were free of shock. As sessions progressed, a weak 900-cps tone was presented throughout the noise signals, and in each session its intensity was progressively increased until its intensity was equal to that of the noise. Finally, in subsequent sessions the noise was gradually reduced in intensity until it was removed altogether, so that at the end of the conditioning procedure these subjects were exposed to the same stimulus configuration as birds subjected to discrimination procedures without fade-in (i.e., an 88-db 1000-cps tone ending with shock and an 88-db 900-cps tone that did not end with shock). Figure 7–18 shows the mean acquisition functions that were generated by these procedures.

In general, these functions are very similar to those obtained in our first fade-in experiment, but the levels of suppression during CS− are lower, especially during the early and middle phase of conditioning.

Figure 7–19 shows the initial gradients generated by this procedure (the solid line) and it also shows a second gradient (the dashed line) obtained during an additional sequence of sessions in which unsignalled shock was administered during periods of total darkness (time-outs) that were presented in the intervals between the several test tones. The purpose of these operations was to determine if the administration of a "stress" condition would cause a recovery of the gradient (as it had in our earlier retention study). As seen in Fig. 7–19, it does, and indeed the gradient obtained during the stress condition is even higher than the

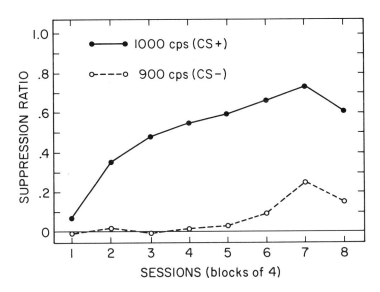

FIG. 7–18.   The development of conditioned suppression to a 1000 cps CS+ during discrimination procedures in which the CS— (900 cps) was gradually faded-in from noise.

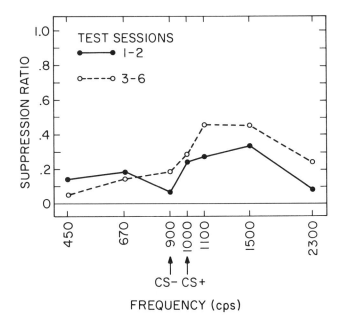

FIG. 7–19.   Gradients of stimulus generalization following discrimination procedures in which the CS— (900 cps) was faded-in from noise.

initial test gradient obtained previously. What at the time seemed even more interesting, however, was the finding that both of the gradients in Fig. 7–19 exhibited the same kinds of unusual trends that were seen in our initial fade-in experiment. Though we still did not understand the mechanisms responsible for the effect, the present independent replication made it perfectly clear that the results were not the product of some undetected artifact.

A Theoretical Treatment of Discrimination Effects in Conditioned Suppression

At the completion of this last fade-in experiment we found ourselves in the uncomfortable position of possessing a considerable amount of reliable and interesting data, but we had no conceptual framework into which this information might fit. Figure 7–20 summarizes the basic problem.

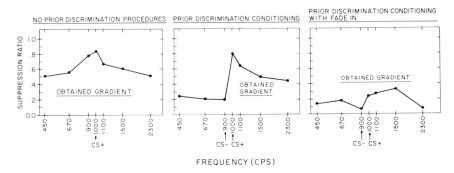

FIG. 7–20.   Gradients of stimulus generalization of conditioned suppression after each of three conditioning procedures. The gradient to the left was obtained after conditioning to a 1000-cps tone only. The middle gradient was obtained after discrimination procedures in which a 1000-cps tone served as CS+ and 900-cps tone served as a safe stimulus (CS−). The gradient to the right was obtained after discrimination procedures throughout which the CS+ (900 cps) was gradually faded-in from noise.

The left panel shows the initial gradient from the control subjects in our first discrimination experiment (Hoffman & Fleshler, 1964). It is typical of the gradients produced by subjects conditioned to suppress to CS+ only. The middle panel shows the initial gradient generated by the discrimination birds from that study. It is representative of the gradient generated by more or less standard discrimination procedures in which the subjects are exposed to both CS+'s and CS−'s throughout the acquisition process. The right panel shows the initial gradient generated by the discrimination procedure in which CS— was faded-in from noise. It illustrates the basic features of the gradient that is generated by the fade-in procedure.

In an effort to explain these very different gradients we carefully reexamined the behaviors that had appeared during acquisition. Figure 7–21 shows the performances during the acquisition procedures. The sequence of boxes under the curves provides a schematic representation of the stimulus configuration for CS— during the several stages of conditioning. The most obvious characteristic of these three functions is that

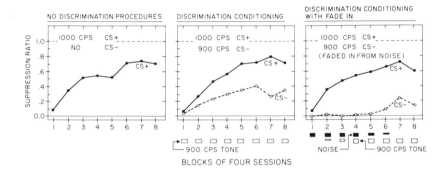

FIG. 7–21. The course of acquisition of conditioned suppression during each of three conditioning procedures. The function to the left was obtained during conditioning to a 1000-cps tone only. The solid line in the middle section indicates suppression to the CS+ (1000 cps) during conditioning procedures in which the CS+ always ended with shock and the CS— (900 cps) never ended with shock. The dashed line indicates the suppression of the CS— throughout these procedures. The solid line to the right indicates the suppression to CS+ (1000 cps) during discrimination procedures in which the CS— (900 cps) was faded-in from noise. The dashed line indicates the suppression to the several CS— stimulus configurations throughout conditioning. The rectangles under the functions provide a schematic representation of the CS— stimulus configuration during the several stages of the conditioning procedures.

acquisition of suppression to the 1000-cps tone is essentially the same under the three conditioning procedures. Apparently, regardless of the conditioning procedure, the development of conditioned suppression to the 1000-cps tone followed a single course. The tone gradually acquired the capacity to suppress ongoing key pecks, and the functions describing the acquisition process appear to approach an asymptote of approximately .8. On the basis of these and the other replications of these procedures (described earlier), it is apparent that during the acquisition of conditioned suppression the presence or absence of a CS— and the use of various discrimination conditioning procedures have essentially no effect on the level of suppression to CS+. Moreover, as seen in Fig. 7–21, the level of suppression to CS— at the end of the fade-in procedure is only slightly lower than the terminal levels obtained when CS− was presented without fade-in. This means that explanations of the differences in the gradients produced by the several procedures must take account of the differential histories of the birds rather than simply noting the performance at the end of those histories.

When we sought to take account of these histories, it quickly became apparent that the major effect of the fade-in procedure was that CS− produced relatively little suppression during the initial phases of conditioning. This was especially evident in the fourth block of sessions. As seen in the right-hand section of Fig. 7–21, the combination of a 900-cps tone and noise produced essentially no suppression. Whereas, at the same stage of conditioning, birds conditioned without fade-in were exhibiting considerable suppression to the same 900-cps tone. (Note the middle section of Fig. 7–21.) At first thought there appeared to be at least two ways to explain this difference. On the one hand, it seemed possible that noise was sufficiently different from the 1000-cps tone so that it controlled very little generalized conditioned suppression. If, in addition, the subject attended only to noise when presented with noise plus tone, very little suppression should occur. The second possibility was that, during presentations of noise and tone combined, the subject attended to both stimuli, but because of its previous history as a "safe" stimulus, the noise was serving to inhibit any generalized suppression tendencies that the 900 cps might control at the time.

In evaluating these possibilities, it seemed quite unlikely that the subjects were failing to attend to tone. The tone was always clearly audible when human observers listened to the several combinations of noise plus tone. Moreover, since the pigeon's audiogram is quite similar to that of the human, there was no *a priori* reason to believe that in the pigeon the tone would be masked by the noise. Finally, the details of the acquisition functions and the findings that the subjects suppressed very little to the 900-cps tone as long as any noise was present (note block 6 in the right section of Fig. 7–21) all suggested that an inhibitory-like phenomenon was involved. Accordingly, we turned to the concept of inhibition in an attempt to comprehend the several facets of our data.

Our theoretical interpretation of the several gradients seen in Fig. 7–20 was based on the proposition that during its pairing with shock, the 1000-cps tone acquires the capacity to control a CER. In accordance with our earlier discussion of the suppression ratio we assumed that the suppression ratio provides a quantitative index of the strength of this control. According to these assumptions the generalization gradient in the left panel of Fig. 7–20 is a reflection of an underlying gradient of excitation for a CER. As was noted above, the differences among the acquisition functions for the several discrimination conditioning procedures had suggested that during discrimination conditioning, CS− may acquire inhibitory properties. The theoretical account of the gradients employs this concept by assuming that when a given stimulus is repeatedly presented without shock, and these presentations occur in the same sessions as other stimuli which are presented with shock, the safe stimulus can acquire the capacity to inhibit the response (CER) that is conditioned to the warning signal.[3] Moreover, it is also assumed that like excitation, inhibition generalizes to stimuli which are like but not identical to the safe stimulus. Finally, it is assumed that when a stimulus on the wing of the generalization gradient of inhibition is repeatedly paired with electrical shock, the stimulus loses its capacity to inhibit the CER, and moreover, stimuli which are like it also lose their inhibitory properties but to a lesser degree. In order to identify the effects of this latter procedure, and to keep it separate from the concept of excitation per se, we have chosen to call the phenomenon "conditioned disinhibition." The term "disinhibition" is used because the procedure counteracts previously developed inhibitory tendencies; the term "conditioned" is used to differentiate the present effect from Pavlovian disinhibition and to take cognizance of the fact that the reduction in inhibition is a result of a procedure in which an inhibitory stimulus is paired with electric shock. As noted above, like excitation and inhibition, conditioned disinhibition

---

[3] Since completing this manuscript, we have performed an additional experiment which bears on these issues. In one aspect of that study, four experimentally naive pigeons were trained to key peck, adapted to tone, and subjected to the same conditioning procedures as the control birds in our first discrimination experiment. Thus, as in the earlier study, the present subjects received 32 sessions in which an 88-db 2-minute 1000-cps tone ending with shock was periodically presented while the birds pecked a key on a VI schedule of food reinforcement. At the completion of the conditioning sessions, the use of shock was discontinued and, in a single test session, each subject was exposed to the CS+ used in training (i.e., the 1000-cps tone), to a novel 2-minute 88-db random noise, and to a complex stimulus consisting of the 2-minute noise and the 2-minute tone presented simultaneously. The three kinds of test stimuli were presented in random order and each kind of stimulus was presented twice.

The course of acquisition of conditioned suppression was similar to that of other birds subjected to these conditioning procedures and like subjects in prior studies, the mean suppression ratio at the completion of conditioning was approximately .80. The mean suppression ratios for the several kinds of test stimuli were as follows:

> 1000-cps tone (0.84)
>
> Noise (0.24)
>
> Noise plus tone (0.76)

Statistical evaluation of the differences in suppression to the several stimuli revealed that although the level of suppression to noise alone was significantly greater than zero, the addition of noise to tone did not produce a statistically significant change in the level of suppression controlled by tone alone.

This finding makes it clear that the occurrence of a novel stimulus (i.e., noise) during a CS+ (tone) does not necessarily produce a reduction in the level of suppression controlled by the CS+; and, what is even more germane to the interpretation of the present sequence of experiments, it means that the reduced suppression in the presence of noise obtained in our second fade-in study cannot be described as an example of Pavlovian external inhibition. If it were, the operations of the present control experiment ought to have maximized the external inhibition effect, and nothing of this sort happened.

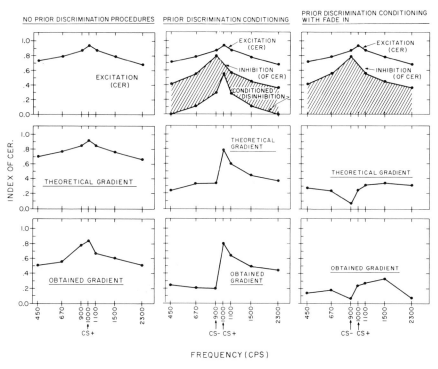

FIG. 7–22. Theoretical analysis of the gradients of stimulus generalization after each of three different conditioning procedures. The obtained gradients are the ones previously shown in Fig. 7–20.

is also assumed to generalize to stimuli similar but not identical to the signal which was paired with shock.

Figure 7–22 shows the set of hypothetical gradients of excitation, inhibition, and conditioned disinhibition that are assumed to result from each of the several conditioning procedures. In generating these hypothetical gradients we made no attempt to employ formal quantitative theory. Rather, we assumed that gradients of excitation, inhibition, and conditioned disinhibition ought to be exponential in form (as Hull's theory asserts). But beyond that, the hypothetical gradients represented our best guess as to the way such gradients ought to look. We did, however, restrict ourselves to using the same hypothetical gradients in all three figures. Thus, the pairing of a 1000-cps tone with shock was assumed to generate the same gradient of excitation whether that pairing occurred in the context of a discrimination experiment or not, and the presentation of a "safe" stimulus during acquisition was assumed to generate the same gradient of inhibition whether those presentations involved fade-in or not.

The conditioning procedure that involved presentation of the 1000-

cps tone with shock and no CS— presumably generates the gradient of excitation seen in the top left section of Fig. 7–22. When, however, the 1000-cps tone is paired with shock and in the same session a 900-cps tone is presented without shock, gradients of excitation, inhibition, and conditioned disinhibition are generated. The gradient of excitation arises because of the pairing of the 1000-cps tone with shock. The gradient of inhibition is generated by the presentation of the 900-cps tone without shock, and the gradient of conditioned disinhibition (centering at 1000 cps) is generated because throughout the acquisition process, a stimulus on the wing of the gradient of inhibition (namely the 1000-cps tone) repeatedly ended with shock.[4] As seen in the top right-hand section of Fig. 7–22, the conditioning procedure in which the CS— was faded-in from noise is assumed to generate a gradient of excitation and a gradient of inhibition, but no gradient of conditioned disinhibition. The rationale here is that during the early stages of acquisition the noise acquired control over inhibition. Fading the 900-cps tone into noise presumably endowed the 900-cps tone with inhibitory capacities. Then, when the noise was finally faded-out, there were very few sessions during which the 900-cps tone was presented alone. Thus, there were relatively few trials in which a stimulus (the 1000-cps tone) on the wing of the generalization gradient of inhibition (around 900 cps) was paired with shock. In essence, the lack of a disinhibitory gradient results from the fact that the 900-cps tone did not become an inhibitor until late in the discrimination procedure, and hence there was little opportunity for conditioned disinhibition to develop.

The middle section of Fig. 7–22 shows the theoretical gradients that

[4] On purely logical grounds it would seem appropriate (though conceptually quite cumbersome) to assume that the standard procedures of conditioning a discrimination generate an infinity of additional gradients of excitation and inhibition. (In one sense the gradient of conditioned disinhibition could be described as a second gradient of excitation.) Thus, it is possible to conceptualize a second gradient of inhibition that is everywhere lower than the gradient of conditioned disinhibition and which has its peak at 900 cps. The repeated presentation of the 900-cps tone without shock would satisfy the requirements for its development since those operations involve the presentation of a stimulus on a wing of the gradient of conditioned disinhibition without an accompanying shock. Accordingly, the conditioned disinhibition should be inhibited at 900 cps and the effect should, theoretically, generalize to other similar stimuli. In a similar manner one could postulate a third gradient of excitation with its peak at 1000 cps and which is everywhere lower than the second gradient of inhibition described above. By extending this line of reasoning one can postulate any number of additional gradients of inhibition and excitation. What is important for present purposes is that each of these "additional" gradients is everywhere lower than its predecessor. As a result, the levels of excitation and inhibition reflected by these gradients soon begin to approximate zero. Moreover, when such gradients are, in fact, added to the three in the top middle section of Fig. 7–22, one discovers that the theoretical gradient which is generated bears an even closer resemblance to the obtained data than the theoretical gradient generated by the simplifying assumption that conditioning a discrimination (without fade-in) yields only the three underlying gradients shown here.

result from the various combinations of excitatory, inhibitory, and disinhibitory gradients. The gradient to the left is simply a repetition of the excitatory gradient since there is assumed to be no inhibitory or disinhibitory tendencies generated by conditioning to a single stimulus. The gradient to the right represents the difference between the excitatory and inhibitory tendencies. The middle theoretical gradient was generated in a comparable manner, except that it was assumed that the conditioned disinhibitory tendency subtracts from inhibition. Thus, to obtain this theoretical gradient, the conditioned disinhibition was first subtracted from the inhibition, and the remainder was then subtracted from excitation.

In order to facilitate visual comparisons, the gradients that were shown in Fig. 7–20 are repeated in the bottom section of Fig. 7–22. As can be seen, the obtained and theoretical gradients bear a marked resemblance to each other. Indeed, when these theoretical gradients were first generated, the fit seemed so good that our initial response was one of disbelief. Like most empiricists, we felt a strong tendency to approach any simple account of a complex process with scepticism. In general, however, the value of any theoretical account lies in its capacity to generate testable predictions, and fortunately the present theoretical treatment can generate a number of rather interesting deductions. For example, an examination of the theoretical gradients in Fig. 7–22 suggested that subjects that have been subjected to discrimination conditioning using fade-in procedures should, if the conditioning is continued long enough, begin to exhibit gradients like those of the subjects that have been conditioned without a fade-in procedure. The assumption here is that during continued discrimination conditioning, the 1000-cps tone would repeatedly end with electric shock, and in this fashion a gradient of conditioned disinhibition would emerge. If, however, a gradient of disinhibition is added to the gradients of excitation and inhibition that are assumed to be generated by discrimination conditioning with fade-in, the resulting theoretical gradient is identical to the one that occurs following discrimination conditioning without fade-in.

In order to evaluate this prediction, the birds that had produced the gradient seen in the lower right-hand corner of Fig. 7–22 were subjected to a series of additional discrimination-conditioning sessions in which the CS+ was a 1000-cps tone ending with shock and the CS− was a 900-cps tone that ended without shock. During this procedure and the tests which followed, both tones were at full intensity (88 db).

It will be recalled that after obtaining the gradients seen in the right panel of Fig. 7–20, we had conducted a sequence of additional test sessions involving the presentation of shocks during time-outs. As was shown in Fig. 7–19, the effect was recovery of the gradient, but the peak was still displaced to the right of 1000 cps. It was following this procedure that the above theoretical analysis was developed and that we set out to test its predictions.

Figure 7–23 again shows the gradient obtained when unsignalled shocks were presented during the intervals between tones (labelled the initial gradient). It also shows the two gradients that were obtained (without the use of shock during time-outs) when 15 additional sessions of discrimination conditioning (i.e., 1000-cps tones with shock, 900-cps tones without shock) intervened between successive generalization tests. As seen in Fig. 7–23, the initial gradient has a peak displaced to the right of 1000 cps. With continued discrimination procedures, however, the peak of the gradient shifted back toward 1000 cps. Thus, the prediction based on the theoretical analysis exemplified by Fig. 7–22 was largely confirmed.

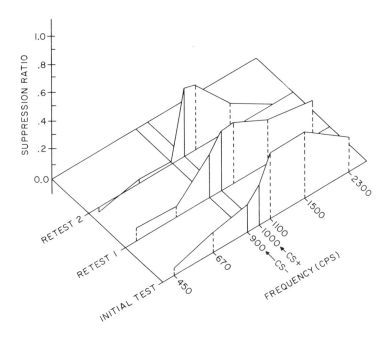

FIG. 7–23.   The effect of additional discrimination conditioning on subjects that previously had been conditioned on the discrimination using fade-in procedures. Fifteen sessions of additional conditioning intervened between the generalization tests.

The next phase of the work represented an attempt to generate empirical gradients of inhibition and of conditioned disinhibition. The success of the theoretical analysis in accounting for the effects of the several conditioning procedures and in predicting the results of continued discrimination conditioning on the fade-in birds made it seem a worthwhile investment of time and energy. Of course, gradients of inhibition have been measured previously, but in every case the behavior inhibited consisted of some form of positively reinforced responding (Jenkins & Harrison, 1962; Honig et al., 1963). In the present circumstances, on the other hand, our interest was focused on inhibition of conditioned suppression where inhibition was to be reflected in an increase in the rate of positively reinforced responses and where inhibition was assumed to represent a mechanism by which CER's could be reduced. To our knowledge, nothing like this had been done before, and we had every anticipation of failure. Still, the postulation of such gradients seemed necessary to account for the effects of discrimination procedures in the conditioned suppression paradigm. And, if these gradients could be empirically derived, they would have important practical implications since basically they would represent a mechanism by which the disruptive effects of anxiety might be reduced. These considerations made the gamble seem worthwhile.

As in previous experiments, four experimentally naive pigeons were trained to peck a key and exposed to a series of 2-minute tones (without shock) so as to adapt them to the stimuli that subsequently were used in the tests for stimulus generalization of inhibition. Next, the birds were exposed to a sequence of 24 conditioning sessions. In each session while the birds pecked the key, a 2-minute 88-db noise ending with electric shock was presented three times, and an 88-db 1000-cps tone ending without shock was presented three times (with the order of stimuli randomized). At the end of this conditioning program, the birds ex-

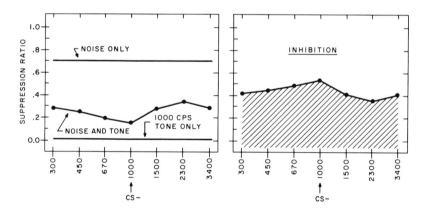

FIG. 7–24.   Empirical gradient of generalization of inhibition. During conditioning of suppression these subjects received a noise ending with shock and a 1000-cps tone (CS−) that never ended with shock. The gradient labelled noise and tone shows the suppression ratios during a sequence of shock-free generalization tests when each of the several tones was presented simultaneously with noise. The lines labelled noise only and tone only indicate the levels of suppression to these stimuli when presented separately during the generalization tests. The gradient to the right shows the degree to which each tone reduced the level of suppression expected from noise only.

hibited a performance in which they suppressed to the noise and showed no suppression to the tone. Moreover, the course of acquisition of suppression to the noise was very similar to that shown for the acquisition of suppression to the 1000-cps tone only, seen in Fig. 7–21. It is also noteworthy that throughout the acquisition process the 1000-cps tone never produced any suppression. As in previous studies, tests for stimulus generalization were conducted without the use of shock. In each test session, the subject was exposed to three kinds of stimuli while pecking the key for food. A given stimulus consisted of either noise alone, tone alone, or a combination of tone plus noise, where both were presented simultaneously.

Figure 7–24 shows the levels of suppression to the noise, to the tone, and to the several test stimuli that consisted of noise plus tone during the four sessions of generalization testing. Noise alone produced a moderate level of suppression. The 1000-cps tone alone produced very little suppression. The combinations of noise and tone produced intermediate levels of suppression, with the lowest level occurring at 1000 cps (the signal which previously served as CS–).[5] The gradient to the right in Fig. 7–24 is based on the difference between suppression to noise alone and suppression to noise plus tone. When plotted in this fashion, the function can be described as an empirical gradient of inhibition of conditioned suppression.

The next step was to determine if it was possible to obtain a gradient of conditioned disinhibition. Following the generalization test upon which Fig. 7–24 is based, the birds were subjected to an additional sequence of four conditioning sessions where in each session they received noise alone ending in electric shock, a 1000-cps tone that did not end in shock, and a 1500-cps tone which ended with electric shock. The rationale here was that inhibition from the 1000-cps tone should generalize to the 1500-cps tone, but since the 1500-cps tone ended with shock, conditioned disinhibition should develop, and this disinhibition should theoretically generalize to tones with higher and lower frequencies. The test for the effects of this procedure involved a sequence of four sessions in which the subjects received noise alone, noise plus tone, or tone alone. As in

---

[5] Wilcoxon matched-pairs signed-ranks tests were used to assess the statistical significance of the observed differences in the levels of suppression to noise only versus the several combinations of noise and tone. The test yielded $T = 0$, $N = 28$, $P<.005$. Thus, it can be concluded that the addition of tone to noise yielded a reliable reduction in the level of suppression. A similar test of the differences between the several combinations of noise and tone versus tone only yielded $T = 9.5$, $N = 28$, $P<.005$. Hence, it can be concluded that the combinations of noise and tone yielded reliably more suppression than tone only. Finally, a Jonckheere test was employed to evaluate the ordered hypothesis that the levels of suppression to the several combinations of noise and tone differ with peak suppression at the extremes of the gradient and minimal suppression at 1000 cps. The test yielded $Z = 1.64$, $P<.05$. Hence, it can be concluded that although the observed differences among the several combinations of noise and tone are small, they are nonetheless statistically significant.

previous tests, no shocks occurred and food was available on the previously established VI schedule of positive reinforcement.

Figure 7–25 shows the levels of suppression to the noise, to the various
combinations of noise plus tone, and to the 1000-cps and 1500-cps tones
presented singly. There is much less inhibition of suppression than was
seen in Fig. 7–24, particularly in the region of 1500 cps. The gradient to
the right in Fig. 7–25 was derived by substracting the gradient to the left
in Fig. 7–24 from the gradient to the left in Fig. 7–25. As would be predicted by the theoretical analyses presented here, the peak of the gradient
of disinhibition is at the tone which was paired with electric shock
(1500 cps).

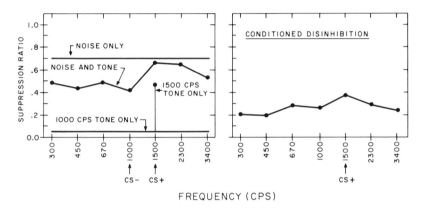

FIG. 7–25.   Empirical gradient of conditioned disinhibition. The gradient marked
noise and tone was obtained from the subjects whose gradient of inhibition was shown
in Fig. 7–24. The lines labelled noise only, tone only, and the point labelled 1500 cps
only show the levels of suppression after a sequence of additional conditioning sessions
during which subjects received noise ending with shock, a 1000-cps tone that did not
end with shock, and a 1500-cps tone that ended with shock. The gradient labelled
conditioned disinhibition was obtained by subtracting the gradient labelled noise and
tone in Fig. 7–24 from the gradient labelled noise and tone in Fig. 7–25.

Figure 7–26 summarizes the results of this last series of procedures and
compares the empirical gradients of inhibition and conditioned disinhibition with the theoretical gradients that were originally used to account
for the effects of the several discrimination procedures. The obtained
gradients of inhibition and those of conditioned disinhibition are flatter
than the theoretical gradients, but they exhibit the same general trends.
In this respect it is noteworthy that the theoretical gradients are assumed
to inhibit different levels of excitation, whereas the obtained gradients
were generated under circumstances where the tones necessarily inhibited
a constant level of excitation (i.e., the level to noise only). Presumably,
given a gradient rather than a constant level of excitation, the similarity

between the obtained functions and those predicated on theory would be even more striking.

These results are still sufficiently new so that their full implications are not yet clear. Nevertheless, our findings seem to suggest new ways of looking at discrimination processes in aversive controls, and at the least

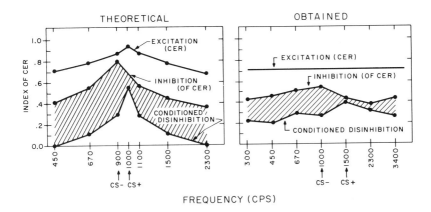

FREQUENCY (CPS)

FIG. 7–26.   Theoretical and empirical gradients of inhibition and conditioned disinhibition. The gradients to the left are from the top middle section of Fig. 7–22. The gradients to the right are from Figs. 7–24 and Fig. 7–25.

they point to questions that need to be explored. For example, our interpretations suggest that a stimulus can become inhibitory in at least two ways: (1) if it serves as CS— from the beginning of acquisition; or (2) if it is faded-in from some other safe signal that was presented during the early phases of acquisition. Are there other ways to make a stimulus inhibitory? Our experiment on late discrimination conditioning (see Figs. 7–16 and 7–17) suggested that if CS— is close to CS+ on the generalization gradient, and if CS— is first encountered well after CS+ has acquired control over suppression, the discrimination is not readily learned. This raises the question of how one might effectively develop a late discrimination. Would, for instance, a late fade-in technique be effective? Or alternatively, might it be appropriate to extinguish suppression to CS+ prior to initiating late discrimination procedures? How stable is the inhibition phenomenon? Would the effects of discrimination procedures be retained as well as the effects of conditioning to CS+ only? Clearly, these and numerous other questions remain to be answered.

In certain respects, the inhibition of conditioned suppression obtained here seems quite comparable to the process Wolpe (1960) describes as reciprocal inhibition. Moreover, Mowrer (1960) has postulated a second type of secondary reinforcement in which the reinforcing properties of the stimulus are based on its capacity to act as a fear reducer. Mowrer noted, however, that at the time, experimental support for the proposition was largely unavailable.

Recent experiments in Solomon's laboratory, however, (Rescorla & LoLordo, 1965) have begun to supply that evidence. Their approach employed a Pavlovian conditioning paradigm in which dogs previously trained to hurdle jump to avoid shock were exposed to a warning signal that ended with shock and a "safe" signal that never ended with shock. It was found that when these signals were subsequently presented during extinction of the avoidance task, the warning signal increased the response rate whereas the "safe" signal yielded a rate decrease. They suggested that the avoidance decrement was a reflection of the "safe" signal's capacity to inhibit the fear reaction that presumably was supporting the avoidance behavior. Our own data are in complete accord with those findings despite the gross differences in experimental technique.

When we initiated our investigations of conditioned suppression we did so in the hope of acquiring information that might ultimately prove useful in the clinical management of anxiety and its related symptoms. The route we took has provided us with a long hard look at the consequences of aversive procedures, and what we saw was seldom encouraging. We found that aversive conditioning could lead to a variety of disruptive behavioral consequences, and apparently, these effects can persist throughout a significant portion of the subject's life. The recent focus on inhibitory processes in our own and other laboratories, however, seems to cast a new light on the area. There is every reason to expect that future work on inhibition will lead to the development of new insights into aversive controls and into practical techniques for alleviating its unfortunate behavioral manifestations.

REFERENCES

BRADY, J. V., & HUNT, H. F. An experimental approach to the analysis of emotional behavior. *Journal of Psychology*, 1955, **40**, 313–324.

BROWN, J. S. The generalization of approach responses as a function of stimulus intensity and strength of motivation. *Journal of Comparative Psychology*, 1942, **33**, 209–226.

CARLTON, P. L., & DIDAMO, P. Some notes on the control of conditioned suppression. *Journal of the Experimental Analysis of Behavior*, 1960, **3**, 255–258.

CHURCH, R. M. The varied effects of punishment on behavior. *Psychological Review*, 1963, **70**, 369–402.

CLARK, F. C. The effect of deprivation and frequency of reinforcement on variable-interval responding. *Journal of the Experimental Analysis of Behavior*, 1958, **1**, 221–228.

ESTES, W. K. & SKINNER, B. F. Some quantitative properties of anxiety. *Journal of Experimental Psychology*, 1941, **29**, 390–400.

FLESHLER, M., & HOFFMAN, H. S. A progression for generating variable-interval schedules. *Journal of the Experimental Analysis of Behavior,* 1962, **5**, 529–530.

GELLER, I., SIDMAN, M., & BRADY, J. V. The effect of electroconvulsive shock on a conditioned emotional response: A control for acquisition recency. *Journal of Comparative and Physiological Psychology,* 1955, **48**, 130–131.

GYNTHER, M. D. Differential eyelid conditioning as a function of stimulus similarity and strength of response to the CS. *Journal of Experimental Psychology,* 1957, **53**, 408–416.

HANSON, H. M. Effects of discrimination training on stimulus generalization. *Journal of Experimental Psychology,* 1959, **58**, 321–333.

HOFFMAN, H. S. A flexible connector for delivering shock to pigeons. *Journal of the Experimental Analysis of Behavior,* 1960, **3**, 330.

HOFFMAN, H. S., & FLESHLER, M. Stimulus factors in aversive controls: The generalization of conditioned suppression. *Journal of the Experimental Analysis of Behavior,* 1961, **4**, 371–378.

HOFFMAN, H. S., & FLESHLER, M. Stimulus aspects of aversive controls: Stimulus generalization of conditioned suppression following discrimination training. *Journal of the Experimental Analysis of Behavior,* 1964, **7**, 233–239.

HOFFMAN, H. S., & FLESHLER, M. Stimulus aspects of aversive controls: The effects of response contingent shock. *Journal of the Experimental Analysis of Behavior,* 1965, **8**, 89–96.

HOFFMAN, H. S., FLESHLER, M., & JENSEN, P. Stimulus aspects of aversive controls: The retention of conditioned suppression. *Journal of the Experimental Analysis of Behavior,* 1963, **6**, 575–583.

HOFFMAN, H. S., & SELEKMAN, W. Stability of response rates maintained by positive reinforcement. *Perceptual and Motor Skills,* 1967, **24**, 91–93.

HOFFMAN, H. S., SELEKMAN, W., & FLESHLER, M. Stimulus aspects of aversive controls: Long term effects of suppression procedures. *Journal of the Experimental Analysis of Behavior,* 1966, **9**, 659–662. (a)

HOFFMAN, H. S., SELEKMAN, W., & FLESHLER, M. Stimulus factors in aversive controls: Conditioned suppression after equal training on two stimuli. *Journal of the Experimental Analysis of Behavior,* 1966, **9**, 649–653. (b)

HONIG, W. K., BONEAU, C. A., BURSTEIN, K. R., & PENNYPACKER, H. S. Positive and negative generalization gradients obtained after equivalent training conditions. *Journal of Comparative and Physiological Psychology,* 1963, **56**, 111–116.

HONIG, W. K., THOMAS, D. R., & GUTTMAN, N. Differential effects of continuous extinction and discrimination training on the generalization gradient. *Journal of Experimental Psychology,* 1959, **58**, 145–152.

HOVLAND, C. I. The generalization of conditioned responses: I. The sensory generalization of conditioned response with varying frequencies of tone. *Journal of General Psychology,* 1937, **17**, 125–148. (a)

HOVLAND, C. I. The generalization of conditioned responses: III. Extinction, spontaneous recovery and disinhibition of conditioned and of generalized responses. *Journal of Experimental Psychology,* 1937, **21**, 47–62. (b)

HOVLAND, C. I. The generalization of conditioned responses: IV. The effects of varying amounts of reinforcement upon the degree of generalization of conditioned responses. *Journal of Experimental Psychology,* 1937, **21**, 261–276. (c)

HULL, C. L. *Principles of behavior.* New York: Appleton-Century, 1943.

JENKINS, H. M., & HARRISON, R. H. Effect of discrimination training on auditory generalization. *Journal of Experimental Psychology,* 1960, **59**, 246–253.

JENKINS, H. M., & HARRISON, R. H. Generalization gradients of inhibition following auditory discrimination learning. *Journal of the Experimental Analysis of Behavior,* 1962, **5**, 435–441.

KALISH, H. I., & GUTTMAN, N. Stimulus generalization after equal training on two stimuli. *Journal of Experimental Psychology,* 1957, **53**, 139–144.

KIMBLE, G. A. *Hilgard and Marquis' conditioning and learning.* (2nd ed.) New York: Appleton-Century-Crofts, 1961.

LITTMAN, R. A. Conditioned generalization of the galvanic skin reaction to tones. *Journal of Experimental Psychology,* 1949, **39**, 868–882.

LYON, D. O. Frequency of reinforcement as a parameter of conditioned suppression. *Journal of the Experimental Analysis of Behavior,* 1963, **6**, 95–98.

LYON, D. O. Some notes on conditioned suppression and reinforcement schedules. *Journal of the Experimental Analysis of Behavior,* 1964, **7**, 289–291.

LYON, D. O., & FELTON, M. Conditioned suppression and variable ratio reinforcement. *Journal of the Experimental Analysis of Behavior,* 1966, **9**, 245–248.

MEDNICK, S. A. A learning theory approach to research in schizophrenia. *Psychological Bulletin,* 1958, **55**, 316–327.

MOWRER, O. H. *Learning theory and behavior.* New York: Wiley, 1960.

RAZRAN, G. H. S. Studies in configural conditioning. VI. Comparative extinction and forgetting of pattern and of single-stimulus conditioning. *Journal of Experimental Psychology,* 1939, **24**, 432–438.

RESCORLA, R. A., & LoLORDO, V. M. Inhibition of avoidance behavior. *Journal of Comparative and Physiological Psychology,* 1965, **59**, 406–412.

SIDMAN, M. Normal sources of pathological behavior. *Science,* 1960, **132**, 61–68.

STEIN, L., SIDMAN, M., & BRADY, J. V. Some effects of two temporal variables on conditioned suppression. *Journal of the Experimental Analysis of Behavior,* 1958, **1**, 153–162.

TERRACE, H. S. Stimulus control. In W. K. Honig (Ed.), *Operant behavior: Areas of research and application.* New York: Appleton-Century-Crofts, 1966. Pp. 271–344.

THOMAS, D. R., OST, J., & THOMAS, D. Stimulus generalization as a function of the time between training and testing procedures. *Journal of the Experimental Analysis of Behavior,* 1960, **3**, 9–14.

WENDT, G. R. Two and one-half year retention of a conditioned response. *Journal of General Psychology,* 1937, **17**, 178–180.

WICKENS, D. D., SCHRODER, H. M., & SNIDE, J. D. Primary stimulus generalization of the GSR under two conditions. *Journal of Experimental Psychology,* 1954, **47**, 52–56.

WOLPE, J. Reciprocal inhibition as the main basis of psychotherapeutic effects. In H. J. Eysenck (Ed.), *Behavior therapy and the neuroses.* New York: Pergamon Press, 1960. Pp. 88–113.

8

Aversive Conditioning and External Stimulus Control[1]

Eliot Hearst

UNIVERSITY OF MISSOURI

The delivery of noxious stimuli to an organism may affect not only the future probability of various responses by the subject, but also the extent to which different stimuli in the external environment control the subject's behavior. Most of the contributors to this volume have focussed on the first of these—what might be called the "response" side—and have shown how aversive events may suppress, facilitate, or shape behavior. In our laboratory the emphasis has been on the "stimulus" side and therefore most of the work has involved procedures traditionally used in the study of stimulus generalization and discrimination. Hoffman's article in this volume reflects a similar and complementary focus.

There are a great variety of questions that someone with this emphasis might innocently ask. For example, what would happen to well-established shock-avoidance behavior if the visual or auditory stimuli present during training were changed? Does behavior controlled by aversive events like electric shock transfer as readily to new stimulus situations as does comparable behavior maintained by food reinforcement? Are discriminations between external stimuli easier to acquire if the behavioral task involves "approach" (delivery of positive reinforcement) or "avoidance" (prevention of an aversive event)? What effects do noxious events have on well-learned discriminations controlled by positive reinforcement? These questions may on the surface appear to be quite amenable to experimental resolution, but unfortunately there are many complications and hidden subtleties that enter the picture. In fact, this chapter is likely to raise more questions than it answers.

Relationships between external stimulus control and noxious stimu-

[1] Many of the experiments described here were performed at the NIMH Clinical Neuropharmacology Research Center, St. Elizabeths Hospital, Washington, D. C. The more recent work has been supported in part by PHS Research Grant MH-12120 from the National Institute of Mental Health. I would like to thank Mrs. Minnie B. Koresko for her assistance in all phases of the research.

lation have received attention in the past. For example, Pavlov (1927) studied one aspect of the problem when he described the "neuropathological disturbances" which develop as a result of extremely powerful and unusual stimuli. Soon after the big storm and flood of September, 1924, in Petrograd had subsided, Pavlov found that not only had well-established salivary CR's been weakened in some of his dogs, but also that formerly excellent discriminations between positive and negative exteroceptive stimuli (such as buzzers, room illumination changes, whistles, and metronomes) were seriously impaired. Some subjects, paradoxically, would salivate the most to negative stimuli, whereas others would drool equally to positive and negative stimuli. Months later, even after recovery of these discriminated salivary CR's, the noiseless presentation of trickling water on the floor of the experimental room sometimes led to a relapse. "Minutest components" of the stimuli associated with the flood thus markedly influenced performance; these minimal cues could evoke "anxious" behavior originally elicited by the flood itself and would also disrupt previously learned appetitive discriminations among a variety of external stimuli in the laboratory.

Naturally, most experimenters have worked with aversive events much less powerful or unusual than Pavlov's flood. Pavlov and his colleagues themselves obtained deteriorations in discriminative performance with electric shock as the noxious event. Some workers have studied the effect of level of "stress" or "anxiety," or clinical grouping, on stimulus generalization gradients (for example, see the experiments reviewed by Mednick & Freedman, 1960, and Kalish, in press). The most frequent conclusion from this work has been that highly anxious human subjects (either classified in that manner by personality test scores or by experimental manipulations such as relatively high shock levels in a classical conditioning paradigm) display flatter exteroceptive generalization gradients than their low-anxious counterparts; in other words, precision of stimulus control often decreases under stress and keen discriminations between external stimuli are impaired. Research with clinical groups has indicated a tendency toward overgeneralization and a difficulty in discrimination tasks for schizophrenic subjects. There is the suggestion from conclusions of this sort, and from pseudoconditioning and sensitization effects with noxious stimuli in classical conditioning (see Kimble, 1961), that aversively-controlled behavior may generalize more widely to new stimuli than other types of behavior.

This general conclusion is in many ways the opposite of what the theory of conflict behavior of Miller (1944, 1959, 1961) would imply. His framework posits a fundamental difference between the stimulus generalization of approach and avoidance behavior, and tests of his notions (primarily performed in the runway apparatus with rats) have repeatedly supported the basic assumption that gradients of approach are flatter than those of avoidance. Thus control by external stimulus dimensions is assumed by Miller to be generally greater for avoidance than for approach behavior and he presents a hypothesis as to why this should occur. But more about that later, since many of our experiments have been designed to isolate factors responsible for the relative slopes of approach and avoidance gradients.

There are two somewhat different aspects of the general area of aversive conditioning and external stimulus control that will be discussed in this chapter. The first section, the longer of the two, concerns a series of experiments to isolate some of the variables important in accounting for the differences in the stimulus generalization of approach and avoidance that we reported some years ago (Hearst, 1960, 1962; Hearst & Pribram, 1964). The second group of experiments involves the effects of contingent and noncontingent shocks on well-learned appetitive discriminations; the resulting phenomena seem somewhat related to the sort of behavioral disruptions that were described by Pavlov following the Petrograd flood, because in both cases aversive events led to a relatively persistent impairment of independently-maintained discriminations based on food reinforcement. There is no basic theory or unitary hypothesis underlying most of the studies I will describe. As of the present time, my colleagues and I prefer the general method (see Platt, 1964) of working simultaneously with several different hypotheses, or "interrelationships among variables," rather than merely testing our favorite one or two.

Stimulus Generalization of Approach and Avoidance

Procedure and Early Results

Initial findings. Our first experiments on this problem proved to require a much more complex analysis than had originally been anticipated. Therefore, several years were subsequently spent in attempts to rule out a variety of confounding factors and alternative explanations for the initial results.

The first study (Hearst, 1960) involved the concurrent determination of appetitive and aversive generalization gradients in individual rhesus monkeys. Each subject was trained to make two responses simultaneously: to press a lever to avoid shock and to pull a chain to obtain food. The monkeys performed both responses in the presence of a bright house light which illuminated the experimental chamber at all times during training. Monkeys first learned to avoid shock on a schedule of the type devised and exhaustively studied by Sidman (see Sidman, 1966, for a complete description), in which each response of the subject postpones shock for a definite period of time(here, 10 sec.); in Sidman's terminology both the response–shock (R–S) and shock–shock (S–S) intervals were 10 seconds. (For convenience we will hereafter abbreviate the Sidman avoidance schedule as SAV.) After avoidance behavior had been acquired, the chain was inserted into the chamber during avoidance sessions and chain pulling was reinforced with food pellets on a variable-interval (VI) schedule with a 2-minute mean interval between reinforcements.

After ten sessions of exposure to these simultaneous schedules of food reward and shock avoidance, monkeys were making both responses at a steady and reliable rate (although absolute rates of avoidance were much higher than variable-interval rates). Then we ran tests for stimulus generalization along the continuum of chamber illumination. During these tests eleven different stimulus illuminations were presented, ten times each in a random order; the brightest one had been the value present during all of training. Extinction was in effect throughout the test and therefore no rewards or shocks were possible. This procedure for studying generalization was very similar to that developed and extensively analyzed by Guttman and Kalish (1956). We tabulated the number of responses at each of the different illuminations during the generalization test. Further details of the training and testing procedures can be secured from previous reports (Hearst, 1960, 1962).

Separate generalization gradients for the two responses are shown in Fig. 8–1 for three monkeys. The results for these monkeys are quite representative of those obtained from subjects in other experiments. Relative generalization (on the ordinates) was scaled by assigning the value of 1.00 to the peak of each gradient and expressing all other response frequencies as decimal fractions of this maximum value.[2]

In every case the avoidance response yielded a very flat gradient and the food-rewarded response a relatively steep gradient along the illumination dimension. Another way of saying the same thing would be to state that the avoidance response generalized strongly to stimuli which are physically different from the training stimulus, whereas the approach response did not. In a purely descriptive sense the dimension of visual illumination appeared to be relevant for one type of response and completely irrelevant for the other.

Effects of differential training.   In the above experiment we utilized the so-called *nondifferential* training procedure (Jenkins & Harrison,

[2] Although the choice of a measure of relative generalization is necessarily somewhat arbitrary, in this chapter we will consistently adopt the method of scaling relative generalization by setting the peak of each gradient equal to 1.00. Another conventional method is to convert each response value on the gradient to a per cent of the total responses at all test stimuli during generalization testing. Conclusions from the studies to be described in this chapter would remain the same if this latter scaling method had been employed instead.

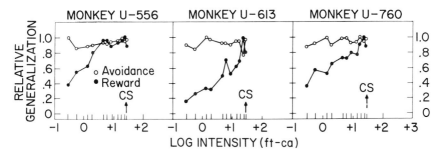

FIG. 8–1.   Gradients of relative generalization following nondifferential training. All three subjects were originally trained in the continuous presence of the brightest light intensity.

From: E. Hearst, "Approach, Avoidance, and Stimulus Generalization," in D. Mostofsky (Ed.), *Stimulus Generalization* (Stanford, Calif.: Stanford University Press, 1965), Fig. 1, p. 333. Reproduced by permission.

1960), in which only one stimulus value is present during training, and responding is reinforced during that stimulus. In order to determine whether a similar difference between gradients for approach and avoidance would occur even after *differential* training, in which reinforcement for responding is possible in one stimulus condition (S+) and extinction is programmed in another stimulus condition (S−), we next gave these three monkeys special discrimination training between two alternately-presented illuminations of the house light.

For two of the subjects a very dim light (S+) signalled the same concurrent schedules of food reward and shock avoidance as before; the former training stimulus (the brightest light) signalled a period (S−) in which the monkey could obtain neither food nor shock. The third monkey continued to have the brightest light as S+; but when the dim intensity (S−) was presented neither food nor shock was possible.

The appetitive half of the discrimination was easy for the monkeys, but many sessions and several procedural changes were required before discrimination indices for the avoidance response reached comparable levels (see Fig. 8–3 for additional data, from a slightly different procedure, on the course of discrimination learning for VI versus SAV responses). When S− rates for both responses were consistently lower than 10% of their respective S+ rates, we tested for postdiscrimination gradients by a procedure very similar to that used in securing Fig 8–1. Figure 8–2 shows these postdiscrimination gradients.

Both gradients were much steeper than before differential training, and the differences between the approach and avoidance gradients diminished greatly. Nevertheless, the same qualitative difference still was present between the two gradients: The avoidance gradient lay above the

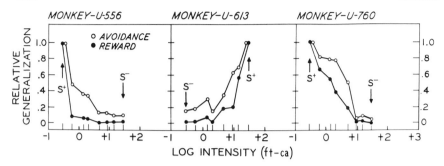

FIG. 8–2.   Postdiscrimination generalization gradients for the three monkeys shown in Fig. 8–1. The dimmest test intensity served as S+ during discrimination training for two subjects, whereas the third subject (U-613) had the brightest test intensity as S+: In all cases the S— intensity was at the opposite end of the intensity continuum.

From: E. Hearst, "Approach, Avoidance, and Stimulus Generalization," in D. Mostofsky (Ed.), *Stimulus Generalization* (Stanford, Calif.: Stanford University Press, 1965), Fig. 2, p. 334. Reproduced by permission.

reward gradient for all subjects. The greater generalization of the avoidance response was particularly apparent in Monkeys U-556 and U-760 for illumination values relatively near S+.

As mentioned above, monkeys were very slow in acquiring the S+ versus S— discrimination for the SAV response; it took a long time for their behavior in S— to extinguish. Relatively slow learning of an avoidance discrimination in the free responding situation has also been reported by others (see, for example, Appel, 1960). Our observation (Fig. 8–1) of the broad initial generalization of SAV certainly implies such an effect on subsequent discrimination learning, since if generalization gradients following nondifferential training are relatively flat, one would predict that subsequent discrimination learning would progress rather slowly. A result supporting this prediction has been obtained by Haber and Kalish (1963) who found in a food-reward situation that pigeons with initially flatter generalization gradients for visual wave length proved harder to train in a subsequent color discrimination than subjects with initially steep gradients.

Some monkeys have served as subjects on a procedure which yielded daily measures of stimulus generalization during the formation of a concurrent approach and avoidance discrimination. These monkeys pressed one lever to avoid shock (RS = SS = 10 sec.), and another lever, mounted below the avoidance lever, to obtain food pellets on a 1-minute VI schedule. Initially the nondifferential procedure was in effect, i.e., the brightest light illuminated the chamber continuously during sessions. After behavior on the two levers had become stable from day to day, we tested for stimulus generalization and obtained results like those in Fig. 8–1; the avoidance gradient was flat and the reward gradient relatively steep.

Next the monkeys were placed on a procedure in which every one of the eight illumination values occurred daily, but the VI and SAV schedules were in force only when the illumination was at its brightest level. The eight stimulus values were presented in a mixed order, approximately 16 times each during 4-hour daily sessions. The procedure was a combination of discrimination training and generalization testing, and consequently gradients could be plotted on each experimental day.

MONKEY #70

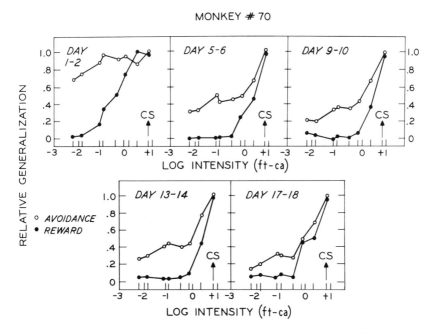

FIG. 8–3. Generalization gradients for concurrent approach and avoidance during successive stages of discrimination training for Monkey No. 70. The S+ was the brightest test intensity (labeled CS on the abscissa); the seven other intensities were S−'s for both approach and avoidance.

From: E. Hearst, "Approach, Avoidance, and Stimulus Generalization," in D. Mostofsky (Ed.), *Stimulus Generalization* (Stanford, Calif.: Stanford University Press, 1965), Fig. 7, p. 340. Reproduced by permission.

Figure 8–3 describes the formation of both discriminations over the course of 18 experimental days in a representative monkey (No. 70). On Days 1–2 the appetitive discrimination was already excellent and after Days 5–6 it did not improve much more. The avoidance discrimination, on the other hand, was quite poor on Days 1–2, it improved gradually throughout the 18 days shown.

Additional controls.   Soon after these initial studies were completed we performed several other experiments in order to eliminate a variety of relatively uninteresting explanations for our observed greater generalization of avoidance than approach. For example, in subsequent studies with rats and monkeys we found that the relative rates of the VI and SAV responses did not matter very much; in tasks with rats, in which VI response rates were higher than avoidance rates (it will be recalled that the opposite held true in Figs. 8–1 through 8–3), gradients still proved significantly flatter for the avoidance response. The type of manipulandum (lever vs. chain) and the relative distance of each from the source of illumination were apparently not critical factors either, nor was the order of training approach or avoidance (i.e., learn-approach-first or learn-avoidance-first). Groups of subjects trained either on approach only or avoidance only (rather than on simultaneous schedules for both responses, as in Figs. 8–1 through 8–3) again yielded flatter gradients for avoidance than for approach. Thus it is also improbable that the earlier results were attributable to unknown response interactions (superstitious chaining) occurring in the two-response situation.

In other experiments, flat reward gradients did not occur even under very high hunger drives; therefore the original slope differences were presumably not due to the specific appetitive motivational levels we happened to select. Experiments with different visual (e.g., dim rather than bright illumination as the training stimulus) or auditory stimuli produced flatter avoidance than approach gradients once again.

These supplementary experiments, and additional data indicating that our initial findings were not merely due to an accidental choice of certain other specific experimental conditions (e.g., shock level, species of subject, etc.), are summarized in Hearst (1965a) in more detail than is possible here.

Experimental Tests of Various Explanations

In a previous discussion of the above results (Hearst, 1965a) several interpretations were suggested which, singly or in combination, might account for our obtained differences between approach and avoidance in the free-operant situation. Since that time additional experiments have been completed in our laboratory to test some of these explanations and their implications for Miller's framework. The emphasis in the following sections will be on recent work, and readers are referred to Hearst (1965a) for more background material and additional discussion of various alternatives.

Internal versus external cues.   Our finding of a greater generalization for avoidance than for approach seems roughly in line with some of the clinical reports and experimental results concerning aversive behavior mentioned in the introduction to this chapter. On the other hand, Miller's theoretical treatment (1944, 1948, 1959) of conflict and displacement, as well as a large number of studies from his laboratory, stress the opposite result; he consistently obtained steeper gradients for avoidance than for approach in a runway situation where he measured the strength of pull of rats toward (approach) or away from (avoidance) a reward-associated or punishment-associated goal box. Miller extended this finding both experimentally and theoretically to exteroceptive gradients other than the spatial one of the runway. The broader generalization of approach than avoidance was attributed by Miller to the relatively greater importance of internal cues in the control of the approach response, i.e., the internal drive stimuli of hunger remain the same at various points in the runway and therefore changes in external stimulation have much less effect than for avoidance behavior, which is said to be principally controlled by external features of the situation.

An explanation in terms of internal cues can be applied to the experiments and diametrically opposite results from our laboratory. Analysts of the dynamics of avoidance behavior, whether or not they are willing to be called two-process theorists, have often stressed non-exteroceptive cues as the important ones controlling the avoidance response. For example, Schoenfeld (1950), Dinsmoor (1954, 1955), and Sidman (1953, 1954) have emphasized the role of proprioceptive or response-produced stimuli as warning signals for avoidance behavior, whereas others like Mowrer (Mowrer, 1960; Mowrer & Keehn, 1958) and Anger (1963) point to the role of temporal discriminations (presumably internally cued) in the Sidman and trace-avoidance situations.[3] Classically-conditioned "fear" is considered by many writers, particularly those labeled two-process theorists (Maier, Seligman, & Solomon, Chapter 10 of this volume; Mowrer, 1960; Rescorla & Solomon, 1967; Solomon & Brush, 1956), to be extremely important in the acquisition, maintenance, and modification of avoidance behavior; sensory feedback from the physiological changes characterizing fear may be another source of conditioned internal stimuli. If a great proportion of the stimuli controlling a given response are in fact internal, then the power of external stimuli might

[3] In a recent series of experiments Rescorla (1968) demonstrated that auditory signals associated with different parts of the R–S interval acquire differential fear-eliciting (late presentation) and fear-inhibiting (early presentation) properties and that a tone which immediately followed ("feedback") each SAV response acts as an inhibitor of fear in subsequent response-independent tests. These results strongly support the idea that temporal factors and proprioceptive feedback from the SAV response can and do function as CS's in a trace conditioning procedure. By this reasoning the stimulus control of SAV behavior ought to be mainly nonexteroceptive in nature.

be expected to be relatively weak. One ought then not be surprised if he obtained a flat SAV gradient along an exteroceptive dimension such as chamber illumination.

Miller has considered the possibility that under certain conditions avoidance gradients may prove to be flatter than approach gradients. He comments (1959, p. 222) that "if the drive motivating avoidance were elicited chiefly by internal cues, which remained relatively constant in different external stimulus contexts, whereas the drive motivating approach was primarily aroused by external cues which changed with the stimulus context," the gradient of approach should be steeper than that of avoidance.

It is clear that Miller's or anyone else's version of the so-called *internal cues hypothesis* is very difficult to test experimentally. Such cues are obviously hard to isolate and independently measure. Therefore, the whole explanation may appear very circular. But certain consequences of the idea are open to test, and we have performed some studies along these lines.

One experimental test (Hearst, Koresko, & Poppen, 1964) involved the realm of positive reinforcement alone. We wanted to determine whether appetitive behavior that is controlled primarily by internal cues exhibits flatter exteroceptive gradients than appetitive behavior that is relatively less dependent on internal cues. An example of food-reinforced behavior that on the surface appears to be greatly dependent on temporal and self-produced stimuli is performance on a differential-reinforcement-of-low-rate (DRL) schedule (Ferster & Skinner, 1957). On this schedule the subject must space or "time" its responses a certain number of seconds apart in order to obtain reinforcement. We compared generalization gradients following DRL training with those following VI training; the latter, it will be remembered, led to relatively steep gradients for the monkeys of Fig. 8–1. Our expectation on the basis of the internal cues hypothesis was that DRL gradients would be the flatter of the two. In a personal communication Miller independently suggested an experimental comparison of this kind as a good indirect test of the internal cues hypothesis for approach-avoidance differences.

Pigeons served as subjects in this study, and they pecked at a disc on which a vertical line (for some subjects) or a horizontal line (other subjects) was projected. The VI birds were trained on a 1-minute VI schedule and the DRL birds on a 6-second DRL schedule. The latter subjects had to pause at least 6 seconds between key-pecking responses in order to obtain grain reinforcement. During generalization testing under extinction conditions, eight tilts of the stimulus line, including the vertical and horizontal orientations, were presented ten times each in a randomized order. The number of key pecks to each stimulus was recorded.

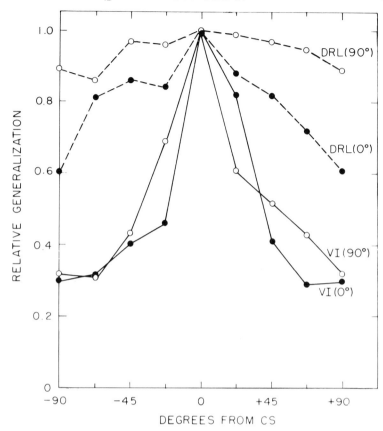

FIG. 8–4.   Gradients of relative generalization for the VI and DRL groups. Each group was composed of two subgroups, one trained with a vertical line as the training stimulus (0°) and the other with a horizontal line (90°).

From: E. Hearst, M. Koresko, & R. Poppen, "Stimulus Generalization and the Response-Reinforcement Contingency," *Journal of the Experimental Analysis of Behavior,* 7, 1964, Fig. 1, p. 371. Copyright 1964 by the Society for the Experimental Analysis of Behavior, Inc., and reproduced by permission.

Figure 8–4 shows that both DRL gradients were much flatter than the VI gradients. Individual gradients for the DRL birds (all included in Hearst et al., 1964) were generally quite flat and irregular, and only 3 out of 16 subjects on DRL actually had the peak of their gradient at the training stimulus value.

These results, in conjunction with very similar findings obtained in an experiment employing a different DRL value (10 sec.) on which birds received a smaller average number of reinforcements than on 1-minute VI (the opposite was true for the 6-second DRL birds), showed clearly that DRL training in a food-reward situation, like SAV training in an avoidance situation, minimizes the control exerted by certain external features of the situation. Visual generalization gradients for both SAV and DRL were much flatter than after 1-minute VI training. The reinforcement schedule during conditioning apparently has a powerful effect on the slope and form of subsequent gradients. Predictions on the basis of the internal cues hypothesis were supported by this experiment.

The above description of DRL performance as a low rate of response does not provide a very complete picture of the behavior of pigeons on this type of schedule. As others have similarly observed (e.g., Wilson & Keller, 1953, for rats; Hodos, Ross, & Brady, 1962, for monkeys; Bruner & Revusky, 1961, for human subjects), collateral or "mediating" behavior developed in most of our birds during the intervals between key pecks. Many subjects performed one or two pirouettes in between pecks at the key, whereas some subjects preened or nodded in a repetitive, stereotyped manner.

Such collateral behavior could have played a role in producing the Fig. 8–4 gradients in at least two important ways. First of all, since the DRL birds usually left the vicinity of the key while engaging in collateral behavior, they presumably had less "exposure" to the training stimulus than the VI birds, which habitually stood in front of the key. Could this relatively limited exposure to the visual properties of the key have directly led to flatter gradients for the DRL birds? This seems to be a good possibility, which is indirectly supported by some recent data from our laboratory (Hearst & Koresko, 1968). In that study both absolute and relative line-tilt gradients became steeper as amount of training on 1-minute VI was increased from two to fourteen daily sessions. Since amount of "exposure" to the response key varies directly with number of training sessions, gradients apparently do steepen with increased exposure to the key-pecking situation. However, "exposure" is confounded with number of reinforcements in most studies of this sort, and a strong conclusion concerning the above argument is therefore not possible at the present time.

Secondly, the stimuli produced by the subject's own stereotyped collateral behavior may gain so much control over key pecking that they completely dominate stimuli from external sources. The pirouetting pigeon, so to speak, is more controlled by its movements than by details of the world around it. Therefore, the visual aspects of the key may constitute a proportionately smaller part of the conditioned stimulus compound than is the case for 1-minute VI, where overt forms of collateral behavior are not usually observed. This interpretation, which is essentially a restatement of the internal cues hypothesis as applied to the DRL situation, seems a reasonable way of analyzing the extremely flat DRL gradients.

There is one other complication in comparing VI and DRL behavior that should be evaluated here. Absolute response rates for VI were much higher than for DRL and the possibility exists that the above gradient differences merely reflect the greater response output of the VI birds. In other words, perhaps subjects trained to respond slowly yield flat gradients and subjects trained to respond rapidly yield steep gradients, regardless of the type of reinforcement schedule involved. Of course, this cannot be the entire story because exactly the opposite result was observed in the data of Fig. 8–1; SAV rates were higher than VI rates there. Nevertheless, we decided to manipulate response rate within a single type of reinforcement schedule, by training different groups of birds on different frequencies of VI reinforcement. It is a well-established finding (Ferster & Skinner, 1957; Clark, 1958; Morse, 1966) that VI schedules with relatively long mean interreinforcement intervals produce lower response rates than VI schedules with relatively short interreinforcement intervals.

Therefore, five groups of birds were each trained for 10–11 sessions on a different VI value (30 sec., 1 min., 2 min., 3 min., and 4 min.) and then tested for line-tilt generalization as in the above VI-DRL comparison. Fig. 8–5 presents relative generalization gradients from that experiment (Hearst, Koresko, & Poppen, 1964, Experiment II).

Generalization gradients for line orientation became much steeper as the VI mean interval during training was shortened (and as absolute response output concurrently increased). This result is analogous to that in Fig. 8–4, where the higher of two response rates yielded the steeper of two gradients. Apparently, various appetitive reinforcement schedules (e.g., DRL and long VI) which lead to low response rates and the frequent development of stereotyped response chains are likely to yield flat generalization gradients. Visual observation of the Fig. 8–5 birds during training did in fact reveal that distinctive response chains (circling the chamber, nodding repetitively, etc.) were much more likely to develop on 3- or 4-minute VI's than on short VI's.

Since Fig. 8–1 displayed opposite results from Figs. 8–4 and 8–5 insofar as the relationship between absolute response rate during training and gradient slope was concerned, it seems that rate per se cannot be the critical factor. Probably more important are the pattern of responding and the relative amount and kind of mediating behavior that emerge on these different appetitive and aversive schedules. Blough (1965) cautions that an understanding of "rate" and its determiners is required before strong conclusions about free-operant generalization should be attempted. Our results reinforce his warning and suggest that a more fine-grained analysis (e.g., interresponse time distributions, quantitative measures of collateral behavior, etc.) is needed than mere calculations of overall response rate.

How useful, then, is the internal cues hypothesis for explaining our

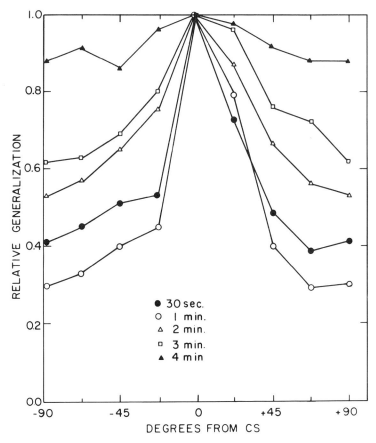

FIG. 8–5.   Gradients of relative generalization for the five different VI groups. The training stimulus (CS) was a vertical line (0°) for all birds.

From: E. Hearst, M. Koresko, & R. Poppen, "Stimulus Generalization and the Response-Reinforcement Contingency," *Journal of the Experimental Analysis of Behavior,* **7,** 1964, Fig. 6, p. 377. Copyright 1964 by the Society for the Experimental Analysis of Behavior, Inc., and reproduced by permission.

obtained differences between the generalization of approach and avoidance behavior? If one considers DRL and relatively long VI schedules to be controlled primarily by proprioceptive or other forms of nonexteroceptive stimuli (for which the observation of frequent stereotyped response chains on both types of schedules seems to provide some independent evidence), then presumably the hypothesis still retains explanatory or integrative power. But there will clearly be a certain amount of circularity in explanations of this sort until the specific internal cues involved in SAV, DRL, etc., are externalized and measured, or some more feasible indirect method is developed to assess their contribution. This is no easy task.

Perhaps the most important, though negative, conclusion to be drawn from Figs. 8–4 and 8–5 is that gradient steepness is obviously dependent on factors that cross the boundaries of approach and avoidance behavior. Fundamental differences do not seem to exist between gradients for approach and avoidance; flat gradients and steep gradients can be produced within the appetitive category itself by appropriately varying the schedule of reinforcement. There is no powerful reason for assuming that internal cues are any more important in approach behavior than in avoidance behavior. Miller's basic assumptions about the generalization of approach and avoidance seem to be severely limited in their applicability.

Generalization testing and the extinction process. Another factor that could be very important in interpreting the approach–avoidance differences of Fig. 8–1 is the relative resistance to extinction of the two types of response (which is admittedly hard to separate from the variables discussed in the preceding section, since schedules of reinforcement themselves have powerful effects on resistance to extinction). Avoidance responses often prove remarkably persistent during extinction, and several writers (e.g., Sheffield & Temmer, 1950; Jacobs, 1963) have attributed this persistence to the greater similarity of conditions during avoidance training and extinction as compared to, let us say, VI training and extinction. In the latter case, subjects experience a discriminable change in the external environment which indicates that extinction has begun (pellets are discontinued) whereas in the case of an established avoidance response there is no comparable environmental change. The beginning of avoidance extinction is presumably difficult for a well-trained subject to discriminate because of the absence of shocks in both conditioning and extinction. In a similar vein, one could also point to the "informative" function of the delivery of pellets, as compared to nonoccurrence of shock, in explaining the differential acquisition rates of exteroceptive discriminations based on approach or avoidance (e.g., see Fig. 8–3).

Since most generalization gradients are obtained during extinction of the conditioned response, one must consider the possibility (as do Prokasy & Hall, 1963) of a complex interaction between the extinction process and the variation of external stimuli during generalization testing. In other words, Miller's effects in the runway and our contrasting results in free-operant situations may primarily reflect differences in the relative extinguishability of approach and avoidance between the two behavioral tasks. In our situation SAV responding typically persisted much longer than VI behavior during the generalization test, whereas in Miller's tests avoidance tendencies often extinguished rather rapidly in the absence of shock. Consequently, it would seem that the fairest test of gradient differences should involve some sort of equation of resistance to extinction for the two types of response.

The development of a method for establishing such a match presents obvious practical and conceptual problems. We decided first to gain some information on the actual influence of the extinction process during generalization testing. Even though most of our experiments on this topic have been performed in an appetitive situation with pigeons, they appear to have implications for comparisons of approach and avoidance gradients obtained during extinction, because they clearly show that the progress of extinction influences gradient slope.

Prior work (Humphreys, 1939; Wickens, Schroder, & Snide, 1954; see also Lewis, 1960) suggests that a variety of factors, e.g., intermittent reinforcement, that increase resistance to extinction tend to flatten generalization gradients. A related finding is that of a progressive steepening of relative gradients while responding extinguishes during generalization testing (e.g., Friedman & Guttman, 1965; Hoffman, Chapter 7 of this volume; Hovland, 1937; Jenkins & Harrison, 1960; Johnson, 1966; Thomas & Barker, 1964; Wickens et al., 1954). One of the most baffling aspects of this finding is that "discrimination" seems to be improving (steepening of gradients around the training stimulus) even though no differential reinforcement is provided during the generalization tests.

We also have consistently observed this steepening-in-extinction effect. Figure 8–6 presents an example of it from one of our experiments. We divided up the generalization tests for the birds in Fig. 8–5 into separate scores for the combined first and second blocks of test trials (i.e., the first two times every stimulus was presented), the combined fifth and sixth blocks, and the combined ninth and tenth blocks. Then relative gradients were plotted for each of these stages of extinction (Blocks 1–2: "initial" stage; Blocks 5–6: "middle" stage; Blocks 9–10: "final" stage).

To save space, complete gradients at each stage are not given in Fig. 8–6, but merely a slope index (Test Responses to the Training Stimulus/Total Test Responses to All Stimuli, expressed as a percent) derived from each of the fifteen different group gradients (five VI groups, three stages of extinction). This slope measure was used by Hiss and Thomas (1963) and Hearst et al. (1964) as an index of the steepness of gradients—the higher the value of this index, the steeper the slope. If the gradients were completely flat, the index would equal 12.5% (the training stimulus was one of eight test stimuli). Figure 8–6 shows that, as extinction progressed, the gradients for all five VI groups became steeper. Stimulus control does appear to be improving in the complete absence of any differential reinforcement.

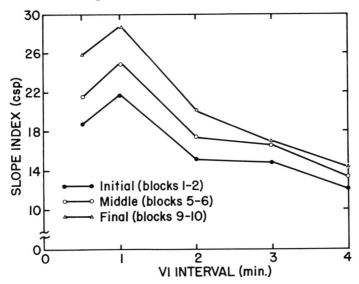

FIG. 8–6.   Steepness of generalization gradients at various stages of testing for the five VI groups of Fig. 8–5. The CSP index refers to the percent of total test responses made to the training stimulus (CS).

It seemed to us that one could further analyze progressive steepening of gradients during extinction by an experiment which separates the two experimental manipulations to which a subject is exposed for the very first time during generalization testing: (1) complete extinction, and (2) the variation of test stimuli. Perhaps such steepening is due to "general effects" of extinction (see Friedman & Guttman, 1965) and would occur even if a variety of different stimuli were not presented during extinction.[4] Poppen and I (Hearst & Poppen, 1965) decided to test this possibility by extinguishing responses at one stimulus value for a set time period before administering a conventional generalization test. If this period of massed extinction leads to steeper gradients than without such preextinction, it would appear that the opportunity for subjects to compare stimuli during testing, and thus to extinguish at differential rates to the various test stimuli (Hull, 1947, p. 125), is not critical in the progressive steepening effect.

Pigeons were the subjects and the entire procedure was very similar to that described in the above pigeon experiments except that, im-

[4] Another possible way of separating these two factors would be to present the various test stimuli without permitting any extinction to occur. We are currently engaged in such a study of auditory generalization in which the response key is inaccessible and the test stimuli are presented to pigeons immediately before the generalization test.

mediately before a standard generalization test, one group of birds was extinguished for 20 minutes to the training stimulus value (vertical line, 0°), and another group for 20 minutes to a value far from the training stimulus (horizontal line, 90°). A third group received the standard generalization test with no previous period of massed extinction.

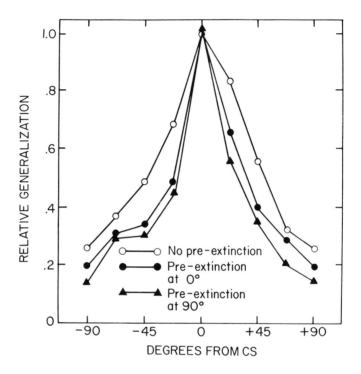

FIG. 8–7.   Gradients of relative generalization for three experimental groups, two given massed extinction at either the vertical line (0°) or horizontal line (90°) before generalization testing, and the other not extinguished before testing. For all subjects the stimulus during training was the vertical line (0°).

From: E. Hearst & R. Poppen, "Steepened Generalization Gradients After Massed Extinction to the CS," *Psychonomic Science*, 2, 1965, Fig. 1, p. 83. Reproduced by permission.

Figure 8–7 presents gradients of relative generalization for the three groups. The groups that had been extinguished at either 0° or 90° both showed significantly steeper gradients than the group that had received no prior extinction. Differences between the two preextinguished groups themselves were not significant.

Thus progressive steepening occurs merely as a result of extinction to a single stimulus; the presentation of a variety of different stimulus values is apparently not necessary for the effect shown in Fig. 8–6. Most interesting is the existence of this effect after preextinction to the training stimulus (0°). Relative gradients produced by successive reinforcement and extinction at the training stimulus are apparently steeper than those produced by reinforcement alone.

What hypotheses could account for the results of both Fig. 8–6 and Fig. 8–7? Currently we are examining two possibilities. The first of these involves the assumption [5] that inhibitory gradients produced by extinction at a particular stimulus value are much flatter than excitatory gradients produced by reinforcement at the training stimulus. If this were true, then a period of preextinction at the training stimulus might reduce response strength fairly equally at all points on the excitatory gradient around the training stimulus, and produce steeper *relative* gradients than would occur without a period of preextinction.

To test this possibility directly we need more information on the shape of inhibitory gradients (see Jenkins, 1965; and Terrace, 1966) as a function of various parameters, particularly the amount of extinction given at the inhibitory stimulus. Farthing and Hearst (1968) have recently completed such a study of inhibitory gradients, which were obtained in pigeons by first establishing a blank key as S+ and a vertical line projected on the key as S— during differential training. Standard generalization tests along the line-tilt continuum were then performed. This method of securing inhibitory gradients was independently developed by Jenkins and Harrison (1962) and Honig, Boneau, Burstein, and Pennypacker (1963). Farthing and Hearst obtained rather flat inhibitory gradients after one or two daily sessions of differential training (15 min. of S+, 15 min. of S— per session), but markedly steeper gradients after four to sixteen sessions. As more data are accumulated on the variables which affect inhibitory as well as excitatory gradients, and on the mathematics of their possible interaction we should be better able to evaluate the feasibility of the above explanation for the preextinction and progressive steepening results (see Hearst, 1968).

Our second working hypothesis to explain these results is closely related to the discussion of internal cues in the preceding section of this chapter. Perhaps as generalization testing proceeds in a free-operant situation, stimulus control from preceding responses (i.e., response-produced or proprioceptive stimulation) weakens more rapidly due to extinction than does control by external stimulation; on this basis exteroceptive gradients ought to steepen during testing. Blough (1963) has shown that key-pecking responses separated by very brief time periods (e.g., approximately 0.5 sec.) from immediately prior key-pecking re-

[5] I wish to thank Dr. Larry Stein for clarifying for me some of the implications of this idea.

sponses on a VI schedule are not affected very much by external stimulus changes, such as wavelength variation on the pigeon's response key. On the other hand, wavelength gradients constructed by including only responses following longer interresponse times (IRT's) exhibit the usual decrements as wavelength on the key is varied. He suggests (as do Crites, Harris, Rosenquist, & Thomas, 1967, and Ray & Sidman, in press) that the stimuli controlling these very short IRT's are derived from the organism's own behavior; the probability of these responses "does not vary with extinction, stimulus change, etc., except indirectly through changes in the probability of the responses on which they depend" (Blough, 1963, p. 245). As applied to our data, the extinction process during generalization testing would have a direct effect on response probability, which results in the gradual elimination of very short IRT's (presumably controlled by stimulation from the organism's immediately prior behavior). This would leave a greater proportion of relatively longer IRT's (presumably controlled by external stimuli) to enter into gradient determination toward the end of generalization testing. Actual measurements of IRT's and stimulus control at various stages of extinction are needed to check directly on these suppositions.

We have tested this idea indirectly by supposing that, besides extinction, some other methods of reducing the occurrence of short IRT's in a free-operant situation should also sharpen external stimulus control. In recent work Koresko and I have found that satiation (by prefeeding grain to subjects 1 hour before an experimental session) leads to an immediate improvement in relative discrimination indices for pigeons performing poorly in a simple successive auditory discrimination task for grain reinforcement. Good as well as poor performers show this improvement which depends, as one would expect, on the amount of grain prefed to the subjects. Other preliminary results indicate that such a satiation procedure also steepens gradients of relative generalization compared to groups of hungrier subjects.

In any event, the separation of response-produced stimulus control and external stimulus control in the Skinner Box situation is an extremely complex task. One wonders, in fact, whether operant base lines are really so ideal for studying external stimulus control, since complications from control by immediately preceding responses or mediating behavior may enter so strongly into the picture. Discrete trial procedures or those involving classical conditioning may thus offer certain advantages.

Most of the above work was triggered by an interest in how the extinction process itself contributed to our obtained differences between VI and SAV. Stage of extinction, relative resistance to extinction, etc., all appear to be important determinants of gradient slope. Therefore, we need more knowledge of the parameters affecting excitatory and inhibitory gradients for both SAV and VI in order to evaluate any differences between them during tests for stimulus generalization or discrimination. The data of Fig. 8–1 may represent an unfair test of approach–avoidance differences because resistance to extinction was not equated in any way for the two responses.

Interactions between Pavlovian and instrumental conditioning. Several influential theories of avoidance behavior (e.g., see Mowrer, 1960; Rescorla & Solomon, 1967; Maier, Seligman, & Solomon, Chapter 10 in this volume) stress the interlocking role of Pavlovian and instrumental conditioning in the development and maintenance of avoidance responses. Solomon and his colleagues have shown how CS+'s from a fear-conditioning paradigm can exercise powerful facilitating effects on SAV responding in the shuttlebox and how CS—'s can often reduce SAV responding. By demonstrating so convincingly that the effects of these CS's on instrumental behavior follow the general laws of Pavlovian conditioning, these experimenters have built a strong case for the critical importance of classically-conditioned responses in the acquisition and maintenance of avoidance behavior.

On an SAV schedule the experimenter makes no changes in the external environment of the subject, except for the delivery of shocks at appropriate times. Since shocks do not consistently follow any discriminable external event, a two-process theorist would presumably postulate that fear becomes conditioned to the large variety of stimuli with which shock UCS is paired: general apparatus cues ("background stimuli"), all nonavoidance behavior of the subject, and "temporal stimuli" which change with passage of time in the response–shock interval. In a sense the subject becomes afraid of everything except making the avoidance response.

An analogous example of classical conditioning probably does not apply in the appetitive operant situation (e.g., 1-min. VI) where the UCS (food) is consistently paired with a specific response of the subject (e.g., lever pressing). This pairing continues throughout all of the subject's exposure to the situation; food is only presented when the subject is in the presence of cues (CS+) closely associated spatially and temporally with the lever. Because of differential conditioning, any initial control by a variety of background or "incidental" stimuli ought to extinguish, or to "neutralize," or to weaken due to the presence of more valid cues (see Hull, 1952, and Wagner, Logan, Haberlandt, & Price, 1968). In contrast, these background stimuli are likely to maintain some higher degree of control at all times in the SAV situation because they still may sometimes be paired with shock on the occasions when the subject fails to avoid. If, in fact, ongoing instrumental behavior is modulated by Pavlovian influences of this kind, one would predict flatter exteroceptive gradients for SAV than for short VI schedules since the distorting influence of incidental stimuli is apparently greater for SAV behavior.

Thus we need more information on the stimulus generalization of classically-conditioned responses. Do generalization gradients for CS+'s and CS−'s in salivary conditioning resemble or differ from those in the fear-conditioning situation? However, this is not an easy question to answer because we have the inescapable problem of how to equate the appetitive and aversive situations for a fair comparison. Within a Pavlovian framework, Bykov (1958, p. 642) found that "when one tone was the signal for a strong conditioned defensive reflex and another tone was the signal for an alimentary reflex, the entire nonreinforced scale of tones provoked the conditioned defensive reflex; the 'food' tone, however, invariably produced only an alimentary conditioned reflex." Here generalization was again greater for the aversively-controlled response but Bykov does not supply enough details to enable evaluation of the generality of his result.

Some of Hoffman's work (Chapter 7 of this volume) is pertinent to the question of generalization effects following classical conditioning. He found that an auditory CER stimulus in pigeons generalized very broadly to other tonal frequencies during the initial sessions of generalization testing, as measured by the amount of suppression of ongoing behavior. If it is typically true that the CER generalizes broadly, then one might expect broad generalization for behavior (avoidance) in which CER's are likely to play an important role.

Novel stimuli and habituation.   Most generalization procedures involve the presentation of novel stimuli to the subject. It is quite conceivable that such stimuli may have different effects on different behavioral base lines. For example, if a novel auditory stimulus such as a buzzer is sounded during ongoing VI behavior, it often results in a depression of responding, perhaps by evoking orienting behavior; similarly, if a novel stimulus is presented during Pavlovian salivary conditioning, it may result in a decrement in amount of salivation (Pavlov's "external inhibition"). On the other hand, when such a stimulus is presented during SAV behavior it frequently has a facilitating effect on behavior. Stone and MacLean (1963) in fact showed that an irrelevant auditory stimulus increased SAV performance, and they suggested that "irrelevant exteroceptive stimulation may energize only aversively-controlled behavior" (p. 264). Solomon and his colleagues have analogously observed that a novel stimulus usually increases SAV jumping rate in the shuttle box.

Such differential effects of novel stimuli could well be involved in the broader generalization of SAV than VI we reported in Fig. 8–1 and elsewhere, since stimulus changes occurred for the first time for all subjects during the generalization test. The tendency for SAV rate to increase during these novel stimuli might have counterbalanced any decremental tendency due to stimulus change, thus producing a flat gradient; whereas in the VI case "stimulus change" and "novelty" would both act to weaken responding, producing a relatively steep gradient. It would be worthwhile to examine the effects of novel stimuli on DRL behavior or long VI schedules in an appetitive situation, because if novel stimuli were to have facilitating effects there, one would be in possession of an interesting fact to ponder in view of the flatness of DRL and long VI exteroceptive gradients. Experiments that involve habituation or preexposure to the forthcoming test stimuli, so they would not be novel in subsequent generalization tests, might enable a better evaluation of the influence of novel stimulation per se in the study of stimulus generalization (see also footnote 4).

Since novel stimulus effects would be expected to be transient, we have found it difficult to conceive of this factor as being critically involved in the relatively permanent VI versus SAV gradient differences discussed above (they usually last through several separate generalization tests). But the actual influence that novelty plays ought to be evaluated experimentally.

Implicit and explicit discrimination training.   When one examines other studies (e.g., Miller, 1944, 1959; Hoffman and Fleshler, 1963) which attempted to compare generalization gradients following approach or avoidance training, numerous procedural differences are apparent which make it difficult to compare these studies to our own. Some of the specific factors that might be critical are: the number of different generalization stimuli presented during testing, duration of generalization testing, the presence or absence of food or shock during testing, the relative resistance to extinction of the approach and avoidance tendencies, the reinforcement schedule during training, locomotor versus manipulative behavior, conflict and nonindependence of approach and avoidance, grouped versus individual data, etc. We have already mentioned some possible reasons why a few of the above could be important in producing different results from ours.

Nevertheless, in recent research we have concentrated on one particular factor among the host of possible differences between the various situations. This factor is the amount of discrimination training, implicit or explicit, given before generalization testing.

In Miller's runway situation, subjects had implicitly received discrimination training along a spatial dimension before the conflict tests were given. During initial training the subjects had traversed the entire runway and therefore had been exposed to all the "stimuli" (distances from the goal) to be presented during subsequent determination of the spatial gradients. In addition, as Donahoe and Schulte (1967) have pointed out, the experiments of Miller and his colleagues were usually conducted in an unilluminated room with a light near the goalbox. Thus, during acquisition, subjects are likely to have learned a visual intensity discrimination, as well as or instead of a spatial one, because dim illuminations (early sectors of the runway) are never correlated with reward or punishment, whereas the brightly-lit goal portion is. The formation of such implicit exteroceptive discriminations may have interacted in some complex way with the approach and avoidance contingencies to affect the relative steepness of subsequent gradients.

Another complication in the runway situation lies in the fact that approach behavior involves the selective reinforcement of high speeds of running, since the faster the subject runs from start to goal box the sooner he is reinforced with food. This seems analogous to the selective reinforcement of high rates that occurs on free-operant FR schedules, where responses often become "firmly locked in a chain." The latter base line is therefore often rejected when a sensitive dependent variable is required, for example, in the study of stimulus generalization. Presumably this same difficulty would arise in the runway and could account partially for the flat approach gradients Miller and his colleagues obtain.

To return to implicit discriminations of the exteroceptive kind, these could also have developed in the design utilized by Hoffman and Fleshler (1963) and others who have used either a single appetitive response or a single avoidance response in studying generalization (see such studies summarized in Mednick & Freedman, 1960). Almost all these experiments have involved conditioning of an operant response to a discrete, "delayed" external stimulus. Differential training of this sort (where S+ is some value along the stimulus dimension and S−, the intertrial interval, is the absence of S+) has been shown to steepen gradients along that dimension, even though differential training to two specific values on the dimension never occurs (Jenkins & Harrison, 1960). Therefore, good exteroceptive control of the avoidance response (and consequently a relatively steep gradient) is much more to be expected in situations involving a delayed conditioning procedure than in situations that involve trace conditioning, or a continuously maintained stimulus as on the SAV procedure which provided the data for Fig. 8–1. In our other SAV work (e.g., Fig. 8–2) we also found that discrimination training (but of an intradimensional variety there) steepened the avoidance gradient and reduced the slope differences between approach and avoidance.

These points suggest that, following delayed conditioning, approach and avoidance gradients ought both to reveal comparatively good exteroceptive control; also, the differences between the gradients should be relatively small. We decided to utilize a procedure similar to Hoffman and Fleshler's to study separate gradients of approach and avoidance in a discrete-trial situation and then to determine what happens when the two tendencies are placed in conflict. This work and some other similar current experiments appear to be more suitable analogs of the Miller-type situation than most of our studies described above.

In the discrete-trial experiments, which involved an auditory intensity dimension, some rats were initially trained in a one-lever box to press the lever to obtain food within 5 seconds after a 4K-cps tone was sounded. Other subjects were trained to press the lever to avoid shock within 5 seconds after the same tone was sounded. Thus, approach subjects learned to make the same response within the same time limit to the same auditory signal as did the avoidance animals. So as to check on the generality of our results and to examine the phenomenon of stimulus intensity dynamism (Hull, 1949; Gray, 1965) for both approach and avoidance, we used different intensities of the 4K-cps tone as the training stimulus for different groups of subjects. Some rats had a loud tone (0-db attenuation in Fig. 8–8), others a tone of intermediate intensity (10-db attenuation), and the third group a rather faint tone (25-db attenuation). Intertrial intervals were silent and averaged about 30 seconds in duration.

All subjects remained on either approach or avoidance training for approximately 25 sessions. Then generalization tests were given to all subjects that had responded to at least 70% of the stimulus presentations on the three sessions preceding the scheduled test day. All approach subjects in the three intensity groups ($N = 5$ in each) easily met this criterion; they responded to more than 98% of the stimuli. Four out of five avoidance subjects in the 0-db group met criterion (averaging 95%), three out of five in the 10-db group (averaging 90%), and three out of five in the 25-db group (averaging 81%). During generalization tests six stimuli, all 4K-cps and spaced at 5-db intervals from 0- to 25-db attenuation, were each presented 12 times in a randomized order. Intertrial intervals averaged 30 seconds, as during training. As usual, no food or shock was possible during the generalization test. It is worth pointing out that Hoffman and Fleshler (1963) continued to give intermittent reinforcement at the training stimulus during their testing period. Through its effects on resistance to extinction, or because discrimination training was occurring during generalization tests, this procedure may have been responsible for the different results they obtained.

Figure 8–8 displays the group gradients for each experimental condition. The value of the training stimulus is indicated by the arrow below

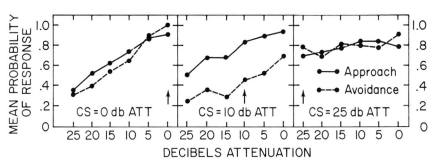

FIG. 8–8.   Gradients of auditory intensity generalization for approach and avoidance in three groups of rats, each trained at a different intensity value (CS).

each pair of gradients. Since only one response per trial was possible (presentations lasted a maximum of 5 sec. and a lever press terminated the stimulus and ended the trial), our dependent variable was the percent of trials at each intensity value to which a response was made. Approach and avoidance gradients were steepest when the training stimulus was of a high intensity, and were both quite flat in the faint stimulus group. This illustrates an effect which Hull would have discussed in terms of "stimulus intensity dynamism."

In terms of approach–avoidance comparisons, however, there is no evidence of systematic slope differences in any of the three pairs of curves (the lower overall performance level for the avoidance group at 10-db attenuation is due to the fact that two rats in that group made comparatively few responses during the generalization test, even to the training stimulus value). Therefore, unlike Hoffman and Fleshler (1963), we obtained no significant differences between gradients of approach and avoidance determined separately in different groups of subjects. As noted above, perhaps Hoffman and Fleshler's procedure of continuing intermittent reinforcement during testing accounts for the flatter approach gradients they obtained.

In the next phase of our experiment, both approach and avoidance rats in the "loud" and "faint" stimulus groups were placed in a two-lever chamber. They learned to press one lever within 5 seconds after a 4K-cps tone was sounded to obtain intermittent food reinforcements and to press the other lever within 5 seconds to avoid shock after a 4K-cps tone at the other end of the intensity continuum was sounded. One of these stimulus–response associations had already been learned in the first phase of the experiment described above, so that the second phase required learning only one new response (approach or avoidance, depending on the subject) to a stimulus at the other end of the continuum. Only the first response to each stimulus had any effect; pressing the wrong lever on an approach trial merely terminated the signal, whereas a wrong first response on an avoidance trial meant that shock could no longer be avoided by making the correct response. Prolonged training and a variety of small changes in the procedure were necessary before a sufficient number of subjects reached the high level of accuracy (approximately 90% correct to each stimulus) necessary before a generalization test could be given.

Stimulus generalization gradients were then determined in two extinction sessions by presenting sound intensities at and in between the two training stimuli. In this way, not only could one evaluate the relative steepness of the two gradients but one could also determine whether the gradients intersect at a point midway between the two training stimuli, which should occur if the slopes of the two gradients are approximately equal. If the avoidance gradient were appreciably flatter, the intersection point would be relatively far from the avoidance-training stimulus; the opposite would occur if the approach gradient were flatter.

The intersecting gradients obtained in this fashion are analogous in some ways to those secured in the Miller-type situation, but here a well-defined avoidance response is established. In Miller's runway, on the other hand, the approach response is specified (a complete run of the alley), whereas the avoidance response is unspecified; only the response that is *punished* [6] (entering the goal box) is clearly defined and any other response avoids shock. Consequently, one might expect a variety of avoidance responses to develop in the situation. At any rate, in our situation we conditioned specific approach and avoidance responses to very different auditory stimuli and tested to see which of the two responses would be made to intensity values in between the original training stimuli. Presumably maximal conflict of response tendencies would occur somewhere in between, just as it is posited to develop somewhere in the runway between start and goal box.

Figure 8–9 presents group curves from two separate experiments with different subjects that we have conducted using this design ($N = 6$ in each experiment). The separate experiments differ in some small details, but essentially the same training procedure was used in both. Generalization gradients were obtained in the same manner as for Fig. 8–8, but of course there were two responses possible here.

Figure 8–9 exhibits a slight tendency for the avoidance gradient to be flatter in both experiments, but neither of these trends stood up to statistical scrutiny. Intersecting gradients for individual subjects also did not reveal any very consistent pattern; some rats showed distinctly

---

[6] Studies involving the stimulus generalization of punishment are clearly relevant here but will not be discussed in this chapter. Readers are referred to the articles by Honig and Slivka (1964), Hoffman and Fleshler (1965), and Honig (1966) for summaries of the findings in this area.

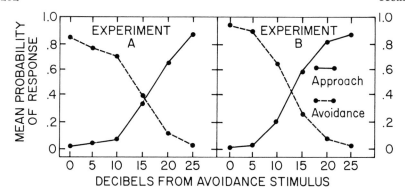

FIG. 8–9.   Intersecting approach and avoidance gradients for auditory intensity in two separate, but very similar experiments (A and B). Data are combined for all groups, some of which had a loud tone as the avoidance stimulus and a faint tone as the approach stimulus, and vice versa.

flatter avoidance gradients, but others showed flatter approach gradients. To summarize, we obtained no significant differences between the two gradients in our discrete-trial situation, whether measured separately (Fig. 8–8) or in conflict (Fig. 8–9).

The differences between approach and avoidance gradients in this experiment may well have turned out to be only minor because two competing responses were used here that were fairly well matched in terms of, among other things,

(1) *Amount of training.* Both received a large number of training trials.

(2) *Response topography.* The two responses were "symmetrical," unlike the usual runway situation where the approach response requires a long sequence of running behavior and fast runs are selectively reinforced. The same is not true for the avoidance response, which involves "pulling away" rather than "pulling toward." But Miller (1959) has described some experiments (e.g., Murray & Miller, 1952) which were designed to analyze response "asymmetry" as an explanation, and he believes the results eliminate this objection.

(3) *Delay of reinforcement.* The auditory stimuli terminate immediately after either a correct approach or avoidance response; however, since no one knows exactly when the "moment of reinforcement" is for each type of response, it is admittedly hard to compare delays or schedules of reinforcement for each.

To reiterate a point implied earlier, when factors such as (1), (2), and (3), are closely equated, as well as opportunities for implicit discrimination training, gradient differences between appetitive and aversive behavior may disappear—a suggestion similar to one made by Kelleher and Morse (1964) in comparing drug effects on the two types of behavior.

Conclusion: Approach, Avoidance, and Stimulus Generalization

Some years ago, when I first began work comparing generalization gradients following appetitive and aversive training, my personal opinion was that fundamental differences might very well appear between the two categories of behavior. Miller had implied such a possibility and the experimental and clinical findings mentioned earlier in this chapter seemed also to suggest that basic differences might exist, even though these findings were often hard to reconcile with Miller's position. During the course of our research, we did find clear effects of reinforcement schedule, level of extinction, and implicit and explicit discrimination training on the slope of gradients *within* the two categories. However, differences *between* the two categories collapsed when changes were made in some specific parameters of the behavioral task. By proper manipulation of certain experimental conditions, one can produce a steep approach gradient or a flat approach gradient, a steep avoidance gradient or a flat avoidance gradient.

Therefore, the original focus and goals of our research have shifted and the most profitable course now seems to me to be a determination of those parametric variations which flatten or steepen gradients, regardless of approach versus avoidance. It must be fairly obvious that I no longer have very much confidence that fundamental differences between the stimulus generalization of approach and avoidance will emerge. The differences that we have obtained, and the ones Miller has described, may be better thought of in terms of certain parametric variations than in terms of any basic dichotomy.

Noxious Stimulation and Discriminative Breakdowns

In a recent report it was found that unavoidable electric shocks may not only lead to a persistent breakdown in the stimulus control of appetitive behavior, but may also result in very large increases in *unreinforced* operant responding (Hearst, 1965b). The second part of this chapter will include a brief summary of those experiments and a new discussion of their possible implications in the light of several related phenomena and concepts investigated in Solomon's laboratory (Rescorla & Solomon, 1967; and Maier, Seligman, & Solomon, Chapter 10 of this volume). Our results seem to fit very nicely into the framework presented in those articles and therefore the following description may be considered a partial supplement to the work reported in Chapter 10.

Procedure and Results

In our experiments, described in much greater detail in Hearst (1965b), rats first learned either an auditory or visual discrimination in which lever pressing was reinforced with food on a 1-minute VI schedule in the presence of one stimulus condition (S+) and extinguished in the other condition (S−). The S− condition involved the presentation of an external signal (a tone or a flickering light, depending on the subject), whereas the S+ condition was simply the absence of this external signal. S+ and S− stimuli alternated frequently during experimental sessions.

When response rates in S+ had stabilized at appreciably higher levels than rates in S−, —i.e., after a good and stable discrimination had been formed—a third stimulus condition (CER), not contingent on the subject's behavior, was occasionally presented. For some rats the CER stimulus was a tone, for others it was a compound stimulus of a light plus clicking sound. The S− and CER stimuli, each 1 minute in duration, occurred in a nonsystemic order and never immediately followed each other; 1–3 minutes of S+ intervened between every S− or CER period. Lever pressing continued to be reinforced with food during the CER stimulus, but at the end of each such stimulus an unavoidable shock was delivered. The entire base line could be classified as a conditioned-suppression procedure (see Hoffman, Chapter 7 of this volume) superimposed upon an S+ versus S− discrimination.

To measure the efficiency of the rat's S+ versus S− discrimination, a *Discrimination Index* (S− response rate/S+ response rate) was calculated. The amount of conditioned suppression was measured by a *CER Index* (response rate in the CER stimulus/S+ response rate). To obtain these indices, total cumulated daily responses in the 1-minute S− and CER components were tabulated and compared to total cumulated daily responses in the immediately preceding 1 minute of S+ ("pre-S−" or "pre-CER"). Low values (e.g., .00–.25) of the Discrimination Index indicate a good discrimination between S+ and S−, whereas low values of the CER Index indicate a large suppression of responding during the CER stimulus.

In Experiment I the behavior of subjects was studied with and without shock at the end of the CER stimulus. Subjects remained on either the shock-on or shock-off procedure for at least five sessions, until inspection of the data indicated that their behavior had stabilized. Stable behavior with and without shock was determined at least three times each in every subject.

TABLE 8-1. Effects of the Shock-off ("OFF") and Shock-on ("ON") Procedures on Several Behavioral Measures When Pre-shock (CER) Periods Were Accompanied by an Exteroceptive Stimulus

Subject	Discrim. Index		CER Index		Rate in S− (rpm)		Rate in S+ (rpm)		Total Reinforcements	
	"OFF"	"ON"	"OFF"	"ON"	"OFF"	"ON"	"OFF"	"ON"	"OFF"	"ON"
No. 60	0.36	0.74	1.20	0.02	4.5	9.2	11.6	10.9	58.5	51.7
No. 62	0.41	0.68	1.22	0.34	10.4	20.3	26.5	29.3	67.3	64.3
No. 63	0.12	0.32	0.89	0.37	6.8	8.1	52.6	23.1	67.8	65.7
No. 64	0.69	0.94	1.06	0.11	7.2	15.3	11.1	15.8	61.8	53.7
No. 65	0.38	0.56	1.04	0.32	15.7	19.5	44.9	32.7	65.0	66.0
No. 66	0.14	0.86	1.36	0.24	2.9	34.5	20.0	38.0	59.3	63.0
Group Mean	0.35	0.68	1.13	0.23	7.9	17.8	27.9	25.0	63.3	60.7

From: E. Hearst, "Stress-Induced Breakdown of an Appetitive Discrimination," Journal of the Experimental Analysis of Behavior, 8. 1965, Table 1, p. 137. Copyright 1965 by the Society for the Experimental Analysis of Behavior, Inc., and reproduced by permission.

Table 8–1 presents various measures of the effects of shock delivery at the end of CER stimuli. The values in the table are means of three or four separate determinations of stable behavior with and without shock.

Every subject exhibited an impairment of the S+ versus S– discrimination whenever shocks occurred at the end of the CER stimulus. More interesting, I think, is the fact that the delivery of shocks produced an increase in the absolute rate of S– responding in every subject, an increment of more than 90% in four of the six rats. The deterioration in the S+ versus S– discrimination index and the loss of inhibitory control by S– were apparently independent of changes in overall response level in S+ or frequency of reinforcement, since these measures rose for some subjects and fell for others. As expected, the delivery of shocks at the end of the CER stimulus caused suppression of behavior during that stimulus.

In the next experiment we were interested in whether shocks alone would disrupt the S+ versus S– discrimination, even if responding in the preshock periods was not selectively suppressed by an external stimulus. To answer this question, the shock warning signal was eliminated but shocks were delivered at exactly the same times as before. Thus subjects would have no warning that shocks were coming and they merely received noncontingent shocks at various times during S+, the absence of external stimulation.

Even after 18 sessions of exposure to this procedure, two of the subjects still exhibited virtually complete suppression in all components of the schedule. The data of the other four subjects under the shock-on and shock-off procedures are shown in Table 8–2. The CER indices given there are merely "dummy" indices, which should average approximately 1.00 under both the shock-on and shock-off conditions since no signal precedes shock on this procedure.

Table 8–2 exhibits an even greater deterioration of the S+ versus S– discrimination than does Table 8–1; the discrimination indices averaged approximately 1.00, which indicates no discrimination between S+ and S–. Two of the four subjects displayed a pronounced facilitation in absolute S– responding when shocks were delivered, whereas the other two rats either showed little effect or a decline. The absence of S– facilitation in the latter subjects may be due to the extremely strong opposing influence of the suppressive factors in the situation, which is evidenced by the marked suppression of S+ rates in these two subjects. Just as Church (Chapter 5 of this volume) has reported, the influence of noncontingent shocks on base rates was more pronounced in most of our subjects when no signal preceded shocks.

Figures 8–10 and 8–11 present day-by-day case histories for two rats on the above procedures (shock-on versus shock-off, with and without an external CER stimulus). There was extremely little overlap in discrimina-

TABLE 8-2. Effects of the Shock-off ("OFF") and Shock-on ("ON") Procedures on Several Behavioral Measures When Pre-shock Periods Were Not Accompanied by an Exteroceptive Stimulus

Subject*	Discrim. Index		CER Index		Rate in S−(rpm)		Rate in S+(rpm)		Total Reinforcements	
	"OFF"	"ON"	"OFF"	"ON"	"OFF"	"ON"	"OFF"	"ON"	"OFF"	"ON"
No. 62	0.43	0.85	0.92	0.90	11.4	11.6	27.1	11.8	63.0	36.0
No. 64	0.64	0.92	0.83	1.01	4.9	30.3	8.3	33.0	54.0	65.0
No. 65	0.31	0.95	0.99	1.01	18.0	11.1	60.4	13.3	67.5	61.0
No. 66	0.30	1.21	1.06	0.99	4.0	12.9	12.8	13.5	59.0	47.0
Group Mean	0.42	0.98	0.95	0.98	9.6	16.5	27.2	17.9	60.9	52.3

* Subjects No. 60 and 63 are not included in this table because under the shock-on procedure their responding continued to be almost completely suppressed throughout experimental sessions, even after 18 sessions of exposure to this procedure.

From: E. Hearst, "Stress-Induced Breakdown of an Appetitive Discrimination," Journal of the Experimental Analysis of Behavior, 8, 1965, Table 2, p. 139. Copyright 1965 by the Society for the Experimental Analysis of Behavior, Inc., and reproduced by permission.

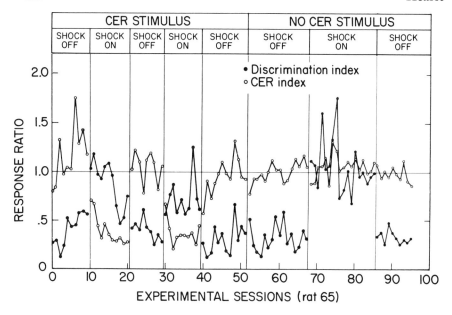

FIG. 8–10.   Day-to-day records of the discrimination and CER indices for rat No. 65 under several different stimulus and shock conditions.

From: E. Hearst, "Stress-Induced Breakdown of an Appetitive Discrimination," *Journal of the Experimental Analysis of Behavior,* 8, 1965, Fig. 2, p. 140. Copyright 1965 by the Society for the Experimental Analysis of Behavior, Inc., and reproduced by permission.

tion indices between the procedures with and without shock. A virtually complete and immediate recovery of discriminative performance occurred whenever shock was eliminated.

In further experiments with these same subjects (also reported in Hearst, 1965b) the intensity of signalled shock proved to be an important parameter of the disruptive effects described earlier. As shock intensity was increased, discrimination indices deteriorated and absolute S— rates progressively increased. Despite these changes, response rates in S+ remained fairly constant with alterations in shock intensity.

In other reported work we found that when response-correlated shocks (punishment) were delivered in the former CER stimulus, behavior was even more suppressed in that stimulus than with unavoidable shocks —a confirmation of Church's (1963) conclusion regarding contingent versus noncontingent shock. However, impairments of the discrimination index and facilitations of absolute S— responding were only temporary under contingent shock and generally disappeared once overall base rate had recovered from extreme suppression. In contrast, the above effects with unavoidable shock were not merely temporary initial effects, but

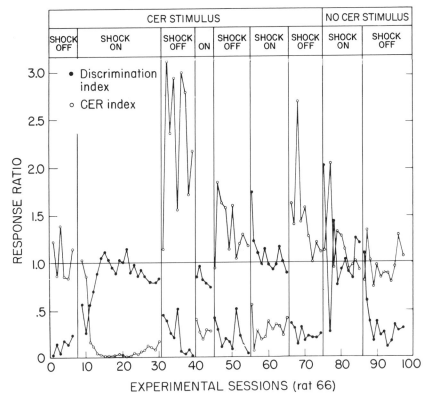

FIG. 8–11.   Day-to-day records of the discrimination and CER indices for rat No. 66 under several different stimulus and shock conditions.

From: E. Hearst, "Stress-Induced Breakdown of an Appetitive Discrimination," *Journal of the Experimental Analysis of Behavior*, 8, 1965, Fig. 3, p. 141. Copyright 1965 by the Society for the Experimental Analysis of Behavior, Inc., and reproduced by permission.

ones which lasted as long as shocks were delivered (see Figs. 8–10 and 8–11).

Discussion and Conclusions

This group of experiments showed that the occasional delivery of strong, unavoidable shocks (whether or not preceded by an exteroceptive warning) produces a marked deterioration in well-established and apparently independently-maintained appetitive discriminations. This impairment can be easily reversed, however, since former levels of accuracy are recaptured as soon as shocks are withdrawn. The dependence of the discriminative breakdown on the presence of persistent noxious stimulation recalls the observations of Pavlov and others (see Dinsmoor, 1960; Broadhurst,

1961) that easy, well-learned discrimination may suffer during periods of conflict, fear, or general stress. The effect also seems related to findings in the field of stimulus generalization, which indicate that highly anxious subjects usually exhibit greater than normal stimulus generalization (Mednick & Freedman, 1960; Kalish, in press). Within an operant conditioning framework Sidman (1958) has interpreted some of his results to indicate that shocks may broaden generalization gradients.

We believe the most interesting feature of this impairment to be the facilitation of S− behavior that occurs with unavoidable shock. One could consider this elevated response rate in S− to be "maladaptive" because such behavior is never reinforced. But how can this effect be interpreted so as to include it within the current systematic body of knowledge on aversive stimulation?

One explanation that seems worthy of some consideration is in terms of certain accidental contingencies of reinforcement. Ray and Stein (1959) observed their highest response rates in a VI-rewarded external stimulus (200-cps tone) that was not followed by shock, as compared to responding in normal VI periods or to responding during an 1800-cps tone (CER) that was followed by unavoidable shock (see Hoffman, 1965, for a discussion of a somewhat similar effect). Ray and Stein discussed the possibility that the higher than normal rates in the nonshocked stimulus might have been due to the fact that responding in this stimulus was never punished by the accidental production of the CER stimulus; the sequence of experimental conditions was such that these two external stimuli never immediately followed one another (as was also true in our experiments). On the other hand, CER stimuli did follow normal VI periods and therefore responding during these periods could have been fortuitously punished by the production of CER stimuli.

An important point is that in our procedure responses we never reinforced in the S− stimulus, whereas Ray and Stein reinforced responses in the 200-cps tone on a VI schedule. As applied to their experiment, an explanation in terms of such accidental contingencies may be a reasonable way to account for the slightly *lower* base-line rates in normal VI than in the nonshocked VI stimulus. But, as applied to our experiment, it is hard to believe that the mere fact that S− responding never produces the CER stimulus would—in the complete absence of any other source of reinforcement—account for the large increases in S− rate observed here. Worth reiterating is the fact that S+ rates (normal VI) did not change in any consistent direction as a result of unavoidable-shock procedures in our experiment (see Table 8–1).

Alternatively, the facilitation of S+ responding under conditions of strong unavoidable shock may be regarded as an emotional effect, akin to the breakdowns in performance, disinhibitions, and maladaptive behavior observed by Pavlov and others during periods of powerful stress. Drugs such as amphetamine, which are sometimes loosely described as increasing emotionality, often produce elevated responding to negative stimuli and inferior discriminative performance (e.g., Hearst, 1964). If loss of inhibitory control by an S— is considered to be an index of increased emotionality or aversiveness, it is interesting that the emotional effects of noncontingent shock (CER) in our experiment proved to be much more persistent and pronounced than those of contingent shock (punishment). Solomon (1964) has similarly remarked that there is often a period of emotionality during the early stages of a discrimination in which wrong responses are punished with electric shock; but after the subject has acquired the discrimination and receives very few shocks, the subject is "well-motivated and happy." It may be that the continued presentation of shocks serves to maintain emotionality, which in turn is correlated with the discriminative breakdowns described above (see also Kimble, 1961, p. 446, for studies on the strength of general anxiety during contingent versus noncontingent shock procedures).

The trouble with the "emotionality" argument is, of course, that the concept is very vague and impossible to measure directly or reliably at the present time. Also, we still would have to determine the variables and laws affecting the development of emotionality before we could account for our present results in any convincing manner. Therefore, we would be more or less back where we started.

The experiments and phenomena described by Solomon and his colleagues (Rescorla & Solomon, 1967; Maier et al., Chapter 10 of this volume) seem to provide the most effective framework in which to deposit our results at the present time. Our signalled-shock procedure fits nicely into their paradigm for studying the effects of differential fear conditioning upon instrumental appetitive learning, since Pavlovian CS+ presentations (the CER stimulus paired with shock) as well as Pavlovian CS— presentations (the S— stimulus not paired with shock) were superimposed on a VI base line in our experiment. Ray and Stein's procedure could be classified in the same way, except that they continued to give positive reinforcement in the CS— and we did not.

Hammond (1966, see also Parrish, 1967) recently confirmed and extended the results of Ray and Stein by showing that the presentation of a CS— established by differential aversive Pavlovian conditioning will facilitate a base line of instrumental behavior maintained by an appetitive reinforcer. As Solomon and his colleagues have shown, such a CS— will reduce responding when the base-line operant behavior involves aversive reinforcement (e.g., SAV). Thus an aversive CS— apparently elevates ongoing instrumental appetitive behavior and depresses ongoing avoidance behavior. This is intuitively appealing and conceptually satisfying, because an aversive CS+ (the CER stimulus) depresses ongoing appetitive behavior and elevates ongoing avoidance behavior (see Sidman, 1960).

The facilitation of behavior in our experiments was of a much greater magnitude (see Table 8–1) than the increases in operant behavior in CS— obtained by Ray and Stein, and Hammond. This may be due to the fact that behavior in S—, being consistently unreinforced throughout our experiment, was relatively weak and therefore there was a great deal of room in which to observe an increase. Perhaps the reason why Hammond was able to observe only a temporary facilitative effect (it persisted only as long as base-line rate was suppressed) is connected with his method of continuing positive reinforcement in CS—; our effect lasted as long as shocks continued to be delivered. Although we never planned it that way, the procedure of instrumental nonreinforcement in CS— may provide a relatively sensitive device for studying the effects on appetitive operant behavior of Pavlovian differential inhibitors established through aversive conditioning.[7]

Viewed in this fashion, the data of Table 8–1 do not really reveal a breakdown of discrimination per se. They merely reflect the effect of an experimental operation (presentation of Pavlovian CS—) which has been shown in several other experiments to facilitate operant appetitive behavior; by increasing S— responding, the presentation of CS— necessarily lowers the index of discrimination between S+ and S—. Also, the temporary nature of the disruption produced by response-contingent shock now begins to make additional sense. After subjects have learned to suppress responding to the punishment-correlated stimulus they receive very few shocks in the CS+, and thus CS— should not serve as a very effective differential inhibitor (since shocks do not occur in either CS+ or CS—). Therefore, facilitation in S— should disappear.

Exactly why an inhibitor of fear, to use Solomon's terminology, should enhance appetitive instrumental behavior is a question that cannot be satisfactorily answered at the present time. Rescorla and Solomon (1967, p. 173) have offered some possible reasons and have pointed out the importance of such phenomena for theories of incentive motivation. The inclusion of our results within their paradigm may not make our findings any more explainable, but at least such an inclusion places these discriminative breakdowns within a category of phenomena similar to those reported by others and apparently affected by the same basic experimental operations.

---

[7] In a recent study Weiss (1968) failed to observe any consistent facilitations of operant behavior in S— when shock was added to a discrimination procedure very similar to the one we used. The reasons for this discrepancy (e.g., different strains of rat, details of apparatus or procedure) are unclear.

REFERENCES

ANGER, D. The role of temporal discriminations in the reinforcement of Sidman avoidance behavior. *Journal of the Experimental Analysis of Behavior,* 1963, **6**, 477–506.

APPEL, J. B. The aversive control of an operant discrimination. *Journal of the Experimental Analysis of Behavior,* 1960, **3**, 35–47.

BLOUGH, D. S. Interresponse time as a function of continuous variables: A new method and some data. *Journal of the Experimental Analysis of Behavior,* 1963, **6**, 237–246.

BLOUGH, D. S. Definition and measurement in generalization research. In D. Mostofsky (Ed.), *Stimulus generalization.* Stanford, Calif.: Stanford Univer. Press, 1965. Pp. 30–37.

BROADHURST, P. L. Abnormal animal behavior. In H. Eysenck (Ed.), *Handbook of abnormal psychology.* New York: Basic Books, Inc., 1961. Pp. 726–763.

BRUNER, A., & REVUSKY, S. Collateral behavior in humans. *Journal of the Experimental Analysis of Behavior,* 1961, 4, 349–350.

BYKOV, K. M. (Ed.) *Textbook of physiology.* (Tr. S. Belsky & D. Myshne.) Moscow: Foreign Languages Publishing House, 1958.

CHURCH, R. M. The varied effects of punishment on behavior. *Psychological Review,* 1963, **70**, 369–402.

CLARK, F. C. The effect of deprivation and frequency of reinforcement on variable-interval responding. *Journal of the Experimental Analysis of Behavior,* 1958, 1, 221–228.

CRITES, R. J., HARRIS, R. T., ROSENQUIST, H., & THOMAS, D. R. Response patterning during stimulus generalization in the rat. *Journal of the Experimental Analysis of Behavior,* 1967, **10**, 165–168.

DINSMOOR, J. A. Punishment: I. The avoidance hypothesis. *Psychological Review,* 1954, **61**, 34–46.

DINSMOOR, J. A. Punishment: II. An interpretation of empirical findings. *Psychological Review,* 1955, **62**, 96–105.

DINSMOOR, J. A. Studies of abnormal behavior in animals. In R. H. Waters, D. A. Rethlingshafer, and W. E. Caldwell (Eds.), *Principles of comparative psychology.* New York: McGraw-Hill, 1960. Pp. 289–324.

DONAHOE, J. W., & SCHULTE, V. G. Effects of stimulus intensity on approach–avoidance conflict behavior. *Psychonomic Science,* 1967, **8**, 355–356.

FARTHING, G. W., & HEARST, E. Generalization gradients of inhibition after different amounts of training. *Journal of the Experimental Analysis of Behavior,* 1968, **11**, 743–752.

FERSTER, C. B., & SKINNER, B. F. *Schedules of reinforcement.* New York: Appleton-Century-Crofts, 1957.

FRIEDMAN, H., & GUTTMAN, N. A further analysis of the various effects of discrimination training on stimulus generalization gradients. In D. Mostofsky (Ed.), *Stimulus generalization.* Stanford, Calif.: Stanford Univer. Press, 1965. Pp. 255–267.

GRAY, J. A. Stimulus intensity dynamism. *Psychological Bulletin,* 1965, **63**, 180–196.

GUTTMAN, N., & KALISH, H. I. Discriminability and stimulus generalization. *Journal of Experimental Psychology,* 1956, **51**, 79–88.

HABER, A., & KALISH, H. I. Prediction of discrimination from generalization after variations in schedule of reinforcement. *Science,* 1963, **142**, 412–413.

HAMMOND, L. J. Increased responding to CS− in differential CER. *Psychonomic Science,* 1966, **5**, 337–338.

HEARST, E. Simultaneous generalization gradients for appetitive and aversive behavior. *Science,* 1960, **132**, 1769–1770.

HEARST, E. Concurrent generalization gradients for food-controlled and shock-controlled behavior. *Journal of the Experimental Analysis of Behavior,* 1962, **5**, 19–31.

HEARST, E. Drug effects on stimulus generalization gradients in the monkey. *Psychopharmacologia,* 1964, **6**, 57–70.

HEARST, E. Approach, avoidance, and stimulus generalization. In D. Mostofsky (Ed.), *Stimulus generalization.* Stanford, Calif.: Stanford Univer. Press, 1965. Pp. 331–355. (a)

HEARST, E. Stress-induced breakdown of an appetitive discrimination. *Journal of the Experimental Analysis of Behavior,* 1965, **8**, 135–146. (b)

HEARST, E. Discrimination learning as the summation of excitation and inhibition. *Science,* 1968, **162**, 1303–1306.

HEARST, E., & KORESKO, M. B. Stimulus generalization and the amount of prior training on variable-interval reinforcement. *Journal of Comparative and Physiological Psychology,* 1968, **66**, 133–138.

HEARST, E., KORESKO, M. B., & POPPEN, R. Stimulus generalization and the response-reinforcement contingency. *Journal of the Experimental Analysis of Behavior,* 1964, **7**, 369–380.

HEARST, E., & POPPEN, R. Steepened generalization gradients after massed extinction to the CS. *Psychonomic Science,* 1965, **2**, 83–84.

HEARST, E., & PRIBRAM, K. H. Appetitive and aversive generalization gradients in amygdalectomized monkeys. *Journal of Comparative and Physiological Psychology,* 1964, **58**, 296–298.

HISS, R. H., & THOMAS, D. R. Stimulus generalization as a function of testing procedure and response measure. *Journal of Experimental Psychology,* 1963, **65**, 587–592.

HODOS, W., ROSS, G. S., & BRADY, J. V. Complex response patterns during temporally spaced responding. *Journal of the Experimental Analysis of Behavior,* 1962, 5, 473–479.

HOFFMAN, H. S. The stimulus generalization of conditioned suppression. In D. Mostofsky (Ed.), *Stimulus generalization.* Stanford, Calif.: Stanford Univer. Press, 1965. Pp. 356–372.

HOFFMAN, H. S., & FLESHLER, M. Discrimination and stimulus generalization of approach, of avoidance, and of approach and avoidance during conflict. *Journal of Experimental Psychology,* 1963, **65**, 280–291.

HOFFMAN, H. S., & FLESHLER, M. Stimulus aspects of aversive controls: The effects of response-contingent shock. *Journal of the Experimental Analysis of Behavior,* 1965, **8**, 89–96.

HONIG, W. K. The role of discrimination training in the generalization of punishment. *Journal of the Experimental Analysis of Behavior,* 1966, **9,** 377–384.

HONIG, W. K., BONEAU, C. A., BURSTEIN, K. R., & PENNYPACKER, H. S. Positive and negative generalization gradients obtained after equivalent training conditions. *Journal of Comparative and Physiological Psychology,* 1963, **56,** 111–116.

HONIG, W. K., & SLIVKA, R. M. Stimulus generalization of the effects of punishment. *Journal of the Experimental Analysis of Behavior,* 1964, **7,** 21–25.

HOVLAND, C. I. The generalization of conditioned responses: I. The sensory generalization of conditioned responses with varying frequencies of tone. *Journal of General Psychology,* 1937, **17,** 125–148.

HULL, C. L. The problem of primary stimulus generalization. *Psychological Review,* 1947, **54,** 120–134.

HULL, C. L. Stimulus intensity dynamism (V) and stimulus generalization. *Psychological Review,* 1949, **56,** 67–76.

HULL, C. L. *A behavior system.* New Haven, Conn.: Yale, 1952.

HUMPHREYS, L. G. Generalization as a function of method of reinforcement. *Journal of Experimental Psychology,* 1939, **25,** 361–372.

JACOBS, B. Repeated acquisition and extinction of an instrumental avoidance response. *Journal of Comparative and Physiological Psychology,* 1963, **56,** 1017–1021.

JENKINS, H. M. Generalization gradients and the concept of inhibition. In D. Mostofsky (Ed.), *Stimulus generalization.* Stanford, Cailf.: Stanford Univer. Press, 1965. Pp. 55–61.

JENKINS, H. M., & HARRISON, R. H. Effect of discrimination training on auditory generalization. *Journal of Experimental Psychology,* 1960, **59,** 246–253.

JENKINS, H. M., & HARRISON, R. H. Generalization gradients of inhibition following auditory discrimination learning. *Journal of the Experimental Analysis of Behavior,* 1962, **5,** 435–441.

JOHNSON, D. F. Determiners of selective discriminative stimulus control. Unpublished doctoral dissertation, Columbia University, 1966.

KALISH, H. I. Stimulus generalization. In M. Marx (Ed.), *Learning processes.* New York: Macmillan, in press.

KELLEHER, R. T., & MORSE, W. H. Escape behavior and punished behavior. *Federation Proceedings,* 1964, **23,** 808–817.

KIMBLE, G. *Hilgard and Marquis' conditioning and learning* (Rev. Ed.). New York: Appleton-Century-Crofts, 1961.

LEWIS, D. J. Partial reinforcement: A selective review of the literature since 1950. *Psychological Bulletin,* 1960, **57,** 1–28.

MEDNICK, S. A., & FREEDMAN, J. L. Stimulus generalization. *Psychological Bulletin,* 1960, **57,** 169–200.

MILLER, N. E. Experimental studies of conflict. In J. McV. Hunt (Ed.), *Personality and the behavior disorders.* New York: Ronald Press, 1944. Pp. 431–465.

MILLER, N. E. Theory and experiment relating psychoanalytic displacement to stimulus–response generalization. *Journal of Abnormal and Social Psychology,* 1948, **43,** 155–178.

MILLER, N. E. Liberalization of basic S–R concepts: Extensions to conflict behavior, motivation, and serial learning. In S. Koch (Ed.), *Psychology: A study of a science*, Vol. 2. New York: McGraw-Hill, 1959. Pp. 196–292.

MILLER, N. E. Some recent studies of conflict behavior and drugs. *American Psychologist*, 1961, **16**, 12–24.

MORSE, W. H. Intermittent reinforcement. In W. K. Honig (Ed.), *Operant behavior: Areas of research and application*. New York: Appleton-Century-Crofts, 1966. Pp. 52–108.

MOWRER, O. H. *Learning theory and behavior*. New York: Wiley, 1960.

MOWRER, O. H., & KEEHN, J. D. How are intertrial "avoidance" responses reinforced? *Psychological Review*, 1958, **65**, 209–221.

MURRAY, E. J., & MILLER, N. E. Displacement: Steeper gradient of generalization of avoidance than of approach with age of habit controlled. *Journal of Experimental Psychology*, 1952, **43**, 222–226.

PARRISH, J. Classical discrimination conditioning of heart rate and bar-press suppression in the rat. *Psychonomic Science*, 1967, **9**, 267–268.

PAVLOV, I. P. *Conditioned reflexes*. (Tr. G. V. Anrep.) Oxford University Press, 1927. (Reprinted, New York: Dover, 1960.)

PLATT, J. R. Strong inference. *Science*, 1964, **146**, 347–353.

PROKASY, W. F., & HALL, J. F. Primary stimulus generalization. *Psychological Review*, 1963, **70**, 310–322.

RAY, B. A., & SIDMAN, M. Reinforcement schedules and stimulus control. In W. N. Schoenfeld (Ed.), *Theory of reinforcement schedules*. New York: Appleton-Century-Crofts, in press.

RAY, O. S., & STEIN, L. Generalization of conditioned suppression. *Journal of the Experimental Analysis of Behavior*, 1959, **2**, 357–361.

RESCORLA, R. A. Pavlovian conditioned fear in Sidman avoidance learning. *Journal of Comparative and Physiological Psychology*, 1968, **65**, 55–60.

RESCORLA, R. A., & SOLOMON, R. L. Two-process learning theory: Relationships between Pavlovian conditioning and instrumental learning. *Psychological Review*, 1967, **74**, 151–182.

SCHOENFELD, W. N. An experimental approach to anxiety, escape, and avoidance behavior. In P. H. Hoch and J. Zubin (Eds.), *Anxiety*. New York: Grune & Stratton, 1950. Pp. 70–99.

SHEFFIELD, F. D., & TEMMER, H. W. Relative resistance to extinction of escape training and avoidance training. *Journal of Experimental Psychology*, 1950, **40**, 287–298.

SIDMAN, M. Two temporal parameters of the maintenance of avoidance behavior by the white rat. *Journal of Comparative and Physiological Psychology*, 1953, **46**, 253–261.

SIDMAN, M. Delayed-punishment effects mediated by competing behavior. *Journal of Comparative and Physiological Psychology*, 1954, **47**, 145–147.

SIDMAN, M. Some notes on "bursts" in free-operant avoidance experiments. *Journal of the Experimental Analysis of Behavior*, 1958, **1**, 167–172.

SIDMAN, M. Normal sources of pathological behavior. *Science*, 1960, **132**, 61–68.

SIDMAN, M. Avoidance behavior. In W. K. Honig (Ed.), *Operant behavior: Areas of research and application*. New York: Appleton-Century-Crofts, 1966. Pp.

SOLOMON, R. L. Punishment. *American Psychologist,* 1964, **19,** 239–253.

SOLOMON, R. L., & BRUSH, E. S. Experimentally derived conceptions of anxiety and aversion. In M. R. Jones (Ed.), *Nebraska symposium on motivation,* 1956. Lincoln: University of Nebraska Press, 1956. Pp. 212–305.

STONE, G. C., & MACLEAN, M. Increased rate of avoidance responding associated with non-contingent auditory stimulus. *Psychological Reports,* 1963, **13,** 259–265.

TERRACE, H. S. Stimulus control. In W. K. Honig (Ed.), *Operant behavior: Areas of research and application.* New York: Appleton-Century-Crofts, 1966. Pp. 271–344.

THOMAS, D. R., & BARKER, E. G. The effects of extinction and "central tendency" on stimulus generalization in pigeons. *Psychonomic Science,* 1964, **1,** 119–120.

WAGNER, A. R., LOGAN, F. A., HABERLANDT, K., & PRICE, T. Stimulus selection in animal discrimination learning. *Journal of Experimental Psychology,* 1968, **76,** 171–180.

WEISS, K. M. Some effects of the conditioned suppression paradigm on operant discrimination performance. *Journal of the Experimental Analysis of Behavior,* 1968, **11,** 767–775.

WICKENS, D. D., SCHRODER, H. M., & SNIDE, J. D. Primary stimulus generalization of the GSR under two conditions. *Journal of Experimental Psychology,* 1954, **47,** 52–56.

WILSON, M. P., & KELLER, F. S. On the selective reinforcement of spaced responses. *Journal of Comparative and Physiological Psychology,* 1953, **46,** 190–193.

9

Predictability, Surprise, Attention, and Conditioning[1]

Leon J. Kamin

PRINCETON UNIVERSITY

The experiments to be described here have no special relevance to the problem of punishment. The studies to be reported do employ the CER procedure (Estes & Skinner, 1941). This procedure, within which an aversive US follows a warning signal regardless of the animal's behavior, has been contrasted to the arrangements employed in response-contingent punishment (Hunt & Brady, 1955). This type of comparison, however, is not germane to the present research. The kinds of results considered in this chapter derive from rats in a CER procedure, with shock as the US; but very similar results have been obtained in the McMaster laboratory by H. M. Jenkins, using pigeons in a food-reinforced operant discrimination. What appears to be involved in these studies is a concern with phenomena often referred to as examples of "selective attention." To the degree that punishment contingencies may be brought under stimulus control, the present work might be related to other contributions in this volume.

The present work arose from an interest in the possible role of attention in Pavlovian conditioning. The usual statement of the conditions sufficient for a Pavlovian CR asserts simply that a neutral, to-be-conditioned CS must be presented in contiguity with a US. What happens, however, when a compound CS consisting of elements known to be independently conditionable is presented in contiguity with a US? Are all elements of the CS effectively conditioned? Does the animal attend, and thus condition, more to some elements than to others? What kinds of experimental manipulations might direct the animal's attention to one or another element?

The first experimental approach to these questions was, in overview, as follows. First, condition an animal to respond to a simple CS, consisting of Element A. Then condition the animal to respond to a compound,

[1] The research reported here was supported by a research grant from the Associate Committee on Experimental Psychology, National Research Council of Canada.

consisting of Element A plus a superimposed Element B. Finally, test the animal with Element B alone. Will it respond to Element B? Put very naively, our primitive notion was that, because of the prior conditioning to Element A, that element might so "engage the animal's attention" during presentation of the compound that it would not "notice" the added Element B. The failure to notice the superimposed element might preclude any conditioning to it. To conclude that the prior conditioning to Element A was responsible for a failure to respond to Element B we must, of course, show that animals conditioned to the compound without prior conditioning to A do respond when tested with B. To control for amount of experience with the US, and variables correlated with it, we ought also to show that, if compound conditioning is followed by conditioning to A alone, the animal will respond when tested with B.

This relatively simple design has since expanded in a number of unexpected directions, and our original primitive notions about attention have been forcibly revised, if not refined. To date, we have utilized over 1200 rats as subjects in more than 110 experimental groups. There has been an earlier report of the first stages of this work (Kamin, 1968); in the present chapter, we shall review the basic preliminary findings, then focus on some of the more recent developments.

The basic CER procedure utilized in all these studies employs naive hooded rats as subjects, reduced to 75% of *ad libitum* body weight and maintained on a 24-hour feeding rhythm. The rats are first trained to press a bar for a food reward in a standard, automatically programmed operant conditioning chamber. The daily sessions are 2 hours in length, with food pellets being delivered according to a 2.5-minute variable-interval reinforcement schedule. The first five sessions (10 hrs.) produce stable bar-pressing rates in individual rats, and CER conditioning is then begun. During CER conditioning, the food-reinforcement schedule remains in effect throughout the daily 2-hour session, but four CS–US sequences are now programmed independently of the animal's behavior. The CS, typically, has a duration of 3 minutes and is followed immediately by a .5-second US, typically a 1-ma. shock. For each CER trial (four trials daily), a suppression ratio is calculated. The ratio is $B/A + B$, where B represents the number of bar presses during the 3-minute CS, and A the number of bar presses during the 3-minute period immediately preceding the CS. Thus, if the CS has no effect on the animal's bar pressing, the ratio is .50; but as the CS, with repeated trials, begins to suppress bar pressing, the ratio drops toward an asymptote very close to .00. We regard the learned suppression produced by the CS as an index of an association between CS and US, much as conditioned salivation to a metronome may be regarded as such an index.

The CS in the experiments to be described was either a white noise (typically 80 db), the turning on of an overhead house light (7.5-w. bulb diffused through milky plastic ceiling), or a compound of noise-plus-light presented simultaneously. The normal condition of the chamber is complete darkness. The various experimental groups received CER conditioning to various CS's, in different sequences. The precise sequences of CS's are detailed in the body of this report. Typically, following the CER conditioning, the animal was given a single test day, during which a nonreinforced CS was presented four times within the bar-pressing session. The data to be presented are suppression ratios for the first test trial. While no conclusions would be altered by including the data for all four test trials, the fact that the test CS is not reinforced means that test trials following the first contribute relatively little to differences between experimental groups.

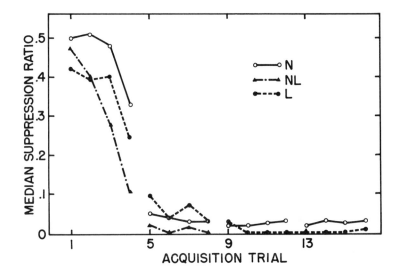

FIG 9–1.   Acquisition of CER by trial, for three groups of rats, trained with either light, noise, or compound CS.

The characteristic outcome of our basic conditioning procedure is depicted in Fig. 9–1, which presents median suppression ratios, as a function of acquisition trial, for three representative groups of subjects. The groups have been conditioned with either noise, light, or the compound as a CS. The major point to note at present is that after a very few trials all groups approach asymptotic suppression. It can also be observed that light has a slightly suppressing effect on the very first trial so that the light group tends to acquire slightly more rapidly than the noise group. Finally, the compound group acquires significantly more rapidly than either of the others.

The first experimental approach to attention is illustrated in the design outlined below. The code letter for an experimental group is indicated at the left of the paradigm. Then the CS employed with that group during consecutive phases of CER conditioning is noted; L, N, and LN refer, respectively, to a light, a noise, or a compound CS. The number of reinforced trials with each type of CS is indicated in parentheses immediately following the CS notation; four reinforced trials are given daily. Finally, the CS employed during the test trial is indicated, together with the median suppression ratio for the group on the test trial. The number of animals per experimental group varies, in the studies to be reported, between 8 and 20.

Group A:	LN (8)	N (16)	Test L	.25
Group B:	N (16)	LN (8)	Test L	.45
Group G:	—	LN (8)	Test L	.05
Group 2-B:	—	N (24)	Test L	.44

There are a number of relevant comparisons which can be made within the above set of four experimental treatments. The basic comparison is that between Groups G and B. The test result for Group G indicates, as a kind of base line, the amount of control normally acquired by the light as a result of eight reinforced compound conditioning trials. This is very significantly different from the result for Group B, within which the same compound conditioning trials have been preceded by prior conditioning to the noise element. Thus, our speculation that prior conditioning to an element might block conditioning to a new, superimposed element receives support. When we next compare Groups A and B, we again observe a significant difference. These two groups have each received the same number of each type of CER conditioning trial, but in a different sequence. Group B, for whom the noise conditioning preceded compound conditioning, is less suppressed on the test trial than is Group A, for whom the noise conditioning followed compound conditioning. This again supports the notion that prior conditioning to A blocks conditioning to the B member of the compound. The further fact that Group A is not as suppressed as Group G is not to be regarded as produced by interpolation of noise conditioning after compound conditioning. It must be remembered that four days elapse for Group A between the last compound trial and the test; appropriate control groups have established that Group A's poor performance on the test, relative to Group G's, can be attributed to the passage of time. This *recency effect,* of course, works counter to the direction of the significant difference we have observed between Groups A and B. The failure of Group B to suppress to light as much as does Group A, even with a strong recency effect working to Group B's advantage, suggests a fundamental failure of conditioning to the light in Group B. This is confirmed when we compare the test results of Groups B and 2-B. These groups each experience 24 times noise followed by shock, but for Group B light is superimposed during the final eight trials. The fact that the test trial to light yields equivalent results for B and 2-B indicates that the superimpositions have produced literally no conditioning to the light. The test ratios for both these groups are slightly below .50, indicating again that, independent of previous conditioning, an initial presentation of light has a mildly disruptive effect on ongoing bar-pressing behavior.

The blocking effect demonstrated by the experimental treatments described above is not specific to the particular sequence of stimuli employed. When four new groups of rats were trained, reversing the roles of the light and noise stimuli, a total block of conditioning to the noise member of a compound was produced by prior conditioning to the light element (Kamin, 1968). Further, it should be pointed out that we have tested many rats, after *de novo* conditioning to the light–noise compound, to each element separately. We have never observed a rat which did not display some suppression to each element. Thus, granted the present intensity levels of light and noise, the blocking effect depends upon prior conditioning to one of the elements; when conditioned from the outset to the compound, no animal ignores completely one of the elements.

We should also note that animals conditioned to noise alone after previous conditioning to light alone acquire at the same rate as do naive animals conditioned to noise alone. Prior conditioning to noise alone also does not affect subsequent conditioning to light alone. It seems very probable that this lack of transfer between the two stimuli, as well as some degree of equivalence between the independent efficacies of the stimuli, are necessary preconditions for the kind of symmetrical blocking effect which we have demonstrated.

The results so far presented indicate that, granted prior conditioning to an element, no conditioning occurs to a new element which is now superimposed on the old. This might mean, as we first loosely suggested, that the animal does not notice (or perceive) the superimposed element; the kind of peripheral gating mechanism popularized by Hernandez-Peon (Hernandez-Peon et al., 1956) is an obvious candidate for theoretical service here. To speak loosely again, however, we might suppose that the animal does notice the superimposed stimulus but does not condition to it because the stimulus is redundant. The motivationally significant event, shock, is already perfectly predicted by the old element. The possible importance of redundancy and informativeness of stimuli in conditioning experiments has been provocatively indicated by Egger and Miller (1962). We thus decided to examine whether, in the case when the superimposed stimulus predicted something new (specifically, nonreinforcement), it could be demonstrated that the animal noticed the new stimulus. The following two groups were examined.

Group Y: N (16)   LN, nonreinforced (8)   N, nonreinforced (4)
Group Z: N (16)   N, nonreinforced (12)

The results for both groups during nonreinforced trials are presented in Fig. 9–2.

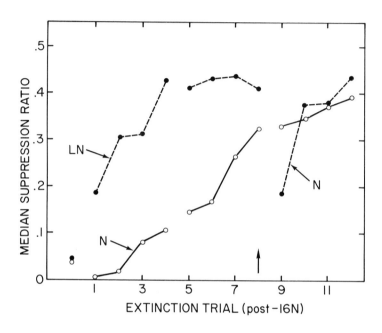

FIG. 9–2.   Extinction of CER, by trial, following conditioning to noise. The groups were extinguished either to noise alone or to the compound. The arrow in the abscissa indicates point at which group extinguished to compound is switched to noise alone.

Through the first 16 CER conditioning trials these groups are treated identically, and on the sixteenth trial the median ratio to noise was .02 for each group. When Group Y was presented with the compound on its next trial, its ratio increased to .18; on the equivalent trial, Group Z, presented with the familiar noise, had a ratio of .01. The difference between groups on this trial fell short of significance, but it is certainly suggestive. The animals in Group Y seem to notice the superimposed light, even before the compound is followed by nonreinforcement. It must be remembered that, until the moment of nonreinforcement on Trial 17, Group Y is treated identically to the blocked Group B in the original experiment. Thus, if this result can be replicated, we have evidence that animals do notice the superimposed element, at least on the first trial of its introduction. The evidence is in the form of an attenuation of the suppression which would have occurred had not the new element been superimposed.

To return to the comparison between Groups Y and Z, on the second nonreinforced trial Group Y's ratio was .31, Group Z's was .02. This difference was significant. Thus a single nonreinforced presentation of the compound was sufficient for Group Y to discriminate between noise (always reinforced) and the compound (nonreinforced). Clearly, the light element had been perceived by Group Y. The very rapid extinction in Group Y cannot be attributed to the mere failure to reinforce the noise element, as Group Z's performance makes perfectly clear. The nature of the discrimination formed by Group Y is further illustrated by comparing performance of the two groups throughout the extinction phase of the experiment. By the eighth nonreinforced trial, the ratios were .41 for Group Y and .33 for Group Z. Then, on the next trial, the stimulus for Group Y was changed to noise alone. The Group Y ratio on this trial was .17, the Group Z ratio was again .33. This was a significantly lower ratio for Group Y than had been observed on the preceding trial. Thus, to some degree, animals in Group Y had learned that it was the compound which was nonreinforced; the noise element per se had been protected from extinction.

We now see that, if the superimposed element provides new information, the animal not only notices the element but can utilize the information which it provides with truly impressive efficiency. Further, the attenuated suppression noted on the transitional trial, when the new element is first superimposed on the old, suggested that, even in the earlier experiments in which the new element was redundant, the animals may have noticed it. This suggestion was confirmed by examining all of our data. We had at last count conditioned 153 animals with 16 trials of noise alone, followed by at least one trial of the compound. The median ratio of these animals on the sixteenth noise trial was .02; on the transitional trial (before reinforcement or nonreinforcement of the compound can exert any differential effect) the median ratio was .15. (When the transitional trial was reinforced, the median ratio on the second compound trial was again .02). There were 106 subjects which displayed higher ratios on the transitional trial than on the sixteenth noise trial; 17 which displayed lower ratios on the transitional trial; and 30 which had equal ratios on the two trials. This is a highly significant effect. There is thus no doubt that, at least on the first transitional trial, an animal previously conditioned to a single element notices the superimposition of a new element.

This observation is clearly fatal to our original theoretical notions. There remains the possibility, however, that in the case when the transitional trial proves the superimposed stimulus to be redundant, some gating mechanism is activated at that point such that the new element is not perceived on subsequent compound trials. Thus, it is at least conceivable that perceptual gating (deficient attention) provides the mechanism through which redundant stimuli are made nonconditionable. This view can be contrasted to the notion that redundant stimuli, though perceived in an intact manner, are simply not conditioned. We shall return to this problem a little later, after reviewing briefly some of the parameters of the blocking effect.

The data gathered to date, much of which has been more fully described elsewhere (Kamin, 1968), indicates such facts as the following. The blocking effect, granted prior conditioning to Element A, remains total even if the number of compound conditioning trials is very substantially increased; on the other hand, if conditioning to Element A is terminated before suppression has become asymptotic, a partial block of conditioning to the B member of the compound occurs. The amount of blocking is very smoothly related to the amount of prior conditioning to Element A. The block can be eliminated by extinguishing suppression to A prior to beginning compound conditioning; if suppression to A is extinguished following compound conditioning (A having been conditioned prior to the compound), the block remains. When blocking experiments were conducted with new groups of animals, holding constant the intensity value of Element B, while varying for different groups the intensity of Element A, the amount of blocking was a clear function of the relative intensities of the two elements. That is, more blocking of conditioning to B occurs if A is physically intense than if A is physically weak. This, however, is confounded with the fact that the level of suppression achieved by conclusion of the conditioning trials to A varies with the intensity of A; and we have already indicated that blocking varies with the level of suppression conditioned to A.

We have, as well, examined the blocking effect under a large number of procedural variations which have had no effect whatever on the basic phenomenon. Thus, for example, if the standard experiment is repeated employing a 1-minute, rather than a 3-minute, CS, a complete block is obtained. The same outcome is observed if the experiment is performed employing a 3-ma., rather than a 1-ma., US throughout. And again, complete blocking is obtained if the first CS, on which light onset is superimposed as a new element, is the turning off of a background 80-db noise, rather than the turning on of an 80-db noise. To put matters simply, the blocking phenomenon is robust, and easily reproducible.

We turn now to consideration of a classical phenomenon to which the blocking effect seems clearly related; we shall later return to a more detailed analysis of blocking itself. The blocking effect demonstrated in these studies seems in many ways reminiscent of the overshadowing of a weak element by a strong element in a compound CS. The basic observation reported by Pavlov (1927, pp. 141 ff.) was that if a compound CS was formed of two stimulus elements differing greatly in intensity or strength, the weaker element, when presented on test trials, failed to elicit any CR, despite repeated prior reinforcement of the compound. This was true although the weaker element was known to be independently conditionable. The major distinctions between the Pavlovian finding and the present blocking effect are: first, that overshadowing was said to occur without prior conditioning of the stronger element; and second, that overshadowing was reported to depend fundamentally on a substantial difference between the relative intensities of the two elements. The available summaries of Russian protocols from Pavlov's laboratory, however, indicate that at least in some of the overshadowing studies the dog had in fact, at an earlier time in its lengthy experimental history, been conditioned to the stronger stimulus. Thus it seemed possible to us that overshadowing might not be obtained if naive animals were, from the outset of an experiment, conditioned to a compound consisting of strong and weak elements.

The data already reported make it clear that complete overshadowing is not obtained when naive rats are conditioned to a compound of 80-db noise plus light. Following sixteen such reinforced compound trials, animals tested either to noise or to light each display clear conditioning; the ratios are .05 to light and .25 to noise. We wished now to see whether overshadowing might be observed if the relative intensities of the light and noise elements were radically changed. To test this, new groups were conditioned (this time for eight trials) to a compound consisting of our standard light plus 50-db noise. The group then tested to light displayed a ratio of .03, while the group tested to noise had a ratio of .42. The weak noise was thus almost completely overshadowed by light. Further, animals conditioned to 50-db noise alone, following conditioning to the compound, did not acquire significantly more rapidly than did naive rats conditioned from the outset to 50-db noise. These results are entirely corroborative of the Pavlovian reports. There remains the problem of relating overshadowing, which is not dependent on prior conditioning to one of the elements, to blocking, which is so dependent.

There is at least one obvious way of incorporating both phenomena within the same framework. We could assume that, during the early trials of conditioning to a compound, independent and parallel associations are being formed between each element and the US. With the further assumption that the association to the stronger element is formed more rapidly than that to the weaker, the overshadowing experiment becomes a case in which, implicitly, precisely the same sequence of events takes place which is explicitly produced in the blocking experiment. That is, in the overshadowing case an association to one element (the stronger) is substantially formed before conditioning to a second element takes place. Thus, conditioning of the second element is blocked.

These assumptions might be made more plausible if we examined the rates at which independent groups of animals acquire the CER when conditioned to either light, noise, or the compound. The relevant acquisi-

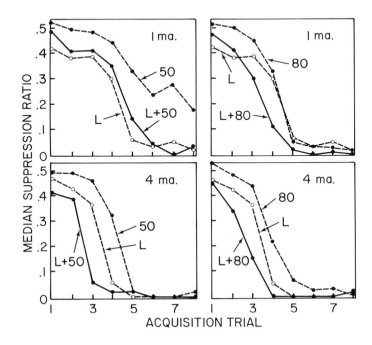

FIG. 9–3.   Acquisition of CER, by trial, for independent groups of rats trained with either 50-db noise, 80-db noise, light, or compound CS. Two upper panels are for groups trained with 1 ma. US, two lower panels for groups trained with 4 ma. US.

tion curves for the first eight trials of conditioning are presented in Fig. 9–3. The upper left-hand panel of the figure presents curves for groups trained with light, 50-db noise, and the compound light plus 50 db, respectively. The group conditioned to light is asymptotically suppressed by Trial 5, before really substantial suppression is observed in the group conditioned to 50 db. The upper right-hand panel indicates that there is relatively little difference in the rates of conditioning to light and to 80-db noise. Thus, assuming the same rates of conditioning to each element within a compound as those observed when the elements are separately conditioned in independent groups, the overshadowing effect would be expected for the 50-db compound, but not for the 80-db compound.

There are further between-group comparisons possible within Fig.

9–3 which seem to support the argument. Within the upper right-hand panel, it can be observed that the compound group acquires significantly more rapidly than does either the light group or the 80-db group. That is, a clear summation of the two stimuli can be detected when conditioning to the compound. However, in the upper left-hand panel, there is clearly no summation; the compound group conditions at the same rate as the group trained to the stronger element, light. The 50-db element cannot be seen to affect in any way conditioning in the relevant compound group. Thus the presence or absence of overshadowing, measurable only after conditioning to a compound, is correlated with the presence or absence of a summation effect, detectable by comparing a compound group to other groups conditioned to single elements. This correlation of summation with overshadowing, it might be noted, seems relevant to Hull's (1943, Ch. 13) early interpretation of Pavlovian overshadowing. Basically, Hull regarded overshadowing as an extreme example of generalization decrement; the weaker member of the compound was assumed to be so dissimilar to the compound that it elicited no response. This view, which regards overshadowing as entirely dependent upon a postconditioning within-subject testing procedure, does not account for the association of overshadowing with the failure to observe summation in between-group comparisons made during conditioning. The very weak element in a compound CS really seems in some sense to be blotted out.

The weaker element in a compound, as has been noted, is one which, at least in independent groups, conditions less rapidly than the stronger element. The question thus arises whether overshadowing is a direct consequence of the relative intensities of the two elements, or whether the effect is mediated by the different rates of conditioning controlled by the separate elements. The finding that the effect depended directly upon relative intensities would be suggestive of perceptual and "attention-like" notions: for example, the weaker stimulus might not be noticed when compounded with a very strong stimulus. To fit overshadowing into the same framework as blocking, however, it would be convenient if the effect depended upon differential rates of conditioning. We have already reported that at least partial blocking of conditioning to a strong stimulus is obtained when the weak stimulus is conditioned prior to its compounding with the strong stimulus.

To decide between the two alternatives, we employed exactly the same pairs of CS elements utilized in the preceding studies, but manipulated the differential rates of conditioning controlled by the elements. This is quite easily done. When an intense US is employed in a CER procedure, differences in the rates of conditioning produced by CS's of different intensities are substantially reduced; all CS's are conditioned very rapidly (Kamin, 1965). We thus assumed that, by repeating the overshadowing studies already reported but now employing a 4-ma., rather than the standard 1-ma., US, the differences in rates of acquisition produced by light, by 50 db, and by 80 db would be reduced, with all groups tending to condition substantially in a very few trials. This in turn should mean that overshadowing, if it is dependent on the formation of a strong association to one element before substantial conditioning has occurred to the other, should be greatly reduced, if not eliminated.

The results were clear cut. The groups conditioned with a 4-ma. US to the compound light plus 80 db, when tested with, respectively, light or 80 db, displayed virtually total suppression. The same result was obtained when groups conditioned with a 4-ma. US to the compound light plus 50 db were tested with either light or 50 db. These CS elements, of course, are identical to those employed in the preceding overshadowing studies. The fact that light does not overshadow 50 db when an intense US is employed makes it clear that overshadowing is not a simple, direct consequence of the relative intensities of conditioned stimulus elements and seems to eliminate a simple attentional interpretation of overshadowing. The alternative interpretation seems quite well supported by examination of the lower two panels of Fig. 9–3. These panels present CER acquisition curves for new independent groups, analogous to the curves in the upper panels, but with US intensity now set at 4 ma. The new groups acquire more rapidly than do corresponding groups conditioned to 1 ma. More important, all new groups acquire rapidly, and none of the single element groups appears to have conditioned substantially before conditioning in another such group was well under way. We do not have enough data to make any precise guess about how much conditioning must occur to one element, in how many trials, before how much conditioning to another element, in order for overshadowing to occur in animals for whom the two elements are compounded. The results do indicate clearly, however, that overshadowing is not the result of a simple interaction of sensory events. They suggest as well that the occurrence of overshadowing can be predicted from examination of the rates of acquisition of independent groups conditioned to the separate elements. We might note, finally, that in each of the lower two panels of Fig. 9–3 clear summation effects are detectable, once again associated with the failure to observe overshadowing.

We return now to some further experimental analyses of the basic blocking effect. Within the work previously reported, substantial prior conditioning to an element has invariably given rise to no evidence of conditioning to the superimposed element. Thus the block has appeared to be a dramatically all-or-none affair. We now ask whether the total block which we observed in our basic Group B was in part an artifact of the relatively blunt measure of conditioning which we employed. The test trial to light, following compound conditioning, measures transfer from the compound to the element. The savings method is known to be extremely sensitive in demonstrating transfer, much more so than is the recall method represented by our test. We now repeated the basic experiment, but the test was no longer a single test trial to light; instead, all animals were given four reinforced conditioning trials to light at the end of the experiment. The focus of interest is on rate of acquisition during this conditioning to light. The two basic groups are outlined below.

Group 2-A:	N (16)	LN (8)	L (4)
Group 2-B:	—	N (24)	L (4)

While Groups 2-A and 2-B have each experienced noise followed by shock 24 times before the conditioning to light alone, the difference is of course that Group 2-A has on the last eight trials experienced the light superimposed on the noise. Will Group 2-A therefore show any savings, relative to Group 2-B, when conditioned to the light alone? Or have the eight superimpositions of light literally left no effect on the animal?

There was, as our earlier results would have suggested, no significant suppression to the light by either group on the first conditioning trial to light. However, Group 2-A displayed significantly more suppression on each of trials 2, 3, and 4 than did Group 2-B. Thus, it is clear that the eight light superimpositions did indeed leave some trace, which was manifested in a significant savings effect. However, we are reminded that our earlier data already demonstrated that, in groups conditioned similarly to Group 2-A, the animals did notice the superimposed light at least on the first, transitional trial. Can it be the case that the significant savings exhibited by Group 2-A is entirely attributable to the first trial on which light is superimposed? Or, do the compound trials following the first also contribute to the savings effect?

To answer this quetsion, Group 2-N was examined. The procedure is sketched below, and should be compared to those diagrammed in the immediately preceding paradigm.

Group 2-N:	N (16)	LN (1)	N (7)	L (4)

Group 2-N differs from Group 2-B only on the transitional trial; though the total number of reinforced experiences of noise is equated across Groups 2-A, 2-B, and 2-N, Group 2-N receives seven fewer light superimpositions than does Group 2-A. Nevertheless, the acquisition curves to light alone in the final phase of the experiment are virtually identical for Groups 2-N and 2-A; like Group 2-A, Group 2-N is significantly more suppressed than Group 2-B on each of Trials 2, 3, and 4. If we compute median suppression ratios over the four trials of light conditioning for each group, they are .28 for each of Groups 2-A and 2-N, but .38 for Group 2-B. Thus it is clear that the savings which we have demonstrated can be entirely attributed to the first, transitional trial. We had in any event independent evidence that the animal noticed the light on that trial, and it is now clear that the reinforcement at the termination of that trial does produce an increment in the associative connection between light and shock. There still, however, is nothing in the data which can allow us to conclude that the animal notices a redundant, superimposed element on any trial after the transitional trial; or at least, we have no indication that reinforced presentations of the superimposed element after the transitional trial in any way affect either the contemporaneous or the subsequent behavior of the animal. These results are obviously consistent with a perceptual gating concept, so long as the gating mechanism is not activated until after the transitional trial.

Where then do we stand now? The fact that the superimposed element proves to be redundant (that the US is already perfectly predicted by Element A) seems to be central to any interpretation of the blocking effect. Presumably, then, blocking would not occur if the superimposed element were made informative. We have earlier demonstrated that, if the compound is nonreinforced, the animal utilizes the information provided by Element B very efficiently. The strategy at this point was to perform a study within the blocking paradigm, reinforcing the compound trials, but at the same time making Element B informative. This was accomplished by radically increasing US intensity during the compound trials above the level employed during the prior conditioning to Element A, as with Group 2-M in the set of experimental treatments outlined below.

Group B:	N-1 ma. (16)	LN-1 ma. (8)	Test L	.45
Group 2-M:	N-1 ma. (16)	LN-4 ma. (8)	Test L	.14
Group 3-U:	N-4 ma. (8)	LN-4 ma. (8)	Test L	.36

The comparison between Groups B and 2-M is instructive. Here at last is a simple procedure which can virtually eliminate the blocking effect. Within Group 2-M, shock intensity is radically increased during the compound trials. The effect of this operation is to allow the formation of a clear association between the superimposed element and the US; Group 2-M, on the test trial, is significantly more suppressed than the standard Group B. This effect is not a simple consequence of employing an intense US during the compound trials. With Group 3-U, the same intense US is employed throughout the experiment, and a clear blocking effect is manifested: the test ratio of 3-U does not differ significantly from that of B, but does from that of 2-M. Thus, it is the change of shock intensity during the compound trials from that employed during prior conditioning which seems responsible for eliminating the block.

These results provide clear support for the assumption that blocking occurs because of the redundancy of the superimposed element. The question remains, how does redundancy prevent the formation of an association between a CS element and a US with which it is contiguously presented?

The most recent conception at which we have arrived seems capable of integrating all the data already presented. The notion is this: perhaps, for an increment in an associative connection to occur, it is necessary that the US instigate some mental work on the part of the animal. This mental work will occur only if the US is unpredicted, if it in some sense surprises the animal. Thus, in the early trials of a normal conditioning experiment, the US is an unpredicted, surprising event of motivational significance and the CS–US association is formed. Within the blocking experiment, the occurrence of the US on the first compound trial is to some degree surprising. This can be deduced, circularly, from the empirical observation that, on the transitional trial only, suppression is moderately attenuated; and some little learning about Element B can be demonstrated to have occurred on the transitional trial, but on no other compound trial. Finally, if in the blocking experiment US intensity is radically increased when compound training is begun, the new US is obviously surprising and no block is observed.

Precisely what mental work is instigated by a surprising US? The language in which these notions have been couched can be made more respectable, as well as more specific. Thus, as a first try, suppose that, for an increment in an associative connection to occur, it is necessary that the US provoke the animal into a backward scanning of its memory store of recent stimulus input; only as a result of such a scan can an association between CS and US be formed, and the scan is prompted only by an unpredicted US, the occurrence of which is suprising. This sort of speculation, it can be noted, leaves perception of the superimposed CS element intact. The CS element fails to become conditioned not because its input has been impeded, but because the US fails to function as a reinforcing stimulus. We have clearly moved some distance from the notion of attention to the CS, perhaps to enter the realm of retrospective contemplation of the CS.

These notions, whatever their vices, do suggest experimental manipulations. With the backward scan concept in mind, an experiment was performed which employed the blocking paradigm, but with an effort to surprise the animal very shortly after each presentation of the compound. Thus, animals were first conditioned, in the normal way, to suppress to the noise CS, with the usual 1-ma., .5-second US. Then, during the compound trials, the animal received reinforced presentations of the light-noise compound, again with a 1-ma., .5-second US. However, on each compound trial, 5 seconds following delivery of the US, an extra (surprising) shock (again 1 ma., .5 sec.) was delivered. When, after compound training, these subjects were tested with the light CS, they displayed a median ratio of .08. That is, the blocking effect was entirely eliminated by the delivery of an unpredicted shock shortly following reinforced presentation of the compound.

We have emphasized the close temporal relation between the unpredicted extra shock and the preceding compound CS. This emphasis is, of course, consistent with the backward scanning notion. There are, however, several alternative interpretations of the efficacy of the unpredicted shock in eliminating the blocking effect. There is the obvious possibility that the extra shock combines with the shortly preceding normal US to form, in effect, a US more intense than that employed during the prior conditioning to the noise element. We have already indicated that a radical increase of US intensity during the compound trials will eliminate the blocking effect. There is in the data, however, a strong indication that the extra shock functions in a manner quite different from that of an intense US. It is true that, if US intensity is increased from 1 ma. to 4 ma. during the compound trials, the blocking effect is eliminated; but it is also true that, if independent groups of naive rats are conditioned, with either a light, noise, or compound CS, paired with a 4-ma. US, they acquire the CER significantly more rapidly than do equivalent groups conditioned with a 1-ma. US. That is, acquisition of the CER is a clear positive function of US intensity. We have conditioned naive groups of animals, with either light or noise CS's, delivering the extra shock, 5 seconds after the normal US, from the outset of conditioning. In each case, the acquisition curve of rats conditioned with the extra shock was virtually superimposed on that of rats conditioned with the normal US. Thus, the extra shock does not appear to increase effective US intensity.

We have stressed the notion that the second, extra shock might cause the animal to scan the preceding sensory input, and that conditioning to the superimposed CS element occurs as a consequence of this scanning. There remains, however, the plausible alternative that the effect of the unpredicted, extra shock is to alert the animal in such a way that it is more attentive or sensitive to subsequent events; i.e., to the following compound trials. Thus, in this latest view, the extra shock does not increase the amount of conditioning taking place to the superimposed CS element on the first compound trial, but it does increase the amount of such conditioning taking place on all subsequent compound trials. Within the experiment already performed, there is unfortunately no way of deciding whether the extra shock facilitates conditioning to the CS which precedes it or to the CS which follows it. We do know, from appropriate control groups, that the extra shock does not cause the animal to suppress to extraneous exteroceptive stimuli which are subsequently presented.

There should be no great experimental difficulty in localizing the effect of the extra shock. We can, for example, deliver the extra shock to different groups at varying temporal intervals following the compound trials. Presumably, backward scanning should be less effective in forming an association when the extra shock is remote in time from the preceding trial. This approach, however, has the disadvantage that moving the extra shock away from the preceding trial moves it toward the subsequent trial. This problem in turn might be overcome by presenting only one compound trial a day. The sensitivity of the procedure seems to be such that, employing a savings technique, we might demonstrate the facilitating effect of a single extra shock, delivered on a single compound trial, with no subsequent compound conditioning. This effect in turn might be related to the temporal interval between the compound trial and the extra shock. There is no dearth of potential experiments to be performed, and not much sense in attempting to anticipate their outcomes.

To sum up, the blocking experiment demonstrates very clearly that the mere contiguous presentation of a CS element and a US is not a sufficient condition for the establishment of a CR. The question, very simply is: What has gone wrong in the blocking experiment? What is deficient? The experiment was conceived with a primitive hunch that attention to the to-be-conditioned stimulus element was a necessary precondition, and many of the results to date are consistent with the notion that the deficiency is perceptual, having to do with impeded input of the CS element. This blocked input was at first conceived as a consequence of a kind of competition for attention between the previously conditioned element and the new element. The results to date, however, make it clear that, if such an attentional deficit is involved, the redundancy of the new element is critical for producing it. The extra shock experiment, most recently, has suggested an alternative conception. The input of the new CS element can be regarded as intact, but the predictability of the US might strip the US of a function it normally subserves in conditioning experiments, that of instigating some processing of the memory store of recent stimulus input, which results in the formation of an association. There is also the possibility, of course, that the predictability of the US, by the time compound training is begun in the blocking experiment, strips the US of the function of alerting the animal to subsequent stimulus input.

There seems little doubt that, as experimentation continues, still other conceptions will be suggested. The experimental procedures are at least capable of discarding some conceptions and of reinforcing others. The progress to date might encourage the belief that ultimately these studies could make a real contribution toward answering the fundamental question toward which they are addressed: What are the necessary and sufficient conditions for the establishment of an association between CS and US within a Pavlovian paradigm?

REFERENCES

EGGER, M. C., & MILLER, N. E. Secondary reinforcement in rats as a function of information value and reliability of the stimulus. *Journal of Experimental Psychology,* 1962, **64,** 97–104.

ESTES, W. K., & SKINNER, B. F. Some quantitative properties of anxiety. *Journal of Experimental Psychology,* 1941, **29,** 390–400.

HERNANDEZ-PEON, R., SCHERRER, H., & JOUVET, M. Modification of electrical activity in cochlear nucleus during "attention" in unanesthetized cats. *Science,* 1956, **123,** 331–332.

HULL, C. L. *Principles of behavior.* New York: Appleton-Century, 1943.

HUNT, H. F., & BRADY, J. V. Some effects of punishment and intercurrent "anxiety" on a single operant. *Journal of Comparative and Physiological Psychology,* 1955, **48,** 305–310.

KAMIN, L. J. Temporal and intensity characteristics of the conditioned stimulus. In W. F. Prokasy (Ed.), *Classical conditioning.* New York: Appleton-Century-Crofts, 1965. Pp. 118–147.

KAMIN, L. J. "Attention-like" processes in classical conditioning. In M. R. Jones (Ed.), *Miami symposium on the prediction of behavior, 1967: Aversive stimulation.* Coral Gables, Fla.: University of Miami Press, 1968. Pp. 9–31.

PAVLOV, I. P. *Conditioned reflexes.* (Tr., G. V. Anrep.) London: Oxford University Press, 1927. (Reprinted, New York: Dover, 1960.)

IV

IMPLICATIONS of PAVLOVIAN
CONDITIONING and
INSTRUMENTAL LEARNING
for PUNISHMENT

10

Pavlovian Fear Conditioning and Learned Helplessness: Effects on Escape and Avoidance Behavior of (a) the CS–US Contingency and (b) the Independence of the US and Voluntary Responding[1]

Steven F. Maier[2]

Martin E. P. Seligman[3]

Richard L. Solomon[4]

UNIVERSITY OF PENNSYLVANIA

Two-process learning theories postulate two kinds of learning: the formation of Pavlovian CR's based on contiguity of CS and US, and the strengthening of instrumental responses resulting from reward and punishment. Beyond this, these theories postulate interrelationships between the Pavlovian conditioning process and instrumental behavior. One postulate is that Pavlovian CR's mediate or motivate instrumental behavior. For example, a CS+, paired with shock in a separate Pavlovian conditioning session, should excite fear. Presentation of this CS+ should energize any instrumental behavior which is motivated by fear. A CS–, previously paired with the absence of shock in a separate Pavlovian conditioning session, should inhibit fear and depress any fear-motivated response. We will discuss evidence which strongly confirms these postulates.

[1] This research was supported by PHS Research Grant MH-04202 from the National Institute of Mental Health and by Grant GB-2428 from the National Science Foundation.

[2] Now at the University of Illinois.

[3] Now at Cornell University.

[4] We wish to thank C. Ransom Gallistel, Francis W. Irwin, M. Frank Norman, and Paul Rozin for their very helpful criticisms of an earlier draft of this chapter.

A procedural regularity characterizes almost all of the experiments which support mediation theory: the CS's are imposed on already established instrumental avoidance responses. First, a subject is trained to avoid. Only then is Pavlovian conditioning carried out. Conditioning can, of course, be carried out before avoidance training. However, we have found it very difficult to produce any escape or avoidance responding at all, if a dog first receives Pavlovian conditioning with shock. This fact led us to think about the voluntary skeletal responses the dog may make while he is being classically conditioned.

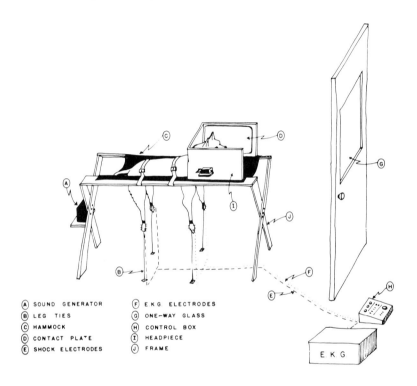

(A) SOUND GENERATOR	(F) E K G ELECTRODES
(B) LEG TIES	(G) ONE—WAY GLASS
(C) HAMMOCK	(H) CONTROL BOX
(D) CONTACT PLATE	(I) HEADPIECE
(E) SHOCK ELECTRODES	(J) FRAME

FIG. 10–1.   Pavlov harness used either for fear conditioning or for escape and avoidance training. The contact plate (D) is the manipulandum for instrumental training. Shock electrodes are attached to hind paws. CS's are presented by tone generator (A).

What skeletal responses does a dog make during conditioning? Consider a dog strapped into the harness shown in Fig. 10–1. He is given a sequence of tones paired with traumatic electric shocks delivered to his hind feet. Figure 10–2 schematizes some of the events that typically occur in such aversive conditioning. Among these events are voluntary skeletal responses. The dog may turn his head, struggle, howl, stiffen, lift his paw, relax, wag his tail, pull in his gut, and so forth. However, the dog's responses do not affect the occurrences of the CS and US. Indeed, this independence between the subject's responses and the occurrence of CS and US distinguishes Pavlovian conditioning from instrumental training. But, surprisingly, nothing more has been made of it beyond using it to make that distinction.

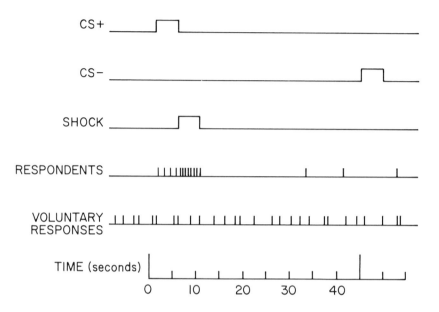

FIG. 10-2.   Diagrammatic representation of typical events during two Pavlovian fear conditioning trials. The CS+ lasts 5 seconds and overlaps with a 5-second shock. The CS−, a contracting, unreinforced CS, comes on after an intertrial interval of 45 seconds. The respondents elicited by CS+ are usually orienting or investigatory reflexes. Respondents elicited by shock are leg-flexion reflexes, vocalization, defecation, urination, piloerection, cardiac acceleration, gasping, etc. Voluntary responses elicited by shock are struggling movements of a wide variety.

It seems naive for us to have thought that the dog might simply ignore the fact that what he does during Pavlovian fear conditioning does not affect what happens to him. It would be a woefully unadaptive organism which was not sensitive to the fact that he is helpless. We shall argue that organisms learn about such independence between responding and reinforcement. We shall further argue that this learning produces profound interference with subsequent instrumental escape and avoidance learning.

In this chapter we discuss two sets of relations among the events of

Pavlovian fear conditioning. First, we describe the effects of the CS–US contingency on avoidance behavior. Later we describe the effects of the dog's helplessness during fear conditioning on his subsequent escape and avoidance learning.

Pavlovian Fear Conditioning: The CS–US Contingency in Aversive Pavlovian Conditioning Controls Already-Learned Escape and Avoidance

The concerted effort in our laboratory to study the effects of aversive Pavlovian conditioning on aversively motivated instrumental performance arose from our interest in the postulates of two-process learning theory. If, indeed, instrumental avoidance responses are mediated by a conditioned emotional reaction (CER) or a conditioned fear state, and if the conditioning of fear obeys the laws of Pavlovian salivary conditioning, then Pavlovian aversive conditioning procedures should predictably influence instrumental avoidance responding. All of the phenomena of Pavlovian salivary conditioning should be demonstrable in Pavlovian fear conditioning; and, in turn, these phenomena should reflect themselves in the control of avoidance responding by Pavlovian CS's. A detailed discussion of this theoretical position has recently been published by Rescorla and Solomon (1967).

The mediation postulate of two-process learning theory can take two forms. The strong form holds that a conditioned fear response *does* in fact mediate all avoidance responding; that is, the subject succeeds in avoiding shock because he learns to escape from the fear-eliciting CS. The weak form holds that a conditioned fear response *can* mediate avoidance behavior. The data we describe will substantiate the weak form of the fear-mediation postulate: fear-producing and fear-inhibiting CSs established by Pavlovian procedures *can* mediate avoidance responding. We have not established whether escape from fear is the mechanism that ordinarily mediates avoidance behavior. Thus, although we lean toward the view that escape from a fear-eliciting CS may mediate the acquisition of early avoidance responses, it is certainly possible that escape from the CS is not necessary for the maintenance of avoidance. At asymptotic avoidance performance (1) subjects often become quite nonchalant responders (Solomon, Kamin, & Wynne, 1953); (2) subjects may not show a CER to the CS (Kamin, Brimer, & Black, 1963); (3) subjects often do not show peripheral autonomic nervous system (ANS) arousal to the CS (Black, 1959); and (4) subjects often respond with an avoidance latency that may be too short to allow significant ANS arousal (Solomon & Wynne, 1953). All these data suggest that the subjects may not be escaping from a fear-eliciting CS when avoidance behavior is well learned. They may be responding in order to avoid the US.

Testing the Fear-Mediation Concept

The difficulty of validating the fear-mediation concept is illustrated by some procedures used by Sidman et al. (1957). While their monkeys were lever pressing at a steady rate in order to avoid shock and were receiving very few shocks each session, the experimenters presented them with a sound which lasted 5 minutes. At the termination of the sound, a brief shock occurred. The monkey could do nothing to change this sound–shock contingency. After many pairings of sound and shock, the onset of the sound alone increased the lever-pressing rate.

Two-process theories of avoidance learning argue that the sound, by association with shock, aroused a conditioned-fear reaction similar to that motivating the lever-press response. Thus, the sound, a CS+, added to the fear-eliciting effect of the training situation, with the result that the total fear was greater in the presence of the CS+ than in its absence. Therefore, the lever-pressing rate increased in the presence of CS+.

There is, however, an alternative to this fear-mediation interpretation. It was put forth by Sidman et al. in explaining their findings. The new sound–shock pairings were imposed on subjects that were already lever pressing at a rapid rate. Shock termination sometimes occurred directly following a lever press in the presence of the sound. It was argued that such pairings should reinforce lever pressing in the presence of the sound. This type of adventitious or superstitious instrumental reinforcement is always a problem when subjects are conditioned "on the base line"; i.e., while they are exercising a free operant. Therefore, although the Sidman et al. procedure suggests that the rate of lever pressing may be a function of the momentary intensity of Pavlovian-conditioned fear, it leaves open the possibility that the lever pressing was actually strengthened via another mechanism, an instrumental reinforcement contingency stemming from shock termination.

Solomon and Turner (1962) attempted to prevent this confounding of Pavlovian and instrumental contingencies. They gave instrumental shock-avoidance training to dogs in the panel-pressing apparatus (see Fig. 10–1). After the dogs had learned to avoid shock by making short-latency responses to a visual S+, they were completely paralyzed by d-tubocurarine. Then they were subjected to Pavlovian discriminative-conditioning procedures in the same apparatus. A tone of one frequency (CS+) was consistently paired with shock, and a tone of another frequency (CS−) was never paired with shock. Two days after recovery from curarization, the subjects were tested in the panel-pressing apparatus. They retained their short-latency avoidance responses to the visual S+. More importantly, when the CS+ was presented, the dogs responded with a short-latency panel press. When CS− was presented, the dogs either did not respond or responded hesitantly. The conditioning procedure thus resulted in immediate discriminative control of previously established instrumental responses by Pavlovian CS's that had not been present during avoidance learning (see Fig. 10–3).

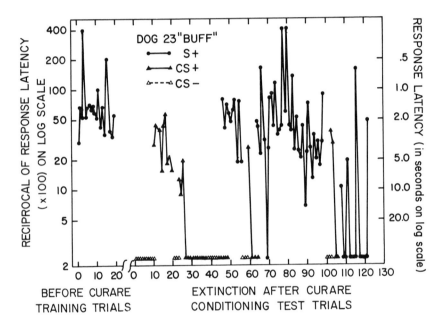

FIG. 10–3.   Control of instrumental avoidance responding by CS's not present during avoidance training but present during a separate Pavlovian fear-conditioning session. Ordinate gives latency of panel-press avoidance response in presence of three different stimuli: (a) the S+, a light used as the danger signal during original avoidance training, (b) CS+, the tonal stimulus always paired with shock during the separate fear-conditioning session, and (c) CS−, the tonal stimulus always presented without a shock during the fear-conditioning session. This figure shows that the first presentation of the CS+ evoked panel-pressing, although the first presentation of CS− did not do so. The successive testing of CS+ under no-shock conditions led to extinction of its evocation power. CS− remained ineffective. In contrast, the S+ retained its evocation power quite well during the long test session.

From: R. L. Solomon & L. H. Turner, "Discriminative Classical Conditioning in Dogs Paralyzed by Curare Can Later Control Discriminative Avoidance Responses in the Normal State," *Psychological Review*, **69**, 1962, Fig. 3, p. 213. Copyright 1962 by the American Psychological Association and reproduced by permission.

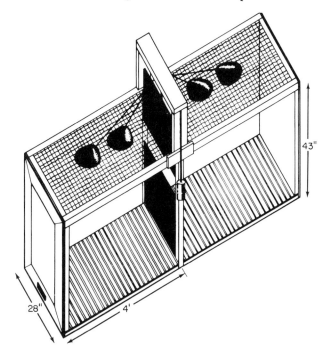

FIG. 10–4.   Schematic diagram of the shuttle box used to train dogs to jump over a barrier in order to escape and avoid shock (see Solomon & Wynne, 1953). Overhead lights can be used as S+. If Pavlovian fear conditioning is carried out in this apparatus, tones are presented by speakers mounted on each end panel. The drop gate is closed during Pavlovian conditioning, preventing escape responses. It is open during escape and avoidance training. The floor of the apparatus is made of steel grid bars for delivery of shocks.

From: R. L. Solomon & L. C. Wynne, "Traumatic Avoidance Learning: Acquisition in Normal Dogs," *Psychological Monographs,* **67** (4, Whole No. 354), 1953, Fig. 1, p. 2. Copyright 1953 by the American Psychological Association and reproduced by permission.

At the time of fear conditioning, the dogs were paralyzed. Therefore, they did not make peripheral skeletal responses which might have been reinforced. Nevertheless, the dogs panel-pressed differentially to CS+ and CS−. Therefore, the instrumental avoidance behavior was probably controlled by Pavlovian contingencies rather than by instrumental contingencies. Adventitious or superstitious reinforcement seems to be a poor explanation for our findings as well as for the Sidman et al. findings.

Nevertheless, consider the possibility that the dogs were trying to press the panel while paralyzed by curare. After all, that is what they had learned to do to escape and avoid shock in the harness. Shock termination might have adventitiously reinforced such attempts at panel pressing in the presence of the CS+. This would transform the CS+ into a Skinnerian S^D. This seems to be a plausible alternative to the fear-mediation explanation. Such an explanation cannot, however, easily be maintained in the light of Leaf's (1964) findings. He trained dogs to avoid shock by jumping over a barrier in the shuttle box shown in Fig. 10–4. Then, in a harness located in another room, he subjected them to discriminative Pavlovian fear conditioning while they were paralyzed by curare. A tone (CS+) was consistently paired with shock, and another tone (CS−) was never paired with shock. Then the tones were separately presented to the dogs in the shuttle box 2 days later, and CS+ evoked short-latency jumps while CS− failed to do so.

It seems most unlikely that Leaf's dogs were trying to jump a non-existent barrier while they were being shocked in the harness. This virtually excludes the possibility that barrier jumping was adventitiously reinforced during the discriminative Pavlovian fear conditioning. Leaf's results therefore are excellent preliminary evidence for the mediational postulate of two-process learning theory.

Fear Conditioning Follows the Laws of Pavlovian Salivary Conditioning

Even stronger evidence for the mediational postulate comes from the work carried out in our laboratory by Rescorla and LoLordo (1965), LoLordo (1967), Rescorla (1967), and Moscovitch and LoLordo (1967). We now know that Pavlovian fear conditioning and Pavlovian salivary conditioning obey the same laws. These laws are revealed in the control of avoidance responding by Pavlovian CS's.

Excitation and differential inhibition.   Rescorla and LoLordo (1965) trained dogs to jump a barrier in a shuttle box to avoid shock on a Sidman schedule. Then they penned the dogs in one side of the shuttle box and carried out discriminative Pavlovian fear conditioning. A tone (CS+) was paired with shock, and another tone (CS−) was paired with absence of shock. Later, in a test session, while the dog was jumping reliably, the experimenters inserted a series of 5-second test presentations of CS+ and CS−. The CS+ produced an immediate tripling of the jumping rate. The CS− reduced the jumping rate almost to zero (see Fig. 10–5). This finding is in agreement with a two-process theory of avoidance behavior. Assume that the fear elicited by apparatus cues maintained the normal rate of Sidman avoidance responding (about seven per min. in Fig. 10–5). The CS+, a conditioned excitor of fear, should have augmented the ambient, conditioned fear level when it was added to the apparatus cues.

Because the CS— was paired with absence of shock, it was a differential inhibitor of fear. Therefore, it should have decreased ambient fear. The fact that these two expectations were confirmed means that conditioned fear follows the Pavlovian law of differential excitation and inhibition.

Excitation and conditioned inhibition.   Rescorla and LoLordo (1965) trained two other groups of dogs to avoid shock on a Sidman schedule in the shuttle box. Then they subjected one group to a Pavlovian fear-conditioning procedure in which CS+ was followed by shock on one

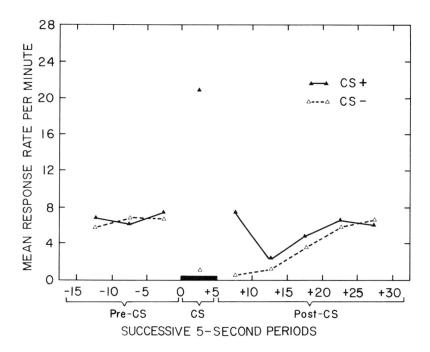

FIG. 10–5.   Differential excitatory and inhibitory control of instrumental avoidance responding by a Pavlovian CS+ and CS—. Prior to testing, subjects had been trained under a Sidman contingency to avoid shocks in the shuttle box. Their typical response rate was about 7 per minute. They were then given Pavlovian differential fear conditioning in the same shuttle box. One tone was CS+, a contrasting tone was CS—. Then, in a test session, while subjects were jumping regularly in the shuttle box, 5-second test prods with each CS were given. The ordinate shows jumps per minute. The abscissa shows time before the test prod, during it, and after it. The rates for CS+ and CS— are compared. This figure shows that the CS+ evoked an increase in rate, and then a decrease and increase after CS+ was withdrawn. CS— produced a decrease in rate which slowly subsided after CS— was withdrawn. Thus the recovery from CS+ was biphasic but the recovery from CS— was monotonic.

half of the trials, but on the other half of the trials CS+ was followed by CS— and no shock. Thus CS— was a temporal substitute for shock. After learning the Sidman avoidance response, the second group was subjected to a different Pavlovian fear-conditioning procedure. CS+ was followed by shock on one half of the trials, but on the other half of the trials CS— was inserted 5 seconds before the CS+, and no shock followed. The CS— in both procedures acquired fear-inhibiting properties. Test presentations of CS— reduced the Sidman avoidance response rate significantly. Presentations of CS+ doubled the response rate (see Fig. 10–6).

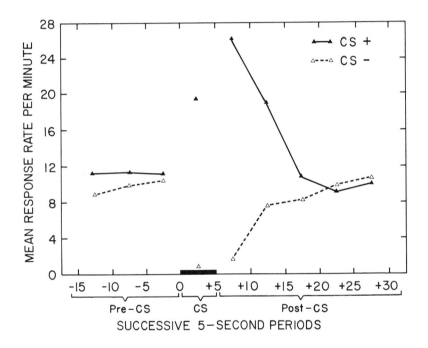

FIG. 10–6.   Conditioned excitatory and inhibitory control of instrumental avoidance responding by a Pavlovian CS+ and CS—. Prior to testing, subjects had been trained under a Sidman contingency to avoid shock in the shuttle box. Their response rate stabilized. They were then given Pavlovian fear conditioning in the same shuttle box, using the Pavlovian conditioned-inhibition procedure. When CS+ occurred alone it was paired with shock. When CS+ and CS— occurred in sequence, no shock was given. Then, in a later test session, while subjects were jumping in the shuttle box, test prods with each CS were given. The ordinate shows jumps per minute. The abscissa shows time before the test, during it, and after it. The rates for CS+ and CS— are compared. This figure shows that the CS+ evoked an increase in rate which continued several seconds after CS+ was withdrawn. The rate subsided monotonically thereafter, until it reached the pre-CS base line. CS— produced a decrease in rate which slowly subsided after CS— was withdrawn. Thus the recovery from both the CS+ and the CS— presentations was monotonic.

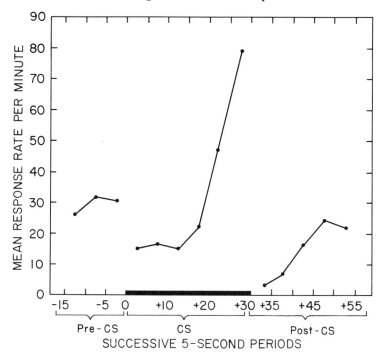

FIG. 10–7.   Inhibition by temporal delay. After avoidance training in the shuttle box under a Sidman schedule, subjects were given simple Pavlovian fear conditioning with a 30-second CS–US interval. There was no CS–. In the test session, while subjects were jumping at a regular rate in the shuttle box, the CS+ was presented from time to time. This figure shows that the onset of CS+ produced a decrease in jumping rate. Then, while CS+ continued, the rate increased until it went above the pre-CS baseline rate. Recovery from the 30-second test prod was biphasic.

From: R. A. Rescorla, "Inhibition of Delay in Pavlovian Fear Conditioning," *Journal of Comparative and Physiological Psychology*, **64**, 1967, pp. 114–120. Copyright 1967 by the American Psychological Association and reproduced by permission.

Inhibition by temporal delay.   Rescorla (1967) trained dogs to avoid shock on a Sidman schedule in the shuttle box. When the dogs had acquired a stable jumping rate, they were subjected to a Pavlovian fear-conditioning procedure in which a 30-second tone (CS+) was followed by shock. Later, while the dogs were performing their avoidance response in the shuttle box, the 30-second tone was presented from time to time. The effects of the tone are shown in Fig. 10–7. The onset of the tone produced a decrease in jumping rate, and in the continued presence of the tone the rate gradually increased. At about 20-second tone duration, the jumping rate went above the normal base-line rate, increasing steadily to the end of the interval, at which time the rate had approximately doubled. Cessation of the tone produced a decrease in jumping rate to a level below the normal base-line rate, followed by slow recovery to the base line rate. The generality of this finding is illustrated by the results in Fig. 10–8. Rescorla (1967) trained dogs to panel-press in the Pavlov harness shown in Fig. 10–1, using Sidman contingencies. When the dogs were pressing at a stable rapid rate, they were given Pavlovian delayed conditioning using a 30-second tone as CS+ and a shock as US. Later, while the subjects were panel pressing, test presentation of the CS+ produced a decrease in responding followed by a gradual increase throughout the CS+ presentation until the rate had doubled (see Fig. 10–8). Here is a

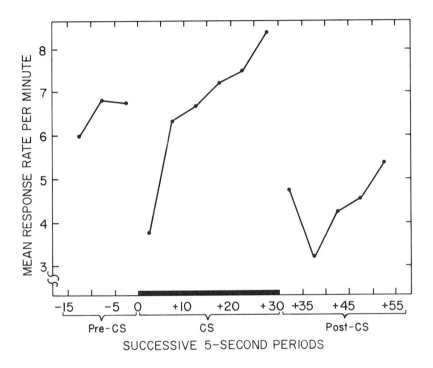

FIG. 10–8.   Inhibition by temporal delay. Subjects were avoidance trained in the Pavlov harness under a Sidman schedule. When they reached a stable panel-pressing rate of about 30 per minute, they were given simple Pavlovian fear conditioning with a 30-second CS–US interval. There was no CS–. In the test session, while subjects were panel-pressing, the CS+ was presented from time to time. This figure shows that the onset of CS+ produced a decrease in panel-pressing rate. Then, while CS+ continued, the rate increased until it went above the pre-CS base-line rate. Recovery from the 30-second test prod was biphasic. The outcome was similar in most respects to that shown in Fig. 10–7.

From: R. A. Rescorla, "Inhibition of Delay in Pavlovian Fear Conditioning," *Journal of Comparative and Physiological Psychology,* **64**, 1967, pp. 114–120. Copyright 1967 by the American Psychological Association and reproduced by permission.

case in which onset of a danger signal decreased avoidance responding. Pavlov found similar inhibition of delay with salivary CR's and long-duration CS's. He argued that the onset of the CS+ is never closely paired with US and functions as a CS−, inhibiting conditioned reflexes. Rescorla's results show that the law of inhibition of delay holds for fear conditioning.

Inhibition from backward conditioning. Backward conditioning might be considered a prime example of an inhibitory Pavlovian procedure. The CS should become inhibitory provided that the intertrial interval is long, because the CS is followed by a US-free time interval. Moscovitch and LoLordo (1967) found this to be true for fear conditioning. They trained dogs to avoid shock on a Sidman schedule in the shuttle box. Then the dogs were penned in one side of the shuttle box and given backward Pavlovian fear conditioning with a tone and shock. The US–CS sequences were followed by a shock-free, variable intertrial interval with a mean of 2.5 minutes. Later, in a test session, short presentations of the tone resulted in a temporary decrease in jumping rate (see Fig. 10–9). We can infer that the backward CS was an inhibitor and therefore reduced the ambient level of fear. This finding confirms Pavlov's belief that backward excitatory conditioning does not occur.

Inhibition by extinction below zero. Pavlov found that a CS+ once paired with a US, took on inhibitory properties after prolonged extinction. It would be interesting to know whether a CS+ for shock, after it has been thoroughly extinguished, would decrease the rate of Sidman avoidance responding. This experiment has not been carried out.

Generalization of excitation and inhibition. Pavlov implied that all gradients of generalization of inhibition are steeper than those of excitation when he postulated that inhibition is transitory relative to excitation. It would therefore be important to determine the shapes of generalization gradients independently for CS+ and CS−. This work recently was carried out in our laboratory by Dr. Otello Desiderato (1969), and Pavlov's expectations were confirmed. There is a true inhibitory gradient for conditioned inhibition of fear.

Induction. Not much is known about the effect of Pavlovian induction procedures on aversive instrumental responding. One might measure the increase in jumping rate produced by (1) a CS+ presentation that followed a CS− presentation, as compared with (2) a CS+ presentation that followed another CS+ presentation. If positive induction were to occur, the jumping rate would be faster to a CS+ that was preceded by a CS− than to a CS+ that was preceded by a CS+. This experiment has

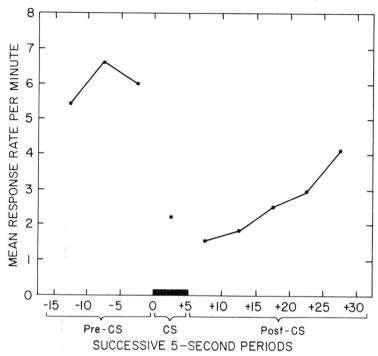

FIG. 10–9.   Inhibition from backward conditioning. After Sidman avoidance training in the shuttle box, subjects were given backward Pavlovian fear conditioning in
the same shuttle box. There were US–CS pairings followed by long intertrial intervals.
Then, during a later test session, while subjects were jumping at a stable rate, 5-second
test prods with CS were given from time to time. This figure shows that the presence
of the CS produced a decrease in jumping rate. Removal of the CS produced a monotonic recovery to the baseline rate. Thus a backward CS can be an inhibitor of fear.

From: A. Moscovitch & V. LoLordo, "Backward Conditioning and Cessation Conditioning Produce Inhibition," paper presented at the meeting of the Eastern Psychological Association, Boston, April, 1967. Reproduced by permission.

not yet been done. Negative induction could also be studied. One would
compare avoidance responding to a Pavlovian CS— when it has recently
been preceded by a CS+ presentation, as compared with its being preceded by a CS— presentation. If negative induction were to occur, the
jumping rate would be slower to a CS— that was preceded by a CS+
than to a CS— that was preceded by a CS—.

External inhibition and disinhibition.   The influence of novel stimuli
upon the power of CS's which are presented during ongoing instrumental
behavior has not been studied. It would be of interest to see whether a
novel (but not aversive) stimulus could disrupt the usual energizing

effect which an aversive CS+ has upon instrumental avoidance behavior (external inhibition). Likewise, we would like to know whether we can remove the inhibitory effect which a CS— has upon instrumental avoidance behavior by presentation of a novel (but not aversive) stimulus (disinhibition).

Other Procedures Affect Conditioned Fear

In the preceding section we showed that fear conditioning obeys the established laws of salivary conditioning. Now we examine other conditioning variables that are important in the control of fear.

Inhibition from a cessation signal.   One relationship not studied by Pavlov, yet of significance to two-process theorists, is that between CS presentation and shock termination. Mowrer (1960) postulated that a cessation signal (a CS inserted shortly before shock terminates) should elicit a relief reaction and thus should be a secondary reinforcer. Actually, evidence on the secondary reinforcing properties of cessation signals is conflicting (see review by Beck, 1961). Furthermore, we do not know whether such signals inhibit fear. To answer this question, Moscovitch and LoLordo (1968) trained dogs to avoid shock with a Sidman contingency in a shuttle box. Then the dogs had a Pavlovian conditioning session, during which 4-, 5- and 6-second shocks were presented in a random sequence. A CS was always presented 1 second before each shock termination and it stayed on for 4 seconds. The shock-free intertrial intervals were either 2.0, 2.5, or 3.0 minutes. Later, in a test session, while the dogs were jumping in the shuttle box, test presentations of the CS produced a small but significant decrease in jumping rate (see Fig. 10–10).

Did the cessation signal inhibit fear during Sidman avoidance responding because it had been paired with termination of shock during conditioning? Or did it inhibit fear because it predicted at least 2 minutes of shock-free time? To answer these questions, Moscovitch and LoLordo (1968) compared the fear-inhibiting properties of backward CS's and cessation CS's. For all dogs the CS predicted the same amount of shock-free time during fear conditioning. There were, however, three experimental groups which differed in the relation between the CS onset and shock termination. In a cessation-signal group, the CS came on 1 second before the shock terminated. In two backward conditioning groups, the CS came on either 1 second or 15 seconds after termination of shock. It was found that the CS in both backward conditioning groups reduced the rate of Sidman avoidance responding more than the CS in the cessation–signal group. This means that the backward CS's were more fear inhibiting than the cessation CS.

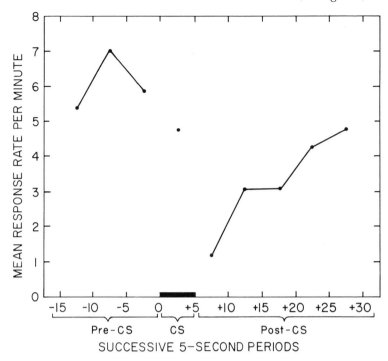

FIG. 10-10.   Inhibition from a cessation signal. After subjects had been trained to jump in the shuttle box in order to avoid shock on a Sidman schedule, they were given a Pavlovian conditioning session. The CS was presented during a 5-second shock. Its onset was 1 second before shock termination. CS duration was 5 seconds. There was no CS signalling the onset of shock. Later, in a test session, 5-second prods with the CS were presented from time to time, while subjects were jumping in the shuttle box. This figure shows that the presence of the CS produced only a slight decrease in jumping rate. However, removal of the CS produced a large decrease in rate followed by slow return to the baseline, pre-CS rate. Thus recovery from the CS test was bi-phasic.

From: A. Moscovitch & V. LoLordo, "Backward Conditioning and Cessation Conditioning Produce Inhibition," paper presented at the meeting of the Eastern Psychological Association, Boston, April, 1967. Reproduced by permission.

This result is paradoxical because the cessation signal predicts both shock termination and 2.0 minutes of shock-free time, while the backward CS's merely predict shock-free time. There is a theoretical resolution of this paradox. Assume that the cessation signal acquired fear-inducing properties because of its temporal overlap with shock. Assume further that this fear-inducing property summated with the fear-reducing properties of prediction of shock termination. Then the backward CS's should have been more fear inhibiting than the cessation CS.

The information value of a cessation CS may be important (Seligman, 1966). If so, then the amount of uncertainty the animal has about the duration of each shock should determine the amount of relief produced by a cessation CS. This suggests an experiment in which, during a fear-conditioning session, the durations of shocks should be more variable than those used by Moscovitch and LoLordo. The CS should reliably predict shock termination. Such a CS might have powerful fear-inhibiting properties and therefore would, if imposed on the subject during Sidman avoidance, greatly reduce the response rate.

Generalization of fear across different US's. If subjects were trained to avoid shock, then were conditioned to fear a stimulus paired with a loud noise, would the CS+ for the noise US have the capacity to raise the shock-avoidance rate? Would the CS— for the noise suppress the shock-avoidance rate? LoLordo (1967) trained dogs in a harness to press a panel to avoid shock on a Sidman contingency. Pavlovian conditioning was carried out "on the base line"; i.e., while the dogs were regularly avoiding shock by panel pressing. The conditioning was discriminative, a CS+ being paired with a loud noise (US) and a CS— paired with no noise. Another group of dogs was conditioned "on the base line" with a CS+ paired with shock and a CS— paired with no shock. The CS+ for the loud noise US acquired excitatory properties; test presentations of it increased the panel-pressing rate. The CS+ for the shock US increased the panel-pressing rate more than did the CS+ for the loud noise. The CS— for shock decreased the panel-pressing rate (therefore showing differential inhibition, in confirmation of the earlier shuttle-box avoidance data of Rescorla and LoLordo). However, the CS— for the loud noise did not decrease the panel-pressing rate.

LoLordo (1967) concluded that both the CS+ for loud noise and the CS+ for shock elicited fear. When the CS+ for loud noise was imposed on the subject while it was avoidance responding, it added to the ambient level of fear and thus increased the response rate. However, we do not understand why the CS— for loud noise did not inhibit fear and decrease the avoidance response rate.

This experiment suggests that the mediational properties of aversive CR's can generalize somewhat across different aversive US's. To this extent, fear of shock and fear of a loud noise summate.

Perseveration of excitation derived from aversive US presentations. Pavlov (1927, p. 59) noted that presentations of meat powder between trials, without pairing them with the CS, enhance salivation to the next presentation of CS+ in well-conditioned dogs. Baum (1967) found similar results with conditioned fear in dogs. The dogs were trained to avoid shock on a Sidman contingency in a shuttle box. Then they were penned up in one side of the shuttle box and were given a series of inescapable shocks. At varying time intervals following the last inescapable shock, the dogs were released and allowed to jump as usual in the shuttle box. The inescapable shocks resulted in greatly increased jumping rates which persisted in some subjects for as long as 35 minutes after the last shock was received. The rates were a monotonic, decreasing function of time since the last inescapable shock. We interpret this to mean that, in a well-trained subject, inescapable shocks produce a transient state of increased fear. Since the rate of Sidman avoidance responding is directly related to ambient fear level, Baum's results seem reasonable. Studies of this type illuminate the role of performance variables in the control of avoidance responding.

US duration and conditioned fear.   What should be the effects of a long-duration US paired with a CS+ as compared with a short-duration US paired with a CS+? We could adopt an S–S drive-induction view and argue that the CS-onset–US-onset relation is all-important (see Mowrer & Solomon, 1954) and that US duration is irrelevant for fear conditioning. Or, we could take a drive-reduction view of conditioning (see Miller, 1951) and argue that a long-duration US represents a long delay of drive-reduction. Such a view would predict better fear conditioning with a short-duration US. Finally, we could argue that a long-duration US is more severe than a short one (see Church et al., 1966) and should produce better fear conditioning than would a short one.

Overmier (1966) trained dogs to avoid shock in a shuttle box whenever a visual S+ was presented. Then the dogs were given Pavlovian aversive conditioning. Conditioning occurred either while the dogs were curarized in the harness or penned up on one side of the shuttle box. One tone (CS_{S+}) was paired with a 0.5-second shock; a contrasting tone (CS_{L+}) was paired with a 50.0-second shock. Later, when the dogs were undergoing avoidance extinction in the shuttle box, test presentations of the two CS's resulted in shorter jump latencies to CS_{L+} than to CS_{S+}. The subjects jumped almost as quickly to both CS's as they did to the original S+, even though the CS's had never been present during the avoidance training (see Fig. 10–11).

We can conclude that a CS+ paired with long-duration shocks is a better conditioned fear-elicitor than is a CS+ paired with short-duration shocks.

The Problem of Independence of Fear Conditioning and Instrumental Learning

We have argued that fear conditioning mediates instrumental avoidance responding and that the laws that govern fear conditioning are identical

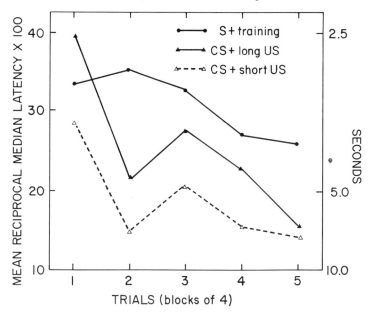

FIG. 10–11.   The effects of US duration during Pavlovian fear conditioning. Subjects
had been trained to jump in order to avoid shock in the shuttle box whenever a visual
S+ was presented. Then they were given discriminative Pavlovian fear conditioning
with one CS+ paired with a long-duration shock and a contrasting CS+ paired with
a short-duration shock. Later, in a test session, each CS+ was presented from time to
time. This figure shows that, in a series of 20 tests of each stimulus, the CS+
paired with the long-duration shock evoked jumping with shorter latencies than did
the CS+ paired with the short-duration shock. The S+ used in original avoidance
training maintained its evocation power during the extinction testing better than the
two Pavlovian CS's did.

From: J. B. Overmier, "Instrumental and Cardiac Indices of Pavlovian Fear Conditioning as a Function of US Duration," *Journal of Comparative and Physiological
Psychology*, **62**, 1966, Fig. 2, p. 18. Copyright 1966 by the American Psychological Association and reproduced by permission.

to those governing Pavlovian salivary conditioning. All of the experiments which have shown this were carried out in two distinct stages:
avoidance training, and then Pavlovian fear conditioning. We have
obviously taken great pains to separate the administration of Pavlovian
CS–US contingencies from the occurrence of Thorndikian response-
reinforcement contingencies in these experiments. Pavlovian aversive
conditioning operations were usually separated from the avoidance training operations both in time and in space. In such experiments, Pavlovian
CS's took control of avoidance responding on their very first presentation
in the avoidance situation. There had been no apparent chance for the

Pavlovian CS+ to have become an S+ for the avoidance operant, nor for the Pavlovian CS− to have become an S−.

Nevertheless, Leaf (1964) and Overmier and Leaf (1965) thought it important to test this assumption further. They pointed out that in the experiments successful in showing the control of avoidance responses by aversive Pavlovian CS's, the instrumental avoidance training had been administered first and the Pavlovian aversive conditioning had been second. Leaf reasoned that if this order were reversed there would exist no already established, and situationally appropriate, avoidance response for the CS+ to control during the conditioning procedure. Therefore, the CS+ could not serve as an S+ for the appropriate operant. Leaf gave naive dogs a Pavlovian discriminative fear-conditioning session while they were curarized in the harness. Three days after this discriminative conditioning, the subjects were taken to another experimental room where they received avoidance training in a shuttle box. After learning, they were tested with a random series of presentations of CS+ and CS−. Both stimuli evoked jumping responses, but the CS+ produced shorter latencies than did the CS−. Because discriminative fear conditioning had preceded avoidance learning, we can be further assured that instrumental contingencies were not responsible for this discriminative control.

Later, Overmier and Leaf (1965) compared the precision of discriminative control of fear for these two orders of events: (1) fear conditioning followed by avoidance training, and (2) avoidance training followed by fear conditioning. One group of dogs received one order of events, and another group received the other order. All subjects in both groups showed immediate, discriminative avoidance responding when they were tested during avoidance extinction with presentations of the Pavlovian CS+ and CS−. However, the sharpness of discrimination was better for the subjects having avoidance learning first than it was for subjects having Pavlovian conditioning first. In addition, the subjects having Pavlovian conditioning first showed a marked extinction trend to all test stimuli over 10 days of testing. In contrast, the subjects having avoidance training first showed no decrement in response to any test stimuli as extinction progressed.

This result requires some supplementary principles not inherent in current two-process learning theories. Although the mediation postulate was again confirmed, order made a difference. This means that Pavlovian fear conditioning and instrumental avoidance learning are not completely orthogonal. A complete two-process theory must therefore contain principles of sequential interaction of fear conditioning and avoidance learning.

There is yet another, and quite unexpected, way in which these two experiments take us beyond existing theory. Leaf (1964) and Overmier and Leaf (1965) [5] noticed that when Pavlovian fear conditioning preceded avoidance training by less than two days, the subjects were initially poor in escaping shock during avoidance training. Sometimes these subjects did not escape shock at all. Aversive Pavlovian conditioning thus can have decremental effects on *to-be-learned* escape and avoidance responses, whereas aversive Pavlovian conditioning has incremental effects on *already learned* avoidance responses. The second section of this paper will examine the nature and cause of the decremental effects.

Learned Helplessness: In Pavlovian Conditioning the US and Instrumental Responding Are Independent; Conditioning Disrupts the Acquisition of Escape and Avoidance

Pavlovian conditioning, by its very nature, establishes a relation between emitted instrumental responding and the US, as well as a relation between CS and US. The relationship between the US and instrumental responding is one of independence; responding neither increases nor decreases the probability of US onset or termination. In other words, the US is inescapable and unavoidable in aversive Pavlovian conditioning. This inescapability of an aversive US interferes profoundly with the subsequent acquisition of instrumental escape and avoidance behavior.

Producing Interference

When an experimentally naive dog receives escape–avoidance training in the shuttle box, the following behavior typically occurs: At the onset of the first electric shock, the dog runs frantically about, defecating, urinating, and howling, until it accidentally scrambles over the barrier and so escapes the shock. On the next trial, the dog, running and howling, crosses the barrier more quickly than on the preceding trial. This pattern continues until efficient avoidance behavior finally emerges. Overmier and Seligman (1967) and Seligman and Maier (1967) found a striking difference between this pattern of behavior and that exhibited by dogs given prior inescapable electric shocks (either unsignaled or preceded by a CS). Such a dog's first reactions to shock in the shuttle box are much the same as those of a naive dog. However, in dramatic contrast to a naive dog, a dog which has experienced inescapable shocks prior to avoidance training soon stops running and howling and remains silent until shock

5 Overmier, J. B., & Leaf, R. C. Personal communication.

terminates. The dog does not cross the barrier and escape from shock. Rather, it seems to give up and passively accept the shock. On succeeding trials, the dog continues to fail to make escape movements and will take as much shock as the experimenter chooses to give.

There is another peculiar characteristic of the escape and avoidance behavior of dogs which have first experienced inescapable shock. Such dogs occasionally jump the barrier and escape or avoid, but then revert to taking the shock; they fail to profit from exposure to the barrier-jumping-shock-termination contingency. In naive dogs a successful escape response is a reliable predictor of future, short-latency escape responses.

We have studied the escape–avoidance behavior of 82 dogs which had received prior inescapable shocks. Two-thirds of these dogs do not escape; the other third escape and avoid in normal fashion. In contrast, only 6% of experimentally naive dogs fail to escape in the shuttle box. So any given dog will either fail to escape on almost every trial or will learn normally. An intermediate outcome is rare.

A typical experimental procedure which produces failures to escape shock is as follows. On the first day, the subject is strapped into the Pavlov harness and given 64 inescapable electric shocks, each 5.0 seconds long and of 6.0-ma. intensity. The shocks occur randomly in time. Twenty-four hours later, the subject is given 10 trials of signalized escape–avoidance training in the shuttle box. The onset of the CS (dimmed illumination) begins each trial, and the CS remains until trial termination. The CS–US interval is 10 seconds. If the subject jumps the barrier (set at shoulder height) during this interval, the CS terminates and no shock occurs. Failure to jump during the CS–US interval leads to a 4.5-ma. shock which remains until the subject jumps the barrier. If the subject fails to jump the barrier within 60 seconds after CS onset, the trial automatically terminates, and a 60-second latency is recorded.

The shuttle-box performance which typically results is plotted in Fig. 10–12, which presents the median latency of barrier jumping on each of the 10 escape–avoidance trials for a group ($N=82$) pretreated with inescapable shocks and a naive control group ($N=35$). The group pretreated with inescapable shocks responds much more slowly than does the group not so pretreated. Sixty-three percent of dogs pretreated with inescapable shock fail to escape on nine or more of the ten trials. Only 6% of naive dogs fail to escape on nine or more of the ten trials. Remember that failure to escape means that the dog takes 50 seconds of severe pulsating shock on each trial.

The interference effect is very general. It does not depend solely on the use of any particular shock parameters. Overmier and Seligman (1967) and Seligman and Maier (1967) varied frequency, intensity, density, duration, and temporal pattern of shocks, and still produced the interference

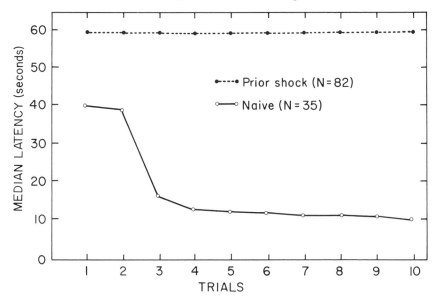

FIG. 10–12.   The effects of inescapable shocks in the Pavlov harness on escape responding in the shuttle box. This figure shows that there is rapid escape learning by 35 naive dogs which received no shocks in the harness. In contrast, the median for 82 dogs which received inescapable shocks in the harness, prior to escape training in the shuttle box, shows failure to escape shock. The arbitrary failure criterion was 50 seconds of shock (a latency of 60 seconds after onset of the S+).

effect. Furthermore, it does not matter if the inescapable shock is or is not preceded by a CS. Finally, it does not matter where the inescapable shocks are given and where the escape–avoidance training takes place. The shuttle box and harness are interchangeable.

Explanations of the Interference Effect

Explaining the interference effect is not easy. Here are some conventional hypotheses which we considered and rejected, together with a new hypothesis which we have confirmed in several ways.

Adaptation.   The adaptation hypothesis maintains that a subject adapts to shock during pretreatment with inescapable shocks and is therefore not sufficiently motivated to escape from shock in the shuttle box. The hypothesis is inadequate: (1) Adaptation to repeated, intense shocks has never been demonstrated (Church et al., 1966). (2) It is unlikely that very much adaptation could persist for as long as 24 hours.

(3) The dogs do not look as though they are adapted; they howl, defecate, and urinate to the first shock presentation in the shuttle box. On later trials, the dogs are passive; but they whimper and jerk with the shock. (4) We have disconfirmed the adaptation hypothesis experimentally. Raising the shock level in the shuttle box should increase motivation to escape. However, Overmier and Seligman (1967) found that increasing the shock level from 4.5 ma. to 6.5 ma. does not eliminate the interference effect. (5) A series of escapable shocks in the harness does not produce failure to escape in the shuttle box (Seligman & Maier, 1967), while the same shocks, if *inescapable,* do produce failure to escape. By this hypothesis, both conditions should lead to equal adaptation to shock and to similar behavior in the test situation, but they do not. (6) Dogs which first escape shock in the shuttle box, then receive inescapable shocks in the harness, later escape and avoid shock normally in the shuttle box (Seligman & Maier, 1967). The inescapable shocks in the harness should produce adaptation to shock, but they do not. (7) Failure to escape can be eliminated by dragging the dog across the barrier in the shuttle box (Seligman, Maier, & Geer, 1967). This exposure of the dog to the escape and avoidance contingencies should not change his degree of adaptation to shock.

Sensitization.   Perhaps the inescapable shocks received in the harness sensitize the subject to shock so that it is too motivated to enable it to make organized responses in the shuttle box. This hypothesis is inadequate. (1) Sensitization explains inefficiency of responding but not the absence of responding. (2) Lowering the shock level in the shuttle box should permit the subject to make organized responses. However, Overmier and Seligman (unpublished data) found that the interference effect is not attenuated when shock in the shuttle box is reduced to 3.0 ma. (3) Arguments (1), (2), and (3) in the previous paragraph, which invalidate the adaptation hypothesis, also invalidate the sensitization argument.

Competing motor responses.   There are three forms which the competing-motor-response explanation takes.

(1) One form, based on the idea of adventitious reinforcement, maintains that a specific motor response occurs at the moment that shock terminates in the harness. This event reinforces the particular response and increases the probability that it will be present when shock terminates on the next trial. In this manner, the response should acquire great strength. If this response is incompatible with barrier jumping, and if shock elicits it in the shuttle box, then the subject will not jump the barrier.

This view is weak empirically. We observed the dogs closely and saw no evidence of superstitious responding. More seriously, the argument is logically unsound. If some response is adventitiously reinforced by shock termination and is thereby more likely to recur, it should be more likely to occur when shock goes on as well as when shock goes off. Thus this response will be punished by shock onset as well as reinforced by shock termination. There is nothing in the adventitious reinforcement notion to suggest that reinforcement will be more effective than punishment. It is, therefore, a mystery why inescapable shock in the harness should establish a specific response. Moreover, even if acquired in the harness, why should the specific response persist in the face of hundreds of seconds of shock during shuttle-box training? It would seem that such a response should disappear. Furthermore, try to imagine a specific response which might have been superstitiously learned in the harness and which would completely prevent barrier jumping in the shuttle box! We doubt that this could be accomplished, even with explicit reinforcement of any specific response in the harness.

(2) A second competing-motor-response hypothesis maintains that active responses are occasionally punished by shock onset. Such adventitious punishment decreases the probability of active responding in the harness, and this transfers to the shuttle box. This hypothesis entails the same logical difficulty as does adventitious reinforcement. Active responding may be adventitiously punished by shock onset, but it should also be reinforced by shock termination. The adventitious punishment hypothesis does not suggest why punishment should be more effective than reinforcement. Furthermore, as active responding is eliminated by punishment, passive responding should increase in frequency. At this point, adventitious punishment should begin to eliminate passive responding, thereby increasing the probability of active responding, and so on. Moreover, even if passive responding were acquired through adventitious punishment in the harness, why should it persist in the face of hundreds of seconds of shock in the shuttle box?

(3) The third version of the competing-motor-response interpretation is that the subject reduces the severity of the electric shocks received in the harness by means of some specific motor response. The transfer of this explicitly reinforced motor response should be mediated by shock in the shuttle box and might interfere with barrier jumping. Because inescapable shocks in the harness are delivered through attached electrodes augmented by electrode paste, it is unlikely that the subject could increase electrical resistance by any particular motor response. It is conceivable, however, that some unknown pattern of muscle tonus or movement may reduce pain. Overmier and Seligman (1967) eliminated this possibility. Their dogs were completely paralyzed by d-tubocurarine during inescapable shocks in the harness, and so could not move or modify their muscle tonus. These dogs subsequently failed to escape shock in the

shuttle box just as do dogs who have received inescapable shocks in the noncurarized state. In contrast, dogs merely curarized in the harness subsequently escaped normally in the shuttle box. If a dog can reduce the severity of shock while curarized, the unknown mechanism for this must be central to the myoneural junction.

This experiment also disconfirms any literal interpretation of the adventitious reinforcement and punishment views. The adventitiously reinforced or punished responses cannot be of a gross, skeletal nature. On the other hand, Black (1967) has shown that electromyographic responses can be explicitly reinforced or punished while the subject is curarized. No one has shown, however, that electromyographic responses in the curarized dog can be established by adventitious reinforcement or punishment. Even if such responses were adventitiously reinforceable, there is no a priori reason to think that they would prevent subsequent barrier jumping in the shuttle box. Finally, it is strange that this type of argument is as widely used as it is (e.g., Herrnstein, 1966; Pinckney, 1967; Sidman et al., 1957). We know of only one demonstration (anecdotal) that any response can be established by adventitious reinforcement (Skinner, 1948) or punishment, although there are a few studies which show that adventitious reinforcement might maintain responses already established by explicit reinforcement.

Emotional exhaustion.   Do the dogs fail to escape from shock because they are emotionally exhausted? This seems plausible because the interference effect has a time course. In all of the experiments discussed so far, 24 hours intervened between the inescapable shocks in the harness and escape training in the shuttle box. Overmier and Seligman (1967) showed that there was no interference effect when escape training came either 48, 72, or 144 hours after inescapable shock. Interference dissipates in time, and this suggests mediation by a time-dependent, physiological state. Perhaps the inescapable shocks produce parasympathetic overshoot (Brush, Myer, & Palmer, 1963; Brush & Levine, 1965). Or, perhaps they produce adrenergic depletion or sympathetic exhaustion.

Simple exhaustion hypotheses are inadequate to explain our findings. (1) The interference effect can be made to last for at least a month. Seligman, Maier, and Geer (1967) showed that if a dog fails to escape in the shuttle box 24 hours after receiving inescapable shocks in the harness, then it will again fail to escape if tested a month later. (2) The dogs are not physically exhausted. They do occasionally jump the barrier during the intertrial interval and at the end of the session in order to leave the shuttle box. They even jump the barrier once in a while during shock, but they do not persist. (3) A series of escapable shocks in the harness does not produce subsequent failure to escape in the shuttle box (Seligman & Maier, 1967). This means that a hypothetical emotional exhaustion state does not arise from shock per se. (4) If a naive dog first receives escape training in the shuttlebox, then receives inescapable shocks in the harness, it will later continue to escape normally in the shuttle box. There is no simple reason why emotional exhaustion should be eliminated by prior escape training. (5) Failure to escape shock, once chronic, is curable. Dragging the dog back and forth across the barrier of the shuttle box during the CS and shock exposes the dog to the escape and avoidance contingencies. After many such draggings, the dog will escape shock on his own (Seligman, Maier, & Geer, 1967). If the dog were emotionally exhausted, merely showing him that he can escape and avoid shock should do no good.

Learned helplessness.   Assume that animals acquire expectations about the outcomes of their acts. They learn that responding produces reinforcement. They also learn that responding does not produce reinforcement (extinction). They can even learn that not responding produces reinforcement (differential reinforcement of other behavior, DRO). In a situation where shock is neither escapable nor avoidable such simple relationships do not hold. Shock termination is not dependent on either the occurrence or the nonoccurrence of a response. Sometimes the dog does something and shock happens to terminate. Sometimes the dog does something and shock does not terminate. Sometimes shock terminates when the dog has not done something. The shock programmer is not influenced by the subject. Can an animal learn in this situation, and if so, how can we describe what it is that he learns?

Consider the time interval between shock onset and shock termination to be broken into a series of small time intervals each of duration Δt. Further, assume that Δt is shorter than the duration of any response that the subject may make. No more than one response can occur in any Δt; therefore, Δt can contain only a response or the absence of a response. In addition to a response (or its absence), Δt can contain shock termination. When shock is inescapable, there is a fixed probability of shock termination in any Δt. For example, our use of a shock of 5-seconds duration determines the probability of shock termination. It will be zero for all Δt's during the shock except the last during which the probability is one. Nothing the subject does in any Δt will effect the probability of shock termination in that Δt. Therefore, the contingencies between responding and shock termination are such that for any Δt the conditional probability of shock termination, given any response, is equal to the unconditional probability of shock termination.

Learning theorists have, with few exceptions (e.g., Skinner, 1938, pp. 163–166), considered only the conditional probability of reinforcement, given a response. However, there is another important conditional probability, that of reinforcement in the absence of a response; in general, reinforcement can occur with any probability when no response is made. When shock is inescapable, this conditional probability is greater than zero. In any Δt it is equal to the unconditional probability of shock termination. It follows that, when shock is inescapable, *the conditional probability of shock termination, given the presence of any response, is equal to the conditional probability of shock termination, given the absence of that response.* Thus, the statement that shock termination is not dependent on responding means that these two conditional probabilities are equal.

We propose that a dog can learn that reinforcement is independent of the presence or absence of responding: "Nothing I do matters." In the case of inescapable shock, the dog learns that shock termination is independent of his behavior. More specifically, we think that the animal is sensitive to the fact that the conditional probability of shock termination, given the presence of any response, does not differ from the conditional probability of shock termination in the absence of that response. Furthermore, we are suggesting that dogs are sensitive to the conjoint variation of these two probabilities. Independence is simply the special case in which these two conditional probabilities are equal.

The procedure of presenting a stimulus independently of the subject's responding is unlike the procedures that most psychologists are used to. It is not an acquisition procedure. In acquisition there is an explicit correlation between a specified response and an outcome. In our procedure there is no specified response and no correlated outcome. It is not an extinction procedure. In extinction procedures some specified response is first strengthened by being correlated with a reinforcing outcome. Then the strengthened response is subsequently weakened by removing the outcome entirely from the experimental treatment. In our procedure this is not the case, because the response (supposedly undergoing extinction) is sometimes correlated with shock termination. Finally, when the experimenter gives the subject inescapable shocks, the procedure is not a partial-reinforcement procedure. In partial reinforcement sometimes the specified response occurs but reinforcement does not occur. Reinforcement never occurs unless the specified response has been made. In our situation shock termination occurs in the absence of a specified response.

Sensitivity to the independence of responding and shock termination could produce the interference effect in the following way: (1) At first the dog makes active responses during shock in the harness. (2) Because shock is inescapable, he learns that shock termination is independent of his behavior. (3) The incentive for the initiation of active responding in the presence of electric shock is partly produced by the expectation that responding will increase the probability of shock termination. When the expectation is absent, the incentive for response-initiation is low. (4) The electric shock in the shuttle box arouses the same expectation that was learned in the harness (i.e., that shock termination is independent of responding). Therefore, incentive for initiating responses in the presence of shock in the shuttle box is low. So the probability of jumping the barrier is low, as is the probability of doing anything active.

The term *learned helplessness* is a convenient label for the expectational and incentive mechanisms we have described.[6]

The prior learning in the harness that shock termination and responding are independent would be expected not only (1) to reduce incentive for barrier jumping, but also (2) to interfere with the formation of the barrier-jumping shock termination association, should the subject happen to jump the barrier and terminate shock. The prior learning of A-B can interfere with learning A-C. This accounts for the fact that a dog, pretreated with inescapable shock, occasionally jumps the barrier but does not "catch on." A small number of response shock-termination pairings is not sufficient to overcome the previous learning of independence between shock termination and responding.

By this hypothesis it is not shock per se that produces helplessness, but rather it is the subject's lack of control over shock. Therefore, learned helplessness should not result from prior escapable shock. Seligman and Maier (1967) performed the obvious test of this prediction. Three groups of eight dogs each were used. An Escape Group was trained in the harness to press a panel with its nose or head in order to turn off shock. A Yoked Group received shocks identical to the shocks delivered to the Escape Group. The Yoked Group differed from the Escape Group only with respect to the degree of instrumental control over shock. Pressing the panel in the Yoked Group did not affect the programmed shocks. A Naive Control Group received no shock in the harness.

The Escape Group learned to terminate shock in the harness and showed decreasing latencies of panel pressing over the course of the session. Towards the end of the session, the response consisted of a single, discrete head movement following shock onset. Subjects in the Yoked Group typically lay motionless after about 30 trials.

Twenty-four hours following the harness treatment, all three groups

---

[6] In this section we are using cognitive terms to describe what is learned. However, in the first section of this paper we used concepts such as conditioned fear and conditioned inhibition of fear to describe performance changes. The reader is entitled to an explanation of this inconsistency. Since the problems covered in Section I have traditionally been described in noncognitive terms, we chose to use noncognitive language. It should be pointed out that concepts like conditioned fear and conditioned inhibition of fear can be translated into cognitive terms such as expectation of shock and expectation of no shock. In this section we face a problem that has not been treated within any theoretical framework. We think the phenomena are most easily understood in cognitive terms. We do not see a simple way of translating our use of expectancy and our explanation of helplessness into the CER, mediational language of Section I. We do not deny the possibility of such a translation.

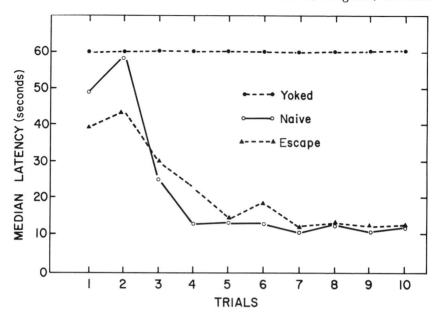

FIG. 10–13.   The effects of matched escapable and inescapable shocks on later escape
learning. This figure shows the median escape response latencies in the shuttle box
for three groups of dogs: (a) those given escape training in the shuttle box as naive
subjects; (b) those given prior escape training in the harness, panel-press apparatus; and
(c) those given prior inescapable shocks in the harness, but matched in duration and
temporal distribution to the shocks for the panel-press, escape-training group. The
arbitrary criterion of failure to jump was a 60-second latency (50 sec. of shock).

received ten trials of escape–avoidance training in the shuttle box.
Shuttle-box performance is summarized in Fig. 10–13, which shows the
median latency of barrier jumping on each of the ten trials for each of
the three groups. The Escape Group did not differ from the Naive Control Group. It suffered no impairment in shuttle-box performance. In
contrast, the Yoked Group showed significantly slower latencies than the
Naive Control Group. Six of the eight subjects in the Yoked Group
failed to escape shock. Thus the helplessness hypothesis was supported.
It is not the shock itself, but rather the subject's inability to control
shock that produces failure to escape.

Immunizing Against Interference

The helplessness hypothesis suggests a way to immunize dogs against the
interfering effects of inescapable shocks. Prior experience with escapable
shocks should do two things: (1) interfere proactively with the dog's ex-

pectation that responding and shock termination are independent, and (2) allow the dog to discriminate between the place where shocks are escapable and the place where they are inescapable. The relevant experiment was done by Seligman and Maier (1967). One group of dogs was given ten trials of escape–avoidance training in the shuttle box before they received inescapable shocks in the harness. Interference with subsequent escape–avoidance behavior was eliminated. That is, such a subject continued to respond normally when placed in the shuttle box 24 hours after inescapable shock treatment in the harness.

Another interesting finding emerged. The dogs which first learned to escape shock in the shuttle box pressed the panels four times as often as did naive dogs during the inescapable shocks in the harness. This happened even though pressing a panel had no effect on the shock. Such panel pressing is probably an index of attempts to control shock.

Is it the escapability of the shock in the shuttle box which prevented the interference effect and the enhanced panel pressing, or is it the subjects' freedom of motion during shock? To answer this question, Seligman and Maier (1967) ran a group of dogs receiving ten trials in the shuttle box on the first day of treatment. However, the subjects' barrier jumping and the termination of shock and CS were independent on these ten trials. On the next day, the subjects received inescapable shocks in the harness, followed 24 hours later by escape–avoidance training in the shuttle box. These subjects failed to escape in the shuttle box and panel pressed infrequently in the harness. Thus, control over shock termination is the crucial determinant of the interference effect.

Breaking Up the Interference Effect

If the subject fails to escape in the shuttle box 24 hours after inescapable shocks, the interference effect will persist in a chronic form; the subject will fail to escape on later opportunities. The helplessness hypothesis suggests a way to eliminate chronic failure to escape. By this hypothesis, the dog does not try to escape because he does not expect that any instrumental response will produce shock termination. By forcibly exposing the dog to the escape and avoidance contingencies, this expectation might be altered. This type of training by "putting through" has been used by others with mixed success (Miller & Konorski, 1928; Loucks, 1935; Woodbury, 1942). Seligman, Maier, and Geer (1967) reasoned that forcibly dragging the dog from side to side in the shuttle box, in such a way that the dog's changing compartments terminated shock, might effectively expose the dog to the response–reinforcement contingency. This was the case. The experimenter pulled three chronically helpless dogs back and forth across the shuttle box with long leashes. This was done during CS and shock, while the barrier was absent. After being pulled across the center of the shuttle box (and thus terminating shock and CS) 20, 35, and 50 times, respectively, each dog began to respond on his own. Then the barrier was replaced, and the subject continued to escape and avoid. The recovery from helplessness was complete and lasting.

The behavior of animals during "leash pulling" was interesting. At the beginning of the precedure, a great deal of force had to be exerted to pull the dog across the center of the shuttle box. Less and less force was needed as training progressed. A stage was typically reached in which only a slight nudge of the leash was required to impel the dog into action. Finally, the subject initiated its own response, and thereafter failure to escape was very rare. The initial problem seemed to be one of "getting the dog going."

Seligman, Maier, and Geer had first tried other procedures with little success. Merely removing the barrier, the experimenter's calling to the dog from the safe side, dropping food into the safe side, kicking the dangerous side of the box—all of these procedures failed. Until the correct response occurs, the dog cannot be exposed to the response–reinforcement contingency. It is remarkable that so many forced exposures were required to "get the dog going." This observation supports our twofold interpretation of the effects of inescapable shock: (1) the incentive for initiating responses during shock is low, and (2) the association of response events and reinforcement is proactively impaired.

Why Does the Interference Effect Dissipate in Time?

As we have mentioned, the interference effect has a time course. Overmier and Seligman (1967) found that if 48 hours or more intervene between inescapable shocks and escape training, the dogs escape normally. In contrast, when a 24-hour interval elapses, dogs fail to escape. In addition, Seligman and Maier (1967) found that if the subject fails to escape shock in the shuttle box 24 hours following inescapable shocks, it will continue to fail at least one month later. Thus, an additional experience with inescapable shock maintains and potentiates the interference effect well beyond the 48-hour interval during which it would otherwise dissipate.

How can we account for this time course? Quite clearly, the helplessness hypothesis alone does not provide for dissipation in time. What mechanism would? The most obvious idea is that shocks per se produce a state of emotional exhaustion from which the dog gradually recovers. We have cited (see pp. 324–325) several lines of evidence to invalidate this simple interpretation. There are, however, three lines of interpretation which, though more complex, seem promising.

Expectation, incentive, and emotional exhaustion. Learning that one's own responses are ineffective in controlling a traumatic situation may produce emotional exhaustion. Weiss (1968) has shown that rats which cannot control shock show more stress, as measured by CER, weight loss, stomach ulcers, and defecation, than do rats which can control shock. The high degree of stress resulting from inescapable shocks might lead to emotional exhaustion. This exhaustion may dissipate in time. Furthermore, like fear, a state of emotional exhaustion might become discriminatively conditioned to external cues. Such a mechanism could explain the perseveration of the interference effect. It is possible that this kind of conditioning occurred when our dogs failed to escape in the shuttle box 24 hours after inescapable shock in the harness. Immunization procedures worked because the emotional exhaustion was discriminatively conditioned only to the harness cues and not to the shuttle box cues. Finally, if emotional exhaustion is produced by the expectation that responding does not control shock, once the dog "sees" a response–reinforcement contingency, emotional exhaustion should disappear. This may be why "dragging" breaks up the interference effect.

Why should inescapable shocks produce more stress than escapable shocks? We lean toward the view that learning that one's responses are independent of traumatic events will itself produce stress over and above that normally caused by the traumatic stimuli themselves. However, there is a good alternative to this explanation. It is possible that learning that one's responses can control traumatic events will reduce the stress normally produced by the traumatic stimuli themselves. With this latter view, one need not postulate that the subject learns that shock is independent of responding. Instead, shock itself sets the level of stress, but learning that one can control shock reduces stress. We have not yet thought of ways of testing directly which of the two positions is correct. There are a number of ways of testing indirectly, and these are described below on pp. 335–337.

There are known physiological mechanisms that might produce emotional exhaustion. We are interested in several of these: (1) exhaustion or inhibition of the adrenergic transmitter involved in the control of aversive motivation; (2) sympathetic exhaustion; and (3) parasympathetic overreaction. Direct manipulation of these systems would test their relevance to the time course of the interference effect. Consider the possibility that exhaustion or inhibition of the adrenergic system mediates failure to escape. If this were so, artificially depleting the adrenergic system, e.g., with reserpine, should produce the interference effect. Preventing depletion of the adrenergic system during inescapable shock, e.g., with chlorpromazine, should prevent the interference effect. Promazine administered along with inescapable shocks prevents the interference effect (Brookshire, Littman, & Stewart, 1962). Direct measurement of catecholamine levels throughout the time course is an alternative strategy. Similar manipulation and measurement of sympathetic and parasympathetic activity would assess their involvement in the interference effect.

There is no necessary incompatibility between such a physiological analysis and our psychological analysis of the interference effect. They might even be complementary. Our analysis holds that the dog's incentive to initiate behavior is undermined by his acquiring the expectation that responding does not control shock. However, incentive processes operate through a physiological medium. Therefore, physiological exhaustion might result from the acquisition of such an expectation. Analysis at both levels would contribute to our understanding of the interference effect.

Proactive inhibition.   The time course of the interference effect can be explained without recourse to an emotionally exhausted state. The dogs in our experiments arrived at the laboratory with a long but unknown history. Probably most of the dogs had experience with aversive events they could control, and such experience should proactively inhibit the failure to escape shock. Because proactive inhibition in both humans (Underwood, 1948) and animals (Maier & Gleitman, 1967) is known to increase in time, the dissipation of the interference effect can be explained. Twenty-four hours after inescapable shock in the harness, the PI is not strong enough to counteract the expectation that responding does not control shock. Forty-eight hours later, it is. Perseveration of the interference effect occurs because the added experience with inescapable shock makes the helplessness too strong to be counteracted by PI.

Prior experience might explain not only the time course but also the individual differences among the dogs in their responses to shock. We reported that 64% of the dogs receiving inescapable shock later failed to escape. Is it possible that the 36% who escaped normally were dogs with long histories of mastery over aversive events? We also reported that 6% of dogs who do not receive inescapable shock will nevertheless fail to escape. These might very well be dogs with a long history of inescapable aversive events. Developmental and controlled life-history experiments should answer these questions.

Retroactive inhibition.   This explanation also does not postulate emotional exhaustion. We returned the dog to his home cage after he received inescapable shock. What the dog does, and how often he does it, may retroactively inhibit what was learned in the harness. More inhibition might result from 48 hours of activity in the home cage than 24 hours. This hypothesis can be tested: simply keep the dog restrained in the harness during the interval between inescapable shock and escape training.

Extinction and spontaneous recovery. The term "extinction" is ambiguously used. It may refer either to a procedure, an outcome, or an inferred process. We have already pointed out (p. 326) that the administration by the experimenter of inescapable shocks is not a conventional extinction procedure. It may, however, produce the same outcome as do normal extinction procedures and it may do so by the same underlying process. Either removing shocks completely or presenting shocks independently of the subject's responses might reduce the subject's incentive to initiate responses. One result of extinction procedures is spontaneous recovery. If extinction procedures and inescapable shocks induce the same process, we should see spontaneous recovery of response-initiation; and since recovery increases over time, more response-initiation should occur after a 48-hour rest than after a 24-hour rest. On the other hand, the usual course of spontaneous recovery for appetitively motivated behavior is over minutes, not hours or days. We know of no evidence on the course of spontaneous recovery for extinguished habits of an aversively motivated sort. It may be that this time course will turn out to be like the one we have observed following inescapable shocks.

Generality of the Interference Effect Across Situations, Responses, and Species

Failure to escape traumatic shock is highly maladaptive. It is important to know whether the behavior is peculiar to the dog and to the situations we have used. We think not. Many experiments conducted for a wide variety of other purposes have incidentally yielded the interference effect. Furthermore, many of these findings can be explained by the helplessness hypothesis.

Species. Deficits in escaping or avoiding shock after experience with inescapable shock has been shown in rats, cats, dogs, fish, and man. Using rats, at least 15 studies have shown an interference effect as a consequence of inescapable shock. For example, Mowrer (1940), Dinsmoor and Campbell (1956a, 1956b), and Dinsmoor (1958), all found that rats which had received inescapable shock were retarded in initiating their first barpress–escape response and were slower to acquire the response once it had been emitted. Brown and Jacobs (1949), Mullin and Mogenson (1963), and Weiss and Conte (1966), all found that fear conditioning that is carried out with inescapable shocks results in escape and avoidance decrements. In addition, the more fear conditioning trials there are, the poorer is the subsequent escape and avoidance performance. Finally, McAllister and McAllister (1962, 1963, 1965) showed a time course for a superficially similar interference effect when fear conditioning and "escape from fear training" took place in different apparatuses; the interference had dissipated after 24 hours.

Inescapable shocks imposed on weanling rats produce escape (and sometimes avoidance) decrements when the rats are adults (Brookshire, Littman, & Stewart, 1961; Levine, Chevalier, & Korchin, 1956; Denenberg & Bell, 1960; Denenberg, 1964). Finally, both Anderson and Nakamura (1964) and Hearst and Whelan (1963) gave inescapable shocks to rats which were performing poorly at wheel-turning avoidance. The treatment did not facilitate avoidance, but rather it produced many failures to escape.

McCulloch and Bruner (1939) found that pretreatment with inescapable shocks later resulted in poor discriminative escape from water when one of the alternative escape routes was punished by shock.

Using dogs (Carlson & Black, 1960) and using cats (Seward & Humphrey, 1967), experimenters have reported interference in escape resulting from previous inescapable shocks.

Behrend and Bitterman (1963) found that inescapable shocks retarded later Sidman avoidance learning by fish in an aquatic shuttle box. Pinckney (1967) found that fear conditioning retarded later shuttle box avoidance learning in goldfish. As did Mullin and Mogenson (1963), Pinckney found that the more fear-conditioning trials he gave, the poorer was the subsequent avoidance performance.

In human subjects, MacDonald (1946) found that inescapable shocks delivered to the finger retarded the later acquisition of finger-withdrawal avoidance.

Many of these studies show facilitation of avoidance performance following inescapable shocks, despite the fact that interference with escaping occurred. This finding is not a paradox for the helplessness hypothesis. Avoidance responding typically emerges only after the subject is escaping reliably. Our hypothesis maintains that inescapable shocks produce deficits in response-initiation and in the association between responding and shock termination. By the time the subject is reliably escaping shock, these deficits must be gone. Then there would be no reason to expect deficits in avoidance performance after escaping is reliable. As a matter of fact, subjects having difficulty in initiating escape behavior will experience more shock following each discriminative stimulus presentation. Conditioned fear of the stimulus should be more intense and therefore should facilitate avoidance.

Situations.   Prior inescapable shocks enhance the suppressive effects of punishment (Kurtz & Walters, 1962; Pearl, Walters, & Anderson, 1964).

If inescapable shocks result in a decrease in the initiation of active responding, then we would expect such a result, provided that the behavioral alternatives to the punished response do not consist of active responses.

Very well-learned escape and avoidance responses are enhanced by subsequent inescapable shock (Baum, 1965, 1966; Kelleher, Riddle, & Cook, 1963; Sidman, Herrstein, & Conrad, 1957; Waller & Waller, 1963). We have discussed the theoretical reason for this in connection with our "immunization" experiment with dogs. Clearly, the ordering of successes and failures in controlling trauma is a major determinant of subsequent escape and avoidance performance.

US's other than shocks can produce effects which may be analogous to failure to escape shock. For example, Richter (1957) produced sudden death in wild rats by forcibly immobilizing them in his hand. When such rats were put in a tank of water from which there was no escape, they gave up swimming after a few minutes and drowned. If, however, (1) Richter repeatedly held the rats in his hands and let them go, or (2) if he put the rats in the water and then took them out, then they swam for approximately 80 hours before dying. Richter attributed the sudden deaths in the first group to loss of hope. Other inescapable US's produce similar effects: death from inescapable tumbling (Anderson & Paden, 1966); passivity from defeat in fighting (Kahn, 1951); and disruption of food getting in very hungry rats as a consequence of inescapable shocks in infancy (Brookshire, Littman, & Stewart, 1961, Experiment 6). Inability to control trauma disrupts a wide range of adaptive behavior in many different species.

The Helplessness Concept Suggests New Lines of Research

Does helplessness occur in appetitive situations? If a subject receives extensive experience in which rewarding brain stimulation is delivered independently of what it does, (1) will it later be retarded in initiating instrumental responses which procure reward? and (2) once it makes the response which procures reward, will it be retarded in associating response with reward?

Does helplessness generalize across different aversive US's? Will prior experience with inescapable shocks retard the subsequent learning to escape a loud noise? It is conceivable that an animal that has learned that it cannot control one aversive event may not attempt to control another aversive event.

Does helplessness generalize from aversive to appetitive situations, and vice versa? If a subject receives inescapable shocks, will it then fail to initiate responses to procure food? If a subject receives food independently of its responses, will it then be poor at escaping shock? If such a result occurred, what mechanism might be involved? Could there be a generalized personality trait of helplessness which arises from long experience with a variety of events over which the subject has no control?

Are there avoidance sets?   We have shown that inescapable shocks received in one situation will interfere with subsequent escape from shock in another situation. Does the opposite occur? Suppose we train a dog to press a panel in order to avoid shock whenever a light flashes. Then would he learn more quickly to avoid shock by barrier jumping in a shuttle box whenever a tone occurs?

Are there analogues of the interference effect in Pavlovian conditioning?
We have argued that the interference effect results from the subject's learning that response events are unrelated to reinforcement events. This not only inhibits response-initiation, but it also retards the association between other response events and reinforcements. If we conceive of a response event as a response-produced stimulus, then the relation is one of CS to US. This led Seligman (1968) to ask whether extended experience with a tone and shock, randomly interspersed, retards the association of a paired light with shock. He found this to be the case in rats. This may mean that an organism exposed to many, varied, unrelated events will have trouble perceiving that new related events are, indeed, related.

The converse may also occur. Seligman (1968) showed that experience with tone and shock pairings facilitated the association of later CS's and shock. This may mean that experience with related events may lower the threshold of conditionability. It may also be the case that such a subject will fail to perceive that events are unrelated when, indeed, they are unrelated. Finally, will a subject that has learned that stimulus events are unrelated, be retarded in the acquisition of an instrumental response because it will have difficulty perceiving the response–reinforcement relationship?

Does the helplessness hypothesis apply to shock onset and shock postponement?   In our experiments, not only did shock termination occur independently of the subject's behavior, but also shock onset and the time to the next shock were not under the subject's control. This raises some interesting questions. Would these subjects fail to initiate responses to postpone shock? If so, they would be poor at Sidman avoidance responding. Would these subjects be poor at initiating responses to prevent the onset of shock? Finally, can a subject be helpless with regard to one mode of controlling shock but not with others? The experimental test of this is as follows: A dog is trained to press a panel in the harness to escape shock which is always signalled by a flashing light, but panel pressing does not change the probability of shock onset during the light–shock interval. Would the dog subsequently escape shock, but fail to avoid it in the shuttle box? Bloom and Campbell (1967) trained rats to avoid shock. They then removed the CS and allowed the rats only to escape. Finally, when the CS was replaced, the subjects made fewer avoidances than before the removal of the CS. Here is a case where removal of the subjects' control over shock onset leads to an avoidance decrement.

Can helplessness be brought under discriminative control? Suppose two dogs can press a panel in order to escape shock in the presence of a constantly present tone. However, when a light is on and the tone is absent, the shocks are inescapable. Now one dog is put in the shuttle box with the tone always present. The other dog is put in the shuttle box with the light present and tone absent. Will the tone dog fail to escape normally and the light dog succeed?

Helplessness and mastery as lasting traits. Our findings suggest a developmental study. Suppose we take one half of a litter of puppies and bring them up under conditions under which they are helpless to control all of the important events in their environment. Food and water come and are removed independently of the puppies' behavior. Long periods of deprivation are interspersed with short periods during which food is abundant. Aversive events come and go, with no relationship to behavior. The other puppies of the litter have the opposite experience. All of their food and water depend only on what they do or do not do. A repertory of specific, instrumental responses is strengthened by repeated response-reinforcement contingencies. How will the litter mates react to new situations which require: (1) the initiation of new responses and (2) the formation of new associations between responses and reinforcements? Will there be important differences between the groups?

Summary

Pavlovian fear conditioning controls escape and avoidance responding in two very different ways:

1. *The contingency between the CS and US gives the CS precise control over already established avoidance responding.* Here, the laws of Pavlovian salivary conditioning reveal themselves in several ways. The phenomena of excitation and differential inhibition, conditioned in-

hibition, inhibition of delay, and inhibition from backward conditioning all are seen in mediation of avoidance responding by conditioned fear. The fear-mediation postulate of two-process learning theory is well supported. In addition, other conditioning phenomena, such as inhibition from a cessation signal, generalization of fear across different US's, perseveration of excitation of fear derived from aversive US presentations, and differential excitation of fear by different US durations all are shown to control avoidance responding.

2. *The independence of shock termination and instrumental responding during Pavlovian fear conditioning subsequently disrupts the learning of escape and avoidance responding.* In conditioning, the subject cannot control shock. This contingency is shown to produce failure to escape shock when escape and avoidance training follow fear conditioning. This interference effect occurs following a wide variety of frequencies and durations of inescapable shocks. It also occurs independently of presence or absence of a signal and independently of the place of conditioning and escape training. In addition, the interference effect has wide generality across species, situations, and responses.

Escapable shocks do not produce the interference effect; moreover, escapable shocks immunize the subject against the interfering effects of inescapable shocks. Failure to escape shocks can be broken up by repeatedly forcing the subject to make the instrumental response which terminates shock.

The interference effect dissipates over time unless it is maintained by an intervening failure to escape shocks.

Several interpretations of all these findings are considered and discarded (adaptation to shock, sensitization by shock, emotional exhaustion, and a wide variety of "competing motor response" interpretations). Alternatively, we suggest a helplessness hypothesis which maintains (1) that inescapable shocks establish in the subject the expectation that responding is independent of shock termination, and (2) that this expectation lowers the subject's incentive to initiate responding in the presence of shock. The helplessness concept suggests many new experiments.

REFERENCES

ANDERSON, D. R. C., & PADEN, P. Passive avoidance response learning as a function of prior tumbling-trauma. *Psychonomic Science,* 1966, 4, 129–130.

ANDERSON, N. H. & NAKAMURA, C. Y. Avoidance decrement in avoidance conditioning. *Journal of Comparative and Physiological Psychology,* 1964, 57, 196–204.

BAUM, M. The recovery-from-extinction of an avoidance response following an inescapable shock in the avoidance apparatus. *Psychonomic Science,* 1965, 2, 7–8.

BAUM, M. Pavlovian generalization of fear measured by changes in rate of Sidman avoidance responding in dogs. Paper presented at the meeting of the Eastern Psychological Association, New York, April, 1966.

BAUM, M. Time course of the perseveration of Pavlovian-conditioned fear measured by changes in rate of Sidman avoidance responding in dogs. Paper presented at the meeting of the Eastern Psychological Association, Boston, April, 1967.

BECK, R. C. On secondary reinforcement and shock termination. *Psychological Bulletin*, 1961, **58**, 28–45.

BEHREND, E. R., & BITTERMAN, M. E. Sidman avoidance in the fish. *Journal of the Experimental Analysis of Behavior*, 1963, **6**, 47–52.

BLACK, A. H. Heart rate changes during avoidance learning in dogs. *Canadian Journal of Psychology*, 1959, **13**, 229–242.

BLACK, A. H. Transfer following operant conditioning in the curarized dog. *Science*, 1967, **155** 201–203.

BLOOM, J., & CAMPBELL, B. A. Effects of CS omission following avoidance learning. *Journal of Experimental Psychology*, 1967, **72**, 36–39.

BROOKSHIRE, K. H., LITTMAN, R. A., & STEWART, C. N. Residua of shock trauma in the white rat: A three factor theory. *Psychological Monographs*, 1961, **75** (10, Whole No. 514).

BROOKSHIRE, K. H., LITTMAN, R. A., & STEWART, C. N. The interactive effect of promazine and post-weanling stress upon adult avoidance behavior. *Journal of Nervous and Mental Disease*, 1962, **135**, 52–58.

BROWN, J. S., & JACOBS, A. The role of fear in the motivation and acquisition of responses. *Journal of Experimental Psychology*, 1949, **39**, 747–759.

BRUSH, F. R., & LEVINE, S. The relationship between avoidance learning and corticosterone levels. Paper presented at the meeting of the Western Psychological Association, Honolulu, April, 1965.

BRUSH, F. R., MYER, J. S., & PALMER, M. E. Effects of kind of prior training and intersession interval upon subsequent avoidance learning. *Journal of Comparative and Physiological Psychology*, 1963, **56**, 539–545.

CARLSON, N. J., & BLACK, A. H. Traumatic avoidance learning: The effects of preventing escape responses. *Canadian Journal of Psychology*, 1960, **14**, 21–28.

CHURCH, R. M., LoLORDO, V. M., OVERMIER, J. B., SOLOMON, R. L., & TURNER, L. H. Cardiac responses to shock in curarized dogs: Effects of shock intensity and duration, warning signals and prior experience with shock. *Journal of Comparative and Physiological Psychology*, 1966, **62**, 1–7.

DENENBERG, V. H. Effects of avoidable and unavoidable electric shock upon mortality in the rat. *Psychological Reports*, 1964, **14**, 43–46.

DENENBERG, V. H., & BELL, R. Critical periods for the effects of infantile experience on adult learning. *Science*, 1960, **131**, 227–228.

DESIDERATO, O. The generalization of excitation and inhibition in the control of avoidance responding by Pavlovian CSs. *Journal of Comparative and Physiological Psychology*, 1969, in press.

DINSMOOR, J. A. Pulse duration and food deprivation in escape from shock training. *Psychological Reports*, 1958, **4**, 531–534.

DINSMOOR, J. A., & CAMPBELL, S. L. Escape-from-shock training following exposure to inescapable shock. *Psychological Reports,* 1956, **2,** 43–49. (a)

DINSMOOR, J. A., & CAMPBELL, S. L. Level of current and time between sessions as factors in "adaptation" to shock. *Psychological Reports,* 1956, **2,** 441–444. (b)

HEARST, E., & WHALEN, R. Facilitating effects of D-Amphetamine on discriminated-avoidance performance. *Journal of Comparative and Physiological Psychology,* 1963, **56,** 124–128.

HERRNSTEIN, R. J. Superstition: A corollary of the principles of operant conditioning. In W. Honig (Ed.), *Operant behavior: Areas of research and application.* New York: Appleton-Century-Crofts, 1966. Pp. 33–51.

KAHN, M. W. The effect of severe defeat at various age levels on the aggressive behavior of mice. *Journal of Genetic Psychology,* 1951, **79,** 117–130.

KAMIN, L. J., BRIMER, C. J., & BLACK, A. H. Conditioned suppression as a monitor of fear of the CS in the course of avoidance training. *Journal of Comparative and Physiological Psychology,* 1963, **56,** 497–501.

KELLEHER, R. T., RIDDLE, W. C., & COOK, L. Persistent behavior maintained by unavoidable shocks. *Journal of the Experimental Analysis of Behavior,* 1963, **6,** 507–517.

KURTZ, K., & WALTERS, G. The effects of prior fear exposure on an approach–avoidance conflict. *Journal of Comparative and Physiological Psychology,* 1962, **55,** 1075–1078.

LEAF, R. C. Avoidance response evocation as a function of prior discriminative fear conditioning under curare. *Journal of Comparative and Physiological Psychology,* 1964, **58,** 446–450.

LEVINE, S., CHEVALIER, J. A., & KORCHIN, S. J. The effects of early shock and handling on later avoidance learning. *Journal of Personality,* 1956, **24,** 475–493.

LOLORDO, V. M. Similarity of conditioned fear responses based upon different aversive events. *Journal of Comparative and Physiological Psychology,* 1967, **64,** 154–158.

LOUCKS, R. B. The experimental delimitation of neural structures essential for learning: The attempt to condition striped muscle responses with faradization of the sigmoid gyri. *Journal of Psychology,* 1935, **1,** 5–44.

MACDONALD, A. Effect of adaptation to the unconditioned stimulus upon the formation of conditioned avoidance responses. *Journal of Experimental Psychology,* 1946, **36,** 1–12.

MAIER, S. F., & GLEITMAN, H. Proactive interference in rats. *Psychonomic Science,* 1967, **7,** 25–26.

McALLISTER, W. R., & McALLISTER, D. E. Postconditioning delay and intensity of shock as factors in the measurement of acquired fear. *Journal of Experimental Psychology,* 1962, **64,** 110–116.

McALLISTER, W. R., & McALLISTER, D. E. Increase over time in the stimulus generalization of acquired fear. *Journal of Experimental Psychology,* 1963, **65,** 576–582.

McALLISTER, W. R., & McALLISTER, D. E. Variables influencing the conditioning and measurement of acquired fear. In W. F. Prokasy (Ed.), *Classical conditioning.* New York: Appleton-Century-Crofts, 1965.

McCulloch, T. L., & Bruner, J. S. The effect of electric shock upon subsequent learning in the rat. *Journal of Psychology*, 1939, **7**, 333–336.

Miller, N. E. Learnable drives and rewards. In S. S. Stevens (Ed.), *Handbook of experimental psychology*. New York: Wiley, 1951.

Miller, S., & Konorski, J. Sur une forme particulière des reflexes conditionnels. *Comptes rendus hebdomadaires des séances et mémoires de la Société de Biologie et filiales*, etc., 1928, **99**, 1155–1157.

Moscovitch, A., & LoLordo, V. M. Role of safety in the Pavlovian backward fear conditioning procedure. *Journal of Comparative and Physiological Psychology*, 1968, **66**, 673–678.

Mowrer, O. H. An experimental analysis of "regression" with incidental observations on "reaction-formation." *Journal of Abnormal and Social Psychology*, 1940, **35**, 56–87.

Mowrer, O. H. *Learning theory and behavior*. New York: Wiley, 1960.

Mowrer, O. H., & Solomon, L. N. Contiguity vs. Drive-reduction in conditioned fear: The proximity and abruptness of drive-reduction. *American Journal of Psychology*, 1954, **67**, 15–25.

Mullin, A. D., & Mogenson, G. J. Effects of fear conditioning on avoidance learning. *Psychological Reports*, 1963, **13**, 707–710.

Overmier, J. B. Instrumental and cardiac indices of Pavlovian fear conditioning as a function of US duration. *Journal of Comparative and Physiological Psychology*, 1966, **62**, 15–20.

Overmier, J. B., & Leaf, R. C. Effects of discriminative Pavlovian fear conditioning upon previously or subsequently acquired avoidance responding. *Journal of Comparative and Physiological Psychology*, 1965, **60**, 213–217.

Overmier, J. B., & Seligman, M. E. P. Effects of inescapable shock upon subsequent escape and avoidance responding. *Journal of Comparative and Physiological Psychology*, 1967, **63**, 28–33.

Pavlov, I. P. *Conditioned reflexes*. (Tr., G. V. Anrep.) London: Oxford University Press, 1927. (Reprinted, New York: Dover, 1960.)

Pearl, J., Walters, G. C., & Anderson, D. C. Suppressing effects of aversive stimulation on subsequently punished behavior. *Canadian Journal of Psychology*, 1964, **18**, 343–355.

Pinckney, G. Avoidance learning in fish as a function of prior fear conditioning. *Psychological Reports*, 1967, **20**, 71–74.

Rescorla, R. A. Inhibition of delay in Pavlovian fear conditioning. *Journal of Comparative and Physiological Psychology*, 1967, **64**, 114–120.

Rescorla, R. A., & LoLordo, V. M. Inhibition of avoidance behavior. *Journal of Comparative and Physiological Psychology*, 1965, **59**, 406–412.

Rescorla, R. A., & Solomon, R. L. Two-process learning theory: Relationships between Pavlovian conditioning and instrumental learning. *Psychological Review*, 1967, **74**, 151–182.

Richter, C. P. On the phenomenon of sudden death in animals and man. *Psychosomatic Medicine*, 1957, **19**, 191–198.

Seligman, M. E. P. CS redundancy and secondary punishment. *Journal of Experimental Psychology*, 1966, **72**, 546–550.

Seligman, M. E. P. Chronic fear produced by unpredictable electric shock. *Journal of Comparative and Physiological Psychology*, 1968, **66**, 402–411.

SELIGMAN, M. E. P., & MAIER, S. F. Failure to escape traumatic shock. *Journal of Experimental Psychology,* 1967, **74,** 1–9.

SELIGMAN, M. E. P., MAIER, S. F., & Geer, J. H. Alleviation of learned helplessness in the dog. *Journal of Abnormal Psychology,* 1968, **73,** 256–262.

SEWARD, J. P., & HUMPHREY, G. L. Avoidance learning as a function of pretraining in the cat. *Journal of Comparative and Physiological Psychology,* 1967, **63,** 338–341.

SIDMAN, M., HERRNSTEIN, R. J., & CONRAD, D. G. Maintenance of avoidance behavior by unavoidable shocks. *Journal of Comparative and Physiological Psychology,* 1957, **50,** 553–557.

SKINNER, B. F. *The behavior of organisms:* An experimental analysis. New York: Appleton-Century, 1938.

SKINNER, B. F. "Superstition" in the pigeon. *Journal of Experimental Psychology,* 1948, **38,** 168–172.

SOLOMON, R. L., KAMIN, L. J., & WYNNE, L. C. Traumatic avoidance learning: The outcomes of several extinction procedures with dogs. *Journal of Abnormal and Social Psychology,* 1953, **48,** 291–302.

SOLOMON, R. L., & TURNER, L. H. Discriminative classical conditioning in dogs paralyzed by curare can later control discriminative avoidance responses in the normal state. *Psychological Review,* 1962, **69,** 202–219.

SOLOMON, R. L., & WYNNE, L. C. Traumatic avoidance learning: Acquisition in normal dogs. *Psychological Monographs,* 1953, **67** (4, Whole No. 354).

UNDERWOOD, B. J. Retroactive and proactive inhibition after five and forty-eight hours. *Journal of Experimental Psychology,* 1948, **38,** 29–38.

WALLER, M. B., & WALLER, P. F. The effects of unavoidable shocks on a multiple schedule having an avoidance component. *Journal of the Experimental Analysis of Behavior,* 1963, **6,** 29–37.

WEISS, J. M. Effects of coping responses on stress. *Journal of Comparative and Physiological Psychology,* 1968, **65,** 251–260. Also available as doctoral dissertation, Yale University, 1967.

WEISS, J. M., & CONTE, R. Effects of fear conditioning on subsequent avoidance and movement. Paper presented at the meeting of the Eastern Psychological Association, New York, April, 1966.

WOODBURY, C. B. A note on "passive" conditioning. *Journal of General Psychology,* 1942, **27,** 359–361.

11

Effects of the Somatic or Visceral Responses to Punishment[1]

Neal E. Miller

Jay M. Weiss

ROCKEFELLER UNIVERSITY

This paper will concentrate on the responses that the subject makes in punishment situations. First, it will discuss the effect of the response the subject makes to the punishment on what he learns. Next, it will discuss the effects of being able to perform a coping response on the psychosomatic effects of punishment. Finally, it will deal with the degree to which specific visceral responses can be instrumentally learned to escape or avoid punishment.

Receiving strong punishment in a situation conditions fear to that situation. Two of the most obvious overt effects of fear present a striking contrast. One is the activation pattern of startle, vocalization, running, leaping, and other escape behavior. The other is the freezing pattern of remaining stationary, motionless, and mute, which reaches its extreme in the death feigning of certain animals (Miller, 1951, p. 441). In addition to these overt behavioral responses, there are many physiological reactions to fear. The foregoing possibilities are presented diagrammatically in Fig. 11–1. We use the word pattern to express the hypothesis that there is a closer functional relationship among the various active responses, such as running and leaping, than between each of these responses and various aspects of freezing. This hypothesis needs to be tested by detailed experimental work. In any event, the pattern is a loose one since different parts of it can be modified separately by learning.

[1] The final section of this paper on visceral responses was written independently by the senior author. Since the paper was delivered informally by the senior author, the personal style is maintained. Much of the research reported, as well as the preparation of this paper, was supported by PHS Research Grant MH-13189 from the National Institute of Mental Health.

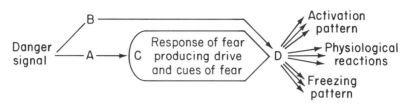

FIG. 11–1.   Theoretical diagram of responses to fear. Responses can be modified by learning at points A, B, and D, and by drugs also at point C.

Thus, a rat can be taught either to run or to leap in order to escape from pain or fear.

We refer to physiological reactions because we do not know the extent to which such reactions are grouped into one or more patterns; it is entirely possible that certain physiological reactions, perhaps tachycardia, are more likely to occur as a part of the activation pattern, and that other ones, perhaps bradycardia, are more likely to occur as a part of the freezing pattern. It is also possible that our use of the word "pattern" has greatly overestimated the degree to which there is some innate tendency for responses given a similar label to be functionally related.

Importance of Response in the Punishment Situation

Let us begin with a consideration of skeletal responses in what we have called the activation pattern. In many situations, the particular one of these responses made to the punishment is crucial in determining its effect. This presumably is because the response that is occurring at the end of the punishment, or of the fear-eliciting danger signal, is the one that is reinforced and learned. Let me give a few illustrations.

As an undergraduate, I heard Guthrie give a characteristically illuminating example. Suppose a dog is jumping out of an open window and you are punishing him for it by a flick from a whip. If at the moment he starts to jump you give him a flick on the rear, which elicits a leap forward, you will probably train him to jump out of the window still faster; but if instead at the same moment you give him a flick on the snout, which elicits rearing back, you probably will train him not to jump out of the window. Fowler and I (1963) designed an experiment somewhat like Guthrie's illustration. Hungry rats were trained to run down an alley to food. The situation at the goal was arranged so that they could be given a mild electric shock either on their rear paws or on their front ones. The shock to the rear paws elicited lurching forward while the shock to the front ones elicited lurching back. And, over a fair range of strength of shocks, the rats punished on their rear paws learned to run faster, while those punished on their front ones learned to slow down. The opposite responses elicited by the different points of application of the punishment produced opposite effects.

In one of the early experiments on conflict behavior, Maritta Davis and I wanted to shock hungry rats halfway to the end of an alley where they found food (Miller, 1944, p. 440). We increased the strength of shock gradually and omitted it on every other trial in order to test for the effects of the preceding shock. We found that if we increased the shock very gradually, some of the animals kept on running down to the goal without stopping, even after they were too excited to eat there. When the shock was increased gradually, the animals learned to respond to it by running forward. In order to make the experiment work, we had to increase the shock more rapidly, so that it would elicit a withdrawal response. Later, Gwinn (1949) performed an experiment specifically de signed for studying the phenomena of running forward into the shock region. But Judson Brown will discuss this kind of work, and some of the complexities involved, in more detail later (see Chapter 15 of this volume). I mention these observations as another example of the fact that the response elicited in the punishment situation is extremely important in predicting the effect of the punishment.

The Role of the Freezing Response

As we have already pointed out, when rats have received painful punishment in a situation, freezing is a response that is high in the hierarchy of responses to the fear which they learn. In many dangerous situations, freezing is a highly adaptive response; it prevents the rat from being noticed and caught. There is considerable evidence suggesting that, other things being equal, the stronger the fear, the more dominant the pattern of freezing becomes over the pattern of actively responding, but that the relative dominance of the two responses can be modified by specific training.

These facts are neatly illustrated in Fig. 11–2, describing data from an experiment which Douglas Lawrence and I performed to show the effect of strength of shock on subsequent learning motivated by fear (Miller, 1951, p. 448). Rats were trained to escape shock from a grid floor in a white compartment by touching a door, thus activating an electronic relay which caused the door to drop so that they could dash into a black compartment with a wooden floor. Different groups received shocks of 90, 180, and 540 volts, respectively, administered through a series re-

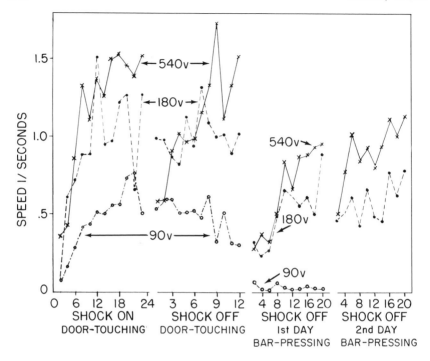

FIG. 11-2.   Effects of strength of shock on subsequent learning without shock. Dur-ing the first 24 trials, rats learned to touch a door which automatically dropped, allow-ing them to escape into a nonshock compartment. During subsequent trials without shock, they first unlearned initial freezing while relearning to touch the door. Subse-quently they learned to press a bar to cause the door to drop.

From: N. E. Miller, "Learnable Drives and Rewards," in S. S. Stevens (Ed.), *Hand-book of Experimental Psychology* (New York: Wiley, 1951), Fig. 6, p. 448. Reproduced by permission.

sistance of 250,000 ohms. As you can see from the extreme left-hand part of Fig. 11-2, all three groups learned, and it is not surprising that the rats receiving the stronger shocks learned to run faster.

The purpose of this experiment was to see how well the animals would learn a new response, pressing a bar, to cause the door to drop during subsequent trials without any electric shock. But, in a previous experiment of this kind (Miller, 1948), I had found that a considerable number of the rats froze, so that they never performed the new response and hence could not learn it. In order to reduce such freezing, we intro-duced a number of trials of running to touch the door with the shock turned off. As you can see from the second part of Fig. 11-2, the rats that had received the weakest shock continued running about as fast as they had before, and then gradually extinguished. The rats that had received the intermediate level of shock also continued running more or less as they had before. But the rats that had received the strongest level of shock, and had been running the fastest before, were the slowest on the first nonshock trials, far below the speed of those that had received the intermediate shocks. This was because they crouched and froze.

Eventually, however, these rats stopped their freezing and hesitantly performed the simple response of touching the door and getting into the safe compartment. We would expect the reduction of fear to reinforce the response of moving, and you can see that, over a series of trials, their speed increased until they were again running faster than any of the other groups.

When we changed the situation so that touching the door was ineffective and the rats had to learn to press a bar to cause it to drop, you can see from the last two parts of Fig. 11–2 that the animals that had received the weakest shock did not learn, while the other two groups did, with the rats receiving the strongest shocks learning to respond the fastest. Since freezing had been eliminated in the preceding stage of training, every rat in the two groups receiving stronger shocks eventually performed the correct response and learned. This was in marked contrast to the earlier experiment (Miller, 1948) in which special pains had not been taken to train rats to run instead of to freeze when the shocks were off.

This experiment shows the effect of strength of shock on a habit reinforced by escape from fear. I want to emphasize that, during the first nonshock trials, the 540-volt group showed more freezing than the 180-volt one. This was not merely helplessness, because both groups had been escaping shock every time during learning to touch the door. In this particular situation, the greater strength of fear during the first nonshock trials produced more freezing which interfered with the response of running.

Specific Training in Activity versus Passivity

In the preceding experiment you have seen speed curves showing that frightened rats were unlearning their passive response of freezing and learning the active one of running to touch the door. This training apparently greatly improved their subsequent learning of a new response, pressing the bar, to open the door, since they responded much better than the rats in an earlier experiment who had not been given special training to eliminate fear.

For some time I have been interested in whether one can train subjects to react to difficult situations by freezing or apathy on the one hand or general activity and striving on the other. On page 132 of Dollard and Miller (1950), we said: "If the child is fed when hungry, it can learn that the one simple thing it can do to get results (i.e., cry) can make a difference in what happens. Learning to cry as a signal for food is one small unit in its control of the world. Such a trait could be the basis of a later tendency to be 'up and doing' when in trouble, or a belief that there is always a way out of a painful situation. If the child is not fed when it is crying, but is instead left to 'cry itself out,' it can, similarly, learn that there is nothing it can do at that time to change the painful circumstances. Such training may also lay the basis for the habit of apathy and not 'trying something else' when in trouble."

Recently, Alfredo Carmona and I have done a little exploratory work in which we trained one group of rats to escape and avoid shock by moving and another group to escape and avoid by freezing. The initial training was in a running wheel in which different groups of rats showed that they could learn to respond differently. We also secured evidence that this training can transfer to a new situation and affect subsequent performance in an alley. I mention these exploratory results more to define an important problem than to state a definite conclusion. Jay Weiss and I are in the process of repeating the experiment with better procedures and controls, and are also following up a suggestive lead in Carmona's data that training in these two different patterns of response may have different psychosomatic effects.

Church (see Chapter 5 of this volume) has already told you about our experiments specifically training rats to resist pain and fear (Miller, 1960; Feirstein & Miller, 1963), so I shall not take the time to describe them. Maier, Seligman, and Solomon have described some beautiful experiments that are also highly pertinent to the problem of training to respond actively or passively (see Chapter 10 of this volume).

Effects of Dexedrine on Freezing

Ever since the first work that Hobart Mowrer and I did on the shuttle box (Mowrer & Miller, 1942), investigators have been plagued by the rat's tendency to freeze in this situation. Apparently, the rat does not like to run back into the place where it has just previously received shock, and the conflict thereby induced increases the relative prepotency of freezing.

Evidence on the inverse relationship between freezing and successful avoidance in the two-way shuttle comes from an experiment in which Krieckhaus, Zimmerman, and I (Krieckhaus et al., 1965) used dexedrine to counteract freezing. The response of freezing can be rated quite reliably by giving rats a score of 4 points if they don't move at all, 3 if they move only their head, 2 if they move either of their front legs, and 1 if they move both of their rear legs. In order to secure an independent measurement of the effects of dexedrine on freezing, rats were placed in a little box and given shocks that they could neither escape nor avoid. When tested after an injection of 2 mg/kg dexedrine, they showed much less freezing than when tested after a control injection of isotonic saline.

Then, in the main experiment, on a new group of rats, we found that the dexedrine improved performance in the two-way shuttle, exactly as one would expect from the reduction that it produces in freezing. Furthermore, for each of the groups receiving electric shocks, there was a reliable negative correlation between the amount of freezing between trials and the number of successful avoidances.

One aspect of the results of this experiment, however, was surprising. I expected the rats that had been rewarded for performing the correct response of shuttling under the drug to do better during a subsequent nondrug session than a control group that had not had this experience. Exactly the opposite happened; when the dexedrine was withdrawn, the performance deteriorated, so that the group that had been performing much better than the controls during learning with a strong dose of the drug performed much more poorly after the drug was withdrawn. Perhaps, if the drug is withdrawn gradually, this decrement can be avoided, but that remains to be seen. At present, these results are similar to those of other experiments showing that drug-induced improvements do not necessarily transfer from the drugged to the nondrugged situation (Miller, 1966).

Effects of Fear Conditioning on Freezing and Avoidance

We have seen that freezing can interfere with avoidance learning, that extremely strong shocks produce more freezing, that the relative dominance of freezing can be reduced by trials during which a simple avoidance response of touching a door is reinforced by escape from fear, and that this reduction in its dominance will help the learning of a new and more difficult avoidance response, pressing a bar. We have also seen that the performance of freezing can be reduced by dexedrine.

In the next experiment, Weiss, Krieckhaus, and Conte (1966), working in my laboratory, showed that giving animals fear conditioning prior to avoidance training interfered with subsequent shuttle avoidance learning. These results are somewhat surprising, since one might very well predict that rats that have already learned to be afraid would subsequently learn an avoidance response faster. However, the investigators also measured movement and showed that if one considers the influence of freezing, the poorer learning can be readily explained.

Figure 11–3 shows the learning of shuttle avoidance. You can see that the Pre-fear group, which before training received fear conditioning consisting of eight unavoidable shocks paired with the warning signal (CS) used in this avoidance training, showed very poor learning com-

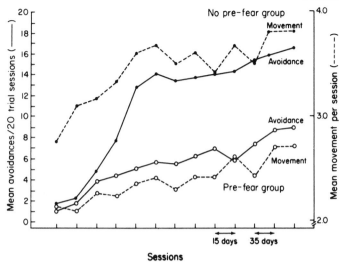

FIG. 11–3.   The effect of fear conditioning before avoidance learning on subsequent movement scores (the converse of freezing) and on avoidance-learning scores. (Data from Weiss et al., 1966)

pared with the No Pre-fear group, which had received no previous shock. The relationship between freezing and poor avoidance learning can be seen from the movement ratings (broken lines) in Fig. 11–3. That the freezing was responsible for the unsuccessful avoidance, rather than vice versa, is indicated by a number of facts. First, Fig. 11–3 shows that the difference in freezing was present from the very beginning of training, clearly preceding the difference in avoidance. Also, the rats that showed the most freezing during the prior fear conditioning, when no avoidance was possible, were the ones which subsequently showed the poorest avoidance learning ($r = -.81$; $p < .01$). That the key variable was indeed freezing to fear rather than general activity is shown by the fact that this correlation for the control group, which did not receive shock before shuttle training, was only $-.20$ and unreliable.

One might suggest that freezing in this experiment is a manifestation of learned helplessness because the animals received eight inescapable shocks during fear conditioning. However, the Pre-fear animals showed a great deal of freezing during the first fear-conditioning session consisting of only two trials, each with a 5-second, 1-ma. shock. It seems very unlikely that the animals would have learned helplessness this quickly. This freezing also correlated highly ($r = -.86$; $p < .01$) with later avoidance.

Another similar experiment showed that the interference with learning after fear conditioning was greater the more the transfer of fear from prior conditioning was mediated by the similarity of the prior shock situation to the subsequent avoidance training one. The results are shown in Fig. 11-4. Shock in avoidance training was preceded by a tone CS. Animals that received prior fear conditioning to this tone showed poor learning, as in the previous experiment. Learning was markedly improved and progressively better across groups that received fear conditioning to a blinking light not used in avoidance training, or shock alone, or no shock.

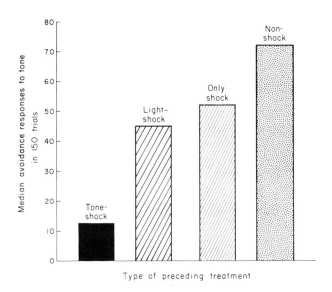

FIG. 11–4.   The effect of the similarity of the previous fear-conditioning situation to the subsequent avoidance-training one on the learning of avoidance. Similarity to the avoidance-training compartment and CS decreases progressively from tone-shock through light-shock to only shock-pretreatment conditions. (Data from Weiss et al., 1966)

Freezing during fear conditioning was again highly correlated ($r = -.83$) with subsequent avoidance behavior. In this experiment, the interval between fear conditioning and shuttle avoidance training was 24 hours, while in the first experiment there was a 4-day interval. The fact that the effect was not transient is further evidence that it was based on a learned response, such as fear, established during the prior fear conditioning.

Continuing our main theme, after the animal has thoroughly learned to shuttle, we would expect the response of running when afraid to be strongly dominant over that of freezing. Thus, fear conditioning administered at this time would be expected to have a different effect than if given before avoidance training. In the next experiment, animals that had already learned to shuttle were given fear conditioning consisting of eight unavoidable shocks preceded by the same CS that had been used in avoidance training. Ratings made while they were receiving these unavoidable shocks showed that they did not freeze but tended to keep moving. As Fig. 11–5 shows, these unavoidable shocks did not

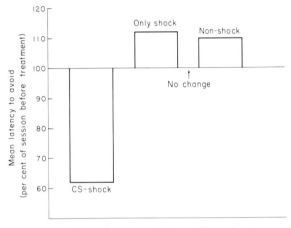

Type of treatment after avoidance learning

FIG. 11–5.   The effect of fear conditioning after the initial avoidance training on the latency of performance during the subsequent session of avoidance training. One group received the same CS used in avoidance training, the other group received only shock, and the third group was kept in the conditioning apparatus without shock. (Data from Weiss et al., 1966)

interfere with performance but, instead, improved it. Animals that were given only the CS without shock, or that received the same shock but associated with different stimulus conditions so that fear would not be expected to transfer as strongly to the avoidance situation, showed no improvement.

Several investigators (Moyer & Korn, 1954; Levine, 1966; Theios, Lynch, & Lowe, 1966) have shown that giving rats training in the two-way shuttle with strong shocks produces poorer learning than using weaker shocks. Presumably this is because strong shocks tend to elicit such strong fear that freezing is dominant. Moyer and Korn (1966) and Theios et al. (1966) found that in the one-way avoidance situation, stronger shocks produced the opposite effect of better learning. In a direct parallel with these effects of strong shock, Weiss et al. (1966) found that the prior fear conditioning which interferes with the learning in the two-way shuttle improves performance in the one-way avoidance. Furthermore, in contrast with the high correlation between freezing during prior fear conditioning and the subsequent performance in the two-way shuttle, there was a very low correlation ($r = - .09$) between such freezing and subsequent performance in the one-way avoidance. This observation indicates that freezing is not as likely to be a significant interfering response in one-way avoidance as it is in the two-way shuttle learning. Weiss et al. suggested that this was why strong fear retarded two-way avoidance learning but not one-way.

One of the reasons why freezing is not an important interfering response in one-way learning may be that, once an animal makes a correct response in the one-way situation, learning to move is reinforced so strongly that it completely out-competes freezing. This could be because this situation does not involve the conflict of running back into the place where the animal was just shocked, which reduces the dominance of moving and increases that of freezing, and/or because escape into a compartment in which the rat has never been shocked is a stronger reinforcement than merely turning off a danger signal and running into a place where he previously has been shocked.

The Role of Coping Responses in the Psychosomatic Effects of Punishment

In conjunction with his exploratory work in the preceding experiments on the effects of fear conditioning on subsequent learning in the shuttle box, Weiss made the incidental observation that certain animals which were yoked to partners running in a shuttle box, and hence had no control over the shocks, lost more weight than did their partners who could control the shocks by making an avoidance response. Since the shocks were administered through grids, he could not be certain that the groups were shocked equally. Therefore, before he could investigate this phenomenon thoroughly, he had to devise some way of making sure that the rats being given the two different treatments actually received the same amount of electric shock to the same place. He did this by developing the ingenious tail electrode which is illustrated in Fig. 11–6. You can see that it is made of a small section of an elastic rubber tube. When it is stretched and slipped over the tail, it clamps a pair of electrodes to the opposite sides of the tail. If a steady shock is applied, the rat is likely to turn around and start biting at the electrode, but if brief pulses of shock are given, the rat's natural response is to move forward to each pulse, and this movement is reinforced by the termination of the pulse. With a little preliminary training, during which the tendency to move forward to the shock is reinforced and any tendency

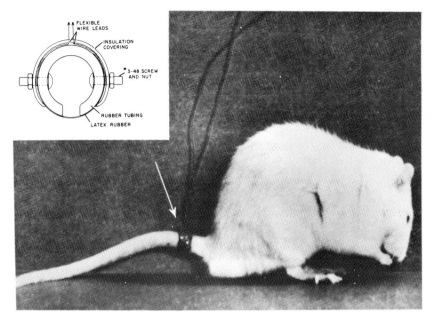

FIG. 11–6.   The electrode used to deliver tail shocks.

From: J. Weiss, "A Tail Electrode for Unrestrained Rats," *Journal of Experimental Analysis of Behavior*, **10**, 1967, Fig. 2, p. 85. Copyright 1967 by the Society for the Experimental Analysis of Behavior, Inc., and reproduced by permission.

to turn and bite the electrode is punished by a momentary increase in the intensity of the shock, it is easy to shape the rat so that he will move about without biting the electrode.

Figure 11–7 shows the apparatus and the general design of Weiss's (1968) first experiment on the psychosomatic effects of a coping response. The tails of two rats were wired in series so that they received exactly the same electric shocks. The third rat received no shocks. The conditioned stimulus consisted of pulling back the plunger which exposed a little platform at the back of the apparatus and turning on a 1000-cycle tone. Ten seconds later, the shock was turned on for the experimental rat and his yoked control. During the first few trials, the shocks were moderate and the experimental rat was shaped to jump onto the platform, at which time the tone and shocks were turned off. At the end of each trial the plunger was gently pushed back so that the rat was forced down onto the floor. After the first few shaping trials, the experimental training began. It consisted of 70 trials spread over a period of approximately 3 hours, during which 0.5-second pulses of 3-ma. shocks were given once every 5 seconds whenever the experimental animal failed to jump up onto the platform within 10 seconds. During all phases of

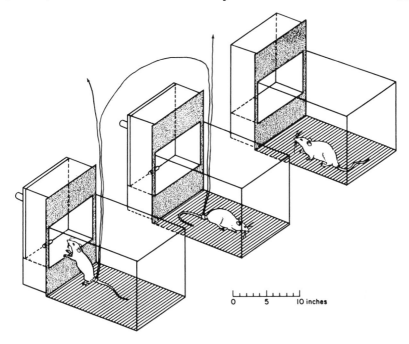

FIG. 11-7.   The apparatuses for the avoidance, yoked, and nonshock rats, respectively, in weight gain experiments. The sides of each box were aluminum, so that rats could not see other other during stress sessions.

From: J. M. Weiss, "Effects of Coping Responses on Stress," *Journal of Comparative and Physiological Psychology,* **65,** 1968, pp. 251–260. Copyright 1968 by the American Psychological Association and reproduced by permission.

the experiment, both rates received exactly the same shocks through their tails which were wired in series.

At the end of the stress session, both shocked animals had lost an equal amount of weight, but you can see from Fig. 11-8 that during the next 24 hours in the home cages the avoidance and the nonshocked rats, which were still young and growing, gained considerable weight, while the yoked control rats, which had received exactly the same shocks without being able to do anything about them, failed to gain weight. During the stress session, yoked rats defecated more than avoidance ones, indicating that they were more afraid, and the amount of defecation correlated −.53 with subsequent weight gain. After 24 hours the curves of weight gain became parallel, which shows that there was no further aftereffect, but that the initial difference, which was highly reliable, persisted throughout the rest period during which no further training was given.

After the rest period, all rats were given brief stress sessions consisting of five trials a day. Again, the yoked control animals, which had no coping response available, failed to gain weight while the other two groups continued to grow at approximately the normal rate. The striking result is that the avoidance animals, which received exactly the same shock, show a weight pattern much more like that of the non-shock group than like that of their yoked partners.

In another part of the experiment, Weiss trained the rats to drink water in a separate boxlike apparatus. Then he put each rat in the training apparatus with water bottles at the corners of the grid com-

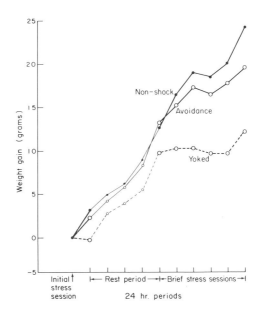

FIG. 11–8.   Curves of weight gain for yoked, avoidance, and nonshock groups following initial stress, during rest periods, and brief stress sessions. (Data from Weiss, 1968)

partment. In two different tests, one during avoidance trials and one without such trials, the avoidance animals drank sooner than the yoked animals, showing that the latter had the greater fear of the apparatus. Thus the results of the behavioral test (CER) for fear yielded the same results as the physiological measure of weight loss.

In the same study, Weiss (1968) also used a different type of situation, illustrated in Fig. 11–9, and a different measure of stress, the amount of stomach lesions produced. Rats were restrained in a little cylindrical device from which they could not back out. Shocks were again delivered to an avoidance and a yoked control animal via tail electrodes wired in series. The conditioned stimulus was the change from darkness to light, an oscillating motion of the entire apparatus, and the sound of the motor driving the cam to produce the oscillation. The avoidance animal could poke his nose out through a little hole and touch a copper plate, thus actuating an electronic relay which turned off both the CS and the shock. If the avoidance rat performed within the 10-second grace period, he turned off the CS and both rats avoided the shock. The

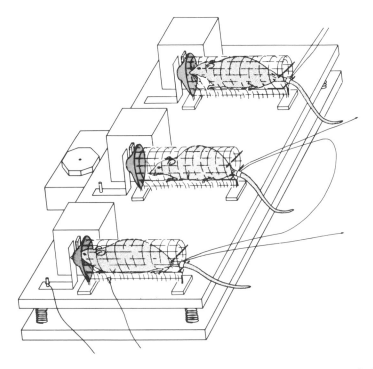

FIG. 11–9.   Apparatus for avoidance, yoked, and nonshock rats, respectively, in stomach-lesion experiments. The avoidance rat can turn off the shock for both himself and his partner by sticking his nose out and touching the plate in front of the cone.

From: J. M. Weiss, "Effects of Coping Responses on Stress," *Journal of Comparative and Physiological Psychology*, **65**, 1968, pp. 251–260. Copyright 1968 by the American Psychological Association and reproduced by permission.

lucky third animal was a nonshock control. After some shaping, to get the avoidance animal to perform the response, Weiss gave 21 hours of training consisting of trials once per minute with shocks for failure to respond gradually increasing from 0.4-ma. pulses 0.1 second long occurring once every 10 seconds to 1.6-ma. steady shock.

Twelve hours after the stress session, the rats were sacrificed, and their stomachs were examined by an independent judge who did not know which rat had received which treatment. Figure 11–10 shows results in terms of average length of lesions in millimeters. You can see that the period of partial restraint without food produced a slight amount of lesions in the nonshock animals' stomachs. The avoidance animals showed slightly more lesions, but again the big difference is between the avoidance animals and their yoked partners who could not do anything about the shocks and showed by far the most stomach lesions. When the judge also made an overall comparison of the three stomachs in each triplet, the yoked animal was rated the worst in all triplets except one. Thus, the results of this second experiment, using a different measure in a different situation, confirm those of the first one.

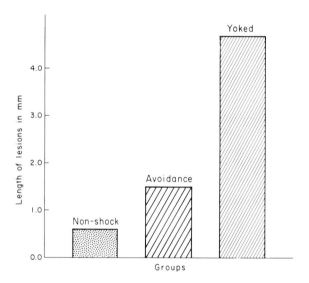

FIG. 11–10.   Mean length of stomach lesions for nonshock, avoidance, and yoked groups. (Data from Weiss, 1968)

The results of these two experiments are, of course, directly opposite to those secured by Brady and his co-workers (Brady, Porter, Conrad, & Mason, 1958). In the light of these opposite results, one is tempted to conclude, "It's easy to be an executive provided you are a rat." On the other hand, the difference could be due to the fact that Brady selected the monkeys who learned the Sidman avoidance to be his executives and put the less able learners in the control group (Brady et al., 1958, p. 70), thus introducing a possible selection for endocrine or personality factors related to good avoidance learning, and perhaps related also to susceptibility to stomach lesions. But it seems more plausible to us that the difference may be a result of the nature and/or the difficulty of the task. Perhaps with a very easy task, being able to perform a coping response reduces the stress; but as the task becomes too difficult, the subject has to worry not only about the shock but also about the task. At present, Weiss and I are investigating the influence of the difficulty of the coping task on its effects of reducing or increasing the stress produced.

Conceivable Mechanisms for Effects of Coping

Whatever the interaction with difficulty of task may be, in the simple situation that Weiss (1968) used, the effects of the coping response were indeed striking. In both experiments, the stress measures used showed the avoidance animals to be more similar to the controls, which received no shocks at all, than to the yoked partners, which received exactly the same electric shocks without being able to do anything about them. Furthermore, these results are in line with those from naturalistic observations of people in realistic danger situations, such as combat, where some of the important factors reducing fear are knowing exactly what to expect, knowing exactly what to do, concentrating on the task at hand, and self-administered reassurance (Miller, 1959, p. 268). In order to stimulate further research, let us speculate briefly on what factors or mechanisms could underlie Weiss's striking results. The various possibilities are, of course, not necessarily mutually exclusive.

Myers (1956) has shown that the predictability of electric shock is an important factor in determining the amount of generalized fear that it produces; at present, Weiss is finding that predictability is also an important factor in the amount of stomach lesions produced. In the first experiment, one might consider that the main variable was not the availability of a coping response, but the predictability of the shocks. Both rats had the promptness with which the tone of the CS was terminated as a cue to predict whether or not they would get shocks. In addition, the avoidance rat had the cues produced by whether or not he jumped up onto the platform. Perhaps these additional cues, available only to the avoidance rat, increased the distinctiveness of the pattern enough to make the occurrence of the shocks considerably more predictable.

But, in the second experiment, the cues of proprioception from shaking plus the noise of the motor plus the change from darkness to illumination were so massive that it seems unlikely that the additional cue of proprioception from merely poking out the nose and touching the plate would add appreciably to the information conveyed by the immediate turning off of this perspicuous pattern of danger signals, the termination of which meant that there was no further possibility of shock for either rat. Similarly, the activity involved in performing the response of poking the nose out was so minimal that there seems to be little likelihood that much relief was produced by the mere exercise involved.

Assuming that the availability of a coping response was indeed a major factor, analogous to knowing what to do for human subjects, how could it operate? Such a response might help by reducing conflict, since it clearly would be dominant over all other responses in contrast to the variety of conflicting responses that would be reinforced for the yoked partner, who would remain in a problem-solving situation. Another closely related possibility is that the dominance of this response and/or the focusing of attention on this response might tend to inhibit emotional responses and even activate corticofugal pathways which might inhibit the reception of pain. Or, it could be that learning a successful response involves the anticipatory activation of a central reward system and that it is this reward system that inhibits fear and perhaps even the perception of pain. Cox and Valenstein (1965) have found that the direct electrical stimulation of a number of rewarding areas in the rat brain reduces the rat's behavioral reactivity to electric shocks to the feet, and Ball (1967) has shown that similar stimulation reduces the evoked potential elicited in the trigeminal nucleus by stimulation of the trigeminal nerve.

When I was first working on fear as a learnable drive in experiments similar to the one with Douglas Lawrence that has already been described, I observed that, as rats learned to avoid shock by running into the safe compartment, they first ran to the far end of that compartment where they eventually started to relax (Miller, 1951, p. 451). Gradually, the relaxation moved forward, until they performed the entire avoidance response in a relaxed manner. That fear had not been completely lost as a potential drive, however, could be shown by disrupting the response sequence that elicited the anticipatory relaxation. For example, if the switch was disconnected so that the door did not open when the rats pressed the bar, they became tense again, pressed the bar much more vigorously, urinated, defecated, and showed other signs of strong fear. Weiss observed similar signs of anticipatory relaxation in his avoidance animals. At first, they relaxed only on the safe platform and remained crouched ready to jump up between trials. Gradually, the jumping posture became more relaxed and was progressively abbreviated until the rats even began exploring between trials, occasionally looking over their shoulders at the general location of the safe platform, as if it gave them reassuring cues of safety. Similarly, during the subsequent CER tests in this apparatus, some of the avoidance rats would freeze at first, and then after they had made their first avoidance response, would immediately jump down off the platform and start to drink. Thus, we suggest that having a coping response makes avoidance animals less afraid because relaxation (or safety) becomes conditioned to the response, and then becomes increasingly anticipatory. Perhaps some of the various hypotheses we have discussed may provide the primitive basis for what, at its cognitively more complex human level, we call hope.

Finally, one must mention the possibility that, after they have learned, the avoidance animals probably received shocks only when they were not frightened enough to have already jumped, while the yoked partners would receive some of their shocks at times when they were frightened. This point is analogous to Church's (1964) criticism of the yoked control technique. While such a possibility cannot entirely be ruled out, it seems rather likely that the strong shocks used had a near maximum effect irrespective of whether they were superimposed on the peaks or the troughs of fluctuations in fear, or were received by tough or timid rats.

Transience of Stress Effects versus Permanence of Memory

Returning to Fig. 11–8, presenting the results of the experiment in which Weiss's rats escaped by jumping up onto a platform, you will remember that the effect of the stress from the single, long session of unavoidable shocks produced a reduced weight gain which showed up at the end of the first 24 hours, after which animals in this group resumed their normal rate of weight gain, so that the curve was parallel to that of the other two groups. The relative transience of this stress effect should be contrasted with the much greater permanence of true learning.

Figure 11–11 shows the results of an experiment in which rats were given a single shock as soon as they stepped out of a narrow starting box into a distinctive larger compartment. When tested the next day, practically none of them stepped out within the maximum available time of 2 minutes, so that the average speed score was greatly reduced. When tested 23 days after this electric shock, their performance remained virtually the same, showing practically perfect retention of the learning produced by a single electric shock. Other experiments, involving training with a longer series of shocks, show similar good retention of avoidance learning or a CER from a month to several years (e.g., Wendt, 1937; Tenen, 1967). The permanence of such learning should be contrasted with the transience of certain acute effects of traumatic stress.

The dogs given inescapable shocks in the excellent experiment by Overmier and Seligman (1967) showed complete failure of escape learning in the shuttle box if tested 1 day later but learned practically as well as nonshocked controls if tested 2 days later. This enormous

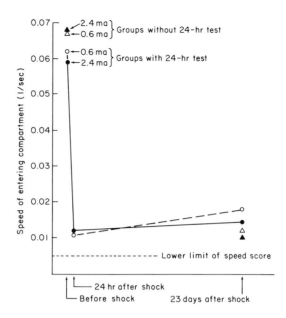

FIG. 11–11.   The memory of rats for a single trial on which they received electric shocks upon entering a distinctive compartment. Learning and retention are shown by reduced speed of entering compartment.

From: N. E. Miller, "Laws of Learning Relevant to Its Biological Basis," *Proceeding of the American Philosophical Society*, **3**, 1967, pp. 315–325. Reproduced by permission.

difference between tests given 1 and 2 days after the unavoidable shock is different from the characteristically good retention of learning and similar to the frequently transient aftereffects of traumatic stress, which strongly suggests that physiological aftereffects of stress may have been a crucial factor in producing the initial failure to learn. As the results of Weiss's experiments on psychosomatic effects have shown, we would expect a series of strong inescapable shocks to have much greater stressful physiological aftereffects than a similar number of avoidable shocks. For these reasons, it seems to us that it would be highly desirable to determine the physiological aftereffects on the dogs of the inescapable shocks used in the experiments on "helplessness." The time course of these aftereffects should be investigated by behavioral measures, such as general activity, and by physiological measures, such as body weight, corticosteroid levels, norepinephrine depletion, and norepinephrine turnover.

Let me be perfectly clear that Weiss and I do not think that the physiological aftereffects of unavoidable shock necessarily are the only factors involved in these striking and unusually significant experiments.

We believe only that some interaction of such physiological aftereffects with other factors is a highly probable explanation of the fact that the failure to learn occurs 1 day, but not 2 days, later, a striking effect for a rest of only 24 additional hours.

Overmier and Seligman describe that the dogs given inescapable shock initially attempt to escape during avoidance training as do normal dogs but soon give up in favor of sitting and howling, whereas normal dogs continue to seek an escape route until they succeed, after which these dogs learn quite rapidly. This suggests that a key variable being affected by inescapable shock is how long the animal will produce active coping attempts prior to success. Part of the explanation for why dogs given inescapable shock stop attempting to escape may be, of course, that they have learned that there is nothing they can do about shock. However, the apparent complete resumption of escape behavior 2 days after treatment, which is difficult to explain on the basis of learning, suggests that a short-lived physiological aftereffect summates with any learning effects that are present, which are by themselves not strong enough to produce failure to escape. Perhaps the dogs typically gave up before they happened to jump over the shoulder-high barrier because of a physiological depression, much as one of us might give up a difficult task more quickly if we were sick with influenza. Under these conditions, one can imagine that stopping effortful escape responses might be immediately reinforced by escape from effort, while sitting would be further reinforced when the shock eventually went off at the end of the trial. Such learning in the shuttle situation should, of course, be relatively permanent, which is what these investigators found.

We are also struck by the fact that occasionally a dog given preceding training with traumatic, inescapable shocks may make a successful response during subsequent escape training but fail to learn it as a naive dog would. A physiological depression and the strength of conflicting responses, like sitting and howling, could contribute to such a failure. But, an informational analysis of the reinforcement situation along the lines of Egger and Miller (1962, 1963) suggests that yet another type of factor could be involved. For the naive dog, the occurrence of a number of unsuccessful responses regularly followed by the continuance of shock and then a single response of hurdle jumping followed by the termination of shock will yield a perfect correlation between the correct response and the termination of shock. For the animal with prior exposure to unavoidable shocks, a number of different responses each will have been associated occasionally with the termination, but usually with the continuation, of shock. Against the background of this noise, the correlation of a single response of hurdle jumping with termination of shock will be considerably lower, yielding less information.

Since such an informational factor is based on learning, however, like any other learning factor it cannot completely explain the failure to escape after 24 but not after 48 hours. It would have to interact with some other factor such as a physiological depression. One basis for such interaction might be a stimulus–generalization decrement in the memory of the unavoidable shock situation as the physiological aftereffects and the cues they produced dissipated with time. Such a stimulus–generalization decrement could, of course, be one of the ways that physiological aftereffects could interact with the habit of sitting and howling, learned effects on the reward mechanism, or other factors involved in learned helplessness.

Escape and Avoidance Learning of Visceral Responses

In the preceding section we have seen that punishment can produce psychosomatic symptoms, such as loss in weight and production of stomach lesions, and that the severity of such symptoms can be a function of the type of learning which is possible for the punished animal. In those experiments, learning presumably affected the psychosomatic symptoms primarily by affecting the amount of fear or stress produced. Can the glandular and visceral responses involved in psychosomatic symptoms be modified more directly by learning?

It has long been known that the training procedure of classical conditioning can be used to transfer a glandular or visceral response from the unconditioned stimulus that innately elicits it to a previously neutral stimulus (Pavlov, 1927; Bykov, 1957). Such conditioning of fear, and possibly of other innate reactions to pain, was one of the factors involved in Weiss's experiments on psychosomatic effects. This procedure has its limitations, however, since the response can be reinforced only by an unconditioned stimulus that has the capacity to elicit the particular response to be learned.

The other type of training procedure, called instrumental learning, trial-and-error learning, or operant conditioning, is much more flexible in that the reinforcement does not have to be able to elicit the response to be learned but, instead, can strengthen any (or perhaps almost any) immediately preceding learnable response. But the strong traditional belief has been that the instrumental learning of glandular and visceral responses mediated by the supposedly inferior autonomic nervous system is impossible, or in other words, that such learning is possible only for skeletal responses mediated by the supposedly superior cerebrospinal nervous system. If true, this difference must have deep significance for the neurological basis of learning; indeed, it has been used as one of the strongest arguments for a two-factor theory of learning, which assumes a fundamental difference between a more primitive mechanism of classical conditioning and a more sophisticated one of instrumental learning. If true, this strong traditional belief also would mean that glandular and visceral responses could not be rewarded by escape from, or avoidance of, punishment.

Recent work from my laboratory has shown that, when the possibility of mediation via overt skeletal responses is eliminated by paralyzing such responses with curare, the instrumental learning of glandular and visceral responses reinforced by direct electrical stimulation of rewarding areas of the brain is possible (Miller & DiCara, 1967; Trowill, 1967). Such learning can be quite specific: when increases or decreases, respectively, in heart rate are rewarded, changes in the appropriate direction are learned but intestinal contractions are unaffected; conversely, when increases or decreases, respectively, in intestinal contractions are rewarded, changes in the appropriate direction are learned but heart rate remains unaffected (Miller & Banuazizi, 1968). Similarly, when increases or decreases, respectively, in the rate of urine formation are rewarded, changes in the appropriate direction are found, but heart rate and blood pressure are relatively unaffected (Miller & DiCara, 1968). The variety and specificity of the glandular and visceral responses that can be learned make it difficult to try to explain away the results as being merely the mediated by-products of the instrumental learning of motor impulses from the brain that would normally have resulted in skeletal responses if the motor endplates of the muscles had not been paralyzed.

The experiments that are most relevant to this conference, however, are those in which the escape from or avoidance of electric shocks was used as the reinforcement. In addition to being relevant to the effects of punishment, these experiments show that the reinforcement of the instrumental learning of glandular and visceral responses is not limited to any peculiar property of the reward by direct electrical stimulation of the brain.

The first experiment was performed by DiCara and me (DiCara & Miller, 1968). Albino rats were injected i.p. with 1.2 mg/kg of d-tubocurarine chloride in a solution containing 3 mg/ml. Then, via a needle inserted subcutaneously after the area had been locally anesthetized, they were constantly infused at a rate of 1.2 mg/kg per hour for the duration of the experiment. They were artificially respirated by a special face mask, and heart rate was recorded via the rat's electrocardiogram which actuated automatic equipment for making the reinforcement contingent upon a specified rate. In order to check on the paralysis by curare, an electromyogram was recorded from the gastrocnemius muscle.

After a period of 30 minutes during which the heart rate was allowed to stabilize, training started. It consisted of 300 trials presented on a 30-second variable-interval schedule and divided equally among shock-signal trials, safe-signal trials, and blank trials. During the blank trials the heart rate was recorded for 5 seconds in order to secure a base line but nothing else happened. For half of the rats, the safe-signal was the onset of light flashing 5 times per second and the shock-signal was a 1000-cps, 82-db steady tone. For the other half of the rats, the functions of these two cues were reversed. During the safe trials, the signal was on for 5 seconds while the heart rate was recorded and nothing else happened.

On shock-signal trials, if the rat achieved the criterion heart rate within 5 seconds of the onset of the shock signal, it was turned off and no shock was delivered. If the rat failed to meet the criterion within the 5 seconds, a 0.1-second pulse of 0.3-ma. electric shock was delivered to the tail until the rat achieved the criterion, at which time both the shock signal and the shock were turned off. Every tenth shock trial throughout training was a special test trial, during the first 5 seconds of which both the criterion and shock circuits were turned off so that heart rate could be measured for the same constant intervals throughout training without any possible contaminating effects from having the shock signal turned off or the shock turned on. At the end of the 5-second interval, the scoring circuit was turned off, the criterion was turned on, and the procedure continued as though this had been the beginning of a regular shock trial.

Half of the rats were assigned to a group which achieved the criterion by slightly slowing down their heart rate; the other half achieved it by slightly speeding up their heart rate. After each rat had learned to meet an easy criterion, he was gradually shaped to meet progressively more difficult ones.

The results are presented in Fig. 11–12. It can be seen that the rats

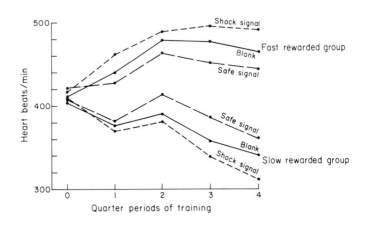

FIG. 11–12.   Changes in heart rate during avoidance training.

From: L. V. DiCara & N. E. Miller, "Changes in Heart Rate Instrumentally Learned by Curarized Rats as Avoidance Response," *Journal of Comparative and Physiological Psychology*, **65**, 1968, pp. 8–12. Copyright 1968 by the American Psychological Association and reproduced by permission.

rewarded by escape or avoidance for speeding up their heart rate learned to increase it, while those rewarded for slowing down their heart rate learned to decrease it. Each of the twelve individual rats changed in the predicted direction; *t*-tests for the reliability of the changes of individual rats yielded one nonsignificant difference, three beyond the .01 level, and eight beyond the .001 level. One could scarcely ask for more convincing evidence.

While part of the learning was a general change in base line, as indicated by the blank trials, in each of the two groups the rats showed highly reliable ($p < .004$) additional changes in the correct direction, which was an increase for one group and a decrease for the other, during the signal for shock. Since these highly reliable changes occurred to the shock signal before the time for delivery of shock and turned off the shock signal and shock circuit, they are avoidance responses. In order to shape the response to secure larger changes and also to control for possible effects of different frequencies of electric shock by holding these relatively constant, the criterion was progressively increased throughout training. Therefore, an increase in the number of successful avoidances cannot be used as an additional indication of avoidance learning. Additional evidence for avoidance learning during training is given by the progressively increasing size of the difference between the blank trials and the shock-signal test trials. Suitable trend tests (Winer, 1962, p. 298) show that this increase in difference is reliable both for the slow and the fast groups ($F = 3.7$ and 5.2; $p < .02$ and .01, respectively; $df = 4, 50$).

During the safe signal, both groups showed a reliable change in the opposite direction, toward the original starting level. This last result, which is like that secured by Rescorla and LoLordo (1965), shows that the stimulus not associated with shock did not function solely as a neutral stimulus but, instead, as a signal for nonshock, producing a relaxation (or inhibition) of the response reinforced by escape or avoidance of shock. Since the animals were always safe in the absence of a shock signal, the only additional function of the safe signal in comparison to a blank trial was to predict that no onset of a shock signal (followed by a 5-second period of grace) was imminent. Nevertheless, there was a difference between the responses during the safe signal and the blank trials which was highly reliable ($p < .01$) for both the fast and slow groups.

Since the rats in each group responded reliably in the reinforced direction to the shock signal and reliably in the opposite direction to the safe signal, it is clear that the instrumental training procedure had brought the heart rate under discriminative stimulus control.

Figure 11–13 shows the percentage in change in heart rate during training for each rat, and also the number of shocks received during

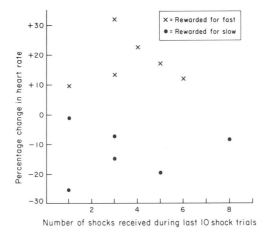

FIG. 11–13.   Heart-rate changes as a function of response rewarded rather than number of shocks received.

From: L. V. DiCara & N. E. Miller, "Changes in Heart Rate Instrumentally Learned by Curarized Rats as Avoidance Response," *Journal of Comparative and Physiological Psychology*, **65**, 1968, pp. 8–12. Copyright 1968 by the American Psychological Association and reproduced by permission.

the last ten shock trials. You can see that, in terms of the number of shocks received, there is considerable overlapping between the two groups but no overlapping in the change in heart rate. The results are similar when analyzed in terms of the total number of seconds of shock received. Therefore, the difference between the groups cannot be a function of the amount of shock received. Since the two groups receiving similar shocks changed in opposite directions, the results cannot be explained on the basis of the classical conditioning of any unconditioned effect of the shock.

Finally, Fig. 11–14 shows a typical electromyographic record of a curarized rat which learned a highly reliable ($p < .001$) increase in the heart rate. This record was taken at a sensitivity of 150 microvolts per centimeter. Throughout training, the records of all rats were flat except for occasional very small denervation potentials, the form of which easily could be distinguished from true muscle potentials. The first minute signs of true muscle action potentials did not appear in this or any of the other rats until at least 1 hour after the end of training. Individual spikes began to be noticed about 1½ hours after the end of training, and full spindle bursts began to be noticed about 2 hours after the end of training, at which time the first slight muscle twitches were observed. By the time appreciable twitching occurred, the gain had to be reduced greatly in order to prevent the pen from going off the paper. It is clear that the rats were completely paralyzed by curare.

In order to determine whether or not these rats were learning to send from the motor cortex impulses that would have resulted in instrumental skeletal responses if the motor endplates of the muscles had not been paralyzed by curare (Miller & DiCara, 1967, p. 17), DiCara and I retested rats from the preceding experiment several days later. We found that the changes in heart rate of both the group trained to speed up and the one trained to slow down were retained and transferred to the noncurarized state. While the two groups showed clear differences in heart rate, they did not show differences in movement that were visually observable or that appeared on a sensitive mechanical movement recorder, on electromyographic records, or on records of breathing. Thus it seeems unlikely that they had learned to send out somatic motor impulses capable of mediating the observed changes in heart rate. Finally, it is difficult for such an hypothesis to explain the specificity of the visceral learning in the experiments on cardiac versus intestinal learning (Miller & Banuazizi, 1968) and on the formation of urine (Miller & DiCara, 1968).

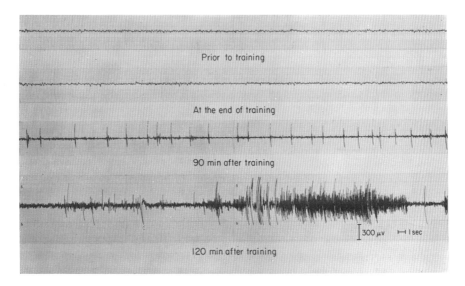

FIG. 11–14. Typical electromyographic record of curarized rat during avoidance-training experiment. These records were obtained from a representative rat which learned a reliable ($p < .001$) increase in heart rate.

In an experiment rather similar to ours on heart rate, Banuazizi (1967) showed that rats can learn to either increase or decrease, respectively, their intestinal contractions in order to escape and/or avoid punishment. Since he did not progressively raise his criterion, he secured a highly reliable ($p < .001$) increase in the number of successful avoidances during learning.

From these experiments it is clear that at least two responses under the control of the autonomic nervous system can be instrumentally learned to escape and/or avoid punishment. These results, and those of the other experiments in the series, remove one of the strongest arguments that has been used for a basic difference between classical conditioning and instrumental learning. Of course, they do not by themselves prove that these two types of training situations involve a single basic mechanism of learning, but it should be noticed that the main facts that have been used in favor of a two-factor (i.e., two-mechanism) theory of avoidance learning could be equally well encompassed in a two-stage, one-mechanism theory.

The results of these experiments open up the possibility that psychosomatic symptoms may be learned as escape and/or avoidance responses. They also open up the possibility that functional disorders of glandular and visceral responses, and perhaps even some organic disorders that are not too severe or are not serving as any physiologically desirable compensation for a defect, can be treated by immediately and specifically reinforcing changes in the therapeutically desired direction.

REFERENCES

BALL, G. G. Electrical self stimulation of the brain and sensory inhibition. *Psychonomic Science,* 1967, **8**, 489–490.

BANUAZIZI, A. Modification of an autonomic response by instrumental learning. Paper read at the Meeting of the Psychonomic Society, Chicago, October, 1967.

BRADY, J. V., PORTER, R. W., CONRAD, D. G., & MASON, J. W. Avoidance behavior and the development of gastroduodenal ulcers. *Journal of the Experimental Analysis of Behavior,* 1958, **1**, 69–72.

BYKOV, K. M. *The cerebral cortex and the internal organs.* (W. H. Gantt, Ed. and Tr.) New York: Chemical Publishing Co., 1957.

CHURCH, R. M. Systematic effect of random error in the yoked control design. *Psychological Bulletin,* 1964, **62**, 122–131.

COX, V. C., & VALENSTEIN, E. S. Attenuation of aversive properties of peripheral shock by hypothalamic stimulation. *Science,* 1965, **149**, 323–325.

DiCARA, L. V., & MILLER, N. E. Changes in heart rate instrumentally learned by curarized rats as avoidance responses. *Journal of Comparative and Physiological Psychology,* 1968, **65**, 8–12.

DOLLARD, J., & MILLER, N. E. *Personality and psychotherapy.* New York: McGraw-Hill, 1950.

EGGER, M. C., & MILLER, N. E. Secondary reinforcement in rats as a function of information value and reliability of the stimulus. *Journal of Experimental Psychology*, 1962, **64**, 97–104.

EGGER, M. C., & MILLER, N. E. When is a reward reinforcing? An experimental study of the information hypothesis. *Journal of Comparative and Physiological Psychology*, 1963, **56**, 132–137.

FEIRSTEIN, A. R., & MILLER, N. E. Learning to resist pain and fear: Effects of electric shock before versus after reaching goal. *Journal of Comparative and Physiological Psychology*, 1963, **56**, 797–800.

FOWLER, H., & MILLER, N. E. Facilitation and inhibition of runway performance by hind- and forepaw shock of various intensities. *Journal of Comparative and Physiological Psychology*, 1963, **56**, 801–805.

GWINN, G. T. The effects of punishment on acts motivated by fear. *Journal of Experimental Psychology*, 1949, **39**, 260–269.

KRIECKHAUS, E. E., MILLER, N. E., & ZIMMERMAN, P. Reduction of freezing behavior and improvement of shock avoidance by d-amphetamine. *Journal of Comparative and Physiological Psychology*, 1965, **60**, 36–40.

LEVINE, S. UCS intensity and avoidance learning. *Journal of Experimental Psychology*, 1966, **71**, 163–164.

MILLER, N. E. Experimental studies of conflict. In J. McV. Hunt (Ed.), *Personality and the behavior disorders*. Vol. 1. New York: Ronald Press, 1944. Pp. 431–465.

MILLER, N. E. Studies of fear as an acquirable drive: I. Fear as motivation and fear-reduction as reinforcement in the learning of new responses. *Journal of Experimental Psychology*, 1948, **38**, 89–101.

MILLER, N. E. Learnable drives and rewards. In S. S. Stevens (Ed.), *Handbook of experimental psychology*. New York: Wiley, 1951. Pp. 435–472.

MILLER, N. E. Liberalization of basic S–R concepts: Extensions to conflict behavior, motivation and social learning. In S. Koch (Ed.), *Psychology: A study of a science*. Study 1, Vol. 2. New York: McGraw-Hill, 1959. Pp. 196–292.

MILLER, N. E. Learning resistance to pain and fear: Effects of overlearning, exposure, and rewarded exposure in context. *Journal of Experimental Psychology*, 1960, **60**, 137–145.

MILLER, N. E. Some animal experiments pertinent to the problem of combining psychotherapy with drug therapy. *Comprehensive Psychiatry*, 1966, **7**, 1–12.

MILLER, N. E. Laws of learning relevant to its biological basis. *Proceedings of the American Philosophcal Society*, 1967, **III**, 315–325.

MILLER, N. E., & BANUAZIZI, A. Instrumental learning by curarized rats of a specific visceral response, intestinal or cardiac. *Journal of Comparative and Physiological Psychology*, 1968, **65**, 1–7.

MILLER, N. E., & DiCARA, L. Instrumental learning of heart-rate changes in curarized rats: Shaping, and specificity to discriminative stimulus. *Journal of Comparative and Physiological Psychology*, 1967, **63**, 12–19.

MILLER, N. E., & DiCARA, L. V. Instrumental learning of urine formation by rats; changes in renal blood flow. *American Journal of Physiology*, 1968, **215**, 677–683.

MOWRER, O. H., & MILLER, N. E. A multipurpose learning-demonstration apparatus. *Journal of Experimental Psychology*, 1942, **31**, 163–170.

MOYER, K. E., & KORN, J. H. Effect of UCS intensity on acquisition and extinction of an avoidance response. *Journal of Experimental Psychology,* 1964, **67**, 352–359.

MOYER, K. E., & KORN, J. H. Effect of UCS intensity on the acquisition and extinction of a one-way avoidance response. *Psychonomic Science,* 1966, **4,** 121–122.

MYERS, A. The effects of predictable vs. unpredictable punishment in the albino rat. Unpublished doctoral dissertation, Yale University, 1956.

OVERMIER, J. B., & SELIGMAN, M. E. P. Effects of inescapable shock upon subsequent escape and avoidance responding. *Journal of Comparative and Physiological Psychology,* 1967, **63**, 28–33.

PAVLOV, I. P. *Conditioned reflexes.* (Tr. G. V. Anrep.) London: Oxford University Press, 1927. (Reprinted, New York: Dover, 1960.)

RESCORLA, R. A., & LoLORDO, V. M. Inhibition of avoidance behavior. *Journal of Comparative and Physiological Psychology,* 1965, **59**, 406–412.

TENEN, S. S. Recovery time as a measure of CER strength: Effects of benzodiazepines, amobarbital, chlorpromazine and amphetamine. *Psychopharmacologia,* 1967, **12**, 1–17.

THEIOS, J., Lynch, A. D., & Lowe, W. F., Jr. Differential effects of shock intensity on one-way and shuttle avoidance conditioning. *Journal of Experimental Psychology,* 1966, **72**, 294–299.

TROWILL, J. A. Instrumental conditioning of the heart rate in the curarized rat. *Journal of Comparative and Physiological Psychology,* 1967, **63**, 7–11.

WEISS, J. M. A tail electrode for unrestrained rats. *Journal of the Experimental Analysis of Behavior,* 1967, **10**, 85–86.

WEISS, J. M. Effects of coping responses on stress. *Journal of Comparative and Physiological Psychology,* 1968, **65**, 251–260. Also available as doctoral dissertation, Yale University, 1967.

WEISS, J. M., KRIECKHAUS, E. E., & CONTE, R. Effects of fear conditioning on subsequent avoidance and movement. Paper read at Eastern Psychological Association, New York, April, 1966.

WENDT, G. R. Two and one-half year retention of a conditioned response. *Journal of General Psychology,* 1937, **17**, 178–180.

WINER, B. J. *Statistical analysis in experimental design.* New York: McGraw-Hill, 1962.

V

PARADOXICAL EFFECTS
of PUNISHMENT

12

The Varied Functions of Punishment in Discrimination Learning[1]

Harry Fowler

George J. Wischner

UNIVERSITY OF PITTSBURGH

Common sense and social practice emphasize the weakening or inhibiting effect of punishment on behavior and reflect the attitude that punishment operates as the counterpart of positive reinforcement. There is much evidence to support this common-sense assumption regarding the weakening or suppressing effect of punishment, but more recently there has been increased recognition of the varied effects that punishment may exert (see Church, 1963). Indeed, there are even experimental situations in which punishment has been found not to have weakening effect on performance but rather, analogous to the operation of positive reinforcement, a strengthening or facilitating effect (e.g., Fowler, 1963; Fowler & Miller, 1963; Martin & Ross, 1964). These diverse effects of punishment on behavior suggest that punishment does not function predominantly in any one way, but that associated with these varied effects are comparably varied functions.

For some investigators, facilitating effects of punishment are viewed as paradoxical exceptions; it is argued that these effects occur not because of but rather in spite of the punishment contingency. We would point out, however, that facilitating effects are paradoxical only insofar as they represent exceptions to the presumed suppressing or inhibiting

[1] The research program reported in this paper was supported initially by National Science Foundation Grant No. G-14312 and subsequently by PHS Research Grant MH-08482 from the National Institutes of Health to George J. Wischner and Harry Fowler. Preparation of this paper was supported by funds from the latter grant. Authorship is alphabetical and there is no implication of seniority.

The authors wish to acknowledge the graduate student research assistants who have served on the project: Louis M. Ascher, George C. Fago, Larry Goldman, Stephen A. Kushnick, and Philip F. Spelt.

function of punishment. In this sense, situations which give rise to facilitation should not be viewed as paradoxical but as representing the bases for elaborating, through experimental analysis, the possibly varied functions of the punishment procedure and the manner in which these functions may relate to or mediate diverse performance outcomes. It seems likely that such an approach can enhance our understanding of punishment phenomena and, as Sandler (1964) has suggested, clarify their extension to such fundamental problems as self-punishment behavior, masochism, and the like.

In line with this orientation, our research has focused on a punishment paradigm that has long been reported to facilitate performance. The research takes as its point of departure the early work by Muenzinger (1934) on the effect of punishment for the correct, food-reinforced response in visual discrimination learning. Although there is much evidence which delimits the generality that this type of punishment procedure (shock-right training) invariably facilitates performance, the phenomenon appears to be generally accepted. Accordingly, various hypotheses have been offered concerning the function of punishment and the mechanisms by which the facilitation is obtained. For example, it has been suggested that (1) punishment serves to slow down the animal at the choice point, making it more sensitive to the discriminanda (Bolles, 1967; Church, 1963; Logan & Wagner, 1965; Woodworth & Schlosberg, 1954); (2) mild punishment may serve as an emphasizer, thus influencing the animal's perceptions of the relevant signs and significates (Hilgard & Bower, 1966; Tolman, Hall, & Bretnall, 1932); and (3) punishment, by virtue of its association with food reinforcement, becomes a discriminative stimulus for food, and thereby functions as a secondary reinforcer (Azrin & Holz, 1966; Freeburne & Taylor, 1952; Logan & Wagner, 1965).

These general interpretations of the phenomenon tend to ignore the equivocal nature of the evidence relating to the generalization that shock for the correct response facilitates performance. Even within the context of a paradigm which has emphasized a facilitating effect of punishment, the data call for an experimental analysis aimed at isolating those conditions which give rise to the effect and those which do not. It is similarly noteworthy that little attention has been given in general accounts of the phenomenon to the fact that, with practically all of the earlier studies assessing the effects of shock-right (SR) training, there was no, or at best, relatively inadequate control of shock parameters, such as the duration of the shock experience, its frequency of occurrence and precise locus with respect to the cues and responses and even the reinforcement with which it was associated. As a consequence, little attention was directed in the earlier work to the relationship between shock parameters and the specific conditions and procedures of training.

The present chapter first reviews the earlier work on SR training in order to point up important methodological and procedural features of this research as well as the restricted bases on which interpretations concerning the function of punishment have been cast. Although critical, the review recognizes the importance of placing the earlier work in appropriate historical perspective. In a following section, our own program of research is presented with an emphasis on the methodology and results of a series of studies that have been designed to assess some of the problems stemming from considerations of the earlier work. Following this, an analysis is offered which suggests the value of differentiating among the effects, functions, and mechanisms of operation of the punishment procedure. Within this framework, an effort is then made to integrate our research findings with those of earlier studies, with the aim of reinterpreting some of the earlier results and of evaluating extant hypotheses concerning the effects of SR training.

History of the Paradox

It has long been the practice in animal discrimination experiments to employ, in addition to the customary food reward for a correct response, some medium of punishment, usually electric shock, for the incorrect response. The logic of such procedure is implied in Thorndike's (1911, p. 244) statement of the Law of Effect:

> Of several responses made to the same situation those which are accompanied or closely followed by satisfaction to the animal, will, other things being equal, be more firmly connected with the situation, so that, when it recurs, they will be more likely to recur; those which are accompanied or closely followed by discomfort to the animal, other things being equal, will have their connections with that situation weakened, so that when it recurs, they will be less likely to occur. The greater the satisfaction or discomfort, the greater the strengthening or weakening of the bond.

In general, early investigations relating to the Law of Effect were in accord with it. For example, studies by Yerkes and Dodson (1908), Dodson (1917), Hoge and Stocking (1912), Warden and Aylesworth (1927), and Bunch (1928) were consistent in showing that punishment administered for the incorrect response led to a relatively more rapid elimination of errors.

Evidence for Facilitation and a General Alerting Function of Punishment

Muenzinger (1934, p. 267) questioned the adequacy of the early discrimination studies when they were offered as support for the generalization that punishment tends to weaken or inhibit the punished response:

It is the so-called "wrong" response that has always been punished in situations in which the conditions of placing the reward favored the performance of some alternative, the so-called "right" response. In order to be sure that the function of punishment is really that of the inhibition of the punished response, we ought to punish the response favored by the reward, the "right" response. In such a case we would expect according to the law of effect that a conflicting tendency be set up in a response that is both rewarded and punished, that is a facilitating and inhibiting tendency which would manifest itself in a slowing down of the course of learning.

Following this rationale, Muenzinger (1934) introduced the technique of administering shock for the correct response, i.e., the response followed by food reinforcement. For rats receiving correction training in a T maze on a simple light-dark discrimination, this shock-right (SR) condition resulted in the reliably faster elimination of errors than a no-shock (NS) condition and an almost equally rapid elimination of errors as in the typically employed shock-wrong (SW) condition. Although the SR group was slightly inferior in performance to the SW group, the difference between the two groups was not statistically reliable. On the basis of these results, Muenzinger concluded that mild shock neither strengthens nor weakens. The facilitating effect of electric shock on discrimination performance is not due to an inhibition of incorrect responses, but rather to a general alerting function of shock "which makes the animal respond more readily to the significant cues in the learning situation irrespective of whether it [shock] accompanies the right or wrong response." (Muenzinger, 1934, p. 274.)

To investigate the possibility that shock applied anywhere in the maze would produce an increased alertness to the relevant cues, Muenzinger and Wood (1935) extended the conditions of the original experiment by administering shock either before or after choice, i.e., either for the approach response in the stem and choice region of a T maze or for *both* correct and incorrect responses. With these procedures, it was felt that any inhibiting effect of the shock would be inconsequential for discrimination performance since such inhibition either antedates choice behavior or is equally applied to both right and wrong responses. On the other hand, the general alerting hypothesis suggested by the original experiment predicted that shock both before and after choice would facilitate performance. Indeed, where shock was applied to both right and wrong responses, there might even be a summation effect. Using the groups of the 1934 experiment as a basis for comparison, Muenzinger and Wood (1935) found, however, that shock after choice or shock-both (SB) facilitated performance only as much as the SR procedure, and further, that shock before choice produced an effect comparable to the NS condition. Thus, these results supported a general alerting function of shock but they required that this interpretation be limited to the condition where shock was administered subsequent to choice.

The same pattern of results prevailed in a study by Muenzinger and Newcomb (1936) where 6-inch gaps in the floor of the maze were substituted for shock. Rats required to jump a gap before choice, i.e., in the stem region, were comparable in performance to the NS group of the 1934 experiment; on the other hand, animals required to jump the gap after choice (actually, in order to make a choice) showed facilitated performance comparable to that of the original SR group. These results illustrated, then, that other stimulus conditions could be substituted for shock in order to facilitate performance; however, they were of import for another reason as well. In contrast to rats of the jump-before-choice condition, rats of the jump-after-choice condition were observed to pause regularly at the choice point before making a choice-jump into one of the T-maze arms. Because this behavior seemed to occur as well in pervious experiments where rats were shocked anywhere after choice, Muenzinger and Newcomb (1936) now proposed that an enforced pause at the moment of choice was the mechanism by which shock exerted its general alerting effect. It is noteworthy that this interpretation of the data has been cited in numerous textbooks and review articles that have appeared on the subject; unfortunately, these general accounts have typically failed to acknowledge an alternative interpretation of the data that Muenzinger and Newcomb (1936) themselves offered.

The gap study (Muenzinger & Newcomb, 1936), as well as the previous shock studies, employed a correction procedure requiring that the rat retrace and enter the correct arm following each error. As a consequence, rats of the gap-after-choice, or gap-both condition, encountered at least three gaps with each error (initially going incorrectly, retracing, and then entering the correct arm), as opposed to only one gap in making an initial correct choice. That jumping a gap may have been unpleasant, perhaps because of the effort involved, is suggested by the pretraining that was required to establish the jump response and the related fact that rats of the jump-before-choice condition *never* returned to the stem having once made their jump. Accordingly, the 3 to 1 differential in favor of the wrong response for rats of the jump-both group may well have been sufficient to produce a rapid elimination of errors, quite independently of any effect of pausing at the choice point.[2] Considered in relation to the Muenzinger and Wood (1935) study in which shock grids extended the full length of the T arms and were charged continuously

[2] A further complication is the differential delay of reinforcement which exists following an incorrect response for rats of the gap-both procedure. These subjects have to pause and jump several times in correcting as compared with those of the jump-before-choice condition, or even those of a control condition—in this case the NS group of the 1934 experiment.

following choice, this differential means that rats of the SB group could receive three times as much shock following an error as for an initially correct response, with the easiest—indeed only—avenue of escape being by way of the correct arm. It should be noted that escape via the correct arm was also the case for rats of the SR and SW conditions of the 1934 experiment.

The role of escape from shock as a potential determinant of the facilitated discrimination performance observed in these earlier studies seems clearly illustrated in the results of an infrequently cited study by Muenzinger and Fletcher (1936). In this study, shock was administered throughout the T maze, i.e., both before and after choice, with the result that the performance of a group so trained was comparable to the facilitated performance of the SB group in the prior Muenzinger and Wood (1935) study. This effect obtained, moreover, for escape-trained rats that were either reinforced or not reinforced with food in the correct goal. (Parenthetically, it may be noted that escape factors also seem responsible for the anomalous pattern of results that prevailed in another study [Muenzinger & Newcomb, 1935] where a buzzer signal was used in place of shock for either the correct or incorrect response. Located directly beneath the choice point and presented when the rat proceeded to make a choice, the buzzer apparently induced escape into the "punished" arm, with the result that facilitation obtained for buzzer-right animals, but not for buzzer-wrong animals.)

These considerations lead one to question the interpretive value of a pause at the choice point, if indeed there can be much of this behavior when rats are escaping shock administered throughout a maze, as in the Muenzinger and Fletcher (1936) study. Nonetheless, a facilitating effect of an enforced pause at the point of choice was demonstrated in a subsequent investigation by Muenzinger and Fletcher (1937). Rats that were delayed at the choice point for 5 seconds by means of glass partitions showed improved performance relative to the NS control group of the original Muenzinger (1934) experiment, although the magnitude of this effect, as measured by trials to criterion, was reliably less than that obtained for the SB group of the Muenzinger and Wood (1935) study. These data point up the importance of a choice-point pause, either enforced directly as in the Muenzinger and Fletcher (1937) study, or induced presumably by shock after choice as in the Muenzinger and Wood (1935) study; however, an important question remains as to what extent such pausing contributes, or actually relates, to the facilitation obtained with SR and SB procedures. On this issue, other investigators were in disagreement with the conclusions drawn by Muenzinger and his co-workers.

In a study by Fairlie (1937) which, like the original Muenzinger experiment, also compared the efficacy of SR and SW procedures, rats received a single half-second shock at the moment of choice, that is, as they appeared to begin to move into one or the other T-maze arm. The

SW procedure was found to be superior to the SR procedure in elim-inating errors, but both procedures seemed to foster comparable if not somewhat retarded performance in comparison with the NS group of the original Muenzinger study. (In this study, as well as in all previously cited experiments, the only NS control group available for comparison was that of Muenzinger's 1934 experiment.) The important data of Fairlie's experiment, however, relate to the percentage of trials on which pauses, accompanied by vicarious trial and error (VTE) behavior (see Goss & Wischner, 1956), were followed by correct choices. Both the SW and SR groups showed a comparable frequency of VTE behavior, but whereas for the SW group correct responses occurred on over 70% of VTE trials, for the SR group there was no consistent relationship be-tween VTE and correct choice.

Drew (1938) offered even more pertinent observations calling into question the relevance of pausing behavior as a mechanism for Muen-zinger's general alerting hypothesis. Investigating the effect of shock locus, Drew compared SR and SW groups that received shock imme-diately after choice with an additional shock-in-food group. The dis-crimination performance of all three shock groups was found to be reliably and comparably facilitated relative to an NS control group that was also employed, but with respect to the amount of VTE shown at the choice point, these groups differed markedly. Drew noted that the SR group engaged in VTE much more than the NS group, whereas the SW group showed no more of this behavior than the control, and even more significantly, the shock-in-food group appeared to show none at all. For this last group, the only hesitation and head turning apparent was that in the vicinity of the food, a finding which suggests that VTE for shocked subjects reflects, at least in part, an avoidance of the specific cues, be they food or choice-point cues, that are associated with the shock. Although Drew did not discuss this possibility, he did conclude that "factors such as increased cautiousness, increased attention, or in-creased alertness likewise have no experimental evidence to prove or disprove them. At present we are justified in saying only that the factor responsible for the acceleration is probably a general rather than a specific one." (Drew, 1938, p. 266.)

Even the positing of a general factor as underlying the effect of shock after choice had to be qualified when, in a study by Muenzinger, Bernstone, and Richards (1938), the important parameters of shock duration and frequency were taken into account. Acknowledging the difference in these parameters which existed for the SR and SW groups of the 1934 experiment, Muenzinger et al. (1938) repeated the original experiment with the addition of an SR group that was yoked with the SW condition. In this experiment, shock was turned off for the SW rats as soon as they turned around to correct, thereby permitting the admin-istration of a comparable duration of shock to SR rats. In accord with the findings of the 1934 study, the SR and SW groups showed facilitated performance in comparison with either the NS group of this study or that of the original experiment.[3] However, the difference between the two shock groups was now reliable with the SR group showing less facilitation than the SW group. In view of this finding, Muenzinger and his colleagues modified their original position and postulated that shock after choice could facilitate discrimination performance through a general mechanism but that it also affected correct and incorrect responses differently through a specific mechanism. For Muenzinger, the general mechanism was revealed behaviorally in VTE activity. All groups receiving shock after choice exhibited a considerable amount of such behavior. The specific factor was suggested by qualitative behavioral differences between SR and SW animals. The latter learned very quickly to turn about before advancing very far into the arm in which they were shocked; the former would continue on to the end of the wrong arm.

Methodological Considerations

It is significant that all of the prior work by Muenzinger and his colleagues, and by other investigators as well, utilized a correction procedure. Wischner (1947) analyzed the complexities associated with the use of correction and emphasized that with such training an error leads to a combination of incentives. He further pointed out that noncorrection training permits a better evaluation of the effects of punishment primarily for the reason that, with this procedure, the time interval between a response and its consequent is better controlled and is relatively constant for all conditions. In addition, all animals must make the same gross response to shock, irrespective of their shock treatments; that is, once committed to a choice, right or wrong, they must cross over the grid to the discriminative cue.

Accordingly, a study was performed in which rats received noncorrection training in a Yerkes-Watson discrimination box. As in prior research, SW rats showed facilitated performance, the difference between this group and SR and NS groups being statistically reliable for both trial and error measures. In contrast, the performance of SR subjects was characterized by a marked initial rise in errors and then a relatively quick drop when the animals finally began to learn, with the resultant that the overall difference between this group and the NS control was not significant. These data were interpreted as seriously questioning Muenzinger's alerting hypothesis of punishment. It was proposed instead that the effect of shock is immediate and specific. It leads very quickly to the

---

[3] The fact that the NS group of this study was also reliably *superior* to the NS group of the original 1934 experiment causes some concern regarding the use of the original control to evaluate treatment effects in all prior research.

building up of avoidance responses to the stimulus cues with which it is associated.

In the discussion which ensued on the interpretive significance of the above findings (Muenzinger, 1948; Wischner, 1948), Muenzinger pointed out that correction and noncorrection procedures differ not only with respect to the consequences of an error but also with regard to terminology and measurement. With the correction method, as used by Muenzinger and his co-workers, a single error (and trial) was recorded irrespective of the number of times the rat actually entered or reentered the incorrect arm before proceeding to the correct goal; with the non-correction procedure, all such entries comprised "additional" errors and trials. Because of this difference, as well as those relating to the char-acteristics of the apparatuses used, Muenzinger and Powloski (1951) attempted to compare the two procedures directly. It is significant, how-ever, that this comparison was effected not by employing noncorrection training as described by Wischner (1947) but by adapting the noncorrec-tion procedure to the general methodology and system of recording utilized with correction. Thus, each time a noncorrection animal entered the incorrect arm of the T maze, it was permitted to return to the start-ing stem via an exterior, adjacent gray alley where it was delayed briefly and then, *with the position of the discriminative stimuli remain-ing the same as on the preceding incorrect choice,* the rat was free to choose again. As for rats of the correction procedure, the position of the discriminative stimuli was varied in accord with a predetermined ran-dom schedule only after a correct response. In this respect, then, the noncorrection procedure employed by Muenzinger & Powloski (1951) actually permitted the animal to correct but via the gray return alley instead of the incorrect maze arm.

With this arrangement, it is perhaps not surprising that Muenzinger and Powloski (1951) found SR groups of both procedures to show facilitated performance relative to their respective NS controls. Never-theless, the magnitude of the facilitation effect under noncorrection training was only marginally reliable. Furthermore, the SW groups of both procedures were superior to their respective SR groups. Since this latter result again pointed up a specific avoidance function of the shock, Muenzinger and Powloski (1951, p. 124) argued that the magnitude of SR facilitation related to differences between correction and noncorrec-tion training which allowed differential adaptation to shock:

> In the corrective situation the frustration in the wrong alley and subsequent retracing towards the positive cue seems to counteract the avoidance tendency towards the shock-producing correct alley thus allowing the accelerating effect to exert itself. In the noncorrective situation on the other hand, the full avoidance effect is present until the animal has somewhat adjusted itself to it when the accelerating effect will gain preponderance.

Following the lead suggested in the previous experiment, Muenzinger, Brown, Crow, and Powloski (1952) sought to adapt animals to shock prior to discrimination training in which shock was applied to either correct or incorrect responses. Rats were pretrained to run in a straight alley where they received food at the goal on each of 120 training trials and shock half-way down the alley on every other trial; other rats were pretrained to run for food alone or were not pretrained at all. Subsequent discrimination training, again with the adapted noncorrection procedure of the prior Muenzinger and Powloski (1951) study, showed, like the results of that study, that SR groups without pretraining or with pretraining for food alone were reliably inferior to their respective SW groups. However, the SR group with shock-food pretraining was comparable in performance to its comparison SW group and therefore presumably facilitated relative to its NS control. (In this study, no statistical comparison was offered on the difference between any SR or SW group and its respective NS control, or for that matter, on the differences, seemingly large, among NS groups of the three pretraining conditions.) These findings led Muenzinger et al. (1952) to argue that by attenuating the aversive, avoidance-producing effect of shock in pretraining, they had enabled the accelerating effect of shock after choice to become manifest within the context of noncorrection training. This interpretation, however, would seem to overlook the likelihood that shock adaptation, especially pretraining to run through shock for food, will decrease the tendency of animals to pause at the choice point and to attend to the relevant cues.

Aside from its effect in attenuating the aversiveness of a shock experience, the procedure of pairing shock with food, as in the pretraining condition of the Muenzinger et al. (1952) study, allows the possibility that shock will acquire reinforcing properties, i.e., become a secondary reinforcer. In relation, then, to discrimination training where shock is administered for the correct food-reinforced response, shock may facilitate performance not because of any alerting function but instead, because as a cue selectively associated with the correct response, it can mediate the effect of food reinforcement. Offering this secondary reinforcement interpretation as an alternative to Muenzinger's general alerting hypothesis, Freeburne and Taylor (1952) sought to determine whether shock would facilitate performance under a condition where it could not serve as a cue to the correctness or incorrectness of a response, i.e., where shock accompanied both correct and incorrect responses. This SB condition had earlier been shown by Muenzinger and Wood (1935) to produce the facilitation required by the alerting hypothesis. However, their study, as well as the comparable gap-both study (Muenzinger & Newcomb, 1936), employed a correction procedure which allowed a differential in the amount of shock (or number of gaps) for right and wrong responses. Using a noncorrection procedure, Freeburne and Taylor (1952) found, nevertheless, that the SB condition facilitated performance relative to their NS control, and thus they interpreted their results as supporting Muenzinger's alerting hypothesis.

Freeburne and Taylor's (1952) results were subsequently questioned by Prince (1956), however, because the difference which they reported was marginally reliable and their discrimination problem so difficult that nearly one third of the animals failed to reach a learning criterion within 500 trials.[4] Under such circumstances, the obtained difference may well have occurred because shock had the effect of disrupting position habits. Moreover, in his own study, which also utilized noncorrection training, Prince (1956) found no difference between SB and NS groups —not even a tendency toward SB facilitation.[5] Prince interpreted this finding as supporting an anxiety-reduction hypothesis that had earlier been offered by Mowrer (1950). According to Mowrer, differences in outcome between correction and noncorrection training related to the availability of responses by which the animal could terminate the fear or anxiety presumably conditioned to the general situation as a consequence of shock. Since, with correction training, only a correct response could remove the animal from the fearful situation, correct responses, even though punished as in the case of SR training, were doubly reinforced; that is, by food reinforcement and fear reduction. With noncorrection training, however, where correct and incorrect responses equally permitted escape from the situation, a differential in favor of the correct response could not exist, at least not early in training while the animal was still making errors. Consequently, neither SR nor SB facilitation should result with noncorrection training as was the case in the Wischner (1947) and Prince (1956) experiments.

All three interpretations, fear reduction, general alerting, and secondary reinforcement, seemed insufficient, however, to account for the results of a second experiment reported by Prince (1956). In previous work by other investigators, several shock-free training trials were administered prior to the introduction of shock after choice, but the effect of this variable had not been systematically explored. Using the noncorrection method and introducing shock after 0, 15, or 25 shock-free discrimination trials, Prince found that both errors and trials for

[4] The heightened difficulty of Freeburne and Taylor's apparently simple black–white discrimination seems to relate to the imposition, following choice, of a 5-second delay in a neutral gray detention chamber; similarly, reinforcement was occasioned away from the discriminative stimuli, again in a neutral gray chamber.

[5] In a fairly recent study comparing the effects of various combinations of food and shock for either the correct or incorrect response, Wischner, Hall, and Fowler (1964) also found no difference between SB and NS groups that were trained with the noncorrection procedure. Equally important was the finding that an SR group, a control absent in the Freeburne and Taylor (1952) and Prince (1956) studies, performed significantly poorer than the NS group.

SR groups were inversely related to the amount of shock-free training. Furthermore, this outcome was such that, relative to an NS control group, the SR group with 0 shock-free trials was poorer in performance (as measured by errors but not by trials), whereas the SR group with 25 shock-free trials was superior in performance (as measured by trials but not by errors). Thus, Prince's second experiment provided some evidence that SR training in a noncorrection context could facilitate performance so long as sufficient shock-free training was administered first. These data seem to complement those of Muenzinger et al. (1952) concerning the effect of shock adaptation. Evidently, by increasing the strength of approach through the administration of shock-free food-reinforced trials, as in the Prince (1956) study, or by decreasing the strength of avoidance through the administration of shock-adaptation trials, as in the Muenzinger et al. (1952) study, a facilitating effect of shock for the correct response could be augmented and made manifest despite the use of correction or noncorrection training. Considered together, the findings of the two experiments clearly suggest the value of parametric studies designed to investigate the determinants of approach and avoidance, i.e., factors such as amount of food deprivation, magnitude of food reinforcement, shock intensity, duration, and frequency.

An interesting parallel to the Muenzinger et al. (1952) study on shock adaptation was provided by the final study in the series conducted by Muenzinger and his students. Attempting to manipulate further the strength of the avoidance reaction to shock, Muenzinger and Baxter (1957) gave rats food-reinforced training in a straightaway where they had either to approach and cross a charged grid "on their own initiative" or, being dropped directly on to the grid, to escape the shock by running into the food compartment. During subsequent discrimination training on a black-white problem, the particular brightness of the straightaway (either black or white) was used as a secondary or substitute cue for shock in order to simulate both SR and SW conditions. As would be expected on the basis of the presumably different reactions that were conditioned during straightaway training, the approach group was found to be superior to the escape group when the substitute cue designated the correct alley and simulated the SR condition; conversely, the escape group was superior to the approach group when the substitute cue designated the incorrect alley and simulated the SW condition. The surprising result, however, was that with either the simulated SR or SW condition, both escape- and approach-trained rats were superior to controls that had also received straightaway training but without shock. These data indicated that apart from the type of motor reaction elicited by shock and conditioned to the cues in a situation, these cues could facilitate performance when designating either a correct or an incorrect alternative. Although not stressed by Muenzinger and Baxter (1957), these findings highlighted the operation of some general accelerating factor, but whether this factor related to an alerting or other function of shock (or conditioned aversive stimulus) was still indeterminant.

A Current Program of Research

The foregoing review indicates a wide range of empirical findings concerning the effect of shock for the correct response in discrimination learning. The results of certain investigators are clearly opposed to those of others; shock for the correct response can facilitate or retard discrimination performance, or have no effect at all. As indicated by our review, these empirical discrepancies relate to procedural and methodological variations in the experimental designs that were employed, and a failure to treat or study the parameters of electric shock per se in a systematic fashion. Thus, while Muenzinger had stated as early as his 1934 experiment that only moderate electric shock would be facilitating, systematic manipulation of shock intensity was never accomplished. Along with this failure to treat shock intensity, there was generally a lack of control of the shock's duration and frequency of occurrence, and consequently its precise locus with respect to the cues and responses with which it was associated. Even in the Muenzinger et al. (1938) experiment, which matched SR and SW conditions on amount of shock received, an animal of either condition could touch a charged grid, withdraw, touch it again, and then finally attempt to run across it.

With the apparent need for parametric studies, the present writers initiated a program of research which was designed to investigate systematically such factors as the intensity, duration, locus, and frequency of the shock administered, along with the ordering of shock and nonshock trials. In addition, a related class of nonshock variables, pertaining to training procedures, performance factors, and variation of the discriminative stimuli was included. These manipulations were treated in a series of studies which utilized a standardized apparatus and procedure. Before turning to a presentation of the specific experiments, we shall present those aspects of our general procedure which have been uniform across studies.

Method of Procedure

Subjects. The subjects for all experiments were 80–100-day-old naive male albino rats of the Sprague-Dawley strain. Upon receipt from the supplier, the subjects were caged individually in the experimental laboratory with the temperature controlled at about 68°–74° F. and the normal day–night cycle reversed through artificial illumination.

Apparatus.   The apparatus was an enclosed T maze of uniform interior dimensions, with start and goal compartments formed by opaque guillotine doors located in the stem and arms. Guillotine doors were also positioned in each arm, just beyond the choice region, to prevent retracing as well as to permit the administration of forced-choice trials as required. The apparatus differed in certain respects from that typically used. Discriminative stimuli were provided through differential illumination of frosted Plexiglas panels serving as the end walls of the goal compartments. Thus, a discriminative stimulus was available to the subject throughout its sequence of responding, i.e., from the choice response to the consummatory response at the goal where food cups were located directly beneath the frosted Plexiglas end panels. It should be noted that, due to general ambient illumination as provided by exterior maze lights, the effective brightness of a discriminative stimulus was unaffected by such factors as reflectance from the opposite goal-box end panel or the operation of a guillotine door.

In place of grid sections located in the stem or arms, the interior of each maze section was comprised of two L-shaped strips of galvanized sheet metal, each L serving as one wall and half of the floor. Being separated at the floor by a ¾-inch gap and connected across the output of a transformer, the two strips of sheet metal within each maze section constituted one large potential grid. Shock was provided by a 60-cps AC source with a series resistance of 0.3 megohms. With this system, the subject received shock as it made contact with both halves of the sheet-metal floor, but only when it interrupted an infrared photoelectric beam crossing the arm at a point typically midway between the choice and goal doors. Because of the narrowness of the maze arms, the subject could not avoid shock by running along only one side of the floor. When shock was delivered, its duration was metered through a timing relay and its intensity set as measured across the output of the transformer.

Procedure.   The general procedure for all experiments included both pretraining and training phases. One week prior to the pretraining phase, the subjects were started and maintained for the duration of the experiment on a daily diet typically of 12 gm. Purina Lab Checkers, with water available *ad libitum*. Pretraining was administered to habituate the subject to the apparatus and to reduce possible position and brightness preferences. Because the latter would relate to the brightnesses of the discriminative stimuli to be employed during training, subjects received pretraining with the frosted goal-box end panels set at brightnesses appropriate to the training phase, i.e., either light–dark or bright–dim.

For pretraining, except where otherwise noted, subjects received a total of 16 forced-choice, food-reinforced trials administered four per day at an intertrial interval of about 15 minutes. During both pretraining and training trials, subjects were kept in individual compartments of a hardware cloth detention cage. The forced-choice pretraining trials were randomly distributed with the restriction that, within each day, they were balanced over right and left arms and bright and dim (or light and dark) goals. Food reinforcement, consisting of P. J. Noyes Formula A rat pellets (4 mm., 45 mg.), was liberally spread throughout a goal compartment on the first pretraining day and thereafter systematically reduced until, on the last pretraining day, the subject received only two pellets per trial.

Training commenced on the day following termination of pretraining and, unless otherwise stated, consisted entirely of free-choice, non-correction trials. The subjects typically received four trials per day for the first 6 days of discrimination training and eight trials per day thereafter. During these trials, food reinforcement was maintained at two pellets per trial, but could be obtained only in the brighter goal, the left–right positioning of which was varied in accordance with a predetermined random schedule. On any trial, detention time in either the correct or incorrect goal was approximately 10 seconds with the interval between trials within a day remaining at about 15 minutes. Discrimination training was typically continued until each subject met a criterion of 15 correct responses out of 16 consecutive choices, with the last 8 being correct, or until a predetermined number of training trials had been administered.

Experimental Studies

Shock parameters. Because of the absence of any systematic exploration of punishment parameters, a first study (Wischner, Fowler, & Kushnick, 1963) was designed to assess the effect of different intensities of shock for either correct or incorrect responses on performance in a simple light–dark discrimination. Shock intensities for SR and SW groups were set slightly above an aversion threshold (30–40 volts, cf. Campbell & Teghtsoonian, 1958) at 45, 60, and 75 volts, with shock duration held constant at .2 second. These shock intensities constituted a range of .15–.25 ma., encompassing the shock values employed in the research by Muenzinger and by Wischner. An effort was also made in this initial study to determine the effect, if any, resulting from equating among groups the number and order of shock and food experiences received over training. Thus, half the subjects of each group were trained under the typically utilized free-choice procedure, and half trained under a forced-choice procedure. With the latter, the first trial of every block of four constituted a free choice; the remaining three trials were forced choices such that after every block of four trials, occasions of reinforcement and of shock for SR and SW subjects were equated across groups and balanced over right and left arms.

To provide a comparable basis for evaluating performances with the two training procedures, error scores were based on the first trial of every block of four, i.e., the comparable free-choice trial for both free- and forced-choice groups. Analysis of these data, which are presented for SR and SW groups as a function of shock intensity in Fig. 12–1,

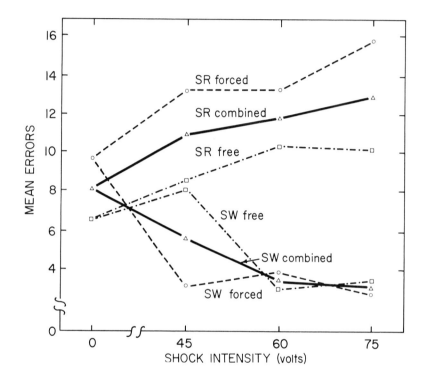

FIG. 12–1.   Mean errors to criterion as a function of shock intensity for SR and SW groups of the free- and forced-choice procedures.

From: G. J. Wischner, H. Fowler, & S. A. Kushnick, "Effect of Strength of Punishment for 'Correct' or 'Incorrect' Responses on Visual Discrimination Performance," *Journal of Experimental Psychology*, **65**, 1963, Fig. 1, p. 134. Copyright 1963 by the American Psychological Association and reproduced by permission.

indicated that the difference in outcome between free- and forced-choice training procedures was not reliable. However, the combined data for the two training procedures, as represented by the solid-line function of Fig. 12–1, showed symmetrical shock intensity effects for SR and SW conditions: whereas errors decreased linearly over increasing SW intensities, they increased linearly over increasing SR intensities, such that all SR groups of both training procedures were inferior to their respective NS controls. These findings were interpreted as supporting an avoidance-producing function of shock and as being opposed to the generalization that shock for the correct response facilitates discrimination performance.

A second study (Wischner & Fowler, 1964), also utilizing a simple light–dark discrimination, attempted to extend assessment of punishment parameters to shock duration. For different SR and SW groups, shock duration was set at .1, .2, and .4 second with shock intensity held constant at 60 volts, the intermediate intensity value employed in the first study. Because of the absence of a difference in the intensity study between free- and forced-choice training procedures, only free-choice discrimination training was employed.

Comparable to the results of the intensity study, the findings of the duration study showed that errors to criterion decreased linearly with increasing durations of shock for SW subjects but, in contrast, errors for SR subjects remained relatively constant across increasing shock durations and did not depart significantly from the performance level of the NS control group. To assess further this finding and its possible relation to sampling factors, additional subjects were trained under the NS and each of the three SR duration conditions. Analysis of the data for these additional subjects, treated either separately or combined with the data for subjects previously run under these conditions, also failed to yield a significant between-groups effect or a reliable trend component. Thus, while the present study demonstrated that shock for the correct response did not facilitate performance, it likewise did not show any significant performance retardation.

It might be suggested that if shock durations longer than the maximum of .4 second had been employed we would have obtained a reliable increasing error trend for the SR condition. However, if this were the only important consideration a significant decreasing error trend as a function of shock duration should not have been found for the SW animals. Furthermore, in our initial study, a shock of comparable intensity (60 volts) but of shorter duration (.2 second) was effective in reducing errors for SW subjects as well as in increasing errors for SR subjects. This discrepancy between the results of the two studies may be reconciled, however, if one reexamines the data presented in Fig. 12–1 for free-choice subjects of the intensity study and uses instead of the NS data, the comparable performance levels of the SR and SW 45-volt groups as an evaluative base line for SR and SW effects. Now it would appear that the findings of the intensity study also show, at least for the free-choice subjects, relatively little of an increasing error trend with the SR condition. Taken together, the data for the free-choice subjects of both the intensity and duration studies indicated that under the SR condition an avoidance-producing effect of the shock was being offset by some additional factor or factors.

Secondary reinforcing factors. A study by Fowler and Wischner (1965b) was suggested by the possibility that the absence of SR retardation in the duration study described above, as well as the seemingly small effect for similarly trained subjects in the intensity study, might relate to a secondary reinforcing function of the shock; that is, its potential role in mediating the effect of food reinforcement. To assess this interpretation, rats were given either NS or SR acquisition training on a light–dark discrimination where, through the use of the previously described forced-choice procedure, occasions of reinforcement were equated across training conditions and balanced (similarly for shock) over left and right maze arms throughout the course of training. All subjects then received free-choice extinction training in which the NS control (NS-C) animals were continued as before without shock. The experimental subjects, however, were now assigned to the following subgroups: SR, shock for the previously correct response; NS, a no-shock condition controlling for the shock experience of acquisition training; and SW, shock for the previously incorrect response. For both acquisition and extinction training, shock intensity and duration were set at the intermediate values, 60 volts, .2 second.

As with the findings of the duration study, no reliable difference occurred in the acquisition performances of NS- and SR-trained groups, even though in this study these groups were trained with a forced-choice procedure. Furthermore, as shown in Fig. 12–2, the extinction data failed to provide any evidence that shock had acquired a reinforcing property via its association with food reinforcement during acquisition training. Instead of protracting responses to the previously correct arm, the SR extinction condition had the opposite effect of rapidly increasing responses to the nonshocked "incorrect" arm. Comparably, as the SW subjects extinguished their "correct" response tendency (hence making more "errors" and thus increasing their receipt of shock), responses to the nonshocked "correct" arm were then abruptly augmented (see Fig. 12–2, trial blocks 6–9). These data indicated that the only apparent effect of shock during extinction was to produce avoidance of the response with which it was associated.

In spite of the avoidance-producing effect of shock during extinction, Fig. 12–2 indicates that prior SR acquisition training had the general effect of facilitating extinction performance, the NS subgroup (or the three experimental subgroups collectively) tending to show a more rapid rate of approach to chance than the NS-C group which received no shock during either acquisition or extinction. The difference between the

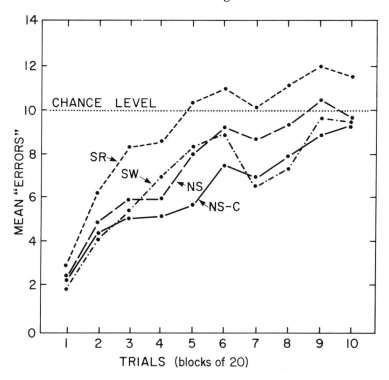

FIG. 12-2. Mean extinction "errors" (responses to the previously incorrect arm) in 20-trial blocks for the no-shock control group (NS-C) and the three experimental subgroups (SR, NS, and SW).

From: H. Fowler & G. J. Wischner, "On the 'Secondary Reinforcing' Effect of Shock for the Correct Response in Visual Discrimination Learning," *Psychonomic Science,* 3, 1965, Fig. 1, p. 210. Reproduced by permission.

NS and the NS-C groups was not reliable, however, and only of marginal significance in a comparison of the NS-C group and the three experimental groups as a whole. This trend pointed up the need for additional assessment of the effect of SR acquisition training on subsequent task performance. A follow-up study employing a reversal paradigm was therefore implemented.

In this as yet unpublished study, rats again received via forced-choice procedure either NS or SR acquisition training on a simple light-dark discrimination. Then, for reversal training, where the correct response of acquisition training was now incorrect and vice versa, subjects of both the SR and NS acquisition conditions were assigned to NS, SR, and SW subgroups, with these conditions indicating, respectively, no shock and shock for correct or incorrect responses of the reversal problem. All subjects received free-choice reversal training with food reinforcement maintained at 2 pellets per correct response and shock set, as in acquisition training, at 60 volts, .2 second.

Comparable to the findings of the previous investigations, the results of the present study showed no difference in the acquisition performances of NS- and SR-trained groups. Similarly, with respect to reversal performance, the NS and SR reversal groups were not different in either errors or trials to criterion, but relative to these two groups, the SW reversal group was reliably superior on both measures. These results on the effects of shock during reversal training were comparable to those generally obtaining for acquisition training; however, these effects were found to be independent of the treatment, either NS or SR, that the subject had experienced during the acquisition phase. With respect, then, to the influence of SR acquisition training in particular, the reversal data also failed to provide any evidence of an acquired reinforcing property of the shock, since the SW reversal subgroup, which received shock for the previously correct response showed the fastest reversal learning, and the SR reversal subgroup, which received shock for the previously incorrect response, exhibited reversal performance that was no better than that shown by the NS subgroup.

Nevertheless, like the results of the extinction study, the reversal study showed that prior SR acquisition training had the general and now reliable effect of facilitating reversal performance. This effect was similarly independent of the presence of shock (NS versus SR and SW) or of the response to which shock was applied (SR versus SW) during reversal training. The data of this experiment, then, are in line with the extinction data in suggesting what appears to be a general sensitizing function of SR training. Taken together with its demonstrated avoidance-producing effect, this sensitizing effect of the shock could account, at least in part, for the absence of a performance difference between NS and SR groups in acquisition training or, as shown by the present study, in reversal training as well.

Distinctive cue factors. The preceding section dealt with the possibility that some of the effects obtained with SR training might be associated with a secondary reinforcing function of shock. An alternative hypothesis suggested itself, namely, that any avoidance-producing effect of shock might be offset, or counteracted in part, merely by its function as a highly discernible stimulus. That is to say, the introduction of shock into one maze arm represents a significant alteration of the complex of stimuli (viz., physical features and discriminative cue) comprising that maze arm, and as such, the arm, e.g. the correct arm, can be more readily perceived by a subject as being different from the similar, incorrect arm which does not include the shock stimulus. Viewed, then, as a distinctive-cue which increases the discriminability of the stimulus alternatives, shock should serve to delimit any generalization of secondary reinforcement from the food-associated correct-arm cues to those in the incorrect arm. In turn, this reduction in the secondary reinforcing properties of the incorrect-arm cues should lead to a reduction in errors.

On the basis of the foregoing considerations, it was reasoned that a distinctive-cue effect of shock would be less predominant in the typically employed light–dark discrimination, where the stimulus alternatives are fairly discriminable and thus generalization of secondary reinforcement already relatively small. We proceeded therefore to assess the distinctive-cue interpretation by using more difficult discriminations. Rats were trained on a set of bright–dim discriminations, where problem difficulty was systematically manipulated by varying the difference in relative brightness of the discriminanda. All other training conditions were in accord with the general methodology outlined previously, shock again being set at 60 volts, .2 second.

The major results of this problem-difficulty study (Fowler & Wischner, 1965a) are presented in Fig. 12–3 along with comparable data for subjects that had received identical training in our initial shock intensity study (Wischner et al., 1963) but on an easy (E) light–dark discrimination. As Fig. 12–3 indicates, performance on the present set of bright–dim discriminations was progressively retarded across increasing levels of task difficulty ranging from moderately easy (ME) through difficult (D) problems. Furthermore, in comparison with NS controls, SR subjects were found to be reliably and comparably facilitated at all problem levels, and the SW subjects even more so. Although Fig. 12–3 indicates a convergence of the SR and SW performance functions at the more difficult problem levels (in part, an artifact of a training cutoff at 400 trials) the overall difference between SR and SW conditions was reliable. Thus, the results of this study indicated both an avoidance-producing and distinctive-cue effect of the shock, the latter presumably providing the basis for the finding obtained for the first time in our laboratory that shock for the correct response could indeed facilitate discrimination learning. It seemed that we now had available conditions for producing either SR facilitation or SR retardation.[6]

In the study just described, problem difficulty was defined by the

[6] Almost coincidental with the publication of these results, Curlin and Donahoe (1965) reported both facilitation and retardation of performance for rats receiving SR training in a free-responding context, i.e., with punishment administered during the S+ period of a discrimination sequence. Because their results related to a manipulation of shock intensity, these investigators suggested that prior, discrepant findings could be attributed to the particular intensity of the shock used. However, the fact that we were able to obtain facilitated performance with the same intensity and duration of shock that had previously led to a retardation of performance (Wischner et al., 1963) indicated that the particular effect of SR training depended not on punishment parameters alone, but on the interaction of these variables with the specific conditions of training. In this regard, the isolation of problem difficulty as a determining factor now provided the opportunity for assaying the influence of *both* shock and nonshock variables in settings where either SR facilitation or SR retardation could be anticipated.

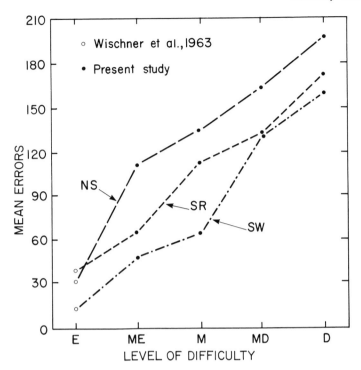

FIG. 12-3.   Mean errors to criterion for SR, SW, and NS groups as a function of
level of problem difficulty ranging from E (easy) to D (difficult). The data presented for
the E problem level are for comparable groups of subjects run in a previous study
(Wischner et al., 1963).

From: H. Fowler & G. J. Wischner, "Discrimination Performance as Affected by
Problem Difficulty and Shock for Either the Correct or Incorrect Response," *Journal
of Experimental Psychology*, **69**, 1965, Fig. 2, p. 417. Copyright 1965 by the American
Psychological Association and reproduced by permission.

degree of similarity between the discriminative stimuli. A question we
asked ourselves was: Is it possible to obtain an SR facilitation effect
within the context of an easy, light–dark discrimination where problem
difficulty is varied in some way which is independent of the similarity
between the discriminanda, and thus independent of a cue effect of
shock? A study, as yet unpublished, manipulated task difficulty at the
easy problem level by varying the amount of balanced, reinforced pretraining with the stimulus alternatives.[7] Such pretraining, when of
sufficient extensity, has elsewhere been shown to produce an increase in
errors and trials to criterion in subsequent free-choice discrimination

[7] This work was initiated as an undergraduate honors project by Douglas A. Bern-
stein.

training (e.g., Bitterman & Elam, 1954; Crawford, Mayes, & Bitterman, 1954). In all of our previous research, pretraining had been set at a total of 16 reinforced trials, balanced via our forced-choice procedure over both positions and stimulus alternatives. In the present study, different groups received 0, 8, 16, 32, or 64 pretraining trials, with the first two conditions being included so as to permit full exploration of the pretraining dimension.

The results of this study showed clearly that discrimination performance was progressively retarded as a consequence of increasing amounts of forced-choice pretraining, but the extent of this retardation was comparable for subjects receiving either NS or SR training. Neither the overall difference between the shock conditions, nor that between respective NS and SR groups at any of the pretraining levels was found to be significant. These findings are particularly important in view of the fact that mean errors to criterion for the NS subjects of the 64-trial pretraining condition approximated the error score obtained in the preceding study for NS subjects trained on a more difficult bright–dim discrimination (the ME level as designated in Fig. 12–3) where the discriminative stimuli were fairly similar. Hence, the noted absence of a performance difference between NS and SR groups of the 64-trial pretraining condition suggests, in accord with the cue interpretation of the function of shock, that the SR facilitation which obtained with the bright–dim discriminations did not relate merely to the increased amount of training required for task mastery at these more difficult problem levels.

An additional question that occurred was whether the SR facilitation that obtained in the problem-difficulty study might not be due in part to the sensitizing function of shock suggested by the findings of the extinction and reversal studies. In an attempt to answer this question we conducted an experiment, as yet unpublished, that used both NS and SR acquisition conditions and, in addition, two new conditions: shock-both (SB) and shock-paired (SP). With the SB condition, the subject received shock for both correct and incorrect responses; with the SP condition, the subject also received shock for both correct and incorrect responses, but only when a paired running mate of the SR condition made a correct response and thus received shock. Hence, while both the SB and SP conditions provided shock, thereby permitting a sensitizing function to be operative, both precluded any cue effect since the shock was not selectively associated with either of the stimulus alternatives. In addition, the SP condition served the necessary function of controlling the number and order of shock experiences received under the SR condition. These four shock conditions, NS, SR, SB, SP, were utilized along with both easy and difficult problems (the light–dark and bright–dim discriminations represented as E and ME, respectively, in Fig. 12–3).

All other conditions of training were consonant with our general methodology.

In support of the cross-study comparison presented in Fig. 12–3 for the E and ME problem levels, the results of the present study showed that performance differences on these two problem conditions were reliable, with superior performance for the easy problem. With respect to the effects of different shock conditions, however, there were no reliable differences for either the error or trials-to-criterion measure between the SB and SP groups, or between these two groups on the one hand and the NS group on the other. Furthermore, the interaction of these group combinations with the problem-difficulty variable also was unreliable. In short, the only significant shock-facilitation effect which prevailed was that relating to a comparison of NS and SR groups and then only for those groups of the more difficult, bright–dim problem condition. Thus, these findings support as well the comparison which Fig. 12–3 presents for NS and SR groups of the E and ME problem levels.

Since the SB and SP training conditions did not exert a facilitating effect on performance at either the easy or difficult problem levels, the present findings (as well as those of the pretraining study) may be interpreted as being opposed to a general sensitizing function of shock and as supporting the previously elaborated cue interpretation. Accordingly, the findings from the extinction and reversal studies, which originally suggested a general sensitizing function of shock, may be reinterpreted in the following manner. It is proposed that the facilitating influence which SR acquisition training exerted on subsequent extinction and reversal performance related, not to any sensitizing function, but rather to the distinctiveness which the positive discriminative stimulus acquired as a consequence of its association with shock during the acquisition phase and thus of the fear that was presumably conditioned to it. During extinction and reversal training, this fear could well have been sufficient to mediate increased distinctiveness of the stimulus alternatives and thereby facilitate performance despite the specific avoidance-producing effect of concurrent shock contingencies.

Performance factors.   As initially considered by Muenzinger (1934), the administration of shock for the correct food-reinforced response provides the conditions for a conflict between the approach tendency to obtain food and the avoidance tendency induced by shock. It is reasonable to expect that the particular effect of SR training will be dependent upon the relative strengths of these approach and avoidance tendencies. This consideration, in fact, was offered earlier in the discussion of the findings of Prince (1956) on the effect of shock-free training trials and the related findings of Muenzinger et al. (1952) on the effect of shock-adaptation trials. Viewing our earlier published work on shock intensity and shock duration as representing an emphasis on avoidance variables, Hawkins (1965) conducted a doctoral study investigating the approach variables of drive (schedule of food deprivation) and incentive (magnitude of food reinforcement).

In all of our prior research, these variables had been held constant at 12 gm. daily ration and two pellets (45 mg.) for each correct response. In the Hawkins study, drive and incentive were manipulated in conjunction with problem difficulty because of the latter variable's significant role as a determinant of SR facilitation in the context of noncorrection training. Specifically, the design comprised a complete factorial of easy (E) and difficult (D) problem levels, high and low drive (10 and 15 gm. daily ration, HD and LD respectively), high and low incentive (four and one pellets, HK and LK, respectively), and NS and SR training. General methodology was simlar to that previously outlined, with shock being set as usual at 60 volts, .2 second and problem difficulty represented by the easy light–dark, and medium-easy bright–dim, discrimination levels designated in Fig. 12–3.

The major findings of Hawkins' study are summarized in Fig. 12–4, which presents mean errors to criterion as a function of drive level (LD and HD) for shock (NS and SR) and incentive (LK and HK) subgroups of the E and D problem conditions. As indicated, the discrimination was acquired with fewer errors (also fewer trials) when the problem was easy, drive level was high, incentive was high, and correct responses were punished. With respect to the last result, however, comparisons of respective NS and SR subgroups showed that the SR facilitation effect was limited entirely to the difficult problem, more specifically, to the HD-LK treatment within this problem condition. Although not indicated in Fig. 12–4, it would seem that comparable SR facilitation for the HD-HK treatment within the D problem condition was precluded by a floor effect; indeed, the general facilitating influence of HK on discrimination performance was so pronounced as to render negligible the effects of drive, shock, and even problem-difficulty manipulations at this incentive level. This suggests, then, that the major performance determinant of SR facilitation at the D problem level was high drive. These findings appear to be amenable to the interpretation that the cue effect of SR training, in delimiting any generalization of secondary reinforcement, operates essentially through the development of differential associative strengths for correct and incorrect response tendencies (i.e., a habit difference) which may be amplified by increased drive.

Still reasoning within the framework of an approach-avoidance conflict paradigm, we turned our attention to the avoidance factor of shock intensity but specifically with respect to its effect in reducing or offsetting the SR facilitation obtaining with more difficult discriminations.

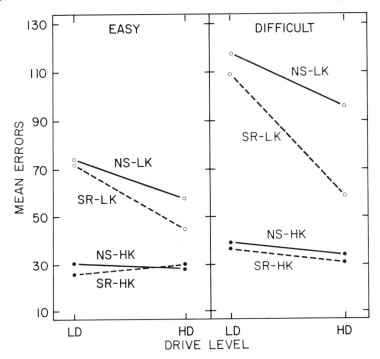

FIG. 12–4.   Mean errors to criterion for shock (NS, SR) and incentive (LK, HK) subgroups of the E and D problem conditions (left and right panels, respectively), as a function of drive level (LD, HD).

Adapted from: R. P. Hawkins, *Effects of Drive, Incentive and Problem Difficulty on the Facilitation of Discrimination Performance by Punishment of Correct Responses*. Unpublished doctoral dissertation, University of Pittsburgh, 1965. Reproduced by permission.

Furthermore, with our research findings suggesting that shock may function both as an avoidance-producing stimulus and as a distinctive cue, we were interested in isolating these two properties of shock. This was attempted in a recent study (Fowler, Goldman, & Wischner, 1968), which assessed the combined effects of sodium amytal and different intensities of shock for the correct response in a bright–dim discrimination. Because sodium amytal has been shown (e.g., Miller, 1961) to reduce the fear or anxiety which motivates avoidance in conflict situations, its utilization in the present study was for the purpose of assessing the cue effect of shock independently of its avoidance-producing property. Specifically then, the design of this study comprised a complete factorial of three drug conditions (20 mg/kg sodium amytal, placebo control, and no-injection control) and five intensities of a .2-second shock for the correct response (0, 50, 60, 80, 120 volts). Training was set at the medium-easy problem level as designated in Fig. 12–3.

Figure 12–5 presents mean errors to criterion for the different drug conditions as a function of log-shock intensity. In this figure, the placebo and no-injection groups have been combined into a single control because the difference between these groups, as well as their interaction with the shock-intensity variable, was not significant. Analysis of the data showed that there was no significant overall difference in errors between the sodium amytal and combined control groups but, as indicated in Fig. 12–5, this effect derived from a reliable interaction of the shock-intensity functions for the drug and control subjects. The effect was particularly pronounced at the higher shock levels: whereas both drug and control subjects exhibited a comparable decrement in errors from 0 to 60 volts, only the control group showed significant retardation as shock intensity was increased from 60 to 120 volts; for the drug subjects, 60 to 120 volts yielded virtually identical performances.

The purpose of introducing sodium amytal was to take advantage of

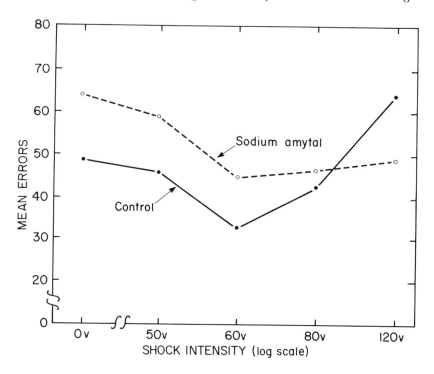

FIG. 12–5. Mean errors to criterion as a function of log shock intensity for the sodium amytal and combined (placebo and no-injection) control groups.

Adapted from: H. Fowler, L. Coldman, & G. J. Wischner, "Sodium Amytal and the Shock-Right Intensity Function for Visual Discrimination Learning," *Journal of Comparative and Physiological Psychology,* **65**, 1968, pp. 155–159. Copyright 1968 by the American Psychological Association and reproduced by permission.

its previously established effect of reducing avoidance and in this way attempting to isolate the cue effect of shock. Although Fig. 12–5 shows that sodium amytal had the general effect of increasing errors at the lower shock voltages,[8] the manipulation was effective in that the SR facilitation effect which obtained at 60 volts did not give way to retardation as shock intensity was increased. As such, the data for the drug subjects suggest that the cue effect of shock is some S-shaped function of shock intensity. In contrast, the findings of our initial shock intensity study (Wischner et al., 1963), which utilized an easy light–dark discrimination wherein the cue effect of shock is presumably absent or minimal, showed that SR retardation, i.e., the avoidance produced, is an increasing linear function of shock intensity. Taken together, this increasing linear avoidance function and the S-shaped cue function suggested by the drug data may thus account for the quadratic relationship between errors and shock intensity which obtained under the control, no-drug condition wherein both cue and avoidance effects of the shock are presumably operative.

Methodological factors.   It will be recalled that Muenzinger and his co-workers consistently obtained SR facilitation with a correction training procedure but always in the context of an easy light–dark discrimination. This may be contrasted with our research findings showing that SR training can facilitate discrimination performance in a noncorrection context but only when the problem is relatively difficult. The isolation of problem difficulty as a dimension influencing SR facilitation suggests that the earlier discrepant findings between correction and noncorrection may relate to a greater difficulty of the correction task as a whole. In support of this assumption, results from investigations comparing correction and noncorrection in different experimental settings have shown the former method to produce significantly more errors both in acquisition and extinction training (Kalish, 1946; Seward, 1943). To assess the relation of problem difficulty and correction training, a recent study (Fowler, Spelt, & Wischner, 1967) compared the effects of SR training on easy and difficult discrimination problems entailing both correction and noncorrection procedures.

     As in prior studies, the easy (E) and difficult (D) problem conditions of the present study comprised light–dark and bright–dim discriminations, respectively. Apart from the correction procedure employed, all other conditions of training were consonant with the general methodology as outlined, shock again being set at 60 volts, .2 second. The cor-

---

8 There is some evidence (see Miller, 1961) that, in addition to reducing the fear-motivating avoidance, sodium amytal can reduce the inhibition produced by nonreinforcement, or much more tentatively, that it affects the rat's ability to discriminate cues. A recent study by Caul (1965), however, showed no effect of sodium amytal on the learning of a black–white discrimination.

rection (C) procedure was similar to our noncorrection (NC) procedure in that all subjects were prevented, via the operation of choice-point doors, from retracing when in the correct T arm; in contrast, however, subjects of the C procedure were permitted to retrace and finally correct following each incorrect response. With both procedures, an error was recorded when the subject's initial choice on any trial was the incorrect arm; further retracing under the C procedure (i.e., prior to the subject correcting on that trial) was scored for entries into the stem or additional entries into the incorrect arm.

Group mean errors to the usual performance criterion of 15 correct responses out of 16 consecutive choices (initial choices for C subjects) are presented in Fig. 12–6. The left panel shows mean errors for SR and NS groups of the NC procedure as a function of E and D problem levels; the right panel shows mean errors for comparable subgroups trained under the C procedure. In line with the trends suggested in Fig. 12–6,

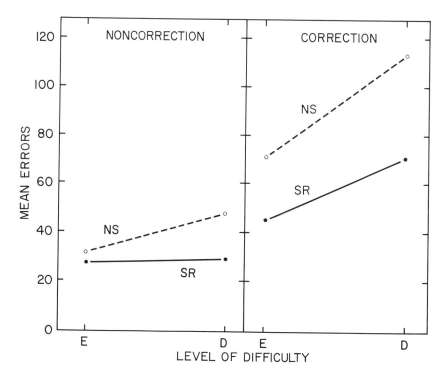

FIG. 12–6.   Mean errors to criterion as a function of easy (E) and difficult (D) levels of discrimination for no-shock (NS) and shock-right (SR) groups trained with either a correction or a noncorrection procedure (right and left panels, respectively).

statistical analysis showed that there were reliably more errors with the C than the NC procedure, more with the D than the E problem, and more with NS than SR training. In addition, there was a reliable training-procedure by problem-level interaction and a marginally reliable procedure by shock interaction. These interactions are particularly important in view of other aspects of Fig. 12–6. First, in accord with our previous findings, SR facilitation did not obtain for NC subjects of the E problem condition; second, the E-C condition, in addition to producing more errors than the D-NC condition, produced greater SR facilitation. Hence, with the conditions ordered as shown in Fig. 12–6 from E-NC to D-C, the data suggest a composite dimension of task difficulty —one which relates positively to the magnitude of SR facilitation. As assessed by trend analysis, this interaction of shock condition (NS versus SR) and composite task difficulty was found to be reliable, indicating that the magnitude of SR facilitation increases across increasing levels of task difficulty as represented by the combined dimensions of discrimination difficulty (E versus D) and training procedure (C versus NC).

The differential magnitude of SR facilitation which obtained for E and D problem subjects of both the C and NC procedures is in accord with our interpretation that shock, as a distinctive cue, may serve to heighten the discriminability of the stimulus alternatives, thereby delimiting the generalization of secondary reinforcement from the correct to the incorrect alternative and thus reducing errors. In view of the composite dimension of task difficulty suggested by the present findings, it would appear that this cue interpretation of the function of shock can be applied to differences between C and NC training as well. With C training, there is, in addition to any generalized secondary reinforcement in the incorrect arm, a related secondary reinforcing effect which derives from a delay of primary reinforcement for each incorrect response; that is, through subjects of the C procedure retracing toward the positive discriminative stimulus and finally correcting. Hence, in comparison with subjects of the NC procedure for which there is an "infinite" delay of primary reinforcement (i.e., no reinforcement) following an incorrect response, subjects of the C procedure should perform more poorly; but with additional or more potent secondary reinforcement available for the incorrect response, additional facilitation from administering shock for the correct response should also occur and now possibly for several reasons.

Upon retracing from the incorrect arm, shocked subjects of the C procedure should be more prone, because of any fear conditioned to the correct-arm cues, to enter the starting stem before going into the correct arm. This behavior, which did indeed occur significantly more frequently for SR and NS subjects, has both the effect of temporally removing the positive discriminative stimulus and of increasing the delay of primary reinforcement contingent upon correcting. As a consequence, secondary reinforcement for incorrect responses of the shocked subjects will be reduced, and in turn, these subjects should perform much better. Moreover, as training progresses, the combination of fear and correct-arm cues should become a more effective stimulus condition (than correct-arm cues alone) in signaling food reinforcement. Accordingly, any anticipatory consummatory responding (i.e., r_g) at the choice point should come sooner under the selective control of the discriminative stimuli for the shocked animals, thereby facilitating appropriate choices earlier in the training sequence. In total, the present findings suggest that as the amount of secondary reinforcement in the incorrect goal arm increases, either by increasing the similarity of the goal arms and/or by using C instead of NC training, the effectiveness of shock for the correct response in differentiating the goal arms and thereby in delimiting secondary reinforcement (or underlying anticipatory responding) will also increase.

In view of the significance of the above results, a related experiment only recently completed was conducted in an effort to explore further the discrepancy existing between our findings and those reported by Muenzinger and his co-workers. Apart from correction training, the discrimination task employed by Muenzinger and by other early investigators as well may have been additionally difficult because the animals, although trained on a simple light–dark or black–white discrimination, were nonetheless reinforced in a *gray* goal box beyond the discriminative stimuli. This procedure has the effect of promoting a temporal dissociation of the positive discriminative stimulus and the food reinforcement (thereby reducing the effectiveness of this stimulus as a secondary reinforcer) and in addition, of promoting a greater similarity in brightness between the gray goal-box cues and those (either black or white) present in the incorrect arm. To assess this form of problem difficulty and the potentially related effect of SR training, the present study utilized a simple black–white discrimination in which the discriminative stimuli were painted wall inserts located (from the choice point) along the first third, two thirds, entire length of the goal arm, or entire length of the arm including the visible end wall of the goal. (Other interior portions of the apparatus were a metallic gray brightness as provided by the internal sheet-metal composition of the maze.) Apart from this manner of presentation of the discriminative stimuli, all other conditions of training were similar to those of our other studies.

Comparable to the results of the initial problem-difficulty investigation (Fowler & Wischner, 1965a), the findings of the present experiment showed that performance was progressively retarded over increasing levels of task difficulty as effected now by the temporal–spatial dissociation of the discriminative stimuli and their respective goal conditions. SR facilitation was also generally observed, and in this experiment, facilitation increased over increasing levels of task difficulty. In fact, a facilitating effect of SR training was absent only when the discriminative-stimulus brightness extended along the entire length of the arm and covered the end wall of the goal as well; that is, when discriminability of the stimulus alternatives was maintained throughout the entire sequence of responding, either correctly or incorrectly.

These results are important not only in illustrating a dimension of problem difficulty common to the work by Muenzinger and his co-workers and other early investigators, but also in pointing up a significant procedural difference between C and NC training. Apparently, if a discriminative stimulus is not selectively and exclusively associated with one response alternative, as for example the correct response, but is present as well during an alternative sequence of responding, as in the case of an animal that is permitted to correct and retrace toward the positive cue, then the presence of that cue can mediate the effect of food reinforcement and thereby impede formation of the discrimination. However, to the extent that SR training can delimit such an effect, as for example, directly, by increasing the discriminability of the stimulus alternatives, or indirectly via fear, causing the animal to enter the stem while it is correcting after an error and thereby be temporally removed from the positive cue, then such training will serve to facilitate discrimination performance.

Functions and Effects of Punishment: An Interpretation

The findings of our research are clear in illustrating that SR training can produce varied effects and that particular performance outcomes are very much dependent upon specific procedural conditions. It is of significance to the analysis to be presented in this section that early work in the area tended to stress a single basic effect and related function of punishment. Thus Muenzinger (1934) emphasized the facilitating effect of SR training and argued that punishment served to slow down the animal at the choice point, making it more sensitive to the cues to be discriminated. Wischner (1947), on the other hand, stressed the retarding effect of punishment for the correct response and proposed that the primary function of punishment was to build up avoidance of the cues associated with it. We would suggest that emphasis on a particular performance outcome and any given function of punishment tends to overlook the varied effects that punishment may exert and the comparably varied functions that may prevail in different situations. In order to understand better the manner in which punishment operates to produce these varied outcomes, we propose that a clearer distinction be drawn among the terms, *effects, functions,* and *principles,* or mechanisms of operation, of the punishment contingency.

The effects of punishment, we suggest, should have reference to the dependent variable under study and the related empirical performance outcome obtaining in a particular situation under specifiable training conditions. Within the context of the present SR paradigm, then, the referent for the term effect is the increment or decrement in the performance measures employed; that is, the basis on which one empirically determines whether shock for the correct response facilitates or retards or perhaps has no effect on performance. The term, function, on the other hand, can have reference to the influence of shock on those behaviors which are not directly involved in the performance-outcome measures but which, it may be hypothesized, account for the measured outcome. These functions of punishment are exemplified in such phrases as: the function of punishment is to cause the animal to slow down at the choice point, to look around, to engage in head-turning movements, and thus become more aware of the relevant discriminanda; or its function is to make the animal jump back, withdraw, cringe, or leap and run ahead; or its function is to instigate autonomic activity thus causing emotional or motivational reactions; or its function is, via its discriminative properties, to provide a discriminative stimulus or a distinctive cue; etc. It seems clear that many of these functions of punishment may be viewed as particular effects that one can study in a variety of situations. Thus, one may investigate choice-point pausing or VTE behavior as measurable performances in their own right. In this sense, the terms, effect and function, are relative, with their utilization in any given context being dependent upon their status relative to the dependent variable or performance that is being measured.

With acknowledgment of these varied functions of punishment, a question arises as to which of these functions will predominate in a particular situation and which, if any, will bear on or relate to the particular effect observed. Thus, the present writers would not deny, for example, that one function of punishment is to slow down the animal at the choice point, but whether this function bears any relation to the measured performance outcome remains an open question. It is important that consideration be given to the manner in which varied functions arise in a given situation, and how, either singly or collectively, they may mediate the observed performance effect. It is proposed, then, that a further distinction be drawn between the effects and functions of punishment and their principles of operation. The latter have reference to such generally accepted principles of behavior theory (and their correlative mechanisms) as reinforcement, learned reward, incentive motivation, fractional anticipatory goal response, or acquired fear. Just as the distinction between functions and effects is relative, so is the distinction between functions and mechanisms of operation. This may be illustrated in the case of the construct, fear. One function of punishment may be to produce the emotional reaction of fear which, by virtue of its association with the discriminative stimuli, may cause the animal to slow down at the choice point. On the other hand, a motivational property of fear might serve to amplify the difference in associative strengths that prevail for correct and incorrect responses as a consequence of differential reinforcement or, as suggested by our findings, as a consequence of SR training delimiting any generalized secondary reinforcement for the incorrect response.

The proposed differentiation of effects, functions, and mechanisms may be viewed as arbitrary and as representing different levels of analysis ranging from the empirical to the theoretical. Nevertheless, such a distinction seems to serve the useful purpose of drawing attention to those varied functions of punishment that may underlie diverse performance effects. So far as the evaluation of different hypotheses offered to account for the effects of SR training is concerned, it would seem that our task is one of determining what functions will predominate, the theoretical bases for their operation, and the manner in which they may relate to or mediate varied performance outcomes.

The general sensitizing or alerting hypothesis.   Muenzinger's (1934) hypothesis that punishment for the correct response facilitated discrimination performance by sensitizing the animal to the discriminanda is coordinate with his judgment that SR facilitation was basically a general effect and as a consequence the function of punishment responsible for this effect was also general. The results of the Muenzinger and Newcomb (1936) gap-after-choice study, the Muenzinger and Wood (1935) shock-both study, and the Muenzinger and Fletcher (1937) enforced-delay study could be most reasonably interpreted as supporting the hypothesis that increased attention to the relevant discriminanda was mediated via pausing behavior in the presence of these cues. The present writers would argue that such observations do not afford an adequate basis for the assumption that jumping a gap after choice and enforcing a delay at the choice point necessarily have the same function or involve the same mechanisms as shock after choice in permitting the operation of a general alerting function. Indeed, it might be argued that for shocked subjects, choice-point pausing is fear-produced and such fear, with its resultant avoidance of the cues associated with shock, may cause the animal to look away and even not to attend to the discriminative stimuli.

The same considerations may prevail with respect to VTE behavior. It is possible that for shocked subjects, such behavior reflects, not increased attentiveness to the cues, but rather an attenuated avoidance of the cues which instigate the fear mechanism. Fairlie (1937), Drew (1938), and Wischner (1947) noted that VTE behavior often was not predictably related to the facilitation of performance obtained with either SR or SW training procedures. In addition, Wischner (1950) presented data in support of the hypothesis that VTE behavior, rather than being associated with facilitation, may be viewed as a vestigial withdrawal response, a remnant of turning around in a nonpreferred alley.

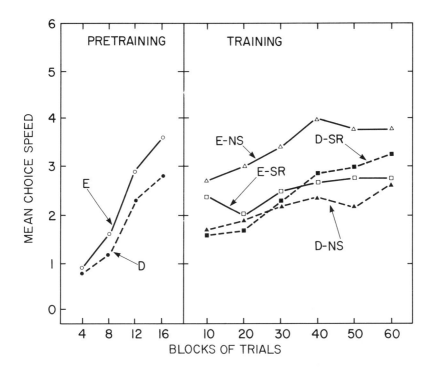

FIG. 12–7.   Mean choice speeds for E and D problem groups in 4-trial blocks over the 16 trials of pretraining (left panel), and the same data for NS and SR subgroups of the E and D problem conditions in 10-trial blocks over the initial 60 trials of discrimination training (right panel).

Adapted from: R. P. Hawkins, *Effects of Drive, Incentive and Problem Difficulty on the Facilitation of Discrimination Performance by Punishment of Correct Responses.* Unpublished doctoral dissertation, University of Pittsburgh, 1965. Reproduced by permission.

An analysis of related data stemming from our own research reveals no consistent relationship between time spent at the choice point and discrimination performance. Figure 12–7 presents the choice-speed data of the Hawkins (1965) study in which the variables of drive and incentive were manipulated in conjunction with NS and SR training on easy (E) and difficult (D) discriminations. The left panel shows mean choice speeds for subjects of the E and D problems over the 16 forced-choice trials of pretraining; the right panel shows comparable data for NS and SR subgroups of the E and D conditions over the initial 60 trials of discrimination training. These data were limited to the initial 60 trials because many animals, especially those of the E problem condition, reached the criterion of learning immediately after this number of trials. As shown in the left panel of Fig. 12–7, speeds increased progressively over the course of forced-choice pretraining with the D problem subjects exhibiting slower speeds, presumably as a consequence of their running always to a lighted (bright or dim) goal, as opposed to the light or dark goal to which E problem subjects ran. With the onset of discrimination training, choice speeds under both problem conditions decreased, probably as a consequence of altered stimulus conditions and

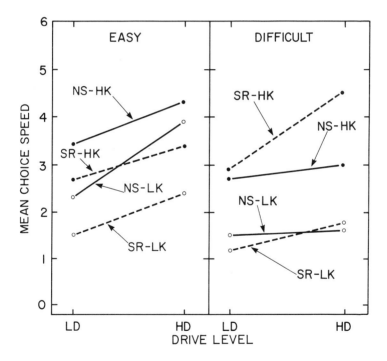

FIG. 12–8.   Mean choice speeds over trials 1–60 for shock (NS, SR) and incentive (LK, HK) subgroups of the E and D problem conditions (left and right panels respectively), as a function of drive level (LD, HD).

Adapted from: R. P. Hawkins, *Effects of Drive, Incentive and Problem Difficulty on the Facilitation of Discrimination Performance by Punishment of Correct Responses.* Unpublished doctoral dissertation, University of Pittsburgh, 1965. Reproduced by permission.

the act of choosing, and then gradually recovered throughout the course of training. Of particular interest is the fact that shocked subjects of the E problem, where SR facilitation was absent (see Fig. 12–4), showed reliably slower choice speeds than the NS control subjects. On the other hand, shocked subjects of the D problem condition, where SR facilitation was manifested, showed speeds that were initially comparable to and then faster than those of the NS controls.

The relation of these effects to performance-factor manipulations (i.e., conditions of drive and incentive) are shown in Fig. 12–8. The left panel presents mean choice speeds as a function of drive level (LD and HD) for shock (NS and SR) and incentive (LK and HK) subgroups of the E problem condition; the right panel presents the same data for comparable subgroups of the D problem condition. With respect to the E problem, Fig. 12–8 indicates that the decremental effect which SR training had on choice-speed performance was essentially additive; that is, the magnitude of the decremental effect was comparable across all levels of drive and incentive. With respect to the D problem, however, Fig. 12–8 indicates that the dynamogenic effect which SR training had on choice-speed performance was limited entirely to the condition of high incentive and was especially amplified under HD. But shock exerted no effect on choice speeds under the LK condition with either LD or HD, and yet the HD-LK condition clearly produced SR facilitation of discrimination performance.

If the itnensity of the shock experience is increased, it can be expected that SR training on the difficult bright–dim problem will produce a decrement in choice speeds under conditions of moderate D and K (i.e., 12 gm., two pellets). This outcome is illustrated clearly in Fig. 12–9 which presents the choice-speed data of the Fowler, Goldman and Wischner (1968) study in which the effect of sodium amytal was also considered. As shown, mean choice speeds over the initial 80 trials of discrimination training for the control no-drug subjects decreased linearly as a function of log-shock intensity; and yet, the only clear instance of SR facilitation for the control subjects was at the 60-volt level (see Fig. 12–5). For the drug subjects, on the other hand, SR facilitation was evident throughout the 60–120-volt range, but as Fig. 12–9 indicates, these voltages were not productive of a reliable decrement in choice speeds. Collectively, our choice-speed data indicate that one very well-established function of shock is to make the animal slow down at the choice point; however, insofar as this effect relates to the particular performance outcome under study, viz., an increment or decrement in errors, the data also show that this function bears no consistent relationship to either SR facilitation or retardation. Consequently, the findings are not reconcilable with an attention, alerting hypothesis presuming only facilitation of performance.

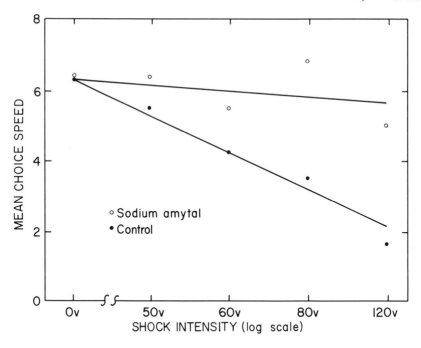

FIG. 12–9.   Mean choice speeds as a function of log shock intensity for the sodium amytal and combined (placebo and no-injection) control groups.

Based on data referred to in H. Fowler. L. Goldman, & G. J. Wischner, "Sodium Amytal and the Shock-Right Intensity Function for Visual Discrimination Learning," *Journal of Comparative and Physiological Psychology*, **65**, 1968, pp. 115–159. Copyright 198 by the American Psychological Association and reproduced by permission.

The fear-reduction hypothesis.   Utilizing an escape or fear-reduction hypothesis, Mowrer (1950) attempted to reconcile the different results obtained with correction (Muenzinger, 1934) and noncorrection (Wischner, 1947). For correction subjects, SR facilitation should occur because correct responses are doubly reinforced, i.e., by food reinforcement and by escape from the fearful situation. Although not elaborated by Mowrer, his interpretation seems applicable as well to the facilitation reported by Muenzinger and Wood (1935) on the effect of shock-both training. It will be recalled, that because of the correction procedure employed in their study, a 3 to 1 differential in the amount of shock existed for incorrect as compared with correct responses.

In the previous section the present writers indicated their acceptance of one function of shock as being the slowing down of the animal at the choice point. We would also accept that another important function of shock is to lead to the development of an emotional reaction which allows the operation of reinforcement via escape or avoidance of the fear-producing cues. There is certainly evidence to support both these functions of shock. But just as the alerting function bears no consistent relationship to SR facilitation and retardation, so also does the fear-reduction hypothesis have difficulty in handling these varied effects, especially those obtaining under conditions of noncorrection training, as observed in Prince's (1956) study and in our research as well.

The secondary-reinforcement hypothesis.   The interpretation that shock, as a cue which is selectively associated with either the correct or incorrect response, can serve as a discriminative stimulus and thus as a secondary reinforcer has received ample support in the literature. Holz and Azrin (1961, 1962) have shown that the discriminative properties of punishment, when selectively designating periods of reinforcement and nonreinforcement during a discrimination sequence, may respectively facilitate and suppress response frequency. Nevertheless, with respect to discrete-trial performance in the SR visual discrimination paradigm, this discriminative-stimulus interpretation of the function of shock would seem to bear little relation to the varied effects that have been obtained, especially those obtaining with the manipulation of problem difficulty. Furthermore, direct assessments of this interpretation, as in our research bearing on extinction and reversal performance, failed to provide any evidence that shock had acquired reinforcing properties.

We would even argue that the discriminative-stimulus interpretation of the function of shock is inapplicable to the SR context on the basis of other considerations. Whereas in the operant work by Holz and Azrin, shock is used as the only cue to the correctness or incorrectness of a bar-press response, in the SR paradigm the visual discriminanda already exist as discernible cues and consequently as effective secondary reinforcers. Thus, in this latter situation, the introduction of a shock stimulus represents the addition of but one other cue, one which is moreover often temporally removed from the act of choosing as well as the act of consuming or not consuming food at the goal. As a counter-argument, it might be proposed that the shock constitutes a more effective secondary reinforcer in that its reinforcing properties may be mediated through the rapid conditioning of a fear reaction (cf. Woodworth & Schlosberg, 1954). It should be considered, however, that such an effect is dependent upon the differential association of a fear reaction to discernible cues, in this case, the visual discriminanda. Hence, in either case, the visual cues must be discriminated for the operation of a differential secondary reinforcing effect and as such these cues can be sufficient as reinforcers in themselves. These considerations provide a basis for expecting retardation of performance across increasing levels of task difficulty as effected, for example, by manipulation of the relative brightnesses of the discriminative cues (Fowler & Wischner, 1965a), and similarly, for the facilitation of performance that prevails as a consequence of the increased discriminability of the stimulus alternatives that is provided by either SR or SW training.

The distinctive-cue hypothesis.   With its emphasis on the extent to which shock increases the discriminability of the stimulus alternatives, the distinctive-cue interpretation of the function of punishment suggests that SR facilitation (and in part SW facilitation) will be highly dependent upon those procedural manipulations that promote secondary reinforcement for the *incorrect* response. As indicated by our research findings, significant variables in this respect include the similarity of the discriminative stimuli, the temporal–spatial dissociation of these stimuli and their respective goal conditions (thereby promoting similarity of the goal conditions) and the extent to which these stimuli may prevail for alternative response sequences, as for example, in correction training. Performance-factor manipulations, such as the level of drive and possibly also the magnitude of reinforcement, can be important in augmenting performance facilitation to the extent that SR (or SW) training can delimit secondary reinforcement for the incorrect response and thereby increase the difference in associative strengths for correct and incorrect response tendencies. Thus, in regard to the differences in outcome that prevailed with earlier research on SR facilitation, our findings point up the necessity of examining the details of the methodology used, in addition to relatively gross procedural characteristics such as correction or noncorrection training.

This point may be illustrated with reference to the Muenzinger and Powloski (1951) study which compared correction and noncorrection procedures. In their study, SR facilitation obtained under both procedures with more facilitation occurring with correction than noncorrection training. More importantly, in contrast to the findings of our research, these effects were demonstrated in a simple light–dark discrimination in which significantly more errors were exhibited by the noncorrection subjects. As noted earlier, Muenzinger and Powloski (1951) employed a modified noncorrection procedure whereby, following an initial incorrect choice, the animal returned to the start compartment via a gray return route and then chose again with the position of the discriminative stimuli unchanged. In effect, with this procedure the animal could also correct; consequently, delayed reinforcement would likewise be available for an incorrect response of the noncorrection animal and would thereby contribute to the SR facilitation obtained with the noncorrection procedure in spite of the use of a simple light–dark discrimination. An additionally important consideration is that the gray return route used by the noncorrection animal following an incorrect response was similar in brightness and physical characteristics to another return route where all animals received food reinforcement following a correct response. Hence, for noncorrection animals which experienced both return routes, as opposed to correction animals which experienced only the correct return route, generalized secondary reinforcement should have been operative in the incorrect route to impede learning of the discrimination. Under these conditions, however, shock could not be expected to facilitate performance more because, being administered in the correct maze *arm,* it could not serve as a distinctive cue to increase the discriminability of the two return *routes.* For noncorrection animals, then, there should have been minimal SR facilitation and yet significantly more errors than for the correction animals.

It should be made clear that the distinctive-cue hypothesis does not require that shock be present in a particular maze arm to exert a cue effect, but only sufficiently associated with some stimulus alternative. That is, via its repeated association with one alternative, shock may provide the basis for the conditioning of fear which itself may effect an increased distinctiveness of the stimulus alternative to which it is conditioned. As will be recalled, this interpretation bearing on the acquired distinctiveness of cues was offered in relation to the findings of our extinction and reversal studies wherein SR acquisition training had the general effect of facilitating subsequent extinction and reversal performance irrespective of concurrent punishment contingencies. Such an interpretation would also seem applicable to the findings of the Muenzinger and Baxter (1957) study wherein the cues associated with escape and approach reactions to shock in a runway had the effect of facilitating subsequent discrimination performance independently of the type of reaction (escape or approach) that was conditioned. Thus, via the association of these cues with shock during preliminary training, any fear conditioned to them and presumably elicited during discrimination training could well serve to delimit generalized secondary reinforcement for the incorrect stimulus alternative.

From the foregoing, it should be clear that the distinctive-cue interpretation of the function of punishment is not independent of other functions of punishment such as that of producing fear. We have already referred to the possible role of fear in correction training, in particular, its presumed effect in causing SR animals to enter the stem upon retracing following an initial incorrect choice and thereby be removed from the postive discriminative stimulus. In this regard, however, it should also be apparent that performance outcomes can be drastically altered and even reversed if the fear-producing function of punishment is made to predominate, as for example, by increasing the intensity of the shock experience. Furthermore, reactions which permit escape and avoidance of the fear-associated correct-arm cues (as in SR training) may be sufficiently strengthened so as to offset any facilitating effect that is mediated by the fear. With these and similar considerations, one begins to understand better the beneficial effect on SR discrimination training (i.e., the heightened facilitation) that is derived from the administration of a drug like sodium amytal (Fowler, Goldman, & Wischner, 1968) or shock-adaptation trials (Muenzinger et al., 1952) or even shock-free training trials (Prince, 1956). This latter manipulation might also be beneficial with respect to the differential in associative strength for correct and incorrect responses that is produced and possibly amplified by fear motivation.

In conclusion, we must emphasize that while the findings of our research are effective in highlighting a distinctive-cue function of punishment, they are equally if not more significant in illustrating that varied performance outcomes are to be understood only in the light of those varied functions of punishment that may prevail in different contexts. Indeed, by considering which of these different functions of punishment can predominate and what performance outcomes they may mediate, it becomes possible to manipulate and structure conditions of training such that punishment is equally effective in producing either performance retardation or facilitation.

Summary

Facilitating effects of punishment have typically been viewed as paradoxical, in so far as they represent exceptions to a presumed, suppressing function of punishment. However, the fact that punishment can produce diverse performance outcomes suggests that facilitation effects may be more appropriately viewed as the bases for elaborating comparably varied functions of punishment. In line with this orientation, the present chapter addresses itself to a classical paradox relating to punishment, viz., the facilitating effect of shock for the correct response in discrimination learning.

A critical review of the literature relevant to this phenomenon is presented, pointing up a wide range of empirical findings, together with the different functions of punishment that have been postulated to rationalize the empirical outcomes. The review gives special attention to procedural and methodological variations in design which appear to underlie different effects showing that shock for the correct response can either facilitate or retard discrimination learning, or even have no effect at all.

A current program of research is presented, addressing those variables relevant to the findings reviewed. Focusing initially on shock parameters, work from our laboratory highlighted an avoidance function of punishment until investigation of specific training conditions yielded a facilitation effect with the same punishing stimulus. Further assessment of the methodological and performance factors relating to this finding demonstrated the conditions under which shock-right training would be effective in producing either performance retardation or facilitation.

An argument is made for the utility of the distinction among the terms *effects, functions,* and *mechanisms of operation* of the punishment procedure. An analysis employing this distinction is applied to extant data and relevant hypotheses, specifically, the general sensitizing hypothesis, the fear-reduction hypothesis, the secondary-reinforcement hypothesis, and the distinctive-cue hypothesis. Although the latter, developed by the present writers, is offered as the one hypothesis most applicable to the bulk of the findings, it is concluded that our research is more significant in illustrating how different functions of punishment can predominate under different training conditions. Accordingly, varied performance outcomes become intelligible only when one considers these varied functions and the mechanisms related to their instigation.

REFERENCES

AZRIN, N. H., & HOLZ, W. C. Punishment. In W. K. Honig (Ed.), *Operant behavior: Areas of research and application.* New York: Appleton-Century-Crofts, 1966. Pp. 380–447.

BITTERMAN, M. E., & ELAM, C. B. Discrimination following varying amounts of nondifferential reinforcement. *American Journal of Psychology,* 1954, **67,** 133–137.

BOLLES, R. C. *Theory of Motivation.* New York: Harper & Row, 1967.

BUNCH, M. E. The effect of electric shock as punishment for errors in human maze-learning. *Journal of Comparative Psychology,* 1928, **8,** 343–359.

CAMPBELL, B. A., & TEGHTSOONIAN, R. Electrical and behavioral effects of different types of shock stimuli on the rat. *Journal of Comparative and Physiological Psychology,* 1958, **51,** 185–192.

CAUL, W. The effects of sodium amytal on discrimination learning in rats. Unpublished doctoral dissertation, Carnegie Institute of Technology, 1965.

CHURCH, R. M. The varied effects of punishment on behavior. *Psychological Review,* 1963, **70,** 369–402.

CRAWFORD, F. T., MAYES, G. L., & BITTERMAN, M. E. A further study of differential afferent consequences in nondifferential reinforcement. *American Journal of Psychology,* 1954, **67,** 717–719.

CURLIN, E. R., & DONAHOE, J. W. Effects of shock intensity and placement on the learning of a food-reinforced brightness discrimination. *Journal of Experimental Psychology,* 1965, **69,** 349–356.

DODSON, J. D. Relative values of reward and punishment in habit formation. *Psychobiology,* 1917, **1,** 231–276.

DREW, G. C. The function of punishment in learning. *Journal of Genetic Psychology,* 1938, **52,** 257–267.

FAIRLIE, C. W. The effect of shock at the 'moment of choice' on the formation of a visual discrimination habit. *Journal of Experimental Psychology,* 1937, **21**, 662–669.

FOWLER, H. Facilitation and inhibition of performance by punishment: The effects of shock intensity and distribution of trials. *Journal of Comparative and Physiological Psychology,* 1963, **56**, 531–538.

FOWLER, H., GOLDMAN, L., & WISCHNER, G. J. Sodium amytal and the shock-right intensity function for visual discrimination learning. *Journal of Comparative and Physiological Psychology,* 1968, **65**, 155–159.

FOWLER, H., & MILLER, N. E. Facilitation and inhibition of runway performance by hind- and forepaw shock of various intensities. *Journal of Comparative and Physiological Psychology,* 1963, **56**, 801–805.

FOWLER, H., SPELT, P. F., & WISCHNER, G. J. Discrimination performance as affected by training procedure, problem difficulty, and shock for the correct response. *Journal of Experimental Psychology,* 1967, **75**, 432–436.

FOWLER, H., & WISCHNER, G. J. Discrimination performance as affected by problem difficulty and shock for either the correct or incorrect response. *Journal of Experimental Psychology,* 1965, **69**, 413–418. (a)

FOWLER, H., & WISCHNER, G. J. On the "secondary reinforcing" effect of shock for the correct response in visual discrimination learning. *Psychonomic Science,* 1965, **3**, 209–210. (b)

FREEBURNE, C. M., & TAYLOR, J. E. Discrimination learning with shock for right and wrong responses in the same subjects. *Journal of Comparative and Physiological Psychology,* 1952, **45**, 264–268.

GOSS, A. E., & WISCHNER, G. J. Vicarious trial and error and related behavior. *Psychological Bulletin,* 1956, **53**, 35–54.

HAWKINS, R. P. Effects of drive, incentive and problem difficulty on the facilitation of discrimination performance by punishment of correct responses. Unpublished doctoral dissertation, University of Pittsburgh, 1965.

HILGARD, E. R., & BOWER, G. H. *Theories of learning.* (3rd ed.) New York: Appleton-Century-Crofts, 1966.

HOGE, M. A., & STOCKING, R. J. A note on the relative value of punishment and reward as motives. *Journal of Animal Behavior,* 1912, **2**, 43–50.

HOLZ, W. C., & AZRIN, N. H. Discriminative properties of punishment. *Journal of the Experimental Analysis of Behavior,* 1961, **4**, 225–232.

HOLZ, W. C., & AZRIN, N. H. Interactions between the discriminative and aversive properties of punishment. *Journal of the Experimental Analysis of Behavior,* 1962, **5**, 229–234.

KALISH, D. The non-correction method and the delayed response problem of Blodgett and McCutchan. *Journal of Comparative Psychology,* 1946, **39**, 91–107.

LOGAN, F. A., & WAGNER, A. R. *Reward and punishment.* Boston: Allyn and Bacon, 1965.

MARTIN, B., & ROSS, L. E. Effects of consummatory response punishment on consummatory and runway behavior. *Journal of Comparative and Physiological Psychology,* 1964, **58**, 243–247.

MILLER, N. E. Some recent studies of conflict behavior and drugs. *American Psychologist,* 1961, **16**, 12–24.

MOWRER, O. H. *Learning theory and personality dynamics.* New York: Ronald Press, 1950.

MUENZINGER, K. F. Motivation in learning: I. Electric shock for correct responses in the visual discrimination habit. *Journal of Comparative Psychology,* 1934, **17**, 267–277.

MUENZINGER, K. F. Concerning the effect of shock for right responses in visual discrimination learning. *Journal of Experimental Psychology,* 1948, **38**, 201–203.

MUENZINGER, K. F., & BAXTER, L. F. The effects of training to approach vs. to escape from electric shock upon subsequent discrimination learning. *Journal of Comparative and Physiological Psychology,* 1957, **50**, 252–257.

MUENZINGER, K. F., BERNSTONE, A. H., & RICHARDS, L. Motivation in learning: VIII. Equivalent amounts of electric shock for right and wrong responses in a visual discrimination habit. *Journal of Comparative Psychology,* 1938, **26**, 177–186.

MUENZINGER, K. F., BROWN, W. O., CROW, W. J., & POWLOSKI, R. F. Motivation in learning: XI. An analysis of electric shock for correct responses into its avoidance and accelerating components. *Journal of Experimental Psychology,* 1952, **43**, 115–119.

MUENZINGER, K. F., & FLETCHER, F. M. Motivation in learning: VI. Escape from electric shock compared with hunger–food tension in the visual discrimination habit. *Journal of Comparative Psychology,* 1936, **22**, 79–91.

MUENZINGER, K. F., & FLETCHER, F. M. Motivation in learning: VII. The effect of an enforced delay at the point of choice in the visual discrimination habit. *Journal of Comparative Psychology,* 1937, **23**, 383–392.

MUENZINGER, K. F., & NEWCOMB, H. Motivation in learning: V. The relative effectiveness of jumping a gap and crossing an electric grid in a visual discrimination habit. *Journal of Comparative Psychology,* 1936, **21**, 95–104.

MUENZINGER, K. F., & POWLOSKI, R. F. Motivation in learning: X. Comparison of electric shock for correct turns in a corrective and non-corrective situation. *Journal of Experimental Psychology,* 1951, **42**, 118–124.

MUENZINGER, K. F., & WOOD, A. Motivation in learning: IV. The function of punishment as determined by its temporal relation to the act of choice in the visual discrimination habit. *Journal of Comparative Psychology,* 1935, **20**, 95–106.

PRINCE, A. I., JR. Effect of punishment on visual discrimination learning. *Journal of Experimental Psychology,* 1956, **52**, 381–385.

SANDLER, J. Masochism: An empirical analysis. *Psychological Bulletin,* 1964, **62**, 197–204.

SEWARD, J. P. An experimental analysis of maze discrimination. *Journal of Comparative Psychology,* 1943, **35**, 17–27.

THORNDIKE, E. L. *Animal Intelligence.* New York: Macmillan, 1911.

TOLMAN, E. C., HALL, C. S., & BRETNALL, E. P. A disproof of the law of effect and a substitution of the laws of emphasis, motivation and disruption. *Journal of Experimental Psychology,* 1932, **15**, 601–614.

WARDEN, C. J., & AYLESWORTH, M. The relative value of reward and punishment in the formation of a visual discrimination habit in the white rat. *Journal of Comparative Psychology,* 1927, **7**, 117–127.

WISCHNER, G. J. The effect of punishment on discrimination learning in a non-correction situation. *Journal of Experimental Psychology,* 1947, **37**, 271–284.

WISCHNER, G. J. A reply to Dr. Muenzinger on the effect of punishment on discrimination learning in a non-correction situation. *Journal of Experimental Psychology,* 1948, **38**, 203–204.

WISCHNER, G. J. VTE and efficiency of discrimination learning involving shock for correct choice. *American Psychologist,* 1950, **5**, 252–253. (Abstract)

WISCHNER, G. J., & FOWLER, H. Discrimination performance as affected by duration of shock for either the correct or incorrect response. *Psychonomic Science,* 1964, **1**, 239–240.

WISCHNER, G. J., FOWLER, H., & KUSHNICK, S. A. Effect of strength of punishment for "correct" or "incorrect" responses on visual discrimination performance. *Journal of Experimental Psychology,* 1963, **65**, 131–138.

WISCHNER, G. J., HALL, R. C., & FOWLER, H. Discrimination learning under various combinations of food and shock for "correct" and "incorrect" responses. *Journal of Experimental Psychology,* 1964, **67**, 48–51.

WOODWORTH, R. S., & SCHLOSBERG, H. *Experimental psychology.* (Rev. ed.) New York: Holt, 1954.

YERKES, R. M., & DODSON, J. D. The relation of strength of stimulus to rapidity of habit formation. *Journal of Comparative Neurology and Psychology,* 1908, **18**, 459–482.

13

The Role of Conflict in Experimental Neurosis

John P. Seward

UNIVERSITY OF CALIFORNIA, LOS ANGELES

A close relation between punishment and conflict has been recognized since Lewin's notable paper on reward and punishment (1935). He identified the types of conflict inherent in two uses of punishment. In the first case, in which a task is imposed under threat of punishment for nonperformance, "the individual finds himself between two approximately equal negative valences" (p. 123); i.e., what Miller (1944) called an *avoidance–avoidance* competition. In the second, probably more typical case, an act is prohibited under threat of punishment. Here a positive and a negative valence give rise to opposed vectors; for Miller this is an *approach–avoidance* competition.

Lewin's treatment was by no means arbitrary. Intuitively, an association between punishment and conflict seems almost inescapable. Two impulses must be involved—to the punished response (or refusal to respond) and to the punishment itself—and they are usually incompatible. From field-theoretical principles Lewin was able to derive a number of commonly observed outcomes of such situations. There is little doubt that the more quantitative conflict models of Miller (1944, 1959) and Hull (1938, 1952), based on stimulus–response principles, would also yield predictions about the effectiveness of punishment under various conditions.

Further implications of this approach may be sought in the area of clinical psychology. Conflicts of some sort figure largely in theories of psychogenic disorders. The same is true of the behavioral abnormalities that sometimes turn up in the laboratory. Deliberate attempts to produce "experimental neuroses" in animals typically try to create conditions of conflict.

From these premises that punishment involves conflict and that conflict is a frequent factor in neurotic behavior it follows that some positive relation should exist between punishment and psychoneurosis.

This paper is concerned with the second premise of the syllogism; with the grounds, both theoretical and empirical, for asserting a causal connection between conflict and psychopathology. It will start by presenting an informal derivation of two types of conflict, including a mechanism for modifying behavior. It will then take up examples of experimental neurosis representing conflicts of both types to see what part conflict may have played in producing symptoms.

A Pretheory of Conflict

Conflict presupposes competing response tendencies that must themselves be accounted for. So the present approach will be found to contain three "mini-theories" for reward, punishment, and escape, but all cut from the same pattern. The one for reward bears a strong family resemblance to the views of Spence (1956), Miller (1963), and Sheffield (1965). Those for punishment and escape find their closest parallels in Mowrer's (1960) revised two-factor theory. Related treatments of punishment were derived from Amsel's (1958) frustration theory by Martin (1963) and Banks (1966) and from Miller's work with fear by Brown and Wagner (1964).

Since formal theorizing is not intended, the following definitions, assumptions, and mechanisms will be asserted quite dogmatically, without the exposition or defense that would otherwise be mandatory.

Definitions

Positive Reinforcement: Application of a stimulus ($S_R - R_R$) that increases the probability of recurrence of a concomitant response.

Reward: A positive reinforcer contingent on a response.

Aversive Stimulus: A stimulus ($S_u - R_u$) that reduces the probability of recurrence of a concomitant response.

Punishment: Application of S_u contingent on a response.

Incentive: Conditioned arousal of a positively reinforcing response ($r_R - s_R$).

Fear: Conditioned arousal of an aversive response ($r_u - s_u$).

Negative Reinforcement: Removal or reduction of an aversive stimulus ($\bar{S}_u - \bar{R}_u$) increases the probability of recurrence of a concomitant response.

Hope: Conditioned arousal of a negatively reinforcing response ($\bar{r}_u - \bar{s}_u$).

Conflict: Simultaneous arousal of antagonistic reactions in the same organism.

Tension: Internal state produced by conflict, consisting of proprioceptive and interoceptive stimuli (S_T).

Note that these definitions include only essential or functional properties. By-products, such as the diffuse autonomic effects of strong aversive stimuli, are omitted.

Basic Assumptions

1. Reinforcement, whether positive or negative, activates a feedback mechanism that facilitates responses in progress.

2. An aversive stimulus activates a drive or arousal mechanism that inhibits recent or ongoing responses and excites a new, incompatible response.

3. Tension has the properties of an aversive stimulus: its increase or maintenance activates a drive mechanism; its reduction, a facilitating mechanism.

These assumptions refer to hypothetical processes mediating reinforcement and response suppression. They owe a debt to Miller: his "go mechanism" (1963) is a forerunner of the first assumption, as his concept of a conflict-produced drive (1944, 1959) antedates the third.

Mechanism of Reward

When a response (R_o) is followed by positive reinforcement, the reinforcing response (R_R) is conditioned to stimuli and stimulus traces producing and produced by R_o. On later occasions, therefore, these stimuli arouse anticipation of reward, or *incentive* ($r_R - s_R$), which, by Assumption 1, facilitates responses in progress, in this case R_o. At the same time s_R becomes a cue to R_o.

Mechanism of Punishment

When a response (R_o) is punished, an aversive response (R_u) becomes conditioned to R_o-correlated stimuli. On later occasions these stimuli arouse anticipation of punishment, or *fear* ($r_u - s_u$). By Assumption 2, fear inhibits recently active responses, notably R_o, and excites a new, incompatible response (R_i).

Mechanism of Escape

When a response (R_{esc}) is followed by negative reinforcement, the reinforcing response ($\overline{R}_u$) becomes conditioned to R_{esc}-correlated stimuli. On later occasions these stimuli arouse anticipation of escape, or *hope* ($\overline{r}_u - \overline{s}_u$); by Assumption 1, facilitating R_{esc} and providing it with an additional cue.

It may be unnecessary to point out that the last two mechanisms apply Mowrer's (1960) theory to two forms of aversive learning, *passive avoidance* and *escape*. It is less obvious but no less true that the same mechanisms will account for *active avoidance*. They will do so if R_o is defined as any response *except* R_{esc}.

Approach—Avoidance Conflict

When R_o has been both rewarded and punished, R_o-correlated stimuli arouse both $r_R - s_R$ and $r_u - s_u$. The simultaneous facilitation and inhibition of R_o and excitation of R_i fulfill the conditions of conflict and produce *tension* (S_T). By Assumption 3, S_T inhibits recent responses (R_o or R_i), excites others, and contributes negative reinforcement to R_{esc}.

Avoidance—Avoidance Conflict

Assume that R_o has been punished and that R_o and R_i are the only responses available. R_o-correlated stimuli will arouse $r_u - s_u$, inhibiting R_o and exciting R_i. If R_i is also punished, R_i-correlated stimuli will arouse $r_u' - s_u'$, inhibiting R_i and exciting R_o. The simultaneous inhibition and excitation of two incompatible responses produce tension; S_T reciprocally inhibits and excites R_o and R_i and adds negative reinforcement to R_{esc} (Assumption 3).

The last two paragraphs state the conditions of conflict. The basis for predicting its effects is to be found in the concept of tension and the aversive properties assigned to S_T. On this basis we should expect conflict to aggravate the effects of punishment; whether these were chiefly inhibitory, excitatory, or reinforcing would depend on specific conditions.

Evidence from Experimental Neuroses
Maier's "Abnormal Fixations"

Method and Results

Since thorough reviews are available (Maier, 1949; Yates, 1962), a brief sketch of the basic procedure will suffice. Rats were first given preliminary training in the Lashley discrimination apparatus to jump from a stand to either of two doors. The doors were covered by cards bearing the cues to be discriminated (e.g., a black circle on white and a white circle on black). The rats were then divided into two groups and trained to a position habit. For one group (position reward) the card on the subject's preferred side was always unlatched, allowing access to food, while the other card was latched, causing the rat to bump its nose and fall into

a net. The other group (position stereotype) was given an insoluble problem; i.e., no matter which side or which card it chose, the rat was
randomly punished on half of the trials. Sooner or later the randomly
punished subject would refuse to jump. When that happened it was
forced to do so by blasts of air, electric shocks, or tail tapping. Most rats
soon started invariably jumping to the same side. When the position
habit was well established, both groups were shifted to a discrimination
problem with one symbol consistently rewarded and the other punished.

The results of this procedure were quite dependable. Most of the
group with rewarded-position habits learned the discrimination. Some
of the group with stereotyped habits also learned. But a sizable proportion of the latter group (i.e., 70% of the pooled subjects from three
experiments) clung to their position habits for the entire 200 trials
allowed them. Because the stereotyped response prevented a more adaptive adjustment to the now soluble problem, Maier called it a *fixation*.

Interpretation

Frustration theory. Maier held that the fixation was abnormal in the
sense that it could not be accounted for by the rules governing normally
motivated behavior. Instead, it expressed a special state of the organism
that he proposed to call *frustration*. This state was activated when
environmental sources of stress (such as the insoluble problem, unavoidable punishment, and forcing of response in Maier's experiments)
crossed the individual's frustration threshold. Frustrated behavior, unlike the normal kind, was not subject to reward and punishment, goal
orientation, or modification by learning. Response selection depended
mainly on availability, as determined by such conditions as physical
nearness, unlearned preferences, the response in progress, and others
(Maier & Ellen, 1959).

To support his claim that such a radical theory was both necessary
and heuristic, Maier presented the following evidence:

1. *Bimodal distribution of trials to learn.* When subjects are distributed by the number of trials they take to learn the discrimination,
the learners and nonlearners form two separate groups, with no scores
between the upper limit of one (about 150 trials) and the lower limit
of the other (some indeterminate number above 200 trials). Such clear-
cut bimodality strongly suggest a qualitative difference.

2. *Effect of 100% punishment.* In one experiment (Maier & Klee,
1943) rats with previously established habits or stereotypes were given
discrimination training such that the original response was punished on
every trial or on half of the trials. It was found, contrary to predictions
from reinforcement theory, that 100% punishment produced more fixations than 50%.

3. *"Latent learning."* In the course of discrimination training, fixated rats developed differential reactions to the positive and negative cues although they refused to abandon their response. They showed progressively greater resistance to jumping at the negative card than the positive one. They also learned to jump so as to soften the fall rather than land on the platform; such abortive jumps came to be made almost exclusively to the negative card. In these ways the subjects betrayed the "compulsive" character of their fixations. An extreme example of the same property was provided by the rat that jumped abortively against the negative card just after inspecting a dish of food in the open door on the nonfixated side.

Conflict theory.   Maier's subversive theorizing was bound to threaten the orthodox. A spate of critical papers appeared, aiming to show that Maier's facts could be handled by concepts familiar to "learning theory" (e.g., Eglash, 1951; Farber, 1948; Mowrer, 1950; Wilcoxon, 1952; Wolpe, 1953). My aim is not to assess these arguments nor the replies from Maier's group (Feldman, 1957; Maier, 1956; Maier & Ellen, 1951). My question is whether the pretheory outlined above contains the rudiments of an adequate explanation of his findings.

The theory assumes that when Maier gave his rats an insoluble problem he put them in an avoidance–avoidance conflict. They had to choose between leaving the jump-stand (R_o), thereby risking a fall $(r_u - s_u)$, and staying where they were (R_i), to be struck by an air blast (r'_u). The conflict generated such a high level of tension that when it was finally resolved by a leap to one door (R_{esc}), that R received exceedingly powerful reinforcement.

This account has two aspects that will be considered separately. First, it contrasts with Maier's view of the role of punishment. For Maier the punishment produces fixations by frustrating the animals so severely that they cannot learn. For conflict theory as for reinforcement theory in general, punishment sets the stage for fixation by lifting the aversive drive level to be reduced by the response. Secondly, and here it goes beyond the ordinary reinforcement position, the theory holds that conflict, by adding tension to fear, makes the resultant negative reinforcement excessive.

The first issue is easier to test. Reinforcement theory implies that if drive reduction were strong enough, it could fixate behavior without assistance from punishment. Wolpe (1953) suggested a crucial experiment to test this implication. He proposed "to give rats the usual preliminary training and then force them by air blast to jump to cards that are always unlatched and never followed by food" (p. 115). Reinforcement theory would predict fixations; frustration theory would not.

This experiment, as far as I know, has never been tried, but an unpublished experiment much like it had actually been done 2 years before. Christie (1951) trained rats on separate occasions to jump through two open doors, each giving access to its own food box. He then tested them to both doors at once, with food only in the box not chosen on the first jump. Both doors were uncovered, and no air blast was needed since the top of the jumpstand was only 3 inches in diameter. Christie's hypothesis, like Wolpe's, was that the dominant escape motive would cause the escape response to be stereotyped. He predicted that in his situation hungry rats would not learn the response to food. As it turned out, 34 of the 38 rats tested confirmed his prediction, although the only punishment for the "wrong" response was the absence of food. Of course the experiment was not really crucial, since Christie's rats did not meet any such rigorous criterion of fixation as Maier's. But it suggested that escape was more important than punishment in Maier's experiments.

To clinch this point it must be shown that unreduced drive is not enough to fixate a response. Three experiments will be cited in evidence.

1. Errett (1948) compared two groups of rats in an E maze with a grid floor and connecting paths from the sides to the starting point. Food was available on both sides during 3 days of training. Two experimental groups received shock; the third group was a no-shock control. Group A had 10 continuous trials a day without being removed and with shock on the grid throughout. Group B had 10 massed trials with shock confined to the middle path and to the choice point. Training was followed by 10 test trials a day for 5 days, with no shock and with food only on the nonpreferred side.

According to the frustration theory, Group A, subjected to inescapable shock, would be expected to learn a stronger and more persistent position habit than Group B, allowed to escape shock by choosing either side. Actually Group A showed no change in degree of side preference over preliminary trials, while Group B increased its choices of one side from 55% to 94%. On test trials Group A learned to reverse its preference significantly ahead of B.

None of Errett's subjects acquired fixations in the sense of an inextinguishable response. But he did test the effect of increased anxiety reduction by running another group with all of the grid except the choice path covered with rubber matting. His aim was to decrease the generalization of fear from the choice path to the side paths. During shock trials the new group showed the same degree of stereotyping as Group B, but on test trials it was clearly more reluctant than the earlier group to abandon the habit.

2. Fowler, Fowler, and Dember (1959) studied the effect of shock intensity on alternation of escape responses. They gave rats massed trials with shock in the stem of a T maze, terminated when the rat made a free choice of either arm. They found a progressive increase in per-

centage of response repetition with increase in voltage. The question arose whether probability of repetition depended on the drive level present at the time of choice or on the drive level reduced on preceding trials. To answer this question the experimenters gave four groups two massed trials in a factorial design. On Trial 1 two of the groups received 20 volts and two received 100 volts. On Trial 2 one group of each pair was given the same voltage as before; the second group was shifted to the other voltage. Interest centers in the percentage of repeated choices on Trial 2.

The authors found that the amount of repetition was determined almost entirely by shock intensity on Trial 1, hardly at all by that on Trial 2. They inferred, soundly, it seems, that strength of preceding reinforcement rather than of present motivation was responsible for increasing the tendency to repeat responses.

3. Knopfelmacher (1953) tested a deduction from Maier's theory, that fixations should increase with the severity and frequency of punishment. He used a Y-shaped water maze, from which rats could escape by swimming to a ladder through either of two identical doors. One door gave immediate access to the ladder; the other gave access only after a delay. For half of the subjects the delay was 8 seconds; for the other half, 80 seconds. In Phase 2 (following the preliminary training of Phase 1) the delay side was shifted randomly from trial to trial with no clue to its location. Thirty-nine of 46 subjects acquired position stereotypes. In Phase 3 the experimenter introduced a discrimination problem by providing a light over the incorrect door. Of 18 subjects with 8-second delay, 15 reached the criterion of 150 trials without breaking their stereotype. None of the subjects delayed 80 seconds failed to learn the discrimination. In Phase 4 the nonlearners were shifted to 80-second delay, and all but four broke the habit.

These results opposed Maier's theory in that the milder punishment proved the more conducive to "fixation." As the author suggests, however, the 8-second delay may not have been enough worse than zero delay to motivate learning. More interesting is the absence of fixations in Phase 3 at the longer delay. An obvious explanation presents itself: the longer escape was delayed, the less reinforcement was received by the choice response. (Contrast this case with Maier's jump stand, in which the choice response *was* the escape response.)

Still to be explained are the "true" fixations of the four rats in Phase 4 that clung to their stereotype in spite of 80-second delay. They conformed to Maier's results in standing apart from the rest of the distribution and displaying the same behavioral symptoms he described. These cases would confound a drive-reduction theory but for one thing: all four of them had developed their position responses with delays of only 8 seconds.

On the whole, the results of this experiment add to the evidence that if punishment fixates a response, it is only by increasing the drive level that the response reduces.

The second hypothesis—that conflict, by producing tension, enhances negative reinforcement—has not been tested in an avoidance–avoidance situation. One difficulty is that this type of conflict is exclusively aversive; a correlated increase of fixation might therefore be due to the punishment that produced it.

An example of the elusiveness of conflict as a factor is provided by Christie's (1951) experiment described above. After test sessions he gave one group of 14 nonlearning rats habit-breaking trials; i.e., he put a block in the preferred door, causing a fall to the floor. The method proved "quickly effective in causing a shift of jump to the open door on the nonpreferred side" (p. 67). This evidence of plasticity could be taken to imply that "true" fixation requires something more than escape from an aversive situation; the "something more" might be escape from conflict. However, it might not. As Christie pointed out, his rats may have seemed less rigid than Maier's because they had never made the escape response "in the face of . . . punishment" (p. 67); i.e., with fear of punishment ($r_u - s_u$) as part of the eliciting situation.

Other kinds of evidence for a drive-producing effect of conflict will be considered later in connection with approach–avoidance conflict.

The question remains if and how the proposed theory can handle Maier's supporting evidence of abnormality. One thing becomes quickly obvious: the need for at least crudely quantitative statements. For example, the higher percentage of fixations occurring with punishment on all trials than on only half of them could be accommodated with the aid of two added assumptions: (1) in the mechanism of punishment, the strength of fear is an increasing function of the number of conditioning trials; and (2) in the definition of negative reinforcement, its strength is an increasing function of the amount of drive reduction.

The wide gap between learners and nonlearners in trials-to-criterion is not so easily derived. One way to "explain" this bimodality would be to assume that a habit becomes irreversible only if the drive it reduces has reached a certain critical level. The circularity of this reasoning could be broken if the hypothetical threshold could be correlated with some independently measured event, such as activation of a subcortical mechanism.

Persistence in jumping to the fixated side in spite of "latent learning" of the discrimination calls for another quantitative provision: that the mechanism of escape can become strong enough to overpower the mechanisms of reward and punishment. Admittedly the argument is strained by the fixated rats' stubborn resistance to the opposite door even when it is open and displaying food. This behavior looks like an extreme case of Tolman's (1948) "cognitive strip-map," or of Murphy's (1958) *canalization*. But these picturesque concepts are largely descriptive: they add little to the speculation that sudden reduction of a high level of arousal may channel all active stimulus energies, including the visual stimulus of food in an open door, into the final response of jumping the other way.

Masserman's Phobic Cats

Methods and Results

Dimmick, Ludlow, and Whiteman (1939) showed how effective punishment could be in disrupting adaptive behavior. In the course of training six cats to open a food box for meat during presentations of a light and bell, they punished intervening responses with a shock through the feet. Five of the cats developed increasing aversion to the food box and signals, displaying panic in the experimental cage and altered behavior outside of it.

Wishing to study "neurotic" behavior under controlled conditions, Masserman (1943) used a similar method. He trained 82 cats to respond to a flash of light and/or bell by lifting the lid of a box and procuring food. Some of them were taught to produce the signals by pressing a switch. When the habits were well established, "as the lid was opened or as the food was being delivered" (p. 67), the cat received a blast of air across its face or an electric shock through its feet or both. One or two applications usually sufficed to produce phobic reactions in most subjects. At the food signals they tried to escape and refused to eat in the apparatus; switch pressers ignored the switch or avoided it. A variety of aberrations appeared in different individuals; e.g., stereotyped escape patterns, compulsive rituals, counterphobic responses, persistent self-grooming, and unusual aggressiveness. These were accompanied by unmistakable signs of anxiety; the cats would crouch, tremble, hide, or become restless and easily startled, with disturbed pulse and breathing. Symptoms persisted for periods ranging from a few days to several weeks, long enough for the experimenters to try different forms of therapy with varying degrees of success.

Prolonged deprivation of food rarely sufficed to overcome the fear, some cats starving themselves for 8 to 22 days. Indeed, panic was likely to be acute on the third day after the initial trauma, when hunger was presumably at its peak, especially if the food box was filled and open. Confining the animal close to the food box produced "claustrophobic" reactions. Interestingly, the same conditions that sometimes produced the most violent efforts to escape (extreme hunger, and forced proximity to displayed food) turned out to be one of the most effective methods of "cure."

Extending the investigation to monkeys, Masserman and Pechtel (1953) produced extreme disturbances by showing the subject a toy snake just as he reached for food. Other workers using Masserman's techniques have reported similar results, if not quite so dramatic. Jacobsen and Skaarup (1955) studied cats under less stressful conditions; their subjects were not severely deprived and were exposed only to the air blast, a milder stimulus than shock. Sooner or later the animals stopped eating, substituting a variety of "displacement activities." Vegetative disturbances (vomiting, diarrhea) were the last to develop. To the authors such behavior expressed more than "mere fright at the disagreeable experience of receiving an occasional air blast on the side of the head" (p. 123).

Watson (1954) repeated Masserman's procedures on 17 cats and reported a typical behavior pattern of three stages: (1) an acute disruption of feeding behavior lasting a day or two; (2) several days of vacillation during which the cats were tense, restless, easily startled, and prone to lick themselves; and (3) adoption of a stable adjustment, either of renewed feeding regardless of occasional blasts or shocks, or of complete withdrawal from the food box. In contrast with Masserman's picture of chronic disturbance, Watson found nothing pathological to report. He suggested that the less-restricted living conditions of his cats might be partly responsible for the difference.

Meanwhile Lichtenstein (1950) did a similar experiment with 14 dogs. After adapting them to a harness and wooden collar and training them to eat the pellets delivered three at a time to a food box, the experimenter introduced the critical treatment. Pellets were delivered as usual, but if and when the dog started to eat, a 2-second shock was applied to his right forepaw. This contingency remained in effect until the dog had refused to eat during three consecutive sessions of 20 trials each.

Most subjects took only one to three shocks before reaching the criterion. A few dogs struggled persistently in the harness, but many became cataleptic. Conditioned gasping was common; tremors, tics, and startle were noted and found to increase during the 3 days of no shocks. Some dogs became more aggressive in their living cages, and one developed a lasting aversion to pellets, although he would eat them if ground into mash.

Interpretation

Masserman interpreted the disorganized behavior of his cats as the result of a conflict of motives involving two mutually exclusive adaptive patterns. In defense of his view he reported several controls, as follows:

A cat that received the air blast following the light and the bell, apart from food, soon ceased to respond with fear to the signals. Cats given unsignaled air blasts became habituated to them in 5 to 30 trials. Omitting food on some trials did not disturb the cats unduly, and locking the food box simply extinguished the food-getting response. Masserman concluded that for traumatic effect the conjunction of aversive stimulus and goal object was essential.

Reviewing studies of this type, including the work of Pavlov, Anderson and Liddell, Maier, Masserman, and others, Russell (1950) attributed experimental neuroses in general to "some variety of conflict" under conditions of limited escape. The importance of the motivational variety was more recently implied in Solomon's (1964) discussion of punishment. Referring to Masserman's and Lichtenstein's observations, he raised the question why consummatory responses seem more vulnerable to punishment than instrumental ones.

Wolpe (1952) took a different position. He held that conflict might be a sufficient condition for neurosis, as shown by Pavlov, Gantt, Dworkin, and others; but that it was not a necessary one. Anxiety aroused by noxious stimuli would account for the results of Anderson and Liddell, Dimmick et al., and Masserman. Criticizing the latter for inadequate controls, Wolpe ran a similar experiment with two groups of six cats each. One group, treated by Masserman's method, was trained to take food at a buzzer; then the animals were shocked just as they tried to seize the pellet. For the other group, acting as a control, the shock followed a whirring noise on a variable-interval schedule independently of buzzer and food. Wolpe described the shock as "very uncomfortable to the human hand" (p. 253). Both groups showed "neurotic" symptoms to about the same degree, though they tended to generalize to different objects, the "Masserman" group to meat, the control group to the experimenter. Wolpe was satisfied that principles governing the conditioning of anxiety and its removal through counterconditioning could account for his and Masserman's findings.

As Smart (1965) pointed out, however, Wolpe's experiment was defective in that the control group had 10 to 20 shocks while the food-shocked group had only the 2 or 3 shocks that sufficed to stop it from eating. In his own experiment Smart trained 30 cats to turn on food signals, open the food box, and eat. For shock training he divided them into three groups: Preconsummatory, shocked after pressing the switch and while lifting the lid of the food box; Consummatory, shocked 1 second after taking food in the mouth; and shock-alone, shocked at least 30 seconds after food-related behavior. All three groups received the same number and distribution of shocks.

For recorded descriptions of behavior Smart substituted ratings of presence or absence of symptom in 16 categories of behavior. Pooling all subjects he found a significant increase of symptoms in all but one category. But in 48 intergroup comparisons only two were significant. He concluded, with Wolpe, that conflict was unnecessary to neurotic behavior; indeed, it even failed to intensify it.

Smart's experiment, like the others, seems not to have closed the issue. He reports using a 1-second shock of 3.5 ma. This is a severe shock, strong enough to suggest that any differences among his groups may well have been hidden by a "ceiling effect." Whether an intensity of shock could be found that would make cats neurotic if used as punishment but not if given separately remains to be seen.

Further Evidence

The foregoing studies, all involving approach–avoidance conflict, produced varying degrees of abnormal behavior but left unsettled the question of how much conflict had to do with it. At this point a change of strategy may help. Turning to the more prosaic investigation of normal behavior, we may ask, what conditions *are* effective in the aversive control of rewarded reactions? If they turn out to be conflict related, they may tell us something about how conflict operates.

Three specific problems will be considered: (1) the role of response contingency; (2) the role of stimulus intensity in generalization; and (3) the role of the consummatory response. Finally, we shall look for more evidence on whether conflict works in the way suggested by Miller (1944, 1959) and adopted here: by functioning as an added source of drive.

The role of response contingency.   Masserman's conflict hypothesis implied that neurotic behavior depended on a close correlation between a noxious stimulus and a response. This was the interpretation challenged by Wolpe and Smart. A closely related question is whether the punished response itself is more effectively suppressed than it would be by a noncontingent stimulus. Church (1963) has reviewed earlier evidence on this question and in his contribution to this conference has presented more. He concludes that with certain qualifications a stimulus is a better suppressor when dependent on a response than when independent or dependent on an uncorrelated stimulus.[1]

For our purpose the qualifications are important. One of them has to do with the intensity of the suppressing stimulus. Of five studies discussed by Church, all using shock, three (Azrin, 1956; Beauchamp, 1966; Camp, Raymond, & Church, 1967), showed stronger suppression by pun-

---

[1] This issue is still unsettled. Church writes: "I have recently found conditions under which the suppression produced by the CER [conditioned emotional response] is greater than that produced by discriminative punishment" (personal communication of July 14, 1967).

ishment than by unavoidable shock. Two of these (Beauchamp, 1966; Camp et al., 1967) used rats and only a moderate shock (.24 ma.). Azrin shocked pigeons with 600 volts through a grid; estimating the resistance of the pigeons' feet as 10 megohms (Azrin, 1959), we can safely assume that the current was quite low, even though he coated the feet with graphite paste. The two remaining studies (Estes, 1944, Experiments B, I; Hunt & Brady, 1955), measuring bar pressing by rats, favored neither method of response suppression over the other. Estes compared scheduled shocks with response-produced shocks during extinction; Hunt and Brady compared conditioned suppression by a 3-minute clicker followed by shock (CER method) with discriminated punishment in which all responses during the clicker were shocked. The point is that strong shocks were used in both studies: Estes called his "severe"; Hunt and Brady gave 3.5 ma. This hint of bimodality suggests that the functions relating suppressive effect to intensity are different for response-contingent and noncontingent shocks. As intensity increases, the effect of punishment may increase rapidly at first and then slowly; the curve for uncorrelated shocks may rise more slowly at first, but then more rapidly. On this assumption a weak shock may inhibit a response provided it is contingent upon it: a strong shock may do so even though it is independent of the response. Church (1963) drew the same inference; such a rule could also handle Smart's (1965) results, as noted above, and, if necessary, Wolpe's (1952).

Unfortunately an exception to the rule has already appeared. Hoffman and Fleshler (1965) trained pairs of pigeons to peck a key for food. After a tone had sounded for 2 minutes, a peck by the experimental bird in the next 2 minutes produced a shock and ended the tone. The "yoked" control bird also received the shock whether or not it pecked. Two pairs of birds completed the experiment. A 2-second shock of 1 ma. suppressed pecking in both yoked controls more than in their punished partners; raising the shock to 2 ma. had no greater effect on the controls but brought the punished birds up to their level of performance. These results neatly reverse predictions from the rule just improvised. To retain the rule would demand more assumptions; e.g., that at the lower intensity the effect of punishment extinguished during the first 2 minutes of the tone. The interaction between intensity and contingency is still unknown.

Church's thesis may also have to be qualified with respect to the degree of generalization of suppression. Hunt and Brady (1955) found that bar-pressing in the absence of clicker or shock was more reduced by the CER procedure than by punishment. Moreover, the CER group was more emotionally disturbed, as indicated by freezing and defecation, than the punished group, both in the bar-pressing box and in a separate grill box with clicker alone.

As a final qualification, there is some tentative evidence (Hunt &

Brady, 1955; Hoffman & Fleshler, 1965) that the inhibitory effect of punishment extinguishes more rapidly than that of the same shock given regardless of the response.

These reservations taken together suggest that punishing shock, although it may be more efficient than a noncontingent one in suppressing a particular response, may prove less likely to produce the widespread and persistent behavioral disturbances referred to as experimental neurosis.

The role of stimulus intensity in generalization.   Generalization of inhibitory effects to other situations and responses is an important byproduct of the use of punishment. Students of "experimental neurosis" have reported behavioral disturbances outside of the experimental cage (Dimmick et al., 1939; Lichtenstein, 1950; Masserman, 1943; Masserman & Pechtel, 1953; Wolpe, 1952). An apparent difference in the generalized effects of punishment and conditioned suppression was noted a few paragraphs back.

A factor thought to be important in the generalization of a conditioned response is the intensity of the US, the reinforcing or inhibiting event. Among students of punishment, Honig (1966; Honig & Slivka, 1964) has studied stimulus generalization and demonstrated the development of gradients of response depression. So far, however, no one seems to have investigated generalization as a function of intensity of punishment. We shall therefore have to consider evidence bearing indirectly on the problem.

In appetitive learning the closest analogue is found in studies manipulating strength of drive by deprivation of food. A common presumption is that generalization is increased as drive is strengthened, but so far it lacks solid support. Brown (1942) trained rats to approach a light for food, then measured starting speed to three brightnesses of the light under 1 and 46 hours of deprivation. Rosenbaum (1951) trained rats with food reward to press a bar presented every 60 seconds, then measured response latencies at varying temporal intervals under two degrees of hunger. Both studies showed flatter gradients with higher drive, but there is serious doubt that differences in starting latency at two drive levels are directly comparable. When Brown, in the same experiment, measured strength of pull toward the stimulus lights under 1 and 46 hours of deprivation, he obtained parallel gradients.

Similar discrepancies appear in the results of two studies measuring the pecking rate of pigeons held at different percentages of normal body weight and reinforced on a variable-interval schedule. Jenkins, Pascal, and Walker (1958) trained their birds to peck a key with a lighted spot and tested generalization to other diameters of spot. Thomas and King (1959) trained theirs to a 550 millimicron-lighted key and tested to 10 other wavelengths. Jenkins et al. found that relative gradients of generalization were flatter at 70% body weight than at either 80% or 90%; Thomas and King found the steepest relative gradient at 80%, with the 90% and 70% groups about equal in slope. (In this connection it is interesting that Hoffman and Fleshler [1961] reported results for the effect of hunger on generalization of *conditioned suppression:* birds tested at 70% body weight showed *steeper* gradients than when retested at 80%.) A second disagreement was of greater theoretical interest. Jenkins et al. presented evidence for the hypothesis that drive level exerted its effect by raising or lowering response strength; Thomas and King, however, found none.

Evidently no ready-made rule is available governing the effect of appetitive drive strength on stimulus generalization that might also hold for intensity of punishment. Turning to aversive stimulation we find one pertinent study. Although it is included in Hoffman's paper, let me call it to your attention in the present context. In the course of their extended investigation of conditioned suppression in the pigeon, Hoffman, Fleshler, and Jensen (1963) had completely extinguished the generalized CER to tonal frequencies in five birds. Only a small residual inhibition to the CS remained. At that point the experimenters introduced stress in the form of shocks during time-out periods between tests. The result was to reinstate the entire suppression gradient as it had stood at an earlier stage of extinction, with no appreciable change of shape. Whether more severe stress would flatten the gradient by lifting its wings is unknown.

The role of the consummatory response.   "Punishment," said Solomon (1964, p. 242), "seems to be especially effective in breaking up this class of responses." He went on to ask "why the same punisher might not appear to be as effective when made contingent on an *instrumental* act as contrasted with a consummatory act." Did it "kill the appetite" more effectively when given for eating than for pressing a lever?

The first question to be considered here is whether Solomon's impression is indeed correct. It could easily be produced by the dramatic results of a few experiments in which eating was punished, compared with the relatively prosaic results of many experiments on the punishment of lever pressing or key pecking. But it should be noted that the aim of the former experiments was to produce chaotic behavior, whereas the latter have been looking for orderly functions. So the investigators of experimental neuroses have pitted hunger against strong shocks abruptly delivered, while students of normal behavior often start with weak shocks and gradually increase them. What looks like a difference between consummatory and instrumental responses might be due to differences in procedure.

Studies directly comparing the effects of punishment on the two types of response are rare. One of the few is reported by Church elsewhere in this volume. He trained rats to shuttle between a lever and food cup on opposite walls of a box. One group was shocked for pressing the lever, the other for seizing the pellet. The first group hesitated longer before pressing, and the second before seizing; but the overall rate of responding was reduced more in the first group than the second.

Two factors may limit the generality of this finding: (1) the shock was quite mild (.16 ma. 0.5 sec.); and (2) as Church points out, the shock at the food-cup preceded the chewing and swallowing of the pellet. It may be recalled, however, that Smart (1965) used a strong shock (3.5 ma. 1.0 sec.) and found little difference between cats shocked while opening the food box and cats shocked 1 second after seizing food. Taken together, these results stir doubts of any intrinsic difference between consummatory and instrumental responses in susceptibility to punishment.

There remains the distinct probability, also stressed by Solomon, that much depends on the precise temporal relationship between reward and punishment. Years ago Miller (1944), using assumptions about gradients of approach and avoidance, drew the following two deductions: (1) a shock encountered on the way to a goal will be more effective the earlier it is met; and (2) encountered after the goal is reached, it will be less effective the longer it is delayed.

Although Miller referred to an early experiment as confirmatory, the only published data bearing on these deductions appeared in Feirstein and Miller's (1963) study, undertaken to test a more complex hypothesis. After training to food in a 6-foot alley, one group of nine rats was given a strong 0.5-second shock at the midpoint on each of ten trials; another group received the same shock 5 seconds after making contact with food at the end. The mean number of trials before refusal to run was 5.0 for the center-shocked group, 7.4 for the end-shocked, a barely significant difference. None of the former and four of the latter were still running at the end of ten trials.

By putting together the two deductions in question, one might intuitively predict some such result; neither of them, however, is clearly confirmed. Needed is a third group shocked at the precise moment of contact with food; or better, two groups, one shocked just before, one just after that moment. Shock given just before food contact should be in the best position to become a conditioned stimulus to the consummatory response; i.e., a secondary reinforcer. The opposite arrangement, with shock occurring just *after* food contact, should be optimal for conditioning fear to food-correlated stimuli. Comparing two such groups we should expect a sharp rise in response suppression from the first to the second, provided, of course, that strength of food motivation and intensity of shock were neither too weak nor too strong. The critical moment of transition, as empirically determined, might not exactly coincide with this prediction; Masserman's traumatic stimuli apparently came just before actual contact with food.

Relevant to the discussion is an incidental finding by Lichtenstein (1950) in the course of producing feeding inhibitions in dogs. As previously noted, his regular procedure was to punish his subjects for eating. Three dogs, however, on the first day received 20 shocks simultaneously with the delivery of food; thereafter they were shocked only after they had started to eat. These three dogs took 35, 44, and 103 trials, not counting the first 20, to reach the criterion of feeding inhibition (refusal to eat during three consecutive sessions of 20 trials each); for ten animals punished that did not receive the 20 shocks simultaneously with the delivery of food, the mean number of trials was 7.8, with a median of 2.

It is unlikely that the effect of an aversive stimulus would so hinge on its temporal relation with an instrumental response. The consummatory reaction, according to the mechanism of reward proposed above, has the unique function of providing the incentive that maintains an instrumental sequence. Conditioned to a preceding punisher it may partially vitiate the suppressive effect. Punished in turn, though no more susceptible than an instrumental response, it substitutes fear for reward expectancy, thereby weakening the entire chain. I believe that intensive study of these temporal relations will provide at least a partial answer to Solomon's question.

The Role of Conflict in Drive Induction

The hypothesis that conflict generates drive, repeatedly advanced by Miller (1944, 1959; Miller & Barry, 1960) and assumed in the present formulation, has so far had to depend for acceptance on intuitive appeal. In this final section an attempt will be made to remedy the situation.

How might conflict increase drive? The readiest answer would be by simple addition, assuming that the drives from two needs active at the same time would summate. But in the case of reward and punishment, where one need is appetitive and the other aversive, this assumption is dubious; if summation occurs, it may well be algebraic, or some process of occlusion may reduce the strength of one or both of the competing drives.

A different answer was suggested by Brown and Farber (1951) in their theory of frustration. They held that frustration resulted when an excitatory tendency was opposed either by a competing excitatory tendency (conflict) or by an inhibitory tendency. As an intervening variable in a Hullian framework, frustration in turn contributed both an increment of drive to the excitatory potentials and a drive stimulus to frustration-linked habits.

Amsel (1958, 1962) assigned a similar dual role to frustration as a source of drive and of cues to specific responses. His theory owes much of its substantial influence to the solid bulk of evidence it was proposed to explain. A series of experiments starting with Amsel and Roussel (1952) and culminating, though by no means ending, with Wagner (1959) demonstrated the motivational effect of reward removal. In the typical double-runway experiment rats were trained in two end-to-end sections of a runway with food in both goal boxes. When the rats were then shifted to a schedule of intermittent reward in Goal Box 1, they ran faster to Goal Box 2 on the trials when Goal Box 1 was empty than when it was baited. In Wagner's experiment they also ran faster than a control group never rewarded in Goal Box 1.

In proposing his theory Amsel (1958) explicitly confined it to situations involving the thwarting of a single response tendency. But his exclusion of conflict is open to question (see, for example, Wagner's contribution to this conference). Time out from positive reinforcement has been found to act as punishment under certain conditions (Azrin & Holz, 1966). It could even be argued that conflict is the more generic term, in that nonreward leads to an avoidance incompatible with approach. From this point of view Amsel's concept of frustration drive would become a special case of the drive induced by conflict.

Evidence from the double runway, however, can be generalized only to other situations blocking a single motive. The reason is that in a conflict involving two motives, such as hunger and fear, an increase of drive could be contributed by the second motive. Suppose, for example, that after training rats in a runway to food, an experimenter applied shock in the goal box, resulting, paradoxically, in an increase of running speed. The result could not be safely attributed to conflict drive, since it might be due to fear.

To establish the reality of a conflict drive other than frustration more evidence is needed. In stating the hypothesis Miller (1944, 1959) suggested a way to test it: Place an animal in a recurrent conflict (e.g., a difficult discrimination) and measure the strength of a response that enables it to escape. If the problem induces a drive to escape, the response will be reinforced; conversely, granted that controls are adequate, if the response is learned, a drive to escape conflict can be inferred. Several lines of evidence, including two experiments of this type, will be evaluated.

Conditioned-reflex method.   Pavlov (1927), who is generally held to have originated the study of experimental neuroses, described several methods of producing them in the conditioning laboratory. Dogs of certain types developed severe disturbances when forced to differentiate closely similar stimuli, or to withstand prolonged delays of the unconditioned stimulus, or to respond to positive and negative conditioned stimuli in rapid succession, or when an exceedingly strong stimulus was used; e.g., an electric shock as conditioned stimulus in alimentary conditioning. Most, if not all, of these situations, according to Pavlov, involved a clash of excitatory and inhibitory processes, destroying the balance between them in the cortex.

Gantt and Liddell, on returning from study with Pavlov, also used conditioned-reflex methods to produce pathological behavior. Of the two, Gantt (1943) adhered more closely to Pavlov in methods and interpretations. The long-standing neurosis of his dog Nick started with the attempt to differentiate an ascending from a descending combination of two similar tones. From its onset Nick accepted no food in the experimental compartment *"throughout practically his whole laboratory life"* (p. 69), although the conditioned stimuli and food were presented over 10,000 times. The laboratory task increased his heart rate more than "the presence of real danger" (p. 129); e.g., a clawing cat on his back.

Liddell (1944) and his associates, working with sheep, goats, and pigs as well as dogs, relied on the conditioned flexion reflex to shock. The mild faradic stimulus, however, was considered of minor significance in producing the disorders observed. Difficult discriminations were useful but unnecessary. The important factors, for Liddell, were (1) the self-imposed restriction of movement built in by long training, and (2) the monotonous repetition of an unvarying routine of stimulation. The "compression chamber-like character of the Pavlovian conditioning situation" (p. 399) was revealed when a well-behaved pig, on having the chain loosened around its neck, went into a tantrum.

Dworkin's (1939) findings suggest a similar interpretation. Testing auditory acuity in cats and dogs, he found dogs much more susceptible than cats to emotional breakdowns, a difference he attributed not so much to species as to the conditions of testing: the dogs were harnessed, while the cats were free to move around.

As evidence for a drive-inducing property of conflict the conditioned-reflex method is of limited value. Except for the use of shock as conditioned stimulus with food as unconditioned stimulus, Pavlov's procedures do not involve the simultaneous arousal of two incompatible needs. At the behavioral level the conflict they produce is between two preparatory adjustments: for food and for no food. The evidence of increased tension reported by Pavlov and Gantt, like that of Amsel, refers to the frustration of one motive rather than the clash of two.

Liddell's interpretation leads to the same conclusion. Most "neurotic" animals try to avoid the experimental situation, but are they avoiding the conflict? If Liddell is correct, the desire to escape, opposed by powerful inhibitions, is a cause of conflict rather than its result. The neurosis can be traced to frustration of what Pavlov (1927) called the "freedom reflex."

Discrimination method. At first glance a choice-reaction method seems more appropriate to the definition of conflict than does Pavlovian differentiation with its "Go, No-go" feature. This is not necessarily the case. Karn (1938) described a cat that "blew up" while performing double alternation in a temporal maze. After 231 trials, in the course of which it had mastered the exceedingly difficult problem to a 90% criterion, the cat suddenly became resistant, regressed to an earlier pattern, and presented a picture of increasing distress. This animal's conflict was between two responses, going right and going left, each of which evoked the same conflict, food reward versus closed door; i.e., a kind of "second-order frustration."

Finger's (1941) experiment, by including punishment for errors, comes closer to meeting the requirements of a test of conflict drive in the narrower sense. He used a Lashley jump stand to train rats in a brightness discrimination. A jump to the correct door led to food, while a wrong jump met a locked card and ended in a fall. Comparing easy discriminations with difficult ones, Finger found that when the differences were subthreshold the rats not only took longer to jump but *jumped with more force*. He showed further that two factors, difficulty of discrimination and punishment, contributed to these effects; and that either could produce them independently of the other. The only remaining question is whether the effect of discrimination difficulty was increased in the presence of punishment for errors by more than the effect of punishment itself.

Approach–avoidance method. Sawrey and Weisz (1956) kept rats for 30 days in a grid-floored box with a food platform at one end and a water bottle at the other. The middle third of the grid was cold, but both end sections were charged, so that a rat could eat or drink only by crossing shock. Every 48 hours the shock was turned off for 1 hour and free feeding and drinking were permitted. Six of the nine animals developed stomach ulcers; in five control rats on a 47-hour total-deprivation schedule for 30 days no ulcers were found.

Primarily to see if conflict contributed anything to ulcer formation beyond hunger, thirst, and shock, Sawrey, Conger, and Turrell (1956) carried out a more elaborate study employing nine groups of rats. Group 1 duplicated the conditions of the previous experiment. The cages were so wired that whenever a Group 1 rat was punished for stepping on the charged grid, a free shock was received by four yoked controls represent-

Seward

ing the possible combinations of hunger and thirst. (The other four groups received no shocks.)

Of many possible comparisons, the one that chiefly concerns us is between Group 1, the conflict group, and Group 2, hungry, thirsty, and noncontingently shocked. Group 1 showed a larger percentage of rats with ulcers and a larger mean number of ulcers per rat. After adjustment for covariance with weight loss the remaining difference was barely significant. Insofar as gastric ulcers are associated with high levels of arousal, this evidence implies that conflict between approach and avoidance induces drive.

Two experiments have appeared embodying in essence Miller's proposed method of testing for a drive produced by conflict. Hearst (1963) presented rats with free food on a 1-minute variable-interval schedule (VI-1) and free shocks on a VI-4 schedule, both in the presence of a continuing stimulus (S+). A bar press would turn off S+ and eliminate both rewards and shocks for 5 minutes. Rates of bar pressing were then compared under different shock intensities with and without reward.

If a state of conflict were aversive, the rats were expected to spend less time in S+ when both reward and punishment were scheduled than when it signaled punishment alone. The opposite occurred except at the highest shock intensities, when the two conditions were equal.

In the earlier study, however (Hearst & Sidman, 1961), both food and shock were made contingent on pressing the same bar, food on a VI-1 or -2 schedule, shock on a fixed ratio. Pressing a second bar turned off S+ and interrupted both schedules for a fixed period. Under these conditions three out of ten rats pressed the second bar to escape from reward and punishment together but not from either one alone, tentatively suggesting an aversive function of conflict.

Discussing the difference in outcome, Hearst (1963) pointed out that in the 1963 experiment escape from conflict was necessarily contaminated by escape from punishment, since the same response was required for both. This was not true of the 1961 study, however, since punishment, but not conflict, could be escaped by not pressing the first bar.

The difference might be more simply explained as follows: Making reward and punishment contingent on the same response is virtually an operational definition of conflict, whereas scheduling them independently and noncontingently may make the situation ambivalent, but the element of conflict is removed.

Summary

Conflict is conceived to be a link between exposure to punishment and neurotic behavior. This paper is concerned with the part played by avoidance–avoidance and approach–avoidance conflicts in experimentally produced abnormal behavior in animals.

A pretheory is first outlined, deriving the two types of conflict from suggested mechanisms of reward, punishment, and escape. It is assumed that conflict affects behavior by producing *tension,* a form of aversive drive with inhibitory, excitatory, and reinforcing properties.

To test the usefulness of this approach, typical examples of "experimental neurosis" are considered. The abnormal fixations of Maier's rats are attributed to powerful reinforcement by escape from a severe avoidance–avoidance conflict. The chief question is whether this theory is *adequate* to handle the evidence. In dealing with the phobias of Masserman's cats, illustrating approach–avoidance conflict, the point at issue is whether the conflict is *necessary* to produce the symptoms. Light is sought by consulting the experimental literature on aversive stimulation with reference to response-contingency, generalization, and the consummatory response.

Central to the discussion is the thesis that conflict enhances drive. Frustration-induced drive seems well established, but conflict, as a separable concept, requires independent evidence. Such evidence proves to be both fragmentary and elusive.

REFERENCES

AMSEL, A. The role of frustrative nonreward in noncontinuous reward situations. *Psychological Bulletin,* 1958, **55**, 102–119.

AMSEL, A. Frustrative nonreward in partial reinforcement and discrimination learning: Some recent history and a theoretical extension. *Psychological Review,* 1962, **69**, 306–328.

AMSEL, A., & ROUSSEL, J. Motivational properties of frustration: I. Effect on a running response of the addition of frustration to the motivational complex. *Journal of Experimental Psychology,* 1952, **43**, 363–368.

AZRIN, N. H. Some effects of two intermittent schedules of immediate and non-immediate punishment. *Journal of Psychology,* 1956, **42**, 3–21.

AZRIN, N. H. A technique for delivering shock to pigeons. *Journal of the Experimental Analysis of Behavior,* 1959, **2**, 161–163.

AZRIN, N. H., & HOLZ, W. C. Punishment. In W. K. Honig (Ed.), *Operant behavior: Areas of research and application.* New York: Appleton-Century-Crofts, 1966. Pp. 380–447.

BANKS, R. K. Persistence to continuous punishment following intermittent punishment training. *Journal of Experimental Psychology,* 1966, **71**, 373–377.

BEAUCHAMP, R. A comparison of the degree of suppression following either a discriminative punishment treatment or a conditioned emotional response treatment. Unpublished master's thesis, Brown University, 1966.

BROWN, J. S. The generalization of approach responses as a function of stimulus intensity and strength of motivation. *Journal of Comparative Psychology,* 1942, **33**, 209–226.

BROWN, J. S., & FARBER, I. E. Emotions conceptualized as intervening variables—with suggestions toward a theory of frustration. *Psychological Bulletin,* 1951, **48**, 465–495.

BROWN, R. T., & WAGNER, A. R. Resistance to punishment and extinction following training with shock or nonreinforcement. *Journal of Experimental Psychology,* 1964, **68**, 503–507.

CAMP, D. S., RAYMOND, G. A., & CHURCH, R. M. Temporal relationship between response and punishment. *Journal of Experimental Psychology,* 1967, **74**, 114–123.

CHRISTIE, L. S. The motivation of behavior on the jump stand. Unpublished doctoral dissertation, University of California, Los Angeles, 1951.

CHURCH, R. M. The varied effects of punishment on behavior. *Psychological Review,* 1963, **70**, 369–402.

DIMMICK, F. L., LUDLOW, N., & WHITEMAN, A. A study of "experimental neurosis" in cats. *Journal of Comparative Psychology,* 1939, **28**, 39–43.

DWORKIN, S. Conditioning neuroses in dog and cat. *Psychosomatic Medicine,* 1939, **1**, 388–396.

EGLASH, A. Perception, association, and reasoning in animal fixations. *Psychological Review,* 1951, **58**, 424–434.

ERRETT, W., JR. An experimental study of fixation in rats. Unpublished doctoral dissertation, University of California, Los Angeles, 1948.

ESTES, W. K. An experimental study of punishment. *Psychological Monographs,* 1944, **57** (3, Whole No. 263).

FARBER, I. E. Response fixation under anxiety and non-anxiety conditions. *Journal of Experimental Psychology,* 1948, **38**, 111–131.

FEIRSTEIN, A. R., & MILLER, N. E. Learning to resist pain and fear: Effects of electric shock before versus after reaching goal. *Journal of Comparative and Physiological Psychology,* 1963, **56**, 797–800.

FELDMAN, R. S. The role of primary drive reduction in fixations. *Psychological Review,* 1957, **64**, 85–90.

FINGER, F. W. Quantitative studies of "conflict": I. Variations in latency and strength of the rat's response in a discrimination-jumping situation. *Journal of Comparative Psychology,* 1941, **31**, 97–127.

FOWLER, H., FOWLER, D. E. & DEMBER, W. The influence of reward on alternation behavior. *Journal of Comparative and Physiological Psychology,* 1959, **52**, 220–224.

GANTT, W. H. Experimental basis for neurotic behavior. *Psychosomatic Medicine Monographs,* 1944, **3** (3–4).

HEARST, E. Escape from a stimulus associated with both reward and punishment. *Journal of Comparative and Physiological Psychology,* 1963, **56**, 1027–1031.

HEARST, E., & SIDMAN, M. Some behavioral effects of a concurrently positive and negative stimulus. *Journal of the Experimental Analysis of Behavior,* 1961, **4**, 251–256.

HOFFMAN, H. S., FLESHLER, M. Stimulus factors in aversive controls: The generalization of conditioned suppression. *Journal of the Experimental Analysis of Behavior,* 1961, **4**, 371–378.

HOFFMAN, H. S., & FLESHLER, M. Stimulus aspects of aversive controls: The effects of response contingent shocks. *Journal of the Experimental Analysis of Behavior,* 1965, **8**, 89–96.

HOFFMAN, H. S., FLESHLER, M., & JENSEN, P. Stimulus aspects of aversive controls: The retention of conditioned suppression. *Journal of the Experimental Analysis of Behavior,* 1963, **6**, 575–583.

HONIG, W. K. The role of discrimination training in the generalization of punishment. *Journal of the Experimental Analysis of Behavior,* 1966, **9**, 377–384.

HONIG, W. K., & SLIVKA, R. M. Stimulus generalization of the effects of punishment. *Journal of the Experimental Analysis of Behavior,* 1964, **7**, 21–25.

HULL, C. L. The goal-gradient hypothesis applied to some "field-force" problems in the behavior of young children. *Psychological Review,* 1938, **45**, 271–299.

HULL, C. L. *A behavior system.* New Haven: Yale University Press, 1952.

HUNT, H. F., & BRADY, J. V. Some effects of punishment and intercurrent "anxiety" on a simple operant. *Journal of Comparative and Physiological Psychology,* 1955, **48**, 305–310.

JACOBSEN, E., & SKAARUP, Y. Experimental induction of conflict behavior in cats: Its use in pharmacological investigations. *Acta Pharmacologica et Toxicologica,* 1955, **11**, 117–124.

JENKINS, W. O., PASCAL, G. R., & WALKER, R. W., JR. Deprivation and generalization. *Journal of Experimental Psychology,* 1958, **56**, 274–277.

KARN, H. W. A case of experimentally induced neurosis in the cat. *Journal of Experimental Psychology,* 1938, **22**, 589–592.

KNOPFELMACHER, F. Fixations, position stereotypes, and their relation to the degree and pattern of stress. *Quarterly Journal of Experimental Psychology,* 1953, **5**, 108–127; 150–158.

LEWIN, K. *A dynamic theory of personality.* (Tr. D. K. Adams & K. E. Zener.) New York: McGraw-Hill, 1935.

LICHTENSTEIN, P. E. Studies of anxiety. I. The production of feeding inhibitions in dogs. *Journal of Comparative and Physiological Psychology,* 1950, **43**, 16–29.

LIDDELL, H. S. Conditioned reflex method and experimental neurosis. In J. McV. Hunt (Ed.), *Personality and the behavior disorders.* Vol. I. New York: Ronald Press, 1944.

MAIER, N. R. F. *Frustration, the study of behavior without a goal.* New York: McGraw-Hill, 1949.

MAIER, N. R. F. Frustration theory: Restatement and extension. *Psychological Review,* 1956, **63**, 370–388.

MAIER, N. R. F., & ELLEN, P. Can the anxiety-reduction theory explain abnormal fixations? *Psychological Review,* 1951, **58**, 435–445.

MAIER, N. R. F., & ELLEN, P. The integrative value of concepts in frustration theory. *Journal of Consulting Psychology,* 1959, **23**, 195–206.

MAIER, N. R. F., & KLEE, J. B. Studies of abnormal behavior in the rat. XII. The pattern of punishment and its relation to abnormal fixations. *Journal of Experimental Psychology,* 1943, **32**, 377–398.

MARTIN, B. Reward and punishment associated with the same goal response: A factor in the learning of motives. *Psychological Bulletin,* 1963, **60**, 441–451.

MASSERMAN, J. H. *Behavior and neurosis.* Chicago: University of Chicago Press, 1943.

MASSERMAN, J. H., & PECHTEL, C. Neuroses in monkeys: A preliminary report of experimental observations. *Annals of the New York Academy of Sciences,* 1953, **56**, 253–265.

MILLER, N. E. Experimental studies of conflict. In J. McV. Hunt (Ed.), *Personality and the behavior disorders.* Vol. I. New York: Ronald Press, 1944. Pp. 431–465.

MILLER, N. E. Liberalization of basic S-R concepts: Extensions to conflict behavior, motivation, and social learning. In S. Koch (Ed.), *Psychology: A study of a science.* Vol. 2. New York: McGraw-Hill, 1959. Pp. 196–292.

MILLER, N. E. Some reflections on the law of effect produce a new alternative to drive reduction. In M. R. Jones (Ed.), *Nebraska symposium on motivation 1963.* Lincoln: University of Nebraska Press, 1963. Pp. 65–112.

MILLER, N. E., & BARRY, H., III. Motivational effects of drugs: Methods which illustrate some general problems in psychopharmacology. *Psychopharmacologia,* 1960, **1**, 169–199.

MOWRER, O. H. *Learning theory and personality dynamics.* New York: Ronald Press, 1950.

MOWRER, O. H. *Learning theory and behavior.* New York: Wiley, 1960.

MURPHY, G. *Human potentialities.* New York: Basic Books, 1958.

PAVLOV, I. P. *Conditioned reflexes.* (Tr. G. V. Anrep.) London: Oxford University Press, 1927. (Reprinted, New York: Dover, 1960)

ROSENBAUM, G. Temporal gradients of response strength with two levels of motivation. *Journal of Experimental Psychology,* 1951, **41**, 261–267.

RUSSELL, R. W. The comparative study of "conflict" and "experimental neurosis." *British Journal of Psychology,* 1950, **41**, 95–108.

SAWREY, W. L., CONGER, J. J., & TURRELL, E. S. An experimental investigation of the role of psychological factors in the production of gastric ulcers in rats. *Journal of Comparative and Physiological Psychology,* 1956, **49**, 457–461.

SAWREY, W. L., & WEISZ, J. D. An experimental method of producing gastric ulcers. *Journal of Comparative and Physiological Psychology,* 1956, **49**, 269–270.

SHEFFIELD, F. D. Relation between classical conditioning and instrumental learning. In W. F. Prokasy (Ed.), *Classical conditioning.* New York: Appleton-Century-Crofts, 1965. Pp. 302–322.

SMART, R. G. Conflict and conditioned aversive stimuli in the development of experimental neuroses. *Canadian Journal of Psychology,* 1965, **19**, 208–223.

SOLOMON, R. L. Punishment. *American Psychologist,* 1964, **19**, 239–253.

SPENCE, K. W. *Behavior theory and conditioning.* New Haven: Yale University Press, 1956.

THOMAS, D. R., & KING, R. A. Stimulus generalization as a function of level of motivation. *Journal of Experimental Psychology,* 1959, **57**, 323–328.

TOLMAN, E. C. Cognitive maps in rats and men. *Psychological Review,* 1948, **55**, 189–208.

WAGNER, A. R. The role of reinforcement and nonreinforcement in an "apparent frustration effect." *Journal of Experimental Psychology,* 1959, **57**, 130–136.

WATSON, R. E. Experimentally induced conflict in cats. *Psychosomatic Medicine,* 1954, **16,** 340–347.

WILCOXIN, H. C. "Abnormal fixation" and learning. *Journal of Experimental Psychology,* 1952, 44, 324–333.

WOLPE, J. Experimental neuroses as learned behavior. *British Journal of Psychology,* 1952, **43,** 243–268.

WOLPE, J. Learning theory and "abnormal fixations." *Psychological Review,* 1953, **60,** 111–116.

YATES, A. J. *Frustration and conflict.* New York: Wiley, 1962.

14

Psychoneurotic Defenses (Including Deception) as Punishment-Avoidance Strategies

O. Hobart Mowrer

UNIVERSITY OF ILLINOIS

The overt acts of living organisms characteristically have two types of consequences. The first of these is purely "informative" or "cognitive" and consists of sensations inherently associated with a response as such. This type of effect, or feedback, may involve both interoceptive and exteroceptive stimuli, i.e., stimuli (e.g., proprioceptive and tactile) produced within the organism's own body by a given response and stimuli of a visual, auditory, or olfactory nature which also impinge (through the distance receptors) upon the organism as a result of its behavior. In contrast to these interoceptive and exteroceptive stimuli, the second type of effect which is produced by the behavior of living organisms involves events which are referred to as pleasurable or painful, rewarding or punishing, reinforcing or aversive.

In this way circumstances are provided which are normally sufficient for the adaptive modifications of behavior called habit formation and response inhibition. If a given response occurs and is soon followed by reward, the stimuli inherently associated with the response acquire the capacity to arouse positive secondary reinforcement or hope and thus facilitate the subsequent occurrence of this response. This is the phenomenon of habit formation. If, on the other hand, a given response occurs and is followed by punishment, the stimuli inherently associated therewith acquire the capacity to arouse fear, and this tends to prevent the subsequent occurrence of the response.

There may be some question as to whether the mechanism of positive and negative behavior modification is precisely that which is here postulated, but the empirical facts are clear: responses which are followed by reward tend to be strengthened, fixated, or, as Thorndike was fond of saying, "stamped-in"; whereas responses which are followed by aversive

stimuli or punishment tend to be weakened, eliminated, "stamped-out."
These facts are subsumed under what is known as the empirical law of
effect. The precise way in which these two types of learning (habit
formation and inhibition) are mediated is perhaps debatable. But the
hypothesis that these changes occur because of the type of conditioning
here suggested seems to be as reasonable as any other and will be accepted as the basis for the ensuing discussion.[1]

However, for completeness of the analysis, it should be noted that,
in addition to habit formation and response inhibition, there are two
other types of learning. As already indicated, habit formation and inhibition are presumed to occur when response-produced stimuli are
followed by reward and punishment, respectively. Now we must ask:
What happens when independent stimuli are followed by reward or by
noxious events? Here are the circumstances in which so-called classical
conditioning occurs. That is to say, independent stimuli (i.e., stimuli
which occur and impinge upon an organism without reference to anything the organism has done), when associated with reward, acquire the
capacity to produce a positive, appetitive reaction (such as salivation)
and to arouse the emotion of hope; whereas such stimuli, when associated
with an aversive noxious event, acquire the capacity to elicit the reaction
of fear. When a stimulus acquires the capacity to arouse hope, the
organism, if properly motivated, tries to get more of it, which often
involves *approach behavior;* and when a stimulus or situation acquires
the capacity to arouse fear, the organism usually tries to get less of it
(cf. Holt, 1931), which may involve flight or other activity which eliminates or lessens the stimulus or stimulus situation which signals the
noxious event. When an organism, in seeking to escape from a danger
signal, also averts the impending aversive stimulus, it is customary to
speak of avoidance learning.

---

[1] The foregoing analysis, like all abstractions, is an oversimplification. Particularly
among human beings, but even to some extent in lower animals, one sees instances
where punishment does not inhibit and reward does not reinforce. For example, among
delinquents and criminals a studied attempt is often made not to be influenced or
changed either by reward or punishment, if meted out by the official representatives
of a social order with which the recipient does not identify. Punishment, stoically
borne, may in fact be a source of prestige in the deviator's own subculture and may
confirm him in his existing way of life. In the religious context it has not been un-
common in the past for individuals, in their loyalty to an ideal, to die rather than
recant. Much depends, obviously, upon the individual's "point of view." If reward or
punishment, approval or disapproval, comes from a "significant other," the effect is
often dramatically effective; but if the person exerting approval or disapproval is an
"outgrouper," the recipient may take pride in stoutly resisting both. Thus the empirical
law of effect is, at best, only a first, general approximation to the facts, which may be
complicated in many ways. Obviously, circumstances alter cases. Here we are concerned with generalizations which hold true under many, but not necessarily all, conditions. The same actions on the part of others may, in one situation, be accepted as
"education," in another interpreted as "brain washing."

Active and Passive Avoidance Learning

The type of learning just described can usefully be designated as active avoidance learning, to distinguish it from response inhibition, which can be designated as passive avoidance learning. If an independent stimulus or signal occurs and is followed by a noxious event, there is a tendency for the organism, when the signal recurs, to do something which will avert the noxious event. That is to say, the fear which has become conditioned to the danger signal motivates the subject to try to eliminate or escape from the signal; and in so doing, the organism may engage in behavior which will prevent the impingement of the noxious event or trauma. Hence, the expression, active avoidance learning.

On the other hand, when punishment is associated with something which the organism itself does, i.e., with response-produced rather than independent stimuli, the fear that gets conditioned to the response-produced stimuli results in conflict which, under certain conditions, produces response inhibition. This sequence of events can appropriately be called passive avoidance learning. Here the subject learns to avoid the noxious-conditioned stimulus by not making the response which would otherwise occur; whereas in active avoidance learning, the subject acquires the capacity to make a response to the danger signal (and thus avoid punishment) which it would otherwise not make.

Although of less immediate relevance in the present paper, a similar distinction can be made between the results of associating a reward with independent stimuli and the results of associating a reward with response-produced stimuli. In these two instances, we speak of approach learning and habit formation, respectively.

All four of the types of learning which have just been described are shown in systematic relation to one another in Table 14–1.

TABLE 14–1.　Schematic Representation of the Four Basic Types of Learning Which Are Produced as a Result of the Various Possible Combinations of the Two Kinds of Reinforcement (Reward and Noxious Event) and Two Types of Stimulation (Response-Dependent and Independent)

	Response-Dependent Stimuli	Independent Stimuli
Reward	Habit	Approach Behavior
Noxious Event	Passive Avoidance Behavior	Active Avoidance Behavior

In other words, when a reward is response-contingent, it results in habit formation; and when a noxious stimulus is response contingent, it results in inhibition. On the other hand, when a reward is contingent upon the occurrence of an external signal, approach behavior is learned; and when a noxious event is contingent upon the occurrence of a signal, active avoidance behavior is learned.

Avoidance Strategies: Primary and Secondary

All four of the types of learning designted in Table 14–1 have been extensively and systematically studied in the animal laboratory and can also be observed in animals under natural conditions. In this paper we are primarily concerned with certain related but more complicated types of learning and ensuing behaviors which are common at the human level but either absent or present only in rudimentary form in subhuman species.

In one sense, both active and passive avoidance learning can be appropriately referred to as avoidance strategies. In the one case, by making a response which it otherwise would not make and, in the other case, by not making a response which it otherwise would make, an organism may be said to be avoiding punishment. In both instances there is an element of loss or sacrifice, and hence conflict. In the case of passive avoidance learning, the organism, in avoiding punishment, also avoids, i.e., forfeits, the satisfaction which a particular response would have brought if it had not been inhibited; and in the case of active avoidance learning, the organism, in responding to a danger signal or command, avoids or forsakes the state of comfortable inactivity which the enforced action at least temporarily interrupts.[2]

---

[2] The foregoing considerations also provide a dynamic for the extinction of both active and passive avoidance learning. Habits and conditioned appetitive respon es extinguish, because, in both instances, *hope* (secondary reinforcement) has become conditioned to response-dependent and independent stimuli, respectively, and when the expected (hoped for) positive reinforcement is not forthcoming, a negative condition of *disappointment* or *frustration* is generated, which then, with repeated trials, gradually counterconditions the hope and reverses, i.e., extinguishes, the prior learning (Mowrer, 1960a, Chapter 7). Sometimes it has been assumed that there is no comparable process in passive and active avoidance learning. In other words, it has been occasionally postulated that these types of learning have a kind of "functional autonomy" and fail to extinguish when the original unconditioned aversive stimulus (punishment) is no longer operative. This assumption has been especially common in the attempts of some writers to account for the failure of maladaptive (pathological) responses to extinguish spontaneously. The considerations advanced above provide grounds for believing that in all instances of passive and active avoidance learning there is a constant (though perhaps slight) pressure or incentive for living organisms to abandon both active and passive avoidance responses, in the absence of the original aversive reinforcement. If this supposition is correct, then some other type of explanation is needed to account for persistent maladjustive behavior (Mowrer, 1960a, Chapter 11).

The situations with which we are here primarily concerned are those in which living organisms try to find, in the one case, a way in which they can go ahead and perform a forbidden act without getting punished or, in the other case, a way in which they may refrain from performing a required response and not get punished. Activities of this kind will be called secondary avoidance responses or defenses, in contradistinction to the primary avoidance responses previously described. In other words, secondary avoidance responses make, or are at least designed to make, primary avoidance responses unnecessary.

Let me give two very simple laboratory illustrations of secondary defense mechanisms. Imagine a Skinner box in which there is the usual small bar, depression of which will produce a pellet of food in a nearby food tray. Let us further suppose that there is also a slightly elevated platform nearby, depression of which will eliminate all illumination within the apparatus for a period of 10 seconds. When a hungry rat is put into the apparatus, it soon learns to press the bar as a means of obtaining food.

The experimenter now decides to inhibit the bar-pressing response by means of an electric shock administered to the subject through the grill which constitutes the floor of the apparatus. While making the next bar response, the rat is shocked. After a brief pause, the rat goes to the food tray and eats, and then returns, somewhat hesitantly to the bar, and presently presses it. Again there is shock. This time the rat is obviously disturbed and delays somewhat longer in eating the available food. Now there is a much longer delay in approaching the lever; and after the third shock, the bar-pressing response is, to all intents and purposes, inhibited. Here is a clear case of passive avoidance learning; and we may also designate it as primary rather than secondary.

Although the rat no longer presses the food lever, it is not entirely inactive and eventually steps on the platform with sufficient force to complete an electrical contact which activates a relay, which turns off the lights for 10 seconds. Circumstances are now changed, bar pressing now seems possibly less dangerous; and presently, in the absence of illumination, the rat again presses the bar, obtains food, and eats. However, since the experimenter does not see the rat perform the forbidden act (and presumably has no other way of knowing that it has occurred), punishment is not forthcoming. Thus heartened or reassured, the rat may now try pressing the bar while the light is on, only to be shocked again. Now a process of discrimination sets in, as a result of which the rat learns that it can safely perform, in the dark (conditions S+), an act which results in punishment if performed openly (under conditions S−). Thus we may say that the subject has developed a secondary defense or avoidance strategy, one which circumvents the aversive reinforcement not by means of the primary strategy of response inhibition but by the strategy of resorting to the cloak of invisibility provided by stepping on the platform.

In a state of nature animals display a wide variety of secondary avoidance strategies, i.e., of managing to perform dangerous but desirable responses (especially in the realm of sex and hunger), without getting caught. They make use of natural cover such as bushes and grass; they move stealthily and are very alert; and they often depend upon the invisibility afforded by darkness, camouflage, protective coloration, mimicry, smoke screens (as in the squid), etc.

The other type of secondary avoidance to which allusion has been made develops in situations calling for active rather than passive primary avoidance. Here is an illustration. Suppose that a rat has learned to shuttle in a Miller–Mowrer apparatus in response to a conditioned stimulus or warning signal such as the sound of a buzzer. Also let us assume that a response to the buzzer not only prevents the occurrence of aversive reinforcement but also terminates the danger signal itself. Further suppose that the apparatus operates automatically and that at a given juncture a small panel becomes available in each end of the apparatus, depression of which will have the same effect on the inanimate programmer as does the shuttling response. In short, by pushing one of the two panels the rat "fools" the programmer into thinking that it has shuttled. And since panel pressing is an easier, less-effortful response than is shuttling, the rat is motivated to resort to such behavior. This type of secondary avoidance behavior may be called "Type-II" to distinguish it from the "Type-I" secondary avoidance exemplified in the first illustration.

Secondary Avoidance Behavior at the Human Level

So far the discussion has been largely couched in the language of the animal learning laboratory. It is, however, immediately obvious that all the paradigms which have been considered here can also be observed in human beings, plus some additional ones. Violations of rules which call for passive or for active avoidance behaviors are commonly referred to at the human level as, respectively, sins of commission and sins of omission. And in both instances, secondary avoidance behavior is not uncommonly manifested. If a rule calls for passive avoidance behavior (i.e., response inhibition) and the subject goes on and performs the forbidden act, this is known as a sin of commission; and often some device, such as hiding, will be used by the subject to conceal the tabooed act. If on the other hand, a rule calls for active avoidance behavior and the subject does not perform the prescribed act, this is known as a sin of omission; and in human beings as well as in lower animals various steps are often taken to make it appear that the prescribed action has indeed occurred. For human beings still another type of secondary defense is possible: namely, verbal denial (in the case of sins of commission) and false affirmation (in the case of sins of omission). In the 1930's one often heard the slang expression, "Let's don't and say we did." Here a sin of omission is covered by verbal deception. And as a corollary, one might say: "Let's do and say we didn't." This would involve the use of verbal deception to cover or protect a sin of commission.

Why, we may now ask, are human beings tempted, despite much social pressure to the contrary, to engage in secondary avoidance behavior in the form of deception? The answer is: because it provides a means of resolving conflict, or at least substantially diminishing it, just as hiding or disguise does. Conflict, as already pointed out, is generated when an organism is prevented under threat of punishment from making some highly motivated response, or when an organism, comfortable and unmotivated, is required to make a response which it otherwise would not make. Thus, the incentive or temptation for human beings to engage in deception is very strong in both instances; and so great and altogether obvious are the advantages of falsehood in many situations that experimentation with this type of behavior can be expected to occur in most children, without either example or encouragement on the part of others.

I recall seeing a little girl (about 2 years old) break a glass tumbler in the presence of her doting and indulgent grandmother from whom the child apparently anticipated no very strong reaction. But 2 or 3 seconds later the child's mother appeared; and, on a sudden inspiration, the child exclaimed, "Gammy boke." This was a very clever—although by adult standards dishonorable—response; for if Gammy (the grandmother) had in fact broken the glass, not only would the little girl herself avoid punishment, the grandmother would also probably be quite safe since the mother would hardly venture to chastize her for breaking, as it happened, one of her own glasses. So far as could be determined, this child had never observed lying on the part of others; and her own ingenious response was apparently an innovation or invention which most bright youngsters probably also hit upon and try out. But just as the representation of reality through language has enormous advantages to human beings, especially as regards their intricate social interaction and common life, so also is misrepresentation (lying) something that must be systematically and powerfully discouraged. This means that when most people resort to deception as a secondary avoidance strategy, they may reduce or eliminate the original conflict only to be plagued by another one: namely, conflict between the guilt associated with the deception as such and fear of the punishment which would ensue if the deception were admitted or refuted by evidence to the contrary.

Because the meaning of the term guilt, as it is used in common speech, is often ambiguous, an attempt will here be made to define it operationally in a way which is consistent with the general tenor of the foregoing discussion. Guilt, we shall assume, is a species of fear; but its defining characteristics are not always precise. The situation as regards passive avoidance learning (response inhibition) is relatively clear; i.e., guilt is the fear experienced by the subject between the performance of a tabooed act and the occurrence of punishment. Guilt is thus distinguished from temptation fear, which occurs before the performance of a tabooed act, and which, if strong enough, prevents the occurrence of the act. (Since living organisms are ordinarily punished after the occurrence of a proscribed act, what is learned first and most strongly is guilt, as just defined; and temptation fear is a generalized form of guilt, i.e., it is guilt which "moves forward" and occurs to a stimulus situation which in some ways resembles, but is by no means identical with, the stimulus situation prevailing after the act when punishment is applied. Just as guilt is an anticipation of punishment, so also is temptation fear an anticipation of guilt, unless punishment has occurred just as the act is being initiated.)

But what is the situation where active avoidance learning is involved? Here a command occurs, arouses fear, and the correct response occurs. Is this merely fear or a form of guilt? Perhaps the concept of guilt is not pertinent in active avoidance–learning situations. Yet we often hear human beings say, "I will feel guilty if I don't do thus and so." Perhaps the fear aroused by a command (danger signal) goes over into guilt when reaction is delayed beyond some point indeterminant in time.

It is obvious that at the human level the circumstances attending both passive and active avoidance learning are more complex than those prevailing in laboratory animals. In human beings, the observation of both restraints and obligations is in some sense voluntary, or at least more so than it is in the case of confined animals (or in the case of human beings who are in bondage, enslaved). Citizens in a free society give assent to the rules (contracts) which govern their conduct and guilt in this situation is almost certainly different, in significant ways, from what it is in the case of either unfree animals or human beings. But it would take use well beyond the scope of this paper to explore this distinction at all adequately (cf. Mowrer, 1960b, Chapter 10).

Against this conceptual backdrop, we are now in a position to suggest a hypothesis concerning the origin and nature of the human condition ambiguously known as neurosis. The two major contemporary theories of personality disorder are: (1) that they are constitional, organic, inherited (Kraepelin); and (2) that they are the residue of traumatic experience which the individual, as a child, has had at the hands of others

(Freud). A third possibility is that, in at least some as yet undetermined percentage of cases, the difficulty is not a neurosis in either of the foregoing senses, but an identity crisis (Erikson) precipitated by the practice of misrepresenting oneself to others, as a secondary avoidance measure, and thus becoming increasingly insecure, fearful, anxious, guilty, lest the fabric of deception be breached and the individual's true identity revealed: hence the apt expression, identity crisis.[3]

Secondary Avoidance Strategies (Hiding and Deception) as Primal Pathogenic Acts

In writing on the origin of neurotic symptoms, Freud often characterized repression as the primal pathogenic act. By this he meant that repression provides the basis for subsequent anxiety (which involves a threatened return of the repressed); and anxiety is always the negative motivating force in symptom formation (the other positive force being an instinct or desire of some sort). Here we shall consider the possibility that in many, perhaps all, so-called neuroses and functional psychoses, the primal pathogenic act is not repression but rather suppression, deception, misrepresentation which is engaged in either as a means of denying the occurrence of a wrong act or of falsely affirming the occurrence of some good act. Excluding from consideration the possible role of constitutional or genetic determinants, let us examine and compare the two remaining hypotheses; namely, that of Freud which implies a crippling false guilt as the basis of neurosis, and the real-guilt theory which has just been sketched.

Figure 14-1 (left panel) represents in highly schematic form the psychoanalytic theory of neurosis. According to Freud, the essence of neurosis and functional psychoses is an emotional disturbance or disorder which has been produced by inappropriate, irrational behavior on the part of others (parents, teachers, husbands, wives, employers, etc.), or perhaps by sheer accidents (impersonal trauma). The resulting abnormal emotions are thus inappropriate, disproportionate, and crippling and the efforts made by therapists, like those of patients, are designed

---

[3] Although systematic deception is found in many instances of psychopathology, the concept of "identity crisis" is not here advanced as a universal explanation of personality disorder. Maier, Seligman, & Solomon (Chapter 10 of this volume) have stressed "helplessness" as a source of self-defeating behavior in animals, with possible implications for human psychopathology. Cf. also the Adlerian conception of "discouragement" and lack of confidence (Dreikurs, 1950). According to Adlerian writers, there are three other major sources of interpersonal disturbance: the desire for attention, for power, and for revenge. It remains to be determined how the concept of identity crisis contrasts with or supplements the four-fold nosology of Adler.

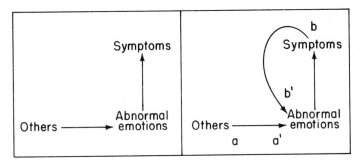

FIG. 14-1.

to lessen or eliminate these unrealistic affective responses (see Fig. 14-1, right panel)· Freud characterized neurotic symptoms as attempts on the part of the individual himself to bind his anxiety (b → b'). And therapists, working at the psychological level, commonly try to reduce or eliminate anxiety in the patient by means of reassurance, advice, suggestion, extinction, counterconditioning, or transference (a → a').[4]

Although psychoanalytic theory has been endlessly elaborated, its underlying assumption is extremely simple: namely, that persons who are destined to become neurotic (develop anxiety) have been inappropriately punished (either by other persons or accidently); and psychotherapy in this frame of reference is simply an attempt to help the individual get rid of the resulting fears, which have not spontaneously extinguished as might have been expected (Mowrer, 1948).

The alternative theory which is being explored here is quite different, and somewhat more intricate. If, in connection with the psychoanalytic approach, attention is drawn to improper, antisocial actions in which the neurotic individual has himself engaged, these actions are often dismissed as merely symptomatic of deep, underlying emotional difficulties and conflicts; and it is argued that they, like other symptoms, will disappear when, and only when, the emotional problems are resolved. Thus, improper behavior on the part of the neurotic individual is regarded as a consequence of his neurosis and in no way its cause. The cause of the neurosis is to be sought in terms of what has been done to the suffering individual, not anything which he himself has done.

The hypothesis with which we are here concerned is schematically represented in Fig. 14-2 (left panel). Here it is assumed that the neurotic

4 There are, of course, many other forms of therapy, including medication, electroconvulsive shock, brain surgery, etc. But they are not included in the above discussion because their use is usually predicated on the assumption that the states which they are designed to change are constitutional, organic, physiological. Without attempting to judge the validity or scope of such approaches, we shall exempt them from discussion. Here we are concerned solely with psychological processes, as they are involved in both causation and correction.

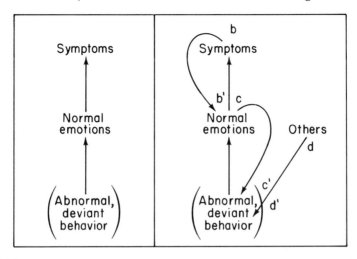

FIG. 14-2.

individual is very largely responsible for the emotional difficulties in which he finds himself and that he has to carry much, perhaps most, of the responsibility for getting out of them. Here abnormal, deviant behavior is taken as the primary datum, which results quite naturally and normally in emotional disturbance; and symptoms (Fig. 14-2, right panel), in this context, are the efforts which the individual makes to relieve himself of tension and distress (b → b') which would be better turned into efforts to bring change in the individual's own life style (c → c'). The therapeutic efforts on the part of others, in this context, consist of their drawing attention to the neurotic's misconduct (d → d') and trying to get his efforts transformed from symptoms to constructive personal change. This involves, first of all, inducing the neurotic individual to take down the barrier of secrecy and deception (see the large parentheses) and then make restitution for the unworthy acts which have thus been kept hidden and denied.

If the concealment of misdeeds is indeed the primal pathogenic act, then confession thereof is the first major step in therapy and change. However, in the past our conception of confession, disclosure, and openness has probably been too circumscribed. Elsewhere (Mowrer, 1967b, pp. 19–20) I have ventured the following observation on this score:

> It now seems that one probably ought to be quite as open about future plans, intentions, "designs," as he is with respect to past mistakes: and if one is meticulous with respect to the former, it follows that there will be little need for the latter. Characteristically, we drift into unfortunate, self-defeating actions which then have to be protected by secrecy, precisely because we have *not shared our intentions* with others and received their counsel and thus been

strengthened in our struggle with temptation. In I.T. groups I hope we shall henceforth put no less emphasis on being open about courses of action which are *merely contemplated* than upon actions which have been performed secretly and thus become a source of guilt and moral apprehension.

In a culture as competitive as ours, it is often regarded as prudent and indeed clever to keep one's plans for future action "to yourself," lest rivals learn of them and act in such a way as to "best" you. But anyone in a position of heavy financial, managerial, or political responsibility usually has at least a few "trusted advisers," with whom he can discuss problems and possible ways of dealing with them. This is a time-tested way of "avoiding mistakes." Here is one of the major functions of a "board of directors" and consultants: to review the plans of executives and help them to be as sure as possible that these plans are practicable and wise. In our private lives, we all probably ought to have a similar "sounding board." In an earlier day, the extended family often performed such a service; and among many primitive peoples, important individual action was taken only after tribal review and approval. The "freedom" which people in our society today have to make decisions without consultation is, it seems, by no means an unmixed blessing.

Neurosis as Learning Not to Learn

In the preceding section of this paper, the hypothesis is set forth that the condition commonly known as neurosis is one in which a human being has engaged in deviant behavior (involving either sins of omission or sins of commission) and has then tried to hide the fact of his deviance by deception. Here deception is called a secondary avoidance response, which is designed to forestall punishment of the individual for deviant behavior. Since the individual is supposed to learn and observe the rules of his society or reference group, secondary defenses can be seen as an instance of learning not to learn; that is, the learning of certain behavior (deception) which will prevent the learning of other behavior (i.e., response inhibition or active response to commands).[5] In a volume which

---

[5] As the conception of psychopathology which is delineated in this paper developed, it was very easy to drop into the practice of using terms such as "hypocrisy," "guilt," "sin," "confession," "restitution," etc. There was, in fact, no other established and widely understood vocabulary in which to refer to the underlying phenomenon. And when one digs back into the history of the church, it becomes clear that Integrity Therapy (I.T.) principles are not new but have, in bygone centuries, been well understood and put into effective practice by religious groups (Mowrer, 1961, 1964, 1966a, 1967a). Accordingly, clergymen were among the first to express interest in I.T.; and this approach has found some of its most effective application and clearest articulation among members of this profession (e.g., Anderson, 1964; Drakeford, 1967). There is, however, a basic difficulty: Because I have often used religious or quasi-religious language, my writings have claimed the attention of clergymen; but since my work is basically naturalistic rather than supernaturalistic in orientation, it has also been the target of much concern and criticism. This fundamental ambivalence on the part of clergymen is reflected, for example, in a book by Klassen (1966).

was published in 1953 [Mowrer (1953a), pp. 146–147], I have previously
set forth this argument in somewhat different terms:

> The Freudian conception of repression holds that this process is the intra-
> psychic equivalent of earlier interpersonal events. The parent apprehends the
> child gratifying tabooed impulses and punishes the child. The parent, being
> more powerful than the child, is thus able to inhibit disapproved behavior.
> But the process does not stop here. Since the child has in some measure identi-
> fied with the parent, i.e., has incorporated ("introjected") many parental values
> into the superego, there is an internal repetition of this drama: the tabooed
> impulses appear in consciousness, are disapproved by the superego, and the ego
> (being poorly developed and inferior to the powerful superego), is compelled
> to reject these impulses and deny them further access to consciousness. Social
> intimidation is thus assumed to be the forerunner of psychic repression, which,
> in turn, sets the stage for subsequent neurotic developments.

> Little attention has been given to another possibility, one which is equally
> logical and indeed clinically better supported. It, too, starts with the observa-
> tion that parents punish their children for displaying certain forms of behavior.
> But there is an immediate divergence. Instead of assuming that parental dis-
> cipline always has the the intended effect of blocking the behavior toward which
> it is directed, the alternative possibility is that very commonly—perhaps uni-
> formly in situations which are to lead to neurosis—parental discipline has the
> effect of merely teaching the child to be *evasive and deceitful!* Gratification of
> the forbidden impulses may in this way be restricted but not entirely stopped,
> and each surreptitious indulgence will now be followed, not only by fear of dis-
> covery, but also by the knowledge that to the first act of disobedience and de-
> fiance has been added a second one of duplicity. Most children are taught that
> they must be truthful and overt with their parents; and if they thus compound
> their disobedience with dishonesty they are likely to have guilt that is all but
> intolerable. Conscience becomes a constant tormenter in such situations, and
> one of two consequences is likely to ensue: the child will either bring his
> suffering to an end by confessing and taking whatever chastisement may be in
> store for him, or he may further extend the strategy of duplicity and social
> isolation by an attempt to deceive the internal representative of parental au-
> thority. This takes the form either of rationalization or repression—but repres-
> sion that is turned toward the conscience, in the interest of preserving the
> possibility of continued impulse gratification, rather than toward the id, as
> Freudian theory would hold.

> Let us examine this point of view in the light of two-factor learning theory.
> We see at once that problem-solving activity which takes the form of social
> duplicity and conscious deception and repression amounts to an attack upon
> the sign-learning (conditioning) functions. Parents are the source of much social
> conditioning, and conscience is the reservoir of that conditioning. Self-protective
> strategies of the kind just described are thus designed to neutralize the second
> form of learning in large and important areas of the individual's life. To put
> the matter somewhat enigmatically: the neurotic is an individual who has
> *learned how not to learn.* What such a statement means is that the neurotic is
> a person in whom solution learning is directed *against* sign learning, instead

of these two forms of learning functioning harmoniously and complementing each other. E. B. Holt once remarked that conditioning, or associative learning, "brought mind into being." It is hardly surprising, therefore, that the individual who systematically attempts to keep this mechanism from operating commonly complains of "poor memory" and of the feeling that he is *losing* his mind. Perhaps a more apt formulation is that he is *destroying* his mind, or at least an essential part of it! [6]

Also in 1953 I published a paper entitled "Some philosophical problems in mental disorder and its treatment." In that paper [Mowrer (1953b), pp. 121–122], I dealt with the phenomenon of "learning not to learn" in the following manner:

Let us now sketch another way other than the Freudian one of looking at neurosis and the therapeutic challenge it offers. Here [see Fig. 14–3] we start, as does Freud, with some drive or desire, D_1, instigating some form of gratification, R_1. Again, with Freud, we assume that this behavior elicits punishment, D_2, and that the fear ($R_2:D_3$) produced by this punishment becomes connected, through conditioning, to the incidental stimulation, S_1, which R_1 produces.

But at this point our views diverge sharply from those of Freud. We assume that the individual headed for neurotic troubles is one who, when impulse and fear are in conflict, tries to resolve this conflict, not by controlling the impulse, but instead by *evasion and deception*. The fear, we assume, results in behavior, R_3, which instead of blocking R_1 tries to prevent punishment, D_2, from occurring; and this strategy commonly involves secrecy and falsehood.

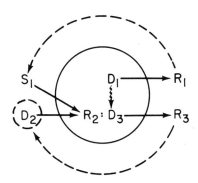

FIG. 14–3.

Thus far the only types of neurotic defenses which have been considered are concealment and deception. While these are probably of greatest importance and frequency of occurrence, it should be noted that there are other related strategies. One of these is the display of

[6] From: O. Hobart Mowrer, "Neurosis, Psychotherapy, and Two-Factor Learning Theory," in O. Hobart Mowrer (Ed.), *Psychotherapy: Theory and Research.* Copyright 1953 by The Ronald Press Company, New York, and reproduced by permission.

anger and belligerence. Instead of protecting their deviant behavior by secrecy, some persons use a strategy of defiance: "Don't you dare try to tell me what to do or not do. Leave me alone or I'll teach you a thing or two." Then there are others who use the plea of extraordinary sensitivity: "Surely you wouldn't want to do or say anything that would hurt my feelings, would you? If you do, I won't like you any more." Other neurotics simply withdraw from human contact and interaction; this can be done physically, as in the case of hermits, and it can also be done by means of behavior which is so bizarre that it causes others to withdraw (Anonymous, 1958; Mainord, 1962). This enumeration is not meant to be exhaustive, but merely illustrative of interpersonal defenses other than concealment and deception which can be and are commonly employed.

Obviously, the notion that psychoneurotic defenses commonly (perhaps always) involve punishment-avoidance strategies is by no means a new one; it was, as we have now seen, explicitly formulated more than 15 years ago. Slowly, during this period, a body of theory and practice which is based on this hypothesis has grown up, the most concise description of which is embodied in a recent book by Drakeford (1967), entitled *Integrity Therapy*. And various writers (e.g., Smith, 1966) have reported favorable results in the use of clinical procedures based on I.T. principles. Therefore, it is now relevant to ask: Are there any hard data to support the hypothesis that neurosis is a state of surreptitious gratification rather than one of overextended inhibition and impulse control? In a monograph entitled "New evidence concerning the nature of psychopathology" (Mowrer, 1968) I have reviewed some 12 or 15 studies which bear upon this issue. The program of Alcoholics Anonymous and of Synanon Foundation (Casriel, 1962; Yablonsky, 1965) and Daytop Village, Inc. (Shelly & Bassin, 1965; Casriel & Deitch, 1966) for drug addicts incorporates, and the success of these organizations tends to validate, the principles here delineated.

Integrity Therapy and Learning Theory

Recently it has repeatedly been suggested that an attempt be made to restate the tenets of Integrity Therapy in the language of learning theory. For a variety of reasons I, personally, have been reluctant to do this. Some 30 years ago (in the late 1930's and early 1940's), I was very much involved in an enterprise of this kind which did not turn out particularly well (Mowrer, 1950). The difficulty, at least in part, was that the clinical concepts which we then had were largely psychoanalytic; and if one starts with a questionable or invalid system (which psychonanalysis now increasingly seems to be), mere translation into another scientific vernacular does not make the original system any truer or more useful. However, as evidence in support of the I.T. conception of neurosis has grown, it has become increasingly feasible to recast it in learning theory terms (Mowrer, 1965, 1966b). Moreover, the kind of learning theory which is today available (cf. Mowrer, 1960a, 1960b) lends itself particularly well, as earlier sections of this paper indicate, to the restatement of I.T. principles.

Although "crazy" and "stupid" are often used more or less synonymously in common language, Dollard and Miller (1950) were among the first scientific writers to make use of the second of these terms in a more or less technical way. For them neurotic stupidity arises when a person fails to discriminate between conditions which once existed (in childhood) but no longer do. Here failure of discrimination is used as more or less equivalent (or at least parallel) to the psychoanalytic conception of repression. In both instances, insight is the remedy, the antidote for stupidity.

In the present paper, a different mechanism has been stressed; namely, that of deviant actions, protected by deception, which then give rise (if corrective action is not taken) to chronic and often incapacitating guilt. This, too, involves a form of stupidity. On an earlier page we have labeled such behavior as learning not to learn. Mainord (1962) makes the related point that deception and other defenses also prevent the individual who manifests them from having access to information that could otherwise be of much value. Lacking this information, the neurotic individual is cognitively and socially disadvantaged, "stupid."

But there is yet a third reason which has been identified as a cause of neurotic stupidity. In 1945 Mowrer and Ullman (1945, p. 61) published a paper entitled "Time as a determinant of integrative learning." Here the problem was identified as follows:

It is a familiar fact that living organisms sometimes manifest behavior which is chronically nonintegrative, i.e., behavior which is consistently more punishing than rewarding. This fact constitutes a major theoretical paradox and is the outstanding characteristic of neurosis and criminality. The present paper attempts to show that the factor of *time* is of special significance in this connection and that only by taking it into explicit account can the problem of persistent nonintegrative behavior be satisfactorily defined and a hopeful way to its theoretical solution be indicated.

And the paper (Mowrer & Ullman, 1945, p. 87) concludes thus:

An experimental paradigm with rats as subjects shows that the tendency for a given action to be perpetuated or inhibited is influenced not only by the nature of the consequences ("effects") of that action but also by the *temporal order* or *timing* of these consequences. Thus, if an immediate consequence is slightly rewarding, it may outweigh a greater but more remote punishing consequence. Living organisms which are not skilled in the use of *symbols* are severely limited in their capacity to resolve behavioral dilemmas of this kind and may, as a result, continue indefinitely to manifest so-called nonintegrative behavior. But by introducing the time element (and the notion of reinforcement "gradients"), it is possible for us to escape from the dilemma which such behavior presents from a theoretical standpoint.

Interestingly, the use of secrecy and deception to conceal and protect deviant behavior can be derived from the foregoing principles. Characteristically, secrecy and deception permit the occurrence of some pleasurable deviant act (or lack of action) which is immediate and pleasurable, and the disadvantages of secrecy and deception usually become apparent only at a much later date—so much later, in fact, that the connection is not always seen. Let us consider, for example, a neurotic defense other than deception, namely, alcoholism. The relief of anxiety afforded by alcohol is certainly not as great as its total negative consequences. But the fact that the relief is immediate and the hangovers, loss of job, and other seriously negative consequences come later, often leads to an addiction which the individual has great difficulty in breaking. If the hangover came immediately after drinking and relief was postponed, there would probably be few alcoholics. Likewise, if the negative results of deception came immediately and its rewards later, there would probably also be very few habitual liars and correspondingly fewer neurotics.

REFERENCES

ANDERSON, P. A. The implication and challenge of O. Hobart Mowrer's position for the church and its ministry. *Minister's Quarterly*, 1964, **20**, 1–8.

ANONYMOUS. A new theory of schizophrenia. *Journal of Abnormal and Social Psychology*, 1958, **57**, 226–236.

CASRIEL, D. *So fair a house: The story of Synanon.* Englewood Cliffs, N. J.: Prentice-Hall, 1962.

CASRIEL, D., & DEITCH, D. New success in permanent cure of narcotics addicts. *The Physician's Panorama*, 1966, 4, 4–12.

DOLLARD, J., & MILLER, N. E. *Personality and psychotherapy.* New York: McGraw-Hill, 1950.

DRAKEFORD, J. W. *Integrity therapy.* Nashville, Tenn.: Broadman Press, 1967.

DREIKURS, R. *Fundamentals of Adlerian psychology.* Chicago: Alfred Adler Institute, 1950.

GOUGH, H. G. *Manual for the California Psychological Inventory.* Palo Alto, Calif.: Consulting Psychologists' Press, 1960.

HOLT, E. B. *Animal drive and the learning process.* New York: Holt, 1931.

KLASSEN, W. *The forgiving community.* Philadelphia, Pa.: Westminster Press, 1966.

MAINORD, W. A. A therapy. *Research Bulletin*, Mental Health Research Institute, Ft. Stilacoom, Washington, 1962, **2**, 85–92.

MOWRER, O. H. Learning theory and the neurotic paradox. *American Journal of Orthopsychiatry,* 1948, **18,** 571–610.

MOWRER, O. H. *Learning theory and personality dynamics.* New York: Ronald Press, 1950.

MOWRER, O. H. Neurosis, psychotherapy, and two-factor learning theory. In O. H. Mowrer (Ed.), *Psychotherapy: —Theory and Research.* New York: Ronald Press, 1953. Pp. 140–149. (a)

MOWRER, O. H. Some philosophical problems in mental disorder and its treatment. *Harvard Educational Review,* 1953, **23,** 117–127. (b)

MOWRER, O. H. *Learning theory and behavior.* New York: Wiley, 1960. (a)

MOWRER, O. H. *Learning theory and the symbolic processes.* New York: Wiley, 1960. (b)

MOWRER, O. H. *The crisis in psychiatry and religion.* Princeton, N. J.: Van Nostrand, 1961.

MOWRER, O. H. *The new group therapy.* Princeton, N. J.: Van Nostrand, 1964.

MOWRER, O. H. Learning theory and behavior therapy. In B. B. Wolman (Ed.), *Handbook of clinical psychology.* New York: McGraw-Hill, 1965. Pp. 242–276.

MOWRER, O. H. *Abnormal reactions or actions?* (An autobiographical answer). Dubuque, Iowa: Wm. C. Brown, 1966. (a)

MOWRER, O. H. The behavior therapies, with special reference to modeling and imitation. *American Journal of Psychotherapy,* 1966, **22,** 439–461. (b)

MOWRER, O. H. Christianity and psychoanalysis: Is a new synthesis needed? In J. C. Feaver & W. Horosz (Eds.), *Religion in philosophical and cultural perspective.* Princeton, N. J.: Van Nostrand, 1967. Pp. 368–413. (a)

MOWRER, O. H. Unpublished manuscript, 1967. (b)

MOWRER, O. H. New evidence concerning the nature of psychopathology. In M. J. Feldman (Ed.), *Studies in psychotherapy and behavioral change.* Buffalo, N.Y.: Unversity of Buffalo Press, 1968.

MOWRER, O. H., & ULLMAN, A. D. Time as a determinant in integrative learning. *Psychological Review,* 1945, **52,** 61–90.

SHELLY, J. A., & BASSIN, A. Daytop Lodge—A new treatment approach for drug addicts. *Corrective Psychiatry,* 1965, **11,** 186–195.

SMITH, V. H. Identity crisis in conversion hysteria with implications for integrity therapy. *Psychotherapy: Theory, Research and Service,* 1966, **3,** 120–124.

YABLONSKY, L. *The tunnel back: Synanon.* New York: Macmillan, 1965.

15

Factors Affecting Self-Punitive Locomotor Behavior[1]

Judson S. Brown
UNIVERSITY OF IOWA

Several relatively recent experiments (e.g., Gwinn, 1949; Whiteis, 1956; Brown, Martin, & Morrow, 1964; Martin & Melvin, 1964; Melvin, 1964; Melvin, Athey, & Heasley, 1965) support the contention that a normally aversive stimulus, if introduced under special conditions during the extinction of a learned response, may speed up responding and prolong extinction. These studies stem from a serendipitous observation by the writer, who noted that rats trained to escape shock in a straight alley by running to a nonelectrified region at one end would continue to do so for many trials after the shock had been disconnected from the starting area but not from an intermediate segment. Mowrer (1947), who was the first to report this observation and to sense its significance, characterized it as an instance of the kinds of viciously circular processes (Horney, 1937) attending the compulsive behavior of the neurotic. Mowrer also provided an insightful theoretical interpretation of the phenomenon which involved the suppositions that the behavior of leaving a safe area was motivated by fear, that fear was strengthened by punishment's onset, and that fear reduction reinforced the locomotor activity that led to punishment. Since then the term vicious-circle behavior has been applied with increasing frequency to such observations, though the labels self-punitive and masochisticlike have also gained some currency.

Although punishment has tended to facilitate performance during extinction in some investigations, in others, in which somewhat different procedures have been followed, the more commonplace inhibitory effect has been obtained. It is the purpose of this review to examine in detail

[1] Incidental expenses incurred in the preparation of the manuscript were defrayed by Grant MH 11734-03 from the National Institutes of Health to Judson S. Brown. The author is indebted to Dr. Eileen M. Beier for a critically helpful reading of the manuscript, to Philip J. Van Bruggen for bibliographic help, and to Mrs. Blanche Knox and Janice Campbell for skillful secretarial assistance.

the procedures associated with these contradictory outcomes with the aim of increasing our understanding of conditions essential to obtaining the vicious-circle effect. In order to keep the task within manageable limits it has been necessary to exclude studies involving the punishment of wheel-turning and lever-pressing avoidance and escape. An excellent summary of much of this material has been provided recently by Azrin and Holz (1966).

Punished Extinction Following Escape Training

Inasmuch as the earliest observations of persisting self-punitive behavior involved shock-escape training followed by what would have been called regular extinction trials had punishment not been present, we begin with studies in which this procedure was employed.

The first systematic study (Gwinn, 1949) was specifically designed to show that an aversive stimulus facilitates rather than inhibits acts motivated by fear whenever the response to the punishing stimulus is compatible with the act that is presumably punished. Rats were first trained (18 trials) to traverse a circular eight-section runway and to jump out of the eighth segment to escape a 60-volt shock. Some of them were then given regular shock-free extinction trials whereas others encountered shock in the sixth and seventh segments only. Therefore, the shocked rats were being punished for responding during extinction. Gwinn's theoretical expectations were confirmed since, under these conditions, the animals often ran forward rather than backward when shock was encountered. Indeed, the shocked subjects ran faster than the non-shocked controls and took a greater number of trails to reach the extinction criterion (taking longer than 10 seconds to traverse the first five sections of the runway). Moreover, of the punished subjects, those receiving 120-volt shocks persisted longer and ran faster than those given 60-volt shocks. This argues against the view that the punishment facilitated performance simply because it increased the similarity of the extinction to the acquisition conditions. Clearly a 120-volt shock during extinction is less like the 60-volt acquisition shock than a 60-volt punishment. The fact that the presence of visually distinctive cues in the alley segments where punishment was administered failed to eliminate the self-punitive (facilitative) outcome also runs counter to expectations derived from similarity or discrimination interpretations. Gwinn's use of a rather lenient extinction criterion of 10 seconds may have been a key factor in his results. As is indicated below, estimates of persistence in these situations vary with the severity of the criterion. It should also be noted that punishment produced inhibitory as well as facilitatory effects since all animals eventually extinguished and some exhibited conflictlike vacillatory movements.

Moyer (1957) used a short, wide, grid-floored, two-compartment apparatus fitted with a small, grid-floored goal box at one end near the corner. Ten trials of escape training were followed immediately by punished and nonpunished extinction trials for separate groups. The rats in the punished group were required to traverse shock in the half of the apparatus adjacent to the goal box in order to reach it. The extinction criterion was one failure to enter the goal box within 2 minutes. The intertrial interval during both acquisition and extinction was 10 seconds. The shocked group required 105 trials on the average to meet the extinction criterion, but the nonshock group extinguished in only 41 trials. While this difference was not significant statistically, the punished subjects failed to extinguish faster than the nonpunished subjects. Punishment, by the usual definition, is supposed to hasten extinction; when it does not, the result merits special attention. The course of extinction for the two groups was similar save that on the last trial before the criterial trial the shock group was running significantly faster than the nonshock group. Moyer concluded that shock during extinction tended to inhibit the goal-running response rather than facilitate it, but the number of trials to extinction and running speeds all favored the opposite conclusion. The only basis for concluding that shock was inhibitory was that the shocked rats showed less spontaneous recovery than the nonshocked controls on a retest.

Seward and Raskin (1960) have reported a group of five experiments in none of which punishment produced a strong facilitative effect. Their fourth study is of interest here since it involved procedures similar to Gwinn's. Immediately after 20 massed, escape-training trials in a three-section straight alley with a 190-volt shock (through 150K ohms) one group of 3-month-old albino rats was extinguished without shock, a second with a shock in the middle segment on 50% of the trials, and a third with shock in the middle section on all trials. The intertrial interval in all cases was 30 seconds (spent in the goal box) plus the time required to traverse the runway. The animals that were shocked on 100% of the trials extinguished significantly more rapidly than those shocked on none or on 50%, but the latter rats were not significantly different from the nonpunished controls. This constitutes another instance in which punishment failed to perform its expected inhibitory function. Some evidence for the facilitative effects of punishment was provided by a comparison of the running times of the three groups over the last five trials before the extinction criterion was met. On those trials the shocked groups ran significantly faster than the control group. The shocked subjects, however, tended to extinguish precipitously, whereas those given no shock slowed down more gradually. This difference in the behavior of punished and nonpunished animals has been frequently observed, and may, in conjunction with the extinction criterion, be of major significance in producing the vicious-circle effect.

Seward and Raskin's failure to replicate Gwinn's findings may have been due primarily to their use of a much stronger shock (190 volts through 150K ohms as compared with 60 or 120 volts through 250K ohms), which would be more likely to evoke backing up or stopping, to their adoption of a slightly more stringent criterion (two 10-second trials in succession rather than one), and/or to the fact that their rats could not leap completely out of the alley into an escape cage as could Gwinn's.

Strong support for the expectation that punishment may, under certain conditions, facilitate extinction performance has been provided by Brown, Martin, and Morrow (1964). Initially, hooded rats were trained with a moderately aversive shock (60–70 volts through 10K ohms) to escape from a light gray, grid-floored, straight alley into a smooth-

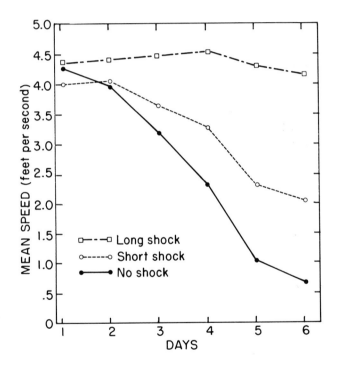

FIG. 15–1.   Mean running speeds of rats receiving shock throughout the entire 6-foot runway (long shock), in the final 2-foot segment (short shock), and at no place in the alley (no shock). These data were derived from running times in the first 2-foot segment. Ten extinction trials were given each day. There were 16 subjects in each group.

From: J. S. Brown, R. C. Martin, & M. W. Morrow, "Self-Punitive Behavior in the Rat: Facilitative Effects of Punishment on Resistance to Extinction," *Journal of Comparative and Physiological Psychology,* **57**, 1964, Fig. 3, p. 131. Copyright 1964 by the American Psychological Association and reproduced by permission.

floored, large, black goal box. Three separate subgroups were then extinguished with shock absent from the start box but present throughout the 6-foot alley, or with shock in the last 2 feet only, or with no shock at all. In the first of two studies, punishment neither accelerated nor retarded extinction. Slightly modified procedures in a second experiment, however, yielded results that unequivocally favored the shocked groups relative to the nonshocked controls. Figure 15–1, reproduced from this study, shows that subjects given the long (6-foot) shock ran substantially faster than animals shocked in only the last 2-foot segment, and these, in turn, maintained a higher running speed than rats that were never punished. The number of animals meeting the extinction criterion of one failure to enter the goal box within 60 seconds was one in the long-shock group, six in the short-shock group, and eleven in the no-shock group. When the data were plotted to indicate speeds in different segments of the runway, it became clear that the long-shock animals maintained a relatively constant high speed throughout the 6-foot space, the nonshocked controls tended to slow down as the goal box was neared, and the short-shock rats tended to speed up as the to-be-encountered shock was neared. These data are shown in Fig. 15–2. The authors' suggestions as to the kind of conditions that might favor finding a facilitative effect of punishment included (1) the gradual reduction of shock in the starting section of the alley during the transition from escape to punished extinction, (2) the initial establishment of a rather strong escape response, and (3) relatively moderate punishment during extinction. In addition (4) the use of a smooth-floored goal box, differing in size and color from the alley, and a unique, two-level, trap-door-floored start box might have been beneficial. With respect to these conditions, it was assumed that the progressive shock reduction (over trials) would facilitate the transition from shock to no shock giving the animals a better opportunity to learn to run to the start-box cues alone. Both vigorous escape response and moderate shock would be expected to reduce the likelihood that the onset of shock would evoke reactions incompatible with running. The distinctive goal box would be expected to increase the probability that fear would be promptly reduced following the crossing of the electrified section and that running would thereby be more powerfully reinforced. Being dropped from the upper level of the starting box may have provided unusually salient external and proprioceptive stimuli to which both running and fear could have become strongly conditioned.

The major findings of the Brown, Martin, and Morrow investigation were quickly confirmed in other experiments. Martin and Melvin (1964) and Melvin, Athey, and Heasley (1965), in studies discussed in more detail below, found that shock near the start box was more efficacious than shock near the goal in maintaining self-punitive run-

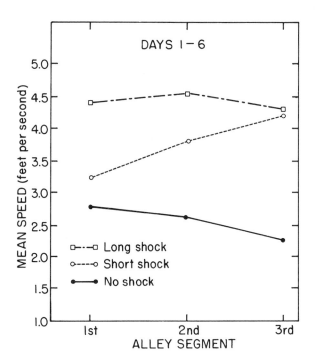

FIG. 15–2.   Mean running speeds exhibited by the three groups in each of the 2-foot segments of the alley. These data indicate that the three groups differed with respect to whether they tended to speed up or slow down in traversing the runway. There were 16 subjects in each group.

From: J. S. Brown, R. C. Martin, & M. W. Morrow, "Self-Punitive Behavior in the Rat: Facilitative Effects of Punishment on Resistance to Extinction," *Journal of Comparative and Physiological Psychology,* **57**, 1964, Fig. 5, p. 132. Copyright 1964 by the American Psychological Association and reproduced by permission.

ning. Martin (1964) reported that shock during extinction facilitated performance save when it was substantially more intense than the shock employed during the initial escape training. And Brown, Anderson, and Weiss (1965) showed that the self-punitive effect could be obtained even when both acquisition and extinction conditions were massed.

Melvin (1964) manipulated percentages of shock trials during the acquisition of escape learning and during punished extinction. He also examined the factor of similarity of percentages of shock trials during training and extinction. Shock was administered on 33, 67, or 100% of the trials during initial escape training and was present in the final 4 feet of the 6-foot runway on 0, 33, 67, or 100% of the trials during extinction. As is evident from Fig. 15–3, groups shocked on all extinction trials extinguished significantly less quickly than subjects given no shock,

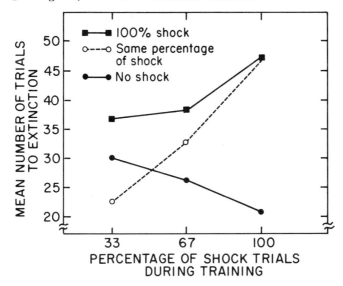

FIG. 15–3.   Mean number of trials to extinction for separate groups of rats given shock on 33, 67, or 100% of their escape-training trials and then tested with the identical percentages of shock in the runway, or with shock on all trials, or with no shock.

From: K. B. Melvin, "Escape Learning and 'Vicious-Circle' Behavior as a Function of Percentage of Reinforcement," *Journal of Comparative and Physiological Psychology,* **58**, 1964, Fig. 1, p. 249. Copyright 1964 by the American Psychological Association and reproduced by permission.

regardless of the percentage of training trials on which shock had previously occurred. Moreover, groups trained under 33% and 67% shock schedules initially and then shifted to 100% were more resistant to extiction than groups maintained on their original schedules. This argues against the view that the similarity of the acquisition and extinction conditions is necessarily the most potent factor controlling extinction (Church, 1963). Further evidence against such an hypothesis was provided by the finding that the 100–100 animals resisted extinction better than the 67–67 group, and these in turn, better than the 33–33 group. As Melvin notes, if maintaining the integrity of the acquisition conditions during extinction were of paramount importance, all three of these groups should have extinguished at an equal rate. That they extinguished in an order paralleling the percentage of shocks during extinction is consistent with expectations derived from Mowrer's theory (1947) and with the findings of Brown, Martin, and Morrow (1964). The three identically trained control groups given no shock (lower curve in Fig. 15–3) extinguished in a reverse order. Martin and Moon (1967) found that rats receiving 33% punishment during extinction continued to run as long as animals given 100% punishment even though both groups were trained under a continuous reinforcement schedule. Once again this would not be an expectation stemming from any simple discrimination hypothesis. Both shocked groups showed greater resistance to extinction than nonshocked controls, again confirming the vicious-circle finding.

At about the time these experiments were reported, however, Seward, King, Chow, and Shiflett (1965) described a study in which shock intensity was systematically varied during the acquisition and extinction of an escape response in a short straight runway. The outcome provided little support for the expectation that punishment can increase resistance to extinction. Nevertheless, 14 of their subjects ran into and across a 215-volt shock (this was the strongest value they used) for more than 40 trials and 12 animals ran to the limit of 60 trials. Moreover, the running-time data were consistent with those of earlier studies since the punished subjects that did not extinguish ran faster than comparable controls. One respect in which this study differed from others was that the shock was turned on throughout the entire alley (when the rats during punished extinction had traversed the first 33 inches of the 53-inch runway) and remained on until the rats had reached the goal box. In experiments involving shock of fixed location and extent, the animal can escape shock by a very slight backward movement at the edge of the shock zone. But the procedure of Seward et al. should have increased resistance to extinction, not the reverse, since their animals should have been punished for backing up. Hence their failure to find facilitation can hardly be attributed to this arrangement. The use by Seward et al. of relatively old albinos may have been a critical factor, but we have no solid basis for this supposition beyond the knowledge that albinos seem to learn wheel-turning avoidance less readily than do hooded rats (Anderson & Nakamura, 1964). Moreover, the thrust of this argument is blunted by the fact that their nonshock controls resisted extinction as well as hooded rats in other somewhat comparable experiments. Aside then from the fact that the shock intensity was not built up gradually during the transition phase from acquisition to extinction (and it is by no means certain that this is essential) we are left without substantial clues as to the reasons for this failure.

In all of the foregoing experiments, shock-escape training was followed by punished extinction, but shock was administered, variously, near the goal box, in the middle of the alley, and throughout the alley. It is of some interest, therefore, to ask whether the position of the shock in the alley and its location within the behavior sequence are of substantial significance.

An unpublished study by Brown, Horsfall, and Van Bruggen (1965) illustrates the problem and the methodology. Specifically, the experiment was slanted toward the question of whether the location of a 1-foot-long electrified zone in a runway would materially affect self-punitive behavior. Following shock-escape training by methods similar to those used by Brown, Martin, and Morrow (1964), the 84 animals were divided into four subgroups of equal size. Three groups designated the near-, middle-, and far-shock groups were destined to be shocked during extinction in the first foot-long segment of the 6-foot runway, in the middle 1-foot, and in the last 1-foot section, respectively. The fourth group was never shocked. Ten trials were devoted to progressive reductions in the intensity of shock in all parts of the runway for the no-shock animals and in all parts save the appropriate 1-foot segment for the to-be-shocked rats. Thereafter, the shocked subjects always encountered a 45-volt shock (through 10K ohms) at the designated spot whereas the no-shock subjects found none.

The median running speeds of the four groups during 60 punished and nonpunished extinction trials are shown in Fig. 15–4. Here it is apparent that the three shocked groups tended to run at a higher speed than the nonshocked controls throughout the course of extinction, an outcome that replicates the basic masochisticlike results reported pre-

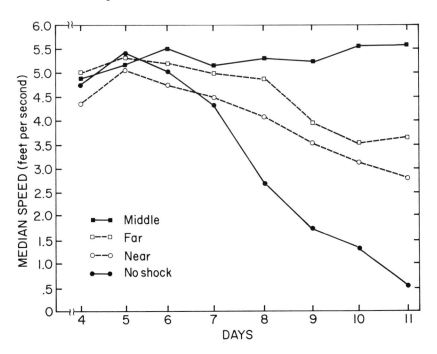

FIG. 15–4.   Runway performance of rats during extinction when a 2-foot segment was electrified either near the start box, in the middle, or far from the start box (near goal box) of the runway. The no-shock subjects were not shocked at any point. (After Brown, Horsfall, & Van Bruggen, 1965)

viously. This figure also shows that the middle-shock group failed to exhibit any speed decrement in 50 trials and was considerably better than the far group. This latter group, in turn was better than the near group, but not significantly. A multivariate analysis of these findings provided statistical support for the visually apparent differences in the figure. More specifically, the days effect, the position-of-shock effect, and the interaction of the two were all highly significant.

Location of shock in the alley thus proved to be a variable of major significance in the self-punitive situation. While the data just presented indicate a substantial superiority in resistance to extinction for the middle-shock group, this superiority diminished when the means were examined and in one of the several replications of the experiment, the far group actually proved to be slightly better than the middle-shock group. Moreover, investigations in other laboratories have also produced somewhat discrepant results, indicating that the question of which location provides optimal facilitative effects is in need of further study. For example, Martin and Melvin (1964) found that shock in an 8-inch zone adjacent to the start box of a 4-foot alley produced greater resistance to extinction and faster running than shock of the same extent adjacent to the goal box. Although the near (immediate) shock group's performance differed markedly from that of a far-shock (delayed) group and from that of a nonshock group, the interaction of trials by groups was not significant. Subsequently, Melvin, Athey, and Heasley (1965) again found that shock in the first foot of their runway led to faster alley speeds as well as to greater resistance to extinction than shock in the final 1-foot segment. However, the most recent studies by Melvin and Stenmark (1968) and Melvin and Bender (1968) indicate that punishment near the middle of the alley is more facilitative than punishment near the goal box. This is consistent with the conclusions of the Brown, Horsfall, and Van Bruggen (1965) experiment, but direct comparisons are hazardous since the investigations of Melvin and his associates involved avoidance training rather than escape. A more complete examination of those studies is included in the next section on punished extinction following avoidance training.

Readily available theoretical interpretations of the probable effects of variations in shock location generate different predictions. If emphasis were placed on the fact that punishment for starting to run is more immediate the nearer its position to the start box, it would be predicted that the near-shock group would extinguish most quickly, followed in order by the middle- and far-shock animals. But in this situation the delay-of-punishment variable is confounded with the length of the response sequence being punished. Shock following several component responses in a sequence may be more inhibitory, in its overall effects, in spite of the delay relative to the beginning of the chain, than a more immediate shock which is preceded by only one or two response units. If the location (delay) of the shock is seen as contributing importantly to the maintenance of conditioned fear then the near (immediate) shock might lead to the greatest resistance to extinction since its usual time of onset following a rat's release from the start box might correspond to the optimal CS–US interval for fear conditioning. But with high running speeds, near shock may result in too short a CS–US interval and the middle- or even the far-shock condition could emerge as the optimum. For the first 3 days, all four groups in the Brown, Horsfall, and Van Bruggen study ran at the same speeds and hence did not differ with respect to duration of exposure to alley cues in the absence of shock. Consequently, degree of extinction attributable to such exposure would be equal across groups. Whether fear extinguishes faster when the CS (e.g., stimulus properties of the alley) extends beyond (in time and space) the US, as in the near-shock condition, or precedes the US, as in the far-shock procedure, is uncertain. Evidently, neither a conditioned-fear interpretation nor a delay-of-punishment conception provides un-equivocal predictions as to the expected outcome of variations in shock position. The conditioned-fear view tends to support the expectation that near-shock will prolong the course of extinction more than far-shock, whereas the punishment-delay principle predicts the reverse outcome. Perhaps the two mutually opposed processes result in the middle-shock's relative superiority to both near- and far-shock conditions. Interpretations are further complicated by the fact that the location of shock offset also varies with shock position so that degree of delay-of-reinforcement must also be considered.

The generality of the original paradigm has recently been extended by Melvin and Martin (1966) who used either a loud buzzer (100 db re .0002 dynes/cm^2) or shock (60 volts, 10K ohms) as the aversive stimulus during escape training and then tested for resistance to extinction with shock, buzzer, or nothing present in the alley. As may be seen from Fig. 15–5, shock was more effective than the buzzer as an aversive stimulus during original training, but both groups learned. The subjects in the two subgroups that were extinguished with shock (Bz-Sk and Sk-Sk), which was presented for 0.3 second as soon as they entered the alley, resisted extinction significantly better than other groups receiving either a buzzer or nothing during extinction. Of these two groups, however, the one trained to escape the buzzer (i.e., Bz-Sk) was substantially better than the one trained with shock (Sk-Sk), in spite of the fact that the shift from acquisition to extinction conditions was more extreme for the former group than for the latter. All of the nine rats in the Bz-Sk group and eight of nine in the Sk-Sk group ran to the limit of 100 trials. The group trained with shock and punished during extinction by means of the buzzer (Sk-Bz) resisted extinction significantly better than a group

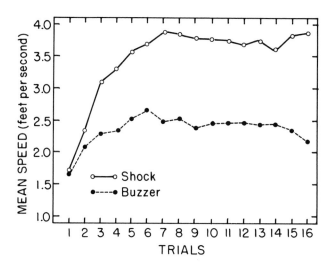

FIG. 15–5.   Mean running speeds of rats in a 4–foot runway to escape an electric shock or a loud buzzer during 16 acquisition training trials. There were 27 subjects in each group.

From: K. B. Melvin & R. C. Martin. "Facilitative Effects of Two Modes of Punishment on Resistance to Extinction," *Journal of Comparative and Physiological Psychology,* **62**, 1966, Fig. 1, p. 492. Copyright 1966 by the American Psychological Association and reproduced by permission.

given no punishment during extinction, but the group trained and extinguished with the buzzer (Bz-Bz) did not differ from the buzzer-trained group given regular extinction (Bz-RE). Alley speeds during extinction, shown in Fig. 15–6, provided additional evidence for the facilitative effect of punishment; the Bz-Sk group proved to be significantly faster than the Sk-Sk group, and both of these groups ran more swiftly than others. The animals in the Bz-Sk group ran faster during punished extinction than during acquisition and showed evidence of new learning, whereas the Sk-Sk group ran more slowly during extinction than during acquisition. This study is of substantial importance in showing that punishment can facilitate resistance to extinction even when it differs qualitatively from the aversive event used to motivate escape. Of the two shock-trained groups, the one extinguished with shock performed better than its counterpart, which accords with a stimulus similarity interpretation, but of the two buzzer-trained groups, the one extinguished with shock was vastly superior to the one extinguished with buzzer. In this case, the lack of similarity to the original training conditions is overridden by the facilitative effect of shock.

One of the variables of potential importance in the maintenance of self-punitive behavior may be the consistency of the intertrial interval, at least when extinction is carried out under massed-practice conditions. Thus Martin (1967) has recently shown that vicious-circle behavior ceases dramatically if an 18-minute delay is introduced during punished-extinction trials administered with a 30-second intertrial interval. The generality of this finding and the boundary conditions necessary to the maintenance of its integrity remain to be determined.

In concluding this review of the effects of punishment during extinction following escape training, it is worth noting that the aversive event may function not only to maintain previously learned activity but

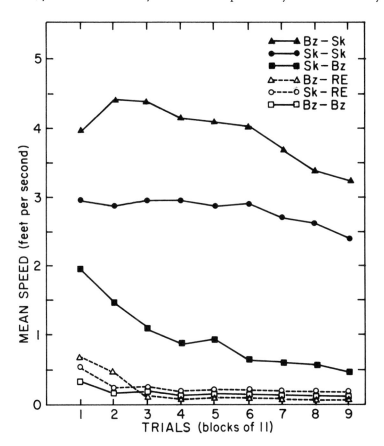

FIG. 15–6.   Mean running speeds for six groups of subjects three of whom had been trained to escape shock and three to escape a loud buzzer. Two were extinguished with shock in the runway (Sk-Sk, Bz-Sk), two with buzzer (Sk-Bz, Bz-Bz), and two under regular extinction conditions (Sk-RE, Bz-RE).

From: K. B. Melvin & R. C. Martin, "Facilitative Effects of Two Modes of Punishment on Resistance to Extinction," *Journal of Comparative and Physiological Psychology,* **62**, 1966, Fig. 2, p. 493. Copyright 1966 by the American Psychological Association and reproduced by permission.

also to produce the kind of improvement in performance that characterizes learning. This outcome has been reported by Melvin and Martin (1966) and studied explicitly by Beecroft and Bouska (1967). The latter investigators trained two groups of rats to escape shock in the apparatus used by Brown et al. (1964) and then punished one of them in the last 2 feet of the runway. The escape training was not extensive, since it involved, after a few shaping trials with shorter runways, only two trials in traversing the entire course of the 6-foot alley. During the following 10-trial extinction session, the nonpunished (no shock) subjects slowed down from about 3 feet per second to less than 2 feet per second whereas

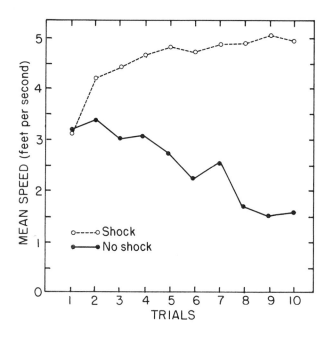

FIG. 15-7. Mean running speeds in the 4-foot shock-free portion of the runway during punished (shock) and nonpunished (no-shock) extinction trials.

From: R. S. Beecroft & S. A. Bouska, "Learning Self-Punitive Running," *Psychonomic Science*, 8, 1967, Fig. 1, p. 107. Reproduced by permission.

the punished (shock) subjects increased their locomotor speed from 3 to almost 5 feet per second (Fig. 15-7). None of the 11 punished animals met the extinction criterion of failing to enter the goal box within 60 seconds whereas three of the nine controls did. The authors suggest that the punished subjects may have been learning to run faster so as to traverse the shock zone with minimum delay or that more fear was being built up during the additional shock trials and that this served as an acquired motivating factor. In either event, it seems likely that reinforcing and/or motivating processes are operative in self-punitive situations and that these influences are capable of counteracting, in some measure, whatever performance-inhibiting effects punishment would normally be expected to exert.

Punished Extinction Following Avoidance Training

In a number of studies of self-punitive behavior, the subjects have been trained to *avoid* rather than *escape* shock. Thus, after an animal has been placed into the apparatus and the CS (if any) has been turned on, the onset of shock is delayed for, say, 5 seconds. If during this period, the subject leaves the to-be-electrified area and runs into the goal box, he receives no shock whatsoever. Subsequently, during the extinction phase, when shock is presented at a fixed (usually) intermediate position in the apparatus, if the animals continue to run into and across the shock longer than nonshocked controls they are said to be evincing the vicious-circle effect. Patently, this procedure differs considerably from that involving escape training. Before examining the experiments proper, therefore, a dissectional analysis is required of some of the conceptual plexuses growing out of these procedural differences.

One of the principal differences between avoidance and escape training lies in the aversive stimulation received by the animals. In avoidance training, the number of shocks, as well as their point of onset in the apparatus and therefore their location and duration, depend on what the animal does. Consequently, these parameters of the shock vary in an uncontrolled manner from animal to animal and from group to group. During escape training, by contrast, the number, location, and spatial extent of the shocks, though not their duration, are under the control of the investigator.

One important consequence of these differences, as Seward and Raskin (1960) have noted, is that the stimulus characteristics of the avoidance-training situation are more like those of the punished-extinction phase than are those of escape training. Avoidance-training methods, like the progressive, shock-reduction procedure described above, provide the subject with repeated opportunities to associate running with start-box and alley cues in the absence of shock-produced stimuli and motivational increments. In effect, the rat is learning essentially the same response that is subsequently required under punished-extinction conditions if the vicious-circle effect is to be observed. Indeed, there are some instances in which the conditions of avoidance training and punished extinction become identical. Suppose, for instance, that an avoidance-trained rat, after a relatively few shock trials, has met a criterion of two successful responses. Now it is entirely possible that, if the avoidance-training procedure were continued without change, he might slow down on the next trial and would encounter shock in, say, the last one-third of the runway. It would be conventional, in this context, to say that "the rat was being punished for slowing down," or that it was getting "an additional reinforcement," or even that it was "testing reality." Few would be surprised, therefore, if the animal were to run faster on the following trial and again avoid shock entirely. On the other hand, if, when an avoidance criterion has been met, the experimenter has chosen to initiate a series of punished extinction trials and has introduced shock in the final one third of the runway, the rat will encounter the shock at the same position in the alley as it would have had it slowed down. In the context of self-punitive studies one would say that the "animal was being punished for avoiding," and the appearance of faster running on the next trial, or a failure to run more slowly would be viewed as "a paradoxical effect of punishment." Evidently, the intensity, duration, position, and spatial extensity of shock may sometimes be precisely the same under an avoidance-training schedule and under punished extinction. Because of this, some of the facilitative effects of punishment following avoidance training might justifiably be construed as instances of further avoidance training in the guise of punished extinction.

Nevertheless, any attempt to explain self-punitive action in terms of factors determining avoidance behavior runs afoul of the fact that our theories of avoidance are themselves regrettably opaque. To assert that the introduction of a fixed-locus shock following avoidance training is facilitatory because it partially reinstates the conditions responsible for avoidance reactions is of little help without a better understanding of avoidance. We have no really satisfactory interpretations of the finding that a rat in avoidance training often runs faster rather than slower on trials after shock has been encountered in the runway. Since shock in the same position during punished extinction also often speeds up running, it is evident that avoidance learning and vicious-circle behavior share some of the same puzzlements.

Part of the difficulty, it seems, lies in vagueness that attends the use of such phrases as "punished for slowing down." Rats in avoidance situations do slow down, to be sure, and hence do receive aversive shock. But since rats do a great many other things during the interval preceding the punishment, one cannot be certain which specific component of the response sequence is being punished. Perhaps on the trial when the rat failed to avoid shock the starting time was long, but the running time was actually shorter than ever before. Is the animal being punished for running swiftly, for starting slowly, or for starting slowly *and* running rapidly? Suppose shock is introduced in the last one third of the runway as punishment following a successful avoidance trial. Although this may be construed as punishment for avoiding, it is evident that the complete avoidance response is not involved but only the first two thirds. And even this is not precisely true save when the rat runs at exactly the same speed that was formerly adequate to avoid shock entirely. If on the first punished trial during extinction the rat runs so slowly as to take longer than the original CS-US interval to reach the shock he has already failed to meet the former avoidance criterion and is being punished, perhaps, for *failing* to avoid. But if the rat speeds up during punished extinction because of shock on the previous trial, then his inevitable encounter with shock may be viewed as punishment for his having run faster. In the punished-extinction situation, it seems, the rat is punished for whatever he does, whether for running faster, or slower, or at the same speed as before, provided he reaches the electrified segment.

There are several additional respects in which the conditions of avoidance training and punished extinction are both similar and different. If, during avoidance training, a rat increases its running speed, the point of shock onset moves toward the goal and shock duration and extent necessarily decrease. The punished-extinction animal, by comparison, cannot alter the point of shock onset or length of the shock zone, but it can, by running more and more swiftly, reduce the effective duration of shock. If the subject slows down during avoidance trials, shock comes on at a progressively earlier position in the alley, until it eventually appears in the start box and the trial becomes one of shock escape rather than avoidance. For the self-punitive subject, however, decreases in speed prolong both the response-shock interval and time in contact with shock, but have no effect on the location or length of the shock zone. Eventually, the animal can sit safely in the start box until the expiration of the criterial time. The two procedures also differ in that the punished-extinction subject that encounters shock can escape it either by continued forward locomotion or by retreating toward the start box. No so for the avoidance subject, since shock is administered throughout the entire alley and can only be escaped by forward locomotion. The point of shock offset may also differ between the two procedures, as for example, when a short shock near the start box is used in punished extinction. In avoidance training, the shock nearly always ends at the junction of the runway and the goal box.

Turning now to the empirical findings themselves, we note that an early study by Solomon, Kamin, and Wynne (1953) of the effects of punishment on the extinction of avoidance behavior provided dramatic evidence for the facilitative influence of punishment. These investigators used a modified Mowrer–Miller shuttle box in which dogs were trained to avoid a very intense shock by leaping over a barrier from one compartment to the other. Since the learned avoidance behavior proved to be unusually persistent, an attempt was made in their fourth experiment to accelerate the process of extinction by introducing a 3-second shock on the side into which the dogs jumped when avoiding. Although 3 of 13 dogs extinguished under these conditions, the remaining 10 failed to extinguish in 100 shock-extinction trials. Indeed, for these animals *shock served to increase the strength of their jumping responses* relative to their previous performance under ordinary extinction conditions. This was reflected in shorter latencies and greater response vigor. As the authors note, the dogs often slammed into the far end of the compartment into which they were jumping. The theoretical interpretation offered by these investigators which stresses the motivational role of fear and the part played by shock in its maintenance, is discussed in our final section below.

Moyer (1955), addressing himself more directly to the vicious-circle phenomenon, construed the problem as one of learning to remain in the safe section of the apparatus (this is currently described as passive avoidance) rather than one of extinguishing the previously acquired avoidance. Preliminary training was carried out in the same apparatus as was used in the escape-training study described above (Moyer, 1957). On each trial the onset of shock was delayed for 10 seconds after the subject had been dropped into the to-be-electrified side and the shock could be avoided provided the rat entered the small goal box in less than that time. A relatively strong, constant-current shock of 1 ma. was applied to both sides of the apparatus during training and, for shock-extinction subjects, to the side between the starting area and the goal box during extinction. The major variables were: (1) number of preliminary avoidance training trials, (2) the time interval between training and testing with (and without) fixed-locus shock, and (3) the similarity between the electrified and the safe regions. Generally speaking, as frequency of avoidance-training trials (and also shocks) increased, resistance to extinction increased. Of two groups given 110 avoidance-training trials, the one that was punished for leaving the starting side during extinction took reliably fewer trials than did the nonshocked controls to reach the stringent criterion of remaining in the no-shock side for 5 minutes. However, when the criterion time was reduced to 10 seconds, the punished group took 39.1 trials to extinguish compared with 20.9 trials for the nonpunished controls. Although this latter difference was not significant, it fits the supposition that the extinction criterion may play an important role in studies of this kind. Moyer also found some evidence to indicate that extinction was accelerated by increasing the distinctiveness of the shock area and by a delay period between avoidance training and extinction. Of special interest was the finding that one animal in a punished group continued to leave the safe starting area and expose itself to shock for 440 trials, thereby providing a striking example of perseverating self-punitive behavior.

Whiteis (1956) trained rats to avoid shock in a short alley and then extinguished them with short, fixed-location shocks near the goal compartment. The results were said to favor the conclusion that punishment produces faster running and greater resistance to extinction than no punishment. No critical evaluation can be made of these findings, however, because of the investigator's failure to report numerical data and procedural details.

Imada (1959), taking special note of the work of Solomon, Kamin, and Wynne (1953), contended that their procedure of administering shock in the jumped-into compartment of a two-way shuttle box should actually have facilitated rather than inhibited performance. This expectation was based on the assumption that this procedure would cause the subjects to confuse punishment administered for successful avoidance with the US for the next trial. It seems equally reasonable, however, to hold that this method should *prevent* the subjects from confusing the two shocks since punishment was administered immediately after an avoidance whereas the US was separated from the response by the intertrial interval. A confusion interpretation of this kind suffers from the same ills that plague any perceptual explanation such as the commonly expressed discrimination hypothesis. In the absence of independent evidence for the kind of confusing or discriminating the organism is doing, any prediction is as justifiable as any other. It should also be noted that in the situation under scrutiny, the punishing shock was not accompanied by the CS, and that punishment could not be terminated by the subject. These differences seem to weigh against the expectation that the training and punishment procedures might be confused.

Imada also believed that it would be inappropriate in studying the effect of punishment on avoidance to introduce the shock into the apparatus in the same section in which it had previously been presented while the avoidance reaction was being established. Although the reasoning behind this restriction was not spelled out, it seems to involve the notion that a true punisher should have no power to evoke the response that is being punished. This mandate is not fulfilled in most of the current investigations in which punishment facilitates behavior during extinction. Indeed, the current practice is to take considerable pains to insure that the punisher *does* duplicate some of the functions of the original aversive stimulus. In addition, contemporary interpretations of persisting self-punitive actions place considerable reliance on the fact that the punishment and the original aversive condition evoke similar kinds of behavior and provide similar stimuli.

Imada's experiment was carried out with a two-compartment, Mowrer–Miller apparatus which was used for one-way avoidance training to obviate the confusion interpretation he had proposed of the study by Solomon et al. This apparatus also satisfied the requirement that punishment should not be introduced into the situation in such a locus as to permit it to function as had the original US since the subjects were always punished in the second compartment after jumping over the hurdle from the first. Upon reaching an acquisition criterion of ten successive avoidance responses, separate groups of rats were punished with 1-second shocks that were both stronger and weaker than that used during avoidance. Consistent with an inhibitory concept of punishment, all shocked animals extinguished more rapidly than non-punished controls. However, the extinction criterion of five successive failures to respond within 2 minutes was unusually stringent. Strangely enough, the weaker the punishment the more the subjects tended to abandon their responses within the first ten trials of extinction. And as punishment decreased in strength the decrement in response speed from the last ten acquisition trials to the first ten extinction trials increased. The two strongest punishment levels actually produced an increase in response speed during extinction, duplicating some of the findings of Solomon et al. Taken as a whole, Imada's study supports the view that punishment is largely inhibitory, though hints are provided of its facilitatory power.

Imada's failure to find stronger evidence of persisting self-punitive behavior may have been due, in part, to the fact that the punishment was introduced after the completion of the avoidance response, thus preventing shock from being terminated by the execution of the final element of the behavioral sequence. Had the punishment been applied, say, to the barrier or to a narrow region adjacent to the barrier in the normally safe side, the outcome might have been more in line with expectations from other self-punitive studies. Under such conditions, the animals would have been able to terminate the shock by leaping forward from the barrier to the far end of the safe compartment. It may be noted, parenthetically, that both compartments of Imada's apparatus were identical in size and in color and both had grid floors. These features would have helped to prevent fear reduction from occurring in the jumped-into compartment.

Negative results have also been reported by Seward and Raskin (1960) in the last of their series of five experiments involving avoidance training and punished extinction. The shocked animals showed no unusual persistence in running, but the shock was rather strong (190 volts through 150K ohms) and the start- and goal-box segments of the apparatus as well as the alley contained identical grid floors. On punishment trials the shock was turned on throughout the length of the 2-foot runway when the rat reached its midpoint and shock could be escaped either by retreating 1 foot or by going ahead 1 foot. As we have noted, this procedure is seldom followed at present, though Gwinn (1949) used a comparable method. In the majority of studies, shock is applied to only a limited section of the grid floor and is not also turned on in the area behind the rat when the point of shock onset is reached. However, such a shock could scarcely explain Seward and Raskin's negative results. Indeed, it should have helped to goad their rats into self-punitive running since slight backward movements at the instant of shock onset would not have terminated the shock. Moreover, this method of presenting the punishing shock would actually heighten the resemblance between the conditions of punished extinction and those the rat would experience during avoidance training if he arrived at the middle of the alley just as the CS-US interval ended.

Seligman and Campbell (1965) have recently conducted a parametric study of the effect of intensity and duration of punishment on the extinction of a one-way avoidance response established with a scrambled 300-volt shock (through 150K ohms) and a 5-second CS-US interval. Training was carried to a criterion of nine consecutive avoidances in a short runway fitted with indistinguishable, interchangeable start and goal boxes. Five intensities of shock (45, 72, 115, 185, and 300 volts), each of one of three durations (0.15, 0.5, and 2.0 sec.), were administered as punishment, the shocks being turned on when the rat interrupted a light beam at the entrance to the goal box. This procedure yielded no facilitation whatever, resistance to extinction decreasing systematically as a function of intensity and duration of punishment.

In discussing their results, Seligman and Campbell noted that they had failed to find facilitative results even though they had met two of the conditions regarded by Brown, Martin, and Morrow (1964) as potentially important for such outcomes. These conditions were (1) that the to-be-punished response should be well established and (2) that the intensity of the punishment should be moderate so as to preclude the evocation of competing reactions. While Seligman and Campbell did indeed fulfill these requirements, any beneficial effects that might have accrued therefrom were evidently offset by other conditions. First of all, the shock was applied to the grid floor of the goal box, and perhaps to the entire alley, though this was not stated, at the instant the rat occluded a light beam at the entrance to the goal box. This would mean that even with the briefest shock (0.15 sec.) some punishment would be received in or near the goal box itself. As a result, the adjacent cues could come to evoke both conditioned fear and incompatible locomotor reactions. Competing movements could have been learned in the goal box or near its entrance especially by rats given the 2-second shock since they would have had time to spin around and move toward the start box before the shock was ended. Second, the use of identical, interchangeable, grid-floored start and goal boxes would probably have made the learning of avoidance difficult since the animals were required to run into goal boxes from which they had just escaped on the previous trial. Consistent with this expectation is the fact that Seligman and Campbell had to discard 22 of 153 rats for failing initially to learn the avoidance response. Lawrence and Miller (1947) have pointed out that interchangeable start and goal boxes, at least in an appetitive situation, lead to paradoxical results; and Denny, Koons, and Mason (1959) and Knapp (1965) have shown that avoidance learning is accelerated and extinction retarded by the use of unlike shock and goal boxes. Finally, Seligman and Campbell's introduction of shock into the goal box, after the manner of Imada, may have prevented their subjects from mastering any response capable of consistently terminating the punishment. Wherever responding during extinction has been prolonged by shock the subjects have usually been able to turn it off by executing the last component of an originally well-learned sequence.

Although Solomon, Kamin, and Wynne (1953) clearly showed that punishment could enhance the speed and vigor of responding of dogs in a two-way shuttle box, Smith, Misanin, and Campbell (1966a) obtained quite different results in an analogous situation with rats. Their procedure was designed to illuminate the view (Mowrer, 1960) that punishment is most likely to facilitate performance when conditions are such as to make it difficult for the organism to discriminate between extinction and training conditions. Thus a two-way shuttle box was chosen in order to maximize the difficulty of the discrimination. How this would operate to achieve the investigators' goals is not clear. Thus, identical compartments would doubtless make it difficult for a subject to discriminate one side from the other as well as increase the difficulty of the avoidance-learning problem by delaying or minimizing fear reduction. But it is far from clear that identical compartments would make it harder for the animal to discriminate acquisition from extinction conditions. Whether the two boxes are the same or different tells the animal nothing as to whether shock will or will not follow the CS. The authors also suggest that the ability to discriminate punished extinction from training should increase with degree of original learning or overlearning. The fact that resistance to extinction increases for a considerable period with practice suggests that the opposite prediction is equally plausible. One of the weaknesses of the discrimination hypothesis, at which we have already hinted, is that it provides no bases for deciding, in advance, whether a rat will or will not perceive or discriminate a difference. Nor does it provide us with rules for deciding just what the rat will do given that it does discriminate.

In their experiment, Smith, Misanin, and Campbell combined five shock intensities (45, 72, 115, 185, and 300 volts) from a matched-impedance source with two shock durations (0.15 and 2.0 sec.) and three degrees of avoidance training (2, 4, or 8 consecutive avoidances). None of the conditions yielded evidence for the facilitative effects of punishment. In general, the stronger the punishment and the longer its duration the fewer the avoidance responses (reactions with latencies of 5 sec. or less) during extinction.

Several reasons may be advanced in explanation of these results. First, as Martin and Melvin (1966) have observed, in this investigation, as in the one by Seligman and Campbell, shock was administered after the animal had completed the avoidance response instead of at an intermediate position. Second, although the 2-second shock could not be escaped by executing the last part of the previously learned avoidance reaction, it could be escaped, as Smith, Misanin, and Campbell (1966b) note in their reply to Martin and Melvin (1966), by a response directly opposed to the movement that produced the shock. That is, when a rat was shocked for having avoided by jumping, say, from left to right it could escape the punishment by a quick movement back through the swinging door from right to left. Such movements would doubtless be strongly reinforced by shock reduction and would compete with the previously learned avoidance reaction. Smith et al. regard their procedure as meeting the requirement that punishment occupy an intermediate position in the behavior sequence since it is preceded by the initial avoidance and followed by escape. Third, as has been true of several studies in which no facilitative effects were observed, the two compartments of the shuttle box were painted the same color, were the same size, and had identical grid floors. As has been noted above, this arrangement minimizes the role of fear reduction in self-punitive behavior and increases the difficulty of the avoidance task. When the environmental cues on the two sides are identical, many additional trials are needed before fear evoked by the apparatus cues can be extinguished, leaving the CS as the sole cue for fear. Finally, as R. S. Beecroft has pointed out to the writer, the procedure followed by Smith et al. during extinction was rather unusual. Initially, the subjects had been trained with a CS-US interval of 5 seconds, and then, on each extinction trial, the CS was presented for 5 seconds. If a member of a to-be-punished group crossed into the opposite compartment within the 5-second period it received either the short or the long shock. But if the animal waited in the first compartment for more than 5 seconds, the trial was terminated by shutting off the CS, and the rat was then free to cross to the opposite side without getting punished. Thus responses with latencies of 5 seconds or less were being punished, but long latency reactions were not. This may explain the fact that the responses of the punished subjects during the latter part of extinction had average latencies of the order of 12 seconds. It is also consistent with the finding that the stronger the punishment and/or the longer its duration, the more quickly the animals learned to wait for the CS to go off before they moved to the opposite side. Waiting, which is incompatible with locomotion, was presumably reinforced by fear reduction attending the cessation of the CS. Apparently, then, the stronger the shock the sooner the subjects gave up making short latency responses, the frequency of which provided the estimate of resistance to extinction. Quite different results might have been obtained if the door between the two compartments had been locked at the end of the 5-second period regardless of the subjects' reactions.

An experiment by Melvin and Smith (1967), involving a one-way avoidance apparatus, provides an interesting contrast to the study by Smith et al. Using a 5-second interstimulus interval, a 4-foot alley, and mild punishment (50 volts through 10K ohms), Melvin and Smith trained two groups of rats to a criterion of five consecutive avoidances, after which one group was given 30 trials of regular extinction (RE) fol-

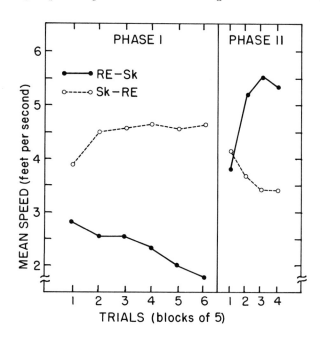

FIG. 15-8.   Mean running speeds for two groups of rats over blocks of five trials (Phase I) and three trials (Phase II). During Phase I, the Sk-RE subjects received a shock during the course of an avoidance response, whereas the RE-Sk animals were given regular extinction trials without shock. The conditions were reversed for the two groups during Phase II.

From: K. B. Melvin & F. H. Smith. "Self-Punitive Avoidance Behavior in the Rat," *Journal of Comparative and Physiological Psychology*, **63**, 1967, Fig. 1, p. 534. Copyright 1967 by the American Psychological Association and reproduced by permission.

lowed by 12 trials of extinction with shock (Sk). The other group received 30 shock-extinction trials first, followed by 12 no-shock, regular extinction trials. The punishment during extinction was provided by a 50-volt shock in the second 1-foot section of the runway. The results, reproduced in Fig. 15–8 indicate clearly that speed of responding was maintained at a high level in the Sk-RE group relative to the RE-Sk animals. Indeed the Sk-RE subjects showed a highly significant improvement in speed over the 30 shock-extinction trials. (Other evidence for the occurrence of new learning during punished extinction following both escape and avoidance training has been cited above). By contrast, the animals given regular extinction trials initially exhibited the orderly decline in speed characteristic of such treatments. Following the reversal of the conditions the performance of the RE-Sk subjects improved dramatically while the Sk-RE animals slowed down progressively. None of the subjects failed to enter the goal box within the criterial time of 40 seconds. The superiority of the RE-Sk subjects relative to the Phase I performance level of the Sk-RE animals suggests the possibility that shock following regular extinction may produce more striking self-punitive effects than when punishment follows avoidance training immediately. The importance of this study lies in its having shown that the facilitative effects of punishment can be studied within subjects and that animals appear to learn to run faster when punishment is interposed between start and goal boxes. As Melvin and Smith suggest, increased running speed minimizes shock duration as well as time in the presence of the CS. Perhaps the strength of the conditioned fear is being maintained in much the manner suggested by Solomon and Wynne's (1954) anxiety-conservation hypothesis.

In the previous section, which was concerned with studies of punished extinction following escape training, some attention was devoted to the question of whether the position of shock in the apparatus would significantly affect self-punitive behavior. Although a similar question can be asked here in the context of avoidance learning, the empirical evidence is too fragmentary to provide an unambiguous answer. In the only study in which a direct comparison of near with far shock has been made, Campbell, Smith, and Misanin (1966) first trained female albino rats to run through a 7-foot long alley to avoid shock during a CS-US interval of 5 seconds. As in the experiment by Seligman and Campbell (1965) the start and goal boxes were grid-floored, were identical in size and color, and were interchanged after each trial. As soon as the acquisition criterion (four consecutive avoidances in 40 trials) was met, the subjects were divided into three groups. One of these was punished near the start of the runway, another was shocked far from the start of the runway near the goal, and the third was not shocked at all. The start-punished animals were shocked at a point 4 inches outside the start box and the goal-punished subjects at a point 8 inches in front of the goal box. The shock was relatively strong (185 volts through 150K ohms) but brief (0.15 sec.). Some of the results of this procedure are summarized in Fig. 15–9, which shows the median percentages of avoidance responses (latencies less than 5 sec.) exhibited by the three groups during the course of extinction.

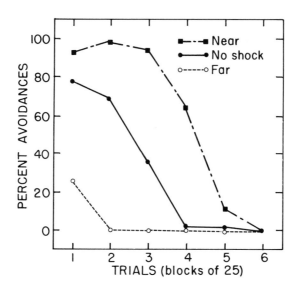

FIG. 15–9.   Median percentages of avoidance responses (i.e., those with latencies less than 5 sec.) for subjects punished near the start of the runway, for those shocked far from the start of the runway (near the goal), and for control subjects that were not shocked at all.

From: B. A. Campbell, N. F. Smith, & J. R. Misanin, "Effects of Punishment on Extinction of Avoidance Behavior: Avoidance–Avoidance Conflict or Vicious Circle Behavior?" *Journal of Comparative and Physiological Psychology*, **62**, 1966, Fig. 1, p. 496. Copyright 1966 by the American Psychological Association and reproduced by permission.

As is evident from this figure, the start-punished subjects showed no evidence of extinguishing at first and indeed over the first 75 trials actually became slightly more proficient at avoiding. Nevertheless, while they were significantly better than the goal-punished subjects they did not differ statistically from the controls. The start-shocked subjects took an average of 79 trials to extinguish compared with 63 for the controls, but again the difference was not significant. (When the goal-punished animals who extinguished in only 12 trials were included the overall analysis was significant. The goal-punished subjects were also significantly poorer than the control and start-punished groups with respect to percent avoidances). As to running time, the start-punished rats showed no signs of extinguishing during the 150 trials and in fact were running slightly faster at the end than at the beginning. On the final trial, in fact, they ran significantly faster than either the goal-punished or control animals. By contrast, both control and goal-punished subjects slowed down significantly during the course of extinction.

Whereas the performance of the start-punished subjects is thus seen to be consistent with data from other vicious-circle experiments, and especially with the findings of Martin and Melvin (1964) indicating that near shock is more effective than far shock, the performance of the far-shock rats relative to the controls is puzzling. Neither the relatively intense shock nor the interchangeable start and goal boxes can account for the inferiority of the goal-punished subjects, though the latter circumstance may explain the fact that it was necessary to discard 18 of 48 animals for failing to learn to avoid initially. The fact that the 0.15-second shock was turned on automatically at a point 8 inches in front of the goal box may have been significant; since if a rat were running at a speed of 6 feet per second, it would have been shocked over the first 4 inches of the goal box as well as the final 8 inches of the runway. This was probably not typical, however, and a speed of 5 feet per second would result in shock in only the first inch of the goal box. We are left, therefore, without a convincing interpretation of the surprisingly poor performance of the far-shock subjects. As we have already noted, shock near the goal should work unusually well following avoidance training since it terminates at about the same point in the apparatus as the shock did during training and may come on at about the same point as it did during training when the rat did not run quite fast enough to avoid it entirely.

The proposition that punishment near the goal can, under somewhat different conditions, lead to self-punitive behavior is amply substantiated by a recent series of experiments by Beecroft (1967), Beecroft, Bouska, and Fisher (1967), and Beecroft, Fisher, and Bouska (1967). In these studies the procedures resembled those of Campbell, Smith, and Misanin (1966), but Beecroft and his associates used the original apparatus of Brown, Martin, and Morrow (1964) rather than one with identical, interchangeable start and goal boxes that were also similar to the alley. In addition, the shock (unscrambled) was confined to the final 1-foot segment of the 6-foot runway, rather than being controlled by a timer, and the voltage (typically) was set at 55 and was applied through a 10K-ohm series resistor. The interval between the rat's being dropped on the grid floor of the double-decker start box and the onset of shock was 3.0 seconds during avoidance training. After the subjects had reached a criterion of three consecutive avoidances (sometimes only one) the shock-extinction and regular extinction trials were introduced.

The results of the first experiment (Beecroft, 1967) are shown in Fig. 15–10. These speed scores were based on only the first 4 feet of the alley so as to provide a shock-free performance measure for both groups. It is evident from this graph that during the first 10 extinction trials, at least, the shocked subjects performed much better than those that were not punished. The mean speeds on the criterial avoidance trial and on

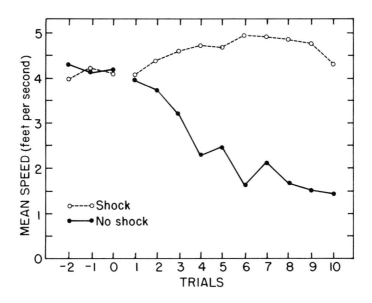

FIG. 15–10.   Mean running speeds in the first 4 feet of the alley during avoidance criterion trials (the first three trials) and the first ten extinction trials on which shock was present near the goal for the punished subjects (shock) and was not present at all for the nonpunished controls (no shock).

From: R. S. Beecroft, "Near-Goal Punishment of Avoidance Running," *Psychonomic Science,* **8**, 1967, Fig. 1, p. 110. Reproduced by permission.

the first extinction trials were essentially the same for both groups. Subsequently, however, the punished (shock) animals increased their speeds from 4 to 5 feet per second whereas the nonpunished (no shock) subjects' speeds declined from 4 to 1.5 feet per second. These findings are supported by the observation that the median number of trials to extinction for the shocked rats was 81 compared with 11 for the controls. Only 2 of the 13 shocked subjects completed less than 41 trials whereas only 2 of 15 controls continued to run for more than 26 trials. Evidently, near-goal shock is substantially better than no shock at all in strengthening resistance to extinction. Beecroft suggests that the facilitative effects of shock in his experiment might have been due, in part, to the faster running, generally, of his animals. This outcome he ascribed, in turn, to his use of a 3-second CS-US interval during acquisition and a fixed-length shock zone. Campbell et al. employed a 5-second interstimulus interval and a fixed-duration shock which could not be minimized by high-speed running.

In the study by Beecroft, Bouska, and Fisher (1967) all subjects were trained to avoid a 55 volt shock, and after the criterion of one avoidance had been met, four subgroups of 12 rats each were extinguished with 0, 40, 55, or 70 volts in the last 1 foot of the alley adjacent to the goal box. Other conditions were the same as in the previous experiment. The mean number of responses made before reaching the extinction criterion were 12, 23, 36, and 25, respectively, for the four groups. All of the various measures, including running speed, number of trials to extinction, and number of subjects still running after 40 trials support the conclusion that shock facilitated resistance to extinction. For example, there was almost no overlap in the extinction distributions of the 0- and 55-volt groups. In addition, speed of running correlated highly with punishment intensity. The subjects given the 70-volt shock took fewer trials to extinguish than those punished with 55 volts, which supports the discrimination hypothesis; but speed of running was directly related to shock intensity, which contraverts the hypothesis.

In a subsidiary experiment, animals extinguished with 55 volts following avoidance training with 70 volts resisted extinction less stoutly than others extinguished with 70 volts. Again, this accords with the view that cues provided by shock during avoidance training become associated with running and that the response is degraded when these cues are either intensified or weakened.

The third study of this series (Beecroft, Fisher, & Bouska, 1967) provided further evidence to indicate that shock near the goal tends to maintain self-punitive behavior and that percentages of shock as low as 20% during extinction are as effective as much higher percentages (up to 100%).

Relative Effectiveness of Avoidance and Escape Training as Antecedents of Self-Punitive Behavior

The foregoing summaries suggest that punishment following avoidance training might be more likely to prolong extinction than punishment following escape. For one thing, if avoidance-trained animals resist extinction better, as the findings of Sheffield and Temmer (1950), Jones (1953), and Santos (1960) suggest, a punishing shock should deter them less. In one of the few experiments bearing on this question, Hurwitz,

Bolas, and Haritos (1961) compared the relative effectiveness of escape and avoidance training in generating vicious-circle behavior. One group of hooded rats was given three trials of escape training in a 4-foot straight alley while a second group received three avoidance trials with a 10-second interval between alley placement and shock onset. During a subsequent punished-extinction phase, shock was present in the second portion of the alley but absent from the escape chamber and the initial alley segment. Two of the 12 subjects in the escape group persisted in self-punitive running for 160 trials while 4 of the 10 avoidance subjects reached the same limit. The mean numbers of trials to the extinction criterion (described by the authors as learning to avoid running) were 89 for the escape subjects and 135 for the avoidance subjects. These differences were not evaluated statistically and may be regarded simply as suggestive. Their direction, however, is consistent with expectations expressed above. Unfortunately, no nonpunished control subjects were included in the design.

As has been noted earlier, subjects given avoidance training learn to run both to the cues present on nonreinforced trials and to stimulus sequences much like those that will be encountered subsequently on punished trials. However, the degree of similarity between events occurring during the acquisition of avoidance and those present during punished extinction depends in some measure on the duration of the CS-US interval used in avoidance training. If the interval is shorter than the subject's reaction time, shock will always be experienced in the start box and throughout the runway and the situation is therefore essentially the same as escape training. With intervals longer than the time the animal usually takes to run the length of the alley, the shock can frequently be avoided entirely. But if the interval is of an intermediate duration, the rat can never run fast enough to avoid shock in some part of the runway near the goal. Since under these conditions the shock is avoided in the first segments of the runway but escaped near the end, the label *avoidance-escape* appropriately describes such composite behavior. Clearly, the stimulus properties of the avoidance-escape training procedure are more like those of the self-punitive situation than they are like those present during either escape or avoidance training.

In a recent experiment by Beecroft and Brown (1967) the CS-US interval used during training in a straight 6-foot runway was varied across groups from 0 second (escape) through intermediate values of 1 and 2 seconds (avoidance-escape) to a maximum of 4 seconds (avoidance). After 5 days of training (10 trials per day), a 55-volt shock was introduced in the last 2-foot section of the alley for all subjects. These punished extinction trials were continued for 4 days. It was expected, following the reasoning just presented and on the basis of related experiments, that the animals in the intermediate delay groups would show superior acquisition and would tend to resist extinction more stubbornly. Representative running-speed data from the middle 2-foot segment of the runway are shown in Fig. 15–11. The curves in the left panel were obtained from performance during acquisition and those at the right during punished extinction. These data make it abundantly clear that the avoidance-escape training procedure with intermediate delays, especially

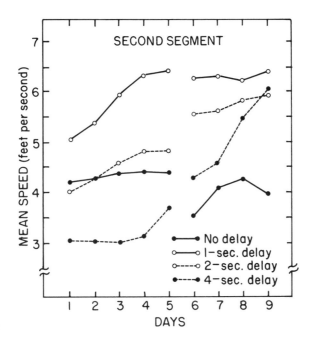

FIG. 15–11.   Mean running speeds in the middle 2-foot segment of a 6-foot runway for four groups of rats that were trained with no delay between being dropped and shock onset (0-sec. group) and with delays, similarly defined, of 1, 2, or 4 seconds. The curves in the left part of the figure represent performance during acquisition; those in the right, the behavior of the same groups during punished extinction with shock in the last 2-foot section of the runway.

From: R. S. Beecroft & J. S. Brown, "Punishment Following Escape and Avoidance Training," *Psychonomic Science*, **8**, 1967, Fig. 2, p. 350. Reproduced by permission.

with a delay of 1 second, results in much faster running speeds than a straight escape condition (0 sec. delay) but that escape tends to be better than avoidance when the delay is long (4 sec.). Evidently avoidance training can yield either better or worse performance than escape training depending on the CS-US interval.

The punished-extinction data (right-hand panel of Fig. 15–11) are of considerable interest in showing that the escape-trained animals slowed

down when shock was confined to a fixed zone near the goal but the
1-second delay group maintained its very high running speed and the
2- and 4-second groups improved dramatically. At the end of the fourth
day all delay groups were running at about the same very high speed
and were all much faster than the escape group. These substantial improvements in performance may have been due to the 2- and 4-second
subjects having learned, during acquisition, to run just fast enough to
avoid shock, and then, during extinction, being forced to adjust to much
the same conditions (i.e., shock in last 2-ft. segment of alley) that
ordinarily lead to substantially faster running as exemplified by the
performance of the 1-second delay animals. With respect to number of
punished-extinction trials completed, the escape-trained subjects were
significantly less resistant to extinction than the shock-delay rats. Similar
findings with respect to the relative efficacy of shock delays of various
magnitudes during acquisition have been reported by Brown and Van
Bruggen (1965). Punished extinction was not, however, investigated in
their study.

A recent study of the relative effectiveness of avoidance and escape
training on self-punitive behavior by Bender and Melvin (1967) again
confirms the basic vicious-circle effect and reveals the superiority of
avoidance- over escape-trained animals in resistance to extinction and
in speed of running during extinction. Within each of the two major
training categories, four different subgroups were extinguished with O,
10, 50, and 100% of the trials involving punishment. Resistance to
extinction was found to be an increasing function of the percentage
of punished-extinction trials for both escape and avoidance subjects.
Moreover, the facilitative effect appeared even when only 10% of the
extinction trials involved punishment. Gwinn (1949) and Melvin (1964)
had previously obtained reliable self-punitive behavior with percentages
of punishment as low as 33%, and Beecroft (1967) observed a similar
effect with only 20% shock during extinction. Consistent with the findings of Sheffield and Temmer (1950), Bender and Melvin's data indicate
that during regular (no shock) extinction avoidance-trained subjects take
longer to extinguish than escape animals. With a CS-US interval of 5
seconds, Bender and Melvin's avoidance subjects were significantly worse
than their 0 second (escape) animals with respect to asymptotic running
speed. This agrees with the observations of Seward and Raskin (1960),
with the data of Beecroft and Brown (1967) and with the conclusion that
escape-trained animals perform worse than avoidance-trained subjects
when the CS-US interval is of the order of 1 second and better than
avoidance subjects when the interval is about 5 seconds or longer. As so
many of the studies we have examined indicate, punishment often improves performance during extinction. Apparently, when the CS-US

interval during avoidance training is quite long, the subject receives too few shocks to maintain his motivation and his performance at a high level.

Miscellaneous Self-Punitive Studies

For convenience, we have classified self-punitive experiments into those that have involved either escape- or avoidance-training procedures followed by shock during extinction. There are several additional studies, however, worthy of attention that do not readily fall into these categories.

Ever since the vicious-circle effect was first reported and analyzed by Mowrer (1947) his theoretical interpretation (see below) with its emphasis on the role of fear has been the reigning conception. The theory has not, however, been subjected to direct test, perhaps because simple, reliable indices of degree of conditioned fear have not yet been developed. Melvin and Stenmark (1968), in a recent study derived from Mowrer's theory, have suggested that if the self-punitive persistence is due to the maintenance by punishment of conditioned fear it should be possible to condition fear first and then maintain it by punishment while a new response is being learned. To this end, hooded rats were given 18 paired presentations of a buzzer and shock in the start box of a runway but were not allowed to escape or avoid. Then, after 3 prepunishment trials on which access to the runway and goal box was permitted, the rats were given 40 conventional punished or nonpunished trials. On each such trial the buzzer was turned on as the rat was dropped into the lower compartment of the start box and remained on until the goal box was reached or until the expiration of the criterial time of 60 seconds. Some animals encountered shock in the middle of the runway, some found shock (55 or 75 volts) at the end, and some were not shocked at all. Figure 15–12 summarizes the results. From these curves, it appears that all animals ran somewhat faster on the trials immediately following the prepunishment experience. Beyond that point, the shocked subjects showed marked additional increases in speed, whereas the nonshocked animals slowed down. Moreover, the groups given a 75-volt shock in the alley ran faster, generally, than those punished with a 55-volt shock. This experiment leaves little doubt that the self-punitive effect is not limited to the maintenance by punishment of a previously learned response during the course of extinction. Here the animals had never learned to run on an electrified grid before punishment was introduced. The only learning that might have taken place would have taken place during the three prepunishment trials and the only reinforcement for such learning would presumably have been fear reduction in the

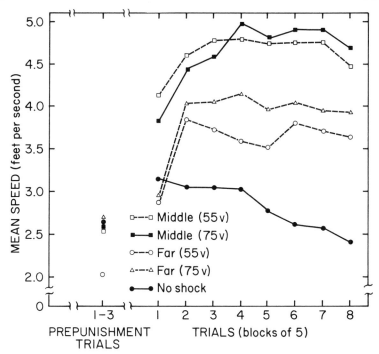

FIG. 15–12.   Mean runway speeds during three prepunishment trials following fear conditioning in the start box and during 40 subsequent trials in which shock was presented in the middle of the runway or far from the start box (near the goal box), or on which, for a third group, no shock at all was presented. The numbers refer to shock voltages in the runway, either 55 or 75.

goal box. But as Fig. 15–12 reveals, the punished subjects, especially, spectacularly improved their speed of running after shock was introduced.

Another study standing aside from the mainstream of those considered heretofore involved an attempt to convert or transmute food-reinforced approach behavior into fear-motivated, self-punitive behavior (Brown, 1965b). In broad outline, the following procedure was followed: (1) rats were trained for about 10 days to run to food in the goal box of the same alley used by Brown, Martin, and Morrow (1964); (2) shocks, the intensity of which was increased progressively from 0 to 40 volts over block of trials, were introduced into the middle 1-foot section of the runway; (3) synchronously with the process of shock escalation, amount of food reward and severity of food deprivation were progressively reduced; and (4) the animals were never rewarded with food for darting across the central shock section to the goal box. It was expected that at least some rats would come under the influence of factors responsible for vicious-circle fixation and would continue to run through shock even in the complete absence of food reward and hunger drive.

The outcome of one of four studies conducted along these lines is

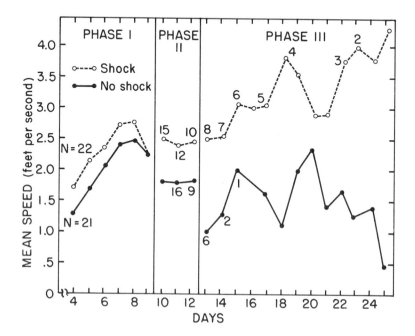

FIG. 15–13.   Mean running speeds for two groups of subjects that were trained in Phase I to run to food reward in a 6-foot alley. During Phase II, rats in the shocked groups were gradually made less hungry, and were given less food in the goal box, while the intensity of shock in the middle of the runway was progressively increased. Nonshocked animals were treated identically except they never encountered shock. Throughout Phase III, none of the rats was fed in the goal box and none was hungry, though the shocked subjects were punished in the middle of the runway. The numbers adjacent to the curves indicate how many subjects had not met the extinction criterion of failing to enter the goal box in 60 seconds. (After Brown, 1965b)

shown in Fig. 15–13. Here it will be seen that the conventional food-rewarded approach training terminated after Day 9 and that shock was introduced on Day 10. The progressive increases in shock for the animals in the shock group and the simultaneous decreases in hunger and food reward for both groups were complete by the end of Day 12. After that none of the animals was hungry, none of them received food in the goal box, and the shocked rats had to run across an electrified zone to reach the goal box. These curves make it clear that from Day 13 on, the punished rats who continued to run tended to run faster and faster, whereas those in the nonpunished group slowed down. The numbers adjacent to the curves indicate how many subjects had not met the extinction criterion of failing to enter the goal box in 60 seconds. On Day 14, for example, seven punished subjects but only two nonshocked subjects were still running. It should be emphasized that none of the rats was ever shocked in the start box and none was ever rewarded with food following a crossing of the electrified zone in the alley. Thus, the few punished subjects that made the transition were avoiding a start box in which they had never been punished, and, though not hungry, were crossing an aversive zone to get to a goal box where they were no longer being fed. Results much like these were obtained in the other three attempts to demonstrate the phenomenon, with about 20% of the animals becoming locked into the vicious circle and the rest not. It is presumed that methods can be worked out for increasing the percentage of subjects that make the transition. However, the balance between forces working toward extinction and those favorable to continued self-punitive actions is extremely delicate.

The interpretation of these studies might proceed along the following lines. First, if the rats develop a strong enough tendency to run to the goal box for food reward they will persist in this activity for a time in the face of shock of mounting intensity. Second, the tactual cues provided by shock become associated with running and fear becomes conditioned to the environmental cues, especially those provided by the grid floor underfoot. Third, fear is aroused as a generalized response to the tactual and visual cues of the start box and provides the motivational increment needed to drive the rats out of that compartment and into the alley even when they are not hungry. Fourth, when shock is encountered in the alley it tends to evoke running and to reinforce the conditioned fear reaction after the manner proposed by Mowrer (1950). Fifth, running is powerfully reinforced by shock reduction when the rat reaches the end of the shock zone. It is difficult, we presume, to set up self-punitive behavior in this manner in every animal because the approach is not always sufficiently strong to maintain the response until shock intensity reaches a level high enough to produce a reasonable degree of conditioned fear. And if the rate at which shock intensity is increased is too high, it may evoke incompatible responses of backing up that negate the approach completely and prevent the response from being transferred to the tactual cues of shock and from being further reinforced by fear reduction.

A final striking example of vicious-circle-like behavior, though it is not identified as such by the investigator, is provided in an experiment by Lohr (1959). In most of the studies we have reviewed thus far, the animals were permitted to choose between sitting in the safe start box and running across shock to the equally safe goal box. But in Lohr's experiment, rats were offered a choice of equivalent left and right alleys leading to the same goal box where food reward was present. When shock of moderate intensity, but above the aversion threshold, was introduced into the preferred pathway after extended approach training (500 trials) and was progressively increased in strength, 12 of 16 subjects chose the side leading to shock 100% of the time in the last 100 trials. Apparently, when training was prolonged, it provided sufficient impetus to carry the animals across the grid a number of times and they acquired what was described as "a compulsion for taking unnecessary punishment." The author's interpretation, which appeals to the secondary reinforcing properties of shock, is discussed below.

Theories of Self-Punitive Behavior

As we have already observed, the first, and probably still the most acceptable interpretation of vicious-circle behavior is that of Mowrer (1947). As originally proposed, his theory involved the assumptions that (1) fear becomes conditioned to the environmental cues because of their repeated contiguous occurrence with shock during training, (2) fear of the starting compartment provides the motivation for running, (3) running is reinforced by fear reduction taking place in the safe goal box, and (4) the acquired, fear-arousing properties of the situation are strengthened on each self-punitive trial when shock is encountered in the runway. The rat runs because he is afraid and continues to be afraid because he encounters punishment when he runs.

The theory in this basic form has substantial merit, to be sure, but it can be strengthened by the addition of propositions relating to the role played by shock itself. First, the act of running is doubtless strengthened by fear reduction, as Mowrer suggests, but it is more immediately and powerfully reinforced by the cessation of shock at the instant the rat steps off the grid. Second, during the original locomotor training, the response of running takes place repeatedly in the presence of tactual stimuli provided by shock to the animal's feet. Therefore, whenever shock is encountered in the runway, whether during avoidance training, escape, avoidance-escape, or punished extinction, it will tend to elicit the response of forward locomotion. It has been pointed out elsewhere (Brown, 1955) that a noxious stimulus tends to lose its power to evoke withdrawal reactions to the degree that it becomes a conditioned stimulus for forward locomotion. The development of such associative connections to shock-produced stimuli may constitute the mechanism for whatever negative adaptation or habituation (Guthrie, 1935) takes place to punishment in self-punitive situations. Third, while shock is being received it provides a substantial increment to the animal's level of drive, and if running is the dominant response it will be further augmented by the increase in motivation. Moreover, residual emotionality from one trial may affect performance on a subsequent trial in ways consistent with motivational theory. Fourth, in those special situations in which appetitive rewards have followed shock it is possible, as Keller and Schoenfeld (1950), Brown (1955), Lohr (1959), and others have suggested, that the shock stimulus acquires secondary reinforcing properties and thereby becomes capable of strengthening the running response. (A secondary reinforcement notion would not serve, of course, in situations involving purely aversive conditions, unless one were to adopt the view that shock onset can become secondarily reinforcing by virtue of its close association with shock offset.)

While the overall value of Mowrer's theory cannot yet be exactly appraised, it seems evident that it can encompass a great many of the findings of self-punitive investigations and that its utility can be increased by the addition of these propositions regarding the motivational and associative roles played by shock. Interpretations consistent with Mowrer's, though not entirely identical therewith, have been espoused by Gwinn (1949), Solomon, Kamin, and Wynne (1953), Whiteis (1956), and Melvin and Martin (1966), to name but a few.

The so-called discrimination interpretation proposed by various writers (e.g., Solomon, Kamin, & Wynne, 1953; Imada, 1959; Mowrer, 1960; Church, 1963; Smith, Misanin, & Campbell, 1966a, 1966b) was not developed with special reference to the self-punitive situation and is too narrow to cover all of the several facets of vicious-circle behavior. In one of the forms the theory takes, changes in environmental conditions of any kind will be followed by correlated changes in behavior whenever the subject is able to "discriminate" or "perceive" or become "aware" of the fact that changes have been made. If the subject cannot discriminate the occurrence of a change, his behavior presumably continues unmodified. For example, if an animal has been receiving shock in the start box of a runway, and shock is then discontinued, the rat may either stop running or continue to run. If he stops running, he is said to have discriminated the change; if he does not, he has not. A subject in the self-punitive situation who "construes" or "interprets" the situation when punishment is being administered in the runway as being the same as it was during acquisition will keep on responding forever. When the discrimination hypothesis is stated in this cognitive, perceptual language with no independent evidence being proffered for the presence or absence of awareness, it is viciously circular and adds nothing to our understanding of the vicious-circle effect. Discrimination, as an activity of an organism, is necessarily a dependent variable not a determinant of the overt responding of interest to the experimenter. A rat that has responded differentially to an objectively definable stimulus pair has indeed discriminated, but until he has so responded we have no basis for talking about how well he discriminates.

Actually this version of the discrimination interpretation has two major weaknesses over and beyond the problem of circularity. The first is its inability to encompass the finding that behavior sometimes gets better (as in some self-punitive experiments) rather than worse when the stimulus situation is drastically altered. This becomes clearer when the hypothesis is couched in its alternate form by referring to degree of "confusion" rather than accuracy of "discrimination." Whenever the subject confuses the conditions of extinction inextricably with those of acquisition he should continue to perform just as though the acquisition regimen were still in force. If the two are not confused completely, the animal is supposed to perform less well during extinction. But there is no way in which the rat can be more confused than completely confused, and there is no way, as a consequence, in which the theory can handle improved performance during extinction. Whenever the second situation differs from the first, the confusion view calls for poorer performance in the second, assuming, of course, that other factors than confusion and similarity are not invoked.

The second, well-nigh fatal weakness of the discrimination conception lies in its complete failure to provide precise statements concerning the theoretical relations holding between discriminations and behavior. Suppose, on the basis of some independent defining operation that it appears appropriate to assert that the rat has indeed been able to discriminate acquisition from extinction conditions. The question now facing the theorist is that of predicting just what the animal will actually do, given that it has discriminated. Obviously, the rat may quit responding completely and entirely, it may continue reacting for a limited period, or it may continue running for an indefinite number of trials, perhaps because of its "desire to please the experimenter." There are no guideposts provided by the cognitive version of the discrimination theory to enable us to choose among these very different alternatives. Knowing that the rat is aware is of no use to the experimenter until the behavioral consequences of such awarenesses are explicitly formulated.

Some proponents of the discrimination hypothesis deny that they are invoking cognitive or perceptual events and insist that reference is being made solely to the *similarity* between two sets of environmental conditions. Framed thus, the theory leads to one and only one expectation; namely, that the more properties of the stimulus situation are changed from one time to another the higher the probability that a decremental effect will be observed in behavior. The conception emphasizes the role of stimulus integrity in the maintenance of behavior and bears a marked similarity to the concepts of empirical stimulus generalization and transfer of training. Like the cognitive view, this version is also unable to handle instances in which behavior improves or continues unchanged in the face of alterations in the environment.

The behavior of animals in self-punitive experiments has sometimes been likened (Mowrer, 1947; Brown, Martin, & Morrow, 1964) to masochistic behavior in human beings. To some this may seem far fetched, but there is ample reason for supposing that the two kinds of activities share some of the same fundamental mechanisms. The principal similarity, of course, lies in the fact that in each instance the organism chooses what may appear to be the more aversive of two alternative courses of action. Both masochistic and vicious-circle behavior may also involve conditioned anxiety or fear, increases in motivation, and the reinforcement of certain responses by anxiety reduction. In a recent discussion of these matters, Brown (1965a) has suggested that the only meaningful way in which the attractiveness or aversiveness of physical events (e.g., electric shocks) can be defined is in terms of the behavior of organisms. Events that elicit escape or withdrawal are definable as aversive and events evoking approach are deemed attractive. But any physical event, object, or situation may be approached by one organism and avoided by another, or approached and avoided by the same organism at different times. Consequently, the noxiousness or attractiveness of any event turns out to be entirely relative to the time, the organism, and the responses used in formulating the definition. This relativistic position, however, provides a solution to the masochistic paradox since the alleged "pleasure in pain" of the masochist can be meaningfully interpreted as involving two incompatible behavior-based definitions concerning the event to which the masochist exposes himself. By one of the definitions the event is aversive, by the other attractive. Self-mutilation by the religious fanatic, for example, can be regarded as attractive when the fanatic's own behavior is woven into the definitional statement, but the event may become aversive when the behavior of others is used as the criterion. In an exactly parallel manner, the shock that is approached by rats in self-punitive demonstrations may be classified either as aversive, because rats normally avoid it, or as attractive inasmuch as it is being approached in the vicious-circle situation. Likewise, although the start box is conventionally described as the safe section of the runway, the fact that the self-punitive rat repeatedly chooses to expose himself to shock rather than remain at the start box permits one to define the start box as more aversive than the shock or the shock as more attractive than the start box. Seen in this light, the rats are not masochistic, but "pleasure bent." By the same reasoning, the shock zone is aversive relative to the goal box, provided the animal whose behavior is to be used as the point of reference rejects the former and accepts the latter. Generally speaking, a relativistic approach of this kind appears to offer some promise as a basic strategy in the interpretation of a variety of puzzling situations involving so-called punishments.

Before turning to our final task of summarizing the several factors that seem to favor the appearance of vicious-circle behavior it is appropriate to comment on two additional theoretical matters, namely, the relation of avoidance–avoidance conflict to self-punitive activity and the issue of what should be included under the vicious-circle rubric.

The question of the relation of vicious-circle behavior to avoidance–avoidance conflict was raised by Campbell, Smith, and Misanin (1966). Specifically, the role played by punishment in increasing vigor of responding and resistance to extinction seems to them to be inconsistent with its capacity to elicit competing responses that could be revealed in a conflict between the tendencies to avoid both the fear-arousing start box and the shock zone. Actually, these need not be regarded as mutually exclusive alternatives. In the typical avoidance–avoidance situation the organism is trained initially to avoid each of two different goals (independently presented) and is then tested by introducing the cues for both reactions at the same moment. In the self-punitive situation, by contrast, the animals are trained to avoid only the start box. They are never deliberately reinforced for running away from the shock zone toward the start box. Indeed, in successful self-punitive experiments considerable care is taken to insure that the subjects always escape shock during training by means of a forward movement. The training program is thus such as to minimize the development of an avoidance-avoidance conflict by reducing the likelihood that avoidance will be built up to the shock region. During the process of extinction, even though shock is present in the runway, the tendency to avoid the now safe start box may weaken. The punishment may then be intense enough to cause the animal to stop, and he may be powerfully reinforced for turning around and retreating. Under the circumstances, one or two occasions of this kind may be adequate to add considerable strength to whatever generalized tendencies may be present to avoid the shock region. In effect, a relatively sudden shift may occur in the apparent strengths of the tendencies to avoid the start box and the shock zone. This is consistent with the observation that when shocked subjects do extinguish in self-punitive experiments, they often do so in a somewhat precipitous manner. Nevertheless, vacillation is not unknown in vicious-circle studies and might be observed more frequently if long alleys were used, if shock were eliminated after the subject's first retreat therefrom, and if the test-trial periods were substantially prolonged. We conclude from this, therefore, that during successful self-punitive trials, the tendency to avoid the start box is strong and tendencies to avoid the intervening shock zone, having not been directly reinforced, are relatively weak. During punished extinction the tendency to avoid the start box may be reduced by the absence of shock, creating a weak avoidance-avoidance conflict, but the subsequent reinforcement of shock-zone avoidance responses abruptly elevates the corresponding reaction tendencies to a position of almost complete dominance. The subject then stays as far as possible from the shock zone and soon meets the extinction criterion.

The issue of precisely what one must do and what outcomes must be observed in order to be able properly to apply the term vicious-circle behavior has been raised in recent discussions (Martin & Melvin, 1966; Smith, Misanin, & Campbell, 1966a). Here there is doubtless no widely acceptable answer since the adoption of either a wide or a narrow view of what comprises vicious-circle activity is more a matter of personal preference than of precedent or convention. Martin and Melvin are correct in assuming that the runway situation, with intermediate fixed-zone shock, provided the original impetus to Mowrer's use of the term in the context of animal behavior. But Mowrer credits Horney (1937) with the prior use of the term in reference to human compulsive behavior. Perhaps the term is appropriate, therefore, whenever perseverative behavior is observed under conditions in which the motivating and reinforcing processes can be shown to have self-maintaining properties.

Factors Relating to the Appearance of Persisting Self-Punitive Locomotor Behavior

In lieu of summarizing the variegated procedures and outcomes of the studies reviewed above, it may be more useful, by way of conclusion, simply to list some of the factors that appear, at the present writing, to contribute significantly to the appearance of vicious-circle behavior. It is not being claimed, incidentally, that the variables in the list, singly or in combination, are necessarily optimal or are capable of counteracting the influence of other, unstated conditions. Nor are we suggesting that noxious stimuli are not often punishing and inhibitory. Clearly, such events are called punishments because on many occasions and under a variety of circumstances they have indeed exhibited behavior-depressing characteristics. But if the basic principle can be accepted that these same physical events may also function, under other conditions and on other occasions, as facilitators of performance, then we need concern ourselves only with the problem of which arrangements favor one outcome rather than the other. The following list, then, constitutes a preliminary catalogue of conditions and relations that tend, within only vaguely prescribable limits, to convert otherwise punishing events into behavior facilitators. Most items should be construed as very tentative guesses rather than firmly established generalizations.

1. The course of extinction of a learned response may be prolonged by the introduction of an otherwise aversive or punishing event provided that event reinstates some of the components of the stimulus complex to which the response had become conditioned during its acquisition.

2. So-called punishing stimuli tend to facilitate behavior during extinction to the degree that they elevate level of motivation, without concurrently eliciting responses that are vigorously incompatible with the ongoing activity.

3. The probability that punishment during extinction will facilitate performance is believed to be an increasing and then decreasing function of the intensity of the punishing stimulus. Extremely weak punishments provide neither appreciable increments in motivation nor usably distinctive relevant cues. Very intense punishing stimuli appear to possess marked motivational properties but are overly likely to evoke inhibitory competing reactions. The variable of intensity of punishment during extinction is expected to interact with intensity during acquisition.

4. The intrinsic qualitative properties of the punishing stimulus may be significant. For example, relatively constant-current shock, because of its tendency to discourage fast running seems less likely than relatively constant-voltage shock to exert facilitative effects on performance during extinction. Scrambled shock may differ from continuous shock in ways that have not yet been determined.

5. Punishment is more likely to retard the rate of extinction of a reasonably strong than of a weak response. The relative dominance of the strong response will be increased by punishment-produced motivational increments, permitting it to compete more successfully with punishment-generated inhibitory tendencies.

6. Responses of intermediate strength are more likely than highly practiced ones to show actual improvement (not just retardation of extinction) during punished-extinction trials. Obviously, if a performance ceiling has been reached, further improvement under any conditions is impossible, and if too little training has been given, the reaction cannot be expected to survive the inhibitory impact of early confrontations with punishment. Furthermore, very weak reactions may extinguish too quickly to provide sensitive indications of the effects of extinction-retarding punishments.

7. So-called punishment during extinction following avoidance training should be more facilitative of performance than punishment following escape training. In the avoidance situation the subject learns to

perform the kinds of responses which will count as self-punitive behavior if exhibited during the test period. Avoidance-escape training, however, which involves interstimulus intervals too short for complete avoidance, may prove to be superior both to ordinary escape and to avoidance training.

8. The interpolation of a few regular extinction trials between acquisition and punished extinction may increase the probability of observing vicious-circle behavior, perhaps because the animal is provided with opportunities to initiate the response under conditions like those encountered during punished extinction. Partial reinforcement during the acquisition of escape responses, though it provides similar opportunities, fails to prolong the course of punished extinction.

9. The punished-extinction phase of a self-punitive study normally involves abrupt transitions from punishment to no punishment (or the reverse) in a given section of the runway or shuttle box. The chances of observing vicious-circle effects may be increased by smoothing the transitions through the use of step-wise increases or decreases in punishment over trials. Such graduated changes should increase the likelihood that running will become conditioned to the new stimulus sets without disruption.

10. The characteristics of the last response that terminates punishment during extinction should affect the strength of the self-punitive phenomenon. The best results should be observed when the direction and general topography of that response is like the one undergoing extinction. If the final movement of the sequence is directed backward toward the start box, little facilitation is anticipated.

11. A fixed-length punishment zone in a runway or shuttle box is probably more beneficial during extinction than a fixed-duration punishment, presumably because the former may be more conducive to high-speed locomotion than the latter.

12. A punishment zone near the middle of the behavior sequence may be more facilitative of performance than one near the beginning or the end, though this will depend on the nature of the previous training. Punishment near the start may be superior following escape training, but punishment near the goal might be better after avoidance or avoidance-escape training.

13. The length of the punishment zone may well be significant. The meagre available evidence favors the conclusion that an extended zone is more facilitative than a short one. Interactions with the position of the zone and with the kind of training preceding extinction are expected. In shifting from escape training to punished extinction the length of the punishment zone decreases whereas in shifting from avoidance training it increases.

14. Extremely long intertrial intervals may diminish the facilitative

role of punishment by providing for the dissipation of its motivational effects.

15. Goal boxes having tactual, visual, and perhaps olfactory cues that are substantially different from those in the punishment zone may enhance vicious-circle behavior by promoting more complete postpunishment relaxation and more abrupt fear reduction. Start boxes and punishment zones should probably be similar, however, so as to guarantee the generalization of fear from the punishment region back to the start.

16. There is reason to believe that running-speed curves for groups that are punished during extinction are higher for a considerable number of trials than those for nonpunished subjects. With continued extinction, however, the curves may cross, with the running speeds of nonpunished subjects exceeding those of the punished animals. If this is the case, a lenient criterion of extinction, such as one failure to enter the goal box in 1 minute will be more likely to provide data favoring the vicious-circle expectations than a more stringent criterion of one failure in 10 minutes. With the lenient criterion, punished subjects will be performing at a higher level than nonpunished controls when the criterion is reached, whereas the reverse may be true if the more stringent criterion is applied.

17. Many other more minor variables may also affect self-punitive behavior. Among these are: the strain of animals (hooded rats appear to exhibit self-punitive behavior more frequently than albinos), the type of start box (trap-door-floored boxes seem to enhance starting latencies and encourage fast running), the presence of irrelevant sources of drive (hungry rats may be more fearful in aversive situations and hence more self-punitive than satiated animals), and the width and length of the runway (wide runways seem to make it easier for animals to turn around and retreat while long runways permit the subjects to attain higher running speeds).

REFERENCES

Anderson, N. H., & Nakamura, C. Y. Avoidance decrement in avoidance conditioning. *Journal of Comparative and Physiological Psychology,* 1964, **57**, 196–204.

Azrin, N. H., & Holz, W. C. Punishment. In W. K. Honig (Ed.), *Operant behavior: Areas of research and application.* New York: Appleton-Century-Crofts, 1966. Pp. 380–447.

Beecroft, R. S. Near-goal punishment of avoidance running. *Psychonomic Science,* 1967, **8**, 109–110.

Beecroft, R. S., & Bouska, S. A. Learning self-punitive running. *Psychonomic Science,* 1967, **8**, 107–108.

Beecroft, R. S., Bouska, S. A., & Fisher, B. G. Punishment intensity and self-punitive behavior. *Psychonomic Science,* 1967, **8**, 351–352.

BEECROFT, R. S., & BROWN, J. S. Punishment following escape and avoidance training. *Psychonomic Science,* 1967, **8**, 349–350.

BEECROFT, R. S., FISHER, B. G., & BOUSKA, S. A. Punishment continuity and self-punitive behavior. *Psychonomic Science,* 1967, **9**, 127–128.

BENDER, L., & MELVIN, K. B. Self-punitive behavior: Effects of percentage of punishment on extinction of escape and avoidance responses. *Psychonomic Science,* 1967, **9**, 573–574.

BROWN, J. S. Pleasure-seeking behavior and the drive-reduction hypothesis. *Psychological Review,* 1955, **62**, 169–179.

BROWN, J. S. A behavioral analysis of masochism. *Journal of Experimental Research in Personality,* 1965, **1**, 65–70. (a)

BROWN, J. S. Experimental masochism and allied phenomena. Progress report on NIH Grants M-4952 and MH-11734, December, 1965. (b)

BROWN, J. S., ANDERSON, D. C., & WEISS, C. G. Self-punitive behavior under conditions of massed practice. *Journal of Comparative and Physiological Psychology,* 1965, **60**, 451–453.

BROWN, J. S., HORSFALL, R. B., & VAN BRUGGEN, P. J. Self-punitive behavior as a function of the position of the shock in the behavior sequence. Unpublished study cited in Brown (1965b).

BROWN, J. S., MARTIN, R. C., & MORROW, M. W. Self-punitive behavior in the rat: Facilitative effects of punishment on resistance to extinction. *Journal of Comparative and Physiological Psychology,* 1964, **57**, 127–133.

BROWN, J. S., & VAN BRUGGEN, P. J. The effect of various CS-UCS intervals upon locomotor avoidance behavior. Unpublished experiment cited in Brown (1965b).

CAMPBELL, B. A., SMITH, N. F., & MISANIN, J. R. Effects of punishment on extinction of avoidance behavior: Avoidance–avoidance conflict or vicious circle behavior? *Journal of Comparative and Physiological Psychology,* 1966, **62**, 495–498.

CHURCH, R. M. The varied effects of punishment on behavior. *Psychological Review,* 1963, **70**, 369–402.

DENNY, M. R., KOONS, P. B., & MASON, J. E. Extinction of avoidance as a function of the escape situation. *Journal of Comparative and Physiological Psychology,* 1959, **52**, 212–214.

GUTHRIE, E. R. *The psychology of learning.* New York: Harper, 1935.

GWINN, G. T. The effects of punishment on acts motivated by fear. *Journal of Experimental Psychology,* 1949, **39**, 260–269.

HORNEY, K. *The neurotic personality of our time.* New York: Norton, 1937.

HURWITZ, H. M. B., BOLAS, D., & HARITOS, M. Vicious circle behaviour under two shock intensities. *British Journal of Psychology,* 1961, **52**, 377–383.

IMADA, H. The effects of punishment on avoidance behavior. *Japanese Psychological Research,* 1959, **1**, 27-38.

JONES, M. B. An experimental study of extinction. *Psychological Monographs,* 1953, **67** (19, Whole No. 369).

KELLER, F. S., & SCHOENFELD, W. N. *Principles of psychology.* New York: Appleton-Century-Crofts, 1950.

KNAPP, R. K. Acquisition and extinction of avoidance with similar and different shock and escape situations. *Journal of Comparative and Physiological Psychology,* 1965, **60,** 272–273.

LAWRENCE, D. H., & MILLER, N. E. A positive relationship between reinforcement and resistance to extinction produced by removing a source of confusion from a technique that had produced opposite results. *Journal of Experimental Psychology,* 1947, **37,** 494–509.

LOHR, T. F. The effect of shock on the rat's choice of a path to food. *Journal of Experimental Psychology,* 1959, **58,** 312–318.

MARTIN, R. C. Vicious circle behavior and escape conditioning as a function of intensity of punishment. Unpublished doctoral dissertation, University of Florida, 1964.

MARTIN, R. C. Stopping self-punitive behavior by prolonging one intertrial interval. Paper presented at the meeting of the Psychonomic Society, 1967.

MARTIN, R. C., & MELVIN, K. B. Vicious circle behavior as a function of delay of punishment. *Psychonomic Science,* 1964, **1,** 415–416.

MARTIN, R. C., & MELVIN, K. B. Punishment-induced facilitation: Comments and analysis. *Psychonomic Science,* 1966, **5,** 269–270.

MARTIN, R. C., & MOON, T. Self-punitive behavior and periodic punishment. Paper presented at the meeting of the Psychonomic Society, 1967.

MELVIN, K. B. Escape learning and "vicious-circle" behavior as a function of percentage of reinforcement. *Journal of Comparative and Physiological Psychology,* 1964, **58,** 248–251.

MELVIN, K. B., ATHEY, G. I., JR., & HEASLEY, F. H. Effects of duration and delay of shock on self-punitive behavior in the rat. *Psychological Reports,* 1965, **17,** 107–112.

MELVIN, K. B., & BENDER, L. Self-punitive avoidance behavior: Effects of changes in punishment intensity. *Psychological Record,* 1968, **18,** 29–34.

MELVIN, K. B., & MARTIN, R. C. Facilitative effects of two modes of punishment on resistance to extinction. *Journal of Comparative and Physiological Psychology,* 1966, **62,** 491–494.

MELVIN, K. B., & SMITH, F. H. Self-punitive avoidance behavior in the rat. *Journal of Comparative and Physiological Psychology,* 1967, **63,** 533–535.

MELVIN, K. B., & STENMARK, D. E. Facilitative effects of punishment on the establishment of a fear motivated response. *Journal of Comparative and Physiological Psychology,* 1968, **65,** 517–519.

MOWRER, O. H. On the dual nature of learning—A reinterpretation of "conditioning" and "problem-solving." *Harvard Educational Review,* 1947, **17,** 102–148.

MOWRER, O. H. *Learning theory and personality dynamics.* New York: Ronald Press, 1950.

MOWRER, O. H. *Learning theory and behavior.* New York: Wiley, 1960.

MOYER, K. E. A study of some of the variables of which fixation is a function. *Journal of Genetic Psychology,* 1955, **86,** 3–31.

MOYER, K. E. The effects of shock on anxiety-motivated behavior in the rat. *Journal of Genetic Psychology,* 1957, **91,** 197–203.

SANTOS, J. F. The influence of amount and kind of training on the acquisition and extinction of escape and avoidance responses. *Journal of Comparative and Physiological Psychology,* 1960, **53,** 284–289.

SELIGMAN, M. E. P., & CAMPBELL, B. A. Effect of intensity and duration of punishment on extinction of an avoidance response. *Journal of Comparative and Physiological Psychology*, 1965, **59**, 295–297.

SEWARD, J. P., KING, R. M., CHOW, T., & SHIFLETT, S. C. Persistence of punished escape responses. *Journal of Comparative and Physiological Psychology*, 1965, **60**, 265–268.

SEWARD, J. P., & RASKIN, D. C. The role of fear in aversive behavior. *Journal of Comparative and Physiological Psychology*, 1960, **53**, 328–335.

SHEFFIELD, F. D., & TEMMER, H. W. Relative resistance to extinction of escape training and avoidance training. *Journal of Experimental Psychology*, 1950, **40**, 287–298.

SMITH, N. F., MISANIN, J. R., & CAMPBELL, B. A. Effect of punishment on extinction of an avoidance response: Facilitation or inhibition? *Psychonomic Science*, 1966, **4**, 271–272. (a)

SMITH, N. F., MISANIN, J. R., & CAMPBELL, B. A. Effect of punishment: Facilitation or inhibition? A reply to Martin and Melvin. *Psychonomic Science*, 1966, **5**, 363–364. (b)

SOLOMON, R. L., KAMIN, L. J., & WYNNE, L. C. Traumatic avoidance learning: The outcomes of several extinction procedures with dogs. *Journal of Abnormal and Social Psychology*, 1953, **48**, 291–302.

SOLOMON, R. L., & WYNNE, L. C. Traumatic avoidance learning: The principles of anxiety conservation and partial irreversibility. *Psychological Review*, 1954, **61**, 353–385.

WHITEIS, U. E. Punishment's influence on fear and avoidance. *Harvard Educational Review*, 1956, **26**, 360–373.

APPENDICES

Summary of the Discussion at the Conference

The Conference on Punishment was held in Princeton, New Jersey, from May 31 through June 4, 1967. Most of the participants at the conference prepared a chapter-length manuscript for distribution several weeks prior to the meeting, so that the conference itself consisted primarily of discussions rather than formal presentations. Since there was no audience, the discussion was informal and candid. Many of the comments and criticisms were directly relevant only to a single chapter, and most of these remarks were considered by the authors in the revision of their chapters, which were completed in the Fall of 1967. Some of the remarks during the discussion, however, were applicable to several chapters, and several types of remarks occurred in more than one context. We have attempted to identify some of the recurrent themes and to organize a summary of the discussion around them.

The discussion of the 15 chapters lasted $1\frac{1}{2}$ to 2 hours for each; all of this was recorded on tape. The complete transcript ran to nearly 600 pages. From the complete transcript we prepared an abbreviated transcript of about 100 pages which included what we considered to be the essential aspects of the discussion at the conference. This served as the basic document for the preparation of this summary. Obviously, considerable editorial discretion was required to prepare a summary of the discussion of 21 psychologists during a 4-day conference. Each participant in the conference, undoubtedly, would have a somewhat different perception of the critical aspects of the discussion. Nonetheless, we hope that this summary provides a reasonably accurate account of the major views that were expressed and that are not included in one or more of the chapters.

We have organized the recorded comments into three sections: (1) a discussion of terminology, which includes an attempt to define punishment and to devise a nomenclature for classical conditioning and instrumental learning paradigms; (2) a discussion of methods, which includes a consideration of experimental designs and apparatus employed in punishment experiments; and (3) a discussion of those results or ideas which have an important bearing on the understanding of the effects of punishment on behavior.

Terminology

One of the repetitive themes of the conference was a concern with terminology and descriptive labels for various experimental procedures. Since the participants came to the conference from many different traditions within experimental psychology, there were frequent questions about the precise meaning of various phrases. As a result, a portion of the last session of the conference was devoted to an effort to achieve some consensus regarding the usage of certain key terms. This session consisted of a free-wheeling discussion during which considerable agreement was achieved regarding various terminological conventions.

Punishment

The discussion was begun by Logan who suggested that we ought to attempt to define punishment. To which Brown replied, "Punishment or punishers?" This precipitated a lengthy discussion and evaluation of the various meanings of the two terms. Some of the highlights of this discussion were as follows:

It was first pointed out that there were two conventional approaches to the definition of punishment (Logan). One is to define punishment in a manner opposite but otherwise analogous to the familiar functional definition of reinforcement; i.e., punishment is the presentation of an event consequent upon a response that reduces the probability of the response. The other is to say that punishment is the presentation of an aversive stimulus consequent upon a response, and then define aversiveness by some other operation. For example, a noxious stimulus could be one that would maintain escape behavior.

Several objections to the use of the escape criterion of a noxious stimulus were raised during the session: (1) Psychologists who believe in the avoidance theory of punishment would not be content with defining aversiveness as just escape, but would require that the stimulus maintain avoidance behavior. Only if it would maintain avoidance behavior would it have the property of leading to avoidance in the punishment context (Logan). (2) An animal does not always escape from some noxious stimuli that are adequate to suppress behavior when they are made contingent upon a response. For example, if the shock is extremely severe (Rachlin) or of very short duration (Church), it may be adequate to suppress behavior when contingent upon a response although an animal cannot learn to escape from it. Further discussion revealed there was general agreement that a punishment procedure necessarily implies a contingency between a response and a noxious stimulus.[1] However, there was no agreement as to whether the criterion of noxiousness should be a reduction in rate of responding or an independent assessment of the noxious properties of the stimulus.

In the course of this discussion Brown suggested that we define a punisher in the same way that we define a reinforcer. In this paradigm "reinforcer" would be used as the equivalent of "reward," and "punisher" as the equivalent of "noxious stimulus." However, there was some dissatisfaction with the ambiguity of the term "reinforcer" since a reinforcer may refer to either an unconditioned stimulus in classical conditioning or a reward in instrumental training. Thus, in a CER experiment, omission of the reinforcer could refer

[1] Thus it would be inconsistent to use the concept of noncontingent punishment (Logan).

to either omission of shock (US) or of food (reward). There was even greater dissatisfaction with the term "punisher." (1) It may lead to confusion since some readers will think of the punisher as the human being who is administering the noxious stimulus (the experimenter) rather than the noxious stimulus itself (Solomon). (2) Furthermore, since we agreed that punishment necessarily implies a contingency of an outcome upon a response, it would be unwise to use the term "punisher" to refer to a noxious stimulus that is not necessarily contingent upon a response.

Brown then pointed out that we must abandon the hope that there is one inviolable definition of a noxious stimulus which can never be changed. A shock of some fixed intensity and duration is not always a punisher. It is a punisher for some organisms, at some times, in some situations. Evidence may be obtained that a given shock has produced escape, and this may then be called a punisher. Or, a given shock in some situation in the past may have been demonstrated to have certain inhibiting effects and this may be called a punisher. In other situations these shocks may not serve as a punisher. It was then generally agreed that the word "punisher" was roughly synonomous with an annoyer, a noxious stimulus, or an aversive stimulus, but there was no clear preference for one term over another. In this case, as in several others, our aim was to eliminate ambiguity (one word with several meanings) and we were not seriously concerned with multiple terms (several words with a single meaning).

Another term that was discussed in this context was "negative reinforcement." Herrnstein pointed out that in some cases it refers to the onset of a noxious stimulus used in a punishment procedure (Skinner, 1938) and in other cases it refers to the termination of a noxious stimulus used in an escape or avoidance paradigm (Skinner, 1953). There was general agreement that "negative reinforcement," if used at all, should refer only to the latter situation.

Classical Conditioning versus Instrumental Learning

Solomon urged that terminological conventions be adopted to strengthen the operational distinction between classical conditioning and instrumental learning. Everyone agreed that it would be extremely useful to be able to identify through terminology the type of procedure used even though the processes underlying the two phenomena may turn out to be the same. The proposal was to reserve the word "conditioning" for procedures in which a contingency between the stimulus and the outcome has been specified, and to reserve the word "training" for procedures in which a contingency between the response and outcome has been specified, and to reserve the word "training" for procedures in which a contingency between the response and outcome has been specified. The outcome of a classical conditioning procedure is an unconditioned stimulus (US); the outcome of an instrumental training procedure is a reward or a noxious stimulus (see Table A–1). Thus, it would be appropriate to say, "The experimenter *trained* the subject to press a lever," if food (an outcome) were contingent upon the lever response. It would be appropriate to say, "The experimenter *conditioned* the subject," if shock (an outcome) were contingent upon a tone stimulus.

TABLE A–1

	Classical Conditioning	Instrumental Training
Other names	Pavlovian conditioning Respondent conditioning	Thorndikian training Operant training
Operational basis for the distinction	Specification of relationship between stimulus and outcome	Specification of relationship between response and outcome
Designation of stimulus	Conditioned stimulus (CS)	Discriminative stimulus (S)
Designation of outcome	Unconditioned stimulus (US)	Reward (also reinforcer) Noxious stimulus (also aversive stimulus, punisher)

To maintain the operational distinction, it was proposed that in conditioning the stimulus should be identified as a conditioned stimulus (CS) and that in instrumental training the stimulus is a discriminative stimulus (S). Further, it was suggested that both CS+ and S+ should refer to those instances in which the probability of an outcome is greater in the presence of a stimulus than in the absence of that stimulus. And, conversely, CS– and S– refer to those instances in which the probability of an outcome is lower in the presence of a stimulus than in the absence of that stimulus.[2]

Discussion of Methods

Nearly all of the evidence presented at the conference, even in discussion, was the result of laboratory experimentation. Although other sources of information were considered, they were frequently criticized. For example, evidence from correlational studies was questioned since it did not lead to inferences regarding the direction of causation, and evidence from case studies was criticized because interpretations may be markedly influenced by the prior beliefs of the investigator (Mowrer). Most of the experiments were relatively simple in design (in contrast to complex factorial designs). Miller said that he had learned from bitter experience not to design an elaborate experiment, with all possible control groups, and then find that the experimental variable is ineffective. In his judgment, an experimenter should discover whether there are differences between two extreme groups and later add the adequate control groups to determine if the phenomenon is what he thinks it is or something else.

[2] S^D and S^Δ have often been used instead of the symbols S+ and S– and are perfectly acceptable.

Experimental Design

Relative versus absolute measures of responding. On several occasions there was discussion of the relative merits of absolute and relative measures of the effect of a treatment. An absolute measure refers to the observed performance of a subject (e.g., response rate); a relative measure refers to the performance of a subject relative to its performance at some other time. Various relative measures were used to describe the performance of rats in punishment, CER, and generalization procedures.

The advantage of a relative measure results from the fact that different animals have very different, but very stable, rates. Hoffman pointed out, for example, that one bird may make about 40 responses per minute while another will make about 65 responses per minute, and that these differences may be maintained for 4 or 5 years.

The major disadvantage of a relative measure is that some information regarding the original performance is lost. If a ratio measure changes, it is extremely useful to know whether this is due to a change in the numerator or the denominator (Miller). From inspection of the change in response rate from a prior response rate (A) to a current response rate (B), the reader can derive a relative measure, but it is impossible to derive the current response rate from the relative measure alone. Of course, the mean of a ratio is not necessarily equal to the ratio of the means. Nonetheless, one can estimate the current response rate from the mean of the relative measure and one other number, the prior response rate (Church). The conclusion was that exclusive reliance upon relative measures would be unfortunate unless some other information were given from which a reader could recapture the raw data (Miller).

In some cases, the conclusions based upon a relative measure may be different from the conclusions based upon an absolute measure (Brown). There was extended discussion of the results of one of the experiments reported by Hearst (Chapter 8 of this volume) in which he concluded that preextinction to the CS produces a steeper generalization gradient. When relative gradients are plotted (percentage of responding to the CS at various stimulus values) there is more control by the CS if preextinction to the CS has been given than if it has not (Hearst). But absolute gradients (response rate at various stimulus values) do not suggest this conclusion (Brown). Nonetheless, it is clear that the proportion of responses to the CS does increase as a result of the treatment, and some method must be used to account for the radically different overall response rates before and after the preextinction procedure (Hearst).

It was also pointed out that in other instances the base rate is reasonably constant, and therefore the conclusions based upon an absolute measure and a relative measure would be the same (Hoffman). The aim should be to find a unit of measurement that gives the simplest total picture (Logan).

Control procedures for experiments using CS+ and CS−. Several of the participants described experiments in which an alleged excitatory stimulus (CS+) produced an acceleration of response rate by subjects performing on an aversive base line. On the first occasion that such an experiment was described, Kamin said that he felt compelled to say that it is absolutely necessary to have a discriminatory control condition (see, for example, Brimer & Kamin, 1963). There was general agreement regarding the necessity for such a condition because of the considerable effects that novel stimuli produce on both appetitive and aversive behavior (disinhibition, external inhibition). Solomon observed that a novel stimulus would cause dogs on a Sidman-avoidance schedule in a shuttle box to increase their response rate—an observation similar to the increase in response rate if the experimenter accidentally dropped a screwdriver on the floor while the animal is Sidman-responding. Hoffman observed that a novel stimulus would cause pigeons in his situation (variable-interval food schedule) to decrease their response rate—a result that may be considered consistent with the acceleration to a novel stimulus produced on an aversive base line. Solomon considered the problem more complex since a stimulus that is exciting to an animal in the shuttlebox may be slightly inhibiting or disruptive to an animal who is panel pressing on a Sidman schedule. In short, appropriate control groups are required in each experiment in which there is a change in response rate as a result of the alleged inhibitory or excitatory aspect of a stimulus.

Yoked control method.   The yoked control design was employed in experiments described by three of the participants: Miller, Maier, and Hoffman. On the first occasion that such an experiment was described, there was an extended discussion regarding the legitimacy of the method. Church attempted to apply the general argument stated in the paper entitled "Systematic effects of random error in the yoked control design" (Church, 1964) to a specific experiment described by Miller (Chapter 11 of this volume). The criticism of the legitmacy of the design of the experiment was clearly separated from an evaluation of the correctness of the conclusions of the experiment; i.e., many experiments that employed this design have come to conclusions that are undoubtedly correct. The general criticism of the yoked-control design is that sources of random error (variability between subjects and within subjects) can lead to systematic differences between an experimental group and a yoked-control group, even in the absence of any treatment effect. An application of the general argument to the experiment described by Miller was as follows: Presumably there are individual differences in reactivity to shock. An experimental animal that is greatly upset by shock may quickly learn an avoidance response and, therefore, receive few shocks. An experimental animal that is not greatly upset may learn an avoidance response slowly and therefore receive many shocks. An experimental animal that is not greatly upset may learn an avoidance response slowly and therefore receive many shocks. This high correlation between emotional reactivity and number of shocks would not appear in the yoked-control group (i.e., in some cases a reactive subject would receive many shocks) and therefore might lead in Miller's experiment to a greater rate of ulceration in the yoked-control group than in the experimental group.

Although Miller believed that this criticism of the yoked-control design might be taken as a possible argument against the conclusions of the experiment, he took special note of the "charitable possibility" that Church had acknowledged that the results are correct in any case. Furthermore, he said that individual differences in susceptibility to electric shocks should be minimal in this experiment because of the high intensity employed. He noted, however, that there could be some individual differences in apprehensiveness as a result of the shock which might lead to individual differences in alertness. There was general agreement that alternatives to the yoked control are needed, but none were proposed. Furthermore, some participants belived that in many instances the yoked-control design was the best available.

Apparatus

Shock sources. The inductorium used in the early punishment experiments produced only single pulses and had to be repeatedly interrupted for shocks of longer duration (Campbell). The Harvard Inductorium, however, had a self-interrupting circuit on the same principle as the vibrator in an automobile that converts the DC voltage of the battery into the AC voltage that is stepped up by a transformer to operate a radio (Brown). Of course, as the contacts wear there are various changes in frequency, and the wave form of such a device is ragged. Mowrer was probably the first individual to use a fixed-impedance source in fear-conditioning studies (Miller). It consisted simply of a step-up transformer, a potentiometer voltage divider, and a series resistor. With this device it was possible to work between the two extremes of constant voltage and constant current. By watching rats, Miller noted, they were lucky to choose a series resistor of about 250K that now appears to be close to ideal. Campbell said there was no question that this work led to the widespread use of fixed-impedance sources.

Grids. Brown noted that the grids that he and Miller built at Yale have not been duplicated. They used a pair of very fine stainless steel wires wrapped around separators in the form of a helix. The advantage of the thin wire was that marked changes in the position of the rat on the wire would not be associated with marked changes in the area of contact so that the current density would be relatively more constant than with the standard-size grids of about $\frac{3}{16}$ inch and far more constant than with the large ($\frac{1}{4}$-in.) diameter grids that have been used in some experiments. Campbell said that he was not familiar with any comparison of the effectiveness of shock with the large and small grids.

Scramblers. Campbell noted that the method of scrambling is probably not a variable of great importance. In one systematic study he compared the aversiveness of various scrambling rates (10 per sec. to 1 per 5 sec.). Only at very slow rates of shifting polarity (e.g., 1 per 5 sec.), when the subject had the opportunity to shift to safe grids, was there a preference among rates. Ideally, a scrambler would put any particular bar at opposite polarity from any other bar exactly half the time. Church contrasted scramblers that do not have all pairs of bars equally often at opposite polarity (e.g., Grason-Stadler Model E1064GS) with those which have only one bar at opposite polarity from all the others at any given time (Lehigh Valley Electronics Model 1311). The percentage of time the animal receives shock, particularly with the latter type of scrambler, is markedly influenced by the number of bars that he is in contact with (Hoffman).

Discussion of Results

The Effectiveness of Punishment

Estes criticized textbook passages that have attributed to him the idea that punishment is a highly ineffective means of influencing behavior. His research on punishment (Estes, 1944) began with the opposite assumption—that people had discounted the effects of punishment because they had not used real punishments. His own first studies, he recalled, introduced electric shocks of appreciable severity and yielded substantial suppression of response.

Studies that show weak shock to be mildly reinforcing have capitalized on the curiosity or exploratory aspect of a novel stimulus (Campbell). In a preference situation a rat may show extensive exploratory behavior of a low shock that he will ultimately avoid 100% of the time.

Contingent versus Noncontingent Shock

Magnitude of suppression. Punishment refers to a noxious stimulus that is contingent upon a response, but a noxious stimulus that is independent of a response may also produce suppression of that response. In general, the literature shows that there is less suppression with noncontingent shock than with contingent shock, and that the suppression is more transient (Herrnstein). Additional sessions with noncontingent shock, at a frequency and intensity that produces permanent suppression with contingent shock may result in complete recovery. Herrnstein noted that some experiments that have compared the magnitude of suppression produced by contingent and noncontingent shocks (e.g., Church, Chapter 5 of this volume) underestimate the magnitude of the difference since the frequency of shocks received by the noncontingent group was greater than that by the contingent group, which markedly reduced the frequency of shock received by not responding. Mowrer described some conditions under which noncontingent shock produced an augmentation of behavior instead of suppression. Ullman (1951) shocked rats during the first 5 seconds of each minute and recorded the amount of eating. At first there was suppression, but eventually there was a substantial increase in the amount of eating.

In addition to the overall degree of response suppression, the kind of behavior produced by contingent shock is sometimes different from that produced by noncontingent shock (Hoffman). A rat may show considerable conflict behavior (approach and avoidance to the lever) if a moderate degree of response suppression was produced by response-contingent shock, but not if it is produced by noncontingent shock (Church). Moreover, under some conditions contingent shock may produce less suppression than a noncontingent shock (Hoffman, Chapter 7 of this volume).

There was some discussion of the appropriate measure of the degree of contingency or dependence of the aversive stimulus upon the response. Herrnstein emphasized the importance of the relationship between the number of responses and the number of shocks; Miller distinguished between this meaning of "dependence" and one based on the amount of information provided by a response about the shock. He suspected that the occurrence of an occasional noncontingent shock would reduce the magnitude of suppression of a rat that received contingent shocks (slightly delayed by some short variable interval to make the situation a bit more confusing to the rat). Miller spoke of this as "spoiling" the contingency correlation.

Level of anxiety. Although the magnitude of suppression is greater with contingent than noncontingent shock, the degree of general emotional upset of an animal may be greater with noncontingent shock than with contingent shock. One general principle may be that the general emotional upset of an animal is greater if the moment of shock is unpredictable than if it is predictable. For example, Azrin (1956) demonstrated there was more general disruption when noncontingent shock came on a VI schedule rather than an FI schedule (Rachlin). Various words were used to describe this emotional state (e.g., generalized fear, free-floating anxiety) and various measures of it were described (breakdown of a discrimination, ulceration, response suppression in the absence of the danger signal). Contingent shocks were assumed to be more predictable than noncontingent shocks. Physiological measures of fear may indicate greater upset if punishment is delayed than if it is immediate (Miller). In discriminative punishment situations the absence of the signal may be considered to be a safety signal, a differential inhibitor of fear (Seligman). In comparison of the avoidance group and a yoked control, a subject in the former group can predict the occurrence of a shock (if the signal occurs and he does not respond), but the yoked-control subject cannot predict the occurrence of a shock since it is independent of its response (Logan). Rachlin said that in the experiments comparing choice between noncontingent and contingent shock (Chapter 4 of this volume), the noncontingent shocks were presented in a regular rather than an irregular manner so that an animal could predict the occurrence of a shock in the noncontingent shock condition as well as in the contingent condition. The difference in performance of groups with regular and irregular noncontingent shock might be substantial if there were a substantial interval between shocks, e.g., 1 minute (Church).

In comparisons between discriminative punishment and CER conditions, subjects in both groups may predict the occurrence of the shock, but only the former group can control the occurrence of a shock. The occurrence of a shock that cannot be controlled may produce more general emotional upset than a shock that can be controlled (Seligman). For example, Hearst reported that shock at the end of a stimulus (CER) produced a breakdown in appetitive discrimination performance, but that response-contingent shock during the stimulus (discriminative punishment) did not do so after the first few days.

An animal that has completely suppressed due to noncontingent shock may show considerably greater generalized anxiety than an animal that has completely suppressed as a result of contingent shock. The latter may not continue to make the instrumental response, but it may be no more afraid than a well-trained avoidance animal (i.e., it is merely doing something which guarantees that there will be no more shock) (Church).

Helplessness versus Incompatible Response

Is it possible explicitly to reinforce any response in the harness which would debilitate a dog to the extent that independence between shock and any response in the harness debilitates a dog in the shuttle box (Maier)? A test between these two bases for interference with subsequent learning would be to compare the avoidance learning of (1) animals that had been trained to perform a directly incompatible instrumental response such as "standing still" with (2) animals that had received the same shock independently of responding (Seligman). This comparison would not, however, be a crucial test, since the two hypotheses are not completely incompatible (Miller). The test might only indicate which of the two factors are stronger given the particular circumstances of the experiment. What would occur if pretraining involved the reinforcement of some active response, but it was always a different one (Miller)?

If shock termination is a critical factor the subjects could, in principle, as easily learn omnipotence rather than helplessness, since anything the subject does is followed by the termination of the shock (Rachlin).

Clinical psychologists may be interested in the results of "helplessness" experiments (this volume, pp. 319–337) because so many patients, particularly depressive patients, keep saying, "Well, it's no use." They are very passive and apathetic. Perhaps they have learned some passive type of response of hopelessness, perhaps some kind of reward learning is involved, or perhaps it is just a physiological change that produces this change in mood and feeling. In any case, the research does seem quite relevant (Miller).

Punishment of Various Responses in a Behavior Sequence

Solomon described the results of some research on the punishment of the consummatory responses of dogs that are consistent with the principle that punishment early in the behavior sequence produces greater suppression of a response than punishment late in the behavior sequence. Eating may be considered as a response chain with constantly repeated components of chewing and swallowing. The most effective way of producing eating inhibition is punishment of an early member of the sequence, and the least effective way to produce the inhibition is to administer the punishment late in the sequence (even though the behavior is still eating). If the dog is swatted with a rolled up newspaper when he starts to eat his first mouthful, he will even starve to death rather than touch food; the same punishment after the dog has taken several mouthfuls, even though he gets hit while eating, does not produce extensive eating inhibition and he will eat the food in a very short period of time. Punishment of eating is not the adequate description, but it is the member of the eating chain that is followed by punishment.

Discriminative and Aversive Aspects of a Signal Associated with Shock

In a signalled Sidman avoidance schedule the rat typically will wait until the onset of the CS before making a response. One of the perplexing problems for theories of "learned aversiveness" is why the animal does not make the response before the CS to postpone the secondarily aversive stimulus as well as the US (Logan). There might be many situations in both avoidance and discriminative punishment where it seems more reasonable to view the informative aspects of that signal as the dominant ones rather than the conditioned aversive aspects (Church).

Contrast

Herrnstein pointed out that the studies of frustration in the double runway (e.g., Amsel & Roussel, 1952) are similar to the studies of contrast effects in the Skinner Box. In the latter experiments extinction in the presence of one stimulus increases the rate of responding to a second stimulus. In the double-runway studies the response speed in the second segment of the runway is greater if there is no reward in the goal box at the end of the first segment than if there is reward in this first goal box. A critical missing group in the runway studies is one that is placed in the first goal box and run in the second segment only (Herrnstein). Wagner said that such a group would provide interesting data, and that it might be quite possible to state frustration theory in terms of a more general theory of contrast.

Fixation

In only a few cases, results of experiments appeared to be directly opposed to those previously reported by others. One such case was the experiment of Fowler and Wischner in which punishment during acquisition decreased resistance to extinction (Chapter 12 of this volume). Logan asked why these results were contrary to about five studies in the literature which obtained the opposite results, starting with Farber's fixation effect (Farber, 1948). Various procedural differences were mentioned, but no satisfactory resolution was offered.

Species Differences

Most of the experiments described at the conference used rats as subjects. Three of the contributors used pigeons (Hearst, Hoffman, and Rachlin-Herrnstein), one used monkeys (Hearst), and one used dogs (Maier, Seligman, & Solomon). An implicit assumption in much of this work may have been that the general conclusions from the research transcends the species differences and that the choice of a particular animal is only a matter of convenience. On several occasions, however, questions arose regarding the generality of conclusions across species. Rats that have acquired an instrumental avoidance response have been observed to decrease the percentage of avoidance responses as a function of repeated sessions of training (Coons, Anderson, & Myers, 1960). Seward asked whether this phenomenon was species specific or whether it has also been observed in cats and dogs. Miller said that he did not believe that Konorski or Solomon had complained about this problem with the avoidance response in dogs. Solomon agreed, adding that once a dog emits an avoidance response in a signalized situation, it is almost certain to learn the avoidance response perfectly. Herrnstein said that an interesting fact in comparative psychology is that a great many people who have some skill in training pigeons to do different things have tried to get them to avoid a shock and that they have, by and large, failed. Thus permanent avoidance, temporary avoidance, and no avoidance is readily observed in dogs, rats, and pigeons, respectively.

Classical Conditioning and Instrumental Learning of Autonomic Responses

The discussion of punishment, avoidance, and the conditioned emotional response primarily concerned the influence of various treatment conditions on learned instrumental responses. During the discussion of Miller's paper, however, there was some consideration of the influence of similar treatment conditions on visceral responses: (1) Solomon noted that cardiovascular physiologists have found that a few seconds before a race, the physiological state of a trackman who intends to run a 100-yard dash is quite different than that of one who intends to run a mile. The whole visceral aspect of the body responds not only to the current muscular state of the body, but also to what the muscular task is going to be. (2) Miller described some studies summarized by Bykov (1957) in which trainmen exposed to a long period of cold in freight cars showed anticipatory changes in body temperature before boarding a train, and differential changes in body temperature depending upon whether they were about to enter a cold or warm station. This suggests the possibility that (in addition to the innate mechanism) some cases of homeostasis may be improved by instrumental learning. (3) Kamin indicated that he was bothered by the question of why an aversive US in a Pavlovian paradigm doesn't act as a punisher of the classically-conditioned response. "To put it absurdly," he said, "I ought to learn not to be afraid, because every time I'm afraid, I'm punished for it." This paradox was not resolved, although Brown suggested that this phenomenon may occur in the GSR, since the magnitude of the classical GSR may decrease as a function of increasing trials of classical conditioning.

Experimental Analogues of Guilt

Mowrer defined "guilt" as "fear precipitated by an act which has been punished." He described the following observation as the best analogue of human guilt in animals that he knew: Food on a stick was presented to a rat in a grill box. The animal took the stick, ate the food, and 10 seconds after it dropped the stick the animal received a shock that it had to terminate by leaping into the air. Eventually, the rat learned to eat the food, drop the stick, and leap off the grid before the shock occurred. Logan said that this was not because the rat was guilty; it was a simple anticipatory response. In reply, Mowrer said, "But maybe that's what guilt is, in the simplest case."

Conditioning of Emotional Reactions

Herrnstein asked the following general questions with respect to the Maier, Seligman, and Solomon paper: "I have three questions: the first is how do you distinguish your effects from the classical association of ideas; the second is how do you prove that the effects you are talking about are emotional; and three, how do you exclude the possibility that the rat is performing syllogisms?" The major point of the question was to determine how the authors could decide that one of their effects was emotional (Pavlovian fear-conditioning) and the other effect was cognitive (learned helplessness). As a general answer, Solomon said: "I think that this is partly a philosophical as well as a scientific matter. I think psychology is plagued by the fact that the laws of cognition for the most part are the laws of conditioned emotion. They are identical in most cases. Tolman was the first to point this out. In his chapter that he wrote for the Moss book on comparative psychology [Tolman, 1934], he argued strongly that the laws of Pavlov were the laws of cognition. He pointed out the real difficulty this poses for psychology in unraveling the emotion–knowledge distinction. I still think Tolman's position on this is essentially the correct one. That is, the laws of conditioning emotional reactions are probably the same as the laws of esablishing cognitions, expectations, and knowledge of what leads to what, with just a few minor exceptions. It seems to me that what we could talk about as conditioned fear reactions could easily be talked about as acquired expectations of shock."

REFERENCES

AMSEL, A., & ROUSSEL, J. Motivational properties of frustration: I. Effect on a running response of the addition of frustration to the motivational complex. *Journal of Experimental Psychology,* 1952, **43**, 363–368.

AZRIN, N. H. Some effects of two intermittent schedules of immediate and non-immediate punishment. *Journal of Psychology,* 1956, **42**, 3–21.

BRIMER, C. J., & KAMIN, L. J. Disinhibition, habituation, sensitization, and the conditioned emotional response. *Journal of Comparative and Physiological Psychology,* 1963, **56**, 508–516.

BYKOV, K. M. *The cerebral cortex and the internal organs.* (W. H. Gantt, Ed. and Tr.) New York: Chemical Publishing Company, 1957.

CHURCH, R. M. Systematic effect of random error in the yoked control design. *Psychological Bulletin,* 1964, **62**, 122–131.

COONS, E. E., ANDERSON, N. H., & MYERS, A. K. Disappearance of avoidance responding during continued training. *Journal of Comparative and Physiological Psychology,* 1960, **53**, 290–292.

ESTES, W. K. An experimental study of punishment. *Psychological Monographs,* 1944, **57** (3, Whole No. 263).

FARBER, I. E. Response fixation under anxiety and non-anxiety conditions. *Journal of Experimental Psychology,* 1948, **38**, 111–131.

SKINNER, B. F. *The behavior of organisms.* New York: Appleton-Century, 1938.

SKINNER, B. F. *Science and human behavior.* New York: Macmillan, 1953.

TOLMAN, E. C. Theories of learning. In F. A. Moss (Ed.), *Comparative psychology.* New York: Prentice-Hall, 1934. Pp. 367–408.

ULLMAN, A. D. The experimental production and analysis of a "compulsive eating symptom" in rats. *Journal of Comparative and Physiological Psychology,* 1951, **44**, 575–581.

Bibliography on Punishment[1]

Erling E. Boe
UNIVERSITY OF PENNSYLVANIA

I. Introduction

The bibliographies presented in the following sections include all relevant articles (and, in some special cases, books) on punishment published through June, 1967.[2] Intentionally excluded are all unpublished manuscripts, papers presented at meetings of learned societies, masters theses, and manuscripts still "in press" on June 30, 1967. Doctoral dissertations, whether or not abstracted in *Dissertation Abstracts,* are included in the bibliographies.

Major problems in compiling bibliographies on behavioral phenomena are (1) establishing an adequate definition of a phenomenon and (2) judging whether specific articles in borderline instances should be included. In the following subsections of the Introduction, the definitions and procedures used in compiling the several bibliographies and the outline are set forth.

The Concept of Punishment

Punishment has traditionally referred to the operation in which an aversive stimulus is presented following the occurrence of a response. The usual, though by no means only, effect of punishment is to reduce the strength of the response upon which the presentation of the aversive stimulus was contingent. An aversive stimulus, in turn, has usually been defined as one which is suitable for the operations of escape learning. That is, it is a stimulus which an organism will seek to terminate. The extent to which the presentation of an aversive stimulus thus defined will reduce the strength of a preceding response depends

---

[1] The compilation of this bibliography was facilitated by a grant from the Faculty Research Fund, University of Victoria, and by material support by the Veterans Administration Hospital (Seattle), the University of Washington, and the University of Pennsylvania.

[2] The phrase "all relevant articles" is used in the sense of all articles identified as relevant after a thorough and systematic search. Although it is almost certain that a few relevant articles have not been found, it is believed that the bibliographies are almost entirely complete.

upon many variables, some of which are parameters of punishment, some are organismic characteristics, and others are situational variables. In a few cases, response-contingent aversive stimulation (i.e., punishment) fails to produce a decrement in response strength. Nevertheless, the punishment operation has been invoked, and other conditions (which may or may not be known) have in these cases nullified its usual effect. Why this should be so may be viewed as just another problem in understanding the behavioral effects of punishment.

Experiments have also demonstrated that the withdrawal of an appetitive stimulus tends to reduce the strength of responses upon which it is contingent, just as the presentation of an aversive stimulus does. Although the stimulus events are different, the behavioral effects are similar. For this reason, it seems appropriate to classify both of these stimulus events as punishers. A similar circumstance obtains for reinforcing events. Both positive and negative reinforcers increase the strength of responses upon which they are contingent. Although the stimulus events differ, the behavioral effects are again similar.

The operations of punishment and reinforcement, along with some of their similarities and differences, are illustrated separately in Fig. B–1. On the left, two reinforcing operations are shown with respect to Response A; on the right, two punishing operations are shown with respect to Response B. Except for the fact that both appetitive and aversive stimuli are involved in punishment and reinforcement, the operations of punishment and reinforcement are independent, and no continuity, temporal or otherwise, is intended.

As Fig. B–1 illustrates, four stimulus events (i.e., changes) are involved in reinforcement and punishment, two for each. The *onset* or presentation of an appetitive stimulus following Response A tends to increase the strength of that

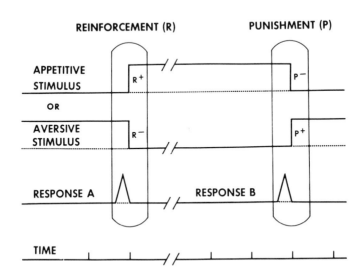

FIG. B–1.   The reinforcement and punishment operations. Although both appetitive and aversive stimuli are involved in reinforcement and punishment, the two operations are independent and no type of continuity should be inferred. It is helpful to consider Responses A and B as being different, and as occurring under different circumstances.

response (or maintains the strength of a response that is already near maximum) and is said to be *positively reinforcing* (R+); the termination or withdrawal of an aversive stimulus following Response A tends to increase the strength of that response and is said to be *negatively reinforcing* (R—). Conversely, the termination or withdrawal of an appetitive stimulus following Response B tends to decrease the strength of that response (or continues to suppress a response that is already near minimum strength) and, by analogy to negative reinforcement which entails the termination of a stimulus, could be said to be *negatively punishing* (P—); the onset or presentation of an aversive stimulus following Response B tends to decrease the strength of that response and, by analogy to positive reinforcement which entails the onset of a stimulus, could be said to be *positively punishing* (P+). The basic behavioral difference between the effects of reinforcement and punishment is that the former tends to increase response strength while the latter tends to decrease it. Although the phrases "positive punishment" and "negative punishment" may sound somewhat odd and unfamiliar, some writers (Logan & Wagner, 1965) have adopted them, and their construction entails the same principles used in formulating the routinely-used concepts of positive and negative reinforcement.

A further useful distinction that is sometimes made occurs between punishment and punishers and between reinforcement and reinforcers. In the empirical sense, punishment and reinforcement can be used to refer to operations; and punisher and reinforcer can be used to refer to stimulus events. The stimulus events defining punishers are the termination of an appetitive stimulus (P—) and the onset of an aversive stimulus (P+); the stimulus events defining reinforcers are the onset of an appetitive stimulus (R+) and the termination of an aversive stimulus (R—). Punishment is the operation in which a punisher is contingent upon the occurrence of a response; similarly, reinforcement is the operation in which a reinforcer is contingent upon the occurrence of a response.[3]

Primary Punishment

Stimulus changes that are punishing or reinforcing without the necessity of being previously associated with other punishing or reinforcing stimuli are appropriate for the operations of primary punishment and primary reinforcement. The Bibliography on Primary Punishment contains references to experiments in which some variation in the punishing condition was introduced by the experimenter. Specifically excluded were studies (1) in which a punishment variable was investigated but not experimentally manipulated, and (2) in which punishment was used but not varied. Among the many experiments falling into the latter category are numerous experiments using the Lashley jumping stand and the step-down response from a platform placed above an energized grid. In the latter instance, for example, a comparison of the step-down latencies of a group of drugged subjects with a control group might be made. Since the variation here is in the drug condition and not in a punishment condition, the experiment would have only used punishment in the investiga-

---

[3] This usage does not include the way in which reinforcement is used in classical conditioning where the reinforcer (i.e., unconditioned stimulus onset) is contingent upon a preceding stimulus instead of a response.

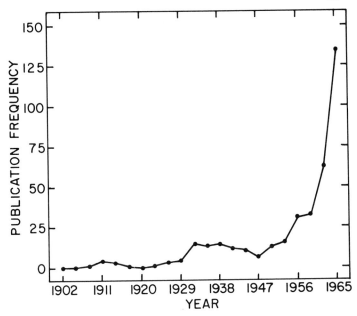

FIG. B–2.   Frequency of publication on primary punishment as a function of year. The years plotted represent the midpoints of class intervals spanning 3-year periods. For example, one publication appeared during the years from 1907 to 1909, four publications during the years from 1910 to 1912, etc. One title (Gates, 1895) included in the Bibliography is not represented in the figure.

tion of a drug effect and, consequently, would be excluded from the bibliography. Only if a systematic variation in a punishment condition were part of the design would the experiment be listed in the bibliography.

Frequently confused with experiments on punishment are avoidance-learning experiments, some of which should be classified under punishment while others should not. Two classes of experiments bearing the word "avoidance" in their title that entail the punishment operation are (1) approach–avoidance conflict experiments (both punishers and reinforcers are contingent upon the occurrence of the same response) and (2) passive avoidance experiments (punishers are contingent upon the occurrence of a response that is usually characterized by a relatively high operant rate and by no history of reinforcement). Active avoidance experiments and escape-learning experiments entail response-contingent *elimination* of aversive stimulation (i.e., either primary or secondary negative reinforcement rather than punishment), and, consequently, are excluded from the Bibliography.[4]

Practically all of the experiments listed in the Bibliography on Primary Punishment entailed positive punishment. The few experiments with negative punishment are identified by an asterisk.

[4] Mowrer (1960) developed the distinction between active and passive avoidance learning in considerable detail.

The publication rate of punishment research has positively accelerated since the first decade of the present century when formal experimentation began (see Fig. B–2). This acceleration would not be noteworthy, however, if it merely kept pace with increases in publication rate in experimental psychology. A comparison of the total number of articles published with the number of primary punishment articles published since 1950 in a group of American journals is shown in Fig. B–3. A high proportion of the total number of articles currently being published on punishment appear in this group of journals. The curves indicate that research on punishment has been increasing at a substantially higher rate than has research in all other areas of experimental psychology covered by the journals. At the descriptive level, one can conclude that punishment research is currently in vogue. Although several hypotheses could be advanced to explain this phenomenon, untestable propositions of this sort could be discussed more appropriately within the context of social philosophy.

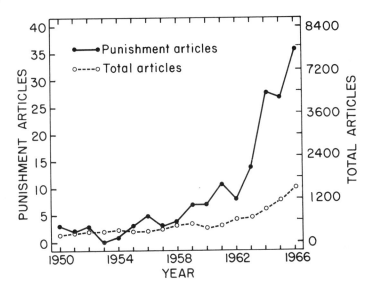

FIG. B–3. Punishment articles and total articles published per year since 1950 in a group of six American journals devoted to research in experimental psychology (i.e., *American Journal of Psychology, Journal of Comparative and Physiological Psychology, Journal of Experimental Psychology, Journal of the Experimental Analysis of Behavior, Journal of Verbal Learning and Verbal Behavior,* and *Psychonomic Science*). The number of punishment articles is read on the left ordinate; the number of total articles is read on the right ordinate. The two ordinates were calibrated so that the average number of punishment articles during the first 6-year period (i.e., 1950–1955) and the average number of total articles during the same period were of equal distance above the abscissa. Thus, the figure shows the relative rates of growth over this base-line period. In short, the number of punishment articles had increased by a factor of 18 over the 1950–1955 base-line period by 1966 while the total number of articles had increased by a factor of only slightly more than five during the same period.

Secondary Punishment

Secondary punishment refers to the operation in which a secondary punisher is contingent upon the occurrence of a response. Secondary punishment is similar to secondary reinforcement in that stimuli which are punishing or reinforcing only as a result of association with other punishers or reinforcers, respectively, are considered to be appropriate for the operations of secondary punishment and secondary reinforcement. Within the class of secondary punishers, two varieties should be distinguished. The first variety is the experimentally produced secondary punisher such as a flashing light which has been paired with the onset of electric shock. When the flashing light is subsequently made contingent upon the occurrence of a response, the strength of that response tends to be reduced, at least temporarily. The second variety of secondary punisher is not experimentally produced. Examples are the spoken word "wrong," and the loss of money. When one of these events is made contingent upon the occurrence of some response, its strength also tends to be reduced, although not so reliably as with experimentally produced secondary punishers. Presumably, the learning history of human subjects has provided these events with an aversive function. Stimulus changes that are not primary punishers are considered to be secondary punishers if a decrement in response strength occurs that is greater than the decrement produced simply by a response-produced change in a comparable neutral stimulus (i.e., one that has not been associated with a primary punisher).

A high proportion of the experiments listed in the Bibliography on Secondary Punishment used nonexperimentally produced secondary punishers. Many of them were included because the experimenters considered them to be punishing even though a punishing effect had not been rigorously demonstrated. The relatively few experiments in which secondary punishers were experimentally produced are identified by a double asterisk in the Bibliography.

Review Articles on Punishment

All theoretical, review, and discussion articles that are directly relevant to or derived from the experimental investigation of punishment are included in the Bibliography on Theoretical, Review, and Discussion Articles on Punishment. Articles on punishment as a means of social control have been excluded. Reasonably extensive textbook treatments have been included even though the book was not primarily on punishment.

Outline of Primary Punishment

An outline has been prepared of all references in the Bibliography on Primary Punishment (Part II). The outline is organized according to independent variable (e.g., intensity of punishment, schedule of punishment) with behavioral categories (e.g., responses at operant level, consummatory responses) as subpoints. The lists of independent variables (identified by Arabic numerals) and behavioral categories (identified by lower-case letters) precede the outline in Part V.

The outline can be conceptualized as a two-dimensional matrix with independent variables heading columns and behavioral categories heading rows, although it is not actually presented in that form. For example, if a list of all experiments on delay of punishment were desired, all references in the delay of punishment column would constitute such a list. Or perhaps all reference on the effect of delay of punishment (i.e., independent variable) on positively reinforced responses undergoing extinction (i.e., behavioral category) might be desired. The cell at the intersection of these two topics would contain that list. In a similar manner, the outline can be used to locate all references to experiments on any combination of independent variable and behavioral category.

The independent variables manipulated in the 406 experiments listed on primary punishment fall into the following two broad classes: (1) variations in the conditions of punishment (e.g., punishment-intensity), and (2) variations in conditions other than punishment (e.g., hours of food deprivation). Items in the latter class, of course, are not parameters of punishment, but they are included because they frequently interact with punishment in determining the degree to which punishment affects behavior. Independent variables numbered 1 through 16 involve variations of the punishing condition, i.e., class (1), while variables numbered 17 through 29 involve variations in nonpunishing conditions, i.e., class (2).

REFERENCES

LOGAN, F. A., & WAGNER, A. R. *Reward and punishment.* Boston: Allyn and Bacon, 1965.

MOWRER, O. H. *Learning theory and behavior.* New York: Wiley, 1960.

II. Bibliography on Primary Punishment [5]

ABT, J. P., ESSMAN, W. B., & JARVIK, M. E. Ether-induced retrograde amnesia for one-trial conditioning in mice. *Science,* 1961, **133**, 1477–1478.

ADER, R., TATUM, R., & BEELS, C. C. Social factors affecting emotionality and resistance to disease in animals: I. Age of separation from the mother and susceptibility to gastric ulcers in the rat. *Journal of Comparative and Physiological Psychology,* 1960, **53**, 446–454. (a)

ADER, R., TATUM, R., & BEELS, C. C. Social factors affecting emotionality and resistance to disease in animals: II. Susceptibility to gastric ulceration as a function of interruptions in social interactions and the time at which they occur. *Journal of Comparative and Physiological Psychology,* 1960, **53**, 455–458. (b)

---

[5] The few experiments in which negative punishment was used are identified by an asterisk. Positive punishment was used in all the other experiments in Section II.

ADLER, N., & HOGAN, J. A. Classical conditioning and punishment of an instinctive response in *Betta splendens. Animal Behaviour,* 1963, 11, 351–354.

AKHTAR, M. The role of counterconditioning in intermittent reinforcement. (Doctoral dissertation, University of Illinois.) Ann Arbor, Mich.: University Microfilms, 1963. No. 63-3196.

ALLYON, T., & AZRIN, N. H. Punishment as a discriminative stimulus and conditioned reinforcer with humans. *Journal of the Experimental Analysis of Behavior,* 1966, 9, 411–419.

APPEL, J. B. Some schedules involving aversive control. *Journal of the Experimental Analysis of Behavior,* 1960, 3, 349–359.

APPEL, J. B. Punishment in the squirrel monkey *Saimiri sciurea. Science,* 1961, 133, 36–37.

APPEL, J. B. Punishment and shock intensity. *Science,* 1963, 141, 528–529.

ASDOURIAN, D. Interaction effects of intracranial stimulation with rewarding and aversive solutions. *Journal of Comparative and Physiological Psychology,* 1962, 55, 685–690.

AZRIN, N. H. Some effects of two intermittent schedules of immediate and non-immediate punishment. *Journal of Psychology,* 1956, 42, 3–21.

AZRIN, N. H. Some effects of noise on human behavior. *Journal of the Experimental Analysis of Behavior,* 1958, 1, 183–200.

AZRIN, N. H. Punishment and recovery during fixed-ratio performance. *Journal of the Experimental Analysis of Behavior,* 1959, 2, 301–305.

AZRIN, N. H. Effects of punishment intensity during variable-interval reinforcement. *Journal of the Experimental Analysis of Behavior,* 1960, 3, 123–142. (a)

AZRIN, N. H. Sequential effects of punishment. *Science,* 1960, 131, 605–606. (b)

AZRIN, N. H., HAKE, D. F., HOLZ, W. C., & HUTCHINSON, R. R. Motivational aspects of escape from punishment. *Journal of the Experimental Analysis of Behavior,* 1965, 8, 31–44.

AZRIN, N. H., & HOLZ, W. C. Punishment during fixed-interval reinforcement. *Journal of the Experimental Analysis of Behavior,* 1961, 4, 343–347.

AZRIN, N. H., HOLZ, W. C., & HAKE, D. F. Fixed-ratio punishment. *Journal of the Experimental Analysis of Behavior,* 1963, 6, 141–148.

*BAER, D. M. Effect of withdrawal of positive reinforcement on an extinguishing response in young children. *Child Development,* 1961, 32, 67–74.

*BAER, D. M. Laboratory control of thumbsucking by withdrawal and re-presentation of reinforcement. *Journal of the Experimental Analysis of Behavior,* 1962, 5, 525–528.

BAILEY, C. J., & MILLER, N. E. The effect of sodium amytal on an approach-avoidance conflict in cats. *Journal of Comparative and Physiological Psychology,* 1952, 45, 205–208.

BANKS, R. K. Persistence to continuous punishment and nonreward following training with intermittent punishment and nonreward. *Psychonomic Science,* 1966, 5, 105–106. (a)

BANKS, R. K. Persistence to continuous punishment following intermittent punishment training. *Journal of Experimental Psychology,* 1966, 71, 373–377. (b).

BANKS, R. K. Intermittent punishment effect (IPE) sustained through changed stimulus conditions and through blocks of nonpunished trials. *Journal of Experimental Psychology*, 1967, **73**, 456–460.

BANKS, R. K., & VOGEL-SPROTT, M. Effect of delayed punishment on an immediately rewarded response in humans. *Journal of Experimental Psychology*, 1965, **70**, 357–359.

BARLOW, M. C. The influence of electric shock in mirror tracing. *American Journal of Psychology*, 1933, **45**, 478–487.

BARNES, G. W., & KISH, G. B. Reinforcing properties of the termination of intense auditory stimulation. *Journal of Comparative and Physiological Psychology*, 1957, **50**, 40–43.

BARON, A. Delayed punishment of a runway response. *Journal of Comparative and Physiological Psychology*, 1965, **60**, 131–134.

BARON, A., & ANTONITIS, J. J. Punishment and preshock as determinants of bar-pressing behavior. *Journal of Comparative and Physiological Psychology*, 1961, **54**, 716–720.

BARRETT, Beatrice H. Reduction in rate of multiple tics by free operant conditioning methods, *Journal of Nervous and Mental Disease*, 1962, **135**, 187–195.

BARRY, H., III, & MILLER, N. E. Effects of drugs on approach-avoidance conflict tested repeatedly by means of a "Telescope Alley." *Journal of Comparative and Physiological Psychology*, 1962, **55**, 201–210.

BARRY, H., III, MILLER, N. E., & TIDD, G. E. Control for stimulus change while testing effects of amobarbital on conflict. *Journal of Comparative and Physiological Psychology*, 1962, **55**, 1071–1074.

BEACH, F. A., CONOVITZ, M. W., STEINBERG, F., & GOLDSTEIN, A. C. Experimental inhibition and restoration of mating behavior in male rats. *Journal of Genetic Psychology*, 1956, **89**, 165–181.

BEECROFT, R. S. Near-goal punishment of avoidance running. *Psychonomic Science*, 1967, **8**, 109–110.

BEECROFT, R. S., & BOUSKA, S. A. Learning self-punitive running. *Psychonomic Science*, 1967, **8**, 107–108.

BERKUN, M. M. Factors in the recovery from approach-avoidance conflict. *Journal of Experimental Psychology*, 1957, **54**, 65–73.

BERNARD, J. A note on non-informative shock. *Journal of Experimental Psychology*, 1941, **29**, 407–412.

BERNARD, J. The specificity of the effect of shock on the acquisition and retention of motor and verbal habits. *Journal of Experimental Psychology*, 1942, **31**, 69–78.

BERNARD, J., & GILBERT, R. W. The specificity of the effect of shock for error in maze learning with human subjects. *Journal of Experimental Psychology*, 1941, **28**, 178–186.

BERRYMAN, R. A technique for the experimental analysis of conflict. *Psychological Reports*, 1962, **10**, 423–426.

BESCH, N. F. Paired-associates learning as a function of anxiety level and shock. *Journal of Personality*, 1959, **27**, 116–124.

BEVAN, W., & DUKES, W. F. Effectiveness of delayed punishment on learning performance when preceded by premonitory cues. *Psychological Reports*, 1955, **1**, 441–448.

BIJOU, S. W. A study of "experimental neurosis" in the rat by the conditioned response technique. *Journal of Comparative Psychology*, 1943, **36**, 1–20.

BINDRA, D., & ANCHEL, H. Immobility as an avoidance response and its disruption by drugs. *Journal of the Experimental Analysis of Behavior*, 1963, **6**, 213–218.

BIRCH, H. The effect of intermittent punishment during acquisition of a barpress habit upon later readiness to accept punishment. (Doctoral dissertation, State University of New York at Buffalo.) Ann Arbor, Mich.: University Microfilms, 1965. No. 65-1293.

BIXENSTINE, V. E. Secondary drive as a neutralizer of time in integrative problem solving. *Journal of Comparative and Physiological Psychology*, 1956, **49**, 161–166.

BLACK, A. H., & MORSE, P. Avoidance learning in dogs without a warning stimulus. *Journal of the Experimental Analysis of Behavior*, 1961, 4, 17–23.

BOE, E. E. Extinction as a function of intensity of punishment, amount of training, and reinforcement of a competing response. *Canadian Journal of Psychology*, 1964, **18**, 328–342.

BOE, E. E. Effect of punishment duration and intensity on the extinction of an instrumental response. *Journal of Experimental Psychology*, 1966, **72**, 125–131.

BOE, E. E., & CHURCH, R. M. Permanent effect of punishment during extinction. *Journal of Comparative and Physiological Psychology*, 1967, **63**, 486–492.

BOITANO, J. J., & ISAACSON, R. L. Effects of variation in shock-intensity on the behavior of dorsal-hippocampectomized rats in two passive-avoidance situations. *American Journal of Psychology*, 1967, **80**, 73–80.

BOLL, T. J., MADISON, H. L., & DOUGLASS, M. C. Probability learning to avoid shock. *Psychonomic Science*, 1966, **6**, 25–26.

BOLLES, R. C., & SEELBACH, S. E. Punishing and reinforcing effects of noise onset and termination for different responses. *Journal of Comparative and Physiological Psychology*, 1964, **58**, 127–131.

BOLLES, R. C., & WARREN, J. A., JR. Effects of delay on the punishing and reinforcing effects of noise onset and termination. *Journal of Comparative and Physiological Psychology*, 1966, **61**, 475–477.

BORN, D. G. Resistance of a free operant to extinction and suppression with punishment as a function of amount of training. *Psychonomic Science*, 1967, **8**, 21–22.

BOROCZI, G., STORMS, L. H., & BROEN, W. E., JR. Response suppression and recovery of responding at different deprivation levels as functions of intensity and duration of punishment. *Journal of Comparative and Physiological Psychology*, 1964, **58**, 456–459.

BOWER, G. H., & MILLER, N. E. Effects of amount of reward on strength of approach in an approach-avoidance conflict. *Journal of Comparative and Physiological Psychology*, 1960, **53**, 59–62.

*BRACKBILL, Y., & O'HARA, J. The relative effectiveness of reward and punishment for discrimination learning in children. *Journal of Comparative and Physiological Psychology*, 1958, **51**, 747–751.

BRADY, J. V. A comparative approach to the evaluation of drug effects upon affective behavior. *Annals of the New York Academy of Sciences,* 1956, **64,** 632–643.

BRADY, J. V. A comparative approach to the study of drug effects on the behavior of higher animals. In A. D. Bass (Ed.), *Evolution of nervous control from primitive organisms to man.* Washington, D. C.: American Association for the Advancement of Science, 1959. Pp. 115–133.

BRETHOWER, D. M., & REYNOLDS, G. S. A facilitative effect of punishment on unpunished behavior. *Journal of the Experimental Analysis of Behavior,* 1962, **5,** 191–199.

BROGDEN, W. J., LIPMAN, E. A., & CULLER, E. The role of incentive in conditioning and extinction. *American Journal of Psychology,* 1938, **51,** 109–117.

BROWN, J. S. Gradients of approach and avoidance responses and their relation to level of motivation. *Journal of Comparative and Physiological Psychology,* 1948, **41,** 450–465.

BROWN, J. S., ANDERSON, D. C., & WEISS, C. G. Self-punitive behavior under conditions of massed practice. *Journal of Comparative and Physiological Psychology,* 1965, **60,** 451–453.

BROWN, J. S., MARTIN, R. C., & MORROW, M. W. Self-punitive behavior in the rat: Facilitative effects of punishment on resistance to extinction. *Journal of Comparative and Physiological Psychology,* 1964, **57,** 127–133.

BROWN, R. L. The effects of aversive stimulation on certain conceptual error responses of schizophrenics. (Doctoral dissertation, Southern Illinois University.) Ann Arbor, Mich.: University Microfilms, 1961. No. 61-2076.

BROWN, R. T., & WAGNER, A. R. Resistance to punishment and extinction following training with shock or nonreinforcement. *Journal of Experimental Psychology,* 1964, **68,** 503–507.

BRUNER, A. Food-based timing behavior sharpened by the selective punishment of short interresponse times. *Psychonomic Science,* 1967, **8,** 187–188.

*BRUNING, J. L., KINTZ, B. L., & MOGRET, M. K. Suppression of a learned response by punishment when an alternative learned response is provided. *Psychonomic Science,* 1965, **3,** 399–400.

BRUNSWIK, E. Probability as a determiner of rat behavior. *Journal of Experimental Psychology,* 1939, **25,** 175–197.

BRUSH, F. R. The effects of shock intensity on the acquisition and extinction of an avoidance response in dogs. *Journal of Comparative and Physiological Psychology,* 1957, **50,** 547–552.

BRUSH, F. R., BRUSH, E. S., & SOLOMON, R. L. Traumatic avoidance learning: The effects of CS-US interval with a delayed-conditioning procedure. *Journal of Comparative and Physiological Psychology,* 1955, **48,** 285–293.

BRUSH, F. R., BUSH, R. R., JENKINS, W. O., JOHN, W. F., & WHITTING, J. W. M. Stimulus generalization after extinction and punishment: An experimental study of displacement. *Journal of Abnormal and Social Psychology,* 1952, **47,** 633–640.

BUNCH, M. E. The effect of electric shock as punishment for errors in human maze-learning. *Journal of Comparative Psychology,* 1928, **8,** 343–359.

BUNCH, M. E. Certain effects of electric shock in learning a stylus maze. *Journal of Comparative Psychology,* 1935, **20,** 211–242.

BUNCH, M. E., & HAGMAN, E. P. The influence of electric shocks for errors in rational learning. *Journal of Experimental Psychology*, 1937, **21**, 330–341.

BUNCH, M. E., & MAGDSICK, W. K. A study of electric shock motivation in maze learning. *Journal of Comparative Psychology*, 1938, **25**, 497–506.

BUNCH, M. E., & McTEER, F. D. The influence of punishment during learning upon retroactive inhibition. *Journal of Experimental Psychology*, 1932, **15**, 473–495.

BUTLER, D. C. Two-choice behavior as a function of the delay between response and punishment. (Doctoral dissertation, Northwestern University.) Ann Arbor, Mich.: University Microfilms, 1959. No. 59-201.

CAMP, D. S., RAYMOND, G. A., & CHURCH, R. M. Response suppression as a function of the schedule of punishment. *Psychonomic Science*, 1966, **5**, 23–24.

CAMP, D. S., RAYMOND, G. A., & CHURCH, R. M. The temporal relationship between response and punishment. *Journal of Experimental Psychology*, 1967, **74**, 114–123.

CAMPBELL, B. A., SMITH, N. F., & MISANIN, J. R. Effects of punishment on extinction of avoidance behavior: Avoidance-avoidance conflict or vicious circle behavior. *Journal of Comparative and Physiological Psychology*, 1966, **62**, 495–498.

CARRAN, A. B. Passive avoidance and strain differences associated with differences in emotionality: A test of Mowrer's theory. *Psychonomic Science*, 1967, **7**, 263–264.

CHOROVER, S. L., & SCHILLER, P. H. Short-term retrograde amnesia in rats. *Journal of Comparative and Physiological Psychology*, 1965, **59**, 73–78.

CHUNG-FANG, N. An experimental study of the influence of punishment for errors during learning upon retention. *Journal of Comparative Psychology*, 1934, **17**, 279–301. (a)

CHUNG-FANG, N. The influence of punishment for errors during the learning of the first maze upon the mastery of the second maze. *Journal of Comparative Psychology*, 1934, **18**, 23–28. (b)

CHURCH, R. M., & RAYMOND, G. A. Influence of the schedule of positive reinforcement on punished behavior. *Journal of Comparative and Physiological Psychology*, 1967, **63**, 329–332.

CHURCH, R. M., RAYMOND, G. A., & BEAUCHAMP, R. D. Response suppression as a function of intensity and duration of a punishment. *Journal of Comparative and Physiological Psychology*, 1967, **63**, 39–44.

CHURCH, R. M., & SOLOMON, R. L. Traumatic avoidance learning: The effects of delay of shock termination. *Psychological Reports*, 1956, **2**, 357–368.

CLARK, R. Retention of a passive avoidance response in mice. *Psychonomic Science*, 1967, **7**, 29–30.

COBURN, C. A., & YERKES, R. M. A study of the behavior of the crow *Corvus Americanus* (Audubon) by the multiple choice method. *Journal of Animal Behavior*, 1915, **5**, 75–114.

COLE, L. W. The relation of strength of stimulus to rate of learning in the chick. *Journal of Animal Behavior*, 1911, **1**, 111–124.

COOK, S. W. The production of "experimental neurosis" in the white rat. *Psychosomatic Medicine*, 1939, **1**, 293–308.

CORNWELL, P. Behavioral effects of orbital and proreal lesions in cats. *Journal of Comparative and Physiological Psychology*, 1966, **61**, 50–58.

CRAFTS, L. W., & GILBERT, R. W. The effect of punishment during learning upon retention. *Journal of Experimental Psychology*, 1934, **17**, 73–84.

CURLIN, E. B., & DONAHOE, J. W. Effects of shock intensity and placement on the learning of a food-reinforced brightness discrimination. *Journal of Experimental Psychology*, 1965, **69**, 349–356.

DALEY, D. A., & COOPER, E. B. Rate of stuttering adaptation under two electroshock conditions. *Behavior Research and Therapy*, 1967, **5**, 49–54.

DALEY, M. F. Punishment and recovery in the rat during three schedules of food reinforcement. (Doctoral dissertation, University of Houston.) Ann Arbor, Mich.: University Microfilms, 1962. No. 62-4205.

D'AMATO, M. R., & GUMENIK, W. E. Some effects of immediate versus randomly delayed shock on an instrumental response and cognitive processes. *Journal of Abnormal and Social Psychology*, 1960, **60**, 64–67.

DARDANO, J. F., & SAUERBRUNN, D. An aversive stimulus as a correlated block counter in FR performance. *Journal of the Experimental Analysis of Behavior*, 1964, **7**, 37–43. (a)

DARDANO, J. F., & SAUERBRUNN, D. Selective punishment of concurrent progresgressive ratio behavior. *Journal of the Experimental Analysis of Behavior*, 1964, **7**, 51–65. (b)

DARDANO, J. F., & SAUERBRUNN, D. Selective punishment of fixed-ratio performance. *Journal of the Experimental Analysis of Behavior*, 1964, **7**, 255–260. (c)

DAVITZ, J. R., MASON, D. J., MOWRER, O. H., & VIEK, P. Conditioning of fear: A function of the delay of reinforcement. *American Journal of Psychology*, 1957, **70**, 69–74.

DE ARMOND, D. Multiple punishment schedule. *Journal of the Experimental Analysis of Behavior*, 1966, **9**, 327–334.

DE ARMOND-EDWARDS, D. Concurrent schedules of reinforcement and punishment. *Psychonomic Science*, 1966, **6**, 219–220.

DELGADO, J. M. R., ROBERTS, W. W., & MILLER, N. E. Learning motivated by electrical stimulation of the brain. *American Journal of Physiology*, 1954, **179**, 587–593.

DELPRATO, D. J., & THOMPSON, R. W. Amnesic and aversive effects of electroconvulsive shock. *Psychological Reports*, 1965, **16**, 561–565. (a)

DELPRATO, D. J., & THOMPSON, R. W. Effect of electroconvulsive shock on passive avoidance learning with high and low intensity footshock. *Psychological Reports*, 1965, **17**, 209–210. (b)

DELPRATO, D. J., & TERRANT, F. R., JR. Effect of ECS on passive avoidance learning with high and low intensity foot shock: Supplementary report. *Psychological Reports*, 1966, **18**, 121–122.

*DESROCHES, H. F. Resistance to weakening influences as a function of the similarity between acquisition and weakening phases. (Doctoral dissertation, University of Tennessee.) Ann Arbor, Mich.: University Microfilms, 1962. No. 62-2300.

DIAMOND, S. Habit formation under non-selective conditions. *Journal of Comparative Psychology*, 1934, **17**, 109–122.

DIMMICK, F. L., LUDLOW, N., & WHITEMAN, A. A study of "experimental neurosis" in cats. *Journal of Comparative Psychology,* 1939, **28**, 39–43.

DINSMOOR, J. A. A discrimination based on punishment. *Quarterly Journal of Experimental Psychology,* 1952, 4, 27–45.

DODSON, J. D. The relation of strength of stimulus to rapidity of habit-formation in the kitten. *Journal of Animal Behavior,* 1915, **5**, 330–336.

DODSON, J. D. Relative values of reward and punishment in habit formation. *Psychobiology,* 1917, 1, 231–276.

DODSON, J. D. The relative values of satisfying and annoying situations as motives in the learning process. *Journal of Comparative Psychology,* 1932, 14, 147–164.

DORCUS, R. M., & GRAY, W. L. The effectiveness of food and electric shock in learning and retention by rats when applied at critical points in the maze. *Journal of Comparative Psychology,* 1932, 14, 191–218.

DREW, G. C. The function of punishment in learning. *Journal of Genetic Psychology,* 1938, **52**, 257–267.

DULANY, D. E., JR. Avoidance learning of perceptual defense and vigilance. *Journal of Abnormal and Social Psychology,* 1957, **55**, 333–338.

EDWARDS, D. D., & DART, G. A. Ply durations in a multiple punishment schedule. *Psychonomic Science,* 1966, **6**, 353–354.

EDWARDS, R. P. The effects of punishment on unpunished responses. Unpublished doctoral dissertation, Harvard University, 1951.

EIGLER, P. The effect of unusual stimulation on motor coordination in children. *Child Development,* 1932, **3**, 207–229.

EISENSON, J. Confirmation and information in rewards and punishments. *Archives of Psychology,* 1935, **27** (No. 181).

EISON, C. L., & SAWREY, J. M. Extinction of avoidance behavior: CS presentations with and without punishment. *Psychonomic Science,* 1967, **7**, 95–96.

FLDER, T. Correlation of two measures of the strength of an approach-avoidance conflict. *Psychological Reports,* 1962, **10**, 510.

ELDER, T., NOBLIN, C. D., & MAHER, B. A. The extinction of fear as a function of distance versus dissimilarity from the original conflict situation. *Journal of Abnormal and Social Psychology,* 1961, **63**, 530–533.

ESSMAN, W. B., & ALPERN, H. Single trial conditioning: Methodology and results with mice. *Psychological Reports,* 1964, 14, 731–740.

ESSMAN, W. B., & JARVIK, M. E. Extinction of a response conditioned in a single trial. *Psychological Reports,* 1961, 8, 311–312.

ESSMAN, W. B., & SUDAK, F. N. Effect of hypothermia on the establishment of a conditioned avoidance response in mice. *Journal of Comparative and Physiological Psychology,* 1963, **56**, 366–369.

ESSMAN, W. B., & SUDAK, F. N. Single-trial avoidance conditioning in rats. *Psychological Reports,* 1964, 15, 775–783.

ESTES, W. K. An experimental study of punishment. *Psychological Monographs,* 1944, **57** (3, Whole No. 263).

EVERALL, E. E. Perseveration in the rat. *Journal of Comparative Psychology,* 1935, **19**, 343–369.

FALLON, D. The durability of a response acquired under conditions of concurrent positive reinforcement and punishment. (Doctoral dissertation, University of Virginia.) Ann Arbor, Mich.: University Microfilms, 1966. No. 66-3179.

FARBER, I. E. Response fixation under anxiety and non-anxiety conditions. *Journal of Experimental Psychology,* 1948, **38**, 111–131.

FARROW, B. J., & SANTOS, J. F. Changes in autokinetic perception as a function of the transfer of conditioning effects. *British Journal of Psychology,* 1962, **53**, 331–337.

FEIRSTEIN, A. R., & MILLER, N. E. Learning to resist pain and fear: Effects of electric shock before versus after reaching goal. *Journal of Comparative and Physiological Psychology,* 1963, **56**, 797–800.

FELDMAN, R. S., & BREMMER, F. J. A method for rapid conditioning of stable avoidance bar pressing behavior. *Journal of the Experimental Analysis of Behavior,* 1963, **6**, 393–394.

FELDMAN, S. M. Differential effects of shock in human maze learning. *Journal of Experimental Psychology,* 1961, **62**, 171–178.

FERRARO, D. P. Suppression and recovery of a regularly reinforced response as a function of probability and frequency of punishment. (Doctoral dissertation, Columbia University.) Ann Arbor, Mich.: University Microfilms, 1966. No. 66-4769.

FERRARO, D. P., SCHOENFELD, W. N., & SNAPPER, A. G. Adrenal hypertrophy in the rat as a function of probability and frequency of punishment. *Psychological Reports,* 1967, **20**, 795–802.

*FERSTER, C. B. Control of behavior in chimpanzees and pigeons by time out from positive reinforcement. *Psychological Monographs,* 1958, **72** (8, Whole No. 461).

*FERSTER, C. B., & APPEL, J. B. Punishment of $S^\triangle$ responding in matching to sample by time out from positive reinforcement. *Journal of the Experimental Analysis of Behavior,* 1961, 4, 45–56.

FILBY, Y., & APPEL, J. B. Variable-interval punishment during variable-interval reinforcement. *Journal of the Experimental Analysis of Behavior,* 1966, **9**, 521–527.

FISCHER, G. J., & CAMPBELL, G. L. The development of passive avoidance conditioning in Leghorn chicks. *Animal Behaviour,* 1964, **12**, 268–269.

FISHER, A. E. The effects of differential early treatment on the social and exploratory behavior of puppies. Unpublished doctoral dissertation, Pennsylvania State University, 1955.

FLANAGAN, B., GOLDIAMOND, I., & AZRIN, N. Operant stuttering: The control of stuttering behavior through response-contingent consequences. *Journal of the Experimental Analysis of Behavior,* 1958, 1, 173–177.

FOWLER, H. Facilitation and inhibition of performance by punishment: The effects of shock intensity and distribution of trials. *Journal of Comparative and Physiological Psychology,* 1963, **56**, 531–538.

FOWLER, H., & MILLER, N. E. Facilitation and inhibition of runway performance by hind- and forepaw shock of various intensities. *Journal of Comparative and Physiological Psychology,* 1963, **56**, 801–805.

FOWLER, H., & WISCHNER, G. J. Discrimination performance as affected by problem difficulty and shock for either the correct or incorrect response. *Journal of Experimental Psychology,* 1965, **69**, 413–418. (a)

FOWLER, H., & WISCHNER, G. J. On the "secondary reinforcing" effect of shock for the correct response in visual discrimination learning. *Psychonomic Science,* 1965, **3,** 209–210. (b)

FOX, S. S., KIMBLE, D. P., & LICKEY, M. E. Comparison of caudate nucleus and septal-area lesions on two types of avoidance behavior. *Journal of Comparative and Physiological Psychology,* 1964, **58,** 380–386.

FREEBURNE, C. M., & SCHNEIDER, M. Shock for right and wrong responses during learning and extinction in human subjects. *Journal of Experimental Psychology,* 1955, **49,** 181–186.

FREEBURNE, C. M., & TAYLOR, J. E. Discrimination learning with shock for right and wrong responses in the same subjects. *Journal of Comparative and Physiological Psychology,* 1952, **45,** 264–268.

FREEDMAN, D. G. Constitutional and environmental interactions in rearing of four breeds of dogs. *Science,* 1958, **127,** 585–586.

FRICK, J. V. An exploratory study of the effect of punishment (electroshock) upon stuttering behavior. Unpublished doctoral dissertation, State University of Iowa, 1951.

GATES, E. The science of mentation and some new general methods of psychological research. *The Monist,* 1895, **5,** 574–597.

GELLER, I. Conditioned "anxiety" and punishment effects on operant behavior of goldfish (*Carassuis auratus*). *Science,* 1963, **141,** 351–353.

GELLER, I., BACHMAN, E., & SEIFTER, J. Effects of reserpine and morphine on behavior suppressed by punishment. *Life Sciences,* 1963, No. 4, 226–231.

GELLER, I., & SEIFTER, J. The effects of meprobamate, barbiturates, d-amphetamine and promazine on experimentally induced conflict in the rat. *Psychopharmacologia,* 1960, **1,** 482–492.

GERBRANDT, L. K. Dissociation of conditioned emotional and avoidance responses due to ECS. *Psychonomic Science,* 1965, **3,** 385–386.

GERBRANDT, L. K., & THOMSON, C. W. Competing response and amnesic effects of electroconvulsive shock under extinction and incentive shifts. *Journal of Comparative and Physiological Psychology,* 1964, **58,** 208–211.

GILBERT, R. W. The effect of non-informative shock upon maze learning and retention with human subjects. *Journal of Experimental Psychology,* 1936, **19,** 456–466.

GILBERT, R. W. A further study of the effect of non-informative shock upon learning. *Journal of Experimental Psychology,* 1937, **20,** 396–407.

GILBERT, R. W., & CRAFTS, L. W. The effect of signal for error on maze learning and retention. *Journal of Experimental Psychology,* 1935, **18,** 121–132.

GOLDIAMOND, I. Stuttering and fluency as manipulable operant response classes. In L. Krasner and L. P. Ullman (Eds.), *Research in behavioral modification: New developments and their clinical implications.* New York: Holt, Rinehart, Winston, 1965. Pp. 106–156.

GOLDSMITH, L. J. Effect of intracerebral actinomycin D and of electroconvulsive shock on passive avoidance. *Journal of Comparative and Physiological Psychology,* 1967, **63,** 126–132.

GURNEE, H. The effect of electric shock for right responses on maze learning in human subjects. *Journal of Experimental Psychology,* 1938, **22,** 354–364.

GWINN, G. T. The effects of punishment on acts motivated by fear. *Journal of Experimental Psychology,* 1949, **39**, 260–269.

HAKE, D. F., AZRIN, N. H., & OXFORD, R. The effects of punishment intensity on squirrel monkeys. *Journal of the Experimental Analysis of Behavior,* 1967, **10**, 95–107.

HAMILTON, J. A., & KRECHEVSKY, I. Studies in the effect of shock upon behavior plasticity in the rat. *Journal of Comparative Psychology,* 1933, 16, 237–253.

HANDE, R. M. Extinction of avoidance behavior in albino rats in an approach-avoidance conflict situation. (Doctoral dissertation, University of Pittsburgh.) Ann Arbor, Mich.: University Microfilms, 1967. No. 67–778.

HARE, R. D. Suppression of verbal behavior as a function of delay and schedule of severe punishment. *Journal of Verbal Learning and Verbal Behavior,* 1965, 4, 216–221.

HARE, R. D. Suppression and recovery of a human response as a function of the temporal order of reward and punishment. *Psychonomic Science,* 1966, **5**, 49–50.

HARVEY, J. A., LINTS, C. E., JACOBSON, L. E., & HUNT, H. F. Effects of lesions in the septal area on conditioned fear and discriminated instrumental punishment in the albino rat. *Journal of Comparative and Physiological Psychology,* 1965, **59**, 37–48.

HAWKINS, R. P. Effects of drive, incentive and problem difficulty on the facilitation of discrimination by punishment of correct responses. (Doctoral dissertation, University of Pittsburgh.) Ann Arbor, Mich.: University Microfilms, 1966. No. 66-8135.

HEARST, E. Stress-induced breakdown of an appetitive discrimination. *Journal of the Experimental Analysis of Behavior,* 1965, **8**, 135–146.

HEARST, E., & SIDMAN, M. Some behavioral effects of a concurrently positive and negative stimulus. *Journal of the Experimental Analysis of Behavior,* 1961, 4, 251–256.

HENDRY, D. P., & VAN-TOLLER, C. Fixed-ratio punishment with continuous reinforcement. *Journal of the Experimental Analysis of Behavior,* 1964, **7**, 293–300.

HERMAN, R. L., & AZRIN, N. H. Punishment by noise in an alternative response situation. *Journal of the Experimental Analysis of Behavior,* 1964, **7**, 185–188.

HOGE, M. A., & STOCKING, R. J. A note on the relative value of punishment and reward as motives. *Journal of Animal Behaviour,* 1912, **2**, 43–50.

HOLDEN, F. A study of the effect of starvation upon behavior by means of the obstruction method. *Comparative Psychology Monographs,* 1926, **3**, No. 17.

HOLZ, W. C., & AZRIN, N. H. Discriminative properties of punishment. *Journal of the Experimental Analysis of Behavior,* 1961, 4, 225–232.

HOLZ, W. C., & AZRIN, N. H. Interactions between the discriminative and aversive properties of punishment. *Journal of the Experimental Analysis of Behavior,* 1962, 5, 229–234. (a)

HOLZ, W. C., & AZRIN, N. H. Recovery during punishment by intense noise. *Psychological Reports,* 1962, **11**, 655–657. (b)

HOLZ, W. C., & AZRIN, N. H. A comparison of several procedures for eliminating behavior. *Journal of the Experimental Analysis of Behavior,* 1963, **6**, 399–406.

*Holz, W. C., Azrin, N. H., & Ayllon, T. Elimination of behavior of mental patients by response-produced extinction. *Journal of the Experimental Analysis of Behavior,* 1963, **6**, 407–412.

Holz, W. C., Azrin, N. H., & Ulrich, R. E. Punishment of temporally spaced responding. *Journal of the Experimental Analysis of Behavior,* 1963, **6**, 115–122.

Holzschuh, R. D. Effects of position of punishment in a fixed-interval schedule of reinforcement. (Doctoral dissertation, Florida State University.) Ann Arbor, Mich.: University Microfilms, 1965. No. 65-15,468.

Honig, W. K. The role of discriminative training in the generalization of punishment. *Journal of the Experimental Analysis of Behavior,* 1966, **9**, 377–384.

Honig, W. K., & Slivka, R. M. Stimulus generalization of the effects of punishment. *Journal of the Experimental Analysis of Behavior,* 1964, **7**, 21–25.

Hudson, B. B. One-trial learning in the domestic rat. *Genetic Psychology Monographs,* 1950, **41**, 99–145.

Hudspeth, W. J., McGaugh, J. L., & Thomson, C. W. Aversive and amnesic effects of electroconvulsive shock. *Journal of Comparative and Physiological Psychology,* 1964, **57**, 61–64.

Hunt, H. F., & Brady, J. V. Some effects of punishment and intercurrent "anxiety" on a simple operant. *Journal of Comparative and Physiological Psychology,* 1955, **48**, 305–310.

Hunt, J. McV., & Schlosberg, H. Behavior of rats in continuous conflict. *Journal of Comparative and Physiological Psychology,* 1950, **43**, 351–357.

Hunter, W. S. The delayed reaction in animals and children. *Behavioral Monographs,* 1913, **2** (1, Whole No. 6).

Hurwitz, H. M. B., Bolas, D., & Haritos, M. Vicious circle behavior under two shock intensities. *British Journal of Psychology,* 1961, **52**, 377–383.

Imada, H. The effects of punishment on avoidance behavior. *Japanese Psychological Research,* 1959, **1**, 27–38.

Isaacson, R. L., Olton, D. S., Bauer, B., & Swart, P. The effect of training trials on passive avoidance deficits in the hippocampectomized rat. *Psychonomic Science,* 1966, **5**, 419–420.

Isaacson, R. L., & Wickelgren, W. O. Hippocampal ablation and passive avoidance. *Science,* 1962, **138**, 1104–1106.

Jackson, D. E. Punishment as a stimulus for conditioned "hope." (Doctoral dissertation, University of Alabama.) Ann Arbor, Mich.: University Microfilms, 1964. No. 64-12,784.

Jacobsen, E., & Skaarup, Y. Experimental induction of conflict-behavior in cats: The effect of some anticholinergic compounds. *Acta Pharmacologia et Toxicologia,* 1955, **11**, 125–134.

Jarvik, M. E., & Essman, W. B. A simple one-trial learning situation for mice. *Psychological Reports,* 1960, **6**, 290.

Jensen, M. B. Punishment by electric shock as affecting performance on a raised finger maze. *Journal of Experimental Psychology,* 1934, **17**, 65–72.

JOHANSON, A. M. The influence of incentive and punishment upon reaction time. *Archives of Psychology,* 1922, **8** (No. 54).

JONES, E. C., & SWANSON, A. M. Discriminated lever-press avoidance. *Psychonomic Science,* 1966, **6**, 351–352.

KAMIN, L. J. The delay-of-punishment gradient. *Journal of Comparative and Physiological Psychology,* 1959, **52**, 434–437.

KARSH, E. B. Effects of number of rewarded trials and intensity of punishment on running speed. *Journal of Comparative and Physiological Psychology,* 1962, **55**, 44–51.

KARSH, E. B. Changes in intensity of punishment: Effect on running behavior of rats. *Science,* 1963, **140**, 1084–1085.

KARSH, E. B. Punishment: Effect on learning and resistance to extinction of discrete operant behavior. *Psychonomic Science,* 1964, **1**, 139–140. (a)

KARSH, E. B. Punishment: Trial spacing and shock intensity as determinants of behavior in a discrete operant situation. *Journal of Comparative and Physiological Psychology,* 1964, **58**, 299–302. (b)

KARSH, E. B., & WILLIAMS, J. P. Punishment and reward in children's instrumental learning. *Psychonomic Science,* 1964, **1**, 359–360.

KATAHN, M., THUNE, L., & DOODY, R. The Effects of shock punishment conditions on the threshold for an associated auditory stimulus. *Psychonomic Science,* 1965, **2**, 353–354.

KAUFMAN, A. Effects of punishment intensity on human operant behavior. *Psychological Reports,* 1964, **15**, 287–294. (a)

KAUFMAN, A. Increased suppression during punishment applied to the responding member. *Psychonomic Science,* 1964, **1**, 311–312. (b)

KAUFMAN, A. Punishment shock intensity and basal skin resistance. *Journal of the Experimental Analysis of Behavior,* 1965, **8**, 389–394.

KAUFMAN, A. Intermittent punishment of responding maintained by variable ratio reinforcement. *Psychonomic Science,* 1966, **4**, 307–308.

KAUFMAN, E. L., & MILLER, N. E. Effect of number of reinforcements on strength of approach in an approach-avoidance conflict. *Journal of Comparative and Physiological Psychology,* 1949, **42**, 65–74.

KAYE, H., COX, J., BOSACK, T., & ANDERSON, K. Primary and secondary punishment of toe sucking in the infant rhesus monkey. *Psychonomic Science,* 1965, **2**, 73–74.

KELLEHER, R. T., & MORSE, W. H. Escape behavior and punished behavior. *Federation Proceedings,* 1964, **23**, 808–817.

KING, R. A. Consolidation of the neural trace in memory: Investigation with one trial avoidance conditioning and ECS. *Journal of Comparative and Physiological Psychology,* 1965, **59**, 283–284.

KINTZ, B. L., & BRUNING, J. L. Punishment and compulsive avoidance behavior. *Journal of Comparative and Physiological Psychology,* 1967, **63**, 323–326.

KLEEMEIER, R. W. Fixation and regression in the rat. *Psychological Monographs,* 1942, **54** (4, Whole No. 246).

KNAPP, R. K., KAUSE, R. H., & PERKINS, C. C., JR. Immediate vs. delayed shock in T-maze performance. *Journal of Experimental Psychology,* 1959, **58**, 357–362.

KNOPFELMACHER, F. Fixations, position stereotypes and their relation to the degree and pattern of stress. *Quarterly Journal of Experimental Psychology,* 1953, **5**, 108–127.

KOSKI, C. H., & ROSS, L. E. Effects of consummatory response punishment in spatial-discrimination learning and response fixation. *Journal of Experimental Psychology,* 1965, **70**, 360–364.

KURTZ, P. S., & SHAFER, J. N. Response contingent shock and avoidance conditioning. *Psychonomic Science,* 1966, **6**, 223–224.

KUSHNER, M., & SANDLER, J. Aversion therapy and the concept of punishment. *Behaviour Research and Therapy,* 1966, 4, 179–186.

LEAF, R. C., & MULLER, S. A. Effects of shock intensity, deprivation, and morphine in a simple approach-avoidance conflict situation. *Psychological Reports,* 1965, **17**, 819–823.

LEBIGOT, L. Influence des sanctions sur l'acquisition et la rétention chez "Blatella germanica." *Journal de Psychologie,* 1954, *47–51*, 349–359.

LEITENBERG, H. Response initiation and response termination: Analysis of effects of punishment and escape contingencies. *Psychological Reports,* 1965, **16**, 569–575.

LEITENBERG, H. Conditioned acceleration and conditioned suppression in pigeons. *Journal of the Experimental Analysis of Behavior,* 1966, **9**, 205–212.

LEVINE, S., & JONES, L. E. Andrenocorticotropic hormone (ACTH) and passive avoidance learning. *Journal of Comparative and Physiological Psychology,* 1965, **59**, 357–360.

LICHTENSTEIN, P. E. Studies of anxiety: I. The production of a feeding inhibition in dogs. *Journal of Comparative and Physiological Psychology,* 1950, **43**, 16–29. (a)

LICHTENSTEIN, P. E. Studies of anxiety: II. The effects of lobotomy on a feeding inhibition in dogs. *Journal of Comparative and Physiological Psychology,* 1950, **43**, 419–427. (b)

LIVERSEDGE, L. A., & SYLVESTER, J. D. Conditioning techniques in the treatment of writer's cramp. *Lancet,* 1955, **1**, 1147–1149.

LOGAN, F. A. *Incentive.* New Haven: Yale University Press, 1960.

LOHR, T. F. The effect of shock on the rat's choice of a path to food. *Journal of Experimental Psychology,* 1959, **58**, 312–318.

LOVAAS, O. I., SCHAEFFER, B., SIMMONS, J. Q. Building social behavior in autistic children by use of electric shock. *Journal of Experimental Research in Personality,* 1965, **1**, 99–109.[6]

LUBAR, J. F. Effect of medial cortical lesions on the avoidance behavior of the cat. *Journal of Comparative and Physiological Psychology,* 1964, **58**, 38–46.

LUTTGES, M. W., & McGAUGH, J. L. Permanence of retrograde amnesia produced by electroconvulsive shock. *Science,* 1967, **156**, 408–410.

MAIER, N. R. F., & WAPNER, S. Studies of abnormal behavior in the rat. XIII. The effect of punishment for seizures on seizure-frequency during auditory stimulation. *Journal of Comparative Psychology,* 1943, **35**, 247–248.

[6] See also: Breger, L. Comments on "Building social behavior in autistic children by use of electric shock." *Journal of Experimental Research in Personality,* 1965, **1**, 110–113.

MALOTT, R. W., & CUMMING, W. W. The differential punishment of inter-response times. *Journal of Scientific Laboratories, Denison University,* 1964, **46,** 91–94.

MARDER, M. The effects of experimenter attractiveness and negative reinforcement on verbal conditioning. (Doctoral dissertation, University of Pennsylvania.) Ann Arbor, Mich.: University Microfilms, 1961. No. 61-3537.

MARTIN, B., & ROSS, L. E. Effects of consummatory response punishment on consummatory and runway behavior. *Journal of Comparative and Physiological Psychology,* 1964, **58,** 243–247.

MARTIN, R. C. Vicious circle behavior and escape conditioning as a function of intensity of punishment. (Doctoral dissertation, University of Florida.) Ann Arbor, Mich.: University Microfilms, 1965. No. 65-5993.

MARTIN, R. C., & MELVIN, K. B. Vicious circle behavior as a function of delay of punishment. *Psychonomic Science,* 1964, **1,** 415–416.

MARTIN, R. F. "Native" traits and regression in rats. *Journal of Comparative Psychology,* 1940, **30,** 1–16.

MASSERMAN, J. H. *Behavior and neurosis.* Chicago: University of Chicago Press, 1943.

MASSERMAN, J. H. Experimental neurosis and group dominance. *American Journal of Orthopsychiatry,* 1944, **14,** 636–643. (a)

MASSERMAN, J. H. Neurosis and alcohol. *American Journal of Psychiatry,* 1944, **101,** 389–395. (b)

MASSERMAN, J. H., ARIEFF, A., PECHTEL, C., & KLEHR, H. The effects of direct interrupted electroshock on experimental neuroses. *Journal of Nervous and Mental Disease,* 1950, **112,** 384–392.

MASSERMAN, J. H., & JACQUES, M. G. Effects of cerebral electroshock on experimental neuroses in cats. *American Journal of Psychiatry,* 1947, **104,** 92–99.

MASSERMAN, J. H., JACQUES, M. G., & NICHOLSON, M. R. Alcohol as a preventative of experimental neuroses. *Quarterly Journal of Studies on Alcohol,* 1945, **6,** 281–299.

MASSERMAN, J. H., & PECHTEL, C. Neurosis in monkeys: A preliminary report of experimental observations. *Annals of the New York Academy of Sciences,* 1953, **56,** 253–265.

MASSERMAN, J. H., & PECHTEL, C. How brain lesions affect normal and neurotic behavior. *American Journal of Psychiatry,* 1956, **112,** 865–872. (a)

MASSERMAN, J. H., & PECHTEL, C. Neurophysiologic and pharmacologic influences on experimental neuroses. *American Journal of Psychiatry,* 1956, **113,** 510–514. (b)

MASSERMAN, J. H., PECHTEL, C., & SCHREINER, L. The role of olfaction in normal and neurotic behavior in animals. *Psychosomatic Medicine,* 1953, **15,** 396–404.

MASSERMAN, J. H., & YUM, K. S. An analysis of the influence of alcohol on experimental neuroses in cats. *Psychosomatic Medicine,* 1946, **8,** 36–52.

McCLEARY, R. A. Response specificity in the behavioral effects of limbic system lesions in the cat. *Journal of Comparative and Physiological Psychology,* 1961, **54,** 605–613.

McCLEARY, R. A., JONES, C., & URSIN, H. Avoidance and retention deficits in septal cats. *Psychonomic Science,* 1965, **2,** 85–86.

McGaugh, J. L., & Alpern, H. P. Effects of electroshock on memory: Amnesia without convulsions. *Science*, 1966, **152**, 665–666.

McTeer, W. A study of certain features of punishment in serial learning. *Journal of Experimental Psychology*, 1931, **14**, 453–476.

McTeer, W. Changes in grip tension following electric shock in mirror tracing. *Journal of Experimental Psychology*, 1933, **16**, 735–742.

Melvin, K. B. Escape learning and "vicious-circle" behavior as a function of percentage of reinforcement. *Journal of Comparative and Physiological Psychology*, 1964, **58**, 251–253.

Melvin, K. B., Athey, G. I., Jr., & Heasley, F. H. Effects of duration and delay of shock on self-punitive behavior in the rat. *Psychological Reports*, 1965, **17**, 107–112.

Melvin, K. B., & Martin, R. C. Facilitative effects of two modes of punishment on resistance to extinction. *Journal of Comparative and Physiological Psychology*, 1966, **62**, 491–494.

Melvin, K. B., & Smith, F. H. Self-punitive avoidance behavior in the rat. *Journal of Comparative and Physiological Psychology*, 1967, **63**, 533–535.

Migler, B. Experimental self-punishment and superstitious escape behavior. *Journal of the Experimental Analysis of Behavior*, 1963, **6**, 371–385.

Miller, N. E. Learning resistance to pain and fear: Effects of overlearning, exposure, and rewarded exposure in context. *Journal of Experimental Psychology*, 1960, **60**, 137–145.

Miller, N. E., & Kraeling, D. Displacement: Greater generalization of approach than avoidance in a generalized approach-avoidance conflict. *Journal of Experimental Psychology*, 1952, **43**, 217–221.

Misanin, J. R., Campbell, B. A., & Smith, N. F. Duration of punishment and the delay of punishment gradient. *Canadian Journal of Psychology*, 1966, **20**, 407–412.

Mowrer, O. H. An experimental analogue of "regression" with incidental observations on "reaction-formation." *Journal of Abnormal and Social Psychology*, 1940, **35**, 56–87.

Mowrer, O. H., & Ullman, A. D. Time as a determinant in integrative learning. *Psychological Review*, 1945, **52**, 61–90.

Moyer, K. E. A study of some of the variables of which fixation is a function. *Journal of Genetic Psychology*, 1955, **86**, 3–31.

Moyer, K. E. The effects of shock on anxiety-motivated behavior in the rat. *Journal of Genetic Psychology*, 1957, **91**, 197–203.

Muenzinger, K. F. Motivation in learning: I. Electric shock for correct response in the visual discrimination habit. *Journal of Comparative Psychology*, 1934, **17**, 267–277. (a)

Muenzinger, K. F. Motivation in learning: II. The function of electric shock for right and wrong responses in human subjects. *Journal of Experimental Psychology*, 1934, **17**, 439–448. (b)

Muenzinger, K. F., Bernstone, A. H., & Richards, L. Motivation in learning: VIII. Equivalent amounts of electric shock for right and wrong responses in a visual discrimination habit. *Journal of Comparative Psychology*, 1938, **26**, 177–186.

Muenzinger, K. F., Brown, W. O., Crow, W. J., & Powloski, R. F. Motivation in learning: XI. An analysis of electric shock for correct responses into its avoidance and accelerating components. *Journal of Experimental Psychology,* 1952, **43**, 115–119.

MUENZINGER, K. F., & POWLOSKI, R. F. Motivation in learning: X. Comparison of electric shock for correct turns in a correction and non-correction situation. *Journal of Experimental Psychology,* 1951, **42**, 118–124.

MUENZINGER, K. F., & VINE, D. O. Motivation in learning: IX. The effect of interposed obstacles in human learning. *Journal of Experimental Psychology,* 1941, **29**, 67–74.

MURPHY, R. E. Effects of threat of shock, distraction, and task design on performance. *Journal of Experimental Psychology,* 1959, **58**, 134–141.

MURRAY, E. J., & BERKUN, M. M. Displacement as a function of conflict. *Journal of Abnormal and Social Psychology,* 1955, **51**, 47–56.

MURRAY, M., & NEVIN, J. A. Some effects of correlation between response-contingent shock and reinforcement. *Journal of the Experimental Analysis of Behavior,* 1967, **10**, 301–309.

MYER, J. S. Punishment of instinctive behavior: Suppression of mouse killing by rats. *Psychonomic Science,* 1966, 4, 385–386.

MYER, J. S. Prior killing experience and the suppressive effects of punishment on the killing of mice by rats. *Animal Behaviour,* 1967, **15**, 59–61.

MYER, J. S., & BAENNINGER, R. Some effects of punishment and stress on mouse killing by rats. *Journal of Comparative and Physiological Psychology,* 1966, **62**, 292–297.

MYERS, A. K. Instrumental escape conditioning to a low intensity noise by rats. *Journal of Comparative and Physiological Psychology,* 1965, **60**, 82–87.

NAGAMACHI, M. The effect of buzzer-shock upon the predictive value of behavior in a two-choice situation. *Psychologia,* 1960, **3**, 159–164.

NELSON, F. B., REID, I. E., & TRAVERS, R. M. W. Effect of electric shock as a reinforcer of the behavior of children. *Psychological Reports,* 1965, **16**, 123–126.

*NIGRO, M. R. Punishment of an extinguishing shock-avoidance response by time-out from positive reinforcement. *Journal of the Experimental Analysis of Behavior,* 1966, **9**, 53–64.

NOBLIN, C. D., & MAHER, B. A. Temporal and physical factors in avoidance reduction. *Journal of Comparative and Physiological Psychology,* 1962, **55**, 62–65.

O'KELLY, L. I. An experimental study of regression. I. Behavioral characteristics of the regressive response. *Journal of Comparative Psychology,* 1940, **30**, 41–53. (a)

O'KELLY, L. I. An experimental study of regression. II. Some motivational determinants of regression and perseveration. *Journal of Comparative Psychology,* 1940, **30**, 55–95. (b)

O'KELLY, L. I., & BIEL, W. C. The effect of cortical lesions on emotional and regressive behavior in the rat. II. Regression behavior. *Journal of Comparative Psychology,* 1940, **30**, 241-254.

OLDS, J. A preliminary mapping of electrical reinforcing effects in the rat brain. *Journal of Comparative and Physiological Psychology,* 1956, **49**, 281–285.

OLDS, J., & MILNER, P. Positive reinforcement produced by electrical stimulation of septal area and other regions of rat brain. *Journal of Comparative and Physiological Psychology,* 1954, **47,** 419–427.

ORZAK, M. H. The effect of punishment on the establishment of a stimulus discrimination. Unpublished doctoral dissertation, Columbia University, 1951.

PARÉ, W. P., & DUMAS, J. S. The effect of insular neocortical lesions on passive and active avoidance behavior in the rat. *Psychonomic Science,* 1965, **2,** 87–88.

PEARL, J. Effects of preshock and additional punishment on general activity. *Psychological Reports,* 1963, **12,** 155–161.

PEARL, J., WALTERS, G. C., & ANDERSON, D. C. Suppressing effects of aversive stimulation on subsequently punished behaviour. *Canadian Journal of Psychology,* 1964, **18,** 343–355.

PEARLMAN, C. A., SHARPLESS, S. K., & JARVIK, M. E. Retrograde amnesia produced by anesthetic and convulsive agents. *Journal of Comparative and Physiological Psychology,* 1961, **54,** 109–112.

PECHTEL, C., & MASSERMAN, J. H. The somatic responses of normal and neurotic monkeys. *Annals of the New York Academy of Sciences,* 1954, **58,** 256–260.

PECHTEL, C., MASSERMAN, J. H., SCHREINER, L., & LEVITT, M. Differential effects of lesions of the mediodorsal nuclei of the thalamus on normal and neurotic behavior in the cat. *Journal of Nervous and Mental Disease,* 1955, **121,** 26–33.

PENNY, R. K., & LUPTON, A. A. Children's discrimination learning as a function of reward and punishment. *Journal of Comparative and Physiological Psychology,* 1961, **54,** 449–451.

PORTER, E. H., & BIEL, W. C. Alleged regressive behavior in a two-unit maze. *Journal of Comparative Psychology,* 1943, **35,** 187–195.

POSCHEL, B. P. Proactive and retroactive effects of electro-convulsive shock on approach-avoidance conflict. (Doctoral dissertation, University of Illinois.) Ann Arbor, Mich.: University Microfilms, 1959. No. 56-1584.

PRINCE, A. I., JR. Effect of punishment on visual discrimination learning. *Journal of Experimental Psychology,* 1956, **52,** 381–385.

QUARTERMAIN, D., PAOLINO, R. M., & MILLER, N. E. A brief temporal gradient of retrograde amnesia independent of situational change. *Science,* 1965, **149,** 1116–1118.

RACHLIN, H. Recovery of responses during mild punishment. *Journal of the Experimental Analysis of Behavior,* 1966, **9,** 251–263.

RACHLIN, H. The effect of shock intensity on concurrent and single-key responding in concurrent-chain schedules. *Journal of the Experimental Analysis of Behavior,* 1967, **10,** 87–93.

RAY, O. S. The effect of central nervous system depressants on discrete trial approach-avoidance behavior. *Psychopharmacologia,* 1964, **6,** 96–111.

RENNER, K. E. Conflict resolution and the process of temporal integration. *Psychological Reports,* 1964, **15,** 423–438.

RENNER, K. E. Temporal integration: Relative value of rewards and punishments as a function of their temporal distance from the response. *Journal of Experimental Psychology*, 1966, **71**, 902–907. (a)

RENNER, K. E. Temporal integration: The relative utility of immediate versus delayed reward and punishment. *Journal of Experimental Psychology*, 1966, **72**, 901–903. (b)

REXROAD, C. N. Administering electric shock for inaccuracy in continuous multiple choice reactions. *Journal of Experimental Psychology*, 1926, **9**, 1–18.

REYNOLDS, G. S. Potency of conditioned reinforcers based on food and on food and punishment. *Science*, 1963, **139**, 838–839.

REYNOLDS, H. E. The disinhibiting effect of an electric shock upon the maze performance of the white rat. *Journal of Comparative Psychology*, 1936, **22**, 187–197.

ROSEN, A. C. Change in perceptual threshold as a protective function of the organism. *Journal of Personality*, 1954, **23**, 182–194.

ROSENBLUM, L. A., & HARLOW, H. F. Approach-avoidance conflict in the mother-surrogate situation. *Psychological Reports*, 1963, **12**, 83–85.

ROTBERG, I. C. Effect of schedule and severity of punishment on verbal behavior. *Journal of Experimental Psychology*, 1959, **57**, 193–200.

SANDER, M. J. An experimental demonstration of regression in the rat. *Journal of Experimental Psychology*, 1937, **21**, 493–510.

SANDLER, J. Some aspects of self aversive stimulation in the hooded rat. *Journal of the Experimental Analysis of Behavior*, 1964, **7**, 409–414.

SANDLER, J., DAVIDSON, R. S., GREENE, W. E., & HOLZSCHUH, R. D. Effects of punishment intensity on instrumental avoidance behavior. *Journal of Comparative and Physiological Psychology*, 1966, **61**, 212–216.

SANDLER, J., DAVIDSON, R. S., & HOLZSCHUH, R. D. Effects of increasing punishment frequency on Sidman avoidance behavior. *Psychonomic Science*, 1966, **5**, 103–104.

SANDLER, J., DAVIDSON, R. S., & MALAGODI, E. Durable maintenance of behavior during concurrent avoidance and punished-extinction conditions. *Psychonomic Science*, 1966, **6**, 105–106.

SAWREY, W. L., CONGER, J. J., & TURRELL, E. S. An experimental investigation of the role of psychological factors in the production of gastric ulcers in rats. *Journal of Comparative and Physiological Psychology*, 1956, **49**, 457–461.

SAWREY, W. L., & WEISZ, J. D. An experimental method of producing gastric ulcers. *Journal of Comparative and Physiological Psychology*, 1956, **49**, 269–270.

SCHAEFFER, A. A. Habit formation in frogs. *Journal of Animal Behavior*, 1911, **1**, 309–335.

SCHMIDT, K. M. The role of alcohol in the production of gastric ulcers in the albino rat placed in an approach-avoidance conflict situation. (Doctoral dissertation, Washington State University.) Ann Arbor, Mich.: University Microfilms, 1966. No. 66-781.

SCHWARTZBAUM, J. S., & SPIETH, T. M. Analysis of the response-inhibition concept of septal functions in "passive-avoidance" behavior. *Psychonomic Science*, 1964, **1**, 145–146.

SEARS, D. O. Punishment and choice in the rat. *Journal of Comparative and Physiological Psychology,* 1964, **57**, 297–299.

SELIGMAN, M. E. P., & CAMPBELL, B. A. Effect of intensity and duration of punishment on extinction of an avoidance response. *Journal of Comparative and Physiological Psychology,* 1965, **59**, 295–297.

SENTER, R. J., & HUMMEL, W. F., JR. Suppression of an autonomic response through operant conditioning. *Psychological Record,* 1965, **15**, 1–5.

SERMAT, V., & GREENGLAS, E. R. Effect of punishment on probability learning in schizophrenia. *British Journal of Social and Clinical Psychology,* 1965, **1**, 52–62.

SEWARD, J. P., KING, R. M., CHOW, T., & SHIFLETT, S. C. Persistence of punished escape responses. *Journal of Comparative and Physiological Psychology,* 1965, **60**, 265–268.

SEWARD, J. P., & RASKIN, D. C. The role of fear in aversive behavior. *Journal of Comparative and Physiological Psychology,* 1960, **53**, 328–335.

SHAPIRO, A. H. Anxiety and the suppressing effect of immediate punishment on a rewarded response. *Psychonomic Science,* 1966, **6**, 373–374.

SHEPARD, R. F., JR. Relative shock intensity and relative grid length in the combined avoidance-escape conditioning procedure. (Doctoral dissertation, Brown University.) Ann Arbor, Mich.: University Microfilms, 1964. No. 64-2008.

SIDMAN, M. By-products of aversive control. *Journal of the Experimental Analysis of Behavior,* 1958, **1**, 265–280.

SIEGEL, G. M., & MARTIN, R. R. Experimental modification of disfluency in normal speakers. *Journal of Speech and Hearing Research,* 1965, **8**, 235–244.

SKINNER, B. F. *The behavior of organisms.* New York: Appleton-Century, 1938.

SMART, R. G. Conflict and conditioned aversive stimuli in the development of experimental neuroses. *Canadian Journal of Psychology,* 1965, **19**, 208–223. (a)

SMART, R. G. Effects of alcohol on conflict and avoidance behavior. *Quarterly Journal of Studies on Alcohol,* 1965, **26**, 187–205. (b)

SMITH, N. F., MISANIN, J. R., & CAMPBELL, B. A. Effect of punishment on extinction of an avoidance response: Facilitation or inhibition? *Psychonomic Science,* 1966, **4**, 271–272.

SNAPPER, A. G., SCHOENFELD, W. N., & LOCKE, B. Adrenal and thymus weight loss in the food-deprived rat produced by random ratio punishment schedules. *Journal of Comparative and Physiological Psychology,* 1966, **62**, 65–70.

SNYDER, D. R., & ISAACSON, R. L. Effects of large and small bilateral hippocampal lesions on two types of passive-avoidance responses. *Psychological Reports,* 1965, **16**, 1277–1290.

SOLOMON, R. L., KAMIN, L. J., & WYNNE, L. C. Traumatic avoidance learning: The outcomes of several extinction procedures with dogs. *Journal of Abnormal and Social Psychology,* 1953, **48**, 291–302.

SPIEGEL, S. The effect of consistent and inconsistent punishment on the exploratory behavior of the white rat. (Doctoral dissertation, University of Florida.) Ann Arbor, Mich.: University Microfilms, 1957. No. 57-3322.

SPIGEL, I. M., & ELLIS, K. Climbing suppression: Passive avoidance in the turtle. *Psychonomic Science,* 1965, **3**, 215–216.

STANLEY, W. C., & ELLIOT, O. Differential human handling as reinforcing events and as treatments influencing later social behavior in Basenji puppies. *Psychological Reports,* 1962, **10**, 775–788.

STECKLE, L. C., & O'KELLY, L. I. The effect of electrical shock upon later learning and regression in the rat. *Journal of Psychology,* 1940, **9**, 365–370.

STEIN, L. Reciprocal action of reward and punishment mechanisms. In R. G. Heath (Ed.), *The role of pleasure in behavior.* New York: Harper & Row, 1964. Pp. 113–139.

STEINER, S. S., & D'AMATO, M. R. Rewarding and aversive effects of amygdaloid self-stimulation as a function of current intensity. *Psychonomic Science,* 1964, **1**, 27–28.

STONE, G. R. The effect of negative incentives in serial learning: I. The spread of variability under electric shock. *Journal of Experimental Psychology,* 1946, **36**, 137–142.

STONE, G. R. The effect of negative incentives in serial learning: II. Incentive intensity and response variability. *Journal of General Psychology,* 1950, **42**, 179–224.

STONE, G. R., & WALTER, N. The effect of negative incentives in serial learning: VI. Response repetition as a function of an isolated electric shock punishment. *Journal of Experimental Psychology,* 1951, **41**, 411–418.

STORMS, L. H., & BOROCZI, G. Effectiveness of fixed ratio punishment and durability of its effects. *Psychonomic Science,* 1966, **5**, 447–448.

STORMS, L. H., BOROCZI, G., & BROEN, W. E., JR. Punishment inhibits an instrumental response in hooded rats. *Science,* 1962, **135**, 1133–1134.

STORMS, L. H., BOROCZI, G., & BROEN, W. E., JR. Effects of punishment as a function of strain of rat and duration of punishment. *Journal of Comparative and Physiological Psychology,* 1963, **56**, 1022–1026.

STORMS, L. H., BOROCZI, G., & BROEN, W. E., JR. Recovery from punishment of bar pressing maintained on fixed and variable interval reward schedules. *Psychonomic Science,* 1965, **3**, 289–290.

SZYMANSKI, J. S. Modification of the innate behavior of cockroaches. *Journal of Animal Behavior,* 1912, **2**, 81–90.

*TATE, B. G., & BAROFF, G. S. Aversive control of self-injurious behavior in a psychotic boy. *Behaviour Research and Therapy,* 1966, 4, 281–287.

TAYLOR, J. A., & MAHER, B. A. Escape and displacement experience as variables in the recovery from approach-avoidance conflict. *Journal of Comparative and Physiological Psychology,* 1959, **52**, 586–590.

TAYLOR, J. A., & RENNIE, B. Recovery from approach-avoidance conflict as a function of escape and displacement experiences. *Journal of Comparative and Physiological Psychology,* 1961, **54**, 275–278.

TERRIS, W., & WECHKIN, S. Approach-avoidance conflict behavior as a function of prior experience with mild or intense electric shock stimulation. *Psychonomic Science,* 1967, **7**, 39–40. (a)

TERRIS, W., & WECHKIN, S. Learning to resist the effects of punishment. *Psychonomic Science,* 1967, **7**, 169–170. (b)

*TOLMAN, C. W., & MUELLER, M. R. Laboratory control of toe-sucking in a young rhesus monkey by two kinds of punishment. *Journal of the Experimental Analysis of Behavior,* 1964, **7,** 323–325.

TOLMAN, E. C., HALL, C. S., & BRETNALL, E. P. A disproof of the law of effect and a substitution of the laws of emphasis, motivation, and disruption. *Journal of Experimental Psychology,* 1932, **15,** 601–614.[7]

TRAVIS, R. C. Comparison of the influences of monetary reward and electric shocks on learning in eye-hand coordination. *Journal of Experimental Psychology,* 1938, **23,** 423–427.

TRAVIS, R. C., & ANDERSON, H. C. The effect of electric shock on learning in eye-hand coordination. *Journal of Experimental Psychology,* 1938, **23,** 101–107.

TUCKMAN, J. The influence of varying amounts of punishment on mental connections. *Teachers College Contributions to Education,* 1933, No. 590.

TUGENDHAT, B. Feeding in conflict situations and following training. *Science,* 1960, **132,** 896–897.

TYLER, V. O., JR., & BROWN, G. D. The use of swift, brief isolation as a group control device for institutionalized delinquents. *Behaviour Research and Therapy,* 1967, **5,** 1–11.

UHL, C. N. Persistence in punishment and extinction testing as a function of percentages of punishment and reward in training. *Psychonomic Science,* 1967, **8,** 193–194.

UNDERWOOD, B. J. The effects of punishment in serial verbal learning. *Proceedings of the Iowa Academy of Sciences,* 1941, **48,** 349–352.

VALENTINE, R. The effects of punishment for errors on the maze learning of rats. *Journal of Comparative Psychology,* 1930, **10,** 35–53.

VAUGHN, J. *Positive versus negative instruction.* New York: National Bureau of Casualty and Surety Underwriters, 1928.

VAUGHN, J., & DISERENS, C. M. The relative effects of various intensities of punishment on learning and efficiency. *Journal of Comparative Psychology,* 1930, **10,** 55–66.

VOGEL-SPROTT, M. D. Suppression of a rewarded response by punishment as a function of reinforcement schedules. *Psychonomic Science,* 1966, **5,** 395–396.

VOGEL-SPROTT, M. D. Alcohol effects on human behavior under reward and punishment. *Psychopharmacologia,* 1967, **11,** 337–344.

VOGEL-SPROTT, M. D., & BANKS, R. K. The effect of delayed punishment on an immediately rewarded response in alcoholics and nonalcoholics. *Behaviour Research and Therapy,* 1965, **3,** 69–73.

WALTERS, G. C. Frequency and intensity of pre-shock experiences as determinants of fearfulness in an approach-avoidance conflict. *Canadian Journal of Psychology,* 1963, **17,** 412–419.

WALTERS, R. H., & DEMKOW, L. Timing of punishment as a determinant of response inhibition. *Child Development,* 1963, **34,** 207–214.

[7] See also: Goodenough, F. L. A note on Tolman's 'disproof' of Thorndike's law of effect. *Journal of Experimental Psychology,* 1933, **16,** 459–462; Tolman, E. C. The law of effect: A reply to Dr. Goodenough. *Journal of Experimental Psychology,* 1933, **16,** 463–470.

WARDEN, C. J. *Animal motivation: Experimental studies on the albino rat.* New York: Columbia University Press, 1931.

WARDEN, C. J., & AYLESWORTH, M. The relative value of reward and punishment in the formation of a visual discrimination habit in the white rat. *Journal of Comparative Psychology,* 1927, **7**, 117–127.

WHEELER, D. R. The inhibitory effects of punishment: An experimental study of the white rat. Unpublished doctoral dissertation, Harvard University, 1933.

WHITE, M. M. Influence of an interpolated electric shock upon recall. *Journal of Experimental Psychology,* 1932, **15**, 752–757.

WHITEIS, U. E. Punishment's influence on fear and avoidance. *Harvard Educational Review,* 1956, **26**, 360–373.

WHITING, J. W. M., & MOWRER, O. H. Habit progression and regression—a laboratory study of some factors relevant to human socialization. *Journal of Comparative Psychology,* 1943, **36**, 229–253.

WIKLER, A., & MASSERMAN, J. H. The effects of morphine on learned adaptive responses and experimental neuroses in cats. *Archives of Neurology and Psychiatry,* 1943, **50**, 401–404.

WILLIAMS, D. R., & BARRY, H., III. Counter conditioning in an operant conflict situation. *Journal of Comparative and Physiological Psychology,* 1966, **61**, 154–156.

WINOGRAD, E., COHEN, P. S., & COLE, B. K. Frequency and latency measures of the generalization of punishment. *Psychonomic Science,* 1965, **2**, 321–322.

WISCHNER, G. J. The effect of punishment on discrimination learning in a noncorrection situation. *Journal of Experimental Psychology,* 1947, **37**, 271–284.[8]

WISCHNER, G. J., & FOWLER, H. Discrimination performance as affected by duration of shock for either the correct or incorrect response. *Psychonomic Science,* 1964, **1**, 239–240.

WISCHNER, G. J., FOWLER, H., & KUSHNICK, S. A. Effect of strength of punishment for "correct" or "incorrect" responses on visual discrimination performance. *Journal of Experimental Psychology,* 1963, **65**, 131–138.

WISCHNER, G. J., HALL, R. C., & FOWLER, H. Discrimination learning under various combinations of food and shock for "correct" and "incorrect" responses. *Journal of Experimental Psychology,* 1964, **67**, 48–51.

*WOLF, M., MEES, H. L., & RISLEY, T. R. Application of operant conditioning procedures to the behavior problems of an autistic child. *Behaviour Research and Therapy,* 1964, **1**, 305–312.

*WOLF, M., RISLEY, T., JOHNSTON, M., HARRIS, F., & ALLEN, E. Application of operant conditioning procedures to the behavior problems of an autistic child: A follow-up and extension. *Behaviour Research and Therapy,* 1967, **5**, 103–112.

---

[8] See also: Muenzinger, K. F. Concerning the effect of shock for right responses in visual discrimination learning. *Journal of Experimental Psychology,* 1948, **38**, 201–203; Wischner, G. J. A reply to Dr. Muenzinger on the effect of punishment on discrimination learning in a non-correction situation. *Journal of Experimental Psychology,* 1948, **38**, 203–204.

Wolpe, J. Experimental neuroses as learned responses. *British Journal of Psychology,* 1952, **43,** 243–268.

Wolpe, J. New therapeutic methods based on a conditioned response theory of neurosis. *Zeitschrift für Psychologie,* 1964, **169,** 173–196.

Wood, A. B. A comparison of delayed reward and delayed punishment in the formation of a brightness discrimination habit in the chick. *Archives of Psychology,* 1933, **24** (No. 157).

Worell, L. The ring of punishment: A theoretical and experimental analogue of repression-suppression. *Journal of Abnormal Psychology,* 1965, **70,** 201–209.

Wynnne, L. C., & Solomon, R. L. Traumatic avoidance learning: Acquisition and extinction in dogs deprived of normal peripheral autonomic function. *Genetic Psychology Monographs,* 1955, **52,** 241–284.

Yerkes, R. M., & Dodson, J. D. The relation of strength of stimulus to rapidity of habit formation. *Journal of Comparative Neurology and Psychology,* 1908, **18,** 459–482.

*Zimmerman, J., & Ferster, C. B. Intermittent punishment of S$^\triangle$ responding in matching to sample. *Journal of the Experimental Analysis of Behavior,* 1963, **6,** 349–356.

Zinkin, S., & Miller, A. J. Recovery of memory after amnesia induced by electroconvulsive shock. *Science,* 1967, **155,** 102–103.

III. Bibliography on Secondary Punishment [9]

Aisenberg, R. B. The cumulative differential effects of reward and punishment on the performance of schizophrenic and normal subjects. (Doctoral dissertation, Boston University.) Ann Arbor, Mich.: University Microfilms, 1957. No. 57-3348.

Alfert, E. "Spread of effect" without guessing sequences. *American Journal of Psychology,* 1963, **76,** 638–643.

Anderson, H. E., Jr., White, W. F., & Wash, J. A. Generalized effects of praise and reproof. *Journal of Educational Psychology,* 1966, **57,** 169–173.

Aronfreed, J. The origin of self-criticism. *Psychological Review,* 1964, **71,** 193–218.

Aronfreed, J., & Reber, A. Internalized behavioral suppression and the timing of social punishment. *Journal of Personality and Social Psychology,* 1965, **1,** 3–16.

Atkinson, R. L., & Robinson, N. W. Paired-associate learning by schizophrenic and normal subjects under conditions of personal and impersonal reward and punishment. *Journal of Abnormal and Social Psychology,* 1961, **62,** 322–326.

Baron, A. Functions of CS and UCS in fear conditioning. *Journal of Comparative and Physiological Psychology,* 1959, **52, 591–593.

Beatty, F. S., Dameron, L. E., & Greene, J. E. An investigation of the effects

[9] The few experiments in which experimentally produced secondary punishers were used are identified by a double asterisk. Stimuli presumed to be secondary punishers but not experimentally produced were used in all the other experiments in Section III.

of reward and punishment on visual perception. *Journal of Psychology,* 1959, 47, 267–276.

BEVAN, W., & DUKES, W. F. Effectiveness of delayed punishment on learning performance when preceded by preliminary cues. *Psychological Reports,* 1955, 1, 441–448.

**BIXENSTINE, V. E. Secondary drive as a neutralizer of time in integrative problem solving. *Journal of Comparative and Physiological Psychology,* 1956, 49, 161–166.

BLANKENSHIP, A. B., & HUMES, J. F. Effect of praise and reproof upon memory span performance. *American Journal of Psychology,* 1938, 51, 527–531.

BOMMARITO, J. W. Conditioning by mild verbal punishment as a predictor of adjustment in kindergarten. (Doctoral dissertation, Wayne State University.) Ann Arbor, Mich.: University Microfilms, 1965. No. 65-1825.

BRACKBILL, Y., & O'HARA, J. The relative effectiveness of reward and punishment for discrimination learning in children. *Journal of Comparative and Physiological Psychology,* 1958, 51, 747–751.

**BRADY, J. V., & HUNT, H. F. An experimental approach to the analysis of emotional behavior. *Journal of Psychology,* 1955, 40, 313–324.

BRANDT, H. The spread of the influence of reward to bonds remote in sequence and time. *Archives of Psychology,* 1935, 27, No. 180.

BRENNER, B. Effect of immediate and delayed praise and blame upon learning and recall. *Teachers' College Contributions to Education,* 1934, No. 620.

BUCHWALD, A. M. Extinction after acquisition under different verbal reinforcement combinations. *Journal of Experimental Psychology,* 1959, 57, 43–48. (a)

BUCHWALD, A. M. Experimental alterations in the effectiveness of verbal reinforcement combinations. *Journal of Experimental Psychology,* 1959, 57, 351–361. (b)

BUCHWALD, A. M. Variations in the apparent effects of "Right" and "Wrong" on subsequent behavior. *Journal of Verbal Learning and Verbal Behavior,* 1962, 1, 71–78.

BUSS, A. H., BRADEN, W., ORGEL, A., & BUSS, E. H. Acquisition and extinction with different verbal reinforcement combinations. *Journal of Experimental Psychology,* 1956, 52, 288-295.

BUSS, A. H., & BUSS, E. H. The effect of verbal reinforcement combinations on conceptual learning. *Journal of Experimental Psychology,* 1956, 52, 283–287.

**CAMPBELL, B. A., & CAMPBELL, E. H. Retention and extinction of learned fear in infant and adult rats. *Journal of Comparative and Physiological Psychology,* 1962, 55, 1–8.

CAVANAUGH, D. K., COHEN, W., & LANG, P. J. The effect of "social censure" and "social approval" on the psychomotor performance of schizophrenics. *Journal of Abnormal and Social Psychology,* 1960, 60, 213–218.

CHAPMAN, J. C., & FEDER, R. B. The effect of external incentives on improvement. *Journal of Education Psychology,* 1917, 8, 469–474.

CHASE, L. Motivation of young children: An experimental study of the influence of certain types of external incentives upon the performance of a task. *University of Iowa Studies: Studies in Child Welfare,* 1932, 5, No. 3.

COURTS, F. A. The alleged retroactive effect of visual stimuli subsequent to a given response. *Journal of Experimental Psychology,* 1937, **20**, 144–154.

Courts, F. A., & Waggoner, D. The effect of "something happening" after a response. *Journal of Experimental Psychology,* 1938, **22**, 383–387.

Cruikshank, R. M., & Feigenbaum, E. A note on the influence of praise and reproof upon size constancy. *Journal of Experimental Psychology,* 1941, **29**, 524–527.

Curry, C. Supplementary report: The effects of verbal reinforcement combinations on learning in children. *Journal of Experimental Psychology,* 1960, **59**, 434.

Dand, A. "Reward" and "punishment" in learning. *British Journal of Psychology,* 1946, **36**, 83–87.

Davis, R. A., & Ballard, C. R. The effectiveness of various types of classroom incentives. *Educational Methods,* 1932, **12**, 134–145.

Duncan, C. P. The action of various after-effects on response repetition. *Journal of Experimental Psychology,* 1950, **40**, 380–389.

Dyal, J. A., & Goodman, E. D. Fear conditioning as a function of CS duration during acquisition and suppression tests. *Psychonomic Science,* 1966, **4, 249–250.

Eisenson, J. Confirmation and information in rewards and punishments. *Archives of Psychology,* 1935, **27**, No. 181.

Evans, W. O. Producing either positive or negative tendencies to a stimulus associated with shock. *Journal of the Experimental Analysis of Behavior,* 1962, **5, 335–337.

Farber, I. Spread of effect of reward and punishment in a multiple choice situation. *Proceedings of the Iowa Academy of Sciences,* 1941, **48**, 313–317.

Filby, Y. M. The effect of punishment on verbal behavior. (Doctoral dissertation, Indiana University.) Ann Arbor, Mich.: University Microfilms, 1963. No. 63-3819.

Forlano, G., & Axelrod, H. C. The effect of repeated praise or blame on the performance of introverts and extroverts. *Journal of Educational Psychology,* 1937, **28**, 92–100.

French, J. R. P., Jr., Morrison, H. W., & Levinger, G. Coercive power and forces affecting conformity. *Journal of Abnormal and Social Psychology,* 1960, **61**, 93–101.

Gardner, J. E. The effects of verbal reprimand on the behavior of young children. (Doctoral dissertation, University of California, Los Angeles.) Ann Arbor, Mich.: University Microfilms, 1964. No. 64-7349.

Gates, G. S., & Rissland, L. Q. The effect of encouragement and discouragement upon performance. *Journal of Educational Psychology,* 1923, **14**, 21–26.

Gilchrist, E. P. The extent to which praise and reproof affect a pupil's work. *School and Society,* 1916, **4**, 872–874.

Goldman, A. R. Differential effects of social reward and punishment on dependent and dependency-anxious schizophrenics. *Journal of Abnormal Psychology,* 1965, **70**, 412–418.

Goodkin, R. Changes in conformity behavior on a perceptual task following verbal reinforcement and punishment. *Journal of Psychology,* 1966, **62**, 99–110.

GRUEN, G. E., & WEIR, M. W. Effect of instructions, penalty, and age on probability learning. *Child Development,* 1964, **35**, 265–273.

HAKE, D. F., & AZRIN, N. H. Conditioned punishment. *Journal of the Experimental Analysis of Behavior,* 1965, **8, 279–293.

HAMILTON, H. C. The effect of incentives on accuracy of discrimination measured on the Galton Bar. *Archives of Psychology,* 1929, **16**, No. 103.

HAMPE, I. E., JR. The modification of the dominance-submission relationship in dyadic groups of school children as a function of various combinations of reward and punishment. (Doctoral dissertation, The Florida State University.) Ann Arbor, Mich.: University Microfilms, 1967. No. 67-291.

HEISTAD, G. T. Effects of chlorpromazine and electroconvulsive shock on a conditioned emotional response. *Journal of Comparative and Physiological Psychology,* 1958, **51, 209–212.

HERRNSTEIN, R. J., & SIDMAN, M. Avoidance conditioning as a factor in the effects of unavoidable shocks on food-reinforced behavior. *Journal of Comparative and Physiological Psychology,* 1958, **51, 380–385.

HETHERINGTON, E. M., & KLINGER, E. Psychopathy and punishment. *Journal of Abnormal and Social Psychology,* 1964, **69**, 113–115.

HICKS, D. J. The effects of various reward and punishment conditions on achievement behavior. (Doctoral dissertation, Stanford University.) Ann Arbor, Mich.: University Microfilms, 1962. No. 62-4055.

HOLLENBERG, E., & SPERRY, M. Some antecedents of aggression and effects of frustration in doll play. *Personality,* 1951, **1**, 32–43.

HOLODNAK, H. B. The effect of positive and negative guidance upon maze learning in children. *Journal of Educational Psychology,* 1943, **34**, 341–354.

HULIN, W. S., & KATZ, D. A comparison of emphasis upon right and upon wrong responses in learning. *Journal of Experimental Psychology,* 1935, **18**, 638–642.

HURLOCK, E. B. The value of praise and reproof as incentives for children. *Archives of Psychology,* 1924, **11**, No. 71.

HURLOCK, E. B. The effect of incentives upon the constancy of the I.Q. *Pedagogical Seminary,* 1925, **32**, 422–434. (a)

HURLOCK, E. B. An evaluation of certain incentives used in school work. *Journal of Educational Psychology,* 1925, **16**, 145–159. (b)

HURLOCK, E. B. The psychology of incentives. *Journal of Social Psychology,* 1931, **2**, 261–290.

JOHANNSEN, W. J. Effect of reward and punishment on motor learning by chronic schizophrenics and normals. *Journal of Clinical Psychology,* 1962, **18**, 204–207.

JONES, H. E. Trial and error learning with differential cues. *Journal of Experimental Psychology,* 1945, **35**, 31–45.

JONES, L. A. M. A comparison of the effects of reward and punishment upon the development of self-control. (Doctoral dissertation, Stanford University.) Ann Arbor, Mich.: University Microfilms, 1966. No. 66-2572.

KARSH, E. B., & WILLIAMS, J. P. Punishment and reward in children's instrumental learning. *Psychonomic Science,* 1964, **1**, 359–360.

KATZ, L. Effects of differential monetary gain and loss on sequential two-choice behavior. *Journal of Experimental Psychology,* 1964, **68**, 245–249.

KAYE, H., Cox, J., BOSACK, T., & ANDERSON, K. Primary and secondary punishment of toe sucking in the infant rhesus monkey. *Psychonomic Science,* 1965, **2, 73–74.

KIPNIS, D. The effects of leadership style and leadership power upon the inducement of an attitude change. *Journal of Abnormal and Social Psychology,* 1958, **57**, 173–180.

LIE, I. Reward and punishment: A determinant of figure-ground perception? *Scandinavian Journal of Psychology,* 1965, **6**, 186–194.

LORGE, I. The efficacy of intensified reward and intensified punishment. *Journal of Experimental Psychology,* 1933, **16**, 177–207. (a)

LORGE, I. The effect of the initial chances for right responses upon the efficacy of intensified reward and of intensified punishment. *Journal of Experimental Psychology,* 1933, **16**, 362–373. (b)

LORGE, I., EISENSON, J., & EPSTEIN, B. Further experiments in the strength of connections where the connection is punished or rewarded or neither punished nor rewarded. *Journal of Experimental Psychology,* 1934, **17**, 412–423.

LORGE, I., & THORNDIKE, E. L. The comparative strengthening of a connection by one or more occurrences of it in cases where the connection was punished and was neither punished nor rewarded. *Journal of Experimental Psychology,* 1933, **16**, 374–382.

LORGE, I., & THORNDIKE, E. L. The influence of delay in the after-effect of a connection. *Journal of Experimental Psychology,* 1935, **18**, 186–194.

LOSEN, S. M. The differential effects of censure on the problem-solving behavior of schizophrenic and normal subjects. *Journal of Personality* 1961, 29, 258–272.

MAJUMDAR, K. An experimental study of the relative influence of reward and punishment on learning. *Indian Journal of Psychology,* 1951, **26**, 67–72.

MALTZMAN, E., HOLZ, W. C., & KUNZE, J. Supplementary knowledge of results. *Journal of the Experimental Analysis of Behavior,* 1965, **8**, 385–388.

MARCHIONNE, A. M. Cognitive and drive properties of censure in schizophrenic learning. (Doctoral dissertation, Washington State University.) Ann Arbor, Mich.: University Microfilms, 1961. No. 61-3241.

MARQUART, D. I., & ARNOLD, L. P. A study in the frustration of human adults. *Journal of General Psychology,* 1952, **47**, 43–63.

MATHIE, J. P. Verbal conditioning by avoidance learning: An experimental analogue to a particular interpersonal situation. (Doctoral dissertation, Michigan State University.) Ann Arbor, Mich.: University Microfilms, 1966. No. 66-418.

MATSUMIYA, Y. The effects of US intensity and CS–US pattern on conditioned emotional response. *Japanese Psychological Research,* 1960, **2, 35–42.

McCARTHY, J. F. The differential effects of praise and censure upon the verbal response of schizophrenics. (Doctoral dissertation, The Catholic University of America.) Ann Arbor, Mich.: University Microfilms, 1964. No. 64-355.

McGAUGH, J. L., & MADSEN, M. C. Amnesic and punishing effects of electroconvulsive shock. *Science,* 1964, **144, 182–183.

McINNIS, T. L., & ULLMAN, L. P. Positive and negative reinforcement with short- and long-term hospitalized schizophrenics in a probability learning situation. *Journal of Abnormal Psychology,* 1967, **72**, 157–162.

McIntire, R. W. Conditioned suppression and self-stimulation. *Psychonomic Science,* 1966, **5, 273–274.

McNamara, H. J. Non-veridical perception as a function of rewards and punishments. *Perceptual and Motor Skills,* 1959, **9,** 67–80.

Melaragno, R. J. Effect of negative reinforcement in an automated teaching setting. *Psychological Reports,* 1960, **7,** 381–384.

Meyer, W. J., & Offenbach, S. I. Effectiveness of reward and punishment as a function of task complexity. *Journal of Comparative and Physiological Psychology,* 1962, **55,** 532–534.

Meyer, W. J., & Seidman, S. B. Age differences in the effectiveness of different reinforcement combinations on the acquisition and extinction of a simple concept learning problem. *Child Development,* 1960, **31,** 419–429.

Meyer, W. J., & Seidman, S. B. Relative effectiveness of different reinforcement combinations on concept learning of children at two development levels. *Child Development,* 1961, **32,** 117–127.

Mischel, W., & Grusec, J. Determinants of the rehearsal and transmission of neutral and aversive behaviors. *Journal of Personality and Social Psychology,* 1966, **3,** 197–205.

Monosoff, H. The comparative effects of rewarding, punishing and counter-conditioning verbal aggressive behavior. (Doctoral dissertation, Stanford University.) Ann Arbor, Mich.: University Microfilms, 1964. No. 64-1639.

Mowrer, O. H., & Aiken, E. G. Contiguity vs. drive-reduction in conditioned fear: Temporal variations in conditioned and unconditioned stimulus. *American Journal of Psychology,* 1954, **67, 26–38.

Mowrer, O. H., & Solomon, L. N. Contiguity vs. drive-reduction in conditioned fear: The proximity and abruptness of drive-reduction. *American Journal of Psychology,* 1954, **67, 15–25.

Muenzinger, K. F., & Dove, C. C. Serial learning: I. Gradients of uniformity and variability produced by success and failure of single responses. *Journal of General Psychology,* 1937, **16,** 403–413.

Murata, K. Punishment: On the effect of verbal punishment upon multiple-selective learning. *Finbun Kenkyu* (Osaka City Univer.), 1957, **8,** 282–320.

Murata, K. The effect of verbal punishment upon selective learning. *Japanese Journal of Psychology,* 1959, **30,** 34–40.

Myers, J. L., & Suydam, M. M. Gain, cost, and event probability as determiners of choice behavior. *Psychonomic Science,* 1964, **1,** 39–40.

Nuttin, J. La loi de l'effet et la finalité du comportement. *Miscellanea Psychologica Albert Michotte,* 1947, 611–633. (a)

Nuttin, J. Respective effectiveness of success and task-tension in learning. *British Journal of Psychology,* 1947, **38,** 49–55. (b)

Offenbach, S. I. Studies of children's probability learning behavior: I. Effect of reward and punishment at two age levels. *Child Development,* 1964, **35,** 709–715.

Parke, R. D., & Walters, R. H. Some factors influencing the efficacy of punishment training for inducing response inhibition. *Monographs of the Society for Research in Child Development,* 1967, **32** (1, Whole No. 109).

Perrine, M. W. Bezugsskalenbildung, Diskrimination, und verbale Verstarkung. *Zeitschrift für Experimentelle und Angewandte Psychologie,* 1966, **13,** 464–483.

POTTER, E. H. The effect of reproof in relation to age in school children. *Journal of Genetic Psychology*, 1943, **63**, 247–258.

PROSHANSKY, H., & MURPHY, G. The effects of reward and punishment on perception. *Journal of Psychology*, 1942, **13**, 295–305.

ROCK, I., & FLECK, F. S. A re-examination of the effect of monetary reward and punishment on figure-ground perception. *Journal of Experimental Psychology*, 1950, **40**, 766–776.

ROCK, R. T., JR. The influence upon learning of the quantitative variation of after-effects. *Teachers College Contribution to Education*, 1935, No. 650.

ROZEBOOM, W. W. Secondary extinction of lever-pressing behavior in the albino rat. *Journal of Experimental Psychology*, 1957, **54, 280–287.

SANDLER, J. The effect of negative verbal cues upon verbal behavior. *Journal of Abnormal and Social Psychology*, 1962, **64**, 312–316.

SCHAFER, R., & MURPHY, G. The role of autism in a visual figure-ground relationship. *Journal of Experimental Psychology*, 1943, **32**, 335–343.

SCHMIDT, H. O. The effects of praise and blame as incentives to learning. *Psychological Monographs: General and Applied*, 1941, **53** (3, Whole No. 240).

SEGAL, E. F. Toward empirical behavior laws: II. Effectiveness of a conditioned reinforcer paired with food and shock. *Psychonomic Science*, 1965, **2, 137–138.

SELIGMAN, M. E. P. CS redundancy and secondary punishment. *Journal of Experimental Psychology*, 1966, **72, 546–550.

SETTERINGTON, R. G., & WATERS, R. H. Effects of concurrent delays of material rewards and punishments on problem-solving in children. *Child Development*, 1964, **35**, 275–280.

SIEGEL, G. M., & MARTIN, R. R. Verbal punishment of disfluencies in normal speakers. *Journal of Speech and Hearing Research*, 1965, **8**, 245–251.

SIEGEL, G. M., & MARTIN, R. R. Punishment of disfluencies in normal speakers. *Journal of Speech and Hearing Research*, 1966, **9**, 208–218.

SIMKINS, L. Scheduling effects of punishment and nonreinforcement on verbal conditioning and extinction. *Journal of Verbal Learning and Verbal Behavior*, 1962, **1**, 208–213.

SIMS, V. M. The relative influence of two types of motivation on improvement. *Journal of Educational Psychology*, 1928, **19**, 480–484.

SNYDERMAN, B. B. The effectiveness of reward and punishment in maintaining children's shift to a non-preferred response. (Doctoral dissertation, University of Pittsburgh.) Ann Arbor, Mich.: University Microfilms, 1966. No. 66-8174.

SOLLEY, C. M., & ENGEL, M. Perceptual autism in children: The effects of reward, punishment, and neutral conditions upon perceptual learning. *Journal of Genetic Psychology*, 1960, **97**, 77–91.

SOMMER, R. Perception and monetary reinforcement: II. The effects of rewards and punishments in the visual modality. *Journal of Psychology*, 1956, **42**, 143–148.

STEPHENS, J. M. Further notes on punishment and reward. *Journal of Genetic Psychology*, 1934, **44**, 464–472. (a)

STEPHENS, J. M. The influence of punishment on learning. *Journal of Experimental Psychology*, 1934, **17**, 536–555. (b)

STEPHENS, J. M. Some anomalous results of punishment in learning. *School and Society,* 1940, **52**, 703–704.

STEPHENS, J. M. The influence of symbolic punishment and reward upon strong and upon weak associations. *Journal of General Psychology,* 1941, **25**, 177–185.

STEPHENS, J. M., & BAER, J. A. The influence of punishment on learning when the opportunity for inner repetition is reduced. *Journal of Genetic Psychology,* 1937, **51**, 209–217.

STEPHENS, J. M., & BAER, J. A. Factors influencing the efficacy of punishment and reward: The opportunity for immediate review, and special instructions regarding the expected role of punishment. *Journal of Genetic Psychology,* 1944, **65**, 53–66.

STEVENS, M. M. The effect of positive and negative reinforcement on specific disfluency responses of normal-speaking college males. (Doctoral dissertation, State University of Iowa.) Ann Arbor, Mich.: University Microfilms, 1963. No. 63-4762.

STEVENSON, H. W., WEIR, M. W., & ZIGLER, E. F. Discrimination learning in children as a function of motive-incentive conditions. *Psychological Reports,* 1959, **5**, 95–98.

STEVENSON, I. The use of rewards and punishments in psychotherapy. *Comprehensive Psychiatry,* 1962, **3**, 20–28.

STONE, G. R. The effect of negative incentives in serial learning: I. The spread of the variability under electric shock. *Journal of Experimental Psychology,* 1946, **36**, 137–142.

STONE, G. R. The effect of negative incentives in serial learning: III. Fixation due to an isolated verbal punishment. *Journal of General Psychology,* 1948, **38**, 207–216.

STONE, G. R. The effect of negative incentives in serial learning: II. Incentive intensity and response variability. *Journal of General Psychology,* 1950, **42**, 179–224.

STONE, G. R. The effect of negative incentives in serial learning: V. Response repetition as a function of successive serial verbal punishments. *Journal of Experimental Psychology,* 1951, **42**, 20–24.

STONE, G. R. The effect of negative incentives in serial learning: VII. Theory of punishment. *Journal of General Psychology,* 1953, **48**, 133–161.

STONE, G. R., & WALTER, N. The effect of negative incentives in serial learning: VI. Response repetition as a function of an isolated electric shock punishment. *Journal of Experimental Psychology,* 1951, **41**, 411–418.

STONE, G. R. & YERRINGTON, F. The effect of various patterns of verbal incentives upon response repetition. *Proceedings of the Oklahoma Academy of Science,* 1948, **29**, 129–131.

SULLIVAN, P. W. The effects of verbal reward and verbal punishment on concept elicitation in children. (Doctoral dissertation, Wayne State University.) Ann Arbor, Mich.: University Microfilms, 1964. No. 64-3325.

TALLARICO, R. B. Effect of punishment on human operant behavior. (Doctoral dissertation, Purdue University.) Ann Arbor, Mich.: University Microfilms, 1957. No. 57-1443.

TAPP, J. T. Strain differences in the acquisition of a conditioned emotional response. *Journal of Comparative and Physiological Psychology*, 1964, **57, 464–465.

TERRELL, G., JR., & KENNEDY, W. A. Discrimination learning and transposition in children as a function of the nature of the reward. *Journal of Experimental Psychology*, 1957, **53**, 257–260.

THOMPSON, D. M. Punishment by S^D associated with fixed-ratio reinforcement. *Journal of the Experimental Analysis of Behavior*, 1965, **8, 189–194.

THORNDIKE, E. L. The law of effect. *American Journal of Psychology*, 1927, **39**, 212–222.

THORNDIKE, E. L. *Human learning*. New York: Century, 1931.

THORNDIKE, E. L. *Fundamentals of learning*. New York: Teachers College, 1932.

THORNDIKE, E. L. An experimental study of rewards. *Teachers College Contribution to Education*, 1933, No. 580. (a)

THORNDIKE, E. L. A proof of the law of effect. *Science*, 1933, **77**, 173–175. (b)

THORNDIKE, E. L. Influence of irrelevant continuing discomfort upon learning. *Journal of Genetic Psychology*, 1934, **44**, 444–448.

THORNDIKE, E. L. *The psychology of wants, interests, and attitudes*. New York: D. Appleton-Century, 1935.

THORNDIKE, E. L. The influence of occurrence, reward and punishment upon connections that had already considerable strength. *Miscellanea Psychologica Albert Michotte*, 1947, 308–322.

THORNDIKE, E. L., & ROCK, R. T., JR. Learning without awareness of what is being learned or intent to learn it. *Journal of Experimental Psychology*, 1934, **17**, 1–19.

TILTON, J. W. The effect of "right" and "wrong" upon the learning of nonsense syllables in multiple choice arrangement. *Journal of Educational Psychology*, 1939, **30**, 95–115.

TILTON, J. W. The relative importance of success and failure in learning, as related to certain individual differences. *Journal of Educational Psychology*, 1943, **34**, 176–180.

TILTON, J. W. "Effect" as determined by initial strength of response. *Journal of General Psychology*, 1944, **31**, 277–281.

TILTON, J. W. Gradients of effect. *Journal of Genetic Psychology*, 1945, **66**, 3–19.

TOLMAN, E. C., & GLEITMAN, H. Studies in learning and motivation. I. Equal reinforcements in both end-boxes, followed by shock in one end-box. *Journal of Experimental Psychology*, 1949, **39, 810–819.

TUCKMAN, J. The influence of varying amounts of punishment on mental connections. *Teachers College Contribution to Education*, 1933, No. 590.

VAN DE RIET, H. Effects of praise and reproof on pained-associate learning in educationally retarded children. *Journal of Educational Psychology*, 1964, **55**, 139–143.

VOGEL-SPROTT, M. D. A classical conditioning procedure to control suppression of a rewarded response punished after delay. *Psychological Reports*, 1966, **19, 91–98.

WAITS, J. V. The law of effect in the retained situation. *Archives of Psychology*, 1937, **30**, No. 208.

WALLACH, H., & HENLE, M. An experimental analysis of the law of effect. *Journal of Experimental Psychology,* 1941, **28**, 340–349.

WALLACH, H., & HENLE, M. A further study of the function of reward. *Journal of Experimental Psychology,* 1942, **30**, 147–160.

WALTERS, R. H. Delay of reinforcement gradients in children's learning. *Psychonomic Science,* 1964, **1**, 307–308.

WALTERS, R. H., PARKE, R. D., & CANE, V. A. Timing of punishment and the observation of consequences to others as determinants of response inhibition. *Journal of Experimental Psychology,* 1965, **2**, 10–30.

WARDEN, C. J., & COHEN, A. A study of certain incentives applied under schoolroom conditions. *Journal of Genetic Psychology,* 1931, **39**, 320–327.

WATERS, T. J. Censure reinforcement, cue conditions and the acute-chronic schizophrenic distinction. (Doctoral dissertation, University of Missouri.) Ann Arbor, Mich.: University Microfilms, 1962. No. 62-6428.

WEINER, H. Some effects of response cost upon human operant behavior. *Journal of the Experimental Analysis of Behavior,* 1962, **5**, 201–208.

WEINER, H. Response cost and fixed-ratio performance. *Journal of the Experimental Analysis of Behavior,* 1964, **7**, 79–81. (a)

WEINER, H. Response cost effects during extinction following fixed-interval reinforcement in humans. *Journal of the Experimental Analysis of Behavior,* 1964, **7**, 333–335. (b)

WEINGOLD, H. P., & WEBSTER, R. L. Effects of punishment on a cooperative behavior in children. *Child Development,* 1964, **35**, 1211–1216.

WEISENBERG, M. Affect and information effects of positive and negative reinforcement as a function of need-achievement. (Doctoral dissertation, New York University.) Ann Arbor, Mich.: University Microfilms, 1966. No. 66-5706.

WEISS, R. F., BUCHANAN, W., & PASAMANICK, B. Delay of reinforcement and delay of punishment in persuasive communication. *Psychological Reports,* 1965, **16**, 576.

WILLCUTT, H. C. The effects of praise and reproof on reaction time in children. (Doctoral dissertation, The Florida State University.) Ann Arbor, Mich.: University Microfilms, 1964. No. 64–3622.

WOOD, T. W. The effect of approbation and reproof on the mastery of nonsense syllables. *Journal of Applied Psychology,* 1934, **18**, 657–664.

WORRELL, L. The preference for conflict: Some paradoxical reinforcement effects. *Journal of Personality,* 1964, **32**, 32–44.

WU, CHING-YI. The autistic effect of reward and punishment on directional perception. *Acta Psychologia Taiwanica,* 1962, **4**, 104–111.

WYER, R. S., JR., & LOVE, J. M. Response speed following failure in a twochoice game as a function of reward, punishment, and response pattern. *Journal of Experimental Psychology,* 1966, **72**, 571–579.

**ZIMMAR, G. P. The effects of secondary punishment on avoidance behavior in extinction. (Doctoral dissertation, State University of New York at Buffalo.) Ann Arbor, Mich.: University Microfilms, 1966. No. 66-7996.

ZIMMERMAN, J., & BAYDEN, N. T. Punishment of S^Δ responding of humans in conditional matching to sample by time-out. *Journal of the Experimental Analysis of Behavior,* 1963, **6, 589–597.

ZIPF, S. G. Resistance and conformity under reward and punishment. *Journal of Abnormal and Social Psychology*, 1960, **61**, 102–109.

ZIRKLE, G. A. Success and failure in serial learning. I. The Thorndike effect. *Journal of Experimental Psychology*, 1946, **36**, 230–236.

IV. Bibliography on Theoretical, Review, and Discussion Articles on Punishment

ANDERSON, N. H. On the quantification of Miller's conflict theory. *Psychological Review*, 1962, **69**, 400–414.

APPEL, J. B. Analysis of aversively motivated behavior. *Archives of General Psychiatry*, 1964, **10**, 71–83.

APPEL, J. B., & PETERSON, N. J. Punishment: Effects of shock intensity on response suppression. *Psychological Reports*, 1965, **16**, 721–730.

AZRIN, N. H., & HOLZ, W. C. Punishment. In W. K. Honig (Ed.), *Operant behavior: Areas of research and application*. New York: Appleton-Century-Crofts, 1966, Pp. 380–447.

BEVAN, W. Reward vs. Punishment: Comment on a confusion. *Journal of General Psychology*, 1957, **56**, 45–50.

BOLLES, R. C. *Theory of motivation*. New York: Harper & Row, 1967. Pp. 416–433.

BROWN, W. The positive effect of punishment. *Journal of Comparative Psychology*, 1939, **28**, 17–22.

BROWN, W. P. The Yerkes–Dodson law repealed. *Psychological Reports*, 1965, **17**, 663–666.

CHAMPION, R. A. Motivational effects in approach–avoidance conflict. *Psychological Review*, 1961, **68**, 354–358.

CHURCH, R. M. The varied effects of punishment on behavior. *Psychological Review*, 1963, **70**, 369–402.

DINSMOOR, J. A. Punishment: I. The avoidance hypothesis. *Psychological Review*, 1954, **61**, 34–46.

DINSMOOR, J. A. Punishment: II. An interpretation of empirical findings. *Psychological Review*, 1955, **62**, 96–105.

DISERENS, C. M., & VAUGHN, J. The experimental psychology of motivation. *Psychological Bulletin*, 1931, **28**, 15–65.

FELDMAN, M. P. Aversion therapy for sexual deviations: A critical review. *Psychological Bulletin*, 1966, **65**, 65–79.

GERBRANDT, L. K. Generalizations from the distinction of passive and active avoidance. *Psychological Reports*, 1964, **15**, 11–22.

GUTHRIE, E. R. Reward and punishment. *Psychological Review*, 1934, **41**, 450–460.

KAUFMAN, A. Recovery or no recovery? *Psychological Reports*, 1965, **17**, 776.

HILGARD, E. R., & BOWER, G. H. *Theories of learning*. (3rd ed.) New York: Appleton-Century-Crofts, 1966. Pp. 29–44.

KNIGHT, N. B. The effect of punishment for errors on learning: An evaluation of the parametric and motivation hypotheses. *Psychological Newsletter, New York University*, 1958, **10**, 76–83.

LEITENBERG, H. Is time-out from positive reinforcement an aversive event? A review of the experimental evidence. *Psychological Bulletin,* 1965, **64,** 428–441.

LOGAN, F. A., & WAGNER, A. R. *Reward and punishment.* Boston: Allyn and Bacon, 1965.

MAIER, N. R. F. *Frustration.* New York: McGraw-Hill, 1949. (Chapter 7).

MARSHALL, H. H. The effect of punishment on children: A review of the literature and a suggested hypothesis. *Journal of Genetic Psychology,* 1965, **106,** 23–33.

MARTIN, B. Reward and punishment associated with the same goal response: A factor in the learning of motives. *Psychological Bulletin,* 1963, **60,** 441–451.

MARTIN, R. C., & MELVIN, K. B. Punishment-induced facilitation: Comments and analysis. *Psychonomic Science,* 1966, **5,** 269–270.[10]

MILLER, N. E. Experimental studies of conflict. In J. McV. Hunt (Ed.), *Personality and the behavior disorders.* Vol. I. New York: Ronald Press, 1944. Pp. 431–465.

MILLER, N. E. Comments on theoretical models illustrated by the development of a theory of conflict behavior. *Journal of Personality,* 1951, **20,** 82–100.

MILLER, N. E. Liberalization of basic S-R concepts: Extensions to conflict behavior, motivation and social learning. In S. Koch, (Ed.), *Psychology: A study of a science.* Study 1, Vol. 2, New York, McGraw-Hill, 1959. Pp. 196–292.

MILLER, N. E., & BARRY, H., III. Motivational effects of drugs: Methods which illustrate some general problems in psychopharmacology. *Psychopharmacologia,* 1960, **1,** 169–199.

MOWRER, O. H. *Learning theory and behavior.* New York: Wiley, 1960.

MUENZINGER, K. F. Reward and punishment. *University of Colorado Studies, General Series,* (A), 1946, **27,** No. 4.

POSTMAN, L. The history and present status of the law of effect. *Psychological Bulletin,* 1947, 44, 489–563.[11]

POSTMAN, L. J. Rewards and punishments in human learning. In L. J. Postman, (Ed.), *Psychology in the making.* New York: Knopf, 1962. Pp. 331–401.

SANDLER, J. Masochism: An empirical analysis. *Psychological Bulletin,* 1964, **62,** 197–204.

SEWARD, J. P. Learning theory and identification: II. The role of punishment. *Journal of Genetic Psychology,* 1954, **84,** 201–210.

SOLLEY, C. M., & MURPHY, G. *Development of the perceptual world.* New York: Basic Books, 1960.

SOLOMON, R. L. Punishment. *American Psychologist,* 1964, **19,** 237–253.

[10] See also: Smith, N. F., Misanin, J. R., & Campbell, B. A. Effect of punishment: Facilitation or inhibition? A reply to Martin and Melvin. *Psychonomic Science,* 1966, **5,** 363–364.

[11] See also: Stone, G. R. A note on Postman's review of the literature on the law of effect. *Psychological Bulletin,* 1948, **45,** 151–160; Postman, L. Discussion of Stone's note on the law of effect. *Psychological Bulletin,* 1948, **45,** 344–345; Stone, G. R. Reply to Postman. *Psychological Bulletin,* 1948, **45,** 536–537; Bernard, J. Note on the Postman–Stone controversy. *Psychological Bulletin,* 1949, **46,** 51–53.

Stone, G. R. The effect of negative incentives in serial learning. II. Incentive intensity and response variability. *Journal of General Psychology,* 1950, **42**, 179–224.

Stone, G. R. The effect of negative incentives in serial learning: VII. Theory of punishment. *Journal of General Psychology,* 1953, **48**, 133–161.

Thorndike, E. L. *Animal intelligence: Experimental studies.* New York: Macmillan, 1911. Pp. 244ff.

Thorndike, E. L. *Fundamentals of learning.* New York: Teachers College, 1932. Pp. 276, 299ff., 311ff.

Thorndike, E. L. *The psychology of wants, attitudes, and interests.* New York: D. Appleton-Century Co., 1935. (Chapters 6, 8, and 10.)

Thorndike, E. L. *Man and his works.* Cambridge, Massachusetts: Harvard University Press, 1943. (Chapter 8.)

Wagner, A. R. Frustration and punishment. In R. N. Haber, (Ed.), *Current research in motivation.* New York: Holt, Rinehart, and Winston, 1966.

Warden, C. J. A note on punishment as a deterrent in animal reactions. *Journal of Genetic Psychology,* 1932, **40**, 203–206.

Waters, R. H. The law of effect as a principle of learning. *Psychological Bulletin,* 1934, **31**, 408–425.

Young, P. T. *Motivation of behavior.* New York: Wiley, 1936. Pp. 278–290.

V. Outline of Experiments on Primary Punishment by Independent Variable and Behavioral Category [12]

As described in the introduction, this outline is organized according to independent variable (identified with Arabic numerals 1 through 29) with behavioral categories as subpoints (lower case letters "a" through "u"). The outline follows a listing of the independent variables and the behavioral categories used.

Independent Variable

1. P group vs. control group

   The first four independent variables entail the comparison of a punishment condition with a control condition. The first of these four is the comparison of a P group with a control group. A typical experimental example is the learning of a right turn in a T maze by rats. Erroneous left turns are punished in the punishment group, while left turns are not punished in the control group. In other respects the treatment of the two groups is identical.

2. P vs. control condition (repeated measures)

   Experiments in which a control condition is compared with a punishment condition on a different occasion in the same subject are included in this category. The approach–avoidance conflict situation is a typical

---

[12] The following abbreviations will be used throughout this outline: punishment (P), reinforcement (R), positive reinforcement (R+), and negative reinforcement (R—).

experimental example. Subjects are first trained to perform a response through R until response strength has stabilized near asymptote. Then P (as well as R+) is made contingent upon the occurrence of the learned response, and changes in response strength caused by the introduction of P are observed.

3. Intracranial P vs. control condition

Experiments classified in this section are similar to those in sections 1 and 2 except that P is applied intracranially.

4. Correlated P group vs. matched control group

The presentation of P may be contingent upon the strength with which a learned response occurs, not just *that* it occurs. For example, only responses occurring at a level of strength below a cutoff point may be punished, while a matched control subject is punished regardless of the strength of its response on that trial. The effect of P on response at specified levels of strength is thereby assessed.

5. P intensity

Variation in P intensity is the most frequent experimental manipulation of a parameter of the punishing stimulus per se. Experiments varying P intensity in which a no-punishment control condition was also included are classified here and are not cross-referenced under one of the four P vs. control categories above. Similarly designed experiments with other parameters listed below are not cross-referenced either.

6. P duration

The temporal duration of the punishing stimulus defines this independent variable.

7. P delay

The temporal delay between the occurrence of a response and the onset of P defines this variable. Comparisons of noncontingent aversive stimulation with punishment are included under this variable since noncontingent aversive stimulation in the experimental setting can be viewed as variable delayed punishment.

8. P schedule

P schedule is analogous to reinforcement schedule. For example, P can be programmed to follow each occurrence of a response (continuous P), or every other occurrence of the response (intermittent P). Experiments in which P schedule was varied are classified in this section.

9. P frequency

Although variations in P frequency have occurred in numerous experiments, very few have specifically examined behavioral changes as a function of P frequency while constant conditions were maintained in other respects. Only experiments which have assessed the effects of varying P frequency are classified in this section.

10. Rate of P intensity or P duration increase

P intensity or P duration may be increased over trials. Experiments which varied the rate of increase are included in this section.

11. Type of P

Experiments which compared the effects of two types of P, such as electric shock and intense noise, are classified under this variable.

12. Length of P period
    The temporal duration of the experimental conditions during which a response is punished defines this variable.
13. Location of P in intermittent schedules of reinforcement
    When a response is reinforced on an intermittent schedule, P can be applied at various points between successively reinforced responses. Variation in these points at which P is applied defines this variable.
14. Segment of running response punishment
    A straight alley can be broken into segments and punishment applied selectively to running responses in different segments. Experimental variation in segment constitutes this variable.
15. Part of body punished
    Experimental variation in the location on the body to which the punisher is applied constitutes this variable. In one experiment, for example, a group of rats was punished on the front feet, while another group was punished on the hind feet.
16. P for errors vs. R+ for correct responses
    One of the earliest questions posed about punishment was: "Is punishment or reward more effective in producing learning?" To answer this question, experiments were designed in which erroneous responses of one group of subjects were punished (e.g., left turns in a T maze), while correct responses of another group of subjects were positively reinforced (e.g., right turns in a T maze). Such experiments are included in this category.
17. Pre-P exposure to aversive stimulation
    Amount of exposure to aversive stimulation prior to punishment constitutes this variable.
18. Amount of training
    Variation in the amount of training or strength of the to-be-punished response defines this variable.
19. Hours of deprivation
    Hours of deprivation or some other measure of drive define this variable.
20. Reinforcement schedule
21. Reinforcement of a competing response
    While punishment is contingent upon one response, a competing response may or may not be punished.
22. Task difficulty
23. Species or strain
24. P of erroneous response vs. P of correct response
    In selective learning, either erroneous or correct response may be punished, while correct responses are reinforced regardless of the P condition.
25. Number of cues presented with P
26. Time interval between post-P recovery periods
27. Drugs
    The comparison of the effect of different drugs with each other or with a control condition defines this variable.
28. Brain surgery
    The comparison of the effect of lesions in different areas of the brain with each other or with a control condition defines this variable.

29. Electroconvulsive shock

Variation in the conditions of electroconvulsive shock constitutes this variable. ECS is not the punisher however.

Behavioral Categories [13]

a. Response at operant level
b. Erroneous response during learning (R+ for the correct response)
c. Erroneous response during learning (R— for the correct response)
d. Erroneous response during learning (no R for the correct response)
e. Correct response during learning (R+ also)
f. Correct response during learning (R— also)
g. Erroneous and correct responses during learning (R+ for the correct response)
h. Learned response (R maintained)
i. Learned response (R+) undergoing extinction
j. Learned response (R—) undergoing extinction
k. Erroneous responses during extinction of correct response learned with R+
l. Consummatory response
m. Exploratory response
n. Instinctive response
o. Social response
p. Psychiatric symptom
q. Unpunished response

All unpunished responses except those described in categories "r" through "u" are included in this category.

r. Competing responses

Unpunished competing responses that could serve as alternatives to instrumental punished responses in attaining reinforcement are classified here.

s. Extinction without P of a response learned when both P and R were contingent upon it.
t. Retention

Tests of retention for correct responses usually learned while erroneous responses were punished are classified here.

u. Physiological response

The Outline [14]

1. P group vs. control group
   a. Response at operant level
   Abet, Essman, & Jarvik (1961); Barns & Kish (1957); Baron & Antonitis (1961); Bolles & Seelbach (1964, Ex. I, II, IV); Essman & Alpern (1964, Ex. I, II, IV); Essman & Jarvik (1961); Essman & Sudak (1963; 1964, Ex.

---

[13] Punishment is contingent upon the responses defined in categories "a" through "p." In the last five categories (q–u), the effect of punishing one response on an unpunished response was observed.

[14] Experiment is abbreviated "Ex" throughout.

II); Gerbrandt & Thomson (1964); Hudspeth, McGaugh, & Thompson (1964); Jarvik & Essman (1960); Leitenberg (1965); Luttges & McGaugh (1967); Marder (1961); McGaugh & Alpern (1966); Myers (1965, Ex. I); Pearl (1963, Ex. Ia); Quartermain, Paolino, & Miller (1965); Sermat & Greenglas (1965); Seward & Raskin (1960, Ex. I, II, III); Siegal & Martin (1965, Ex. I, II); Stone (1950); and Zinkin & Miller (1967).

b. Erroneous response during learning (R+ for the correct response)
Barlow (1933); Bernard (1941); Besch (1959); Brackbill & O'Hara (1958, Ex. I); Brown (1961); Brunswick (1939); Bunch (1928, 1935); Bunch & Hagman (1937); Bunch & Magdsick (1938); Bunch & McTeer (1932); Chung-Fang (1934a, 1934b); Crafts & Gilbert (1934); Dodson (1932, Ex. I, II); Drew (1938); Fowler & Wischner (1965a); Freeburne & Schneider (1955); Gilbert (1936, 1937); Gilbert & Crafts (1935); Hoge & Stocking (1912); Hunter (1913); Jensen (1934); McTeer (1931, 1933); Muenzinger 1934a, 1934b); Muenzinger, Bernstone, & Richards (1938); Muenzinger, Brown, Crow & Powloski (1952); Muenzinger & Powloski (1951); Muenzinger & Vine (1941); Murphy (1959); Nagamachi (1960); Nelson, Reid, & Travers (1965); Penny & Lupton (1961); Rexroad (1926); Rosen (1954); Stone & Walter (1951); Tolman, Hall & Brentnall (1932); Underwood (1941); Valentine (1930); Warden & Aylesworth (1927); Wischner (1947); and Wischner, Hall, & Fowler (1964).

c. Erroneous response during learning (R— for the correct response)
LeBigot (1954).

d. Erroneous response during learning (no R for the correct response)
Travis & Anderson (1938).

e. Correct response during learning (R+ also)
Diamond (1934); Drew (1938); Fowler & Wischner (1965a, 1965b); Freeburne & Schneider (1955); Hawkins (1966); Karsh & Williams(1964); Koski & Ross (1965); Muenzinger (1934a, 1934b); Muenzinger, Bernstone, & Richards (1938); Muenzinger, Brown, Crow & Powloski (1952); Muenzinger & Powloski (1951); Muenzinger & Vine (1941); Tolman, Hall, & Brentnall (1932); Wischner (1947); and Wischner, Hall, & Fowler (1964).

f. Correct response during learning (R— also)
Kurtz & Shafer (1966); LeBigot (1954); and Migler (1963, Ex. II).

g. Erroneous and correct responses during learning (R+ for the correct response)
Freeburne & Taylor (1952); and Rosen (1954).

h. Learned response (R maintained)
Akhtar (1963); Banks (1966a, 1966b, 1967); Birch (1965); Bolles & Seelbach (1964, Ex. I and II); Brown & Wagner (1964); Church & Raymond (1967); Fallon (1966); Farber (1948); Goldsmith (1967, Ex. I); Jackson (1964); Jones & Swanson (1966, Ex. I); Karsh & Williams (1964); Kelleher & Morse (1964); King (1965); Masserman, Arieff, Pechtel, & Klehr (1950); Masserman & Jacques (1947); Pearlman, Sharpless, & Jarvik (1961); Pechtel, Masserman, Schreiner & Levitt (1955); Poschel (1959); Rosenblum & Harlow (1963); Sandler, Davidson, & Holzschuh (1966); Sandler,

Davidson, & Malagodi (1966); Smart (1965a, 1965b); and Warden (1931).

i. Learned response (R+) undergoing extinction
Akhtar (1963); Baer (1961); Born (1967); Desroches (1962); Edwards (1951); Estes (1944, Ex. A, B, C, D, G, K); Fallon (1966); Fowler & Wischner (1965b); Freeburne & Schneider (1955); Jackson (1964); Skinner (1938); and Uhl (1967).

j. Learned response (R—) undergoing extinction
Beecroft (1967); Beecroft & Bouska (1967); Brown, Anderson, & Weiss (1965); Brush, Brush, & Solomon (1955); Campbell, Smith, & Misanin (1966); Church & Solomon (1956); Eison & Sawrey (1967); Melvin & Martin (1966); Melvin & Smith (1967); and Moyer (1955, Ex. I; 1957).

k. Erroneous responses during extinction of correct response learned with R+
Fowler & Wischner (1965b); and Freeburne & Schneider (1955).

l. Consummatory response
Delprato & Thompson (1965a); Drew (1938); Hudson (1950); Hunt & Schlosberg (1950); Lichtenstein (1950b); Martin & Ross (1964); and Terris & Wechkin (1967b).

m. Exploratory response
Bolles & Seelbach (1964, Ex. III); Fisher (1955); Pearl, Walters, & Anderson (1964, Ex. II); and Spiegel (1957).

n. Instinctive response
Adler & Hogan (1963, Ex. II).

o. Social response
Fisher (1955).

p. Psychiatric symptom
Prince (1956).

q. Unpunished response
Chung-Fang (1934b); Everall (1935, Ex. I); Farrow & Santos (1962); Hamilton, & Krechevsky (1933, Ex. I, II); Kleemier (1942, Ex. II); Koski & Ross (1965); O'Kelly (1940b); and Smart (1965a, 1965b).

r. Competing responses
Whiting & Mowrer (1943).

s. Extinction without P of a response learned when both P and R were contingent upon it
Akhtar (1963); Brown & Wagner (1964); Church & Raymond (1967); Fallon (1966); Jackson (1964); Karsh (1964b); Karsh & Williams (1964); and Martin & Ross (1964).

t. Retention
Bunch & McTeer (1932); Chung-Fang (1934a); Crafts & Gilbert (1934); Gilbert (1936); Luttges & McGaugh (1967); and White (1932).

u. Physiological response
Barlow (1933); Katahn, Thune, & Doody (1965); Sawrey, Conger, & Turrell (1956); Sawrey & Weiz (1956); and Schmidt (1966).

2. P vs. control condition (repeated measures)
a. Response at operant level
Feldman & Brenner (1963); and Szymanski (1912).

b. Erroneous response during learning (R+ for the correct response)
Bernard (1942); Bernard & Gilbert (1941); Eigler (1932); Eisenson (1935, Ex. I); Herman & Azrin (1964); and Stone (1946).

d. Erroneous response during learning (no R for the correct response)
Dulany (1957); Gates (1895); Johanson (1922); and Vaughn (1928).

f. Correct response during learning (R— also)
Isaacson, Olton, Bauer, & Swart (1966).

h. Learned response (R maintained)
Appel (1960, 1961); Ayllon & Azrin (1966); Azrin (1958, 1960b); Azrin, Hake, Holz, & Hutchinson (1965, Ex. I, II); Berkun (1957); Berryman (1962); Bruner (1967); Brush, Bush, Jenkins, John, & Whiting (1952); Dimmick, Ludlow, & Whiteman (1939); Dinsmoor (1952); Edwards (1951); Elder (1962); Elder, Noblin, & Maher (1961); Estes, (1944, Ex. H.); Ferster (1958, Ex. V); Fischer & Campbell (1964); Geller (1963); Geller, Bachman, & Seifter (1963); Hearst & Sidman (1961); Hendry & VonToller 1964); Herman & Azrin (1964); Holz & Azrin (1961, 1962b); Holz, Azrin, & Ayllon (1963); Honig (1966); Honig & Slivka (1964); Isaacson & Wickelgren (1962); Jacobson & Skaarup (1955); Levine & Jones (1965); Masserman (1943, 1944a, 1944b); Masserman, Jacques, & Nicholson (1945); Masserman & Pechtel (1953, 1956a, 1956b); Masserman, Pechtel, & Schreiner (1953); Masserman & Yum (1946); Migler (1963, Ex. I, III); Miller & Kraeling (1952); Mowrer (1940); Murray & Berkum (1955); Noblin & Maher (1962); Pare & Dumas (1965); Pearl, Walters, & Anderson (1964, Ex. I, III); Pechtel & Masserman (1954); Rachlin (1966, Ex. I, II); Sears (1964, Ex. I, II); Skinner (1938); Stein (1964); Storms, Boroczi, & Broen (1962); Taylor & Maher (1959); Taylor & Rennie (1961); Tyler & Brown (1967); Vogel-Sprott (1967); Whiting & Mowrer (1943); Wikler & Masserman (1943); Winograd, Cohen, & Cole (1965); and Wolpe (1952).

i. Learned response (R+) undergoing extinction
Holz & Azrin (1961); Racklin (1966, Ex. I); Sidman (1958); and Skinner (1938).

j. Learned response (R—) undergoing extinction
Appel (1960); Black & Morse (1961); Brogden, Lipman, & Culler (1938, Ex. III); Nigro (1966, Ex. I); Solomon, Kamin, & Wynne (1953); and Wynne & Solomon 1955.

k. Erroneous responses during extinction of correct response learned with R+
Dulany (1957).

l. Consummatory response
Cornwell (1966, Ex. I. IV); Fox, Kimble, & Lickey (1964, Ex. I); Freedmen (1958); Lichtenstein (1950a); Lubar (1964, Ex. I); McCleary (1961, Ex. I); McCleary, Jones, & Ursin (1965); Pearl, Walters, & Anderson (1964, Ex. III); Schaeffer (1911); Snyder & Isaacson (1965, Ex. II); and Stanley & Elliot (1962).

n. Instinctive response
Myer (1966); and Myer & Baenninger (1966).

    p. Psychiatric symptom
       Baer (1962); Barrett (1962); Daly & Cooper (1967); Flanagan, Goldia-
       mond, & Azrin (1958); Frick (1951); Goldiamond (1954); Kaye, Cox,
       Bosack, & Anderson (1965); Kushner & Sandler (1966); Liversedge & Syl-
       vester (1955); Lovaas, Schaeffer, & Simmons (1965); Maier & Wapner
       (1943); Tate & Baroff (1966); Tolman & Mueller (1964); Wolf, Risley,
       Johnston, Harris, & Allen (1967); Wolf, Risley, & Mees (1964); and
       Wolpe (1964).

    q. Unpunished response
       Everall (1935, Ex. II); Kleemeier (1942, Ex. I); Martin (1940, Ex. II);
       O'Kelly (1940a, 1940b); O'Kelley & Biel (1940); Porter & Biel (1943);
       Reynolds (1936); Sander (1937); Sidman (1958); and Steckle & O'Kelly
       (1940).

    t. Retention
       Worell (1965).

3. Intracranial P vs. control condition
    a. Response at operant level
       Olds (1956); and Olds & Milner (1954).

    h. Learned response (R maintained)
       Steiner & D'Amato (1964).

    l. Consummatory response
       Asdourian (1962); and Delgado, Roberts, & Miller (1954).

4. Correlated P group vs. matched control group
    e. Correct response during learning (R+ also)
       Logan (1960, Ex. 58B).

    h. Learned response (R maintained)
       Logan (1960 Ex. 57C, 58B, 59A).

5. P intensity
    a. Response at operant level
       Bindra & Anchel (1963. Ex. II); Delprato & Thompson (1965b, 1966);
       Essman & Sudak (1964, Ex. I); Renner (1964, Ex. II); Rothberg (1959);
       and Spigel & Ellis (1965).

    b. Erroneous response during learning (R+ for the correct response)
       Boll, Madison, & Douglass (1966); Curlin & Donahoe (1965); Feldman
       (1961); Gurnee (1938); Lohr (1959, Ex. II); Vaughn & Diserens (1930);
       and Wischner, Fowler, & Kushnick (1963).

    c. Erroneous response during learning (R— for the correct response)
       Cole (1911).

    d. Erroneous response during learning (no R for the correct response)
       Dodson (1915, 1917); and Yerkes & Dodson (1908).

    e. Correct response during learning (R+ also)
       Curlin & Donahoe (1965); Fowler (1963); Fowler & Miller (1963); Karsh
       (1963, Ex. I); Logan (1960, Ex. 57B); and Wischner, Fowler, & Kush-
       nick (1963).

    f. Correct response during learning (R— also)
       Shepard (1964).

    h. Learned response (R maintained)
       Appel (1963); Azrin (1959, 1960a); Azrin & Holz (1961); Azrin, Holz, &

Hake (1963); Barry & Miller (1962); Barry, Miller, & Todd (1962); Boroczi, Storms, & Broen (1964); Brethower & Reynolds (1962); Brown (1948); Bruning, Kintz, & Morgret (1965); Camp, Raymond, & Church (1967, Ex. I) ; Carran (1967, Ex. I, II); Church, Raymond, & Beauchamp (1967); Daley (1962); Dardano & Sauerbrunn (1964a, 1964b, 1964c); Edwards & Dart (1966); Filby & Appel (1966); Geller & Seifter (1960); Hake, Azrin, & Oxford (1967); Hande (1967); Harvey, Lints, Jacobsen, & Hunt (1965, Ex. VI, VII); Holden (1926); Holz & Azrin (1962a, 1963); Holz, Azrin, & Ulrich (1963); Jones & Swanson (1966, Ex. II); Karsh (1962, Ex. I, II, III; 1963, Ex. II; 1964a; 1964b); Kaufman (1964a, 1964b, 1965); Logan (1960, Ex. 57B); Lohr (1959, Ex. I); Murray & Nevin (1967); Rachlin (1967, Ex. I); Ray (1964); Reynolds (1963); Sandler, Davidson, Greene, & Holzschuh (1966); Schwartzbaum & Spieth (1964); and Walters (1963).

i. Learned response (R+) undergoing extinction
   Azrin & Holz (1961); Boe (1964; 1966, Ex. I, II); Boe & Church (1967, Ex. I); and Edwards (1951)

j. Learned response (R−) undergoing extinction
   Brush (1957); Gwinn (1949); Hurwitz, Bolas, & Haritos (1961); Imada (1959); Martin (1965); Sandler, Davidson, Greene, & Holzschuh (1966); Seligman & Campbell (1965); Seward, King, Chow, & Shiflett (1965); and Smith, Misanin, & Campbell (1966).

l. Consummatory response
   Beach, Conovitz, Steinberg, & Goldstein (1956); Boitano & Isaacson (1967); Cook (1939); Fowler (1963); Fowler & Miller (1963); Hunt & Schlosberg (1950); Leaf & Muller (1965, Ex. I); Terris & Wechkin (1967a); Tugendhat (1960); and Walters (1963).

n. Instinctive response
   Myer (1967).

q. Unpunished response
   Brethower & Reynolds (1962); and Dardano & Sauerbrunn (1964b).

r. Competing response
   Boe (1964); and Bruning, Kintz, & Morgret (1965).

s. Extinction without P of a response learned when both P and R were contingent upon it
   Shepard (1964).

u. Physiological response
   Ader, Tatum, & Beels (1960a, Ex. I); and Kaufman (1965).

6. P duration

a. Response at operant level
   Chorover & Schiller (1965); Clark (1967); and Essman & Sudak (1964, Ex. III).

b. Erroneous response during learning (R+ for the correct response)
   Coburn & Yerkes (1915); Ferster & Appel (1961); Wischner & Fowler (1964); and Zimmerman & Ferster (1963).

c. Erroneous response during learning (R− for the correct response)
   Knopfelmacher (1953).

e. Correct response during learning (R+ also)
Wischner & Fowler (1964).

f. Correct response during learning (R— also)
Migler (1963, Ex. VII).

h. Learned response (R maintained)
Boroczi, Storms, & Broen (1964); Church, Raymond, & Beauchamp (1967); Church & Solomon (1956); Storms & Boroczi (1966); and Storms, Boroczi, & Broen (1963, 1965).

i. Learned response (R+) undergoing extinction
Boe (1966, Ex. I, II).

J. Learned response (R—) undergoing extinction
Misanin, Campbell, & Smith (1966); Seligman & Campbell (1965); and Smith, Misanin, & Campbell (1966).

t. Retention
Clark (1967).

7. P delay

a. Response at operant level
Bindra & Anchel (1963, Ex. I); Bolles & Warren (1966); Essman & Alpern (1964, Ex. III); Hare (1965); Renner (1964, Ex. II, III; 1966a); and Siegal & Martin (1965, Ex. III).

b. Erroneous response during learning (R+ for the correct response)
Bevan & Dukes (1955); Rosen (1954); and Wood (1933).

c. Erroneous response during learning (R— for the correct response)
Butler (1959).

g. Erroneous and correct responses during learning (R+ for the correct response
Rosen (1954).

h. Learned response (R maintained)
Azrin (1956); Banks & Vogel-Sprott (1965); Baron (1965); Brady (1956, 1959); Camp, Raymond, & Church (1967, Ex. I, II, III, IV); D'Amato & Gumenik (1960); Hare (1966); Hearst (1965, Ex. III, V); Hunt & Brady (1955); Knapp, Kause, & Perkins (1959); Leitenberg (1966, Ex. I); Renner (1966b); Vogel-Sprott & Banks (1965); and Walters & Demkow (1963).

i. Learned response (R+) undergoing extinction
Boe & Church (1967, Ex. II); and Estes (1944, Ex. J1, J2).

j. Learned response (R—) undergoing extinction
Kamin (1959); Kintz & Brunning (1967); Martin & Melvin (1964); Misanin, Campbell, & Smith (1966); and Nigro (1966, Ex. II).

l. Consummatory response
Bixenstine (1956); Davitz, Mason, Mowrer, & Viek (1957); Mowrer & Ullman (1945); and Wheeler (1933).

u. Physiological response
Senter & Hummel (1965).

8. P schedule

a. Response at operant level
Hare (1965); and Rothberg (1959).

b. Erroneous response during learning (R+ for the correct response)
Zimmerman & Ferster (1963).

    c. Erroneous response during learning (R— for the correct response)
       Knopfelmacher (1953).

    d. Erroneous response during learning (no R for the correct response)
       Travis & Anderson (1938); and Vaughn (1928).

    e. Correct response during learning (R+ also)
       Logan (1960, Ex. 57B).

    f. Correct response during learning (R— also)
       Whiteis (1956).

    h. Learned response (R maintained)
       Azrin (1956); Azrin, Holz, & Hake (1963); Banks (1957, 1966b); Camp,
       Raymond, & Church (1966); De Armond (1966); Ferraro (1966); Kauf-
       man (1966); Logan (1960, Ex. 57B); Sandler (1964); Sandler, Davidson,
       & Malagodi (1966); Shapiro (1966); Snapper, Schoenfeld, & Locker (1966,
       Ex. I); Storm & Boroczi (1966); Uhl (1967); and Vogel-Sprott (1966).

    i. Learned response (R+) undergoing extinction
       Estes (1944, Ex. E, K); and Uhl (1967).

    j. Learned response (R—) undergoing extinction
       Gwinn (1949); Melvin (1964); and Seward & Raskin (1960, Ex. IV, V).

    m. Exploratory response
       Spiegel (1957).

    s. Extinction without P of a response learned when both P and R were
       contingent upon it
       Logan (1960, Ex. 57B); and Whiteis (1956).

    u. Physiological response
       Ferraro, Schoenfeld, & Snapper (1967); and Snapper, Schoenfeld, &
       Locke (1966, Ex. I).

9. P frequency

    b. Erroneous response during learning (R+ for the correct response)
       Boll, Madison, & Douglass (1966); Bunch (1935); Muenzinger, Bern-
       stone, & Richards (1938); and Tuckman (1933, Ex. II, III).

    h. Learned response (R maintained)
       Akhtar (1963); Brush, Bush, Jenkins, John, & Whiting (1952); Ferraro
       (1966); and Kaufman & Miller (1949).

    u. Physiological response
       Ferraro, Schoenfeld, & Snapper (1967).

10. Rate of P intensity or P duration increase

    h. Learned response (R maintained)
       Bower & Miller (1960); Feirstein & Miller (1963); and Miller (1960, Ex.
       I, II, III).

    j. Learned response (R—) undergoing extinction
       Kintz & Brunning (1967).

    l. Consummatory response
       Miller (1960, Ex. I).

11. Type of P

    a. Response at operant level
       Gerbrandt (1965); and Gerbrandt & Thomson (1964).

    b. Erroneous response during learning (R+ for the correct response)
       Bijou (1943).

    h. Learned response (R maintained)
       Leitenberg (1966, Ex. I).
12. Length of P period
    b. Erroneous response during learning (R+ for the correct response)
       Orzak (1951).
    h. Learned response (R maintained)
       Edwards & Dart (1966).
    i. Learned response (R+) undergoing extinction
       Edwards (1951).
    u. Physiological response
       Ader, Tatum, & Beels (1960b, Ex. II).
13. Location of P in intermittent schedules of reinforcement
    h. Learned response (R maintained)
       Dardano & Sauerbrunn (1964c); De Armond-Edwards (1966); Holz & Azrin (1962a); Holzschuh (1965); Malott & Cumming (1964); and Williams & Barry (1966).
14. Segment of running response punishment
    j. Learned response (R−) undergoing extinction
       Brown (1964, Ex. I, II); Campbell, Smith, & Misanin (1966); and Melvin, Athey, & Heasley (1965).
15. Part of body punished
    b. Erroneous response during learning (R+ for the correct response)
       McTeer (1931).
    e. Correct response during learning (R+ also)
       Fowler & Miller (1963).
    h. Learned response (R maintained)
       Kaufman (1964b).
    l. Consummatory response
       Fowler & Miller (1963).
16. P for errors vs. R+ for correct responses
    b. Erroneous response during learning (R+ for the correct response)
       Dorcus & Gray (1932); and Tolman, Hall, & Bretnall (1932).
    d. Erroneous response during learning (no R for the correct response)
       Dodson (1917); Hoge & Stocking (1912); Penny & Lupton (1961); Travis (1938); and Warden & Aylesworth (1927).
    e. Correct response during learning (R+ also)
       Tolman, Hall, & Bretnall (1932).
17. Pre-P exposure to aversive stimulation
    a. Response at operant level
       Baron & Antonitis (1961); and Pearl (1963, Ex. Ia, III).
    b. Erroneous response during learning (R+ for the correct response)
       Muenzinger, Brown, Crow, & Powloski (1952).
    e. Correct response during learning (R+ also)
       Muenzinger, Brown, Crow, & Powloski (1952).
    h. Learned response (R maintained)
       Banks (1966b); Fallon (1966); Pearl, Walters, & Anderson (1964, Ex. I, III); and Walters (1963).

     i. Learned response (R+) undergoing extinction
        Birch (1965); and Fallon (1966).

     l. Consummatory response
        Freedman (1958); Pearl, Walters, & Anderson (1964, Ex. III); Terris & Wechkin (1967a, 1967b); and Walters (1963).

     m. Exploratory response
        Pearl, Walters, & Anderson (1964, Ex. II).

     q. Unpunished response
        Steckle & O'Kelly (1940).

     s. Extinction without P of a response learned when both P and R were contingent upon it
        Fallon (1966).

18. Amount of Training

     b. Erroneous response during learning (R+ for the correct response)
        Bunch (1935); and Valentine (1930).

     e. Correct response during learning (R+ also)
        Karsh & Williams (1964); Koski & Ross (1965); and Prince (1956).

     f. Correct response during learning (R— also)
        Isaacson, Olton, Bauer, & Swart (1966).

     h. Learned response (R maintained)
        Karsh (1962, (Ex. II, III); Kaufman & Miller (1949); Lohr (1959, Ex. I); Miller (1960, Ex. III); and Schwartzbaum & Spieth (1964).

     i. Learned response (R+) undergoing extinction
        Boe (1964); Born (1967); and Estes (1944, Ex. F).

     j. Learned response (R—) undergoing extinction
        Moyer (1955, Ex. I); and Smith, Misanin & Campbell (1966).

     n. Instinctive response
        Myer (1967).

     q. Unpunished response
        Everall (1935, Ex. I); Martin (1940, Ex. II); and Porter & Biel (1943).

     r. Competing responses
        Boe (1964).

19. Hours of deprivation

     e. Correct response during learning (R+ also)
        Hawkins (1966).

     f. Correct response during learning (R— also)
        Shepard (1964)

     h. Learned response (R maintained)
        Azrin, Holz, & Hake (1963); Dinsmoor (1952); Holden (1926); and Warden (1931).

     i. Learned response (R+) undergoing extinction
        Edwards (1951).

     l. Consummatory response
        Leaf & Muller (1965, Ex. II).

     s. Extinction without P of a response learned when both P and R were contingent upon it
        Shepard (1964).

u. Physiological response
Sawrey, Conger, & Turrell (1956).

20. Reinforcement schedule
   b. Erroneous response during learning (R+ for the correct response)
      Hoge & Stocking (1912); Penny & Lupton (1961); and Warden & Aylesworth (1927).
   d. Erroneous response during learning (no R for the correct response)
      Hoge & Stocking (1912); Penny & Lupton (1961); and Warden & Aylesworth (1927).
   h. Learned response (R maintained)
      Church & Raymond (1967); Daley (1962); Edwards (1951); Estes (1944, Ex. B); Migler (1963, Ex. IV); and Uhl (1967).
   i. Learned response (R+) undergoing extinction
      Dinsmoor (1962); Estes (1944, Ex. B); and Uhl (1967).
21. Reinforcement of a competing response
   h. Learned response (R maintained)
      Holz, Azrin, & Ayllon (1963).
   i. Learned response (R+) undergoing extinction
      Boe (1964); and Desroches (1962).
   r. Competing responses
      Boe (1964).
22. Task difficulty
   b. Erroneous response during learning (R+ for the correct response)
      Fowler & Wischner (1965a).
   d. Erroneous response during learning (no R for the correct response)
      Dodson (1915); and Yerkes & Dodson (1908).
   e. Correct response during learning (R+ also)
      Fowler & Wischner (1965a); and Hawkins (1966).
   r. Competing responses
      Whiting & Mowrer (1943).
23. Species or Strain
   h. Learned response (R maintained)
      Masserman & Pechtel (1956b); Masserman, Pechtel, & Schreiner (1953); and Storms, Boroczi, & Broen (1963).
   l. Consummatory response
      Freedman (1958).
   m. Exploratory response
      Fisher (1955).
   o. Social response
      Fisher (1955).
24. P of erroneous response vs. P of correct response
   b. Erroneous response during learning (R+ for the correct response)
      Curlin & Donahoe (1965); Drew (1938); Feldman (1961); Fowler & Wischner (1965a); Freeburne & Schneider (1955); Gurnee (1938); Muenzinger (1934a, 1934b); Muenzinger, Bernstone, & Richards (1938); Muenzinger, Brown, Crow & Powloski (1952); Muenzinger & Powloski (1951); Muenzinger & Vine (1941); Nelson, Reid, & Travers (1965); Wischner

(1947); Wischner & Fowler (1964); and Wischner, Fowler, & Kushnick (1963).

    e. Correct response during learning (R+ also)

Curlin & Donahoe (1965); Drew (1938); Feldman (1961); Fowler & Wischner (1965a); Freeburne & Schneider (1955); Gurnee (1938); Muenzinger (1934a, 1934b); Muenzinger, Bernstone, & Richards (1938); Muenzinger, Brown, Crow, & Powloski (1952); Muenzinger & Powloski (1951); Muenzinger & Vine (1941); Nelson, Reid & Travers (1965); Wischner (1947); Wischner & Fowler (1964); and Wischner, Fowler, & Kushnick (1963).

25. Number of cues presented with P

    f. Correct response during learning (R— also)

Whiteis (1956).

    j. Learned response (R—) undergoing extinction

Moyer (1955, Ex. III).

    s. Extinction without P of a response learned when both P and R were contingent upon it

Whiteis (1956).

26. Time interval between post-P recovery periods

    a. Response at operant level

Pearl (1963, Ex. Ia vs. Ib).

    i. Learned response (R+) undergoing extinction

Estes (1944, Ex. C).

27. Drugs

    a. Response at operant level

Abt, Essman, & Jarvik (1961); and Bindra & Anchel (1963, Ex. III).

    h. Learned response (R maintained)

Barry & Miller (1962); Barry, Miller, & Todd (1962); Brady (1956, 1959); Geller, Bachman, & Seifter (1963); Geller & Seifter (1960); Goldsmith (1967, Ex. I); Hendry & VonTeller (1964); Kelleher & Morse (1964); Levine & Jones (1965); Masserman (1944b); Masserman, Jacques, & Nicholson (1945); Masserman & Pechtel (1956b); Masserman & Yum (1946); Pearlman, Sharplers, & Jarvik (1961); Smart (1965b); Vogel-Sprott (1967); Vogel-Sprott & Banks (1965); and Wikler & Masserman (1943).

    l. Consummatory response

Leaf & Muller (1965, Ex. III).

    q. Unpunished response

Smart (1965b).

    u. Physiological response

Schmidt (1966).

28. Brain surgery

    f. Correct response during learning (R— also)

Isaacson, Olton, Bauer, & Swart (1966).

    h. Learned response (R maintained)

Harvey, Lints, Jacobson, & Hunt (1965, Ex. VI, VII); Isaacson & Wickelgren (1962); Masserman & Pechtel (1956a, 1956b); Masserman, Pechtel,

& Schreiner (1953); Pare & Dumas (1965); Pechtel, Masserman, Schreiner, & Levitt (1955); and Schwartzbaum & Spieth (1964).

l. Consummatory response

Boitano & Isaacson (1967); Cornwell (1966, Ex. I, IV); Fox, Kimble, & Lickey (1964, Ex. I); Lichenstein (1950b); Lubar (1964, Ex. I); McCleary (1961, Ex. I); McCleary, Jones, & Ursin (1965); and Snyder & Isaacson (1965, Ex. II).

q. Unpunished response

O'Kelly & Biel (1940).

29. Electroconvulsive shock

a. Response at operant level

Chorover & Schiller (1965); Delprato & Thompson (1965b, 1966); Hudspeth, McGaugh, & Thompson (1964); Luttges & McGaugh (1967); McGaugh & Alpern (1966); Quartermain, Paolino & Miller (1965); Zinken & Miller (1967).

h. Learned response (R maintained)

King (1965); Masserman, Arief, Pechtel, & Klehr (1950); Masserman & Jacques (1947); and Poschel (1959).

l. Consummatory response

Delprato & Thompson (1965a).

t. Retention

Luttges & McGaugh (1967)

Subject Index

Author Index

Numbers in italic indicate the page in which the full reference appears.